Italy For Dummies, 2nd Edition

Train Routes through Italy

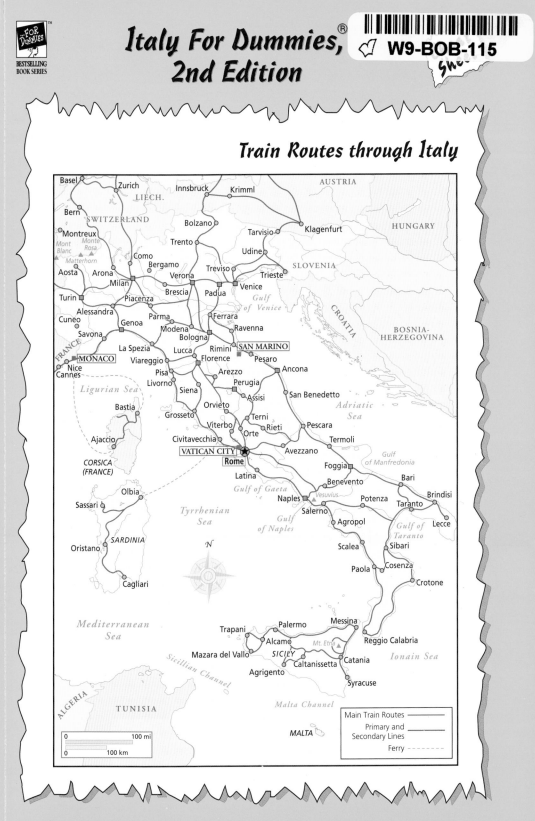

Main Train Routes ———
Primary and ————
Secondary Lines
Ferry - - - - - -

Venice Vaporetto System

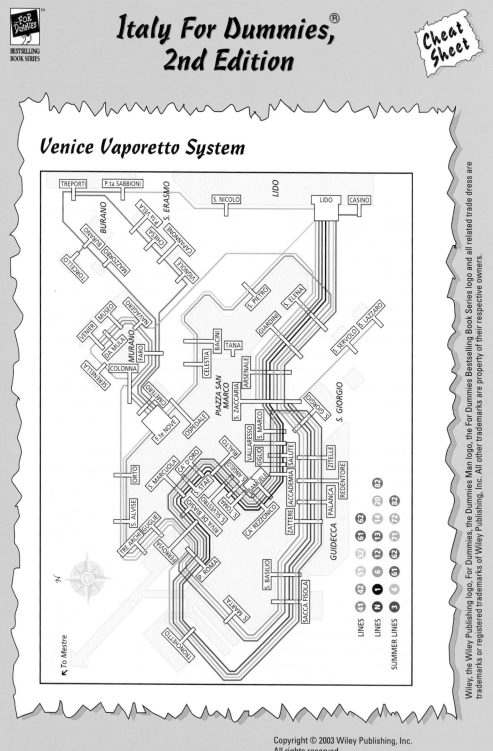

For Dummies: Bestselling Book Series for Beginners

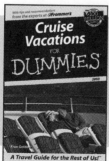

Italy
FOR
DUMMIES®
2ND EDITION

by Bruce Murphy and Alessandra de Rosa

WILEY

Wiley Publishing, Inc.

Italy For Dummies,® 2nd Edition

Published by
Wiley Publishing, Inc.
909 Third Avenue
New York, NY 10022
www.wiley.com

Copyright © 2003 by Wiley Publishing, Inc., Indianapolis, Indiana

Published simultaneously in Canada

No part of this publication may be reproduced, stored in a retrieval system, or transmitted in any form or by any means, electronic, mechanical, photocopying, recording, scanning, or otherwise, except as permitted under Sections 107 or 108 of the 1976 United States Copyright Act, without either the prior written permission of the Publisher, or authorization through payment of the appropriate per-copy fee to the Copyright Clearance Center, 222 Rosewood Drive, Danvers, MA 01923, 978-750-8400, fax 978-750-4744. Requests to the Publisher for permission should be addressed to the Legal Department, Wiley Publishing, Inc., 10475 Crosspoint Blvd., Indianapolis, IN 46256, 317-572-3447, fax 317-572-4447, or e-mail permcoordinator@wiley.com.

Trademarks: Wiley, the Wiley Publishing logo, For Dummies, the Dummies Man logo, A Reference for the Rest of Us!, The Dummies Way, Dummies Daily, The Fun and Easy Way, Dummies.com and related trade dress are trademarks or registered trademarks of Wiley Publishing, Inc., in the United States and other countries, and may not be used without written permission. Frommer's is a trademark or registered trademark of Arthur Frommer. Used under license. All other trademarks are the property of their respective owners. Wiley Publishing, Inc., is not associated with any product or vendor mentioned in this book.

For general information on our other products and services or to obtain technical support, please contact our Customer Care Department within the U.S. at 800-762-2974, outside the U.S. at 317-572-3993, or fax 317-572-4002.

Wiley also publishes its books in a variety of electronic formats. Some content that appears in print may not be available in electronic books.

Library of Congress Control Number: 2002112139

ISBN: 0-7645-5453-0

ISSN: 1531-1805

Manufactured in the United States of America

10 9 8 7 6 5 4 3 2 1

2B/RV/RR/QS/IN

®Wiley Publishing, Inc. is a trademark of Wiley Publishing, Inc.

About the Authors

Bruce Murphy: Bruce Murphy was born in New York City, where he continues to live when not traveling and working on projects as a freelance writer.

Alessandra de Rosa: Alessandra de Rosa is a world traveler and professional tourist who has also worked for the United Nations.

Bruce and Alessandra also collaborated on *New York City For Dummies* (published by Wiley).

Dedication

To Ron Boudreau

Publisher's Acknowledgments

We're proud of this book; please send us your comments through our Dummies online registration form located at www.dummies.com/register/.

Some of the people who helped bring this book to market include the following:

Editorial

Editors: Alexis Lipsitz Flippin, Elizabeth Kuball

Cartographer: Roberta Stockwell

Editorial Supervisor: Michelle Hacker

Editorial Assistants: Melissa Bennett, Carol Strickland

Senior Photo Editor: Richard Fox

Front Cover Photo: © Marc Romanelli/ The Image Bank

Back Cover Photo: © Dave Bartruff Photography

Cartoons: Rich Tennant, www.the5thwave.com

Production

Project Coordinator: Erin Smith

Layout and Graphics: Amanda Carter, Carrie Foster, Joyce Haughey, Tiffany Muth, Barry Offringa, Jacque Schneider, Julie Trippetti, Scott Tullis

Proofreaders: Andy Hollandbeck, Susan Moritz, Carl Pierce, TECHBOOKS Production Services

Indexer: TECHBOOKS Production Services

Publishing and Editorial for Consumer Dummies

Diane Graves Steele, Vice President and Publisher, Consumer Dummies

Joyce Pepple, Acquisitions Director, Consumer Dummies

Kristin A. Cocks, Product Development Director, Consumer Dummies

Michael Spring, Vice President and Publisher, Travel

Brice Gosnell, Publishing Director, Travel

Suzanne Jannetta, Editorial Director, Travel

Publishing for Technology Dummies

Andy Cummings, Vice President and Publisher, Dummies Technology/General User

Composition Services

Gerry Fahey, Vice President of Production Services

Debbie Stailey, Director of Composition Services

Contents at a Glance

Maps at a Glance

Table of Contents

Introduction

So you've decided to visit Italy. *Molto bene!* But where will you go? The Eternal City of Rome? The Serene Republic of Venice? The Renaissance glory of Florence? The charming hill towns of Tuscany? The dramatic island of Sicily? What interests you most — paintings, sculptures, frescoes, ancient ruins, baroque churches, beaches, vineyards, food, fashion, grand *palazzi,* natural beauty, opera?

That's the problem with visiting Italy: You have far too many wonderful things to see and choices to make. And to make it that much harder, Italians pride themselves on being very individualistic, so each region has its own particular character and flavor. This applies to each city within each region, each neighborhood within each city, and so on.

It seems that everyone wants to visit Italy these days, especially because of the tremendous efforts (both public and private) to restore, refurbish, and modernize the country to celebrate the Papal Jubilee in 2000. These efforts have saved monuments from years of neglect and made Italy even more glorious. In addition, you'll find an even greater awareness of visitors' needs, with many attractions staying open late in summer and accommodations offering more (and improved) services. A language barrier remains, of course — unless you know Italian — but that's hardly insurmountable if you remember a few key words and phrases. You'll find the Italian people warm and welcoming and ready to help ease you into *la dolce vita.*

About This Book

With a history stretching from the dawn of time through the Roman Empire, the Middle Ages, the Renaissance, and up to the new Europe, Italy offers too much to see in one visit, unless your visit is a long one, and we mean *really* long. Whether you're a first-timer or making a repeat visit to see sights you missed the first go-round, *Italy For Dummies,* 2nd Edition, is designed to give you all the information you need to help you make savvy, informed decisions about your trip.

Some people spend more time planning their trip than they do taking it. We know your time is valuable, and Italy has too much to see to waste a lot of time sorting out the endless details. So here we happily do the work for you, to help ease you painlessly into a memorable Italian vacation. Unlike some travel guides that read more like a phone-book-style directory listing everything and anything, this book cuts to the chase. We've done the legwork for you, offering our expertise and not-so-humble opinions to help you make the right choices for your trip. This book is a reference work as well as a guidebook — the place where you can quickly look up information as you travel and that you can refer to again and again.

Conventions Used in This Book

The structure of this book is nonlinear: You can open it at any point and delve into the subject at hand. The information is concentrated, not spread out all over the map, and we use icons to guide you toward particular kinds of tips and advice (see "Icons Used in This Book" later in this Introduction for a full list).

We list the hotels, restaurants, and sights alphabetically, not jumbled up by area, with prices and our frank evaluations. We use this series of abbreviations for credit cards in our hotel and restaurant reviews:

AE: American Express

DC: Diners Club

MC: MasterCard

V: Visa

Note that Discover is not listed. The Discover Card is unknown in Italy, so having one or more of the big three — American Express, Visa, MasterCard — is best.

How This Book Is Organized

The book is broken down into eight parts. The first two parts cover everything you need to consider to plan your trip and get organized. The other parts of the book concern the several regions of Italy that we've chosen to cover, which are the major tourist destinations and their environs, as well as the island of Sicily. You can read each of these parts independently if you want to zero in right away on the areas that attract you. Following are brief summaries of each of the parts.

Part 1: Getting Started

Part I gives you a preview of your choices in Italy. Think of it as our rundown of the best of Italy. In this part, we give you a flavor of the country, climate, special events, and the particular aspects that make traveling in Italy unlike traveling elsewhere. We also suggest some itineraries in case you don't want the hassle of working out your own. Likewise, we help you come up with a workable budget and provide some advice on cutting costs.

Part II: Ironing Out the Details

This part takes you through the nuts and bolts of your journey — making the travel arrangements — that you can do through an agent, on the Internet, or on your own. We help you decide if an escorted or a guided tour is right for you and address the special concerns of families, seniors, travelers with special needs, and gays and lesbians. We also cover details like getting a passport, making reservations, and handling money.

Part III: The Eternal City: Rome

The Eternal City was magnificently spiffed up for the Papal Jubilee, and we guide you through its wonderful maze of ancient and modern treasures. We also take you on side trips to Tivoli and its villas, the ancient seaport of Ostia Antica, and the Castelli Romani.

Part IV: Florence and the Best of Tuscany and Umbria

Tuscany is currently Italy's most popular region. Ask just about anyone where he or she would like to have a little hideaway, and you can bet the answer will be "Tuscany!" Part IV deals with the cultural and artistic treasures of Renaissance Florence as well as the most appealing aspects of the surrounding Tuscan towns, such as Lucca, Pisa, Siena, and San Gimignano. It also introduces you to the beauties of Umbria, a small, green neighboring region highlighted by such famous towns as Assisi, Spoleto, and Perugia.

Part V: Venice and the Best of the Pianura Padana

La Serenissima (the Serene Republic, the old nickname of the Republic of Venice) is the mysterious and lovely city of canals that's sinking slowly year after year in the lagoon it was built upon. Part V takes you through Venice, perhaps the most magical place in the world, as well as to the top cities of the Pianura Padana: nearby Verona and Padua, and the business and fashion capital of Italy, Milan.

Part VI: Naples, Pompeii, and the Amalfi Coast

Part VI covers one of the most diverse corners of the country. Naples is as frenetic and fascinating as ever, chock-full of wonderful art, food, and people. Pompeii and Herculaneum are centers of ancient history, while the Amalfi Coast and Capri are part of one of Italy's most beautiful natural areas and most visited resorts.

Part VII: Sicily

To many, Sicily is the heart of Italy. In fact, Goethe called it the "key to everything." Part VII shows you how this intense land has changed and how it proudly retains the past. From the region's capital, Palermo, we take you around the island to Taormina, Syracuse, and Agrigento, as well as to some smaller destinations such as Segesta and Cefalù.

Part VIII: The Part of Tens

This special section is part handy reference, part troubleshooting guide, part summary of key points, and part signpost for where to go for more information.

Icons Used in This Book

Throughout this book, you'll notice these four icons intended as signposts and flags for facts and information of a particular nature or interest:

This icon signals advice on do's and don'ts, shortcuts, and how to make the most of your time.

With the Heads Up icon, we tell you about tourist traps, pitfalls, rip-offs, and things and places to avoid.

If you're bringing your children along, look for the Kid Friendly icon to read about venues that families love. When the icon is used in conjunction with a restaurant listing, it means that high chairs and *mezza porzione* (half portions) are available. When it's used with a hotel listing, it means that the staff is ready to meet your children's special needs.

This icon signals a way to save money, as well as special deals that you shouldn't overlook.

Where to Go from Here

Now you can dig in wherever you want. If you've already decided which cities you're going to visit (maybe you've even bought your plane tickets), you can get down to selecting hotels, sights, and restaurants. But if you first need to decide where in Italy you want to go, start with Chapter 1.

Part I
Getting Started

The 5th Wave   By Rich Tennant

Magnifico!

Molto bello!

"I insisted they learn some Italian.
I couldn't stand the idea of standing
in front of the Trevi Fountain and
hearing, 'gosh', 'wow', and 'far out'."

In this part . . .

So you know you want to go to Italy, but exactly when and exactly where? What sort of weather are you hoping for? Do you want to see the major destinations and have to deal with tourist hordes? Or are you looking for off-the-beaten-path places where you can relax in relative solitude? How much can you afford to spend? In this part, we sort through your options, showing the advantages and drawbacks of each choice and mentioning special considerations. We even suggest smart choices to reduce the cost and enjoy your trip even more. (We also list less-expensive hotels and restaurants throughout the book and offer tips for pinching a euro here and there without sacrificing.)

In Chapter 1, we highlight Italy's most interesting features so that you can choose what you like the most. In Chapter 2, we describe the characteristics of each region covered in this book and the best season in which to travel. We also give you a calendar of the most important festivals and events and tips on planning your itinerary. If you don't want to plan your own trip, you can follow one of the five itineraries we provide in Chapter 3. In Chapter 4, we deal with budget-related questions, and in Chapter 5, we list some tips for travelers with special interests and needs.

Chapter 1

Discovering the Best of Italy

● ●

In This Chapter

▶ Gaining an Italian perspective

▶ Savoring Italy's culture and cuisine

▶ Shopping for that quintessential Italian memento

▶ Reveling in the country's natural beauty

▶ Reviewing a brief history of Italy

● ●

*I*taly was probably the first place in the world to become a tourist destination. It has been a pilgrimage site ever since Rome ascended as the seat of papal power. In the 15th century, artists and scholars of the northern Renaissance were drawn to the country's burgeoning centers of art and learning, and disseminated a new way of thinking — humanism — to the rest of Europe. In the 19th century, Americans made taking the *Grand Tour* — the classic, months-long, European tour undertaken by the rich and satirized by Mark Twain in *The Innocents Abroad* — a rite of passage for the well-heeled. Anyone who has seen a Merchant-Ivory film (*A Room with a View,* for one) knows that Italy was among the most popular stops along the Grand Tour.

Italy today remains a giant cultural and religious pilgrimage site. But even more, it retains an almost mythical status in the minds of many who believe its groundbreaking artistic heritage, voluptuous natural beauty, deceptively simple yet elegant cuisine, and *la dolce vita* perspective have no equals on earth. But this is no cookie-cutter homogenous culture. From the Teutonic undertones in the Dolomites mountain range in the north to the earthy sensuousness of Sicily in the south, Italy offers a fantastic range of natural and cultural attractions. Selecting your destinations from among these riches is a real challenge, whether you're a first-timer or a regular. In *Italy For Dummies,* 2nd Edition, we give you our vision of the best Italy has to offer.

Where Modern Civilization Began

In Italy, history is present in everyday life everywhere you go, but the remains of the Roman and Greek civilizations are probably the most striking relics from ancient times. In Rome, you'll find the bare bones of the **Colosseum (Colosseo),** the ancient theater/stadium where hundreds of men fought with ferocious animals to amuse the crowds — among other popular sports and games. You can take a stroll in the impressive archaeological park of the **Roman Forum (Foro Romano),** the **Imperial Forums (Fori Imperiali),** and the **Palatine Hill (Palatino),** which cover much of the ancient center of Imperial Rome: its main street and temples, its marketplace, and its most exclusive residential area. The **Pantheon** is a still-perfect Roman temple that was transformed into a church during Christian times. And nearby Rome is **Ostia Antica,** the ancient seaport that's now a massive archaeological site.

In Verona, you can attend an opera in the **Roman Amphitheater (Anfiteatro Romano),** giving life to the ancient ruins. The cities of **Herculaneum (Ercolano)** and **Pompeii,** on the other hand, are monuments to a lost culture that was smothered by lava, volcanic ash, and pumice during the A.D. 79 eruption of Vesuvius; the volcanic inundation eerily preserved the sites to a degree that is unique for ancient ruins. Sicily boasts even more Roman and Greek sites, paramount among them the magnificent **Greek temples of Agrigento.** In **Syracuse (Siracusa)** and **Segesta,** Greek tragedies are still performed in the amphitheaters where Greek colonists who founded these cities saw them more than 2,000 years ago. Performances are also mounted in **Taormina** in a fabulous ancient theater overlooking the sea and with views of Mount Etna.

Paintings: The Old Masters Live On

There's something about seeing paintings at their original source of origin, rather than in an institution in a faraway place, that makes the visitor's connection to the painter and the era that much more profound. What's amazing is that even though collectors pillaged Italy for centuries, carrying off its treasures to remote points of the globe, the country still contains a rich trove of homegrown masterpieces. If you gave each truly great painting and fresco and mosaic and sculpture in Italy your full attention, you'd return home without a spot of color from the glorious Italian sun.

Begin your tour of masterpieces by gazing upward in the Vatican's **Sistine Chapel (Cappella Sistina),** whose breathtaking ceiling frescoes by Michelangelo were freshly (and controversially) restored in the 1990s and now glow with vivid color. The Sistine Chapel is but one of the many great works in the **Vatican Museums (Musei Vaticani).** In **St. Peter's Basilica (Basilica di San Pietro),** you can't miss the unearthly beauty of Michelangelo's *Pietà.*

The Regions of Italy

The etiquette of standing in line

Italian rules for lining up at museums differ from what you may be used to. You may think that people are packed together, trying to push their way through, but each person is more or less aware of who was there first. Even if the mass of people doesn't look like a line, it's sort of structured like one. Note the faces of who's around you when you arrive so you know where you stand, and be ready to slightly modify your posture so the person behind you knows that *you* know when it's your turn. (Get used to the fact that body language is important in Italy!)

In Rome, dozens of churches hold wonderful paintings that never travel to foreign museums or shows (among them **Santa Maria sopra Minerva** and **Santa Maria del Popolo**), and hundreds more are scattered throughout the country. For example, Padua's **Cappella degli Scrovegni** contains a cycle of marvelous Giotto frescoes (restored in 2001), and Assisi's **Basilica of St. Francis (Basilica di San Francesco)** — recently restored and reopened after suffering severe damage from earthquakes in 1997 — contains Giotto's celebrated fresco cycle on the life of St. Francis.

During high season, you may have to grit your teeth and stand in long lines at Venice's **Academy Gallery (Gallerie dell'Accademia).** Thanks to a newly installed system at Florence's **Uffizi Gallery (Galleria degli Uffizi),** however, you can reserve tickets ahead and avoid the lines. Lines or not, the treasures inside both are more than worth the wait. Virtually every Italian master from the Renaissance onward is represented (Titian, Veronese, Tintoretto, Andrea del Sarto, Raphael, Leonardo, Perugino, Cimabue, Botticelli, and Bellini, to name a few). In Florence's **Accademia Gallery (Galleria dell'Accademia),** you will find Michelangelo's unsurpassed *David.*

Architecture: From Ruins to Rococo

Italian architecture encompasses a vast array of styles, each magnificently represented — from Roman and Greek ruins to the finest examples of the Romanesque, medieval, Gothic, Renaissance, baroque, and rococo.

In a country full of spectacular *duomos* (cathedrals), basilicas, and *chiese* (churches), Rome's **St. Peter's Basilica (Basilica di San Pietro)** is the largest and most imposing, crowned by Michelangelo's dome. The marble beauty of Florence's **Duomo** (with its dome by Brunelleschi), as well as its **Baptistry (Battistero),** and **Bell Tower (Campanile)** by Giotto, rival Siena's **Duomo** and **Battistero** as the top must-sees in Tuscany. In addition to ancient monuments and ruins, many Italian cities boast monumental *piazze* (squares), with beautiful buildings surrounding a fountain or ruin and denying the passage of time. A few of the best are

Rome's **Piazza San Pietro, Piazza di Spagna,** and **Piazza Navona;** Florence's **Piazza della Signoria;** and Venice's **Piazza San Marco.**

If you don't know a baptistry from a basilica or a loggia from a lozenge, see the appendix.

Every Italian city seems to have a famous symbolic landmark, like Rome's **Colosseum (Colosseo)** and Florence and Siena's **Duomos.** In Pisa, of course, it's the **Leaning Tower,** the delicate marble bell tower that has been tipping for centuries. The 13 noble towers of **San Gimignano** (remaining from the original 70 or so) are the source of its nickname, the "Manhattan of Tuscany." Venice's **St. Mark's Square (Piazza San Marco)** and its fantastical **St. Mark's Basilica (Basilica di San Marco)** are among the most recognizable public spaces in the world. And Naples's **Castle of the Egg (Castel dell'Ovo)** rises against the surrounding gulf, one of the largest and most scenic harbors in Italy.

The variety of Italy's architecture from region to region is amazing. In Tuscany and Umbria, the picturesque hill towns are like unique works of sculpture. Venice has a style all its own, including the delicate and almost mystical **Venetian Gothic** — reflected in the water, the buildings are even more magical. You can also see the explosive **Sicilian Barocco,** a captivating and ornate style that is found in many cities in Sicily and contrasts with the stark beauty of Norman architecture in Palermo.

Food and Drink: The Bounty of the Cucina Italiana

Italians talk about eating the way other people talk about . . . well, other things. Indeed, Italian food constitutes one of the world's great cuisines, and variations of Italian traditional dishes have become fundamental parts of other cultures. What would the world be like without pizza, that specialty of Naples; pasta in its many forms and sauces; espressos and cappuccinos; gelati; and Chianti Classico, Lambrusco, and Asti Spumante?

You can have a bad meal in any country, but in Italy you really have to work hard to find one. To satisfy your hunger in Italy, stop into one of the innumerable *pizzerie,* trattorie, and *osterie.* The choices can be overwhelming, so throughout this book we recommend sure-fire restaurants where, for a reasonable amount of money, you can satisfy your hunger and quench your thirst.

A taste of the land, region by region

Italian cuisine is really many different styles of cooking that vary in subtle and not-so-subtle ways from region to region. Of course, you'll find spaghetti, penne, tagliatelle, and innumerable other varieties of fresh pasta *everywhere* in Italy — prepared with *vongole* (clams) in the south, *cinghiale* (wild boar sauce) in Tuscany, sardines in Sicily, and an abundance of seafood in Venice. You can also find fresh filled pasta, such as tortellini, ravioli, and lasagne — the richest pasta specialties of all. For Italians, fresh filled pasta is reserved for special days, but as a visitor you can indulge any day you choose.

Neapolitan pizza, the *real* thing, the original from which all other pizzas have descended (and we mean *descended*), is lovingly prepared with fresh tomato, locally produced buffalo-milk mozzarella, and anchovies. ***Beware:*** This pizza may spoil you and make it hard for you to eat any lesser version.

As for dessert, the Italians continue their culinary brilliance. Don't miss the local *gelato* (rich, creamy ice cream), *granita* (frozen coffee or lemon ice and, in Sicily, almond ice), creamy *zabaglione* (made with sugar, egg yolks, and Marsala wine), or *tiramisù* (layers of mascarpone cheese and espresso-soaked ladyfingers).

Of course, all Italian cooks share one thing in common: proximity to some of the finest locally grown and produced foodstuffs in the world: sublime olive oils and herbed vinegars; delicious fresh fruits and vegetables like grapes, figs, and tomatoes; locally made cheeses such as mozzarella, including the famous *mozzarella di bufala* (buffalo mozzarella) and *parmigiano reggiano* (the original Parmesan cheese), which makes the commercial stuff taste like sawdust; and cured meats, such as the incomparable *prosciutto di Parma* air-cured ham.

Check out the appendix if you can't tell cannelloni from calzone or pesto from polenta.

A taste of the grape

Italy is also the homeland of some of the best wines in the world. From the world-famous Chianti to crisp Frascati to *Lachrymae Christi* (Tears of Christ, a wine made from grapes grown on the slopes of Mount Vesuvius), you're sure to find a flavor that pleases your palate. In the introduction to the restaurant section in each chapter, we give you suggestions for some of the best local wines.

Made in Italy: Shopping Around

Italy is famous for its style and for the care it puts into crafting goods, whether leather shoes, exquisite glassware, or ceramic plates. And not only are Italian goods tops in quality, but you can also expect to save money on big-name Italian brands while you're here, especially if the exchange rates are favorable.

The etiquette of drinking

Don't expect to order a martini before dinner. In restaurants, but more particularly in trattorie, _osterie,_ and _pizzerie,_ you probably won't find a full bar, because Italians simply don't drink liquor before dinner. And unless they're in a pub, Italians don't drink alcohol at all without eating something. You're likely to find liquor in larger, more touristy restaurants, where you can ask for a scotch and water and won't be rewarded with a perplexed stare. Elsewhere, follow the "when in Rome" rule: Start with wine and have a _grappa_ (a clear brandy) or an _amaro_ (a 60– to 80-proof bitter drink, made with herbs) _after_ your meal.

Getting the goods

Although you can find many Italian designer-goods in the United States, plenty of interesting things rarely make it out of the country. An example is housewares: Alessi and other manufacturers produce an incredible range of cool-looking coffeemakers, corkscrews, kitchen implements, and every conceivable device you may need. Glassware is similarly varied. Italians are also crazy about accessories. Look for a big range of fountain pens, watches, sunglasses, gloves, and other tools of personal style-building.

You can certainly save some money buying Italian clothes in Italy, but you can really save on Italian shoes. You can get a nice pair of good-quality leather-soled shoes for under $100.

Only in Italy

Alas, one of Italy's greatest products — food — isn't something you can bring home, given most customs regulations. But there are many other specialties from which to choose. Venice is known for blown glass, Florence for leather goods, and both for beautiful paper and lace. All roads lead to Rome, where you can find shops that sell antique furniture, prints, paintings, glassware, and china. Hand-painted ceramics are also an Italian specialty. Deruta in Umbria; Vietri in Campania; Santo Stefano, Sciacca, and Caltagirone in Sicily; and Faenza in Emilia-Romagna (famed for _faïence/majolica_) produce colorful ceramics of every shape and size. At each of the major shopping points, we help steer you toward the good deals and away from the tourist traps. So if you buy a glow-in-the-dark plastic gondola, it's because you really want one!

Bella Italia: Italy's Natural Beauty

Italy has been a settled, cultivated, civilized land for thousands of years, so there isn't much real wilderness left. But you'll find the country has natural beauty in abundance, as well as lovely places where human constructions fit harmoniously with the land.

Buon giorno, baby!

Italians offer a salutation whenever they enter shops, so follow suit and say *Buon giorno* (bwon *jawr*-know; "Good day") as you enter. Doing so gives you the double advantage of making your presence known (you're given attention as soon as it's your turn) and making the shop owner well disposed toward you. If you change your mind, just say *Grazie* (*grah*-tzieh; "Thank you") and exit.

You feel this beauty when you inhale the enigmatic calm of the **Venetian lagoon** from the abandoned island of Torcello or from the tip of the slim, sandy island of the Lido. (It's balanced by the infamous odors and humidity of Venice in summer, and that shiny stuff reflecting the basilica after the high water has abated is mud.) You will instantly fall in love with the landscapes of **Tuscany** and **Umbria,** whose rolling green plains, cypress trees, olive groves, walled hill towns, and terraced vineyards look as if they were lifted from a Renaissance painting. And who can resist the **Amalfi Coast (Costiera Amalfitana),** the gorgeous coastline south of Naples rising at breathtaking heights above the sea? This sea-coast is cut by deep gorges, where towns like Positano and Amalfi nest on the steep rocks. Just 4.8km (3 miles) off the Amalfi Coast is the island of **Capri,** where Roman emperors like Tiberius once sought amusement. The star of Capri is the stunning **Blue Grotto (Grotta Azzurra).**

If your interest in nature is truly elemental, note that Italy boasts two major volcanoes, one apparently sleeping and the other very much alive. You can climb eerie **Mount Vesuvius,** which towers over Naples, to admire the view and wonder what's happening in the depth of its cavities. You won't find a single tree on the upper slopes, and you'll be hot and thirsty after your climb, but it's an awesome experience. In Sicily, you find the imposing beauty of **Mount Etna,** smoking under the snow on its summit (it's three times the height of Vesuvius). When you see this volcano, you'll know why the Greeks believed Hephaestus, the god of fire, lived under it.

Don't forget that all around this long peninsula are beautiful beaches and the perfect blue waters of the Mediterranean!

An Italian History Lesson, in Brief

If Mesopotamia is the cradle of civilization, Italy is the cradle of Western culture (well, there was Greece, too, but that's another book). The Roman Empire borrowed heavily from both Mesopotamia and Greece as well as from every other culture that it absorbed. The principles of Roman civilization and the Renaissance still play a great role in our modern ways of thinking, our values, and our institutions. Summarizing Italy's history in anything less than a book-length study is impossible, but you'll need at least a taste of it in order to understand what you're looking at as you explore the country.

Around 1000 B.C., Italy began developing into the vital cultural center it would become for the following 3,000 years. The **Etruscans** had already developed a sophisticated culture in southern Tuscany when Rome was still a collection of shepherd's huts. But then, they were integrated in the **Roman Republic,** founded in 509 B.C. The Roman government was headed by two consuls and a senate, all controlled by the upper or *patrician* (aristocratic) class. The *plebeians* (working class) later obtained their own council and were represented by tribunes.

The Romans have been called the "Prussians of the ancient world" for their militarism, and they first showed their might in two decades of bloody war against Carthage (in North Africa) and Hannibal over possession of Sicily. After defeating Carthage, Rome spread its influence across the Mediterranean.

The end of the Roman Republic and the beginning of the **Roman Empire** occurred largely through the antagonism of two great generals, **Pompey** and **Julius Caesar,** who became a tyrant after his defeat of Pompey. Following Caesar's murder on the Ides of March in 44 B.C., civil war ensued and was won by Caesar's grandnephew and adopted son, Octavian, who became the first emperor, **Caesar Augustus.** His regime turned Rome into a glowing marble city the likes of which the world had never seen, but he was followed by a string of mostly debauched and even insane rulers: **Tiberius, Caligula, Claudius** (an exception, even though his third wife, Nero's mother, was also his niece), and **Nero.**

In the early centuries of the first millennium, the empire reached its greatest size, extending from the Caspian Sea in the east to Scotland in the west. However, a chaotic period of war, plague, barbarian advances, and inflation spelled the beginning of the bitter end. As **Emperor Constantine** converted to Christianity and founded Constantinople in A.D. 330, Rome's wealth shifted east, and, shortly after, the empire was swept by Barbarian invasions: the **Goths** sacked Rome in A.D. 410; the Huns came next under **Attila,** and were followed by the **Vandals** of North Africa. In A.D. 476, the German chief Odoacer deposed the western Roman emperor, in effect signaling the end of the once invincible Roman Empire.

Independent local governments developed along the peninsula, while Rome and central Italy became the seat of the Christian Catholic church: the Papal States, ruled by the worldly popes. The French king **Charlemagne** tried to revive the Western Empire in A.D. 800 when the pope crowned him emperor but instead found the forerunner of the **Holy Roman Empire.** This historical oddity profoundly affected Italy's history during the Middle Ages and Renaissance. The German emperor was elected by the German princes, but only the pope could crown him Holy Roman Emperor. For the next 1,000 years, Italian politics were defined by the struggle among the Holy Roman Emperor (who was German), the Pope, Spain, and France (aspiring to the imperial crown). During the height of the Renaissance, city-states like Florence and Siena sought the help of these powerful large states in their local wars, thus inviting foreign intervention in Italy.

In the 13th century, Italy was the crossroads of the Mediterranean; a banking and commercial culture was based on the great seafaring empires of Venice and Genoa and powerful Florence. It was here at this time that the Renaissance was born, an explosion of magnificent artistry and the spread of *humanism,* a new philosophy promoting the dignity of the human individual and developing secularism. Only in the south and in Sicily, where the **Normans** (Viking descendants) founded a kingdom in the 11th century, did medieval feudalism take root. Later, the Spanish rulers used feudalism for their own political aims and induced it to hang on — one of the causes of north-south cultural and economic disparities that still persist.

The *Risorgimento* (resurgence) movement, secret societies such as the Carbonari, and revolutionaries like Giuseppe Mazzini and Giuseppe Garibaldi brought about Italian unification in the 19th century (completed in 1870). A liberal state was formed around the House of Savoy, the rulers of Piedmont and Sardinia. Between 1870 and World War I, Italy saw massive emigration to the United States and Argentina. The country was tempted by territorial promises to join the Allies in 1915 (mainly in order to get Venice back from the Austrians). After World War I, discontent and economic depression helped Mussolini rise to power. Mussolini's imperialist adventures abroad were matched by repression at home, and his alliance with the Nazis was disastrous. Italians turned against him in 1943 and then continued in World War II on the Allied side while suffering under German occupation.

Italy rebuilt after the war and became a modern democratic state. Today, unemployment is a persistent problem, and many Italians — even those educated in such professions as law, academics, and architecture — work for free for years just to get a foot on the employment ladder. Corruption has also been a nagging problem, but in the 1990s, a series of scandals and dramatic trials of key Mafia leaders led to major housecleaning. Still, Italy is famous for its numerous changes of government in the postwar period; its current prime minister was reelected after being ousted in 1994 during corruption investigations. The ramifications of the ongoing European unification are yet to be seen.

Chapter 2

Deciding When and Where to Go

In This Chapter

▶ Exploring Italy's main areas of interest

▶ Knowing the right time to visit

▶ Scanning a calendar of the best festivals and events

*I*n this book, we give you lots of options from which to choose, taking you through the various and varied regions, cities and towns, attractions and distractions, cuisines, and subcultures, as well as giving you the lowdown on the best times of the year to travel.

Italy has never been better: Motivated by the Papal Jubilee of the year 2000, a great wave of renovation fever swept the country, and many museums, attractions, hotels, and restaurants have been handsomely spruced up and smartly reorganized, all of which makes it that much easier to enjoy the array of choices ahead of you — whether you're sipping a cup of espresso on Venice's St. Mark's Square or a glass of Chianti in a trattoria in Florence, visiting the Uffizi Gallery in Florence or the Sistine Chapel in Rome, taking in a performance in the Greek-Roman theater in Taormina, or making a day-trip to the isle of Capri. Wherever you go, you'll meet friendly people and find yourself immersed in a fascinating culture — one in which we guarantee you'll never starve and never find yourself bored.

Checking Out Italy's Points of Interest

In this book, we've selected the best Italy has to offer, those places you simply won't want to miss. Following is a quick sketch of each area included in the book. Of course, there is much, much more — a whole country's worth! We know many people who keep coming back after their first "cover-it-all" trip to Italy to explore further and pursue their special tastes and inclinations. Lucky them — and lucky you!

To view the makeup of Italy by region, check out the map "The Regions of Italy" in Chapter 1.

Romancing Rome: From the Colosseum to Vatican City

Rome is the capital of modern Italy, as it was the capital of the vast Roman Empire in ancient times. It's saturated with fantastic things to see from those ancient times, most of which are world famous: the **Colosseum (Colosseo),** the **Roman Forum (Foro Romano)** and **Imperial Forums (Fori Imperiali), St. Peter's Basilica (Basilica di San Pietro)** and the **Vatican Museums (Musei Vaticani),** the **Pantheon** . . . the list goes on and on. There are even things to see underground, like the **Catacombs** (including the famous ones on the **Appian Way**) and a number of archaeological excavations.

At one time or another, you've probably used the expression "When in Rome, do as the Romans do." Well, there are many fun things you can do around Rome that Romans have been doing for centuries. For example, you can explore the **Castelli Romani** (the hill towns at the east of Rome), where it's pleasurably cool in summer and the food and wine are superb. You can also immerse yourself in ancient times at **Ostia Antica**'s ruins near the sea or at **Hadrian's Villa** in Tivoli at the north of Rome, where you can also visit the cool fountain gardens of the Renaissance **Villa d'Este** and enjoy a nice meal.

Rome is a major modern city: It offers a varied and exciting nightlife, a huge selection of restaurants, plentiful comfortable hotels, and world-famous shops. But with it come big-city problems. The traffic in Rome is as eternal as the Eternal City itself: Buses and metros are crowded at rush hour, and the streets are filled with pedestrians and motorbikes jostling for space.

An important feature of Rome is its position, which makes it easy to use as a base for a visit either farther south to Naples and the Amalfi Coast (Sicily is a bit of a stretch) or north into Tuscany and Umbria (Venice is a bit of a stretch). See Part III for our coverage of Rome and its environs.

Exploring Florence and the best of Tuscany and Umbria

No question: **Tuscany** is *the* destination for Americans, who, like many travelers around the world, are attracted to the lush Italian countryside (where most people would love to own a villa). **Florence,** with its beautiful **Duomo (cathedral)** and museums overflowing with art treasures — such as the **Uffizi Gallery (Galleria degli Uffizi)** — is the main city in Tuscany and has been drawing visitors for centuries. Other important cities in Tuscany include **Pisa,** with its newly reopened **Leaning Tower** (Galileo Galilei made his experiments with gravity here, a few centuries back); **Siena** (where the exciting **Palio delle Contrade** horse race occurs twice a year); **San Gimignano,** with its medieval towers; and **Lucca,** a medieval and Renaissance jewel. Also in Tuscany is the region of **Chianti,** renowned for its beautiful hill towns and delicious food and wine. A little farther afield, and actually in the region of Liguria, are five ancient fishing/farming villages nestled along a stretch of coast that rivals the more famous **Amalfi Coast** in steepness and natural beauty: the **Cinque Terre.**

Neighboring Tuscany is the smaller region of **Umbria.** Its attractions include the monuments and chocolate of **Perugia,** a city known for its medieval architecture and culinary traditions; the churches and monasteries of **Assisi,** with the famous frescoes by Giotto celebrating the life of St. Francis; and the medieval town of **Spoleto,** acclaimed for its music-and-arts festival as well as its architectural beauty.

Although you may not find the climate of Tuscany and Umbria ideal (it's baking hot in summer and chilly and damp in winter), its main attractions are hardly a secret, so you may have to vie for space with people from all over the planet. However, most people prefer to give up almost anything else in Italy before they cut this region from their itinerary. See Part IV for our coverage of Florence, Tuscany, and Umbria.

Viewing Venice and the best of the Pianura Padana

Many artists and writers have been utterly smitten by **La Serenissima (the Serene Republic),** as Venice called itself when it was an independent state. Imagine riding along the **Grand Canal** in a gondola maneuvered by a skilled oarsman, passing beneath bridge after bridge, seeing magnificent *palazzi* and medieval buildings mirrored on the lagoon. No place promotes dreaming like **Venice.** The **Doge's Palace (Palazzo Ducale), St. Mark's Basilica (Basilica di San Marco),** and **St. Mark's Square (Piazza San Marco)** are magical, and the **Academy Gallery (Gallerie dell'Accademia)** offers countless art treasures.

Although summer humidity, crowds (which completely block the narrow streets on weekends and in high season, with the result that you have to line up as at the post office and wait your turn to pass), and the stench of the canals in hot weather can be a bit much, Venice is always captivating. If you're planning an especially romantic vacation, don't miss Venice.

The surrounding **Pianura Padana** region is also full of interesting sights. **Verona** is a delightfully romantic town where (supposedly) Romeo and Juliet lived out their tragic affair. Speaking of tragedy, you can also see an opera in the Roman amphitheater in Verona, still in use after a couple thousand years. Nearby **Padua,** another charming Renaissance town, features Giotto's most celebrated frescoes in the **Chapel of the Scrovegni (Cappella degli Scrovegni)** and is the perfect start for a captivating river cruise toward Venice. See Part V for our coverage of Venice and the Pianura Padana.

Visiting Naples, Pompeii, and the Amalfi Coast

Naples seems more Italian than the rest of Italy, if such a thing is possible. It's an intense city, perhaps too much so for some people. Naples's somewhat sorry reputation has improved markedly in recent years, thanks to a steady program of renovations, and the city is full of often overlooked art and cultural treasures. The **National Archaeological Museum (Museo Archeologico Nazionale)** is the richest in Italy, and the many churches and museums hold important Renaissance art. Naples is also the jumping-off point for exploring some of southern Italy's most popular sites.

The **Amalfi Coast** is a scenic area with beautiful seaside resorts, such as Positano and Amalfi, nestled along plunging cliffs. Closer to Naples, **Herculaneum** and **Pompeii,** Roman cities wiped out by Vesuvius in A.D. 79, are among the country's most important archaeological attractions. And, of course, there's **Mount Vesuvius** itself, the volcano's eerie presence towering over Naples.

Off the coast of Naples — less than an hour away — is one of the most famous islands in Italy. **Capri,** a green hill that rises steeply from the sea, has been a trendy resort since the days of the Roman Empire, when Tiberius and Caligula sought "amusement" there. See Part VI for our coverage of Naples and the Amalfi Coast.

Seeing Sicily

The farther south you go, the more intense and lively Italy becomes. **Sicily**'s rugged beauty, bountiful waters, and rich soils have been fought over for millennia. The region's reputation as headquarters of the Mafia and its bloody vendettas used to scare people away, but a government crackdown has spawned a Sicilian renaissance, and even though getting there takes extra time, it's worth the trip. You won't find such an exciting and pleasing mix of sights, cultures, and flavors anywhere else in Italy. Early Greek settlers left behind the magnificent temples in **Agrigento,** in the appropriately named **Valley of the Temples,** and in **Segesta.** The Normans (a name that comes from Norsemen) created a uniquely beautiful style of art in the capital of **Palermo** as well as all over the island. You can also admire the splendors of the Sicilian baroque and Liberty (Art Nouveau) styles in Palermo. The towering snow-capped volcano **Mount Etna** dominates the island and in particular the fashionable city of

Taormina, which is home to both well-preserved ancient sites and a modern resort. Down the coast is **Syracuse,** with its dark and fascinating history — the early part of which is still visible in the excavations of the **Archaeological Zone** and on the island of **Ortigia.**

See Part VII for our coverage of Sicily.

Knowing the Secret of the Seasons

When you're planning your trip to Italy, consider the weather during each season to best determine the right time for you to schedule your vacation.

Italy's climate

In general, Italy has a warm, dry climate, with well-defined seasons. Spring and fall are the most pleasant times, with mild weather and moderate temperatures; summer is quite hot, especially in the south; and winter can get quite cold in the north.

Of course, because the peninsula is 1,100km (700 miles) long, the weather can vary greatly between north and south, from the rugged limestone Dolomites to Sicily's Scirocco-swept fields (Scirocco are strong windstorms that blow in from Africa). Because the Apennine mountains run down the middle of Italy, the weather also varies between the coast and inland areas.

 You know your limits, so if you find waiting in line for two hours in the hot sun to get into the Vatican Museums unendurable, don't come to Italy in July or August. Make sure that you check the average temperatures we list in Table 2-1.

Table 2-1	Italy's Average High and Low Temperatures							
Region	Winter Average Low/ Average High				Summer Average Low/ Average High			
	°C	°F	°C	°F	°C	°F	°C	°F
Florence	2.5	36.5	11	52	16.4	61.5	29.7	85
Naples	4.9	41	13.2	56	17.6	64	28.5	83
Palermo	10.6	51	15.4	60	22	71	27.7	82
Rome	3	37	13	55	16.1	61	29.9	86
Venice	1.5	35	8.3	47	15.4	60	24.5	79

Remember that official temperatures are taken at the airports; the temperatures in towns are higher. In summer, places near the sea (such as Naples), even if farther south, are sometimes cooler than places farther north. For example, Florence, which sits in a valley, is notorious for the summer heat that reverberates off the stone *palazzi*. Nearby Siena sits atop a hill, so you won't find much shade there. The sea cools Venice somewhat, but the summers there are famous for the stench of the canals and the large crowds. And, after June, Sicily is sunstroke territory unless you're used to such conditions. Frankly, when it's hot, you may want to do as the Italians do: They either go to the beach and soak in the water, or they simply don't go anywhere.

Humidity in Italy isn't nearly as bad as it is in parts of the United States, such as the Mid-Atlantic and the Midwest. However, remember that enduring the summer in your air-conditioned office and apartment in Chicago or New York is a lot different from spending a few weeks in a (mostly) non–air-conditioned country, living out of a suitcase in a rented room.

Winters, on the other hand, are fairly mild everywhere except in the mountains and the far north. Of course, if you come from Florida, you may find it chilly!

In our opinion, the best times to visit Italy are April through June and late September through October. The worst times to visit Italy are July and August.

When to avoid the crowds

Italy used to have a well-defined off-season in winter, but more and more tourists are coming in winter, taking advantage of the off-season's lower prices, often better and more attentive service, and fewer crowds at the country's favorite attractions. (Consider that the wait to get into Florence's Uffizi in summer can last as long as three hours — if you don't reserve your tickets ahead.) During the off-season, however, you may have fewer lodging choices in some areas because of seasonal closures — most hotels and restaurants in Italy take a winter break of about two to three weeks.

We still think that Italy has a midwinter lull (February) and a spring high (around Easter), when an influx of Catholic pilgrims and large school groups from around Europe often take trips (mainly to Florence and Rome). One strategy for avoiding crowds is to choose destinations away from Rome, Venice, and Florence. Smaller towns and areas are usually untouched by pilgrims and large school groups.

In general, August is one of the least attractive months to visit Italy. The heat is at its peak, and most Italians are also on vacation, crowding destinations generally along the coast (many offices and businesses close in August, causing most Italians to take their vacation in this month), and leaving the large cities empty. If August is the only time that you can travel, however, remember that although the seashore will be crowded, you may find fewer people (and cooler temperatures) in the mountains.

Labor Day (Festa del Lavoro) is celebrated in Italy and the rest of Europe on May 1. Be prepared for businesses to be closed all across the country. Also, **Ferragosto,** which takes place on August 15, is a good holiday to know about, though it's for Italians, not visitors. The Italians, like the French, go on holiday en masse, and many shops and businesses close.

Getting the Lowdown on Italy's Special Events

Many people plan their vacations around Italy's many exciting festivals, whether celebrated across the country or in individual cities and towns. Some want to attend Venice's Carnevale or Siena's Palio so badly that they don't give a hoot about the weather or having to face an onslaught of revelers. Others want to know when all the big events are being held so that they can avoid being there during the celebrations. Either way, here's a helpful rundown of Italy's primary festivals and events — plus a few unusual choices.

January

Regata sull'Arno (Regatta on the Arno). January 1; Florence. Celebrate the new year in Firenze with a boat race. ☎ 055-23320.

Epifania (Feast of the Epiphany). January 6; countrywide. This religious holiday is very important for children, because they receive their Christmas gifts on this day, not on December 25. On the days preceding Epiphany, open-air fairs selling children's toys and gifts are held in most towns. Full of carts and stands selling gifts and sweets, the fair on Rome's Piazza Navona stays open till dawn on feast day.

Midday: When the country closes shop

Generally speaking, everything in Italy closes between lunchtime and about 4 p.m., when nobody does anything. You may find shopping at those times difficult, but you can still find a museum to prowl through. Restaurants, of course, are open at lunchtime. Keep in mind that the midday tradition of closing up shop is changing, slowly, as tourism-driven businesses adapt to visitors' schedules and expectations. As a result, many stores stay open all day long, especially in large cities.

February

Carnevale. The week before Ash Wednesday, culminating on Fat Tuesday or *Martedi Grasso;* countrywide. You can best observe this well-established holiday (formerly a pagan rite of the coming of spring) in Venice, where people dress up in spectacular costumes and participate in masked balls and a variety of events (music, concerts, fireworks, and so on) organized by the city. Contact the Venetian Tourist Office, A.P.T. Venezia, Castello 4421, 30100 Venezia (☎ **041-529-8711;** Fax: 041-523-0399) for a calendar of events. Every town in Italy celebrates Carnevale to one degree or another — at least by making *frappe,* thin slices of crunchy fried dough with powdered sugar, and *castagnole,* deep-fried balls of dough, often filled with custard. The famous parade of floats in Viareggio in Tuscany, culminates celebrations that last a whole month (☎ **0584-47-503**). In Rome, you can find concerts and organized events, as well as lots of people parading around the city (particularly along Via Veneto) in costume on Fat Tuesday evening. Call the tourist office at ☎ **06-4889-9253** or 06-4889-9255, or check www.comune.roma.it for details.

March/April

Venerdì Santo (Good Friday). Friday before Easter Sunday; countrywide. The Catholic rite of the procession of the stations of the cross *(Via Crucis)* is presented in many towns as a reenactment with costumes. In Rome, the procession takes place at night, led by the Pope, between the Colosseum and Palatine Hill. Other spectacular processions are the ones in Assisi and in several towns in Sicily.

Pasqua (Easter Benediction). Sunday, between the end of March and mid-April; countrywide. In Rome, the Pope gives his traditional benediction in Piazza San Pietro.

Scoppio del Carro (Explosion of the Cart). Easter Sunday, Florence. Florentines celebrate Easter with a bang. During morning Mass, a cart laden with fireworks covered with flowers and led by white oxen is blown up by an effigy of a dove that slides down a wire from the Duomo. ☎ **055-290-832.**

Mostra delle Azalee (Exhibition of Azaleas). A week in mid-April, weather dependent; Rome. During this exhibition, more than 3,000 azalea plants are exhibited on the Spanish Steps to celebrate the beginning of spring. Concerts are held in Trinità dei Monti at the head of the steps. ☎ **06-4889-9255** or 06-4889-9253.

Anniversario della Liberazione (Anniversary of the Liberation of Rome in 1944). April 25; Rome. This event commemorates the massacre in the Fosse Ardeatine on Via Appia perpetrated by the German occupiers: Hundreds of randomly captured Italians (including women and children) were executed in reprisal for a partisan attack. The event is commemorated by a gathering on the site. ☎ **06-4889-9255** or 06-4889-9253.

Festa di San Marco (Festival of St. Mark). April 25; Venice. This religious holiday is marked by a procession to St. Mark's Basilica in honor of the patron saint of Venice. Also, the Venetian men mark the day by giving women a red rose.

May

Festa del Lavoro (Labor Day). May 1; countrywide. The whole country shuts off for a day as every person who holds a job takes a deserved rest. Minimal services are assured in hospitals and transportation. Plan ahead and inquire at your hotel for what services are going to be available locally; you don't want to be stuck without lunch or transportation back to your hotel.

Calendimaggio. First weekend after May 1; Assisi. This pagan celebration of spring includes singing, dancing, medieval costumes, and competitions. ☎ **075-812-450.**

Concorso Ippico Internazionale (International Horse Show). Near the end of May; Rome. For this horse show, the best riders and mounts from Italy, the rest of Europe, and beyond compete in the Villa Borghese's beautiful Piazza di Siena for over 50,000€ ($45,000) in prizes. At the gate, you can buy tickets, which start at 11€ ($11) For details, contact the Federazione Italiana Sport Equestri at ☎ **06-3630-8547** or visit www.fise.it.

International Rose Show. A week in mid-May, weather dependent; Rome. As many as 5,000 roses of more than 1,000 varieties, many very rare, serve as the background to this international competition among new varieties. The show takes place in the Roseto Comunale di Valle Murcia all'Aventino. ☎ **06-4889-9255** or 06-4889-9253.

Maggio Musicale Fiorentino (Florentine Musical May). May into June; Florence. Italy's oldest and most prestigious music festival, this concert and dance series includes famous performers and world premiers. ☎ **055-211-158** or 055-213-535; Internet: www.maggiofiorentino.com. You can buy tickets online.

Regata delle Grandi Repubbliche Marinare (Regatta of the Great Maritime Republics). Second or third weekend in May; each year by turns in Venice, Amalfi, Genoa, or Pisa. These four cities take turns hosting this competition between the great Medieval Maritime Republics. For details, call the tourist office of Pisa at ☎ **050-42-291,** Venice at ☎ **041-529-8711,** or Amalfi at ☎ **089-871-107.**

Vogalonga. Second half of May; Venice. Rowers train year-round for this "long row," a major competition. ☎ 041-529-8711.

June

Festival di Spoleto (Spoleto Festival). All month; Spoleto. This program of concerts, opera, dance, and theater (formerly called the Festival dei Due Mondi) is now in its fourth decade. For details, contact the Associazione Spoleto Festival (☎ 0743-44-325; Fax: 0743-40-696; Internet: www.spoletofestival.net).

Arena di Verona (Verona Amphitheater). Beginning of June through September; Verona. This festival features opera performed in the city's well-preserved Roman arena. For details, call ☎ 045-800-5151 or check the Web at www.arena.it.

Gioco di Calcio Storico Fiorentino. June 16, 24, and 30; Florence. For the feast of San Giovanni, patron saint of Florence, Florentines hold a tournament of rough-and-tumble Renaissance soccer among the city's four traditional neighborhoods, played on Piazza di Santa Croce (packed with dirt). Fireworks are set off on the Arno River at night. ☎ 055-261-6050, 055-261-6051, or 055-261-6056.

Estate Romana (Roman Summer). Mid– to late June through August; Rome. The Roman Summer is a program of concerts, theater, special exhibits, and other events. Performances held inside Roman ruins are particularly dramatic. For details, call ☎ 06-4889-9255 or 06-4889-9253 or check on the Web at www.comune.roma.it.

Biennale di Venezia (Venice Biennial). June through October; Venice. One of the premier art expositions in the world, the Biennial takes place in odd-numbered years (2003, 2005, and so on) in the Giardini, Venezia's public park and exhibition center. ☎ 041-521-8838; Internet: www.labiennale.it.

July

Palio delle Contrade of July 2nd. June 29 through July 3; Siena. The first of the two palios, this is one of Italy's most famous spectacles. Horses and riders wearing the colors of their Sienese neighborhoods ride around Piazza del Campo in a wild, dangerous race. The event is preceded by much fanfare and pageantry lasting for days, culminating in a giant costume party all over the city the night before. Celebrations of the winner follow the final. ☎ 0577-42-209.

Festa di Santa Rosalia (Festival of St. Rosalia). July 11 through July 15; Palermo. This festival celebrates the anniversary of the rediscovery of the saint's remains in 1624. Niece of King Guglielmo II, Santa Rosalia abandoned the riches of her palace for a cave. When her remains were discovered on Mount Pellegrino and brought down through the city, the plague epidemic, which had been going on at that time, miraculously stopped. A religious procession with a decorated triumphal carriage carrying an orchestra parades through the city, and a candlelight procession ascends the mountain overlooking the harbor.

Umbria Jazz. Mid– to late July; Perugia. This is one of Europe's top jazz events. Contact the Associazone Umbria Jazz for more information (☎ 075-573-2432; Fax: 075-572-2656; Internet: www.umbriajazz.com).

Festa del Redentore (Feast of the Redeemer). Third Saturday and Sunday of July; Venice. The Feast of the Redeemer includes boating and fireworks in Venice's lagoon to mark the lifting of the plague in 1571.

August

Ferragosto. August 15; countrywide. This pagan holiday celebrates the culmination of the summer. Italians vacation on the seashore and on the mountains. Most businesses are closed that day; check your destination in advance to know what will be open.

Palio delle Contrade of August 16th. August 13 through August 17; Siena. This second *palio* is held between the finalists of the previous *palio* in July. The program is the same as the one in July, except that the number of participating *contrade* is smaller — but the celebrations are as grand as ever. ☎ 0577-42-209.

September

Venice International Film Festival. First two weeks of the month; Venice. Held at the Palazzo del Cinema on the Lido, this is one of the top film festivals in the world. Despite the proliferation of bigwigs, hangers-on, and wannabes, you can actually get tickets to screenings. Getting a room in town is another matter, however — book early. ☎ 041-521-8838; Internet: www.labiennale.it.

Regata Storica (Historic Regatta). First Sunday of September; Venice. This rowing event is held in the Grand Canal, and you need tickets to see it. ☎ 041-529-8711.

Settembre Lucchese. The whole month of September; Lucca. This opera festival celebrates the memory of Puccini in his hometown, and all his operas are performed in the original theater where they were first shown. ☎ 0583-419-689; Fax: 0583-442-505; E-mail: luccadgt@tin.it.

October

Festa di San Francesco d'Assisi (Feast of St. Francis of Assisi).
October 4; countrywide. This celebration for the patron saint of Italy is
observed in various towns and cities, notably Rome and Assisi, with
processions, special masses, and other religious events.

November

Tutti Santi (All Saints' Day). November 1; countrywide. This national
holiday is a feast honoring all Christian saints.

Presentation of Mary in the Temple. November 21; Venice. This religious
holiday is celebrated with a procession that crosses the city, including a
bridge made of boats strung across the Grand Canal at La Salute.

December

Crèche Exhibit. The three weeks before Christmas; Rome. For this
event, more than 50 nativity scenes are displayed in the Villa Giulia,
and many others are on view in churches around Rome; particularly
nice are the ones in the Basilica di Santa Maria Maggiore, Santa Maria
d'Aracoeli (see Chapter 12), Santa Maria del Popolo (Piazza del Popolo
12; ☎ 06-361-0487), and Chiesa del Gesù (Piazza del Gesù, off Via del
Plebiscito; ☎ 06-679-5131).

Christmas Blessing. December 25; Rome. On Christmas Day, the pope
blesses Rome and the world from St. Peter's Square at noon. The event
is broadcast all over the world.

New Year's Eve. December 31; countrywide. Italians love New Year's
Eve, the occasion for a big celebration. Partying reaches its climax at
midnight when the country explodes — literally — with fireworks.
There are organized public displays in some towns and cities, but
everybody gets into the act, shooting fireworks from every window and
roof of the country. By tradition, fireworks are accompanied by the symbolic throwing away of something old to mark the end of the old year
(some people get carried away — in the past, items like old TVs and
refrigerators have been thrown from upper-story windows). Watch out
for falling UFOs if you take a stroll in major cities shortly after midnight!

Planning a Cool Trip

On your visit to Italy, you may be tempted to try to cram too much into
your trip because of the wealth of things to see and do. You can, however, make your trip more comfortable and enjoyable. Here are a few
tips to help you plot a satisfying, stress-free itinerary for Italy:

✔ **Be realistic.** You know your stamina, aversion or tolerance for crowds and hot weather, level of interest in culture (just how many museums can you walk through before burnout?), and budget. Don't overextend yourself (or your kids, if they're coming along) and possibly ruin your trip.

✔ **Limit the north-south distance you cover.** If money is not an object, you can fly and see more distant destinations (fly to Venice and stay a few days, fly off to Naples and see Capri and the towns on the Amalfi Coast, and then fly down to Sicily for the final leg of your trip), but if you're planning to move by car or train, don't expect to get from one tip of the Italian peninsula to the other in one week. Keep your exploring limited, especially for your first trip to Italy — perhaps visiting only Tuscany/Umbria or Rome/Florence or Florence/Venice. Doing so is more practical and probably a lot more fun, because you'll be cutting down travel times, costs, and the attendant hassles.

✔ **Park and ride.** Throughout this book, we remind you that driving in the major cities and finding a place to park can be a major pain. Don't try it. Public transportation is highly developed in the big cities, and you don't need a car. If you happen to arrive in a big city by car, either return it to the rental agency (because you won't need it anymore) or garage it if you want to use it again when you leave. For example, you can pick up a car at Pisa's airport, drive through Tuscany's hill towns for several days, and then continue on to Florence, where you can immediately drop off the car.

✔ **Allow time for delays and serendipitous discoveries.** Italy has a reputation for being disorganized, which is partly undeserved: A positive way to look at it is that the Italians have a high tolerance for change — of bus schedules, museum hours, prices, arrangements, you name it. Don't set a schedule in which you *must* get from Florence to Venice in five hours, because traffic or a railroad delay may intervene; or, more likely, you may see a villa, a vineyard, a trattoria, a ruin, or a hill town that you just have to investigate along the way. Give yourself permission to take a little extra time out to go with the flow. Traveling is about enjoyment, not running up a list of accomplishments.

✔ **Remember that quality is more important than quantity.** Don't try to cram in so many sights and sounds that everything blurs in your mind at your return. Perhaps you've heard someone say about a trip, "I was there once but don't remember much," or you've looked at a vacation picture from years ago and said, "I know I saw this, but I just can't remember the experience." If so, you know the gap that exists between simply seeing something the time a picture was taken and really knowing that you've been there: recalling what it meant to you to stand there and experience it.

✔ **Be honest with yourself.** Perhaps our most heretical advice is this: Don't force yourself to see things you're not really interested in just because *everybody* (including us) says you should. If you're blown away by the first five rooms of Florence's Uffizi, impressed by the next five, and really dazed by the next five, leave and get some yummy gelato. Or if you'd rather shop for a neat leather purse than see one more basilica, go for it. It's your trip, your money, and your life.

Chapter 3

Five Great Italian Itineraries

M any guidebooks take a connect-the-dots approach to tourism: Here are a thousand hotels and restaurants, a ton of important and secondary sights to see, and a stack of maps . . . now go figure out your trip. This approach can leave many first-time or time-pressed travelers feeling overwhelmed and frustrated, especially in a country like Italy, which offers so much to see.

Where you should go in Italy depends, above all, upon your interests. Sometimes being self-indulgent is also being smart: If you don't like the beach, don't go there; if you get bored in museums, spend more of your time strolling along the streets or in parks and gardens and lounging in cafes. One thing you'll discover is that, as D. H. Lawrence observed, "Italy does not judge." Choose what you like from the endless banquet that Italy provides, and feel free to enjoy.

Okay, so you're just like everyone else and want to see a whole bunch of Italy anyway, even though your time is limited. You still have to make choices, such as how many hours you can stand in a museum (if you're zonked out from the last one, you're just wasting your time in the next, regardless of how good the art is), how much walking and standing in line in the hot sun you can take, and how much time you'd like to set aside for sitting and contemplating what you've seen, resting your weary feet, and breathing in the beautiful surroundings. You decide.

In this chapter, we give you some sample itineraries that won't break your budget or your back. If you choose to develop a tour to fit your special interests, we give you a couple of suggestions for that, too. Read on.

Exploring Italy in One Week

Use the following itinerary to make the most of your week in Italy, but be aware that you'll see only the highlights of this rich country.

Fly into Rome, check into your hotel and take a rest. Then get to Termini train station and take the three-hour **ATAC bus tour** to get a general city orientation (see Chapter 12 for details). The bus makes slightly extended stops at **St. Peter's (San Pietro)** and the **Colosseum.** Following the tour, enjoy a leisurely stroll and dinner in the funky medieval neighborhood of **Trastevere,** on the south side of the river Tiber, and call it a day; you'll be jet-lagged and need to get to bed early.

On each of Days Two and Three, see one major and two minor sights of your choice (check out Chapter 12 for detailed information on Rome's sights). Major sights include the **Vatican Museums/Sistine Chapel (Musei Vaticani/Cappella Sistina), Roman Forum/Imperial Forums/Palatine Hill (Foro Romano/Fori Imperiali/Palatino),** and **Borghese Gallery (Galleria Borghese).** Minor attractions (in terms of time commitment, not importance) include the **Spanish Steps (Scalinata di Spagna)** and **Spanish Square (Piazza di Spagna), Trevi Fountain (Fontana di Trevi),** the **Pantheon,** and **Piazza Navona.** You can work in other *piazze* (squares) at night using our restaurant choices in Chapter 11.

On Day Four, take an early train (leaving no later than 8 or 9 a.m.) to **Florence,** where you will arrive about two hours later. Check into your hotel, and then head for the **Duomo, Giotto's Bell Tower,** the **Baptistry,** and the **Duomo Museum (Museo dell'Opera del Duomo).** Have dinner in one of our recommended restaurants.

On Day Five, get up early and run to the **Uffizi Gallery (Galleria degli Uffizi)** — of course, you've reserved tickets in advance so you won't have to stand in line for hours (see Chapter 14 for details). In the afternoon, go to the **Accademia Gallery (Galleria dell'Accademia)** — make sure that you reserve tickets here as well — to see Michelangelo's *David,* and then stop by the leather market and test your bargaining skills. Take a pre-dinner stroll on the **Ponte Vecchio.** Don't forget to see the **Palazzo Vecchio** (from the outside only) and **Piazza della Signoria** on the way back (see Chapter 14 for more information on Florence's sights, hotels, and restaurants).

On Day Six, take an early two-and-a-half-hour train ride to Venice, and check into your hotel. Then catch vaporetto no. 1 (see Chapter 18 for details on public transportation in Venice) for a slow cruise down the **Grand Canal,** noting the *palazzi* (palaces) lining the canal and the **Rialto Bridge** as you pass under it. Get off to explore **St. Mark's Square (Piazza San Marco)** and **St. Mark's Basilica (Basilica di San Marco).** In the afternoon, go to the **Academy Gallery (Gallerie dell'Accademia)** for a tour of several hundred years of Venetian art.

On the morning of Day Seven, visit **Santa Maria Gloriosa dei Frari** and the nearby **Scuola di San Rocco.** After lunch, see the **Doge's Palace** and the **Bridge of Sighs.** (For more details, see Chapter 18.) You can then either head back to Rome by train that night (about five hours) and fly out the next day, or spend your last night in Venice and fly home from there the next morning. If you don't have that extra day, use the afternoon and evening of Day Six to walk around the city (you may even want to skip the visit to the Accademia Galleries altogether), and just skip Day Seven.

Seeing Italy in Two Weeks

With two weeks to explore Italy, you'll be able to breathe a little and have the luxury of free time (when you can meet people and have unforgettable experiences). For the whirlwind two-week tour, you can tack another day each onto Rome, Florence, and Venice (see "Exploring Italy in One Week," earlier in this chapter). Doing so allows you to see more of the sites that we list throughout the book, sample more of the great food, and walk around more to get a feel for the cities.

Spend Days One through Four in Rome (see "Exploring Italy in One Week" in this chapter). From Rome, you can also take a side trip to Tivoli and see the **Hadrian's Villa** and **Villa d'Este,** or go to **Ostia Antica** to see the ruins of Rome's ancient seaport (see Chapter 13).

Early on Day Five, take the two-and-a-half-hour train ride from Rome to Naples, and check your luggage at the station. Transfer to the train to **Pompeii** (a 45-minute trip), and visit the archeological park in the late morning and early afternoon (see Chapter 21). Returning to Naples, spend the rest of the afternoon strolling the waterfront and historic neighborhood nearby, seeing the **Castle of the Egg (Castel dell'Ovo), Riviera di Chiaia, New Castle (Castel Nuovo),** and **Palazzo Reale** (see Chapter 20). Get back to the train station for your luggage and take a taxi to the Molo Angioino, where you will catch the Tirrenia overnight ferry for Sicily (see Chapter 23). Check into your cabin and enjoy the cruise (if you wake up at the right time in the night, you may catch a glimpse of Stromboli, an active volcano of the Eolian Islands, spewing fireworks into the evening sky); the ferry will arrive the next morning in Palermo.

Check into your hotel and spend the morning of Day Six seeing Palermo's **Palazzo Reale, Palatine Chapel (Cappella Palatina),** and the **Duomo.** After lunch, take the bus to the **Duomo di Monreale** and the **Cloister,** where you can see some of the world's most incredible mosaics (see Chapter 23 for more details). Return to Palermo for a family-style Sicilian dinner and crash early.

On the morning of Day Seven, take a train to **Agrigento** and the **Valley of the Temples (Valle dei Templi),** some of the finest Greek ruins any-where. If you have a rental car, you can drive and make a detour to see the Doric temple in **Segesta** as well. You can then come back to spend the night in your hotel in Palermo.

On Day Eight, fly directly from Palermo to Florence on an early flight. (Alternatively, but only during the summer, you can catch the SNAV morning ferry back to Naples — a four-hour trip — and enjoy the rest of the day visiting what you missed in Naples on Day Five. Spend the night there and catch a very early train to Florence on the morning of Day Nine — about a five-hour trip. In that case, you'll have one less half-day each in Florence and Venice.) Spend Days Eight and Nine visiting Florence (see Chapter 14).

On Day Ten, explore one of the charming towns of Tuscany — **Siena** is an excellent choice (see Chapter 16 for tour companies).

On Day Eleven, take an early train to Venice (or an early-afternoon train if you arrived in Florence on Day Nine) and spend Days Eleven and Twelve exploring this magical city (see Chapter 18).

On Day Thirteen, journey beyond the city center to visit some of the other islands: **Murano, Torcello,** and the **Lido.** On Day Fourteen, mourn the end of your vacation and get ready to take an afternoon flight home.

Enjoying Italy with Kids

The great thing about traveling to Italy with kids is that Italians love children and will often go out of their way to help you and make things easier for you, especially if your children are well behaved. Also, Italy offers many attractions and sights that kids will enjoy. One of the big issues that only you can answer, though, is how much museum time your children can take. In general, we think that Rome and Venice are better destinations than Florence for families with children. Why? Mainly because many of their major attractions are outdoor experiences, easy and enjoyable for children of all ages, whereas in Florence, most of the major attractions are actually museums or churches. In Rome, for example, your kids can run off some energy at the **Roman Forum, Imperial Forums,** and **Palatine Hill;** the **Villa Borghese;** the **Spanish Steps;** and the **Spanish Square** (see Chapters 11 and 12); in Venice, **St. Mark's Square**, boat rides on the *vaporetto* transportation system, and the **lagoon** are other great outdoor attractions. In addition, Rome is a bustling modern city that offers your kids all the stuff they like to do at home, and in Venice the **Rolling Venice** program is designed especially for teenagers (see Chapter 18 for more details).

One possibility we recommend is taking the itinerary "Seeing Italy in Two Weeks," earlier in this chapter, and cutting out the trip to Sicily. Instead, spend Days Five and Six based in Naples, and take Day Seven to show your kids the **Amalfi Coast,** where you can spend some time playing on the beach and enjoying the warm Mediterranean (see Chapter 22). Then get to Florence on Day Eight (flying is the fastest, but you can also take a train or drive). If you decide to have only a quick look at the town, use Days Nine and Ten to explore the landscape: the **Chianti** countryside, and some nearby destinations such as **Pisa,** and its newly restored Leaning Tower, and the **Cinque Terre** (literally, "five towns"), known as the Italian Riviera. (If you rent a car in Rome, you can drive through **Siena** on the way to Florence on Day Eight.) You can then continue the itinerary and spend the rest of your vacation in Venice.

Taking the Ancient History Tour

If archeology, ancient history, and culture are your thing, the focus of your visit to Italy should be the center and southern parts of the country — Rome, Naples and Sicily, where the main intersection of Etruscan, Greek, Carthaginian, Roman, Norman, and Arab influences took place. You will skip the Renaissance cities of Florence and Venice.

To begin this week-long itinerary of ancient history sights, fly into Rome and, during your three-day stay, make sure you see the **Roman Forum, Imperial Forums,** and **Palatine Hill,** as well as the very rich **Roman National Museum (Museo Nazionale Romano)** in the **Palazzo Massimo** and the **Palazzo Altemps** for Greek and Roman sculpture, and the **Etruscan Museum (Museo Etrusco di Villa Giulia).** You may also want to take the side trips to Tivoli's **Villa Adriana** and to **Ostia Antica,** Rome's ancient seaport (see Chapters 12 and 13).

Take a very early train to **Naples** on Day Four, and on Days Four and Five visit **Pompeii** and, back in Naples, the **National Archaeological Museum (Museo Archeologico Nazionale),** where many of the frescoes and other treasures from Pompeii are on display, alongside a rich collection of Greek and Roman art. Try to squeeze in a visit to **Herculaneum** as well; or, like Tiberius, you can holiday on **Capri** (see Chapters 20 and 21). You can then take the night ferry to **Sicily** on the evening of Day Five (see Chapter 23).

If you want, spend part of Day Six in Palermo, visiting the **Palazzo Reale** with its **Palatine Chapel (Cappella Palatina),** and the **Duomo di Monreale** with its **Cloister;** otherwise, rent a car and start directly for **Agrigento,** for its **Valle dei Templi,** making the detour by **Segesta** on your way (see Chapters 24 and 25). Continue to **Syracuse,** and plan to spend the night there.

Early on Day Seven, in Syracuse, make sure to visit the **Zona Archeologica** with its spectacular ruins and the harbor and the island of **Ortigia.** From there, head to **Taormina** and its beautifully preserved Greek/Roman theater, which hangs over an azure sea in the shadow of **Etna** (into which the philosopher Empedocles is said to have thrown himself). Spend the night there and fly back home on Day Eight, from the Catania airport (the closest) or from Palermo.

Taking the Art Buff's Tour of Italy

If you're an art buff and want an itinerary that highlights the master-pieces of Italy, you'll want to focus on the Renaissance and skip the ancient history. Your key destinations will be Palermo, Naples, Rome, Florence, and Venice. Of course, that is far too much if you only have a week. In that case, you have to make the difficult decision of what to skip: Sicilian Baroque is unique and very interesting, but Sicily is far away. On the other hand, you could easily squeeze in Palermo if you take the time to visit the rich collection of the **National Museum and Gallery of the Capodimonte (Museo e Gallerie Nazionali di Capodimonte)** in Naples.

For a one-week tour, we suggest you follow the "Doing Italy in One Week" itinerary (earlier in this chapter) with the following changes: Skip the bus tour and the ancient Roman attractions, focusing on the **Vatican Museums/Sistine Chapel (Musei Vaticani/Cappella Sistina)** and the **Borghese Gallery (Galleria Borghese).** Make sure you visit **Palazzo Barberini** and the **Caravaggios** in some of the churches, such as **San Luigi dei Francesi.** In Florence, you can shorten your tour of the **Duomo** and spend an hour or two at the **Palazzo Pitti.** Try to squeeze in the **Basilica di San Lorenzo** and the **Medici Chapels (Cappelle Medicee)** as well. When you get to Venice, curtail your visit to the Palazzo Ducale (skip the New Prisons and the nonart parts) to make time to go to the **Peggy Guggenheim Collection.**

If you have two weeks, follow the "Seeing Italy in Two Weeks" itinerary earlier in this chapter, with the following changes: Use your extra day in Rome to catch one of the special art exhibits (see Chapter 12) and visit **Villa d'Este** in Tivoli (see Chapter 13). Otherwise, spend your extra time in Naples, a town well worth three days. Take a day to visit the **National Museum and Gallery of the Capodimonte (Museo e Gallerie Nazionali di Capodimonte),** which have reopened after a complete overhaul, and the rest of the time to take in the art in the churches of **Sant'Anna dei Lombardi, Santa Chiara,** and the **Certosa di San Martino.** See the **Teatro San Carlo** and the **Galleria Umberto I** (see Chapter 20). When you head to Sicily, skip Agrigento in favor of more time in Palermo in order to make room for a visit to the **Palazzo Abbatellis,** which contains, among other things, the famous *Madonna* by Antonello da Messina, and for a visit to the **Teatro Massimo** (see Chapter 23). At this point, you'll head for Florence by air. There, spend your extra time seeing the paintings by Fra Angelico in the **St. Mark's Museum (Museo San Marco)** and the Masaccio in the church of **Santa Maria del Carmine** (see Chapter 14). On the way to Venice, stop in **Padua** (see Chapter 19) to see Giotto's masterpiece, the **Scrovegni Chapel (Cappella degli Scrovegni).** In Venice, use your extra day to visit the city's churches, like the **Madonna del'Orto** and **La Salute,** filled with masterpieces by Tintoretto, Tiziano, and other Venetian masters (see Chapter 18).

Chapter 4

Planning Your Budget

In This Chapter

▶ Devising a realistic budget

▶ Determining traveling, lodging, and dining expenses

▶ Remembering the extras: shopping and entertainment

▶ Tipping, Italian style

▶ Saving money

*B*udgeting your trip isn't always easy. In this chapter, we give you some pointers on being realistic and keeping track of all the costs that you'll have to bear in mind.

Adding Up the Elements

When it comes to planning a trip, you usually deal with two different numbers: what you'd *like* to spend and what you *can* spend. Your budget will have a good number of variables. By deciding what's most important to you, you can trim here and there on the incidentals and splurge on the things that really matter. Airfare, of course, is one of the biggest components, so if your budget is limited, follow the money-saving tips we give you at the end of this chapter and in Chapter 6 to save on airplane seats. Examine the range of choices that we offer in dining, lodging, and so on, including estimated costs, and work out a budget that's right for you. Use the worksheets at the end of this book to help you get an idea of what your trip will cost.

Getting to and around Italy

Chances are that your airfare to Italy will be one of the largest items in your budget, but the actual cost depends on the time that you travel. In high season, you're lucky to find a round-trip ticket for less than $800, but at other times, you may find tickets for as low as $350. Airfare is the least flexible of your budget's elements, unless your traveling time is very flexible. Make sure that you check out our money-saving tips before you buy an airline ticket (see Chapter 6).

Transportation within Italy offers many more choices. To explore cities in the United States and many other countries, you either absolutely *shouldn't* rent a car (in New York City, for example) or absolutely *must* rent one (in the wilds of the U.S. West). In Italy, the question is less clear-cut: Because the country's train and bus systems are highly developed and because gasoline (call it *benzina* in Italy) is so expensive (about $4 per gallon), you don't save much by driving. Renting a car is also likely to be more expensive than you're used to back home. Because of car theft, some agencies may demand that you take theft insurance, regardless of what your credit card may cover. (Other issues may keep you from driving abroad as well, such as high speeds and hair-raising curves.)

Without a car, you don't have the hassle of trying to find parking and paying for it. And, if you arrive in Venice, Florence, or Rome with a car, you have to keep it garaged during your entire stay: Venice has no roads at all, Florence is small and bans cars from the historic center, and Rome has too many roads and drivers for you to want to deal with, and also bans nonresidents from the historic center. Taking public transportation can definitely save you money and trouble. Think how much more you'll enjoy looking out the window at the countryside instead of the cars speeding by you.

The only time you may want to have a car in Italy is when you have the time to see more than just the highlights, and when you're planning to visit smaller towns and countryside areas (see Chapter 7 for the details on renting). For example, say you're a return visitor to Italy and want to spend your ten-day vacation exploring the nooks and crannies of Tuscany/Umbria or Sicily. In this case, a car gives you further flexibility and scope. Keep in mind that you'll probably be picking up and returning your car in a major city, but in most cities, rental agencies have locations on the edge of town, making exiting and entering a snap. If your destinations are Rome, Florence, or Venice, however, renting a car is really not necessary.

Finding lodging

Most likely, finding a place to stay in Italy isn't the same as finding a hotel or motel where you live. For one thing, your lodging in Italy may be in a building that went up when your hometown was still a big empty spot on the map. And originally, the building may have been a princely *palazzo,* a grand townhouse, or a spartan monastery. We list many renovated hotels in this book, but keep in mind that space is at a premium in Italy. For a detailed discussion of what you can expect in Italy's hotel rooms, see Chapter 8.

Here's something that may surprise you: Hotel bathrooms in Italy are often tiny. Buildings are much older than in the United States, and private bathrooms were added to preexisting rooms, creating sometimes funky results. Be aware that in many smaller hotels, rooms still exist with a shared bath down the hall and just a sink (or nothing) in the room itself. If you absolutely want a nice bathroom, be willing to fork over extra euros for a more expensive hotel. On the other hand, you can save a lot of money if you don't mind smaller private facilities or even going down the hall for a shower.

Keep in mind that hotel rates vary from region to region and from city to city: Florence and Venice are pricier than Rome, but Naples, and even more so Sicily, are cheaper. Figure that 130€ ($120) buys you a decent double room with private bath anywhere (though a much better room in the south than in the north), but 180€ ($160) buys you a nice room all over the country. From 210€ ($190) and up, you're buying a luxury room. Of course, the amount that these estimates represent in dollars always changes according to the current currency rates.

You can save money if you renounce the breakfast that your hotel serves, unless it's included with your room rate. Breakfast is worth paying for only at the more expensive hotels ($$$ and above), where you find a buffet with a variety of foods, usually including eggs, sausage, cheese, cold cuts, yogurt, fruit, and cereal. This kind of breakfast may run about 15€ ($13.50), so you have to decide if what you get is worth the money.

In all the hotel reviews in this guide, we supply the *rack rates* (the off-the-shelf rate that hotels quote you). See Chapter 8 for the price categories.

Tables 4-1 and 4-2 give you a sampling of costs that you may encounter on your trip.

Table 4-1	What Things Cost in Rome
A metro or city bus ride	0.77€ (69¢)
Can of soda	0.77€–1.30€ (69¢–$1.17)
Pay-phone call	0.10€ (9¢)
Movie ticket	6.50€ ($5.85)
Caffè lungo (American-style espresso)	0.62€–0.83€ (56¢–75¢)
Cappuccino (or something similar)	1.14€ ($1)
Ticket to the Galleria Borghese	6.19€ ($5.57)
Gallon of gasoline	1.14€ ($1) per liter = 4.33€ ($4) per gallon ($4)
Average hotel room	130€ ($120)
Liter of house wine in a restaurant	4.15€ ($3.74)
Individual pizza in a pizzeria	5.16€–9.30€ ($5–$8)
First-class letter to U.S. (or any overseas country)	0.67€ (60¢)

Table 4-2	What Things Cost in Greve in Chianti
A subway or city bus ride	0.62€ (56¢)
Can of soda	0.62€–1.03€ (56¢–93¢)
Pay-phone call	0.10€ (9¢)
Caffè lungo (American-style espresso)	0.52€–0.67€ (47¢–60¢)
Cappuccino (or something similar)	0.83€ (75¢)
Gallon of gasoline	1.14€ ($1) per liter = 4.33€ ($4) per gallon
Average hotel room	80€ ($72)
Liter of house wine in a restaurant	3.62€ ($3.26)
Individual pizza in a pizzeria	4.13€–7.75€ ($4–$7)
First-class letter to U.S. (or any overseas country)	0.67€ (60¢)

Eating out

As in most places in the world, you can spend a lot or a little in restaurants in Italy, but what may surprise you is that less-formal restaurants (called *pizzerie,* trattorie, *osterie,* and *rosticcerie*) often offer the best combination of quality and price. You can generally count on all of these having traditional fare served in simple surroundings. *Pizzerie* (obviously) specialize in pizza; trattorie and *osterie* are casual, family-run restaurants serving full, hearty meals at relatively inexpensive prices; and *rosticcerie* are cafeterias with pre-prepared hot dishes and roasting chickens in the window. Of course, you can find some famous *ristorantes* (restaurants) that are elegant and pricey and serve fantastic food, but the equation *high price=good food* is not at all a certain bet in Italy. And to confuse the issue even further, the names have become interchangeable: Many high-price joints take the name trattoria for it's homey, feel-good vibe, and smaller places anoint themselves as *ristorantes* to try to class up the place. When in doubt, always go for the simpler option. Chances are you'll get homemade cooking for only a few dollars.

Although things are changing, *pranzo* (lunch) used to be the big meal in Italy, where lunch hour is more like one and a half to two hours. Lunch prices may also be cheaper, so in most cities two people can eat a nice lunch with a half-liter of wine for about 24€ to 38€ ($22 to $34) if they don't eat in a touristy piazza or a glitzy restaurant. Dinner in the same type of place will be 42€ ($38) and up for two.

Most restaurants impose a basic **table-and-bread charge,** called *pane e coperto,* of about 1.50€ to 4€ ($1.40 to $3.60), and you'll probably like to drink mineral water (fizzy or not, it's much cheaper than in the United States). On the other hand, service is usually included (look for the words *servizio incluso* on the menu) unless otherwise noted. If it's not, leave a 10 to 15% tip on the table if service was satisfactory.

Here are the price categories we use in this book:

$	Up to 15€ ($13.50)
$$	15€–20€ ($13.50–$18)
$$$	20€–30€ ($18–$27)
$$$$	30€–45€ ($27–$40)
$$$$$	More than 45€ ($40 and up)

If your budget is limited, you can find many other ways to cut costs besides eating in simple trattorie or *pizzerie.* We like to take a splurge-and-save approach to dining in order to even out our costs. If we really want to try a particular expensive restaurant, we make up for the extra outlay by eating a lunch or dinner of fresh bread, locally cured prosciutto, regional cheeses, raw or cooked vegetables, and local wine or mineral water, all of which can be found at Italy's great markets and *rosticcerie.* You can save a lot by making a few meals of your own this way, especially lunch. Having a picnic lunch is also a great way to visit some of the outdoor sights.

Discovering What Italy Has to Offer

Museums and other sights cost anywhere from 2€ to 9€ ($1.80 to $8) for admission. Most churches are free (avoid visiting during services unless you're attending the service, however). Frankly, sightseeing isn't an area where you can save a lot of money, and you'll probably be sorry if you try. On the other hand, the attractions aren't that expensive to begin with, so your budget won't be stretched to its limits by daily sightseeing expenditures.

A pocketful of change

In many of Italy's churches, fragile paintings are kept in semi-obscurity, but you will often find a light box nearby. When you insert a coin or two, a light pops on to illuminate a painting, fresco, or sculpture for a limited amount of time. Therefore, carrying a pocketful of coins is always a good idea.

In the specific destination chapters, we note whenever you can find special combination discount tickets and special discount cards. (In Venice, for instance, people under 30 can receive a discount for shopping, accommodation, and sightseeing with the Rolling Venice pass.)

 Beware that many special discounts are available based on reciprocity between countries. Therefore, many discounts — senior and children discounts especially — aren't available to Americans but are available to British and other residents of European Union (EU) countries.

 Because of the long lines at times of great tourist influx, many major museums in Italy have started offering advance ticketing. You can now make reservations before you leave, thus bypassing waits of up to three hours. The list of museums for which you can make reservations includes Rome's **Galleria Borghese** (see Chapter 12) and Florence's **Uffizi Gallery** and **Accademia Gallery** (see Chapter 14).

Shopping to your heart's content

Shopping is the most personal and flexible part of your budget's bottom line. You can spend hundreds on a full-length leather coat for yourself or for a friend or loved one, or you can skip shopping completely. Throughout this book, we give you our recommendations for the best shops and items that each city offers.

Italy is famous for its artwork, design, and crafts — art glass, pottery, leather, gold, and lace, among many other fine wares. Italian fashion isn't half-bad either — Versace, Dolce and Gabbana, and Armani are some of the world-famous Italian firms.

You'll also save by buying Italian goods in Italy. Use your trip as a chance to pick up that special something you have an irresistible craving for — maybe a Murano chandelier, a pair of leather boots, a Gucci handbag, or even a Ferrari. And even if you only save a little, you can find a much bigger selection here than you'll find in your hometown.

Italy's **value-added tax** (known as the IVA) is a steep 19%, but you can get a refund for purchases costing more than 155€ ($140). The value-added tax is included in all the prices that you're quoted. Stores displaying a "Tax Free" insignia can give you an invoice that you can cash at the airport's Customs office as you leave Italy. Otherwise, you have to take the invoice from the store, have it stamped at the airport by Customs, and then mail it back to the store, which will then send you a check or credit your charge account.

Don't sit to sip

Be aware that any time you sit down in a *caffè* or bar in Italy, things cost more. Coffee at an outside table in Piazza del Popolo or Piazza San Marco may cost the same as lunch anywhere else. Most Italians stand at the bar while they have a coffee or a beer.

Experiencing the Italian nightlife

Visiting the opera, going out for a drink, listening to music in a jazz club, and dancing the night away are all extra pleasures that make your time in Italy that much more memorable. You can spend big bucks in this area of entertainment, or you can cut your costs down by doing those serendipitous little things that are free or nearly so, such as people-watching on a beautiful floodlit piazza or ordering a coffee or drink in a classic *caffè* and soaking in the atmosphere.

If you want to attend a performance of an ancient Greek tragedy or a Verdi opera, we give you the best options for getting tickets at each venue and tips for saving money at the same time. Nightclubs in Italy are about as expensive as anywhere else, but you may be able to avoid a cover charge by sitting or standing at the bar rather than taking a table, or by arriving before a certain hour. If you happen to be in Italy during a public holiday or festival, you may enjoy abundant free entertainment, much of it in the streets.

Getting Tips on Tipping

Tipping isn't a big extra cost in Italy the way it is in some destinations. Because waiters are better paid and employers can't wriggle out of paying them a wage by assuming they'll get tips, gratuities aren't a big part of their income. (Leaving a few euros as a token of appreciation is always a polite gesture, though.) If, on the other hand, you eat in the restaurants of big glitzy hotels in major cities, keep in mind that such places may expect you to fork over the usual American 15 to 20%. Check for the words *servizio incluso* (service included) on the menu; if they aren't there, expect to pay a full gratuity.

You do have to tip bellhops who carry your bags, and you should give cab drivers a small tip as a token of appreciation, much like you would waiters.

Keeping a Lid on Hidden Expenses

Remember *Frommer's Europe on $5 a Day?* Do you also remember how long ago that book came out? Well, these days the title is *Frommer's Europe from $90 a Day*.

Count on a rock-bottom cost (without transportation) of $50 to $75 per day per person. If you shoot for $50, you'll probably hit $75. Of course, everything depends on the exchange rate of the euro, which, at press time, is quite favorable to the dollar, making a lot of prices cheaper than they used to be, even a couple years ago. In any case, you can save some money here and there if you follow the tips we give you in this section and throughout the book.

Note, however, that we aren't of the save-a-buck-at-any-cost school. Sometimes paying more makes sense. For example, if you're facing sightseeing overload and are dead tired, you may not want to take an hour-long bus ride to the other side of town to your hotel. Why not take a cab instead? And why not grab a bite to eat in the slightly expensive cafe near where you are rather than deal with crossing town to an extra-cheap restaurant? Plus, there are areas where you shouldn't make cuts, because they'll kill your trip. Not seeing Florence's Uffizi, Venice's Accademia, Rome's Vatican Museums and Sistine Chapel, or some other major sights, just because they cost more, would be a tragedy. We'd rather skip lunch and take the opportunity to go to one of these must-sees twice. Who knows when you'll be back that way again? Decide what's most important to you as you plan your trip and where to splurge or save.

Getting the most bang for your buck

There are many ways to trim your budget down to a size that you can stand. One place to start is your plane ticket. If you buy a relatively expensive ticket, you'll have to sacrifice in other areas to make up for the extra expense. We like the idea of saving a big chunk of change by reserving your ticket early and traveling off-peak, and then spreading the saved money around to make the rest of your trip more enjoyable.

Another thing that you can do to save money is to start thinking like an Italian. Italians have relatively less disposable income than Americans. The closer you mirror the way Italians live and travel, the cheaper your trip will be — and the closer you get to the Italians themselves. Staying in a huge hotel designed for foreign tourists with all the fixings will cost you a lot. The luxury of renting a big car will cost you, too. Likewise, eating in five-star restaurants instead of exploring local eateries is more expensive. If you can live for a week without your own private bathroom, make big healthy sandwiches from delicious stuff you bought in a market, and pass on the postcards, trinkets, and things that you pick up just to say that you've been to Italy, you can seriously cut your costs and have money left over for splurges here and there. As the management gurus say, don't think of cost-cutting as a limitation but as an opportunity!

Cutting costs

Throughout this book, you can find Bargain Alert icons that highlight money-saving tips and/or great deals. Here are some additional cost-cutting strategies:

- ✔ **Visit during the off-season.** If you can travel at nonpeak times (usually winter, with the exception of the Christmas/New Year's holidays), you can find airfares and hotel prices as much as 20% less than during peak months.

- ✔ **Travel during off-peak days of the week.** Airfares vary depending not only on the time of the year but also on the day of the week. In Italy, weekend rates are often cheaper than weekday rates. When you inquire about airfares, ask if you can obtain a cheaper rate by flying on a different day.

- ✔ **Surf the Web.** Airlines often have special Internet-only rates that are appreciably cheaper than rates quoted over the phone. Also, you can find good hotel packages online.

- ✔ **Try a package tour.** For popular destinations like Italy, you can book airfare, hotel, ground transportation, and even some sightseeing by making just one call to a travel agent or packager, and you may pay a lot less than if you tried to put the trip together yourself. But always work out the prices that you'd pay if you arranged the pieces of your trip yourself, just to double check. See the section on package tours in Chapter 6 for specific suggestions.

- ✔ **Pack light.** Packing light enables you to carry your own bags and not worry about finding a porter (don't forget to tip yourself). Likewise, you can take a bus or a train rather than a cab from the airport if you pack light, saving you a few more euros.

- ✔ **Always ask for discount rates.** Membership in AAA, frequent-flier plans, trade unions, AARP, or other groups may qualify you for discounts on plane tickets, hotel rooms, or even meals. Ask about everything — you may be pleasantly surprised with the answer you receive.

- ✔ **Get out of the center of town.** In many places, you may find that staying in hotels just outside the city center or across the river aren't quite as convenient but are a great bargain. You may only need to do a little more walking or take a short commute. See the chapter on each destination for hotel information. On the other hand, if you pick a hotel out of the way, you'll waste precious time in transportation and you may well ruin your trip. The key is always to have a short commute to the attractions you want to visit.

✔ **Ask if your kids can stay in your room with you.** Many hotels won't charge you the additional-person rate if your extra person is pint-sized and related to you. You can save much more if you don't take two rooms, even if you have to pay some extra for a rollaway bed.

✔ **Try expensive restaurants at lunch instead of dinner.** At most top restaurants, prices at lunch are usually considerably less than those at dinner, and the menu often offers many of the same specialties.

✔ **Have a picnic.** You can put together some delicious and inexpensive meals at an Italian grocery store, and then enjoy your feast in a garden or park.

✔ **Use the public transportation system.** In Italy, moving from one destination to another by train is cheap and easy. (We include a map of Italy's train system on the inside front cover of this book to get you started.) Using the local bus system in large cities like Venice and Rome is a little more complicated, but it's also a great way to visit the city.

✔ **Walk.** A good pair of walking shoes can save you money in taxis and other local transportation. Remember that the historic center of most cities and towns is pretty small, so you can actually walk almost anywhere you need to go. You'll save money, get your exercise for the day, and get to know the city more intimately.

Chapter 5

Planning Ahead for Special Travel Needs

Do you want to bring your kids with you on your trip to Italy? Are you a single woman traveling alone and concerned about safety? Are you worried about wheelchair accessibility? Are you interested in special programs and activities for seniors? Do you have concerns about attitudes toward gays and lesbians? In this chapter, we discuss the challenges — and opportunities — that travelers with special needs may encounter in Italy.

Traveling with Kids

Italy has a very family-oriented culture, so you shouldn't have any qualms about traveling with your kids. In fact, Italians love children, and you'll find that people will often talk and play with your child on public transportation and in public areas. The Italian society is also a more traditional one, however. Italians, in general, believe that children should be well behaved (act politely like little adults in museums and other public places), and they aren't worried that disciplining their children will give the kids a complex. Tantrums, whining, and other such behavioral outbursts are frowned upon.

Opting for child care

Child care in Italy is also handled in a traditional way. Members of the extended family — grandparents and other relatives — often help care for children during the day if both parents work. And having one parent stay home taking care of the kids (usually the mother) is more common in Italy than in the United States. As a result, Italy doesn't have a major infrastructure of day care and child care. In fact, finding a hotel with day-care service is rare. However, many hotels can arrange for a sitter from a baby-sitting service, and in a few small family-run places, a daughter or son may pitch in and watch your kids. You can find standard day-care service only at the more expensive, larger hotels in the big urban areas. Thus, if you have a very small child, you may find that you wind up paying more for lodging simply because you need the amenities of the higher-priced hotels.

Keeping kids in the know

Kids can have a great time in Italy, and if they know some of the special things in store for them, they'll be as excited about the trip as you are. Before you leave, sit down with your children and plan a family strategy. Go over the list of sights and activities in the cities and areas that you plan to visit, particularly noting those with the Kid Friendly icon. Let your kids list a few of the things they'd like to see and do, in order of preference, and make a similar list of your own. You may also want to let your older children research Italy on the Internet (see the appendix for a list of Web sites). Together, you can then plot out a day-by-day schedule that strikes a balance between your desires and those of your offspring. Following are several resources to consider when traveling with kids:

  ✔ **Check out some books that offer tips to help you travel with kids.** Most of these books concentrate on travel in the United States, but *Family Travel & Resorts: The Complete Guide* by Pamela Lanier (Lanier Publishing International) and *How to Take Great Trips with Your Kids* by Sanford and Joan Portnoy (Harvard Common Press) are full of good general advice that can apply to travel anywhere. Another reliable book with a worldwide focus is *Adventuring with Children: An Inspirational Guide to World Travel and the Outdoors* by Nan Jeffrey (Foghorn Press).

  ✔ **Consider a special magazine subscription.** *Family Travel Times,* published six times a year by TWYCH (Travel with Your Children; ☎ 888-822-4388 or 212-477-5524; Internet: www.familytravel times.com), includes a weekly call-in service for subscribers. Subscriptions are $40 per year for quarterly editions. Call to receive a free publication list and a sample issue.

✔ **Try out a university-sponsored program abroad.** The University of New Hampshire runs **Familyhostel** (☎ 800-733-9753; Internet: www. learn.unh.edu/familyhostel), an intergenerational alternative to standard guided tours. In Italy, the affiliated university is the Art Institute of Florence, Lorenzo de Medici. There are two– or three-week programs during which you attend lectures and seminars, take lots of field trips, and sightsee with a team of experts and academics. The program is designed for children ages 8 to 15, parents, and grandparents.

Seeing Italy in Senior Style

In general, Italy accords older people a great deal of respect, probably because of the continued existence of the extended family as well as the nature of the Italian language (there are polite forms of address you use when talking to someone older than yourself). Therefore, you're unlikely to encounter ageism.

People older than 60 are traveling more than ever before, and being a senior entitles you to some terrific travel bargains. If you're not already a member of **AARP** (formerly known as the American Association of Retired Persons), 601 E St. NW, Washington, DC 20049 (☎ **800-424-3410** or 202-434-2277; Internet: www.aarp.org), do yourself a favor and join ($8 per year or $20 for three years) to receive discounts on car rentals and hotels.

Elderhostel (☎ 877-426-8056; Internet: www.elderhostel.org) arranges study vacations for those ages 55 and over (and a spouse or companion of any age) in more than 80 countries around the world. Recent program offerings for Italian trips included arts and culinary explorations in Rome, Central Tuscany, Padua and Venice, and the Bay of Naples.

Most major domestic airlines, such as American, United, Continental, US Airways, and TWA, offer discount programs for seniors. Make sure that you ask about discounts whenever booking a flight.

Senior discounts on admission at theaters, museums, and public transportation are subject to reciprocity between countries. Because the United States hasn't signed the bilateral agreement (you discount us and we'll discount you), Americans aren't eligible for senior discounts in Italy. (The same rule applies to the under-17 discount.) All discounts apply if you're a citizen of a European Union country.

You can find *101 Tips for the Mature Traveler* from **Grand Circle Travel,** 347 Congress St., Suite 3A, Boston, MA 02210 (☎ **800-221-2610** or 617-350-7500; Fax: 617-350-6206; Internet: www.gct.com). Grand Circle

Travel is also one of the literally hundreds of travel agencies specializing in vacations for seniors. But beware: Many agencies are of the tour-bus variety, with free trips thrown in for those who organize groups of 20 or more.

Traveling without Barriers

A disability shouldn't stop anybody from traveling, and more options and resources are available than ever before. However, Italy isn't as advanced as some other countries in its accessibility. Part of the problem is the age of the housing stock and the difficulty of retrofitting medieval buildings with elevators or ramps. Some of the major buildings and institutions have been converted; others have not. Calling ahead is always best, especially because, although special entrances may exist for the disabled, you may need to be met there by an attendant. Italy is working to make its treasures more accessible, but application is proceeding slowly (remember, Rome wasn't built in a day). Public transportation reserves spaces for the disabled, but getting in and out of the train or bus can prove difficult, even impossible, if you're in a wheelchair.

If you're a traveler with a disability, you may want to consider joining a tour that caters specifically to your needs. The **Society for Accessible Travel and Hospitality,** 347 Fifth Ave., Suite 610, New York, NY 10016 (☎ **212-447-7284;** Internet: www.sath.org), can give you the names and addresses of other tour operators. Annual membership is $45 ($30 for seniors and students).

Vision-impaired travelers should contact the **American Foundation for the Blind,** 11 Penn Plaza, Suite 300, New York, NY 10001 (☎ **800-232-5463;** Internet: www.afb.org), for information on traveling with seeing-eye dogs.

Getting Advice for Gay and Lesbian Travelers

Italy is a fairly tolerant country, and violent displays of intolerance such as gay bashing are extremely unusual. If you're polite to people, they'll generally be polite to you, regardless of your orientation, race, beliefs, or sex. All major towns and cities have an active gay life, especially Florence, Rome, and Milan, which considers itself the gay capital of Italy and is the headquarters of **ARCI Gay** (Internet: www.gay.it), the country's leading gay organization with branches throughout Italy. Capri is the gay resort of Italy, rivaled only by the gay beaches of Venice and Taormina.

The first-ever World Pride event was held in Rome in July 2000, to coincide with the Jubilee celebrations.

The **International Gay & Lesbian Travel Association (IGLTA)** (☎ 800-448-8550 or 954-776-2626; Fax: 954-776-3303; Internet: www.iglta.org) links travelers with the appropriate gay-friendly service organization or tour specialist. With approximately 1,200 members, the IGLTA offers quarterly newsletters, marketing mailings, and a membership directory that's updated quarterly. Membership often includes gay or lesbian businesses but is open to individuals for $150 yearly, plus a $100 administration fee for new members. Members are kept informed of gay and gay-friendly hoteliers, tour operators, and airline and cruise-line representatives. Contact the IGLTA for a list of its member agencies, who are tied into its information resources.

General gay and lesbian travel agencies include **Above and Beyond Tours** (☎ 800-397-2681; Internet: www.abovebeyondtours.com).

If you're looking for a guidebook written specifically for you, you can't do better than *Frommer's Gay & Lesbian Europe,* 2nd Edition, by David Andrusia and Haas Mroue (Wiley Publishing). Two biannual English-language books, focusing on gays but also including information for lesbians, are the *Spartacus: International Gay Guide* (Bruno Gmünder Verlag) and the *Odysseus* guide (Odysseus Enterprises LTD). You can order these from most gay and lesbian bookstores, like **Giovanni's Room** (☎ 215-923-2960; Internet: www.giovannisroom.com).

Out and About, 8 W. 19th St., Suite 401, New York, NY 10011 (☎ 800-929-2268 or 212-645-6922; Internet: www.outandabout.com), offers guidebooks and a monthly newsletter packed with information on the global gay and lesbian scene. A year's subscription is $49.

Traveling Tips for Women

If you're a woman traveling alone in Italy — especially if you're young and fair-haired — you'll attract young Italian men. In fact, they'll approach you and try to charm you; however, it's unlikely that someone will touch you, let alone harm you. Guidebooks tend to exaggerate pinching, groping, and the like (though on crowded buses these occurrences aren't unheard of). Conditions aren't the same as 20 or 30 years ago, and the younger generation of Italians is much less prone to this kind of behavior.

Wearing the proper outfit generally will help you avoid annoying situations. Italians have a stricter dress code than Americans do, and, although women can generally wear more casual clothing than men, only dressy and longish shorts are accepted. The farther south you go, the more traditional the society is. In Sicily, men may bother you if you go around in short shorts and revealing tops; Sicilian women simply don't dress this way. You have two choices in such situations: One is to dress however you feel like dressing (and steel yourself for the occasional look of disapproval or suggestive remark), and the other is to adapt your mode of dress to fit in with local traditions, even if you don't agree with them. The choice is yours.

The **Women's Travel Club** (☎ **800-480-4448;** Internet: www.womens travelclub.com) was designed by a woman in search of female travel companions because her husband preferred work to travel. Now the group organizes some 30 trips a year, with the emphasis on foreign culture, scenery, and safety.

Going It Alone

Many people prefer traveling alone. Unfortunately, the solo traveler is often forced to pay a punishing *single supplement* charged by many resorts, cruise lines, and tours for the privilege of booking a single room, which is usually well over half the price of a double.

Travel Companion Exchange (☎ **631-454-0880;** Internet: www.travel companions.com) is one of the oldest roommate finders for single travelers. Register with them and find a trustworthy travel mate who'll split the cost of the room with you and be around as little, or as often, as you like during the day.

Travel Buddies (☎ **800-998-9099** or 604-533-2483; Internet: www.travel buddiesworldwide.com) runs small, intimate, single-friendly group trips and will match you with a roommate free of charge, saving you the cost of single supplements.

Part II
Ironing Out the Details

The 5th Wave   By Rich Tennant

"And how shall I book your flight to Italy — First Class, Coach, or Medieval?"

In this part . . .

In this part, we get down to the nuts and bolts of booking your trip. Chapter 6 concerns the various ways of getting to Italy and saving some money, and Chapter 7 gives you information about getting around Italy after you arrive. Chapter 8 covers hotel options and booking your room. Chapter 9 discusses money; there are more options than ever before concerning how you handle your cash and pay your expenses. Chapter 10 takes care of the details that travelers too often leave to the last minute, such as getting a passport, thinking about medical and travel insurance, making reservations for special events, and packing.

Chapter 6

Getting to Italy

· ·

· ·

*1*f you live near a major city, getting to Italy may be even easier than reaching another destination in your own country. Direct flights go to and from the major cities of the world and the two international airports in Rome and Milan on a daily basis. But getting to Italy will probably take the biggest chunk out of your budget: Airfares to Italy are significantly higher than those from the U.S. to England, for example, and a round-trip ticket during peak times can range between $800 and $1,000 per person. Of course, with the cutthroat competition among airlines, you may be able to lock in a much better deal — especially if you book well in advance and have a flexible itinerary. In this chapter, we outline all the ways and means you have at your disposal to make getting to Italy a snap.

Using a Travel Agent

Any travel agent can help you find bargain airfares, a hotel room, or a rental car. The best travel agents can do even more: They can tell you how much time you need to budget for a destination, find a cheap flight that doesn't require you to change planes in Atlanta and Chicago, book you a better hotel room for about the same price as an average room, and give recommendations on restaurants. Another plus is that the agent can issue your tickets and vouchers on the spot.

The best way to find a good travel agent is to do so the same way you find a good plumber, mechanic, or doctor — by word of mouth. It's also wise to pick an agent who knows Italy.

Travel agents have traditionally worked on commissions paid by the airlines, accommodations, and tour companies. In the past few years, many airlines and resorts have begun limiting or eliminating travel agent commissions altogether. The immediate result has been that travel agents don't bother booking these services unless the customer specifically requests them. Some travel-industry analysts predict that if other airlines and accommodations follow suit, travel agents will have to start charging customers for their services.

To make sure you get the most out of your travel agent, do a little homework. Read about Italy (you've already made a sound decision by buying this book) and pick out those hotels and attractions you think you'll like. Go on the Web for available offers from airlines and tour companies (see "Getting the best airfare," later in this chapter). Then take your guidebook and Web information to a travel agent and ask him or her to make the arrangements for you.

The Ins and Outs of Package Tours

Package tours are not the same thing as escorted tours (see "The Ins and Outs of Escorted Tours," later in this chapter). Package tours are simply a way to buy the airfare, accommodations, and other elements of your trip (such as car rentals, airport transfers, and even activities) at the same time and often at discounted prices — kind of like one-stop shopping.

Package tours do have their advantages — someone else does most of the arranging for you, and you almost always save money. Some packages let you choose between escorted vacations and independent vacations; others allow you to add on a few guided excursions or escorted day-trips (also at prices lower than if you booked them yourself) without booking an entirely escorted tour. But among the disadvantages are limited choices, such as where you stay (some packages offer a better class of hotels than others), or a fixed itinerary that doesn't allow for an extra day of shopping.

Which package is right for you depends entirely on what you want; the time you spend shopping around will be well rewarded.

How to tell the deals from the duds

When you start looking at packages, use these tips to help you distinguish one from the other and figure out the right package for you.

✔ **Read this guide.** Decide what attractions you want to visit, and pick the type of accommodations you think you'll like. Compare the rack rates we quote in the hotel listings throughout this book against the discounted rates being offered by the packagers to see if you're actually being given a substantial savings. And remember:

Don't just compare packagers; compare the prices that packagers are offering on similar itineraries. The amount you save depends on the deal; most packagers can offer bigger savings on some packages than others.

✔ **Read the fine print.** When you're comparing packages, you don't want to be comparing apples to oranges. Make sure that you know exactly what's included in the price you're being quoted, and what's not. Don't assume anything: Some packagers include everything but the kitchen sink — with lots of extra discounts on restaurants and activities — while others don't even include airfare (packagers know better than anybody how fares can fluctuate, and they may not want to get locked into a yearlong airfare promise).

✔ **Know what you're getting yourself into — and whether you can get yourself out of it.** Before you commit to a package, make sure that you know how much flexibility you have. Some packagers require ironclad commitments, while others charge minimal fees for changes or cancellations. Ask the right questions: What's the cancellation policy if my kid gets sick at the last minute and we can't go? What if the office calls me home three days into my vacation? What if we have to adjust our vacation schedule — can we do that?

✔ **Use your best judgment.** If a package appears to be too good to be true, it probably is. Go with a reputable firm with a proven track record or one your travel agent recommends.

Where to find the packager for you

The best place to start looking is the travel section of your local Sunday newspaper. Also check the ads in the back of national travel magazines like *Travel + Leisure, National Geographic Traveler,* and *Condé Nast Traveler.* The biggest hotel chains also offer packages. If you already know where you want to stay, call the hotel and ask if they offer land/air packages.

Airlines also often package their flights together with accommodations. Although you can book most airline packages directly with the airline itself, your local travel agent can also do it for you. Prices are usually comparable to what you can get from other packagers.

Recommended packagers include **Kemwell** (☎ **800-678-0678;** Internet: www.kemwell.com) and **Central Holidays** (☎ **800-611-1139;** Internet: www.centralholidays.com). **Italiatour** (☎ **800-845-3365** or 212-675-2183; Internet: www.italiatour.com), associated with Alitalia, the Italian state airline, offers interesting packages and specializes in tours for independent travelers, who take a car or train between destinations for which Italiatour books accommodations at a discounted rate.

The Ins and Outs of Escorted Tours

Many people love escorted tours. Escorted tours — whether by bus, motor coach, train, or boat — let you sit back and enjoy your trip without having to spend lots of time behind the wheel. All the little details are taken care of, you know your costs up front, and there are few surprises. Escorted tours can take you to the maximum number of sights in the least amount of time with the least amount of hassle — and you don't have to sweat over the plotting and planning of a vacation schedule.

What you give up when you choose to take an escorted tour is a certain freedom of movement and spontaneity — the opportunity to discover a destination on your own or stumble upon a gem of a restaurant. That's why you may want to schedule an escorted tour with some flexibility in the schedule to allow you time to explore on your own.

How to tell the deals from the duds

If you choose an escorted tour, ask the following questions before you buy:

- **What is the cancellation policy?** Do I have to place a deposit? Can the tour organizers cancel the trip if they don't secure enough people? How late can I cancel if I'm unable to go? When do I pay? Do I receive a refund if I cancel? If they cancel?

- **How jam-packed is the schedule?** Do tour organizers try to fit 25 hours into a 24-hour day, or is there ample time for relaxing and/or shopping?

- **How big is the group?** The smaller the group, the more flexible the schedule and the less time you'll spend waiting for people to enter and exit the bus. Tour operators may be evasive about this, because they may not know the exact size of the group until everybody makes their reservations, but they should be able to give you a rough estimate. Some tours have a minimum group size and may cancel the tour if they don't book enough people.

- **What is included in the package?** Don't assume that anything is included. For example, you may have to pay to get yourself to and from the airport. Or an excursion may include a box lunch, but drinks may cost extra, or the meal may include beer but not wine. How much choice do you have? Can you opt out of certain activities, or does the bus leave once a day, with no exceptions? Are all your meals planned in advance? Can you choose your entree at dinner?

With an escorted tour, think strongly about purchasing travel insurance, especially if the tour operator asks you to pay up front. But don't
buy insurance from the tour operator! If they don't fulfill their obliga-
tion to provide you with the vacation that you've paid for, don't expect
them to fulfill their insurance obligations either. Buy travel insurance
through an independent agency.

Escorted tours to Italy

Some companies specialize in escorted Italian tours. Here's a brief list:

- ✔ **Italiatour** (☎ 800-845-3365 or 212-675-2183; Internet: www.
  italiatour.com) is associated with Alitalia (Italy's national
  airline) and offers a variety of tours and excellent expertise.

- ✔ **Perillo Tours,** 577 Chestnut Ridge Rd., Woodcliff Lake, NJ 07675-9888
  (☎ 800-431-1515 or 201-307-1234; Internet: www.perillotours.
  com), has been in business for more than half a century. Its itineraries range from 8 to 15 days and are very diverse. From April
  through October, you can choose among nine itineraries. In the
  off-season, Perillo Tours visits only the big cities — Rome, Florence,
  and Venice.

- ✔ **Central Holidays** (☎ 800-935-5000; Internet: www.central
  holidays.com) offers fully escorted tours in addition to their
  packages.

- ✔ **Insight International Tours,** 745 Atlantic Ave., Suite 720, Boston,
  MA 02111 (☎ 800-582-8380; Internet: www.inusa.insight
  vacation.com), runs luxury motor-coach tours lasting from a
  week to a month.

- ✔ If you're interested in luxurious, classy tours of Italy, you can also
  try **Abercrombie & Kent,** 1520 Kensington Rd., Oak Brook, IL
  60523 (☎ 800-323-7308; Internet: www.abercrombiekent.com;
  London address: Sloan Square House, Holbein Place, London
  SW1W 8NS; London ☎ 020-7730-9600).

- ✔ If you're only interested in one specific area of Italy, you can also
  check out Italian companies that specialize in one Italian region.
  For example, **Compagnia Siciliana Turismo (CST),** Via E. Amari
  124, 90139 Palermo (☎ 091-582-294; Fax: 091-582-218; Internet:
  http://web.tin.it/cst; E-mail: cstmail@tin.it), offers a
  number of organized tours of Sicily, lasting from a few days to two
  weeks. **Authentic Sicily,** 300 W. 23rd St., Suite 8G, New York, NY
  10011 (☎ 212-741-2258; Internet: www.authenticsicily.com)
  takes small groups on tours of "authentic" Sicily, promising a
  family-style environment and a relaxed pace.

Wine, antiques, and hunting for mush-rooms: Specialty tours on the Internet

You can find tours in Italy centered around just about any– and everything — antiques, archaeology, art history, cooking, cycling, gay life, nudism, religion, walk-ing, wineries, and more — at **InfoHub Specialty Travel Guide** (www.infohub. com). Two other good resource sites for specialty tours and travels are the **Specialty Travel Index** (www.specialtytravel.com), which offers a com-prehensive selection of Italian tours from ballooning to mushroom hunting to river cruises, and **Shaw Guides** (www.shawguides.com), with links to a substantial volume of trips to Italy, from archaeological programs to falconry trips to tours for opera fans.

The Independent Traveler: Making Your Own Arrangements

Whether you're committed to going it alone and planning your trip yourself, or you're just pricing out the pieces to see how much of a deal you're really getting with a package tour (see "The Ins and Outs of Package Tours," and "The Ins and Outs of Escorted Tours," earlier in this chapter), making your own travel arrangements is a step-by-step process. First, of course, you need to know which airlines fly to Italy from where you are.

Finding a suitable flight

Rome and Milan are the only two Italian cities to which you can fly non-stop from North America. For Florence, Venice, Naples, or Sicily, you have to take a connecting flight in Rome or Milan. Fly into Milan if you're focusing on northern Italy, and fly into Rome if you're focusing on the south.

Because Italy is long and skinny in shape, flying into one airport and leaving from the other makes a lot of sense, especially if you have only a week or ten days to travel and you want to see sights in both north-ern and southern Italy. If, for example, you landed in Milan, you could take a train to Venice, then pick up a car and drive down through Tuscany, loop around the near south taking in Rome and some other sites, and then fly out of Rome. For the right price, this plan may save you hundreds of miles of driving or sitting on the train.

Alitalia, the Italian national airline, offers flights from every major city in the world to every destination in Italy by way of Rome or Milan

(☎ **800-223-5730** in the U.S., 800-361-8336 in Canada, 020-7602-7111 in London or 0990-448-259 in the rest of the U.K., 1300-653-747 or 1300-653-757 in Australia, toll-free 1478-65-643 or 06-65643 in Italy; Internet: www.alitalia.it or www.alitaliausa.com). Alitalia also offers daily flights to all European capitals. Direct daily flights are scheduled from a number of cities in the United States and from Toronto and Montreal in Canada. Likewise, Alitalia offers direct service between Sydney and Melbourne and Italy, but not every day. At press time, Alitalia offers three flights a week from Sydney to Rome and three to Milan, as well as one flight a week from Melbourne to Milan and Melbourne to Rome.

In addition to Alitalia, from the United States, **American Airlines** (☎ **800-433-7300;** Internet: www.aa.com) runs nonstop flights to Italy out of Chicago. **Delta** (☎ **800-241-4141;** Internet: www.delta.com) flies from New York City to Italy, whereas United (☎ **800-538-2929;** Internet: www.ual.com) flies to Milan from Washington, D.C. **US Airways** (☎ **800-428-4322;** Internet: www.usairways.com) flies from Philadelphia to Rome; **Continental** (☎ **800-525-0280;** Internet: www.continental.com) flies to Rome from Newark, New Jersey; and Northwest/KLM Airlines (☎ **800-447-4747;** Internet: www.nwa.com) flies from its hub in Detroit.

In Canada, you can fly **Alitalia** (☎ **800-361-8336;** Internet: www.alitalia.it) from Montreal or Toronto. In addition, you can also fly **Air Canada** (☎ **888-247-2262;** Internet: www.aircanada.ca).

From Britain, your best bet other than Alitalia is **British Airways** (☎ **0345-222-7111** in the U.K.; Internet: www.britishairways.com), though smaller charter companies also offer flights.

From Australia and New Zealand, **Cathay Pacific** (☎ **131-747** toll-free in Australia, 0508-800454 in New Zealand; Internet: www.cathaypacific.com) offers three flights a week to Rome from Melbourne and Sydney, connecting through Hong Kong. The airline also offers two flights from Perth and Cairns, connecting through Hong Kong, and one flight from Brisbane connecting through Hong Kong. Auckland is also served thrice weekly, also with a connection through Hong Kong. Another option is **Qantas** (☎ **13-13-13;** Internet: www.qantas.com), which offers some direct flights — daily from Melbourne to Rome and several days a week from Sydney. **Air New Zealand** (☎ **800-737-000;** Internet: www.airnz.com) doesn't fly directly to Italy. You have to change in another European city to a national carrier — most likely in London or Frankfurt.

On any day of the week, you can get a connecting flight through a major European capital, where you switch to the national carrier — connecting through London with British Airways or through Paris with Air France. European airlines include **British Airways** (☎ **800-247-297;** Internet: www.britishairways.com), **Air France** (☎ **800-237-2747;**

www.airfrance.com), **KLM** (☎ **800-374-7747**; Internet: www.klm.nl), and **Lufthansa** (☎ **800-645-3880**; Internet: www.lufthansa-usa.com).

All European carriers will make you stop over in their own country before you fly on to Italy. In order to encourage the public to choose a non-direct alternative, round-trip rates are often handsomely discounted, and direct connections sometimes involve no more than an hour or two of layover. By connecting in major European hubs, you may be able to avoid Milan and Rome by flying into Italy's secondary airports, such as Venice, Turin, or Genoa. If you plan to travel on one of the European carriers, you may also want to consider combining a stop of a few days in a major European city en route to Italy.

Getting the best airfare

For Italy, the high season is long and getting longer, and snagging low fares is increasingly more difficult; at certain times, you may be lucky just to get on any plane heading for Italy. But fear not: There are myriad ways to avoid paying top dollar for your airline seat.

If you need the flexibility to purchase your tickets at the last minute, change your itinerary at a moment's notice, or want to get home before the weekend, you'll pay the premium rate, known as the *full fare* — many business travelers fall into this category. If, on the other hand, you can book your tickets far in advance, don't mind staying over Saturday night, or are willing to travel on a Tuesday, Wednesday, or Thursday, you'll pay the least, usually a fraction of the full fare.

Keep in mind that European national airlines (Alitalia, Lufthansa, Air France, and so on) may cost more, but they also seem to have more legroom and better service. This may be an important consideration, given that the flight from New York to Rome is about eight hours compared with five hours to London.

Here are some tips on snagging the best airfare:

✔ **Book in advance and be flexible.** Passengers who can book their ticket long in advance, who can stay over Saturday night, or who are willing to travel on a Tuesday, Wednesday, or Thursday after 7 p.m., for example, will pay a fraction of the full fare. If your schedule is flexible, say so — ask if you can secure a cheaper fare by staying an extra day, by flying midweek, or by flying at less-trafficked hours. Buying in advance makes a big difference as well: If you can book your airfare more than 21 days in advance, you may be able to snag supersaver seats.

✔ **Shop around for seasonal or promotional specials.** You'll almost never see a sale during the peak summer vacation months of July and August or during the Thanksgiving or Christmas seasons; but in periods of low-volume travel, look for sales or fare wars, when airlines periodically lower prices on their most popular routes. If you already hold a ticket when a sale breaks, exchanging your ticket, which usually incurs a $100 to $150 charge, may pay off. Keep in mind that the lowest-priced fares are often nonrefundable, require advance purchase of one to three weeks and a certain length of stay, and carry penalties for changing dates of travel.

✔ **Use the Internet.** The benefits of researching your trip online can be well worth the effort. Airlines often offer discounts on fares or incentives like extra frequent-flier miles just for booking online.

Some sites will send you e-mail notification when a cheap fare becomes available to your favorite destinations. Some will also tell you when fares to a particular destination are lowest. Among the most popular are **Travelocity** (www.travelocity.com or www.frommers.travelocity.com), Frommer's online travel planning/ booking partner, which offers reservations and tickets for more than 400 airlines, plus reservations and purchase capabilities for more than 45,000 hotels and 50 car-rental companies; and **Expedia** (www.expedia.com), another comprehensive planning/booking site. Travelers search by destination, dates, and cost. **Orbitz** (www.orbitz.com) is a popular site launched by United, Delta, Northwest, American, and Continental Airlines. **Priceline** (www.priceline.com) lets you "name your price" for airline tickets, hotel rooms, and rental cars. For airline tickets, you can't say what time you want to fly — you have to accept any flight between 6 a.m. and 10 p.m. on the dates you've selected, and you may have to make one or more stopovers. Tickets are nonrefundable, and no frequent-flier miles are awarded.

✔ **Use consolidators.** Also known as *bucket shops,* consolidators are a good place to find low fares. Consolidators buy seats in bulk from the airlines and then sell them back to the public at prices usually below even the airlines' discounted rates. Their small ads usually run in Sunday newspaper travel sections. Before you pay, request a confirmation number from the consolidator and then call the airline to confirm your seat. Be aware that bucket-shop tickets are usually nonrefundable or rigged with stiff cancellation penalties, often as high as 50 to 75% of the ticket price. Protect yourself by paying with a credit card rather than cash. Also check out the name of the airline; you may not want to fly on some obscure airline, even if you're saving money. **Council Travel** (☎ 800-226-8624; Internet: www.counciltravel.com) and **STA Travel** (☎ 800-781-4040; Internet: www.sta.travel.com) cater especially to young travelers, but their bargain-basement prices are available to people of all ages. **The TravelHub** (☎ 888-AIR-FARE; Internet: www.travelhub.com) represents nearly 1,000 travel agencies, many of whom offer consolidator and discount fares. Other reliable consolidators include **1-800-FLY-CHEAP** (Internet: www.1800flycheap.com); **TFI Tours International** (☎ 800-745-8000 or 212-736-1140; Internet: www.lowestprice.com), which serves as a clearinghouse for unused seats; or "rebators," such as **Travel Avenue** (☎ 800-333-3335; Internet:

www.travelavenue.com) and the **Smart Traveller** (☎ 800-448-3338 in the U.S. or 305-448-3338), which rebate part of their commissions to you.

✔ **Join frequent-flier clubs.** Accruing miles on one program is best, so you can rack up free flights and achieve elite status faster. But opening as many accounts as possible makes sense, no matter how seldom you fly a particular airline. It's free, and you get the best choice of seats, faster response to phone inquiries, and prompter service if your luggage is stolen, if your flight is canceled or delayed, or if you want to change your seat.

Spinning Wheels: Getting to Italy by Train, Ferry, Bus, or Car

If you're coming to Italy from continental Europe and don't want to fly, taking a train is your best alternative. Italy has an excellent rail system, and there are several long-distance trains to and from everywhere in Europe. You can even take the Orient Express to Venice!

Paris is connected by high-speed TGV trains to Torino-Novara-Milan. From Paris, you can also take the famous Palatino, the overnight train to Rome. You can also catch overnight trains from Germany (Hanover, Düsseldorf, Köln, Bonn, and Frankfurt). For more on taking the train in Italy, see Chapter 7.

Another way to arrive in Italy from continental Europe is by ferry. There are several ferry services to Genoa from France (for example, from Sète), from Patras in Greece to Brindisi and Ancona, and from Croatia to Ancona. One such line is Naples-based **Grimaldi Ferries** (☎081-496-444; Internet: www.grimaldi-ferries.com), which offers ferry service to and from Salerno to Palermo (Sicily), Malta, and Valencia (Spain).

You can even get to Italy by bus. **Eurolines** (☎ 0990-143-219; Internet: www.eurolines.com) is the leading operator of scheduled coach services across Europe, and services to Italy depart from London's Victoria Coach Station. Its comprehensive network of services includes regular departures to destinations throughout Italy, including Turin, Milan, Bologna, Florence, and Rome — plus summer services to Verona, Vicenza, Padua, and Venice.

If you love driving very long distances and have plenty of time, you can also drive a car to Italy. Crossing the Alps is quite an experience. The highway takes you through one of the major passes, depending on where you're coming from, or you can take the newly reopened tunnel under Mont Blanc. You then arrive at one of three main cities: Milan (central Italy), Genoa (western coastal), or Venice (eastern coastal). All roads headed south converge in Florence and Rome. For more on renting a car — and knowing the rules of the road — in Italy, see Chapter 7.

Chapter 7

Getting Around Italy

• •

In This Chapter

▶ Flying to and fro

▶ Traveling on land

• •

*T*he first thing that you notice in Italy is that everybody speaks *Italiano*. Luckily, signs are often *nonlingual* (using international symbols) and bilingual in major tourist areas. Among the most common signs — and most useful to a tourist — are the square black-and-yellow signs indicating a tourist information office or booth (a lowercase black italic *i* on a yellow background; sometimes white on brown), and the skirted and panted stick figures indicating women's and men's restrooms.

As a land of tourism, Italy has developed a set of special signs that indicate sights, which are different from the regular road signs. These signs have white lettering on a brown background, or black lettering on a yellow background, and they often have a little picture (a box with a cross on it for a church, two columns and one lying down for a Greek or Roman ruin, and so on). Likewise, they may even include the distance to the attraction in meters.

In this chapter, we give you the information you need to travel throughout Italy and tips for choosing the type of transportation that best adapts to your plans and destinations. We also give you a comparison of travel times between major destinations using different modes of transportation.

Traveling by Plane

The Italian national airline is **Alitalia** (☎ **800-223-5730** in the U.S., 800-361-8336 in Canada, 020-7602-7111 in London, 0990-448-259 in the rest of the U.K., 1300-653-747 or 1300-653-757 in Australia, and toll-free 1478-65643 or 06-65643 in Italy; Internet: www.alitalia.it or www.alitaliausa.com). Alitalia offers flights to every destination in Italy.

However, you can choose from regional airlines as well. **Air Sicilia** (☎ 06-6501-71046) flies to Sicily from other Italian cities and sometimes offers better rates than Alitalia. Other private airlines include **Air One** (☎ 1478-48-880 toll-free or 02-5832-5035 in Italy; Internet: www.air-one.it), which flies to several destinations in Italy, including between Venice and Rome, and **Meridiana** (☎ 078-952-600; Internet: www.meridiana.it), which also flies to several destinations in Italy and Europe, including from Palermo to Milan, Florence, Pisa, and Verona, and from Verona to Catania, Naples, Palermo, and Rome.

When traveling on domestic flights in Italy, you can receive a 30% fare reduction if you take a flight that departs at night.

Table 7-1 provides the travel times between major Italian cities using different modes of transportation.

Table 7-1	Travel Times between the Major Cities			
Cities	**Distance**	**Air Travel Time**	**Train Travel Time**	**Driving Time**
Florence to Milan	298km/185 miles	55 min.	2½ hrs.	3½ hrs.
Florence to Venice	281km/174 miles	2 hrs., 5 min.	4 hrs.	3 hrs., 15 min.
Milan to Venice	267km/166 miles	50 min.	3½ hrs.	3 hrs., 10 min.
Rome to Florence	277km/172 miles	1 hr., 10 min.	2½ hrs.	3 hrs., 20 min.
Rome to Milan	572km/355 miles	1 hr., 5 min.	5 hrs.	6 hrs., 30 min.
Rome to Naples	219km/136 miles	50 min.	2½ hrs.	2½ hrs.
Rome to Venice	528km/327 miles	1 hr., 5 min.	5 hrs., 15 min.	6 hrs.
Venice to Naples	747km/463 miles	1 hr., 45 min.	7 hrs., 45 min.	8 hrs., 30 min.

Taking the Train

Train travel in Italy is often a preferred choice. The network is large, distances are relatively small, the express trains are fast and comfortable, it's not very expensive, and you depart and arrive right from and to the center of town. To check how well your chosen destinations are served by rail, see the Italian train routes map on the inside front cover of this guide.

One train-travel option is buying a pass from the **Rail Europe Group** (☎ **800-438-7245** in the U.S. and 800-361-7245 in Canada; Internet: www.raileurope.com). The Rail Europe Group offers several options, based on how many days you want to travel and whether you want to travel consecutively for several days or stop in between. For example, the eight-consecutive-day pass for Italy is $227 (second class) and gives you unlimited travel all over Italy for those eight days. Another possibility is the Flexi Rail Card, which allows you to travel in Italy on a specific number of days within a month; for example, you can get a four-day Flexi Rail Card for $191 and have the right to unlimited travel during any four days of your choice. You can also choose other options for longer periods of time. The interesting Rail 'n Drive pass includes an automatic Hertz car rental for two days (with unlimited mileage) as well as three days of unlimited rail travel within a month for $444 for two people. Not bad!

Another train-travel option is buying the special kilometric ticket directly from the **FS (Ferrovia dello Stato),** Italy's national rail company. With a kilometric ticket, you buy a number of kilometers that you can use as you wish for as many as four passengers. Several amounts are available; for example, you can buy 3,000km (1,860 miles) for 108€ ($97). You can use as many kilometers as you want at a time and use the ticket for two months; shorter distances are available, too. Using the kilometric ticket, you save about 15% over what you'd spend buying individual tickets. You can also sign more than one person onto the ticket, so you don't have to buy one for each person in your party. If you're a couple traveling from Rome to Venice (528km), you'll use up a little over a third of your ticket. Each time you travel, go to the train-station window and have the pass validated. The teller will calculate the distance and write down how many kilometers you have left. You can also ask the teller to write "Roma to Venezia, via Firenze" so you don't have to go to the ticket booth at your through-stops. However, after the ticket is validated for a trip, you do have to complete the trip within four days. Surcharges apply to the super-fast Eurostar trains, and in the high travel season, you have to reserve your seat (at a slight extra charge); you can buy the surcharge at the time you validate your ticket.

You can buy kilometric tickets and rail passes at all train stations in Italy. Likewise, you can also buy rail passes before you leave the United States through a travel agent or Rail Europe (see the contact information earlier in this section). In the United States, you can buy kilometric tickets from the official U.S. representative of the Italian national rail company, **CIT Tours,** 15 W. 44th St., Suite 104, New York, NY 10036 (☎ **800-248-8687;** Fax: 800-338-3964; Internet: http://cit-tours.com). You can also find FS rail info or buy tickets online at www.fs-on-line.com.

Getting Around by Bus

In Italy, you can get virtually anywhere with public transportation. If you are up to it and have the time, you don't really need to rent a car even to reach remote destinations in the middle of nowhere. Where the train system stops, the bus system takes over and gets you even into the smallest hamlets in the countryside. For example, **SITA,** Viale del Cadorna 105, Firenze (☎ **055-47821**), operates an extensive bus network in central Italy. You often see people from the countryside taking the bus to and from Florence, Siena, and other major centers. In this book, we list other companies for each destination where taking a bus makes sense and is a better way of transportation. You won't see too many tourists on buses, however, which is good if you want to meet real Italians and get a feeling for what life is really like in Italy.

Be sure to call the bus company in advance and inquire about the schedules, which change frequently. Tickets must be bought at the bus station in advance, because drivers don't have cash to make change. Do not plan to use the bus, though, if you need to reach several small towns in a day — that's not what the system is geared for (it's meant for people who need to commute between the small town where they live and the larger towns of the area), and schedules will not work very well.

Floating by Ferry

The only ferries you're likely to use in Italy are the ferries to Capri (see Chapter 21) and Sicily (see Chapter 23) from Naples, and the ferry to Capri from Positano (see Chapter 22); ferries to Sicily take cars. For more information, see the relevant chapters.

If you want to bring your car on a ferry, you must make a reservation well in advance — especially during the high season. Taking your car on a ferry also means that you'll have to pay more. In some cases, you may save money renting your car on arrival rather than taking it on a ferry.

Driving Around in a Car

In order to drive in Italy, you need to get an International Driver's License before leaving the United States. Any branch of the **American Automobile Association (AAA)** (☎ **800-222-4357** in the U.S. or 613-247-0117 in Canada) issues International Driver's Licenses. You have to fill out the AAA application form and provide a 2-x-2-inch photograph, a photocopy of your U.S. driver's license, and $10. Don't forget to bring your U.S. license with you in Italy, though, because the International license is valid only in combination with your regular license. An alternative to the International Driver's License is to take an

Italian translation of your U.S. license (prepared by AAA or another organization) to an office of the **Automobile Club d'Italia** (☎ **06-4477** for 24-hour information and assistance) in Italy to receive a special driving permit.

Likewise, if you're planning to drive in Italy, make sure that you have a good road map. The best maps are published by the Automobile Club d'Italia and the Italian Touring Club and are widely available in bookstores and at newsstands in Italy. A lot of highway building is going on in Italy, so maps change often.

Knowing the rules of the road

You need to know two very important rules when driving in Italy: Drive defensively, and always be ready to get out of the way.

It's a myth that Italians drive badly or at least worse than anyone else. They drive fast and are usually skilled drivers. For one thing, you won't see (as you often do in the United States) someone driving along a major highway reading a book or newspaper or putting on makeup. (If you tried that in Italy, you'd be killed.) Italians love to drive, but they drive fast and aren't very patient. If you're going 90kmh (56 mph) and passing a car going 80kmh (50 mph), someone may zoom up behind you going 140kmh (87 mph) and flashing his lights (a perfect time to apply Rule 2). People do, however, follow the rules of the road (even at 100 mph), because the penalty for doing something dumb at that speed is often dire; at slower speeds, at the very least, people yell and make obscene gestures.

Road signs in Italy for the *autostrada* (limited access, national or international toll road) are white on green; signs for local roads are white on blue. A white-on-blue sign saying "SS119" means that you're on the *strada statale* (state road) number 119.

A puzzling sign placed close to the ground is the white arrow on a blue circle; it points you to the lane that you should enter or the correct way around an obstacle, a traffic island, and so forth. Another important sign is No Parking — a blue-and-red circle with a diagonal stripe pointing to the side of the street where you can't park. If the sign shows two stripes (an X), you can't park on either side of the street. *Senso Unico* written on a white arrow on a blue background means a one-way street, and the white-on-red stop sign is obvious. Another useful sign to know is *Stazione* or *Stazione FS* or only *FS,* indicating the direction of the local train station (the sign may also include the name of the station).

Keep your eyes peeled for exits (each marked *Uscita*). They're often indicated on the highway far in advance and then right on top of the ramp — not a few hundred yards in advance, where it's helpful.

The following three rules are rigidly obeyed on the highway in Italy (again, unlike in the States):

Rule 1: Pass only on the left.

Rule 2: Never stay in the passing lane unless you're going faster than everybody else. Just pull out, pass, and get back in the slow lane right away.

Rule 3: When you're entering on a highway and you have a sign to yield, you *do* have to yield, which may mean stopping and waiting for the merging lane to be available. Do not assume people will move over; they won't (chances are there is a very fast car coming up behind them that you cannot see) and they know they have the right of way over you and take it for granted that you'll wait your turn (they won't expect you to force your way into their lane, so if you do, they may very well lack the time to react). That is true of any merging intersection between a minor and a major road and when you come out of a gas station or rest area. At regular intersections, the person on the right always has the right of way unless otherwise indicated, and except in traffic circles, where the cars already in the circle have priority over those trying to enter.

Naples deserves special mention with respect to driving — even other Italians won't drive there. Consider that on our first visit, in one block we saw a motorcyclist riding a wheelie the length of the street and a tiny car that drove up on the sidewalk and around the signal pole to avoid a red light! If you arrive in Naples by car, find a garage or parking space fast, and then walk or take the bus.

If you're used to highways that run in straight lines and city streets that follow neat grids, prepare yourself for twisting roads (plunging cliffs optional), paved ancient Roman roads, city streets with kidney-shattering cobblestones, big broad piazze without lines indicating lanes, and streets only as wide as one Italian car. (We once saw a Corvette with New York plates plug up a small street in Rome.) In Italian cities, you also find swarms of *motorini* — what Americans call mopeds (but in Italy they're much faster). If you're first at a stoplight, a swarm of 15 can easily surround you by the time the light changes. Look out for *motorini,* because they certainly aren't looking out for you.

The driving situation in Italy probably isn't as bad as we've made it sound. But we will go against the other guidebooks and make the following claim: Unless you're really going to spend time off the beaten track, don't rent a car. If the focus of your trip is the big three cities (Rome, Florence, and Venice), traveling by train is faster, less stressful, and cheaper. Even if you want to explore the Tuscan countryside, a large fleet of buses serves the territory between Florence and Siena, for example, and you can take trains to smaller cities like Perugia and Assisi in Umbria.

If you aren't in shape or very mobile, however, a car makes sense. Here's a good compromise: Plan your itinerary so that you can either spend a few days in a city, and then pick up your car when you're ready to leave (not at the airport upon your arrival), or plan your rural driving first, and then dump your car as soon as you get to the city where you'll spend the most time.

In Italy, driving a car is often more expensive than traveling by train or bus, because tolls are high and gas is very expensive (about 4.5€/$4 per gallon). Driving from Rome to Florence and back, for example, can cost you two tanks of gas ($80 plus) and another $10 to $20 in tolls depending on how much of the *autostrada* you use. To that you have to add what you pay for parking.

If, after our warnings, you still can't wait to load up a Cadillac with your steamer trunks and do the Amalfi Coast, think again. Italian cars are small, and Italian roads are designed for Italian cars; even the big ones are never larger than an American midsize and the trunk has half the capacity of American cars. Keep your luggage to a minimum; you don't want to drive around and park with your extra suitcase sitting in the back seat — a sure way to have your car broken into.

If you don't know how to drive a standard shift car (that is, with a manual transmission), consider learning how before leaving for Italy. Most Italian cars are standard. The country is very mountainous, and a car with an automatic shift is often a pain. Likewise, automatics cost more to rent, and rental agencies may run out of them sooner. Standard cars also get better gas mileage, especially crawling up and down steep grades. Keep in mind that gas stations often close for lunch and shut down all day on Sunday (except along the *autostrada*), so don't let your gas gauge get too low, especially if you're cruising the rural countryside.

Understanding the rules of renting

Car-rental rates vary more than airline fares. The price you pay depends on the size of the car, the length of time you keep it, where and when you pick it up and drop it off, where you take it, as well as a host of other factors. Reserving the car before leaving home is usually best.

When renting a car, asking a few key questions can save you hundreds of dollars. Are weekend rates lower than weekday rates? Is the rate the same for pickup Friday morning as it is for Thursday night? If you're keeping the car five or more days, you may find that a weekly rate is cheaper than the daily rate. Does the company assess a drop-off charge if you don't return the car to the same renting location? Is the rate cheaper if you pick up the car at the airport or at a location in town? Does the rate include a set number of miles you're allotted to drive?

If you see an advertised price in your local newspaper, make sure that you ask for that specific rate; otherwise, the company may charge you the standard (higher) rate. And don't forget to mention membership in AAA, AARP, frequent-flier programs, and trade unions. These memberships usually entitle you to discounts of 5 to 30%. And remember, most car rentals are worth at least 500 miles on your frequent-flier account!

Internet resources can make comparison shopping for rental cars easier. For example, Yahoo!'s partnership with Flifo Global travel agency allows you to look up rental prices for any size car at more than a dozen companies in hundreds of cities. It will even make your reservation for you, if you choose. Point your browser to http://travel. yahoo.com/travel and choose "Reserve car" from the options. Travelocity.com also offers a car-rental component, and on Priceline.com, you can bid the price you want to pay for a rental.

On top of standard prices, optional charges apply to most car rentals. Most rental companies require that you pay for theft protection insurance, because car theft is unfortunately common in Italy. (International gangs operate in Italy and ship stolen cars to Eastern Europe.) Many credit cards cover you for damage to a rental car, so that you don't have to take the rental company's collision insurance. However, check with your company to see if your card's benefit extends outside the United States so that you can avoid paying this hefty fee (as much as $10 per day).

Car-rental companies also offer additional liability insurance (if you harm others in an accident), personal accident insurance (if you harm yourself or your passengers), and personal effects insurance (if your luggage is stolen from your car). If you have insurance on your car at home, you're probably covered for most of these unlikelihoods. (However, check to see if your insurance covers overseas rentals.)

Some companies also offer refueling packages, in which you pay for an entire tank of gas up front. If you reject this option, you pay only for the gas you use, but you have to return the car with a full tank or face expensive fuel charges. If a stop at a gas station on the way to the airport will make you miss your plane, take advantage of the fuel-purchase option. Otherwise, skip it.

The most well-known car-rental companies operating in Italy are **Avis** (☎ **800-331-1212** in the U.S., or 06-41-999 in Italy; Internet: www.avis. com); **Hertz** (☎ **800-654-3001** in the U.S., or 199-112-211 in Italy; Internet: www.hertz.com); **National/Maggiore** (☎ **800-227-7368** in the U.S., or 1478-67-067 toll-free in Italy; Internet: www.maggiore.it/eng/ Master_Eng.htm); **AutoEurope** (☎ **800-223-5555** in the U.S., or 800-334-440 toll-free in Italy; Internet: www.autoeurope.com); **Kemwel** (☎ **800-678-0678** in the U.S; Internet: www.kemwel.com); **Europe by Car** (☎ **800-223-1516** in the U.S.; Internet: www.europebycar.com); and **Europcar** (☎ **800-014-410** toll-free in Italy, or 06-6501-0879; Internet: www.europcar.it).

Chapter 8

Booking Your Accommodations

● ●

In This Chapter

▶ Choosing among Italy's hotels

▶ Booking a room

▶ Saving money on hotel costs

▶ Avoiding getting stuck without a place to sleep

● ●

Despite the recent currency consolidation in Europe and the push toward globalization, hotels are not the same all over the world. International chains are moving toward a certain standardization of services, but you can still find plenty of individuality and quirky charm out there, especially in countries where hostelry and hospitality are long-standing traditions. Italy is certainly one of those places.

Travelers have journeyed to Italy for the past 3,000 years (at least), and more than a few inns can claim several centuries of service. This history creates an enormous variety in Italy's hotels, from romantic 15th-century hostels and 17th-century *palazzi* with frescoes to simple 19th-century farmhouses and modern luxury hotels. In this chapter, we give you all the important tips you need to make your accommodations choices.

Knowing What to Expect: From Albergo to Agriturismo

Many hotels in Italy simply don't resemble hotels in the United States. In most American hotels, you'll find spacious, air-conditioned rooms, equally big bathrooms with tub/shower combos, beds that come in a variety of sizes, and amenities galore, in even the most basic rooms.

Italy, however, is different. Because the buildings that house guest accommodations are sometimes centuries old, there often isn't room to fit all the modern amenities. The average room is smallish with a relatively tiny bathroom with shower only and twin beds that can be made into a double. If you must have American-style amenities, you will have to opt for a super-deluxe hotel (often operated by a chain, and either housed in modern buildings or ancient villas and *palazzi*); if you can adapt to simpler accommodations, you can stay in a more modest *albergo* (hotel) or *pensione* (a small, family-run hotel offering basic rooms and services). Out in the countryside, you can opt to stay in a farmhouse, apartment, or bedroom on a working Italian farm as part of a nationwide program known as *agriturismo* (wine-producing estates make up a large part of these), or at a villa-resort (usually a patrician country residence transformed into a hotel and featuring swimming pools, spas, and beautiful gardens).

Amenities: The bare facts

Not long ago, a friend asked us to help her choose a hotel in Florence and complained of the high prices. "We only need a private bathroom," she said. She then added with surprise, "Does this mean some hotels don't have private baths?" Well, the sooner you know the bad news, the better: In Italy, a private bathroom is an *option* and not a basic amenity, although it is slowly becoming one. If you don't like having your bath outside your room (not necessarily shared) or sharing it with another room or two, you have to pay extra. We hasten to add that this rule is rapidly changing, however. Hotels are adding private baths wherever they can, but in some historic buildings, room isn't available to put in a big bathroom or even a tub. Therefore, it's not at all unusual for the shower to be a wall fixture over part of the tiled floor, with a curtain around it (not a door) and the drain below it. (Prepare yourself for wet floors.) Renovating buildings that are pro-tected as historic sites can be difficult.

If you absolutely must have a big comfortable room or a bathroom with all the amenities, prepare to fork over extra euros for a room in a bigger, newer, more expensive hotel.

Throughout this guide, we include recently built hotels that provide modern amenities (including bathrooms) at good prices. Some accom-modations are a little outside the city center or away from fashionable neighborhoods. Face it: You may not want old-world charm every night; sometimes reading in a decent-sized tub or crashing early and comfortably is more important.

Another difference in accommodations between the U.S. and Italy is beds. The majority of hotels in Italy have only one kind of bed — a large twin. In a double room, you usually find two separate twin beds. If you ask for a double bed, the host or hostess puts together the two twins into a *matrimoniale* (large bed), making the bed up tight together with sheets. You may think this practice is unusual, but you'll discover that it's not uncomfortable. On the good side, most hotels in Italy, and certainly all the ones in our listings, are proud of the quality of their bedding, providing good mattresses with a medium degree of firmness.

Besides the differences between beds and bathrooms, other hotel features in Italy also differ from U.S. hotel standards. For example, despite often sweltering summers, air-conditioning isn't common in Italy, and its installation is still in the early stages. Usually, only the more expensive hotels are air-conditioned; many hotels have air-conditioning only in specific rooms, for which you must pay more, of course. Regular TVs are standard, but these simple TVs don't offer English-language programs. For English-language programming, you need satellite TVs, which are available only in the higher-category hotels. All rooms usually have telephones. In fact, only in smaller villages or very simple accommodations will you not have a phone in your room. Another difference is floors: Often you'll find tiles or marble and sometimes wooden floors, whereas carpeting is more rare. Bring slippers to get around the room and go to the bathroom in the cooler months if you don't want to get cold feet!

The best room — and how to get it

To increase your chances of getting a good room, ask for a corner room. They're usually larger, quieter, and have more windows and light than standard rooms. And they don't always cost more. On the other hand, in some buildings 500 or more years old, corner rooms may not be the most spacious.

The prevalence of old buildings raises another issue: renovations. When you make your reservation, ask if the hotel is renovating. If it is, request a room that's already been renovated or, failing that, a room away from the renovation work. If the hotel is on a busy street, request a room away from the street. If a hotel has a garden or courtyard, ask if rooms that overlook it are available. Likewise, inquire about the location of restaurants, bars, and discos in the hotel — and if noise or smoke bothers you, ask for a room as far away from them as possible.

Speaking of smoke, in Italy, don't count on getting a nonsmoking room; most hotels have only one such room, if at all. On the other hand, because rooms usually have hard floors instead of carpeting and it's a common practice to wash curtains often, even a regular room rarely smells of old tobacco.

And finally, remember that if you aren't happy with your room when you arrive, you can talk to the front desk about moving to another one.

Checking out rooms online

To look at Italian hotels online and even make reservations, we recommend the following sites:

www.giroscopio.com

www.initaly.com

www.italyguide.com

www.italyhotel.com

www.italyhotelink.com

www.italyincoming.com

www.itwg.com

www.venere.it

www.wel.it

More and more, hotels are offering their own Web sites, and we note these sites in the hotel listings.

Getting the Most for Your Money

Getting the room you want at the right price is the name of the game. In this section, we go over the variety of prices, the price scale used in this book, and what you can expect to get for your money in each category. We also tell you how to make a reservation and how to cut your hotel costs.

The *rack rate* is the maximum rate a hotel charges for a room. The rack rate is the rate you get if you walked in off the street and asked for a room for the night. You see this rate printed on the fire/emergency exit diagrams posted on the back of guest room doors. We quote the rack rate for each of our hotel listings throughout this book.

Hotels are happy to charge you the rack rate, but you don't always have to pay it. Perhaps the best way to avoid paying the rack rate is surprisingly simple: Ask for a cheaper or discounted rate. You may be pleasantly surprised.

The price offered for a room may often be lower than the rack rate, because that refers to high season and full hotel occupancy, whereas you may have scheduled your trip during a slightly less mobbed time.

Knowing the price categories

In this book, we list our favorite hotels, using cleanliness, comfort, and the most amenities at the best prices as essential criteria. Each listing includes a key indicating the cost of the hotel with a number of dollar signs that correspond to the following amounts:

$	Up to 90€ ($80)
$$	90€–160€ ($80–$145)
$$$	160€–210€ ($145–$190)
$$$$	210€–260€ ($190–$235)
$$$$$	More than 260€ ($235 and up)

A typical hotel with a $ is basic and cheap, with no private baths or air-conditioning. A $$ hotel has some rooms with private baths and some without; some may have air-conditioning as well. To have a more spacious bathroom with a modern-style shower, as well as the general certainty of air-conditioning, you need a $$$ hotel. Hotels in the $$$$ and $$$$$ ranges are luxury places, sometimes part of international chains; they offer basic amenities plus special touches, ranging from antique furniture and minibars to luxurious bathrooms with deluxe toiletries and pools and gyms.

Room prices are subject to change without notice, so the rates that we quote in this book may differ from the actual rates that you receive when you make your reservations. And remember that the exchange rate varies from day to day, so the U.S. dollar amounts that we quote may be slightly different when you get to Italy.

Reserving in advance

In all but the smallest accommodations, the rate you pay for a room depends on many factors, not the least of which is how you make your reservation. With certain hotels, travel agents may be able to negotiate better prices than you can get on your own. (Hotels give the agents discounts in exchange for steering business their way.) And if you reserve your hotel rooms as part of a package, you may be able to save a bundle (see "Being part of a package," later in this chapter).

If you're traveling during high season (Easter to the end of summer, though in August large cities tend to be slightly less crowded because of the heat), reserve your hotel rooms as soon as you've finalized your itinerary and know definitely where you're going. The longer you wait, the fewer choices you'll have. In the city and regional chapters in this book, we note those highly-sought-after hotels where you should make reservations months in advance. Reserving your rooms as far as possible in advance for stays in Venice and Florence is an especially good idea; Rome is much larger and has many more hotels, but if you have your eye on a particular place, jump on it as soon as you can.

Making reservations can get complicated when you buy an E-fare or other last-minute bargain ticket. This cost-effective approach leaves you with relatively little time to get organized and make reservations, so you may end up booking into a large chain hotel that has lots of rooms or a more expensive hotel with vacancies. (In our opinion, the higher cost for accommodations is worth it. If the money evens out, we'd rather spend more on the place we stay than on our plane tickets.)

After you've reserved your rooms in whichever cities you plan to visit, remember to request faxed confirmations from the hotels, and then make sure that you bring these with you to Italy. If you check into a hotel that suddenly says they have no record of your reservation — mistakes occur everywhere — you can produce your faxed confirmation.

If you don't reserve your accommodations before leaving home, remember that in the train station(s) of each major city you can find a hotel desk whose staff will call around town and find you a room, if one is available. (In the high season, there's always the risk that rooms aren't available.) Sometimes this service is free and sometimes you have to pay a small fee.

Being part of a package

Joining a group tour or purchasing a package tour (see Chapter 6) almost ensures that you'll be staying in a fairly modern large hotel at a reasonable rate. That's because packagers don't make deals for five rooms here and three rooms there; they tend to use large hotels that give them good deals for bringing in so many customers. However, always price out the offers to see if the deal that you're getting is really as good as it seems. The packager should provide you with some pretty detailed information about the hotel options that the package offers, and if the hotel is online, you may be able to see pictures of your room choices.

Even if you don't sign up with a tour or a package, you may want to investigate their offerings to see which hotels they feature. Some packages offer a better class of hotels than others. Some offer the same hotels for lower prices than their competitors. Some offer no flexibility on hotel selections at all.

Finding tips on getting a room

Here are some additional strategies for finding the right room for you at the right price:

✔ **Surf the Web.** You can find good hotel packages online. See "Checking out rooms online," earlier in this chapter.

✔ **Go during off-peak times.** Your best chance of getting a deal or a discount is, of course, during the off-season, which generally means January and February, with the exception of Carnevale in towns where the celebrations attract many tourists (see Chapter 2 for a calendar of events). Starting with Easter, the travel season gets busy again. Room rates also change depending on occupancy rates. Obviously, you stand a better chance of receiving a discount if the hotel is almost empty than if it's booked solid. Resorts are most crowded on weekends, so they usually offer discounts for midweek stays. However, the reverse is true for business hotels in downtown locations.

✔ **Rely on a qualified professional.** Certain hotels give travel agents discounts in exchange for steering business their way, so if you're shy about bargaining, an agent may be better equipped to negotiate discounts for you.

✔ **Make use of your member rewards programs.** Mention your membership in AAA, AARP, frequent-flier programs, and any other corporate rewards programs when making your reservation.

✔ **Just ask for a better rate, especially in the off-season.** The magic words at many hotels are, "Is that your best rate?" You can also ask if the hotel offers a smaller room or a room with a shared bath (if you're willing to go that route) for a better rate.

Finding Alternative Housing: From Roughing It in a Camp to Luxuriating at a Spa

Italy offers several other accommodations options, ranging from camping under the stars to staying at a luxurious spa. If you plan to stay in one place for a week or more, you can also rent an apartment. Another option is to stay at one of the many convents and other religious houses that rent out rooms (they allow couples — the rooms aren't monastic cells). However, in this book we don't list religious houses that accept guests because they usually have curfews (10 to 11 p.m., sometimes even earlier), and we don't think that you want to deal with a curfew, especially if your trip is relatively short.

Likewise, campsites are usually located outside the cities and aren't convenient. If you have a car and camping gear, contact the **Federazione Italiana Campeggiatori,** Via Vittorio Emanuele 11, 50041 Calenzano (☎ **055-882-391;** Fax: 055-882-5918; Internet: www.federcampeggio.it), or ask at the accommodations desk in the city train stations for prices and directions to nearby campsites.

If you want to rent an apartment, consult an organization that specializes in such arrangements. Here are a few:

✔ **Hideaways International,** 767 Islington St., Portsmouth, NH 03801 (☎ **800-843-4433** or 603-430-4433; Internet: www.hideaways.com)

✔ **At Home Abroad,** 405 E. 56th St., Suite 6H, New York, NY 10022 (☎ **212-421-9165;** Fax: 212-752-1591; Internet: http://hometown. aol.com/athomabrod)

✔ **Rentals in Italy,** 1742 Calle Corva, Camarillo, CA 93010 (☎ **800-726-6702** or 805-987-5278; Fax: 805-482-7976; Internet: www.rentvillas.com)

To rent something really ritzy, like a *palazzo* or a castle, try **Abitare la Storia,** Località L'Amorosa, 53048 Sinalunga, Siena (☎ **0577-632-256;** Fax: 0577-632-160; Internet: www.abitarelastoria.it).

Another option — a favorite with Italians — is *agriturismo* (staying on a working farm or former farm somewhere in the countryside). *Agriturismo* (agricultural tourism) is particularly popular in Tuscany. Contact **Italy Farm Holidays,** 547 Martling Ave., Tarrytown, NY 10591 (☎ **914-631-7880;** Fax: 914-631-8831; Internet: www.italyfarmholidays.com) for information on some of the farms that offer this type of accommodation. Your lodging usually includes breakfast and at least one other meal (your choice of dinner or lunch), most likely prepared and produced on the farm or by other local small farms.

No Room at the Inn?

What if you find yourself stuck in a town with no vacant rooms and it's getting late? Don't panic. Italy isn't that big. Ask the hotel desk in the train station if there are good hotels outside of town or in the town next door. For example, some people who are visiting Venice stay in Padua because it's cheaper and only 30 minutes from Venice by train. If you have a car, you can stay at a hotel in the countryside between towns.

If you're planning to travel without hotel reservations, don't wait until dark before you start thinking about where you're spending the night. Try calling ahead by midday; hotels will know of cancellations at that time and you'll be ahead of other travelers looking for a room later in the day.

Chapter 9

Money Matters

In This Chapter

▶ Saying goodbye to the lira and hello to the euro

▶ Using cash, credit, or check

▶ Knowing what to do in case of loss or theft

Money, money, money makes the world go 'round and makes the vacation machine run. In this chapter, we help you make sense of the newly introduced euro and give you tips to help you decide on which form of money you're going to rely on during your travels.

Making Sense of the Euro

Italy's currency is now the *euro* (the plural is also *euro* and it's abbreviated as € in this guide — as in 15€). The new currency was introduced in January 2002 in Italy and in 11 other European countries. Now you can use the same currency in Austria, Belgium, Finland, France, Germany, Greece, Ireland, Italy, Luxembourg, the Netherlands, Portugal, and Spain. The old lira (plural lire) was removed from circulation but can still be changed at major banks until late 2002.

You may still see signs of the old lira in receipts and tickets that have not been updated. Should you come across a price still only in lire, know that the fixed exchange rate between lira and euro is 1,936.27 lire for 1 euro. Simply remove the three zeros and get your price in euro.

The transformation to euro has made things much easier for Americans, because 1 euro exchanges at about $1 (the exchange rate at press time is about 1€ for 90¢). Therefore, you can say goodbye to complicated calculations of exchange rates! Exchange rates, of course, vary daily. In this guide we use a *conversion rate* of 1€ = 90¢ U.S., and we round off all dollar values above $5.

Paper bills come in 5€, 10€, 20€, 50€, 100€, 200€, and 500€ denominations. All bills are brightly colored and have a different shade for each denomination. In addition, the higher the value, the larger the physical size of the bill. A 50€ bill is bigger than a dollar bill, and even the smaller denominations are taller than dollar bills; if you have a bunch, you'll find stuffing them in your wallet a bit difficult. Remember that shops are always short of change, and breaking those large bills to buy a soft drink is sometimes difficult. Think ahead and try to have enough 10€ bills with you as you travel in Italy.

Coins come in 2€ and 1€ (both thin and brass-colored); 50-cent, 20-cent, and 10-cent (all brass colored); and 5-cent, 2-cent and 1-cent (all copper-colored) denominations.

For more information and pictures of the new currency, check online at the official Web site of the **European Union** (http://europa.eu.int/euro) or at the site of the **European Central Bank** (www.euro.ecb.int).

Don't be surprised to see different country names on euro bills and coins: One face is the European side, common to each of the 12 participating countries, and the reverse face is the national side, where each country has printed its own design. All are valid and accepted in each of the countries.

You can exchange money at the airport, at banks, and at exchange bureaus, which usually display multilingual signs ("Change/Cambio/Wechsel"). Rates may vary to some degree. For example, some bureaus advertise "no fee," but then give you a lower rate so you come out the same anyway. Arriving with a small supply of euro, at least enough to pay for a cab to your hotel, is a good idea.

After you're in Italy, the best way to exchange money is at an ATM. (Make sure your ATM is affiliated with the Cirrus network, however; the only two networks that work in Europe are Plus and Cirrus, but Plus is much rarer.) If you prefer to exchange cash or traveler's checks, the exchange bureaus at airports usually offer the best rates.

Choosing Traveler's Checks, Credit Cards, ATMs, or Cash

In what form should you bring your money? Now that ATMs have gone international, this question is a matter of choice. Some people prefer the security of traveler's checks, though it means standing in line to get the checks at your bank and then standing in line while you're traveling in order to redeem them (and remember that you must show your passport every time you cash one). But, on the other hand, if you get your money out of ATMs in Italy you have to deal with nagging questions like: What if I lose my card? What if my card gets demagnetized? What if the network is down and I have ten minutes to buy my ticket and get on the train?

Using ATMs

In major cities, ATMs are never far away, so you can walk around with 100€ in your wallet (about $90) and you should be set to dine and pay your museum admissions (but not your hotel bill). Before going off on a driving tour of the countryside, however, such as in Sicily or Chianti, make sure that you have a good stock of cash in your wallet; banks and ATMs are rarer outside the big cities.

How much cash you carry around daily also depends on how much of your trip you've prepaid and whether the hotels and restaurants you choose accept credit cards (hotels usually do, whereas for restaurants it depends on their size and policy).

ATMs are linked to a network that most likely includes your bank at home — but not always. **Cirrus** (☎ **800-424-7787;** Internet: www.mastercard.com/atm) is the most common international network in Italy. The **Plus** network (☎ **800-843-7587;** Internet: www.visa.com/atms) also exists in Italy but is rarer. The Banca Nazionale del Lavoro (BNL) is one of the few banks that offers Plus in its ATMs; you can find BNL branches all over Italy, but not in every small town. The NYCE network is unknown in Italy. Check the back of your ATM card to see which network your bank belongs to and ask your bank for a list of overseas ATMs or go online to the networks' Web sites for locations.

 Before departing for Italy, make sure that you check the daily withdrawal limit for your ATM card and ask whether you need a new personal identification number, or PIN. (You need a four-digit PIN for Europe, so if you currently have a six-digit PIN, you must get a new one.)

 Not all ATM keypads in Italy display letters as well as numbers. Some have only numbers. Therefore, if your PIN is "SPOT," you need to know how it translates into numbers (check this before you leave home!).

If you have linked checking and savings accounts and you're in the habit of moving relatively small amounts of money from savings to checking as you need it, beware: Italian ATMs won't show you the transfer-between-accounts option, and they won't allow you to withdraw money directly from your savings account. If your checking account runs dry, you must call or write your bank to move money from savings to checking. (We did so, and our bank charged us $30. Ouch!)

Many banks now charge a fee ranging from 50¢ to a whopping $3 whenever a non-account-holder uses their ATMs. Your own bank may also assess a fee for using an ATM that's not one of their branch locations. With many banks, these extra fees don't apply when you travel abroad; the fee is included in the exchange rate. Also, you usually get a better exchange rate with your ATM card than what you'd get changing currency or traveler's checks at an exchange bureau. Still, check in advance with your own bank to avoid surprises. Unless the fees are really huge, we find that the convenience of using our ATM card outweighs the cost.

Paying with plastic

Credit cards are invaluable when traveling. They provide a safe way to carry money and pay for things as well as a convenient record of all of your travel expenses when you arrive home. If you really need it, you can also receive cash advances from your credit cards at any bank; bear in mind, though, that you begin paying a sizable interest on the advance the moment you receive the cash, and you won't receive frequent-flier miles on an airline credit card for cash advances.

At most banks, you don't need to go to a teller; you can get a cash advance at an ATM if you know your PIN. (Make sure that it's four digits long, not six digits, or it won't work with European ATMs!) If you've forgotten your PIN, call the phone number on the back of your credit card and ask the bank to send it to you. Receiving your PIN usually takes five to seven business days, although some banks will give you the number over the phone if you tell them your mother's maiden name or pass some other form of security clearance. Better yet, just call your bank before you go, and set up a PIN for cash advances.

The most commonly accepted credit card in Italy is Visa, closely followed by MasterCard, American Express, and Diners Club.

Taking traveler's checks

Traveler's checks are something of a relic from the days when people used to write personal checks all the time instead of going to ATMs. In those days, travelers weren't sure of finding a place that would cash a check for them on vacation. Because you can replace them if they're lost or stolen, traveler's checks were a sound alternative to stuffing your wallet with cash at the beginning of a trip.

These days, however, traveler's checks are less necessary because most cities have 24-hour ATMs. You can withdraw only as much cash as you need every couple of days, so you don't feel insecure carrying around a huge wad of cash.

If you prefer the security of traveler's checks, you can find them at almost any bank. **American Express** offers checks in denominations of $20, $50, $100, $500, and $1,000. You pay a service charge ranging from 1 to 4%, but AAA members can obtain checks without a fee at most AAA offices. You can also call ☎ 800-221-7282 to get American Express traveler's checks over the phone.

Visa (☎ 800-227-6811) also offers traveler's checks, available at several banks across the country. The service charge ranges between 1.5 and 2%; checks come in denominations of $50, $100, $500, and $1,000.

MasterCard also offers traveler's checks. Call ☎ 800-223-9920 for a location near you.

Getting cash before you leave

Buying some euro to have with you before you leave for Italy is a good idea. Get at least enough to cover your initial expenses, so that you don't have to line up at the exchange bureau at the airport when you're tired, jet-lagged, and struggling with your luggage.

Nowadays, though, you don't even need to go to your bank to buy euro: You can get foreign currencies (including euro) delivered to your door before you leave. This beats any ATM at the airport! **Chase Manhattan** offers this service by phone or online (☎ 888-CHASE-84; Internet: www.currencytogo.com) to Chase Manhattan customers. Others have to contact a Chase branch near them. The minimum purchase is $100 worth, and you get free delivery if you buy over $500. You can use your credit card (MasterCard or Visa only) for the purchase, and the sale is processed as a regular purchase, not as a cash advance. This makes the rates better even than at ATMs in Italy.

Also offering the same service is OANDA (a company linked to Thomas Cook). It's online at www.oanda.com, but its prices are somewhat higher than Chase Manhattan's. The minimum purchase is $200 and the maximum is $1,500; shipping is free if you buy over $500, and you'll probably want to pay by debit card. (If you pay by credit card, you're charged as you would be for a cash advance, with the consequent fees.)

Knowing What to Do if Your Wallet or Purse Gets Stolen

Being on vacation is a blissful time of distraction and discovery. Unfortunately, this makes a tourist a ripe target for those whose profession is pickpocketing. In this section, we deal with the unpleasant occurrence of being robbed. Note, though, that in Italy violent crime is rare; most of the wallets are lost to pickpockets, not muggers.

To minimize the risk of having your money or credit cards stolen, keep your wallet or purse out of sight, in inner pockets but not in your back pocket or in your backpack. Don't leave your purse, briefcase, backpack, or coat unattended in any public place. Don't flash around your money or credit cards. When walking on the streets, keep your purse on the side away from traffic, so a thief on a motorscooter can't speed by and grab it from you.

In the unlikely event that your wallet or purse is stolen, you need to cancel all your credit cards. Almost every credit card company has an emergency toll-free number that you can call if your card is stolen. The issuing bank's toll-free number is usually on the back of the credit card, but that doesn't help much if your card is stolen. So be sure to write down the number before you leave home and keep it in a safe place (away from your wallet), just in case. The company will cancel your card number immediately so someone else can't use it. They also may wire you a cash advance off your credit card immediately so you have some money. And, in many places, credit card companies can get you an emergency replacement card within a day or two.

The numbers to call if your credit card gets lost or stolen are: **MasterCard** (☎ **800-870-866** in Italy or 800-307-7309 in the U.S.); **Visa** (☎ **800-819-014** in Italy or 800-847-2911 in the U.S.); **American Express** (☎ **06-72-282** in Italy (301-214-8228 collect from Italy) or 800-554-AMEX in the U.S.; and **Diners Club** (☎ **702-797-5532** in Italy or 800-525-7376 in the U.S.).

If you opt to carry traveler's checks, make sure that you keep a record of all their serial numbers (keep the record separate from the checks, of course), and write down the numbers of the checks as you cash them. If your checks are stolen, you must report exactly which checks are gone in order to get them replaced. The check issuer will tell you where to pick up the new checks.

Odds are that if your purse or wallet is gone, you've seen the last of it, and the police aren't likely to recover it for you. However, after you cancel your credit cards, you should call to inform the police. You may need the police report number for credit card or insurance purposes later.

A taxing matter: The IVA

The value-added tax in Italy is called the IVA and is a whopping 19%. The tax is always already included in prices, so you don't need to calculate it as an additional expense. You do get some of that money back, however: At the airport, you can get reimbursed for taxes paid on items you're bringing out of the country that cost over 155€ ($140). See the appendix for details.

Chapter 10

Taking Care of Last-Minute Details

· ·

In This Chapter

▶ Getting your documents in order

▶ Purchasing insurance — or not

▶ Making reservations in advance

▶ Knowing what to pack — and what you can bring home

· ·

*E*ven after you have a destination, an itinerary, and a ticket, you'll find that every trip has last-minute details to attend to. Forgetting about some of them — such as getting a passport — could put a real crimp in your plans to visit Italy. In this chapter, we tell you where to apply for a passport, whether to get traveler's insurance, how to make reservations, and even what to pack (and what to leave at home).

All About Passports

Losing your passport may be worse than losing your money. Why? Because a passport shows (and proves to authorities) that you are you. Safeguard your passport in an inconspicuous, inaccessible place like a money belt.

Always carry a photocopy of your passport with you and keep it in a separate pocket or purse. If you lose your passport, visit the nearest consulate of your native country as soon as possible for a replacement.

If you don't already have a valid passport, you can download an application from the Internet sites that we list later in the chapter, or you can get one by mail or in person.

For residents of the United States

If you're applying for a first-time passport, you need to do so in person at one of the 13 passport offices throughout the United States; at a federal, state, or probate court; or at a major post office. You need to present a certified birth certificate as proof of citizenship; also, bringing along your driver's license, state or military ID, and social security card is a good idea. You also need two identical passport-size photos (2 x 2 inches), which you can have taken at any photo shop. (You can't, however, use strip photos from a photo-vending machine.)

When you get your passport photos taken, ask for six to eight total if you're planning to also apply for an International Driving Permit and an international student or teacher ID, which may entitle you to discounts at museums. Take the extra photos with you. You may need one for random reasons on the road, and if — heaven forbid — you ever lose your passport, you can use them for a replacement request.

For people over age 15, a passport is valid for ten years and costs $60 ($45 plus a $15 handling fee); for those 15 and under, it's valid for five years and costs $40. If you're over 15 and have a valid passport that was issued within the past 12 years, you can renew it by mail and bypass the $15 handling fee. Allow plenty of time before your trip to apply, however; processing normally takes three weeks but it can take longer during busy periods (especially spring). You can take advantage of expedited service by paying an extra fee and presenting yourself in person to the passport office (usually only in major cities). For general information, call the **National Passport Agency** at ☎ **202-647-0518.** To find your regional passport office, call the **National Passport Information Center** at ☎ **900-225-5674** or check the Web at http://travel.state.gov.

For residents of Canada

You can pick up a passport application at one of the 28 regional passport offices or most travel agencies. The passport is valid for five years and costs C$85 for those 16 years and older and C$35 for children 3 to 15. For children under 3, a passport costs C$20 and is valid for three years. As of December 11, 2001, Canadian children who travel will need their own passport. However, if you hold a valid Canadian passport issued before December 11, 2001, that bears the name of your child, the passport remains valid for you and your child until it expires. You can pick up applications, which must be accompanied by two identical passport-size photos (2 x 2 inches) and proof of Canadian citizenship, at travel agencies throughout Canada or from the central **Passport Office,** Department of Foreign Affairs and International Trade, Ottawa, Ontario K1A 0G3 (☎ **800-567-6868**). You can also find applications on the Web at www.dfait-maeci.gc.ca/passport. Processing takes five to ten days if you apply in person or about three weeks by mail.

For residents of the United Kingdom

As a member of the European Union, you need only an identity card, not a passport, to travel to other EU countries. However, if you already have a passport, carrying it is always useful. To pick up an application for a regular ten-year passport (the Visitor's Passport has been abolished), visit your nearest passport office, major post office, or travel agency. You can also contact the **London Passport Office** at ☎ **0870-521-0410** or search its Web site at www.ukpa.gov.uk. Passports are £30 for adults and £16 for children under 16.

For residents of Ireland

You can apply for a ten-year passport, which costs 57€, at the **Passport Office,** Setanta Centre, Molesworth Street, Dublin 2 (☎ **01-671-1633**) or on the Web at www.irlgov.ie/iveagh/services/passports/passportfacilities.htm. If you're under 18 or over 65, you must apply for a three-year passport that costs 16€. You can also apply at 1A South Mall, Cork (☎ **021-272-525**), or over the counter at most main post offices.

For residents of Australia and New Zealand

In Australia, apply at your local post office or passport office or check out the government Web site at www.dfat.gov.au/passports. Passports for adults are A$128 and A$64 for those under 18.

In New Zealand, you can pick up a passport application at any travel agency or Link Centre or download it from their Web site. For more information, contact the **Passport Office,** P.O. Box 805, Wellington (☎ **0800-225-050; Internet:** www.passports.govt.nz). Passports for adults are NZ$80 and NZ$40 for people under 16.

Travel and Medical Insurance: Do You Need It?

Check your existing insurance policies before you buy travel insurance to cover trip cancellation, lost luggage, medical expenses, or car-rental insurance (see Chapter 7 for more on the last of these). You're likely to have partial or complete coverage. But if you need some, ask your travel agent about a comprehensive package. The cost of travel insurance varies widely, depending on the cost and length of your trip, your age and overall health, and the type of trip you're taking.

And keep in mind that in the aftermath of the terrorist attacks of September 11, 2001, a number of airlines, cruise lines, and tour operators are no longer covered by insurers. The bottom line: Always, *always* check the fine print before you sign on; more and more policies have built-in exclusions and restrictions that may leave you out in the cold if something does go awry.

For information, contact one of the following popular insurers:

- **Access America** (☎ 800-284-8300; Internet: www.access america.com)

- **Travel Guard International** (☎ 800-826-1300; Internet: www.travelguard.com)

- **Travel Insured International** (☎ 800-243-3174; Internet: www.travelinsured.com)

- **Travelex Insurance Services** (☎ 800-228-9792; Internet: www.travelex-insurance.com)

Trip-cancellation insurance

There are three major types of trip-cancellation insurance (TCI): one, in the event that you prepay a cruise or tour that gets cancelled, and you can't get your money back; a second when you or someone in your family gets sick or dies, and you can't travel (but beware that you may not be covered for a preexisting condition); and a third, when bad weather makes travel impossible. Some insurers provide coverage for events like jury duty; natural disasters close to home, like floods or fire; and even the loss of a job.

Always check the fine print before signing on, and don't buy trip-cancellation insurance from the tour operator that may be responsible for the cancellation; buy it only from a reputable travel-insurance agency. And don't overbuy. You won't be reimbursed for more than the cost of your trip.

Medical insurance

Most health-insurance policies cover you if you get sick away from home — but check, particularly if you're insured by an HMO. With the exception of certain HMOs and Medicare/Medicaid, your medical insurance should cover medical treatment — even hospital care — overseas. (For specifics on coverage in Italy, see the next section, "What to Do if You Get Sick Away from Home.") However, most out-of-country hospitals make you pay your bills up front, and send you a refund after you've returned home and filed the necessary paperwork. Members of **Blue Cross/Blue Shield** can now use their cards at select hospitals in most major cities worldwide (☎ 800-810-BLUE or www.bluecares.com for a list of hospitals).

The cost of travel medical insurance varies widely. Check your existing policies before you buy additional coverage. If you require additional insurance, try one of the following companies:

✔ **MEDEX International**, 9515 Deereco Rd., Timonium, MD 21093-5375 (☎ **888-MEDEX-00** or 410-453-6300; Fax: 410-453-6301; Internet: www.medexassist.com)

✔ **Travel Assistance International** (☎ **800-821-2828**; Internet: www.travelassistance.com), 9200 Keystone Crossing, Suite 300, Indianapolis, IN 46240 (for general information on services, call the company's Worldwide Assistance Services, Inc., at ☎ **800-777-8710**).

Lost-luggage insurance

On international flights (including U.S. portions of international trips), baggage is limited to approximately $9.07 per pound, up to approximately $635 per checked bag. If you plan to check items more valuable than the standard liability, you may purchase excess-valuation coverage from the airline, up to $5,000. Be sure to take any valuables or irreplaceable items with you in your carry-on luggage. If you file a lost-luggage claim, be prepared to answer detailed questions about the contents of your baggage, and be sure to file a claim immediately, because most airlines enforce a 21-day deadline.

Lost luggage may also be covered by your homeowner's or renter's policy. Many platinum and gold credit cards cover you as well. If you choose to purchase additional lost-luggage insurance, be sure not to buy more than you need. Buy in advance from the insurer or a trusted agent (prices will be much higher at the airport).

What to Do if You Get Sick Away from Home

Getting sick on vacation is no fun, and finding a doctor and obtaining medication can be difficult. But you can take certain precautions to minimize your risk.

Bring all your medications with you, as well as prescriptions for more (in generic — not brand-name — form) if you worry that you'll run out. If you have health insurance, make sure that you carry your ID card in your wallet.

If you have a chronic illness, talk to your doctor before taking your trip. For conditions such as epilepsy, diabetes, or a heart condition, you may want to wear a Medic Alert Identification Tag, which immediately alerts any doctor to your condition and gives him or her access to your medical records through Medic Alert's 24-hour hot line. A worldwide toll-free emergency response number is on the tag, so if you become ill in Italy, you know exactly whom to call. Membership is $35, plus a $15 annual fee. Contact the **Medic Alert Foundation,** P.O. Box 1009, Turlock, CA 95381-1009 (☎ **800-825-3785;** Internet: www.medicalert.org). If getting sick away from home worries you, buy medical insurance (see the section on travel insurance earlier in this chapter).

If you do get sick, ask the concierge at your hotel to recommend a local doctor — even his or her own doctor, if necessary. If you can't locate a doctor, try contacting your embassy or consulate — they maintain lists of English-speaking doctors. For an emergency dial ☎ 113 for the police or ☎ 112 for the *carabinieri* (army police corps): They can call an ambulance or help you in many ways. If your situation is life-threatening, go to the *pronto soccorso* (emergency department) at the local hospital.

Under the Italian national health-care system, you're eligible only for free *emergency* care. If you're admitted to a hospital as an in-patient, even from an accident and an emergency department, you're required to pay (unless you're a resident of the European Economic Area). You're also required to pay for follow-up care. For the names, addresses, and phone numbers of hospitals offering 24-hour emergency care, see the "Fast Facts" section at the end of each destination chapter.

If you do end up paying for health care, especially if you're admitted to a hospital for any reason, most health-insurance plans and HMOs will cover at least part of the out-of-country hospital visits and procedures. Be prepared to pay the bills up front at the time of care, however. You'll get a refund after you've returned to your country and filed all the paperwork.

How to Make Reservations and Get Tickets in Advance for Events and Sightseeing

You'll want to reserve tickets in advance — as far in advance as possible — to get into certain museums. If you call ☎ **055-294-883** or visit www.firenzemusei.it, you can reserve tickets for several museums in Florence, including the **Uffizi Gallery (Galleria degli Uffizi),** where lines are so bad it may take you more than three hours to get in, and the **Accademia Gallery (Galleria dell'Accademia),** which houses Michaelangelo's *David.* In Rome, you may want to make reservations in advance for the **Galleria Borghese,** which accepts a restricted number of visitors at a time (☎ **06-32810;** Internet: www.ticketeria.it). When you reserve tickets in advance, remember that you're given a date and a time for your visit, so you have to arrange your sightseeing schedule around those reservations.

You can now check schedules and programs and make reservations for a number of exhibits, museums, and shows (from concerts to soccer matches, including the Greek Theater in Agrigento and Taormina and other important venues throughout Italy) through **TicketOne.** This service allows you to make all your reservations and purchase your ticket online at www.ticketone.it (the Web site is very good, and although it is in Italian only, it is self-explanatory) or on the phone (☎ **02-392-261** for an English-speaking operator). If you're already in Italy, you can go in person to one of their many local offices (call ☎ **06-6141-6108** for an automated list of locations in Italy, or check the list of their agents online).

Musical and theatrical events that you should get advance tickets to see include the following:

- **Umbria Jazz Festival** (☎ **075-573-2432**; Fax: 075-572-2656; Internet: www.umbriajazz.com).

- **Spoleto Festival** (☎ **06-321-0288** or 0743-44-325; Fax: 06-320-0747 or 0743-40-696; Internet: www.spoletofestival.it).

- **Operas performed in Verona's Anfiteatro Romano** (☎ **045-800-5151**; Internet: www.arena.it). You can now book your ticket online. In the U.S., you can also contact the Global Tickets agency at ☎ **800-223-6108** or 914-328-2150.

- **The alternating performances of Greek tragedies at Selinunte and Syracuse in Sicily.** Instituto Nazionale per il Dramma Antico (☎ **0931-67-415** or toll-free within Italy 1478-82211).

- **The performances at Taormina.** Taormina Arte (☎ **0942-21142**).

- **The Maggio Musicale concert and dance series in Florence** (☎ **055-211-158** or 055-213-535; Internet: www.maggio fiorentino.com).

In order to get more information about happenings during the time of your visit, check the Web sites that we list in the Calendar of Events in Chapter 2, the appendix, and the Web sites we recommend in the "Fast Facts" section at the end of each destination chapter.

Pack It Up and Hit the Road

Italy is a crowded country where space is always at a premium. Buses and trains are crowded — lots of people will be competing for the luggage bins — so you won't be very popular with your four duffle bags. In trains, limited room is available near the doors for oversized bags; you won't have much room for luggage in a car either. If you rent a car, it will probably be quite compact — gas is horrendously expensive, so cars are light, small, and efficient. And really: Why would you want to be lugging pounds and pounds of clothes and stuff halfway around the world when you could be saving room for all the goodies you're bringing back? That's why, when it comes to packing for a trip, we say, "Lighten up."

The bare essentials

Here are some key items that are essential for your trip to Italy:

- ✔ Comfortable walking shoes (make it two pairs)

- ✔ Versatile sweater and/or jacket

- ✔ Hat or sun visor

- ✔ Sunscreen (the Italian sun is cruel)

- ✔ Sunglasses (or you can treat yourself to an Italian pair when you arrive)

- ✔ All daily prescription medications (pack these in your carry-on bag so you have them if the airline loses your luggage)

- ✔ Over-the-counter medications and supplements (vitamins and health preparations are often more expensive in Italy)

- ✔ Small binoculars or opera glasses (use these to get a closer look at faraway frescoes, particularly important in the Sistine Chapel)

- ✔ Corkscrew and bottle opener (these come in handy for those great picnics among Roman ruins, but remember to bring a small one and put it in your checked luggage — you can't bring it on an airplane in a carry-on bag)

Leave it at home

It's easier said than done, but take it from us: You'll be glad you didn't overpack. Come on: Do you really need five pairs of pants? Will you actually use three different sweaters? Must you carry all your favorite doodads around with you? If you're having trouble paring down, take a look at the following suggestions:

- ✔ **Don't bring it if you plan to buy it.** Italy is famous for fashion, so an obvious tip is not to bring anything you intend to buy while you're on your trip, such as a pair of Italian-made shoes, an Armani jacket, or even sunglasses. Alternatively, you can bring your least favorite clothes and accessories (such as a handbag) and discard them after you make your purchase.

- ✔ **Light and easy does it.** You probably won't need heavy clothing unless you're going to Northern Italy in winter. (In the warm months, the south is gloriously sunny most of the time.) Being too hot is more of a concern than getting too cold. Breathable fabrics like cotton and rayon work nicely.

✔ **Leave the ballgowns at home.** Unless you're attending a board meeting or wedding, or dining at one of the city's finest restaurants, you probably won't need a very fancy suit or dress. On the other hand, you should prepare to dress up your everyday wear (see the next section, "Dress Like the Locals").

✔ **Go small.** Use travel-size products whenever you can. You can also save little travel-size bottles, wash them out, and pour your favorite shampoo, lotion, or whatever in them to take with you.

✔ **Leave the appliances at home.** We recommend that you leave all your electronic gadgetry at home. But if you really, really need to bring those appliances, read "Electric Conversions: Don't Get Shocked," later in this chapter.

Dress Like the Locals

Italians dress more formally than Americans. No matter what your age, you'll stand out if you spend your vacation wearing a sweat suit. (We know one Italian man who puts on a sports coat to go for a walk around the block.) Leave the active wear at home. You'll get more use out of a pair of jeans or khakis, a shirt with a collar, and a comfortable cotton sweater.

What you can carry on — and what you can't

The Transportation Security Administration (TSA), the government agency that now handles all aspects of airport security, has devised new restrictions for carry-on baggage, not only to expedite the screening process but to prevent potential weapons from passing through airport security. Passengers are now limited to bringing just one carry-on bag and one personal item onto the aircraft (previous regulations allowed two carry-on bags and one personal item, like a briefcase or a purse). For more information, go to the TSA's Web site (www.tsa.gov). The agency has released an updated list of items passengers are not allowed to carry onto an aircraft:

Not permitted: Knives and box cutters, corkscrews, straight razors, metal scissors, golf clubs, baseball bats, pool cues, hockey sticks, ski poles, ice picks.

Permitted: Nail clippers, nail files, tweezers, eyelash curlers, safety razors (including disposable razors), syringes (with documented proof of medical need), walking canes and umbrellas (must be inspected first).

The airline you fly may have additional restrictions on items you can and cannot carry on board. Call ahead to avoid problems.

Italians don't wear sneakers very much either; sneakers can get very hot. An option we like for summer is a pair of comfortable walking sandals — they keep your feet cooler, you don't need socks, and (perhaps best of all) they pack flat.

At the other end is your headgear. In the United States, people accept Academy Awards wearing baseball caps, but that goofy-cool look in Italy is just goofy. So you may want to bring something a bit more upscale to keep the sun off your head — or buy a hat in Italy, home of the famous Borsalino hats and beautiful straw hats.

Are your kids in the habit of wearing enormously baggy hip-hop clothes? If so, encourage them to keep such attire at home. Some young Italians have adopted this look, but it isn't popular. Italians of all ages like to look trim and not sloppy, and Italian kids ride *motorinis* (motor-bikes) — which voluminous hip-hop clothes could make impossible or even dangerous.

Churches in Italy have a strict dress code — no bare shoulders and no bare legs (this goes for men as well as women, by the way). This fact annoys some people, but when was the last time you saw someone wearing a tank top in your church, synagogue, or mosque? Therefore, if you're visiting St. Peter's, St. Mark's, or other churches, bring along something to throw over your shoulders (it's pretty cold inside some of the churches, which have walls several feet thick, so you'll appreciate having something to keep you warm).

Cultural variances among regions can also dictate an appropriate dress code. The farther south you go, the more traditional people are, especially out in the country. You'll see that women and men tend to cover themselves more. You can either try to look like a local or just do whatever you want; however, if you're a woman, you may risk being bothered by young men if you're less covered (see Chapter 5 for tips for women travelers).

Electric Conversions: Don't Get Shocked

American current runs 110V, 60 cycles. The standard voltage throughout Italy is 220V, from 42 to 50 cycles. ***Translation:*** You can't plug an American appliance into an Italian outlet without frying your appliance and/or blowing a fuse. You need a current converter or transformer to bring the voltage down and the cycles up. In Italy, the prongs of plugs are round, so you also need a plug adapter. Plug adapters and converters are available at most travel, luggage, electronics, and hardware stores. Remember to get them before you leave. (You may find a plug adapter that also doubles as a current converter, saving you a step.)

Travel-sized versions of hair dryers, irons, shavers, and so on are dual voltage, which means that they have built-in converters (usually you have to turn a switch to go back and forth). Likewise, most contemporary laptop computers automatically sense the current and adapt accordingly. (Check the manual, the bottom of the machine, or with the manufacturer first to make sure you don't burn out your computer.)

Size Conversions: The Large and the Small of It

Face it: You're probably going to be tempted to buy some clothes while in Italy. Shopping for clothes in Italy has become a bit easier, now that S, M, and L are used in some cases. Hats and shirt collars, however, are measured in centimeters. To find your correct size, multiply the number of inches you require by 1.34.

Consider that Italians are often smaller — and thinner — than Americans. Many women's clothes come in a maximum size of 48 (a U.S. size 12), so you have to go to specialty stores to find the larger sizes, with a very marked change in style. For men, the advantage is that pants are sold without a hem, so you can have them custom tailored for your height (usually done in a few hours).

Table 10-1 is a size conversion chart to help you with your purchases. However, remember that sizes aren't standardized among different makers. Always try on clothes before you buy.

Table 10-1	**Size Conversion Chart**						
Women's Clothes							
Italy	38	40	42	44	46	48	50	52
U.S.	2	4	6	8	10	12	14	16
Men's Clothes							
Italy	46	48	50	52	54	56	58	60
U.S.	36	38	40	42	44	46	48	50
Women's Shoes							
Italy	35	36	37	38	39	40	41
U.S.	4	5	6	7	8	9	10
Men's Shoes							
Italy	39	40	41	42	43	44	45
U.S.	8½	9	9½	10	10½	11	11½

Customs Regulations: What Can You Bring Home?

Another part of packing is packing to return home. Buying something in Italy, bringing it back on the plane, and then having it confiscated would really be a drag. Therefore, you need to know as much as you can about Customs regulations before you go.

The "no agricultural products" policy is strictly enforced in the United States. That means *absolutely no meat.* Don't buy prosciutto, sausage, or any other meat product that you don't plan to eat before you return. In addition, the threat from agricultural pests means that vegetables and plants — including dried flowers — aren't allowed into the States. You can, however, bring back some products in vacuum-packed sealed plastic bags or in cans and jars — like *parmigiano reggiano* (Parmesan cheese). In general, whatever you can buy in a duty-free shop at the airport is legal.

For residents of the United States

Returning U.S. citizens who've been away for 48 hours or more are allowed to bring back, once every 30 days, $400 worth of merchandise duty-free, including all gifts. If you expect to go over this limit, think about mailing some of your goodies back. You can send yourself $200 worth of goods per day and $100 worth of gifts to others — alcohol and tobacco excluded. On the plane, you can bring with you 1 liter of alcohol and 200 cigarettes or 100 cigars. The $400 ceiling doesn't apply to artwork or antiques (items must be at least 100 years old to be considered antique), for which you have to pay duty. You're charged a flat rate of 10% duty on the next $1,000 worth of purchases. Make sure that you have your receipts handy. On gifts, the duty-free limit is $100.

For more information, contact the **U.S. Customs Service,** 1301 Constitution Ave. (P.O. Box 7407), Washington, DC 20044 (☎ **202-927-1770;** Internet: www.customs.ustreas.gov) and request the free pamphlet "Know Before You Go." You can also find the pamphlet on the Web at www.customs.ustreas.gov/travel/kbygo.htm.

For residents of Canada

If you're a Canadian citizen, write for the booklet "I Declare," issued by **Revenue Canada,** 2265 St. Laurent Blvd., Ottawa K1G 4KE (☎ **613-993-0534; Internet:** www.ccra-adrc.gc.ca). Canada allows its citizens a C$750 exemption, and you can bring back duty-free 200 cigarettes, 2.2 pounds of tobacco, 40 imperial ounces of liquor, and 50 cigars. In addition, you can also mail gifts to Canada from abroad at the rate of C$60 per day, provided they're unsolicited and don't contain alcohol or tobacco (write on the package "Unsolicited Gift, Under $60 Value"). Declare all valuables on the Y-38 form before departure from Canada, including the serial numbers of valuables that you already own, such as expensive foreign cameras. *Note:* You can use the C$750 exemption only once a year and only after an absence of seven days.

For residents of the United Kingdom

U.K. citizens returning from a European Union country go through a separate Customs Exit, called the "Blue Exit." In essence, there's no limit on what you can bring back from an EU country, as long as the items are for personal use (this includes gifts) and you've already paid the necessary duty and tax. However, Customs law sets guidance levels. If you bring in more than these levels, you may be asked to prove that the goods you're bringing back are for your own use. Guidance levels on goods bought in the EU for your own use are 800 cigarettes, 200 cigars, 1kg of smoking tobacco, 10 liters of spirits, 90 liters of wine (of this not more than 60 liters can be sparkling wine), and 110 liters of beer. For more information, contact **HM Customs & Excise,** Passenger Enquiry Point, 2nd Floor Wayfarer House, Great South West Road, Feltham, Middlesex, TW14 8NP (☎ **0181-910-3744,** or 44-181-910-3744 from outside the U.K.; Internet: www.hmce.gov.uk).

For residents of Australia

The duty-free allowance for Australian citizens is A$400 or, for those under 18, A$200. Mark personal property that you mail back home "Australian Goods Returned" to avoid payment of duty. Upon returning to Australia, citizens can bring in 250 cigarettes or 250 grams of loose tobacco, and 1,125mL of alcohol. If you're returning with valuable goods that you already own, such as foreign-made cameras, file form B263. A helpful brochure, available from Australian consulates or Customs offices, is "Know Before You Go." For more information, contact **Australian Customs Services,** GPO Box 8, Sydney NSW 2001 (☎ **02-9213-2000; Internet:** www.customs.gov.au).

For residents of New Zealand

The duty-free allowance for New Zealand citizens is NZ$700. Citizens over 17 can bring in 200 cigarettes or 50 cigars or 250 grams of tobacco (or a mix of all three if their combined weight doesn't exceed 250 grams), plus 4.5 liters of wine and beer, or 1.125 liters of liquor. New Zealand currency doesn't carry import or export restrictions. Fill out a certificate of export, listing the valuables you're taking out of the country; that way, you can bring them back without paying duty. Most questions are answered in a free pamphlet available at New Zealand consulates and

Customs offices, "New Zealand Customs Guide for Travellers," Notice no. 4. For more information, contact **New Zealand Customs,** The Customhouse, 17–21 Whitemore St., Box 2218, Wellington (☎ **04-473-6099; Internet:** www.customs.govt.nz).

Part III
The Eternal City: Rome

The 5th Wave   By Rich Tennant

"It says, children are forbidden from running, touching objects or appearing bored during the tour."

In this part . . .

Yes, we've devoted a whole part to Rome. Rome is not only Italy's largest city, but it's also the hub from which you'll probably do most of your traveling. The treasures of Rome stretch from pre-Republic ruins to Bernini's baroque marvels to the stylish, convulsive Rome depicted by Fellini in his famous movies. Though modern, today's sprawling city still breathes to the rhythm of its history and is set in a beautiful country-side, where affluent Romans have been building palaces and villas since . . . well, the Romans.

Chapter 11 provides everything you need to know to get to Rome, get oriented in the city, find a comfortable place to stay, and order a delicious Italian meal. Included are rundowns of the best hotels and the best restaurants, plus some runner-up choices. In Chapter 12, we describe the major sites and activities (not only how to see the Colosseum and the Vatican Museums but also where to shop and where to go for fun after dark). Chapter 13 takes you into Rome's countryside, the renowned Castelli Romani—the towns that dot the hills surrounding the city—where Romans go for a meal, a walk, and magnifi-cent views.

Chapter 11

Settling Into Rome

. . . .

In This Chapter

▶ Arriving in Rome

▶ Finding your way around the city

▶ Choosing your Roman villa (or at least a room with a view)

▶ Enjoying Roman cuisine

. . . .

The seven hills of Rome (Roma) and the surrounding area have been continuously inhabited for the past 3,000 years or so. The Roman Empire, centered in the Eternal City, may not have been the world's first great empire, but it was certainly the longest lasting, and by borrowing liberally from its subject states — particularly Greece — it created the foundation for a cosmopolitan European culture.

What does this history mean for you? It means that nowhere else will you find such a density of amazing things to see. For instance, Rome has 913 churches, many packed to the rafters with great art. The renovations and refurbishings for Papal Jubilee 2000 made Rome even more glorious, which means that during the high season you may have to share the city with a good number of other fellow travelers. Not to worry: This shimmering city of fountains, medieval alleyways, and papal riches has magic enough for all to share.

Getting There

Although Italy is steeped in history, it's also a contemporary country, boasting all the conveniences of modern transportation. Getting to Rome isn't difficult, and you can make your way there in numerous ways.

By air

Italy has two international ports of entry by air: Rome and Milan. Rome has two airports: **Fiumicino** and the smaller **Ciampino.**

Arriving at Fiumicino/Leonardo da Vinci

Rome's international airport is officially called Leonardo da Vinci (☎ **06-659-51** or 06-6595-3640), though it's better known as Fiumicino, after the nearby town. This airport is also the point of departure for flights to all other Italian cities. **Alitalia** (☎ **1478-65-643** or 06-65643; Internet: www.alitalia.it or www.alitaliausa.com), Italy's national airline, offers daily flights from Rome to all major Italian towns as well as to major European and world cities.

Despite being Italy's main airport, Fiumicino is relatively small but well organized. It has just gone through a growth spurt, with a new terminal serviced by a monorail. While at the airport, you may also note the high level of security: Don't be concerned if you see police officers with submachine guns walking around — it's routine.

The heightened security at Fiumicino hasn't yet been able to completely eradicate theft. Therefore, watch over your belongings like a hawk and don't leave anything precious in your check-in luggage.

Navigating your way through passport control and Customs

After your plane lands, you arrive at passport control. As in other European cities, there are two passport-control lines — one for European Union citizens and one for non–EU citizens. After the passport check, you proceed to the baggage-claim area and then through Customs. Items for personal use enter duty-free. When you leave Customs, you're in the main concourse, where information booths and rental-car desks are located. Taxis and public transportation are right outside.

Only two ATMS are located inside the airport, so it's rare not to find a long waiting line of travelers withdrawing cash. The only currency-exchange desk also gets very crowded. If you don't like standing in line after a long trip, you may want to arrive with some euro in your pockets to get you to your hotel (see Chapter 9); you can also change more money later in the city. If you aren't planning to use your credit/debit cards, you may want to stand patiently in line for the exchange office — its rates are usually the best in town.

On your way out to ground transportation, you'll also find a very good **tourist information desk** (☎ 06-6595-4471 or 06-6595-6074); at one end they answer questions about Rome, and at the other they answer questions about all of Italy. The tourist desk is also a good place to pick up maps and other details. Nearby is a help desk for last-minute hotel reservations — the service, however, doesn't cover all the hotels in town.

Getting from the airport to your hotel

Fiumicino lies about 30km (18 miles) from Rome and is well connected by highway, train, shuttle train, and bus.

The easiest way to get to your hotel, of course, is taking a **taxi;** expect to pay about 44€ ($40) for a ride. The regular taxi line is just outside the terminal. Your taxi ride will take about 50 minutes at good times, but at rush hours, when traffic is at its worse, you risk being in the car a while longer. Also note that taxis charge a per-bag luggage fee of about 1€ (about $1) for everything that goes in the trunk, so keep your purse or any small bags with you inside the car.

Beware of gypsy-cab drivers who offer you a taxi right at the exit from the arrival gate. They don't have meters and will often charge you more than regulation cabs.

Another option is one of the minivan services to and from most hotels. From the airport to town you don't need a reservation; just walk to the desk near the tourist information area. The **CON.CO.RA. Autonoleggio** (☎ **06-6595-3934;** Fax: 06-6595-3932) is reliable and will take you from the airport to your hotel for a flat rate of about 10€ (about $9) per person, plus a surcharge for luggage. The company offers discounts on return trips.

You can also take the **train.** The railroad terminal is connected to the air terminal through a corridor on the second floor. There you can take the airport shuttle to **Termini** (Rome's central rail station) or the local train to one of the other railroad stations in Rome. The shuttle costs 9€ ($8), takes about 35 minutes, and runs about every half-hour. The local commuter train costs 4€ ($3.60), takes 30 to 40 minutes depending on the station where you get off, and runs every 20 minutes. Tickets are sold at the ticket booth in the terminal. If you're planning to use public transportation later on that day, you may want to buy a day-pass ticket for 4.40€ ($4) valid for your train ride into Rome plus unlimited **bus** and **Metro** (short for Metropolitana) subway rides for 24 hours. Note, though, that the ticket is good only for the local commuter train and not the airport shuttle train.

If you take the local commuter train, get off at **Roma Ostiense** if your hotel is in the area of the Aventino, the Colosseum, St. Peter's (San Pietro), or the Centro; alternatively, you can get off at **Roma Tiburtina,** if your hotel is in the Porta Pia or Villa Borghese area.

From the Termini, Ostiense, or Tiburtina stations, you can catch a taxi or even take the Metro or a bus.

Arriving at Ciampino

A number of international charter flights arrive at **Ciampino** (☎ **06-794-941**), the second airport of Rome, 16km (10 miles) from the center. This airport is far from being a large air terminal, and the reception structures in Ciampino are very limited. It's almost like an American civil aviation airport.

The easiest way to get to town from Ciampino is by taking a **taxi.** Expect to pay about 30€ ($27): Your ride will take about 45 minutes. You can also take the **bus** (a Cotral blue bus) to Ciampino Stazione (train station of Ciampino), and from there you take a ten-minute **train** ride to Termini (Rome's central rail station). The bus costs about 1€ (90¢), and so does the train. This method is the fastest and cheapest but can be done only if you have little luggage. From Termini, you can then take a taxi to your final destination.

By car

All roads lead to Rome, said the ancient Romans, and that statement is still true. Rome is the big transportation hub of Italy, and getting lost and confused is easy. Having a good map and precise driving directions is imperative. All highways converge onto a circular highway that runs around the outer limits of Rome, the **G.R.A. (Gran Raccordo Anulare),** also known as just the *Raccordo.* All the highways empty onto the G.R.A., while some of them (in particular the *consular roads,* state roads built by ancient Roman consuls and still in use) cross it and lead into town. Before approaching Rome, make sure you know which of the main roads that cross the G.R.A. brings you closest to your destination; note that they bear names, not numbers (the consul's name, quite often). If you arrive by highway, you must then get onto the G.R.A. and exit at the main access road that you need to arrive at your destination (for example, exit at the Aurelia if you're going to San Pietro or the Nomentana if you're going to Via Veneto). The signs on the G.R.A. don't mention all the exits, just the few upcoming exits. Therefore, you have to know which exit comes next when you enter the G.R.A. in order to enter the G.R.A. going in the right direction. When you have made it to your main access road into the city, you still have to tackle the labyrinthine layout of the city streets and its *senso unico* (one-way) streets to get to your destination.

 Rome is large, with an extremely complicated layout. Many Italians dread using their cars in the city because of the constant traffic, the aggressive driving style (for Romans it's survival, because they'd never get home otherwise), the impossibility of parking even when you've fig-ured out how to get where you want to go, and so on. If you really like to drive, you may take the challenge and drive yourself to your hotel in Rome, but otherwise we recommend that you visit Rome without a car and only rent one when you leave. Heading out of town is much easier, and you can rent a car from one of the many rental points near the out-skirts of Rome, head directly out of the city, and return the car at the airport — that way, you avoid having to drive into Rome again.

By train

Rome's central rail station is **Stazione Termini (☎ 06-4730-6559,** or 1478-880-881 for train information). It is the major public transportation hub of the city, with many bus lines starting and ending in the large square in front of the station (Piazza dei Cinquecento), and with the two Roman subway lines crossing underneath (see "Getting Around Rome," later in this chapter).

Italy's train service is excellent: cheap, reliable, and frequent. Rome is its central hub, and trains arrive and depart for every destination in Italy and Europe every few minutes.

After a renovation that lasted several years, the station looks spanking new; on the ground level are the tracks, a merchant gallery with bars, a pharmacy, newsstands, information booths, the large entrance hall with ticket tellers and ticket vending machines, and a bookstore that extends to the lower level. Public toilets and luggage checking are at either end of the track area. On the lower level you'll find a complete mall, with a supermarket (with an excellent food selection, given its size), a cosmetics shop, and several smaller services and shops, from stationery to flowers to shoe repair.

All **ground transportation** is on Piazza dei Cinquecento in front of the station's main entrance. The head of the taxi line is outside the station near the metro sign on the right. For some mysterious reason, the line forms at the end farthest from the exit of the train station, so you have to walk a bit. Take your cab from the line of taxis (taxis are white, with a checkered line on the side in yellow and black).

Although they've basically disappeared, a few pirate cabbies hang around the station and will approach you on your walk from the train to the taxi line. Reject their offers, be firm, and get in line for a regulation ride.

Orienting Yourself in Rome

Rome spreads out like a starfish. From the older central body springs arms of newer urban development that have logically formed along the *consular roads* (the roads built by the ancient Roman consuls that head out of Rome). The central body corresponds to Rome's medieval perimeter — marked by the city walls — and to the ancient Roman center. An interesting fact is that Rome didn't spread beyond its walls until the end of the 19th century — the medieval walls were built basically on top of the ancient Roman ones. The city has therefore occupied pretty much the same area for about three millennia, and consecutive layers of urban development have created a confused layout of streets, with tiny medieval roads crossed by larger — and more recent — avenues. The central body is still the heart of the city today and the part that you'll want to visit.

Rome Orientation

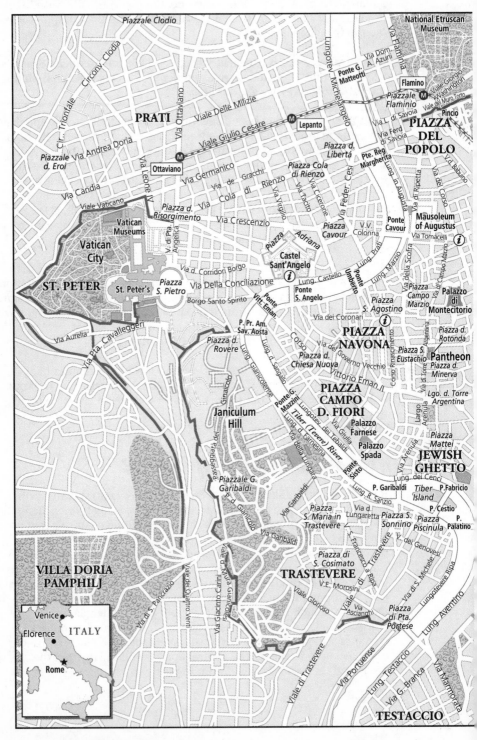

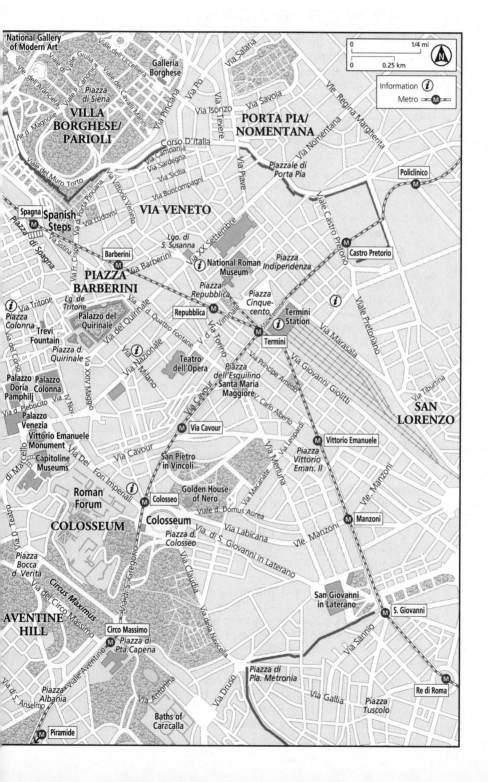

Roma by neighborhood

Rome is divided by the river **Tiber (Tevere)** that runs — or rather meanders — north-south, leaving about a third of the city's central body on its western bank and the rest on its eastern bank. Rome is divided into districts that are named after the original seven hills on which the city was built 3,000 years ago, with some other areas added afterward. However, people usually refer to much smaller neighborhoods within a district by the name of the monument or important building at their core.

An important fact is that the historical hills of Rome are no myth: They are real — and steep. The one myth is that there are only seven. Rome looks flat on a map but is very hilly — you'll soon understand why locals use mopeds (or cars, unfortunately) and why there are so few bicycles around!

The center (Il centro)

On the eastern bank of the Tevere, the *centro* is the political, cultural, commercial, and tourist heart of the city, with many of its most famous monuments, elegant shopping areas, and key political institutions. The government and the two chambers of the Italian Parliament are housed in beautiful Renaissance buildings in this area, while the presidential offices and residence are on the northeastern edge of the area. The *centro* is bordered by the Tiber to the west, Villa Borghese and the city walls to the north, the Termini railroad station to the east, and Piazza Venezia to the south. Note that there is a little confusion about *il centro* in Rome: The word is used by those living outside the city walls to refer to the whole central body of Rome within the city walls, but, of course, there is a center of the center, and that is the traditional meaning.

Among the attractions (and neighborhood-defining monuments) in this area are **Piazza del Popolo, Piazza di Spagna** (with its famous Spanish Steps), and **Via Veneto** to the north; **Piazza Navona** and **Campo de' Fiori** to the west; the **Jewish Ghetto** and **Piazza Venezia** to the south; the **Quirinale** (Presidential headquarters and residence) and **Piazza Barberini** to the east; and the **Pantheon** and the **Trevi Fountain (Fontana di Trevi)** in the center.

The main streets are **Corso Vittorio Emanuele II** running east-west from the Tiber to Piazza Venezia (technically it changes its name to Via del Plebiscito at Largo Argentina) and **il Corso** (actually Via del Corso), running north-south from Piazza del Popolo to Piazza Venezia.

All the neighborhoods within the *centro* are very desirable places to stay, with lively nightlife, restaurants, cafes, and most of the attractions within easy reach. The drawback is that everybody shows up here, so you have to contend for your space with all the Romans as well as the hordes of foreign and Italian tourists. The Ghetto and Campo de' Fiori are more authentic — and still residential — neighborhoods, while Piazza di Spagna, Via Veneto, and the Pantheon are mostly frequented by tourists — but you won't find more romantic areas. If crowds and high prices don't scare you, *il centro* is the place to be.

Colosseum (Colosseo)

Referred to by its most famous monument, this area covers the heart of the ancient Roman center, bordered by Piazza Venezia and the Fori Imperiali to the north, Capitoline Hill (the Capitolino) to the west, Circus Maximus (Circo Massimo) to the south, and the Basilica di San Giovanni in Laterano and the city walls to the east. You'll find here the most famous monuments of ancient Rome, including **Palatine Hill (the Palatino)**, the **Roman Forum (Foro Romano)** and the **Campidoglio**, and, of course, the **Colosseum.** Most of the area is occupied by archaeological parks, and there are very few hotels and restaurants, but the atmosphere is exotic: It's quiet at night but also a little eerie. This area is only steps away from all the major attractions.

Aventine Hill (Aventino) and Testaccio

This area to the south of the Colosseum was already a residential neighborhood at the time of the ancient Romans — only in those days plebeians resided in what has now become a rather patrician area. It is bordered by the Circo Massimo to the north, the Baths of Caracalla (Terme di Caracalla) to the east, the city walls to the south (with the Pyramid of Caius Cestius and the Protestant Cemetery), and the Tiber to the west. The **Aventine Hill (Aventino)** is indeed a hill, with beautiful medieval churches and monasteries at its top, while **Testaccio** is a flatter area famous for its nightlife.

Villa Borghese/Parioli

Just at the north of the *centro,* on a hill overlooking the heart of modern Rome, this residential neighborhood is among the most elegant in Rome, if not *the* most elegant. The **Villa Borghese** park fills the air with fragrance, and the neighborhood sits atop a hill. Of course, prices are at the top, too. If you can afford it, this is a great place to be — just a short walk away from many attractions, yet quiet and off the beaten path.

Porta Pia/Nomentana

Pia Gate (Porta Pia) opens at the northeast of Rome's city walls onto **Via Nomentana,** one of the oldest of the consular roads. This traditional Roman residential area is not as upscale as the Parioli, but it's more of a mix of beautiful villas from the 18th and 19th centuries, elegant buildings, and more middle-class ones. Very close to both Stazione Termini (the central rail station), and Via Veneto, it is also very well connected by public transportation and has many restaurants, cafes, and pubs that are popular with the locals. It is an excellent choice for quieter accommodations that are still quite central to the big attractions.

Trastevere

Located on the western bank of the Tiber at the foot of the Janiculum Hill (Gianicolo), Trastevere is just across the river from the Aventino and the Colosseum areas. Literally meaning "on the other side of the Tiber," this was the traditional residence of poorer artisans and workers from Roman times. Its character was preserved during the Middle Ages and the Renaissance and to some extent up to the last century. In recent times, though, it has become an artsy neighborhood, famous for its restaurants and nightlife and popular with younger and not so young Romans and visitors.

St. Peter (San Pietro)

On the western bank of the river Tiber, this area is mainly occupied by the walled city of the **Vatican** (seat of the *Holy See* — the seat of the Pope — and including the Vatican Museums and the Sistine Chapel) and dominated by the grandiose **St. Peter's Basilica (Basilica di San Pietro).** Flanking the basilica are two small, ancient residential neighborhoods that are quite picturesque.

Prati

This "new" residential neighborhood — it was developed only at the beginning of the 20th century — stretches between St. Peter's Basilica and Castel Sant' Angelo to the south to the river Tiber to the north and east. Streets are wide and straight and lined with trees. The area is pleasant and close to the *centro;* it is the seat of a relatively active if subdued nightlife, with restaurants and jazz clubs and an important shopping area along **Via Cola di Rienzo.**

Street smarts: Where to get information after you arrive

The main office of the **Rome tourist office (Azienda di Promozione Turistica di Roma) is** at Via Parigi 5 (☎ **06-4889-9253** and 06-4889-9255; Fax: 06-4889-9228; Internet: www.informaroma.it), two blocks north off Piazza della Repubblica, just north of Stazione Termini. Open Monday through Saturday from 9 a.m. to 7 p.m., the office offers a choice of material on Rome and on side trips from the city, plus a free map and a calendar of events, published monthly.

The **City of Rome** maintains two tourist information desks at main points of arrival; one at the international arrivals in the **Fiumicino Airport** (☎ 06-6595-6074; open daily 8:15 a.m. to 7:00 p.m.) and one in the **Stazione Termini** (the central railroad station) at the front of track 4 (☎ **06-4890-6300;** open daily 8 a.m. to 9 p.m.). It also maintains ten information kiosks at key points around the city, near major attractions; the staffs at these kiosks are usually less overwhelmed and more available than the staff in the main tourist office and offer free city maps, a calendar of events, and much more. Open daily 9 a.m. to 6 p.m., the kiosks are at the following addresses:

✔ **Termini,** Piazza dei Cinquecento, in front of the railroad station (☎ **06-4782-5194;** Metro: Termini)

✔ **Via Giolitti,** along the southern side of Stazione Termini, the railroad station (☎ **06-4740-028;** Metro: Termini)

✔ **Largo Goldoni,** off Via del Corso (☎ **06-6813-6061;** Metro: Piazza di Spagna)

✔ **Fontana di Trevi,** Via Minghetti (☎ **06-6782-988;** Metro: San Giovanni)

✔ **San Giovanni in Laterano,** on the Piazza (☎ **06-7720-3535;** Metro: San Giovanni)

✔ **Via Nazionale,** across from the Palazzo delle Esposizioni (☎ **06-4782-4525;** Bus: 64)

✔ **Piazza delle Cinque Lune,** just north of Piazza Navona (☎ **06-6880-9240;** Minibus: 116)

✔ **Castel Sant'Angelo,** Piazza Pia, to the east of the Castel Sant'Angelo (☎ **06-6880-9707;** Metro: Ottaviano–San Pietro)

✔ **Piazza Tempio della Pace,** off Via dei Fori Imperiali, just across from the entrance (☎ **06-6992-4307;** Metro: Colosseo)

✔ **Trastevere,** Piazza Sonnino (☎ **06-5833-3457;** Tram: 8)

✔ **Santa Maria Maggiore,** Via dell'Olmata, on the southeastern side of the church (☎ **06-4788-0294;** Metro: Termini)

The **Holy See,** being a separate state, maintains its own tourist office. It is located in Piazza San Pietro (☎ **06-6988-4466;** open Monday through Saturday 8:30 a.m. to 7:00 p.m.), just left of the entrance to the Basilica di San Pietro, and has information on the Vatican and all its tourist attractions and religious events. You can get a plan of the basilica and make reservations for a visit to the Vatican gardens; you can also get the form to participate in a papal audience, but making a reservation to do so before you leave home may be better.

Another source of information is the friendly staff at **Enjoy Rome** (Via Varese 39, three blocks north of Stazione Termini; ☎ **06-445-1834;** Internet: www.enjoyrome.com), which also offers a free room-finding service and walking tours of the city (see Chapter 12). Enjoy Rome is open Monday through Friday 8:30 a.m. to 7:00 p.m. and Saturday 8:30 a.m. to 2:00 p.m.

For further tips and to find out what's going on around town, you can buy *Roma C'è,* which has a section in English and comes out on Thursdays, and *Wanted In Rome,* an all-English publication. Both are available at newsstands.

Getting Around Rome

You'll have your choice of several modes of transportation, public and private, to help you get around Rome. Our favorite is on foot, because you see the most; remember that the city is more than 2,000 years old, so much of it isn't designed for any mode of conveyance other than the human foot. Streets curve, merge, narrow to almost shoulder-width, change names, and meander among beautiful old buildings. There are times, however, when you'll welcome public transportation. Taxis, for example, are great at night.

Rome is generally very safe, especially in its most central areas, and you can get around following the same precautions that you'd use in any large city. The most common form of crime is pickpocketing, practiced extensively at crowded locations — such as on buses and at markets — by a variety of characters. Often the perpetrators are Gypsies, a nomad people originally from central Europe. Gypsy women and children can be seen around the city begging for change. Roving gangs of Gypsy children will virtually surround you, distract you in all the confusion, and pick your pocket in the mayhem. Hold tight to your wallet and purse, and brush your way through with a stern "no." In addition, try to stay away from the curbs when walking — thieves on motor scooters sometimes speed by and yank bags or purses from people's shoulders.

On foot

Probably the best way to visit any Italian city is on foot, and Rome is no exception. The center of town is relatively small, and you can visit many attractions in one long stroll. Rome has many centers, however, and to get from one to the other — unless you're reasonably fit — you may want to catch some form of public transport (see the following sections).

To enjoy this delightful labyrinth, you need a good map. Making your way around Rome without a map is very difficult; the layout of the city is quite complicated. The free tourist-office map is pretty good as is the free bus and Metro map you can get at the bus information stand in front of the Termini station, when it is available. If you want to do more-serious exploration, however, buying one of the detailed city maps available at any newsstand and many bookstores around town is a good idea.

By Metro (subway)

Rome has only two Metropolitana (Metro for short) subway lines, **Line A** and **Line B,** which connect and cross each other at the Termini station, which is also the head of many bus lines. Line A runs near San Pietro, passing Piazza di Spagna and the Palazzo Barberini (Via Veneto) on one side and San Giovanni on the other. Line B is the one you take to the Colosseum. The Metro runs Sunday through Friday from 5:30 a.m. to 11:30 p.m. and Saturday from 5:30 a.m. to 12:30 a.m.

Tickets for public transportation

Metro, trams, and buses belong to the same system (ATAC, the city transport system), so your ticket is valid for all public transportation in Rome. A regular *biglietto* (ticket) for the bus/metro is valid for 75 minutes and costs .77€ (70¢). As elsewhere in Italy, you need to buy tickets before boarding the metro, tram, or bus, and you can buy them at most bars, tobacconist shops (signed *tabacchi* or by a white *T* on a black background), and newsstands. Tickets and passes are also sold at the ticket booths in the metro, at the ATAC bus information booth in front of Stazione Termini (near Platform C), and from machines at many locations. Within the 75 minutes of validity, you can take as many buses and trams as you want, but you can take only one Metro (subway) ride. Remember that you need to stamp the ticket at your first ride, using the machine inside the bus or tram and always before your ride in the subway; without the stamp, the ticket isn't valid. If you're still on the bus when you approach the expiration of the 75 minutes of validity — let's say after 65 minutes — stamp your ticket again at its other end; it will show that you boarded the bus during the period of validity of your ticket and not after it expired, so you'll be in the clear if a ticket inspector boards the bus. Also available is a daily pass costing 3.10€ ($2.80) and a weekly pass costing 12.39€ ($11).

The Colosseum, Circus Maximus, and Cavour stops on line B don't offer full elevator/lift service and aren't disabled-accessible. (For tips for travelers with disabilities, see Chapter 5.)

By bus (autobus)

The ATAC bus system is large and under continuous improvement. However, Rome's ancient layout resists any real modernization, so things don't always go smoothly: Buses are very crowded at rush hours, and traffic jams are common. Still, buses remain an excellent resource because they go absolutely everywhere in Rome. The buses you're more likely to use are the **64** (which runs from Termini to San Pietro, crossing the *centro*) and the two small electric buses that go around the area of limited circulation in the heart of Rome (full of tiny narrow streets), the **116** and **117**. A very large number of bus lines service Rome, however, and many of them overlap in the center of town, giving you many opportunities to climb aboard.

When you arrive in Rome, one of the first things you should do is pick up an updated bus map from the bus information booth outside the main train station in Piazza dei Cinquecento or from the tourist information office inside the station.

Most buses run daily from 5:30 a.m. to 12:30 a.m., but some stop at 8.30 p.m. A few nighttime lines are marked with an *N* for *notturno* (night); they usually run every hour, leaving the ends of the line on the hour.

In the continuous effort to improve circulation, bus routes and some-times lines are changed; be sure to double-check that some of the bus numbers we give you in this chapter and Chapter 12 haven't changed by the time you get to town.

By tram

Rome still has a few tram lines (they belong to the same system as the buses); they aren't as spectacular as the cable cars in San Francisco, but they're fun to ride. Also, trams have a separate lane, so they're less frequently stopped by traffic. The routes are long, however, and you may have an extended — though scenic — ride. A line we like a lot is the **30,** which passes by the Basilica di San Giovanni and the Colosseum. Trams are indicated on the bus map.

By taxi

Taxi rates are reasonable in Rome, but taking a taxi can be expensive during those busy times of day when you're stuck in traffic. They're a great resource for getting to your hotel from the train station at your arrival, traveling around at night after the buses and Metro stop run-ning, and getting to some areas that are poorly served by public trans-port, such as the Gianicolo. A taxi is always the best option if you have a lot of luggage, but if you don't and it's rush hour, the bus is probably a better idea. It depends on your budget.

Taxi fare starts at 2.32€ ($2), and then the meter adds .10€ (9¢) for every kilometer or minute, whichever comes first, and there is a night surcharge (between 10 p.m. and 6 a.m.) of 2.60€ ($2.30), and a Sunday and holiday surcharge of 1€ (90¢). There also is a supplement of 1€ (90¢) for each piece of luggage put in the trunk.

Hailing a taxi on the street is possible but not that easy, particularly at night. Taxis don't cruise the streets as they commonly do in most major U.S. cities but return to taxi stands and wait for a call. Luckily, there are many taxi stands around Rome, especially in the center of town. Look for them near major monuments, at places like **Piazza Barberini** (at the foot of Via Veneto), **Piazza San Silvestro,** and **Piazza SS. Apostoli** (both not far from the Trevi Fountain). You can identify taxi stands by a smallish telephone on a pole marked "TAXI"; usually a few cabs are lined up and waiting. Always go to the first taxi in the line. If you're starting from a place with a phone — a hotel, restaurant, and so on — ask the staff to call the nearest station or one of the radio taxis for you. For a **24-hour radio taxi,** call ☎ **06-88-177,** 06-66-45, or 06-49-94.

By motor scooter

Yes, most Romans travel around via moped, or so it seems when you're on a street corner waiting for the signal to turn green. If you want to do as the Romans do, you can find a number of places to rent a *motorino*. The best spot is **Treno e Scooter (TeS)** just outside Stazione Termini by the taxi stand and Metro entrance (☎ **06-4890-5823**). TeS gives you a 10% discount if you've traveled by train that day. The scooters are very good quality and the prices (for example, 52€/$46 for the weekend) include insurance, taxes, and a free map. To get there, take the Metro to Termini.

Of the many other scooter-rental places, here are a few good ones: **Rent a Scooter Borgo,** Via delle Grazie 2, just off Via di Porta Angelica, on the right side of the Vatican (☎ **06-687-7239**; Metro: Ottaviano); **Roma Solutions,** Corso Vittorio Emanuele II 50, just off Piazza Navona (☎ **06-687-6922**; Minibus: 116); and **New,** Via Quattro Novembre 96/a, just up from Piazza Venezia (☎ **06-679-0300**; Bus: 64).

Remember that riding a scooter can be quite dangerous in Rome's most busy areas and that you need to be passably fit (to squeeze in between parked cars and other obstacles). Accidents are increasingly common. It is a great mode of transport on Sundays and holidays, when there are fewer buses and little traffic, or to explore quiet neighborhoods.

Where to Stay in Rome

Rome has a variety of accommodations choices, ranging from the very basic to the supremely elegant. Though the city holds lots of rooms, in high tourist season you may find it difficult to find the type of lodging you prefer. Papal Jubilee 2000 brought both good and bad things: Many hotels were refurbished for the event and several new ones opened, but at the same time hoteliers raised their rates, sometimes steeply (offset somewhat by a better exchange rate). Following is a rundown of the best places to stay, followed by some acceptable alternatives if you have trouble booking a room. Unless otherwise specified, all rooms in the hotels that we list in this section come with private bathrooms. Note that many of the hotels in historical areas are housed in ancient buildings and have relatively few rooms, so reserve well in advance.

If you arrive without a room reservation (something we advise against), remember that there's a hotel desk at the airport and that Enjoy Rome (see "Street smarts: Where to get information after you arrive," earlier in the chapter) offers a free room-finding service.

Rome Accommodations and Dining

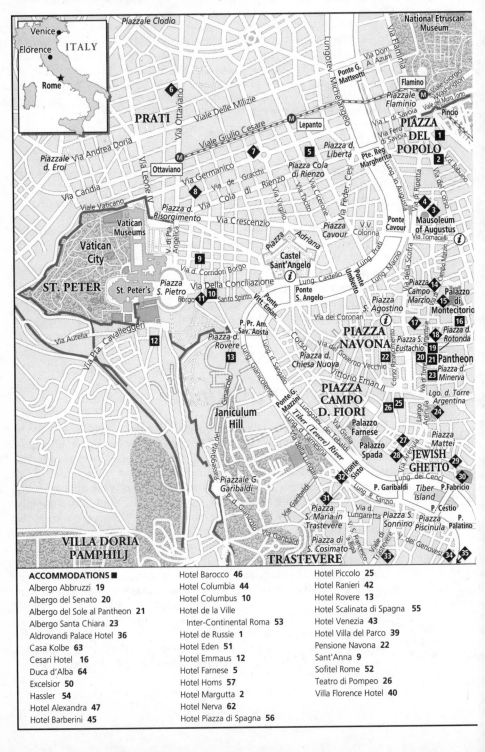

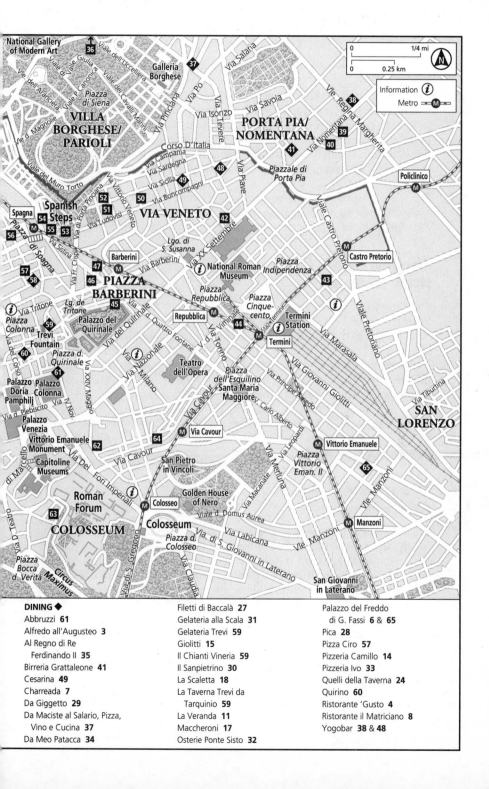

DINING ◆

Abbruzzi **61**

Alfredo all'Augusteo **3**

Al Regno di Re
Ferdinando II **35**

Birreria Grattaleone **41**

Cesarina **49**

Charreada **7**

Da Giggetto **29**

Da Maciste al Salario, Pizza,
Vino e Cucina **37**

Da Meo Patacca **34**

Filetti di Baccalà **27**

Gelateria alla Scala **31**

Gelateria Trevi **59**

Giolitti **15**

Il Chianti Vineria **59**

Il Sanpietrino **30**

La Scaletta **18**

La Taverna Trevi da
Tarquinio **59**

La Veranda **11**

Maccheroni **17**

Osterie Ponte Sisto **32**

Palazzo del Freddo
di G. Fassi **6** & **65**

Pica **28**

Pizza Ciro **57**

Pizzeria Camillo **14**

Pizzeria Ivo **33**

Quelli della Taverna **24**

Quirino **60**

Ristorante 'Gusto **4**

Ristorante il Matriciano **8**

Yogobar **38** & **48**

The top hotels

Albergo Abbruzzi

$ Pantheon

This very basic hotel offers roomy and immaculate guest rooms, but the real draw is that you're right at the Pantheon. The prices for this fantastic location are extremely low because you have to share a bath and there's no air-conditioning or elevator. The view, however, is unbeatable. The Abbruzzi is much in demand — reserve well in advance to get a room with a view. Rooms in the back without the view are quieter, though.

Piazza della Rotonda 69 (just across from the Pantheon). ☎ *06-679-2021. Bus: 116 to Pantheon or 64 or 70 to Largo Argentina, and then walk north. Rack rates: 73€–95€ ($66–$86) double, including breakfast. No credit cards.*

Albergo del Sole al Pantheon

$$$$$ Pantheon

Claiming to be Rome's oldest hotel — there are accounts of it being a hostelry as far back as 1467 — the Albergo del Sole al Pantheon didn't steal its name: It sits just in front of the famous monument. The original coffered ceilings are hand-painted, and the confusing layout is typical of medieval Rome, with a few steps to climb up and down to the slightly different levels. The guest rooms are individually decorated and air-conditioned. The suites offer baths with hydromassage.

Via del Pantheon 63. ☎ *06-678-0441. Fax: 06-6994-0689. Internet:* www.hotel solealpantheon.com. *Bus: 116 to Pantheon or 64 or 70 to Largo Argentina, then walk north. Rack rates: 309€–325€ ($280–$290) double. AE, DC, MC, V.*

Albergo Santa Chiara

$$$ Pantheon

This is one of Rome's oldest hotels, run since 1838 by the Corteggiani family, and a great value. Just behind the Pantheon and a few steps from Piazza della Minerva, it's functional and comfortable. From the beautiful entry hall, with its statuary and porphyry columns, to the breakfast room with its skylights, the Santa Chiara offers a feeling of elegance. All the guest rooms are air-conditioned and have small safes.

Via Santa Chiara 21. ☎ *06-687-2979. Fax: 06-687-3144. Internet* www.albergo santachiara.com. *E-mail:* stchiara@tin.it. *Bus: 116 to Pantheon or 64 or 70 to Largo Argentina, then walk north. Rack rates: 152€–244€ ($140–$220) double, including buffet breakfast. AE, DC, MC, V.*

The big splurge

In this chapter, we supply entries for several deluxe ($$$$$) hotels, among them the Albergo del Sole al Pantheon, the Aldrovandi Palace Hotel, and the Hotel Scalinata di Spagna. If you're looking for the plushest of the plush, here are a few more suggestions:

- **Excelsior.** Via Vittorio Veneto 125; ☎ 800-325-3589 in the U.S. or 06-47-081; Fax: 06-482-6205; Internet: www.luxurycollection.com; Metro: Line A to Barberini.

- **Hassler.** Piazza Trinità dei Monti 6; ☎ 800-223-6800 in the U.S. or 06-699-340; Fax: 06-678-9991; Internet: www.hotelhasslerroma.com; E-mail: hassler roma@inclink.it; Metro: Line A to Spagna.

- **Hotel de la Ville Inter-Continental Roma.** Via Sistina 67–69; ☎ 800-327-0200 in the U.S. and Canada or 06-67-331; Fax: 06-678-4213; Internet: www.interconti.com; E-mail: rome@interconti.com; Metro: Line A to Spagna or Barberini.

- **Hotel de Russie.** Via del Babuino 9; ☎ 06-32-8881; Fax: 06-32-8888; Internet: http://hotelderussie.it; E-mail: reservations@hotelderussie.it; Metro: Line A to Flaminio.

- **Hotel Eden.** Via Ludovisi 49; ☎ 800-225-5843 in the U.S. or 06-478-121; Fax: 06-482-1584, Internet: www.hotel-eden.it; E-mail: reservations@hotel-eden.it; Bus: 119.

Aldrovandi Palace Hotel

$$$$$ Villa Borghese

Opened in 1981, the Aldrovandi Palace is housed in an elegant villa facing the park of the Villa Borghese. Although pricey, the hotel offers many extras that you wouldn't expect to find in Rome: a large free parking area, pool, private park, gym and health club, and restaurant with park views. Above all, it's extremely quiet at night — a rare advantage in Rome. All the guest rooms are air-conditioned and have satellite TVs, and a number of them are disabled-accessible. Don't forget to ask about any special offers the hotel is running, which may bring the steep prices down a bit.

Via Ulisse Aldrovandi 15 (behind the Villa Borghese). ☎ *06-322-3993. Fax: 06-322-1435. Internet:www.aldrovandi.com. E-mail:hotel@aldrovandi.com. Tram: 19 or 30 to Via Ulisse Aldrovandi. Parking: Free. Rack rates: 400€–500€ ($360–$450) double. AE, DC, MC, V.*

Casa Kolbe

$ Teatro di Marcello

Near the Jewish Ghetto, steps from the major classical sites — the Capitoline Hill, Palatine Hill, Roman Forum, and Colosseum — this is an old-fashioned hotel in a former convent; it offers room-and-board combinations if you want. The guest rooms are clean but sometimes a little worn and the furnishings simple. For the price, however, you can't beat it. This is a peaceful area, and the quietest rooms overlook the small inner garden. Many tour groups book here, so reserve in advance. A number of rooms are disabled-accessible.

Via San Teodoro 44. ☎ *06-679-8866. Fax: 06-6994-1550. Bus: 60 or 81 to Bocca della Verità, and then walk east to Via San Teodoro. Rack rates: 80€ ($70) double. AE, DC, MC, V.*

Cesari Hotel
$$ Pantheon

Housed in a building from the first half of the 18th century that was renovated in 1999, this hotel lies between the Pantheon and the Corso; the Trevi Fountain is only steps away. Most of the guest rooms have been soundproofed, and all offer air-conditioning and satellite TVs. If you have a large party, inquire about the triple and quad rooms.

Via di Pietra 89a. ☎ *06-674-9701. Fax: 06-674-97030. E-mail:* cesari@venere.it. *Bus: 60 or 116 to Via di Pietra, just south of Piazza Colonna on the Corso. Parking: Free nearby. Rack rates: 125€–202€ ($110–$180) double. AE, DC, MC, V.*

Duca d' Alba
$$ Colosseo

Near the Colosseum and the Roman Forum, this hotel offers guest rooms that are soundproofed, have air-conditioning, and come with safes. They're decorated with classic accents, and a few even have private balconies.

Via Leonina 12. ☎ *06-484-471. Fax: 06-488-4840. Internet:* www.hotelduca dalba.com. *E-mail:* info@hotelducadalba.com. *Metro: Line B to Cavour, and then walk a block north; Via Leonina is on your left. Parking: Nearby garage 20€–26€ ($18–$24) per day. Rack rates: 100€–255€ ($90–$230) double, including breakfast. AE, DC, MC, V.*

Hotel Alexandra
$$$ Via Veneto

The Alexandra is a good value, considering that it's on famous Via Veneto — you couldn't ask for a more glamorous location. The hotel is very well kept and has undergone a renovation and expansion. All the guest rooms are air-conditioned and nicely furnished. The pleasant breakfast room was designed by the famous Italian architect Paolo Portoghesi.

Via Vittorio Veneto 18. ☎ *06-488-1943. Fax: 06-487-1804. E-mail:* alexandra@ venere.it. *Metro: Line A to Barberini, then walk up Via Veneto. Parking: Nearby garage 26€ ($24) per day. Rack rates: 202€ ($180) double, including breakfast. AE, DC, MC, V.*

Hotel Barocco
$$$$ Via Veneto

Right off Piazza Barberini, this charming small hotel has a fantastic location on one of the quieter streets behind Via Veneto, both a little removed from its noise and yet still close by and near major attractions. Its guest rooms are tastefully furnished in cherry wood and have marble baths and stuccoed ceilings. The refined ambience is pleasant without being stuffy.

Via della Purificazione 4. ☎ *06-487-2001. Fax: 06-485-994. Internet:* www.hotelbarocco.com. *E-mail:* info@hotelbarocco.com. *Metro: Line A to Barberini, and then walk up Via della Purificazione, on the west side of the piazza. Rack rates: 191€–326€ ($170–$295) double, including breakfast. AE, MC, V.*

Hotel Columbia
$$$ Piazza della Repubblica

Renovated in 1997, this hotel dates back to 1900. The Murano chandeliers are nice touches in otherwise simple, modern guest rooms (with air-conditioning). The service is good, and there's a nice rooftop garden with a bar. The Hotel Venezia (later in this section) is under the same management.

Via del Viminale 15. ☎ *06-474-4289 or 06-488-3509. Fax: 06-474-0209. Internet:* http://hotelcolumbia.com. *E-mail:* info@hotelcolumbia.com. *Metro: Line A to Repubblica, and then walk toward Stazione Termini. Rack rates: 195€ ($176) double, including breakfast. AE, DC, MC, V.*

Hotel Columbus
$$$$ San Pietro

Only steps from St. Peter's Basilica, this wonderful hotel in the Palazzo della Rovere was built in the late 1400s by Cardinal Domenico della Rovere and surrounds a garden courtyard. Charles VIII is one of the many notables who have occupied it at one time or another. Both the public spaces and the air-conditioned guest rooms are beautifully furnished; you'll feel as if you're a guest in an aristocrat's palace. Some of the frescoes were done by Pinturicchio. **La Veranda** restaurant offers refined Roman and Italian cuisine and tables in the garden in the summer. The hotel is disabled-accessible.

Via della Conciliazione 33. ☎ *06-686-5435. Fax: 06-686-4874. Internet:* www.hotelcolumbus.net. *E-mail:* columbus@hotelcolumbus.net. *Bus: 64 to last stop, and then walk south to Via della Conciliazione and turn left. Parking: Free. Rack rates: 237€–307€ ($213–$276) double, including breakfast. AE, DC, MC, V.*

Hotel Farnese
$$$$ Prati

Tucked between the Castel Sant'Angelo and Piazza del Popolo in a quiet neighborhood, this hospitable hotel occupies a 19th-century patrician palace and was recently completely renovated. The Farnese is steps from one of Rome's best shopping streets — Via Cola di Rienzo — and within walking distance from the Vatican and the medieval center. The decor in the air-conditioned guest rooms is one of subdued elegance. The hotel also has a roof garden.

Via A. Farnese 30. ☎ *06-321-2553 or 06-321-2554. Fax: 06-321-5129. Metro: Line A to Lepanto, and then walk northeast on Via degli Scipioni to Via A. Farnese. Parking: Free in private garage. Rack rates: 258€ ($230) double. AE, MC, V.*

Hotel Margutta
$$ Piazza di Spagna

On one of the charming old streets between Piazza del Popolo and Piazza di Spagna, in perhaps the most chic area of the *centro,* the Margutta is a very good value. If you can put up with the lack of air-conditioning and not having a phone in your room, you're compensated by having most of the main attractions — including the Spanish Steps — only a walk from your doorstep. A couple of guest rooms have terraces (they're more expensive). Ask if the rooms have been soundproofed.

Via Laurina 34. ☎ *06-322-3674. Fax: 06-320-0395. Metro: Line A to Spagna; if walking from Piazza del Popolo, Via Laurina is the second street on your left. Rack rates: 110€–155€ ($100–$140) double, including breakfast. AE, DC, MC, V.*

Hotel Nerva
$$ Colosseum

Renovated in 1997, this hotel occupies a building from the 16th and 17th centuries situated above the archaeological area of the Roman Forum. The guest rooms are comfortable and pleasantly decorated in a modern style, all with air-conditioning and other amenities.

Via Tor de' Conti 3–5. ☎ *06-678-1835. Fax: 06-6992-2204. E-mail:* hotelnerva@ libero.it. *Bus: 75 to Via Tor de' Conti, which runs between Via Nazionale and Via dei Fori Imperiali. Rack rates: 62€–217€ ($56–$195) double, including breakfast. AE, DC, MC, V.*

Hotel Piazza di Spagna
$$$$ Piazza di Spagna

This hotel is only a stone's throw from Piazza di Spagna. The Giocondi family (now the third generation) completely renovated and redecorated the place in 2001. The guest rooms are small but comfortable; each is personalized with special furnishings and touches, and all have air-conditioning, satellite TVs, and minibars; a few have Jacuzzis and/or private terraces. Because the hotel is small and in a prime location, make your reservations well in advance.

Via Mario de' Fiori 61. ☎ *06-679-6412. Fax: 06-679-0654. Internet:* www.hotel piazzadispagna.it. *E-mail:* info@hotelpiazzadispagna.it. *Metro: Line A to Spagna, and then walk a block southeast to Via Mario de' Fiori. Rack rates: 180€–260€ ($165–$235) double, including buffet breakfast. AE, DC, MC, V.*

Hotel Scalinata di Spagna
$$$$$ Piazza di Spagna

This clean, pleasant hotel is just above the Spanish Steps and is loaded with character: Your guest room may have exposed ceiling beams and quaint old furniture, or a private small terrace. It feels more like a country inn on a hill — the view from the roof garden is spectacular — than a hotel smack-dab in the middle of Rome. It's a perfect spot from which to explore the *centro*.

Piazza Trinità dei Monti 17. ☎ *06-679-3006. Fax 06-6994-0598. Internet* www.hotelscalinata.com. *E-mail:* info@ hotelscalinata.com. *Metro: Line A to Spagna, and then walk up the Spanish Steps. Rack rates: 250€–350€ ($225–$315) double, including buffet breakfast. AE, MC, V.*

Hotel Villa del Parco
$$$ Porta Pia

This family-run hotel is housed in one of the elegant villas on Via Nomentana and is surrounded by a garden. Although it's outside the historic center, the area boasts beautiful 19th-century villas, parks, and quiet tree-lined streets and is well connected by public transportation. The Bernardini family treats its customers as personal guests, so you feel as if you're staying in a refined home. A recent renovation included the installation of an elevator. The guest rooms are decorated in muted tones, with comfortable furnishings.

Via Nomentana 110. ☎ *06-4423-7773. Fax: 06-4423-7572. E-mail:* villaparco@ mclink.it. *Bus: 60 or 62 to third stop after Porta Pia on Via Nomentana. Rack rates: 195€ ($176), including breakfast. AE, DC, MC, V.*

Pensione Navona
$$ Piazza Navona

This family-run *pensione* is just off Piazza Navona, and the location is its great plus. Otherwise, the guest rooms are simple, with functional modern furniture — this is a *pensione* after all, not a hotel. About two-thirds of the rooms offer private baths. Air-conditioning is available on request (and for an extra fee), but the high ceilings keep the house quite cool even on the hottest days.

Via dei Sediari 8. ☎ *06-686-4203. Fax: 06-6880-3802. E-mail:* navona@posta 2000.com. *Bus: 70, 81, or 116 to Via dei Sediari, which is east of the southern tip of Piazza Navona, just off Corso Rinascimento. Rack rates: 98€ ($90) double; air-conditioning 16€ ($15) per day. No credit cards.*

Sant'Anna
$$$ San Pietro

Set in one of Rome's most authentic and charming neighborhoods, this hotel is in a 16th-century building surrounding a courtyard. Tasteful and elegant, the spacious guest rooms are air-conditioned and include marble baths. The Sant'Anna has a brightly decorated breakfast room, offers wheelchair access, and allows pets.

Via Borgo Pio 134. ☎ *06-6880-1602. Fax: 06-6830-8717. Internet:* www.hotel santanna.com. *E-mail:* santanna@travel.it. *Bus: 64 to the next-to-last stop, and then walk north to Borgo Pio. Parking: Free. Rack rates: 159€–197€ ($143–$180) double, including buffet breakfast. AE, MC, V.*

Sofitel Rome
$$$$$ Via Veneto

From the roof garden on the sixth floor of this palatial residence of the Roman nobility, you can enjoy one of the best views over the Eternal City. The hotel has been completely restored with sumptuous period furniture and luxurious marble baths that wouldn't have displeased Nero. The hotel is wheelchair accessible.

Via Lombardia 47. ☎ *06-478-021. Fax: 06-478-022. Internet:* www.sofitel.com. *Metro: Line A to Barberini, and then walk up Via Veneto, turn left on Via Cadore and walk two blocks to Via Lombardia. Parking: Free. Rack rates: 284€–490€ ($256–$450) double, including buffet breakfast. AE, DC, MC, V.*

Teatro di Pompeo
$$ Campo de' Fiori

The name of this hotel indicates that the building sits on top of the remains of a 55 B.C. Roman theater, some of which you can still see in the breakfast room. The rest of the building is from the 15th century, as revealed by the beamed ceilings in the rooms, which are matched by tasteful furnishings in the old style. All the guest rooms are air-conditioned. The hotel is small, so reserve your room early.

Largo del Pallaro 8. ☎ *06-6830-0170. Fax: 06-6880-5531. E-mail:* hotel. teatrodipompeo@tiscalinet.it. *Bus: 64 to Sant'Andrea della Valle, then walk east on Via dei Chiavari and turn right. Rack rates: 95€–190€ ($86–$170) double, including breakfast. AE, DC, MC, V.*

Villa Florence Hotel
$$$ Porta Pia

This recently renovated hotel occupies an 1860 patrician villa with its own garden. Just outside the walls at Porta Pia on Via Nomentana in an area of elegant villas and embassies, the hotel is well connected by public transportation and just a 20-minute walk from Via Veneto. The guest rooms vary in configuration and size (there are some triples and quads), and all come with trouser presses and baths with Jacuzzis. The continental breakfast is served in the garden or in your room.

Via Nomentana 28. ☎ ***06-440-3036*** *or 06-440-2966. Fax: 06-440-2709. Internet:* www.charmingrome.com/villaflorence. *E-mail:* villa.florence@ flashnet.it. *Bus: 60 or 62 to the first stop after Porta Pia on Via Nomentana. Parking: 11€ ($10). Rack rates: 207€ ($186) double, including breakfast. AE, DC, MC, V.*

Runner-up accommodations

Albergo del Senato
$$$$ Pantheon

A good-value hotel near the Pantheon. All the guest rooms are air-conditioned.

Piazza della Rotonda 73. ☎ ***06-678-4343.*** *Fax: 06-699-40297. Internet:* www.albergo delsenato.it. *E-mail:* info@albergodelsenato.it.

Hotel Barberini
$$$$ Via Veneto

This hotel is expensive but beautiful, with elegant reproduction furniture and luxurious baths. It's located just off Via Veneto near the Fontana di Trevi.

Via Rasella 3. ☎ ***06-481-4993.*** *Fax: 06-481-5211. Internet:* www.hotel barberini.com. *E-mail:* info@hotelbarberini.com.

Hotel Emmaus
$$ San Pietro

This recently renovated hotel is only a hundred yards from the Basilica di San Pietro. All the guest rooms have modern but tasteful furnishings, and some enjoy views over St. Peter's dome.

Via delle Fornaci 23. ☎ ***06-635-658.*** *Fax: 06-635-331.*

Hotel Homs
$$$ Piazza di Spagna

Only a short walk from the Spanish Steps, the Hotel Homs offers nice amenities and reasonably large guest rooms (some of them disabled-accessible) with contemporary furniture, as well as a roof terrace with a view where you can have breakfast.

Via della Vite 71. ☎ **06-679-2976.** *Fax: 06-678-0482.*

Hotel Piccolo
$ Campo de' Fiori

The Piccolo lives up to its name — a small hotel squeezed into the narrow streets not far from Campo de' Fiori. Price is the attraction in this popular area, but the guest rooms are nice but quite basic.

Via dei Chiavari 32. ☎ **06-6880-2560** *or 06-689-2330.*

Hotel Ranieri
$$$ Termini

This hotel is within walking distance of Via Veneto and was renovated in the last ten years. The guest rooms offer modern baths and air-conditioning.

Via XX Settembre 43. ☎ **06-4201-4531.** *Fax: 06-4201-4543. E-mail:* `hotel.ranieri@italyhotel.com`.

Hotel Rovere
$$$ San Pietro

Set on the lower slope of the Gianicolo on a quaint side street, the Rovere is close to Trastevere and the Vatican. It's a clean, quiet place, with pleasant modest rooms of comfortable size. A buffet breakfast is also included.

Vicolo Sant'Onofrio 4–5. ☎ **06-6880-6739.** *Fax: 06-6880-7062.*

Hotel Venezia
$$$ Termini

In a residential district near the university, this hotel boasts relatively large guest rooms decorated with Murano chandeliers. It also has a very helpful staff.

Via Varese 18. ☎ **06-445-7101.** *Fax: 06-495-7687. Internet:* `www.hotelvenezia.com`. *E-mail:* `info@hotelvenezia.com`.

Where to Dine in Rome

Italian gourmands maintain that there isn't a really good restaurant in Rome. And they're right — sort of. However, you can find hundreds of excellent *trattorie, osterie,* and *pizzerie* — small joints, simple in decor (often even basic), offering delectable preparations of typical Roman cuisine. Other than a few exceptions, truly good food is served only in mom-and-pop places with real homemade cuisine. Rome offers many excellent trattorie, and if you want to find your own preferred spot, the best areas to search are *il centro* (the center) between the Corso and the river Tiber and Trastevere. Local wines are from the nearby Castelli Romani (hill towns to the east of Rome).

Primi, secondi, and contorni

Roman cuisine is rich in regional specialties. *Primi* (first courses) include *pasta all'amatriciana* (a tomato-and-bacon sauce with pecorino cheese), *pasta all'arrabbiata* (tomato and lots of hot red pepper), the famous Thursday specialty *gnocchi* (potato dumplings usually in a tomato-based sauce), *spaghetti alle vongole* (spaghetti with clams), and *cannelloni* (pasta tubes filled with meat or fish and baked).

Secondi (second courses) are dominated by the delicious *abbacchio* (young lamb), prepared *alla cacciatora* ("hunter's style" — sautéed with herbs and wine) or *scottadito* (literally "finger burning" — small grilled cutlets served crispy and hot to eat with your hands); the traditional *contorno* (vegetable side dish) is succulent roasted potatoes. Another justly famous *secondo* is *saltimbocca alla romana* (literally "jump in your mouth" — veal or beef stuffed with ham and sage and sautéed in a Marsala sauce). If you're adventurous, try *trippa alla romana* (tripe Roman style) and *coda alla vaccinara* (oxtail stew). Other favorites include a variety of dishes such as roast pork, fried fish and calamari, and *baccalà* (codfish).

Pizza, with all the toppings

The most common food that Romans head out to eat is pizza. Pizza in a pizzeria is strictly an individual-size round pizza (not by the slice — for that, see "Snacks on the run and picnic fare" later in this chapter) with a variety of toppings. Traditional toppings include (but are not limited to) the following:

- *Margherita:* Tomato and mozzarella
- *Napoletana:* Margherita, plus anchovies
- *Capricciosa:* Tomato, mozzarella, and mushrooms with artichoke hearts, olives, ham, and an egg

- *Rugola e parmigiano:* Fresh arugula — called "rocket" on many menus — and thin slices of Parmesan cheese
- *Funghi:* Mushrooms, tomato, and mozzarella

In addition, *pizzerie* typically serve the following appetizers:

- *Supplì:* Rice balls stuffed with a small piece of mozzarella and deep fried
- *Filetti di baccalà:* Deep-fried codfish
- *Bruschetta:* Toasted peasant-style bread topped with oil and garlic and, on request, tomatoes, olive caviar, ham, and so on
- *Olive ascolane:* Large green olives stuffed and deep fried
- *Fiori di zucca:* Zucchini flowers stuffed with a small piece of anchovy and mozzarella and then deep fried

If you don't want pizza, try a *crostino* (several slices of bread with mozzarella and a variety of toppings, toasted in the oven). The Roman *crostino* is different from the Tuscan variety, discussed in Chapter 14.

Sweet stuff

Typical *dolci* (desserts) in Rome are *torta della nonna* (a pie filled with custard and pine nuts), *torta di crema e visciole* (pie with custardy ricotta and sour cherries), *tiramisù* (layered espresso-soaked ladyfingers and mascarpone cheese), and of course *gelato* (ice cream — see the sidebar "Looking for a gelato break?" later in this chapter).

If you're in the mood for a sweet snack, try **Limentani** (Via Portico d'Ottavia 1; ☎ **06-686-0011**), in the Jewish Ghetto, where you can stop for some of the best traditional Roman treats at the pastry shop. Another place to grab a pastry or treat to fill your stomach is **Valzani** (Via del Moro 37a in Trastevere; ☎ **06-580-3792**).

Snacks on the run and picnic fare

Of one thing you can be sure in Rome: You won't starve! You can always get good food while you're on the go.

You can have lunch or a quick snack for little money if you go to a take-out pizzeria. The sign usually says *pizza a taglio* (by the slice) or *rustica* (rustic). On the display counter you can see a number of large square pans containing a variety of pizzas: *rossa* (tomato and mozzarella), *bianca* (oil, salt, and rosemary), *funghi* (tomato and mushrooms), as well as the chef's own inventions. The person serving will cut out a hunk for you (you can indicate if you want it larger or smaller) and sell it by weight. They sometimes also have a *calzone*

(baked turnover filled with a varying assortment of ham, cheese, and vegetables).

Another option is to make a sandwich and have a picnic in Villa Borghese or on the Gianicolo (see Chapter 12). An excellent place to buy farm-fresh food for your picnic is the **Fattoria la Parrina** (Largo Toniolo 3, between Piazza Navona and the Pantheon; ☎ 06-6830-0111), which offers wonderful cheese, wine, and veggies.

The top restaurants

Alfredo all'Augusteo
$$ Piazza del Popolo   ROMAN/ITALIAN

Just behind the Mausoleum of Augustus between Via del Corso and the river, this restaurant is where the original Alfredo sauce (a classic cream sauce) was invented. The fettuccine Alfredo will set you back 12€ ($11) here. Besides excellent fresh pasta, the menu includes a number of Italian specialties, with *secondi* like lamb, beef, pork, and fish (though pasta is the real attraction). The dining room is more upscale than most in Rome, and the service is very professional.

Piazza Augusto Imperatore 30. ☎ 06-687-8734. Reservations recommended on weekends. Metro: Line A to Piazza di Spagna. Secondi: 12€–20€ ($10–$18). AE, MC, V. Open: Lunch Tues–Sat.; dinner Mon–Sat.

Al Regno di Re Ferdinando II
$$ Testaccio   NEAPOLITAN

In one of the historic cellars of Monte Testaccio — the hill formed by discarded pottery shards under Nero — this restaurant offers excellent Neapolitan food. The choice of fresh pasta is superb and the *Sfizietto del Re* (a huge portion of linguine with a mountain of shellfish from the nearby Tirrenian Sea) delights any palate and leaves an everlasting memory after you finish — *if* you can finish. All the appetizers are delicious and the *secondi* (particularly the fish) are excellent. This restaurant also makes pizza, but the pasta is much better. If you visit in the summer, bring a jacket — the place isn't air-conditioned, but the cellar maintains an icy temperature inside.

Via di Monte Testaccio 39. ☎ 06-578-3725. Reservations recommended. Metro: Line B to Piramide, but taking a cab is best. Secondi: 10€–18€ ($9–$16). AE, DC, MC, V. Open: Lunch Tues–Sat; dinner Mon–Sat.

Birreria Grattaleone
$ Porta Pia   ITALIAN/PIZZA/BIRRERIA

Much care and money made this spacious *birreria* (like a Bavarian beer hall, but with a wood-fired pizza oven and typical Italian specialties) stylish and welcoming. The American-trained chef presents the food — from traditional fried fish to *bistecca alla fiorentina,* the enormous and tender Florentine steak — with a flair learned in New York and Miami. The restaurant features live music on Thursday, Friday, and Saturday.

Via Messina 42. ☎ *06-4424-2379. Reservations recommended on weekends. Bus: 60 or 62 to Porta Pia and Via Nomentana; then turn left on Via Ancona, and then right on Via Messina. Secondi: 7€–13€ ($5–$12). AE, DC, MC, V. Open: Lunch and dinner daily.*

Cesarina
$$$ Via Veneto   ROMAN/BOLOGNESE

Offering a nice selection of specialties from Rome and Bologna, this restaurant is an excellent choice in the residential area north of Via Veneto, away from the crowds. The food is wonderful and perfectly prepared. Go for the many homemade pastas and/or the choice of meat dishes. The *bollito misto* (variety of boiled meats) is delicious.

Via Piemonte 109. ☎ *06-488-0828. Reservations recommended. Metro: Line A to Barberini. Bus: 56 or 58 to Via Piemonte (the fourth street off Via Boncompagni coming from Via Veneto). Secondi: 9€–23€ ($8–$21). AE, DC, MC, V. Open: Lunch and dinner Mon–Sat.*

Charreada
$$ Cola di Rienzo   MEXICAN

Mexican food in Rome? Sure! But check your wallet before going because this restaurant is trendy and, therefore, expensive. Charreada is located in one of Rome's prettiest squares and is a popular place — especially late at night — to have guacamole or a nice steak.

Piazza dei Quiriti 4. ☎ *06-3600-0009. Reservations recommended. Metro: Line A to Lepanto, and then walk up Viale Giulo Cesare and take the second left on Via Duileo to the piazza. Secondi: 12€–20€ ($11–$18). AE, MC, V. Open: Dinner daily.*

Da Giggetto
$ Teatro Marcello   JEWISH ROMAN

This famous restaurant has for decades been the destination of Romans who want to taste some of the specialties of Jewish Roman cuisine. Some Romans say Gigetto is a little past its prime, but we think it's still a good place to sample such typical specialties as *carciofi alla giudia* (crispy fried artichokes), as well as traditional Roman dishes like *fettuccine all'amatriciana* (pasta with a tomato-and-bacon sauce).

Via del Portico d'Ottavia 21. ☎ *06-686-1105. Reservations recommended. Bus: 60 to last stop, and then walk north behind the synagogue. Secondi: 10€–14€ ($9–$13). AE, DC, MC, V. Open: Lunch Tues–Sun; dinner Tues–Sat; closed two weeks in Aug.*

Da Maciste al Salario, Pizza, Vino e Cucina
$ Villa Borghese   ROMAN/PIZZA

A great place to go for lunch before or after your visit to the Galleria Borghese, this large basement eatery gets really busy with locals from nearby offices and shops. The food is simple but excellent, and the pizza is one of the best Roman-style pizzas around — thin and crispy and sea-soned to perfection. At lunch, it's cafeteria style — you walk up to the counter and choose from the buffet. Get there early because the best choices disappear fast, and definitely take the side bread dish with a few pieces of pizza *bianca* (focaccia). At dinner they offer a large choice of great antipasto, hearty primi, and pizza.

Via Salaria 179/a. ☎ *06-884-8267. Reservations only necessary for dinner. Bus: 52 or 53 to Via Salaria; or exit Galleria Borghese in the rear and take Via Pinciana, bearing right on Via Giovannelli to reach Via Salaria. Secondi: 5€–9€ ($4.50–$8). AE, DC, MC, V. Open: Lunch Mon–Sat; dinner Tues–Sun.*

Da Meo Patacca
$ Trastevere   ROMAN

Probably Rome's most famous restaurant among locals, Meo Patacca was an ancient inn and stagecoach stop. Romans come here today for spe-cial occasions and to enjoy the traditional music and clowning around. The restaurant attracts loads of visitors as well, but the place is huge, with two terraces and a labyrinth of tavern rooms. Food choices include a large selection of grilled meats — the pork is excellent — homemade pastas and staples like *frittata* (Roman omelet), *saltimbocca alla romana* (veal or beef stuffed with ham and sage and sautéed in a Marsala sauce), *lepre in salmì con la polenta* (hare with polenta), and *melanzane alla parmigiana* (eggplant parmigiana).

Piazza dei Mercanti 30. ☎ *06-581-6198. Internet:* www.dameopatacca.com. *Reservations not necessary. Tram/Bus: Tram 8 or bus 23 to Trastevere; from Piazza Sonnino, turn left on Via dei Genovesi and then right on Via de' Vascellari. Secondi: 6€–15€ ($5–$14). AE, DC, MC, V. Open: Dinner daily.*

Filetti di Baccalà
$ Campo de' Fiori   ROMAN

Hidden in a courtyard (or overgrown side street), this restaurant has been famous for decades for one specialty: *filetti di baccalà,* delicious slabs of deep-fried salt cod. The *filetti* are so good, it's almost all they serve, but the menu also includes salad, beans, *puntarelle* (one of the typ-ical fresh greens of Rome) when in season and some reasonably good choices of wine. The desserts are few but homemade. Go early, because lines begin even before darkness falls in the warm months.

Largo dei Librari 88. ☎ *06-686-4018. Reservations not accepted. Bus: 116 to Campo de' Fiori; Largo dei Librari is just off Via dei Giubbonari, down from Campo de' Fiori. Secondi: 2.60€ ($2.50) per filetto. No credit cards. Open: Dinner Mon–Sat.*

Looking for a gelato break?

Italian ice cream is among the best in the world. It's called gelato and comes in a variety of flavors, divided between fruits and creams. In addition to *limone* (lemon), *arancio* (orange), and other fruits, you can choose from specialties such as *mora* (blackberry) and *frutti di bosco* (mixed berries). The best cream flavors are *zabaglione* (a rum-and-egg combo, like eggnog), *bacio* (hazelnut chocolate), and *stracciatella* (vanilla with chocolate chips).

The oldest ice-cream parlor in Rome is **Giolitti,** Via Uffici del Vicario 40 (☎ 06-699-1243; Minibus: 116), which offers a huge selection of flavors — the fruit and chocolate flavors are usually excellent. The second oldest is the **Palazzo del Freddo di G. Fassi,** with two locations: one on Viale Angelico off San Pietro (Metro: Line A to Ottaviano), and the main store on Via Principe Eugenio 65–67 (☎ 06-446-4740; Metro: Line A to Piazza Vittorio). (We think that the main store is much better.) In Trastevere, try the **Gelateria alla Scala,** Via della Scala 5 (☎ 06-581-3174; Tram: 8), for excellent homemade ice cream. Off Campo de' Fiori, go to **Pica,** Via della Seggiola 12 (☎ 06-6880-3275; Tram: 8) , which prepares one of the best ice creams in Rome. Near the Fontana di Trevi, don't miss the **Gelateria Trevi,** Via del Lavatore 84–85 (☎ 06-679-2060; Bus: 52, 53, 61, 62, 63, 116, or 492).

A new passion in Rome is frozen yogurt, made with real fresh yogurt and fruit. You can find some of Rome's best at **Yogobar,** with several locations, including Viale Regina Margherita 83b, just north of Via Nomentana (☎ 06-855-1374; Bus: 61 or 63; Tram: 19 or 30), and Via Lucania 23–27, off Via Boncompagni, east of Via Veneto (☎ 06-4288-3001; Minibus: 116).

Il Chianti Vineria

$ Fontana di Trevi   TUSCAN

Sharing an outdoor terrace with La Taverna Trevi (see the restaurant's listing, later in this chapter) and located in a *largo* (widening of a street, like a small square) behind the Trevi Fountain, Il Chianti is a wine bar with a buffet that specializes in Tuscan cuisine and offers a variety of light choices. The typical cheese and cold cuts are excellent. Savor the tasty menu choices with a glass from the excellent wine list.

Via del Lavatore 81. ☎ 06-678-7550. Reservations recommended. Bus: 85, 60, 116, or 117 to Via del Tritone, and then turn right on Via Poli, pass in front of the Fontana di Trevi, and turn right on Via del Lavatore. Secondi: 7€–11€ ($5–$10). MC, V. Open: Lunch and dinner Mon–Sat.

Il Sanpietrino

$$ Teatro Marcello   ROMAN

This restaurant, located in the Jewish Ghetto, is just steps from all the sites of ancient Rome. In its stylish dining rooms, you can taste innovative interpretations of Roman cuisine with an emphasis on seafood. An ample choice of seafood appetizers (such as fresh anchovies baked between slices of eggplant), seafood ravioli, and other delicacies surprises and satisfies the most demanding palates.

Piazza Costaguti 15. ☎ *06-6880-6471. Reservations recommended. Bus: 60 to last stop, and then walk up Via del Portico d'Ottavia and turn right on Via Progresso to the piazza. Secondi: 12€–17€ ($11–$16). AE, DC, MC, V. Open: Lunch Mon–Fri; dinner Mon–Sat.*

La Taverna Trevi da Tarquinio
$ Fontana di Trevi   ABBRUZZESE/ROMAN

Opening into a courtyard-sized square shared with Il Chianti, the Taverna is a great spot to dine outdoors in nice weather. Given its location, you'd expect one of those touristy prix-fixe places, but Romans love the center as much as visitors, and this restaurant has so far maintained its quality standards. The food is good traditional Abbruzzese and Roman, with a variety of delicious homemade pastas, *abbacchio* (lamb roast), and a choice of grilled meats.

Via del Lavatore 82. ☎ *06-679-2470. Reservations recommended. Bus: 85, 60, 116, or 117 to Via del Tritone, and then turn right on Via Poli, pass in front of the Fontana di Trevi, and turn right on Via del Lavatore. Secondi: 9€–15€ ($8–$14). MC, V. Open: Lunch and dinner Mon–Sat.*

La Veranda
$$$ San Pietro   CONTEMPORARY ITALIAN

This restaurant is in the Palazzo della Rovere, which also houses the Hotel Columbus (see "Where to Stay in Rome," earlier in this chapter). When the weather's fine, you can eat in one of Rome's nicest garden courtyards. The changing menu offers seasonal specialties and regional dishes, mainly Roman and Tuscan. Of particular interest are the *piatti della storia,* dishes made from recipes from Renaissance Rome. Of these, try the soup of porcini mushrooms and pears or the rabbit with pistachio sauce. For an appetizer, try the crêpes with chestnuts and radicchio.

Borgo Santo Spirito 73. ☎ *06-687-2973. Reservations recommended on weekends. Bus: 62 to San Pietro, and then turn right on Borgo Santo Spirito. Secondi: 14€–21€ ($13–$19), including contorno. AE, MC, V. Open: Lunch and dinner Fri–Wed; closed Aug.*

Osteria Ponte Sisto
$ Trastevere   ROMAN

Offering traditional Roman fare, this famous *osteria* has been a long-standing destination for locals and tourists alike. Try the delicious *risotto al gorgonzola* (Italian rice cooked with Gorgonzola cheese) or, if you dare, some truly Roman specialties such as *trippa alla romana* (tripe in a light tomato sauce) or beef roasted on a charcoal grill.

Via Ponte Sisto 80. ☎ *06-588-3411. Reservations recommended. Bus/Tram: Tram 8 or bus 23 to Trastevere, then turn right and walk along the river to Piazza Trilussa and turn left on via di Ponte Sisto. Secondi: 6€–13€ ($5–$12). AE, MC, V. Open: Lunch and dinner Thurs–Tues; closed Aug.*

Pizzeria Camillo

$ Pantheon   PIZZA A TAGLIO/SPAGHETTI

This tavern with simple wooden tables and benches serves some of the best pizza in Italy. The pizza is sold by weight, and going to the counter, ordering, and then taking it to your table is best. The restaurant also prepares a variety of pasta dishes served at the table and a choice of *rosticceria* (roastery) specialties. One of the most delicious pizzas offers sausages and mushrooms, or you can try the pizza with peppers when it's available.

Via Campo Marzio 45a. ☎ *06-687-1161. Reservations not accepted. Bus: 116 to Pantheon, and then walk north on Via della Maddalena to Via Campo Marzio. Pizza: 2€–4€ ($1.75–$4.50) per pound. MC, V. Open: Lunch and dinner Mon–Sat.*

Pizzeria Ivo

$ Trastevere   PIZZA

One of Rome's most established pizzerias, Ivo is as popular with locals as it is with visitors. Luckily, the place is big! Here you can enjoy an entire range of pizzeria appetizers, pizzas, crostini, and calzones. All the pizzas are good, but we love the seasonal one with *fiori di zucca* (zucchini flowers) and the *capricciosa* (prosciutto, carciofini, and olives).

Via di San Francesco a Ripa 158. ☎ *06-581-7082. Reservations not necessary. Tram: 8 to Via di San Francesco a Ripa (on the right off Viale Trastevere). Secondi: 5€–8€ ($4.50–$7). DC, MC, V. Open: Lunch and dinner Wed–Mon.*

Quelli della Taverna

$ Campo de' Fiori   ROMAN

In a quiet street in the middle of a very busy area, the Taverna is a quality restaurant in a touristy sector of town where it's sometimes difficult to choose a place to eat. The very moderate prices and hearty portions are the draw, and the well-prepared Roman specialties are served in a country-style ambience. The *antipasto misto* is a must, with a choice of savory vegetables, cheese, and cold cuts from the nearby hills. The primi are superb; go for fresh *pasta all'amatriciana* (tomato-and-bacon sauce) or *pasta all'carbonara* (egg-and-bacon sauce). For a secondo, the *involtini di melanzane* (stuffed rolled eggplant) is delicious. There's also a selection of homemade desserts.

Via dei Barbieri 25. ☎ *06-686-9660. Reservations recommended. Bus: 58, 60, or 62 to Largo Argentina; Via dei Barbieri is just off Largo Argentina behind the theater. Secondi: 6€–9€ ($5–$8). MC, V. Open: Lunch and dinner Mon–Sat.*

Ristorante 'Gusto

$$ Piazza del Popolo   ITALIAN/INTERNATIONAL

If an establishment can be all things to all people, this is it: a restaurant, an *enoteca* (a kind of wine shop and bar), a pizzeria, a wine bar, and a cigar club. It even has a store that sells cookbooks and kitchenware. The restaurant offers several prix-fixe options, and you can order the self-service lunch buffet for 9€ ($8). The pastas are good, as are the pizzas (like *chicoria* and *funghi*), and the menu even features items like couscous, wok-prepared Asian dishes, and continental choices. The restaurant is popular with workers during the day and young people at night — especially on weekends, when you can get pizza until 1:30 a.m. The wine bar in back offers a large choice of drinks, whiskies, and *grappas* (Italian brandy). Romans are even learning about brunch from the great buffet served here on Saturdays and Sundays.

Via della Frezza 23. ☎ *06-322-6273. Reservations recommended for dinner. Bus: 117 or 119 from Piazza del Popolo to Via della Frezza/Piazza Augusto Imperatore. Secondi: 9€–18€ ($8–$16). AE, MC, DC, V. Open: Lunch and dinner daily.*

Ristorante il Matriciano

$$ San Pietro   ROMAN

This family-run restaurant is a wonderful place to eat outside in the summer, but you must have a reservation because it's well known and popular. The name reflects one of the specialties, *bucatini all'amatriciana* (thick spaghetti with a hollow center served with a tomato-and-bacon sauce). You can also find excellent versions of other typical specialties of Roman cuisine, such as *abbacchio al forno* (baked lamb casserole) .

Via dei Gracchi 55 ☎ *06-321-2327. Reservations required. Metro: Line A to Ottaviano/San Pietro, and then walk on Via Ottaviano south toward San Pietro and turn left on Via dei Gracchi. Secondi: 12€–16€ ($11–$15). AE, DC, MC, V. Open: Winter, lunch and dinner Thurs–Tues; Summer, lunch and dinner Sun–Fri. Closed three weeks in Aug.*

Runner-up restaurants

Abbruzzi

$$ Fontana di Trevi

At this moderately priced and popular Roman/Abbruzzese trattoria off the Fontana di Trevi, the big attraction is the large selection of cold appetizers.

Via del Vaccaro 1. ☎ *06-679-3897. Bus: 62 or minibus 116 or 119.*

La Scaletta
$ Pantheon

A rustic *birreria* (beer pub) and *vineria,* it offers a huge selection of wine, and you can find something to eat for as little as 4€ ($3.60). Try the polenta with mushrooms for 8€ ($7). The restaurant stays open until 2 a.m., and it's only a stone's throw from the Pantheon.

Via della Maddalena 46–49. ☎ *06-679-2149. Bus: 116.*

Maccheroni
$$ Pantheon

This clean, bright, nouveau trattoria has great food, including excellent pastas and wines, just north of the Pantheon.

Piazza delle Coppelle. ☎ *06-6830-7895. Internet:* http://italmarket.com/ rm/maccheroni. *E-mail:* maccheroni@italmarket.com. *Bus: 116.*

Pizza Ciro
$ Piazza di Spagna

This pure Neapolitan pizzeria opened in Rome in 1996, after 100 years of service in Naples. It offers an unbeatable 5€ ($4.50) lunch special including a margherita pizza and a beer.

Via della Mercede 43–45. ☎ *06-678-6015. Bus: 62.*

Quirino
$$$ Piazza di Spagna

A traditional Roman restaurant with some Sicilian influence, Quirino's focus is on seafood, from *fritto di paranza* (mixed deep-fried small fish and calamari) to grilled fish.

Via delle Muratte 84. ☎ *06-679-4108. Bus: 62.*

Chapter 12

Exploring Rome

The Eternal City awaits, enigmatic as ever. Its thousands of years of history have left imprints everywhere you look, but this is no lifeless museum of the past. A couple million people live and work in a place designed for chariots instead of cabs and hordes of kids on motorbikes. They walk on ruins from the days of Caesar, turn along the same alleyways trod by masters of the Renaissance, and thrill to the same lighted fountains that were reflected in the eyes of Fellini's beautiful debauchers.

Rome also contains a state — the **Vatican,** the world's second-smallest sovereign state, its vast complex of museums, apartments, grottoes, chapels, and gardens filled with masterpieces and riches beyond your wildest dreams. This, along with the city's many other historic sights, will make you understand why they say that Rome wasn't built in a day. And don't think you can *see* it all in a day: Set aside several days to do the city right.

There's No Place Like Rome, There's No Place Like Rome: The Top Sights

Ticket booths at the sights mentioned in this section usually stop selling tickets about an hour before closing. The city of Rome has been making an effort to accommodate ever-growing numbers of tourists, and as a result, late-evening days have been added and hours have been extended in summer. Some sights are staying open on Monday as well, a day when most attractions traditionally are closed.

To appreciate fully the Roman Forum, the Colosseum, and other ruins, buy a copy of the small book entitled *Rome Past and Present* (Vision Publications), sold in bookstores or on stands near the Forum. Its plastic overleafs show you how Rome looked 2,000 years ago.

Rome Attractions

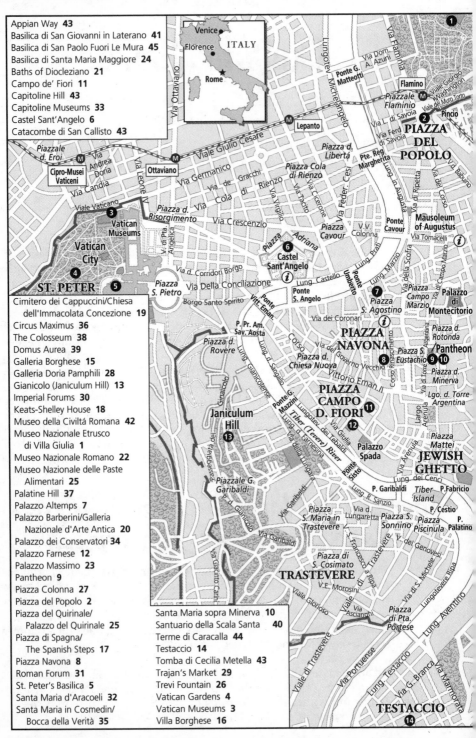

Appian Way **43**
Basilica di San Giovanni in Laterano **41**
Basilica di San Paolo Fuori Le Mura **45**
Basilica di Santa Maria Maggiore **24**
Baths of Diocleziano **21**
Campo de' Fiori **11**
Capitoline Hill **43**
Capitoline Museums **33**
Castel Sant'Angelo **6**
Catacombe di San Callisto **43**

Cimitero dei Cappuccini/Chiesa
   dell'Immacolata Concezione **19**
Circus Maximus **36**
The Colosseum **38**
Domus Aurea **39**
Galleria Borghese **15**
Galleria Doria Pamphili **28**
Gianicolo (Janiculum Hill) **13**
Imperial Forums **30**
Keats-Shelley House **18**
Museo della Civiltá Romana **42**
Museo Nazionale Etrusco
   di Villa Giulia **1**
Museo Nazionale Romano **22**
Museo Nazionale delle Paste
   Alimentari **25**
Palatine Hill **37**
Palazzo Altemps **7**
Palazzo Barberini/Galleria
   Nazionale d'Arte Antica **20**
Palazzo dei Conservatori **34**
Palazzo Farnese **12**
Palazzo Massimo **23**
Pantheon **9**
Piazza Colonna **27**
Piazza del Popolo **2**
Piazza del Quirinale/
   Palazzo del Quirinale **25**
Piazza di Spagna/
   The Spanish Steps **17**
Piazza Navona **8**
Roman Forum **31**
St. Peter's Basilica **5**
Santa Maria d'Aracoeli **32**
Santa Maria in Cosmedin/
   Bocca della Verità **35**

Santa Maria sopra Minerva **10**
Santuario della Scala Santa **40**
Terme di Caracalla **44**
Testaccio **14**
Tomba di Cecilia Metella **43**
Trajan's Market **29**
Trevi Fountain **26**
Vatican Gardens **4**
Vatican Museums **3**
Villa Borghese **16**

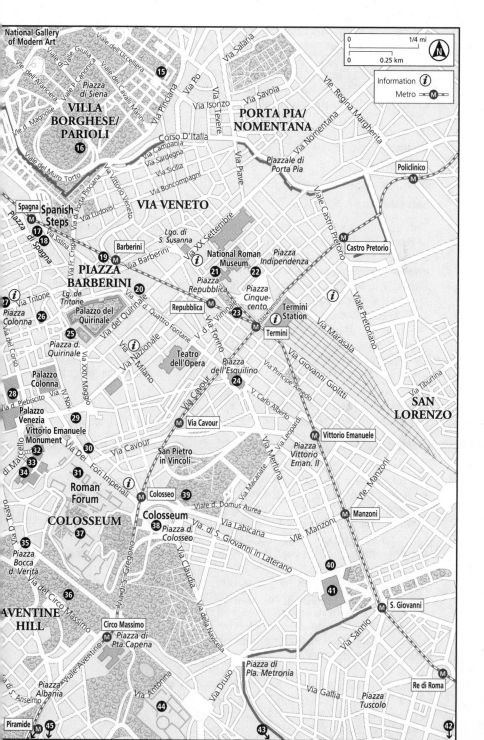

National Gallery of Modern Art

Viale dell'Uccelliera

Via Salaria

Via Po

Via Isonzo

Via Savoia

1/4 mi

0.25 km

Information ⓘ
Metro Ⓜ

15

VILLA BORGHESE/ PARIOLI

Piazza di Siena

16

Vle. d'Magnolie

Vle. del Muro Torto

PORTA PIA/ NOMENTANA

Via Nomentana

Corso D'Italia

Via Campania

Via Sardegna

Via Sicilia

Via Boncompagni

Piazzale di Porta Pia

Vle. Regina Margherita

Vle. Castro Pretorio

Policlinico Ⓜ

Spagna Ⓜ **Spanish Steps**

17 Ⓜ 18

Piazza di Spagna

VIA VENETO

Lgo. di S. Susanna

Barberini

19 Ⓜ

PIAZZA BARBERINI

Via Barberini

Via XX Settembre

National Roman Museum ⓘ

21

Piazza Indipendenza

Piazza Repubblica

Castro Pretorio

Vle. Pretoriano

7 ⓘ

Via Tritone

26

Piazza Colonna

Lgo. de Tritone

20

Palazzo del Quirinale

Via del Quirinale

Via d. Quattro Fontane

Republica Ⓜ

22

Piazza Cinquecento

23

Termini Station

ⓘ Ⓜ

Termini

Via Marsala

25

Piazza d. Quirinale ⓘ

Via XXIV Maggio

Via Nazionale

Teatro dell'Opera

Piazza dell'Esquilino

24

Via Milano

Piazza Vittorio Eman. II

Via Giovanni Giolitti

V. di Torino

Via Cavour

V. Principe Amedeo

Via Tiburtina

SAN LORENZO

28

Via d. Plebiscito

Palazzo Colonna

Palazzo Venezia

29

Vittorio Emanuele Monument

Via IV Nov.

30

Via Dei

Via Cavour Ⓜ

Via Cavour

San Pietro in Vincoli

V. Carlo Alberto

Via Merulana

Vittorio Emanuele Ⓜ

Piazza Vittorio Eman. II

Vle. Manzoni

32 Ⓜ

33

34

31

Roman Forum

Fori Imperiali ⓘ

Colosseo Ⓜ

39

Viale d. Domus Aurea

Via Labicana

Manzoni Ⓜ

Via Macanate

Vle. Manzoni

COLOSSEUM

37

Colosseum

38

Piazza d. Colosseo

Via di S. Giovanni in Laterano

35

Piazza Bocca d. Verità

Via Claudia

Via della Navicella

40

41

S. Giovanni Ⓜ

36

Via del Circo Massimo

AVENTINE HILL

Circo Massimo Ⓜ

Piazza di Pta. Capena

Via Sannio

Piazza di Pla. Metronia

Via Gallia

Piazza Tuscolo

Re di Roma Ⓜ

Piazza Albania

Via Antonina

Via Druso

44

Piramide Ⓜ 45

43

42

There are three special tickets for visiting the sites of ancient Rome. A **five-day, four-sight pass** includes Palazzo Altemps, Collegio Massimo, Terme di Diocleziano, and Cripta Balbi (7.75€/$7). A **five-day, seven-sight pass** includes these sights plus the Colosseum, Palatine Hill, and Terme di Caracalla (15.50€/$14). The most comprehensive ticket is the **Archaeologia Card,** which costs 20€ ($18); it's a seven-day pass that includes all of these sites plus the Villa dei Quiriti and the Tomba di Cecilia Metella on the Via Appia Antica (see "More Fun Stuff to Do").

Here is a rundown of Rome's top attractions (see Chapter 11 for neighborhood locations).

Basilica di San Giovanni in Laterano
San Giovanni

This church, and not St. Peter's Basilica, is the cathedral of the diocese of Rome. Built in A.D. 13 by Constantine, it suffered many indignities, including being sacked by the *Vandals* (a barbarian tribe whose name has given us the word *vandalism*), burned, and then damaged in an 896 earthquake. The basilica was restored and rebuilt at various times by various architects. The facade, designed and executed by Alessandro Galilei in 1735, is crowned by **15 giant statues** (7m/22-feet tall) representing Christ, St. John the Baptist, John the Evangelist, and other Doctors of the Church; you can see them from many parts of Rome. Outside is an **Egyptian obelisk,** the tallest in Rome (32m/105 feet), consecrated in the fourth century as a symbol of Christianity's victory over pagan cults.

The interior of the basilica as you see it today was redesigned by Borromini in the 17th century. The **papal altar** — under a beautiful 14th-century *baldacchino* (canopy) — conserves an important relic: the wooden altar on which Peter and the other paleo-Christian popes after him are said to have celebrated mass in ancient Rome's catacombs. In the left transept is the altar of the **Santissimo Sacramento,** decorated with four giant gilded bronze columns that are the only remains of the original basilica. Under the *baldacchino* of this altar is another important relic: It is said to be the table of Christ's last supper. The apse was redone during the 19th century, and its mosaics are copies of the original medieval mosaics. However, the fresco fragment depicting Pope Boniface VIII, who declared the first Papal Jubilee in 1300, is from the 13th century. The **Baptistry** was built by Constantine in the fourth century, making it the first of the Western world. (The walls are still original, although the interior was restored several times and the present form was designed by Borromini.) The 13th-century cloister was designed by Vassalletto and is a showcase for remains and art from the older basilica, including paleo-Christian inscriptions.

Piazza di San Giovanni in Laterano. ☎ *06-6988-6433. Metro: Line A to San Giovanni. Bus: 81, 85, 850, or minibus 117. Tram: 3. Open: Basilica and cloister daily 7:00 a.m.– 6:00 p.m. (in summer to 6:45 p.m.); Baptistry daily 9 a.m.–1 p.m. Admission: Basilica free; cloister 2.07€ ($1.86).*

Basilica di San Paolo Fuori Le Mura
Ostiense/San Paolo

According to tradition, the body of St. Paul was buried after his martyrdom on this road (Via Ostiense) leading out of Rome. As early as the time of Emperor Constantine in the fourth century, a church was built around St. Paul's tomb (below the high altar). Consecrated in A.D. 324 but later vastly enlarged, this magnificent church, second in size only to St. Peter's, was almost totally destroyed by fire in 1823 and rebuilt using marble from the original structure. (The apse and triumphal arch are the most ancient parts.) The mosaic in the apse is a faithful copy of the 13th-century one, reconstructed using parts of the original damaged by the fire. The *baldacchino* (canopy) — a masterpiece by Arnolfo di Cambio from 1285 — miraculously escaped the fire. Under the altar is the **sepulchre of St. Paul,** the tomb containing the saint's remains; it's accessible via a staircase. The interior is vast and impressive (divided by 80 granite columns), regardless of its age; the windows may look like stained glass, but they're actually made of translucent alabaster. The **cloisters** are original, and you'd have to go to Sicily to find such distinctively carved and decorated columns of so many diverse patterns.

Via Ostiense 184. ☎ *06-541-0341. Metro: Line B to Basilica di San Paolo. Bus: 23. Open: Church daily 7:00 a.m.–6:30 p.m.; cloister daily 9 a.m.–1 p.m. and 3–6 p.m. Admission: Free.*

Basilica di Santa Maria Maggiore
Termini

This church's history stretches back 1,600 years, and though it's undergone many changes over the centuries, Santa Maria Maggiore remains one of the city's four great basilicas. Ordered constructed by Pope Sisto III, it was built as a sanctuary for Mary (mother of Jesus) and was originally referred to as Santa Maria della Neve (St. Mary of the Snow) because its outline was drawn in the snow that had miraculously fallen in the summer of A.D. 352. The facade of Santa Maria Maggiore looks like your typical baroque church (Rome is full of them); the current facade was designed by Ferdinando Fuga, who sandwiched it between two palaces that had been built in the meantime (one in the 17th and the other in the 18th century). The walls, though, are original, as are the mosaics of the apse and side walls. Although restored, the floors are the original 12th-century Cosmatesco-style, and the 15th-century coffered wooden ceiling is richly decorated with gold (said to be the first gold brought back from the New World and donated by the Spanish queen). One of the church's main attractions is in the loggia: the **13th-century mosaics** preserved from the old facade. Look carefully to the right side of the altar for the **tomb of Gian Lorenzo Bernini,** Italy's most important baroque sculptor/architect. In the crypt are relics of what many people say are pieces of Jesus's crib.

Piazza di Santa Maria Maggiore. ☎ *06-488-1094. Metro: Line A or B to Termini, and then walk south on Via Cavour. Bus: 70. Open: Daily 7 a.m.–7 p.m. Admission: Free.*

Campo de' Fiori
Centro

Surrounded by cafes, restaurants, and bars, the lovely square of Campo de' Fiori boasts many attractions. Its **fruit-and-vegetable market** is one of the city's best and certainly one of the liveliest. Though popular with working people as a lunch spot, the campo is even more popular with young people (both Romans and foreigners) at night. The **central statue of the hooded Giordano Bruno** hints at the more sinister parts of the campo's history — it was the site of executions in the Middle Ages and the Renaissance, and Bruno was burned at the stake here in 1600. Bruno was a philosopher who championed the ideas of early scientists like Copernicus and maintained such heretical ideas as his theory that the earth revolved around the sun. Nearby is the delightful **Piazza Farnese,** dominated by the **Palazzo Farnese** (currently the seat of the French Embassy), surely one of Rome's most dramatic buildings, designed by Sangallo and Michelangelo. The cleaning completed in 1999 turned its somber gray color into a startling pale yellow. It can be visited on selected Sundays; call the French embassy at ☎ **0668-6011.**

Off Largo Argentina, roughly between Via Arenula and Corso Vittorio Emanuele II. Bus: 62 or 64 to Corso Vittorio Emanuele at Largo san Pantaleo or minibus 116 to Campo de' Fiori.

Capitoline Museums (Museo Capitolino)
Centro/Campidoglio

On the Capitoline Hill (Capitolino), the **Capitoline Museums (Musei Capitolini)** open onto the beautiful **Piazza del Campidoglio,** designed by Michelangelo. The oldest public collections in the world, the museums hold a treasury of ancient sculpture and an important collection of European paintings from the 17th and 18th centuries. The first masterpiece you see stands in the middle of the square, the famous **equestrian statue of Marcus Aurelius** (this is a copy; the original second-century bronze is inside for protection). The statue was saved only because early Christians thought it was the first Christian emperor Constantine. In the **Capitoline Museum (Museo Capitolino)** (housed in the Palazzo Nuovo), the other famous sculptures are the *Dying Gaul,* a Roman copy of a Greek original, and two statues of female warriors known as *The Amazons* (under restoration at press time) that were originally in Hadrian's Villa.

Across from the Palazzo Nuovo is the **Palazzo dei Conservatori Museum.** You may have already seen photos of the huge head, hands, foot, kneecap, and other dismembered pieces of an ancient 40-foot **statue of Constantine II** that stands in the courtyard and of the famous *Lupa Capitolina,* the wolf suckling Romulus and Remus, a fifth-century-B.C. bronze. Another famous work is the bronze of a **boy removing a thorn from his foot**. These artworks are ones that will likely appeal to children (especially in the fresh air of the courtyard). On the top floor is the

Capitoline Picture Gallery (Pinacoteca Capitolina). The paintings in the Pinacoteca are amazing, including Caravaggio's *Fortune Teller* and *John the Baptist,* Titian's *Baptism of Christ*, and works by Veronese, Rubens, and others.

Between the Palazzo Nuovo and the Palazzo dei Conservatori, closing Piazza del Campidoglio to the south, is the **Senatorial Palace (Palazzo Senatorio).** This palace was used for administrative purposes until recently, when it was included in the Capitoline Museums to provide additional expository space and show the results of the recent excavations under it. It was built in the Middle Ages over the **Tabularium,** an imposing Roman building that housed the public archives of the Republic in Roman times. The Tabularium was built of massive stone blocks with Doric columns in the facade. You can clearly see its remains from the Forum (3 of the original 11 arcades remain). It's now part of the museum complex, and its admission is included in the ticket.

When the Palazzo Nuovo was recently restored, the Greek and Roman sculpture collection was permanently moved to a new site, the **Centrale Montemartini.** The first electrical plant built in Rome (1912), it was transformed into a multimedia center in 1990 and is a beautiful setting for the art collection. Among the most important pieces are a beautiful **giant mosaic with hunting scenes** (20 x 40 feet) from an imperial Roman residence and some of the best examples of Roman sculpture.

Piazza del Campidoglio 1. ☎ *06-6710-2475. Internet:* www.museicapitolini. org. *Bus: 60, 81, or minibus 117 to Campidoglio (on the right around the monument to Vittorio Emmanuele II). Open: Tues–Sun. 9:30 a.m.–8:00 p.m. Admission: 7.74€ ($7) for both museums and Tabularium, free last Sun of the month.*

Extension of Museo Capitolino at the Centrale Montemartini. Via Ostiense 106. ☎ *06-574-803. Metro: Line B to Pyramide; walk down Via Ostiense. Bus: 23 to Via Ostiense. Tram: 3 to Piazza di Porta San Paolo (Stazione Ostiense, Piramide). Open: Tues–Sun 9:30 a.m–7:00 p.m.. Admission: 4.13€ ($3.70); integrated ticket for museum, Tabularium and Montemartini 8.26€ ($7.50).*

Castel Sant'Angelo
San Pietro/Vatican

This "castle" began as a mausoleum to house the remains of Emperor Hadrian and other important Romans. However, it may have been incorporated into the city's defenses as early as 403 and was attacked by the Goths (one of the barbarian tribes who pillaged Rome in its decline) in 537. Later, the popes used it as a fortress and hideout and connected it to the Vatican palace with an elevated corridor, which you can still see near Borgo Pio stretching between St. Peter's and the castle. Castel Sant'Angelo now houses a museum of arms and armor; you can also visit the papal apartments from the Renaissance as well as the horrible cells in which prisoners were kept (among them sculptor Benvenuto Cellini).

Lungotevere Castello 50. ☎ 06-687-5036 or 06-3996-7600. Bus: 23, 62, or 64 to Lungotevere Vaticano, and then walk north along the river. Open: Tues–Sun 9 p.m.–8 p.m.; closed last Tues of each month. Admission: 5.16€ ($4.70) adults, children 17 and under and adults 60 and over free.

Catacombe di San Callisto
Via Appia

There are several places to visit the catacombs in Rome (including the catacombs of St. Sebastian and those of Domitilla farther along Via Appia Antica), but this one is among the most impressive, with 20km (12½ miles) of tunnels and galleries underground and organized on several levels. (It's cold down there at 60 feet, so bring a sweater.) The catacombs began as quarries outside ancient Rome where travertine marble and the dirt used in cement were dug. Early Christians, however, hid out, held mass, and buried their dead in the catacombs. The Catacombs of St. Callixtus (Callixtus III was an early pope, elected in 217) have four levels, including a crypt of several early popes and the tomb where St. Cecilia's remains were found. Some of the original paintings and decoration are still intact and show that Christian symbolism — doves, anchors, and fish — was already developed.

Via Appia Antica 110. ☎ 06-513-6725. Metro/Bus: Line A to Colli Albani (on Sun to Arco di Travertino), and then bus 660 to Via Appia Antica. Open: Thurs–Tues 8:30 a.m. to noon and 2:30–5:00 p.m. (in summer to 5:30 p.m.). Admission: 5.16€ ($4.70).

The Colosseum (Colosseo)
Colosseum

The Colosseum, along with St. Peter's Basilica, is Rome's most recognizable monument. However, the "Colosseum" isn't its official name. Begun under the Flavian emperor Vespasian, it was named the Amphiteatrum Flavium and finished in A.D. 80. The nickname came from the colossal statue of Nero that once stood nearby — it was part of the grounds of Nero's Domus Aurea (see the following listing). Estimates show that the Colosseum could accommodate as many as 50,000 spectators. The entertainment included fights between gladiators, battles with wild animals, and naval battles where the arena was flooded (these gory details appeal to kids). In the labyrinth of chambers beneath the original wooden floor of the Colosseum, deadly weapons, vicious beasts, and unfortunate human participants were prepared for the mortal combats. (Historians now believe, however, that Christians were never fed to lions here.) The Colosseum was damaged by fires and earthquakes and eventually abandoned; it was then used as a marble quarry for the monuments of Christian Rome, until Pope Benedict XV consecrated it in the 18th century. Next to the Colosseum is the **Arch of Constantine,** built in 315 to commemorate the emperor's victory over the pagan Maxentius in 312. Pieces from other monuments were reused, so Constantine's monument includes carvings honoring Marcus Aurelius, Trajan, and Hadrian.

In the summer of 2000, for the first time in centuries, the Colosseum was brought to life again with performances under the aegis of the Estate Romana (see Chapter 2 and "Nightlife," later in this chapter).

Via dei Fori Imperiali. ☎ *06-700-4261. Metro: Line B to Colosseo. Bus: 81, 85, 850, or minibus 117; Tram: 3. Open: Daily 9 a.m.–6 p.m. (in summer to 7 p.m.). Admission: 5.16€ ($4.70).*

Domus Aurea
Colosseum

The Domus Aurea (Golden House) was the brainchild of the infamous emperor Nero. Although it once covered more than 200 acres, after the decline of Rome, this grandiose structure fell into ruin and disappeared from history. It was stumbled upon in the 18th century when Romans digging in the "hill" across from the Colosseum found caves that turned out to be ceilings of ancient rooms decorated with Roman frescoes. Only since 2000, however, have tourists been allowed to visit these cavernous spaces, some of which still have traces of the elegant interior paintings of the Roman artists of Nero's time.

Via dei Fori Imperiali. ☎ *06-3974-9907. Metro: Line B to Colosseo. Bus: 81, 85, 850, or minibus 117; Tram: 3. Open: Daily 9 a.m.–7 p.m. Admission: 5.16€ ($4.70), 1.03€ (93¢) for advance reservation.*

Trevi Fountain (Fontana di Trevi)
Centro

The massive Trevi Fountain in its own little piazza became one of the sights of Rome following the opening of the film *Three Coins in the Fountain,* though today it seems that many of the thousands who clog the space in front of it don't take the time to *really* look at it — instead, they throw coins in it, have their pictures taken in front of it, and go away. You'll be lucky if you have a tranquil moment to actually appreciate the artwork. The fountain was begun by Bernini and Pietro da Cortona, but there was a 100-year lapse in the works and the fountain wasn't completed until 1751 by Nicola Salvi. The central figure is Neptune, who guides a chariot pulled by plunging sea horses. *Tritons* (mythological figures that live in the ocean) guide the horses, and the surrounding scene is one of wild nature and bare stone.

Of course, you have to toss a coin in the Trevi. To do things properly, hold a lira coin in your right hand, turn your back to the fountain, and toss the coin over your shoulder (being careful not to bean anyone behind you). Then the spirit of the fountain will see to it that you return to Rome one day — or that's the tradition, at least.

Piazza di Trevi. Bus: 62 or minibus 116 or 119 to Via del Tritone, then walk right on Via Poli.

Imperial Forums and Trajan's Market (Fori Imperiali and Mercati Traianei)
Centro

During the first century A.D., each Roman emperor added luxurious public constructions to the original Roman Forum. Today, the whole area is being excavated after much of it was covered in the 1920s to build Via dei Fori Imperiali, a major transportation artery of modern Rome. Many of the temples were dismantled during the Middle Ages and the Renaissance, when the marble was used for other constructions, but the archaeological remains are still fascinating. Walking north along the Via dei Fori Imperiali from the Colosseum, you can see the remains on your right. The best, though, is a visit to **Trajan's Market (Mercati Traianei),** the impressive brick building rising behind and above **Trajan's Forum.** Several stories tall, this second-century structure once housed stalls and small boutiques — sort of an ancient mall. From it you also have access to part of the Imperial Forums below.

If you're an ancient-architecture aficionado, we recommend that you take one of the guided tours offered from the **Forum Information Center** (see address below), which will bring the stones back to life (something we recommend with all ancient Roman ruins); the tour, led by a live guide, will also give you access to some of the newly excavated parts under Via dei Fori Imperiali which are otherwise invisible. You can also get an audio guide machine and do the tour by yourself.

Imperial Forums information center: Via dei Fori Imperiali 7. ☎ *06-3996-7850. Metro: Line B to Colosseo and walk to your right (towards Piazza Venezia). Bus: 85, 850, or minibus 117. Open: Daily 9:00 a.m.–6:30 p.m; guided tour in English at 11 a.m., 12 p.m., and 4 p.m. Admission: Guided tour 5.16€ ($4.70); audio guides 4.13€ ($3.70) single, 6.20€ ($6) double.*

Trajan's Market: Via 4 Novembre. ☎ *06-679-0048. Open Tues–Sat 9 a.m.–4 p.m. and Sun 9:00 a.m.–1:30 p.m.. Admission: 2.60€ ($2.40).*

Roman Forum and Palatine Hill (Foro Romano and Palatino)
Centro

Rome has many forums. The original, the **Roman Forum,** lies in the valley between the Palatine and Capitoline hills (Palatino and Capitolino). The **Via Sacra** ("sacred way") runs through it. This area was the heart of Rome for more than a thousand years, and a stone discovered under the Forum in 1899 bears an inscription from the time of the Roman kings (sixth century B.C.). The Forum has many ruins (some, like the sanctuary of the sewer goddess Venus Cloaca, are just a mark on the ground) as well as a few standing buildings. The most important (but only a "restored" structure from 1937) is the square **Curia,** on the spot where the Senate once met. (Pop inside to see the third-century marble-inlay floor.) The **Temple of Antoninus and Faustina** (Antoninus Pius succeeded Hadrian in 138)

The Roman Forum and Imperial Forums

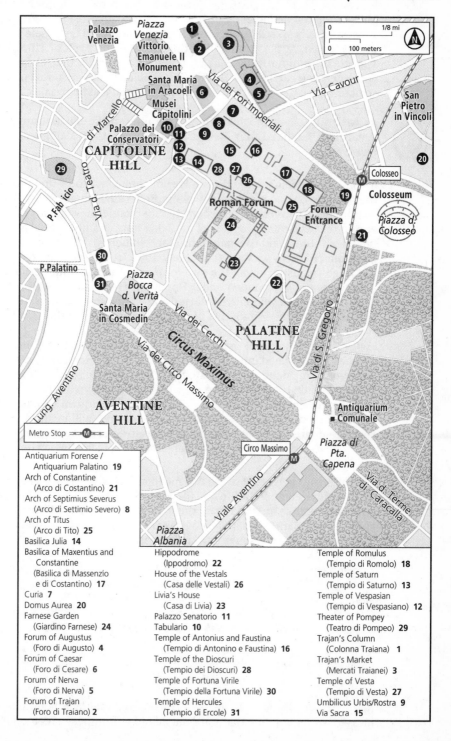

Antiquarium Forense /
 Antiquarium Palatino **19**
Arch of Constantine
 (Arco di Costantino) **21**
Arch of Septimius Severus
 (Arco di Settimio Severo) **8**
Arch of Titus
 (Arco di Tito) **25**
Basilica Julia **14**
Basilica of Maxentius and
 Constantine
 (Basilica di Massenzio
 e di Costantino) **17**
Curia **7**
Domus Aurea **20**
Farnese Garden
 (Giardino Farnese) **24**
Forum of Augustus
 (Foro di Augusto) **4**
Forum of Caesar
 (Foro di Cesare) **6**
Forum of Nerva
 (Foro di Nerva) **5**
Forum of Trajan
 (Foro di Traiano) **2**

Hippodrome
 (Ippodromo) **22**
House of the Vestals
 (Casa delle Vestali) **26**
Livia's House
 (Casa di Livia) **23**
Palazzo Senatorio **11**
Tabulario **10**
Temple of Antonius and Faustina
 (Tempio di Antonino e Faustina) **16**
Temple of the Dioscuri
 (Tempio dei Dioscuri) **28**
Temple of Fortuna Virile
 (Tempio della Fortuna Virile) **30**
Temple of Hercules
 (Tempio di Ercole) **31**

Temple of Romulus
 (Tempio di Romolo) **18**
Temple of Saturn
 (Tempio di Saturno) **13**
Temple of Vespasian
 (Tempio di Vespasiano) **12**
Theater of Pompey
 (Teatro di Pompeo) **29**
Trajan's Column
 (Colonna Traiana) **1**
Trajan's Market
 (Mercati Traianei) **3**
Temple of Vesta
 (Tempio di Vesta) **27**
Umbilicus Urbis/Rostra **9**
Via Sacra **15**

was later turned into a church and given a baroque facade (Chiesa di San Lorenzo in Miranda). Near the Curia is the **Arch of Septimius Severus,** built in 203 to commemorate his victories. The arch mentioned his two sons, Caracalla and Geta, but after Caracalla murdered Geta, Geta's name was removed. At the other end of the Forum is the **Arch of Titus.** Titus reigned as emperor from 79 to 81. If you buy a map of the Forum when you enter, you can identify the sometimes faint traces of a host of other structures (also see the map "The Roman Forum and Imperial Forums").

As with any archaeological site, things often make much more sense if you take a guided tour. Ask at the ticket booth or call ahead for a reservation.

If you find the ruins in the Roman Forum confusing, you'll find those on the **Palatino** behind it sometimes incomprehensible. Huge blocks of brick surrounded by trees and greenery testify mutely to what was once an enormous residential complex of patrician houses and imperial palaces, built under the grandiose ambitions of the emperors. The throne room of the **Domus Flavia** was approximately 100 feet wide by 131 feet long. Although Augustus began the development of the Palatine residences, they were vastly expanded under Domitian. The Palatino is also where the first Roman developments started and where Romulus drew the original square for the foundation of Rome. Excavations in the area found remains that date back to the eighth century B.C. **Livia's House** (Casa di Livia) is one of the best-preserved homes. During the Middle Ages, the site was transformed into a fortress, and during the Renaissance it again became the residence of the aristocracy, who built large villas (the **Horti Palatini,** built by the Farnese on top of the palaces of Tiberius and Caligula, for example). From the hill, you can look down behind to the **Circus Maximus (Circo Massimo),** where a quarter-million Romans once watched chariot races. Unfortunately, the structures flanking the arena were plundered for their stone, as happened with many Roman buildings.

Also interesting to visit are the two museums, the **Antiquarium Forense** and **Antiquarium Palatino,** inside an ex-convent. The Antiquarium Forense contains vestiges from the necropolis underneath the Forum, and the Antiquarium Palatino showcases art from the excavations of the Palatino, including frescoes and sculptures.

Foro Romano: Via dei Fori Imperiali; Palatino: Via di San Gregorio 30; Antiquariums: Piazza Santa Maria Nova 53. ☎ 06-699-0110. Metro: Line B to Colosseo, cross the street to the entrance to the right of the Colosseo. Bus: 85, 850, or minibus 117. Open: Summer daily 9 a.m.–6 p.m. (Sun to 1 p.m.); winter daily 9 a.m.–3 p.m. (Sun to 1 p.m.). Admission: Forum free; Palatino and Antiquariums 6.19€ ($5.60).

Galleria Borghese
Villa Borghese

Reopened in 1997 after 13 years of restoration, the Galleria Borghese is housed in the building that Cardinal Scipione Borghese created for his art collection inside the Villa Borghese (now a large public park; see "More Cool Things to See and Do"). Only a limited number of visitors is allowed inside at one time, so reservations are essential (see the phone number at the end of this listing). Your visit is limited to two hours, but the large number of truly amazing works makes you long for more time (or a second visit). The ground floor focuses on sculpture, including Canova's sensual reclining *Paulina Borghese as Venus Victrix* (Paulina was Napoleon's sister) and dramatic works by the young Gian Lorenzo Bernini showing breathtaking stone carvings. His David is in the middle of a slingshot wind-up and full of charmingly boyish concentration; his *Apollo and Daphne* captures the moment when Daphne turns into a laurel tree, her fingers bursting into leaves and bark climbing her legs. In the *Rape of Proserpine,* a sculpture he executed in collaboration with his father, the god's fingers seem actually to press into her marble flesh. The extensive painting collection contains countless masterpieces: Caravaggio's haunting self-portrait as *Bacchus* and his *St. Jerome Writing,* Antonello da Messina's subtle and mysterious *Portrait of a Man,* a young Raphael's *Deposition,* and Tiziano's *Sacred and Profane Love.* Andrea del Sarto, Coreggio, Lucas Cranach, Bronzino, Lorenzo Lotto, and many other artists are also represented.

Piazzale Scipione Borghese 5. ☎ 06-8424-1607 or 06-32810 for reservations; otherwise, 06-854-8577 or 06-841-6542. Bus: 52, 53, or 910 to Via Pinciana behind the villa, 490 to Viale San Paolo del Brasile inside the park or minibus 116 to the Galleria Borghese. Metro: Line A to Spagna; take the Villa Borghese exit and walk up Viale del Museo Borghese. Internet: www.ticketeria.it. *Open: Tues–Fri 9:00 a.m.–7:30 p.m., Sat 9 a.m.–11 p.m., Sun 9 a.m.–8 p.m. Admission: 6.19€ ($5.57).*

Museo Nazionale Etrusco di Villa Giulia
Flaminio/Villa Borghese

This museum, housed in a papal villa built by the most prominent architects of the 16th century, boasts the world's best Etruscan collection. Originally from Asia Minor, the Etruscans were a mysterious people who preceded and ruled over the Romans up to the fifth century B.C. Many of the objects in this museum came from Cerveteri, an important Etruscan site northwest of Rome. One of the most spectacular objects is the **bride and bridegroom sarcophagus** from the sixth century B.C., upon which two enigmatic figures recline. You can also see a fairly well-preserved **chariot** and impressive sculptures. Some of the most amazing works are the tiniest: The Etruscans made **intricate decorative objects** from woven gold. (How they managed to do so is still a mystery today.) In the summer, the garden is the site of musical events (see "Nightlife" later in this chapter).

Piazzale di Villa Giulia 9. ☎ 06-841-2312 or 06-321-7224. Tram: 3 or 19 to last stop, and then walk down Viale delle Belle Arti to Piazzale di Villa Giulia or 225 to Via di Villa Giulia. Open: Tues–Sun 8:30 a.m.–7:30 p.m. Admission: 4.13€ ($3.72).

Museo Nazionale Romano
Termini

The National Roman Museum is actually housed in three separate locations, one of which is the Palazzo Altemps (see the next listing). The two
other locations are the **Terme di Diocleziano (Baths of Diocletian)** and
the nearby **Collegio Massimo.** Many of the objects in the National Roman
Museum originally came from the Terme, parts of which were later used
to build **Santa Maria degli Angeli on Piazza della Repubblica** (☎ 06-
488-0812). Other pieces of ancient art and sculpture have been added
from excavations in Rome's environs. The museum was founded in 1889,
and its heart is the **Ludovisi Collection** — much of which is now housed
in the reopened Palazzo Altemps (going here first is a good idea).

Among the pieces in the Museo Nazionale are a **satyr pouring wine,** a
Roman copy of the original by Greek sculptor Praxiteles; the *Daughter
of Niobe from the Gardens of Sallust;* and an *Apollo* copied from a
sculpture by Phidias, one of the greatest Greek sculptors. These few
examples are only highlights — the museum's collection includes literally
hundreds of statues, including an interesting series showing how the
style of representation changed under various emperors. The basement
of the museum contains a **rare Roman mummy,** as well as an extensive
and well explained **numismatic display** (containing coins from earliest
times through the 19th century) based on the collection that once
belonged to the king of Italy.

Audio guides are available and are free for the first three hours.

Terme di Diocleziano: Via G. Romita 8. ☎ *06-488-0530. Metro: Line A to Repubblica;
Bus: 60, 62, or minibus 116T to Piazza della Repubblica. Collegio Massimo: Largo di
Villa Peretti 1.* ☎ *06-4890-3500 or 06-3996-7700. Metro: Line A and B to Termini; Bus:
64 or 70. Open (both museums): Tues–Sat 9 a.m.–7 p.m., Sun 9 a.m.–8 p.m.
Admission: Terme 5€ ($4.50); Collegio Massimo 6.19€ ($6).*

Palazzo Altemps
Centro/Piazza Navona

Behind Piazza Navona, the Palazzo Altemps was begun sometime before
1477; continued by the cardinal of Volterra, Francesco Soderini, from 1511
to 1523; and finished by Marco Sittico Altemps, who enlarged it at the
end of the 1500s. The palace was restored in such a way that you can see
the layers of medieval, Renaissance, and later decoration. Inside is the
Ludovisi Collection, one of the world's most famous private art collections, particularly strong in Greek and Roman sculpture, as well as
Egyptian works from the collection of the Museo Nazionale Romano (see
earlier listing).

The most important piece from the Ludovisi Collection is the **Trono
Ludovisi,** a throne thought to be the work of a fifth-century-B.C. Greek
sculptor brought to Rome from Calabria. One side depicts Aphrodite

Urania rising from the waves, another shows a female figure offering incense, and another side features a naked female playing a flute. The remarkable **statue of a soldier** apparently committing suicide with a sword was commissioned by Julius Caesar and placed in his gardens to commemorate his victories in Gaul. The *Ares Ludovisi,* a statue restored by Bernini in 1622, is believed by art historians to be a Roman copy of an earlier Greek work and shows a warrior (possibly Achilles) at rest. The colossal **head of *Hera*** (also known as Juno) is one of the best-known Greek sculptures; Goethe wrote of it as his "first love" in Rome and said it was like "a canto of Homer." It has been identified as an idealized portrait of Antonia Augusta, mother of Emperor Claudius.

Piazza Sant'Apollinare 44. ☎ *06-683-3759. Bus: 70, 81, or minibus 116 to Via dei Coronari, walk northeast away from Piazza Navona. Open: Tues–Sat. 9 a.m.–2 p.m., Sun 9 a.m.–1 p.m. Admission: 5.16€ ($4.70).*

Palazzo Barberini and Galleria Nazionale d'Arte Antica
Centro/Via Veneto

Finished in 1633, the Palazzo Barberini is a magnificent example of a baroque Roman palace. Bernini decorated the rococo apartments in which the gallery is now housed, and they're certainly luxurious. Also preserved in the Palazzo Barberini is the wedding chamber of Princess Cornelia Costanza Barberini and Prince Giulio Cesare Colonna di Sciarra, exactly as it was centuries ago. Although the structure itself is an attraction, the collection of paintings that make up the Galleria Nazionale d'Arte Antica is most impressive, including Caravaggio's *Narcissus,* Tiziano's *Venus and Adonis,* and Raphael's *La Fornarina,* a loving informal portrait of the bakery girl who was his mistress (and the model for his Madonnas). The galleria's **decorative-arts collection** contains not only Italian pieces but also fine imported objects, including some from Japan. In addition to the regular collections, the gallery frequently houses special exhibits of great interest.

Via delle Quattro Fontane 13. ☎ *06-481-4430. Metro: Line A to Barberini. Bus: 62 or minibus 116 to Quattro Fontane. Open: Tues–Fri 9:00 a.m.–7:30 p.m., Sat 9 a.m.–11 p.m., Sun 9 a.m.– 8 p.m. Admission: 6.19€ ($6).*

Pantheon
Centro

Rome's best-preserved monument of antiquity, the imposing Pantheon was built by Marcus Agrippa in 27 B.C. (though later rebuilt by Hadrian) as a temple for all the gods (from the ancient Greek "pan-theon," meaning "all Gods"). It was eventually saved from destruction by being transformed into a Christian church. The adjective that all descriptions of the Pantheon should contain is *perfect:* The building is exactly 142 feet wide and 142 feet tall. The portico is supported by huge granite columns, all but three of which are original, and the bronze doors weigh 20 tons each. Inside, the empty niches surrounding the space once contained marble statues of Roman gods. Animals were once sacrificed beneath the beautiful **coffered dome** with an 18-foot hole *(oculus)* in the middle through which light (and sometimes rain) streams. An architectural marvel, this dome inspired Michelangelo when he was designing the dome of St. Peter's, though he made the basilica's dome 2 feet smaller. Buried here are the painter Raphael and two kings of Italy. Crowds always congregate in the square in front, **Piazza della Rotonda** (Piazza del Pantheon for Romans). The square contains a Giacomo della Porta fountain and many cafes — though the eyesore of a McDonald's and the attendant greasy smell make the place less attractive.

Piazza della Rotonda. ☎ 06-6830-0230. Bus: 62, 64, or 70 to Largo Argentina or minibus 116 to Piazza della Rotonda. Open: Mon–Sat 9:00 a.m.–6:30 p.m., Sun 9 a.m.–1 p.m. Admission: Free.

Piazza Colonna
Centro

The focus of Piazza Colonna is the imposing **Colonna di Marco Aurelio,** 83 feet tall and decorated with bas-reliefs. The column was erected in honor of Marcus Aurelius, who ruled from 161 to 180, and the reliefs recount his exploits in battles against the German tribes. A statue of the emperor once adorned the top, but in the 16th century, Pope Sixtus V replaced it with the statue of St. Paul that you see today. The **Palazzo Chigi** on one side of the piazza is the residence of the Italian prime minister, so don't be surprised if you see intense guys standing around with submachine guns.

At the intersection of Via Tritone and Via del Corso. Bus: 62, 85, or minibus 116, 117, or 119 to Piazza Colonna.

Piazza del Popolo
Centro

The "piazza of the people" really lives up to its name: Romans like to meet here to talk, have a drink, hang out, and people-watch. You can do the same, though be warned that the two cafes fronting the piazza gouge you unmercifully if you sit at an outdoor table (or even an indoor one) instead of taking your coffee at the counter like a Roman. **Santa Maria del Popolo** (☎ 06-361-0836) stands by the gate leading out to busy **Piazzale Flaminio** (where you can catch lots of buses). Founded in 1099, the church contains magnificent Caravaggios as well as a Pinturicchio. The brace of baroque churches directly across the square is the work of Carlo Rainaldi, Bernini, and Carlo Fontana. In the center is an **Egyptian obelisk,** one of Rome's most ancient objects, dating from 1200 B.C. It came from Heliopolis, where Ramses II set it up, and was brought during Augustus's reign (it stood in the Circo Massimo until one of the popes, in their nearly endless reshuffling and meddling with monuments, moved it here). When you leave the piazza, head up the steps into the trees on the east side.

This path leads to the Pincio, the park overlooking the square, which is one of the best places to see the sun set over Rome.

Intersection of Via del Babuino, Via del Corso, and Via de Ripetta. Metro: Line A to Flaminio. Bus: 490 to Piazzale Flaminio; Minibus 117 or 119 to Piazza del Popolo; Tram: 225 to Piazzale Flaminio.

Piazza del Quirinale and Palazzo del Quirinale
Centro

Now the home of Italy's president, the Palazzo del Quirinale was the residence of the king up until the end of World War II, and earlier in history, the pope lived here — or rather hid, in the case of Pius VII, who locked himself in after excommunicating Napoleon (soldiers broke in and carted him off to Fontainebleau for the duration of the Napoleonic era). The **fountain (the Fontana di Monte Cavallo)** has two giant statues of Castor and Pollux, the founders of Rome. The **Egyptian obelisk** adorning the square was taken from the Mausoleum of Augustus by Pius VI in 1793. For this attraction, you need to bring your passport so you can prove who you are. You may also get to see the changing of the guard.

End of Via XX Settembre. Metro: Line A to Barberini. Bus: Minibus 116 or 117 to Via del Quirinale. No telephone. Open: Sun 9 a.m.–1 p.m.

Piazza di Spagna and the Spanish Steps (Scalinata di Spagna)
Centro

The Piazza di Spagna and the Spanish Steps (Scalinata di Spagna) rising from the piazza are the meeting place of Rome. In spring, the steps are decorated with colorful azaleas, but in any season the square is a wonderful place to hang out — if you can find space among the wall-to-wall tourists, lovers, backpackers, Roman youth, and so on. The atmosphere is festive and convivial, though. The piazza's name comes from the 16th century, when the Spanish ambassador made his residence here. In those days, the piazza was far less hospitable. (People passing through the piazza at night sometimes disappeared. Because it was technically Spanish territory, the unwary could be pressed to join the Spanish army.) The area's most famous resident was English poet John Keats, who lived and died in the house to the right of the steps, which is now the **Keats–Shelley House** (☎ 06-678-4235; open daily 9 a.m. to 1 p.m. and 2:00 to 5:30 p.m.; admission 5.16€/$4.70). The real name of the steps isn't the Spanish Steps but the Scalinata della Trinità del Monte, because they lead to the **Trinità del Monte church,** whose towers loom above; the steps were funded almost entirely by the French as a preface to their church. At the foot of the steps, the **boat-shaped fountain** is by Pietro Bernini, father of Gian Lorenzo.

Via del Babuino and Via dei Condotti. Metro: Line A to Spagna. Bus: Minibus 117 or 119 to Piazza di Spagna.

Piazza Navona

Centro

One of Rome's most beautiful piazze and also one of its most popular hangouts, Piazza Navona was built on the ruins of the **Stadium of Diocletian,** where chariot races were held (note the oval track form). In medieval times, the popes flooded the square for mock naval battles. Besides the twin-towered facade of the 17th-century **Santa Agnes,** the piazza boasts several baroque masterpieces, the greatest being Bernini's **Fountain of the Four Rivers (Fontana dei Quattro Fiumi),** with massive figures representing the Nile, Danube, della Plata, and Ganges — the figure with the shrouded head is the Nile, because its source was unknown at the time. The **obelisk** is Roman, from Domitian's time. At the piazza's south end is the **Fountain of the Moor (Fontana del Moro),** also by Bernini; the **Fountain of Neptune (Fontana di Neptuno),** which balances that of the Moor, is a 19th-century addition.

On the east side of the square is the famous **Palazzo Braschi,** which opened its doors in May 2002 after 15 years of closure and an $8-million restoration. It houses the **Museo di Roma,** covering the cultural, social, and artistic life of the city from the Middle Ages to the first half of the 20th century. The *palazzo* is also an attraction in itself, a baroque palace with a grand staircase (☎ **06-8207-7304;** Internet: www.museodiroma. commune.roma.it; Open: Tuesday through Sunday, 9 a.m. to 7 p.m; Admission: 6.20€/$6).

Just off Corso Rinascimento. Bus: 70 or 116 to Piazza Navona.

Santa Maria d'Aracoeli

Centro/Campidoglio

Next to Piazza del Campidoglio (see the listing for the Capitoline Museums), Santa Maria d'Aracoeli dates from 1250 and is reached by an impressive high flight of steps. It stands on the site of an ancient Roman temple. The exterior of the church is austere yet boasts two rose windows, and inside are a number of interesting works of art. The floor is an excellent example of **Cosmati marblework** (the Cosmati were Roman stoneworkers of the Middle Ages). The **Cappella Bufalini** is decorated with Pinturicchio masterpieces, frescoes depicting scenes from the life of St. Bernardino of Siena and St. Francis receiving the stigmata.

Piazza d'Aracoeli. ☎ **06-679-8155.** *Bus: 60, 81, or minibus 117 to Campidoglio; then walk to the right around the Vittorio Emanuele II Monument. Open: Daily 7 a.m. to noon and 4–7 p.m. Admission: Free.*

Santa Maria in Cosmedin and Bocca della Verità

Centro/Circo Massimo

Although this orthodox church is very pretty inside and outside — it's one of the few Roman churches to have escaped baroque restoration — the real attraction is the famous **Bocca della Verità (Mouth of Truth),** a Roman marble relief of a head with an open mouth that sits against the wall under the porch outside the church. The round marble piece used to be a manhole cover, but legend has it that if you put your hand inside the mouth while lying, it will bite off your hand. (Remember the scene with Gregory Peck and Audrey Hepburn from *Roman Holiday?*) Kids get a kick out of putting their hands in the mouth. The church opens on **Piazza Bocca della Verità,** one of the nicest squares in town — at its best during off hours — with two small Roman temples still standing, believed to be a temple of Vesta and a temple of Castor and Pollux.

Piazza Bocca della Verità. ☎ *06-678-1419. Bus: 81. Open: Daily 7:00 a.m.–6:30 p.m. Admission: Free.*

Santa Maria sopra Minerva
Centro/Pantheon

The construction of this church started in the eighth century on the foundation of an ancient temple to Minerva (goddess of wisdom), but the present structure dates from 1280. This is the only Gothic church in Rome (though you wouldn't know it from the facade, due to a 17th-century revision — one of many). The treasures inside include Michelangelo's *Cristo Portacroce* in the sanctuary, as well as frescoes by Filippino Lippi. Under the altar are the **relics of St. Catherine of Siena.** The church also houses the **tomb of the painter Fra Angelico.** On the square in front of the church is the much-photographed Bernini **elephant sculpture** that serves as the base for a sixth-century-B.C. Egyptian obelisk.

Piazza della Minerva. ☎ *06-679-3926. Bus: 62, 64, 70, or 81 to Largo Argentina, or minibus 116 to Piazza della Minerva. Open: Daily 7 a.m. to noon and 4–7 p.m. Admission: Free.*

The Vatican

San Pietro

In 1929, the Lateran Treaty between Pope Pius XI and the Italian government recognized the independent state of the Holy See, with its physical seat in Vatican City (St. Peter's Basilica and adjacent buildings). Politically independent from Italy, the Vatican is the world's second-smallest sovereign state, with its own administration, post office, and tourist office. Making the **tourist office** (☎ **06-6988-4466;** open Monday through Saturday 8.30 a.m. to 7:00 p.m.) the first stop on your visit is a good idea — it's just to the left of the entrance to St. Peter's. In the tourist office, you can get a plan of the basilica — very useful given the sheer size of the thing — and make a reservation for a tour of the Vatican Gardens. You can also find the **Vatican Post Office** — nice stamps and faster service than the Italian one — and public restrooms.

How to attend a papal audience

An interesting event to attend is a *papal audience,* during which the pope addresses a crowd of people gathered in the Vatican. To attend a papal audience on Wednesdays (entrance between 10:00 and 10:30 a.m.), you must get free tickets from the **Prefecture of the Papal Household** (☎ **06-6988-3017**) at the bronze door under Piazza di San Pietro's right-hand colonnade (Monday through Saturday 9 a.m. to 1 p.m.). To get tickets in advance, write to the Prefecture of the Papal Household, 00120 Città del Vaticano, indicating your language, the dates of your visit, the number of people in your party, and (if possible) the hotel in Rome to which the office should send your tickets the afternoon before the audience.

Leave your hot pants behind in your visit to the Vatican. Here even the men wear ankle-length gowns. Bare shoulders, halter tops, tank tops, shorts, and skirts above the knee will have you turned away from the basilica — no kidding. This is, after all, the heart and brain of the Catholic Church and not just a tourist extravaganza.

St. Peter's Square: The entrance to the Vatican is through one of the world's greatest public spaces — Bernini's **St. Peter's Square (Piazza San Pietro).** As you stand in the huge piazza (no cars allowed), you're in the arms of an ellipse partly enclosed by a majestic Doric-pillared colonnade, atop which stand statues of some 140 saints. Straight ahead is the facade of **St. Peter's Basilica (Basilica di San Pietro)** (the statues represent Sts. Peter and Paul, Peter carrying the Keys to the Kingdom), and to the right, above the colonnade, are the dark-brown buildings of the **papal apartments** and the **Vatican Museum (Musei Vaticani).** In the center of the square is an **Egyptian obelisk,** brought from the ancient city of Heliopolis on the Nile delta. Flanking it are two 17th-century **fountains** — the one on the right by Carlo Maderno, who designed the facade of St. Peter's, was placed here by Bernini himself; the other is by Carlo Fontana. The piazza is particularly magical at night in the Christmas season, when a *presepio* (Nativity scene) and a large tree take center stage.

Beneath the basilica are **grottoes,** extending under the central nave of the church, that have been the site of archaeological excavations. You can visit them and wander among the tombs of popes. In addition to the papal tombs, **paleo-Christian tombs** and **architectural fragments of the original basilica** have been found here.

To visit **Michelangelo's dome** and marvel at the astounding view, you have to climb some 491 steps. Make sure that you're ready and willing to climb, however, because after you've started up you're not allowed to turn around and go back down. If you want to take the elevator as far as it goes, it'll save you 171 steps. You have to make a reservation when you

The Vatican

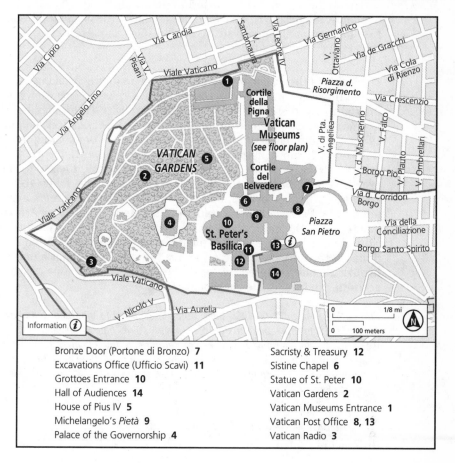

Bronze Door (Portone di Bronzo) **7**	Sacristy & Treasury **12**
Excavations Office (Ufficio Scavi) **11**	Sistine Chapel **6**
Grottoes Entrance **10**	Statue of St. Peter **10**
Hall of Audiences **14**	Vatican Gardens **2**
House of Pius IV **5**	Vatican Museums Entrance **1**
Michelangelo's *Pietà* **9**	Vatican Post Office **8, 13**
Palace of the Governorship **4**	Vatican Radio **3**

buy your ticket to go up in the dome (you'll pay an additional .60€/54¢). On busy days, you have to wait in line because the elevator can't accommodate all the people who want to use it.

St. Peter's Basilica (Basilica di San Pietro)
Piazza San Pietro

In 324, Emperor Constantine commissioned a sanctuary to be built on the site of St. Peter's tomb. The first Apostle was thought to have been buried here under a simple stone, and excavation and studies commissioned by the Vatican have produced additional proof that the tomb is indeed St. Peter's. You can find the tomb in the present basilica's central nave, under the magnificent altar by Bernini.

The original basilica stood for about 1,000 years — undergoing remodeling, pillaging, sacking, and rebuilding — until it was on the verge of collapse.

The basilica you see today, mostly High Renaissance and baroque, was born with the renovation begun in 1503 following designs by Sangallo and Bramante. Michelangelo was appointed to finish the magnificent dome in 1547 but wasn't able to do so; he died in 1564, and his disciple Giacomo della Porta completed it.

The inside of the basilica is almost too huge to take in; walking from one end to the other is a workout, and the opulence will overpower you. On the right as you enter is Michelangelo's exquisite *Pietà*, created when the master was in his early 20s. (Because of an act of vandalism in the 1970s, the statue is kept behind reinforced glass.) Dominating the nave is Bernini's 96-foot-tall *baldacchino* (canopy), supported by richly decorated twisting columns. Completed in 1633, it was criticized for being excessive and because the bronze was supposedly taken from the Pantheon. It stands over the papal altar, which in turn stands over the tomb of St. Peter. A bronze statue of St. Peter (probably by Arnolfo di Cambio — 13th century) marks the tomb, and its right foot has been worn away by the thousands of pilgrims kissing it in the traditional devotional gesture to salute the pope. By the apse, above an altar, is the bronze throne sculpted by Bernini to house the remains of what is, according to legend, the chair of St. Peter.

Piazza San Pietro, ☎ *06-6988-4466. Bus: 23, 62, or 64 to Via della Conciliazione. Metro: Line A to Ottaviano/San Pietro; then walk down Viale Angelico to the Vatican wall. Open: Winter daily 7 a.m.–6 p.m., summer daily 7 a.m.–7 p.m.; Grottoes daily 8 a.m.–5 p.m.; Dome winter daily 8:00 a.m.–4:45 p.m., summer daily 8:00 a.m.–5:45 p.m.; Admission: Basilica free; Dome 2.60€ ($2.40), with elevator 3.10€ ($2.80).*

The Vatican Museums (Musei Vaticani)
Piazza San Pietro

This enormous complex of museums could swallow up your entire vacation — with tons of Egyptian, Etruscan, Greek, Roman, paleo-Christian, and Renaissance art. After admittance, you must choose which of the four color-coded itineraries (A, B, C, or D) you want to follow — they range from 1½ to 5 hours. Don't worry: All the itineraries end at the Sistine Chapel.

Along the way you'll come across highlights such as these: the Borgia Apartments (Appartamento Borgia), designed for Pope Alexander VI (the infamous Borgia pope), and the Chapel of Nicholas V (Cappella di Nicholas V), with floor-to-ceiling frescoes by Fra Angelico; the Pinacoteca (Picture Gallery), with treasures like Raphael's *Transfiguration,* Leonardo da Vinci's *St. Jerome* (which had to be pieced back together — it was somehow mislaid and cut into two pieces; one piece ended up as a stool top in a shoemaker's shop, the other as a table top in an antiques shop), and Giotto's *Stefaneschi Triptych;* and the Raphael Rooms (Stanze di Raffaello), the private apartments of Pope Julius II frescoed wonderfully by the artist.

The Vatican Museums

Borgia Apartments & Collection
of Modern Religious Art **10**
Chapel of Nicholas V **17**
Galleria degli Arazzi **14**
Galleria del Candelabri **13**
Galleria delle Carte Geografiche **15**
Galleria Lapidaria **9**
Library **7**
Museo Chiaramonti **8**

Museo Gregoriano Egizio **6**
Museo Gregoriano Etrusco **12**
Museo Gregoriano Profano **1**
Museo Missionario Ethnologico **2**
Museo Pio-Clementino **5**
Museo Storico **4**
Pinacoteca **3**
Sistine Chapel **11**
Stanze di Raffaello **16**

But what most people can't wait to see is the **Sistine Chapel (Cappella Sistina),** Michelangelo's masterpiece. Restoring and cleaning Michelangelo's frescoes took a dozen years, and the brilliant colors that were uncovered have amazed some and horrified others who believe that too much paint was removed, flattening the figures. Whether you like the colors of the drapery or not, Michelangelo's modeling of the human form is incredible. The *Creation of Adam* and the temptation and fall of Adam and Eve are the most famous scenes. Michelangelo also painted a terrifying and powerful *Last Judgment* on the end wall.

Binoculars or even a hand mirror will help you appreciate the Sistine ceiling better; your neck tires long before you can take it all in. Just think how poor Michelangelo must have felt while painting it flat on his back atop a tower of scaffolding.

The Vatican Gardens (Giardini Vaticani): People often think that the Vatican is made up of only the basilica and the neighboring buildings, but the grounds behind the main structures are actually quite large. Although you can't visit most of the Vatican (you need a special permit to enter the Vatican grounds), guided tours take small numbers of visitors to admire the beautiful Vatican Gardens. If you enjoy touring gardens, you can sign up for a tour at the ticket office of the Vatican Museums.

Viale Vaticano, walk around the walls of the Vatican to the right of the basilica. ☎ *06-6988-3333. Internet:* www.vatican.va *or* www.christusrex.org. *Museums Mon–Fri 8:45 a.m.–4:45 p.m., Sat 8:45 a.m.–1:45 p.m., closed all Catholic religious holy days. Admission: 9.29€ ($8.50) adults, 6.19€ ($5.57) children (last tickets to the museums sell an hour before closing — though an hour is hardly enough time to scratch the surface).*

More Cool Things to See and Do

There's a lot more to see in Rome than the sights we mention in the previous section detailing the city's top sights. If you're traveling with children, for example, you know that they weary of going from one museum to another. Fortunately, Rome offers plenty of other activities, sights, and attractions for any– and everyone.

✔ The **Cimitero dei Cappuccini/Chiesa dell'Immacolata Concezione** (Via Veneto 27, not far from the U.S. Embassy; ☎ 06-487-1185; Metro: Line A to Barberini; Bus: 62 or minibus 116 or 119 to Largo Tritone) holds one of the most chilling sights you'll ever see. A Capuchin monk used the bones of 4,000 of his brothers to create a monument to death. There are corpses dressed in monk's robes, and the ceilings and walls are decorated with pieces of skeletons (for example, rows of spinal vertebrae trace the vaults). In an age that confronted death in a more head-on fashion than most societies, this monument may have been somehow comforting, and it's definitely a sight you won't soon forget. Admission is free but a donation is expected (2.50€/$2.30 per person is nice). The monument is open daily from 9 a.m. to noon and 3 to 6 p.m.

✔ The **Galleria Doria Pamphili** (Piazza del Collegio Romano 1/A; ☎ 06-679-7323 or 06-7707-2842; Internet: www.doriapamphilj.it; Bus: 62, 85, 850, or minibus 117 or 119 to Piazza San Marcello on the Corso or 116 to Piazza del Collegio Romano) is the place to come if you want to know what it was like to live in an 18th-century Roman palace. The Doria Pamphili family traces its history back to Admiral Andrea Doria. The _palazzo_'s richly decorated apartments are filled with tapestries, beautiful furnishings, and artworks from the 16th to 18th centuries. The gallery has paintings by Filippo Lippi, Raphael, Caravaggio, Tiziano, and others. Velázquez's portrait of Pope Innocent X is a true masterpiece. The gallery is open Friday through Wednesday from 10 a.m. to 5 p.m. It is also open selected evenings for classical music concerts, which you can combine with a visit to the galleries. Admission is 7.23€ ($6.50); private apartments 3.09€ ($2.80).

✔ The **Gianicolo (Janiculum Hill)**, overlooking Trastevere, is one of the two best places to see the panorama of Rome, the other being the **Pincio** (see the entry for Piazza del Popolo under "There's No Place like Rome, There's No Place like Rome: The Top Sights"). You can take the 870 bus to the top of the hill (though the best idea is taking a cab up and walking down, rather than waiting for the bus and possibly missing the sunset). On the hill is a monument to Giuseppe Garibaldi, and a little farther down is a unique equestrian statue of his wife, Anita, pistol in hand (she fought alongside him and was killed in battle). Perhaps the most beloved figure of the 19th-century Italian struggle for self-determination, Garibaldi invaded Sicily in 1860 with 1,000 men, his famous "Red Shirts," opening the way to the unification of Italy. On his statue is his slogan, _Roma o morte_ (Rome or death). For some reason, there's also a lighthouse atop the Gianicolo, but we can't find anyone who knows why it's there (it photographs nicely, though).

✔ The **Museo della Civiltá Romana** (Piazza Giovanni Agnelli 10; ☎ 06-592-6141; Metro: Line B to EUR Fermi) houses an excellent miniature reconstruction of ancient Rome showing the great buildings intact, which helps you make sense of all the broken columns and holes in the ground. Other models display facets of daily life in antiquity. Admission is 3.09€ ($2.80) for adults and free for children under 18. The museum is open Tuesday through Saturday from 9 a.m. to 7 p.m. and Sunday from 9:00 a.m. to 1:30 p.m.

✔ The **Museo Nazionale delle Paste Alimentari** (Piazza Scanderbeg 117; ☎ 06-699-1119; Internet: www.pastainmuseum.com; Bus: 116 or 117 to Piazza del Quirinale; Admission: 7.75€/$7.00) is a unique museum covering 800 years of — you guessed it — pasta. Here you can find out about everything having to do with the production of pasta, from the ancient and traditional to the modern. The museum is open daily from 9:30 a.m. to 5:30 p.m.

✔ Just above Piazza del Popolo and extending north beyond the city walls is the **Villa Borghese,** one of Rome's most beautiful parks. It's famous for the Galleria Borghese (see "There's No Place like Rome, There's No Place like Rome: The Top Sights") and the **Pincio,** the terrace above Piazza del Popolo offering a beautiful view over Rome, which is particularly striking at sunset. Inside the park is also the **Piazza di Siena,** a picturesque oval track surrounded by tall pines, used for horse races and particularly for the **Concorso Ippico Internazionale di Roma** (Rome's international horse-jumping event), held in May (see Chapter 2). This park is perfect for a family picnic, especially in summer, when its beautiful Roman pines offer relief from the heat.

✔ **Testaccio** (Metro: Line B to Piramide; Bus: 23 or tram 3 to Via Marmorata) is a neighborhood named for Monte Testaccio, a hill made out of broken pots collected in A.D. 55. The Romans stacked the shards *(testae)* 200 feet high after Nero whimsically ordered that they be collected here. Though the top of this dangerouly shifting mountain is closed to visitors, dwellings that were dug into its lower slopes over the centuries still exist, and some of them house restaurants and jazz clubs. Testaccio is a real Roman neighborhood, with a reputation for being less safe after dark. However, in summer big crowds of young people flock here, and we doubt that you'll have any problems. Other landmarks here are the **pyramid of Caius Cestius,** a Roman praetor and tribune who died in 12 B.C., and the **Protestant Cemetery** next door (☎ 06-574-1141), a kind of pilgrimage site for fans of poets John Keats and Percy Bysshe Shelley, who are buried here, along with the murdered anti-Fascist Antonio Gramsci. Admission to the cemetery is free; hours of operation are Tuesday through Sunday 9 a.m. to 5 p.m.

✔ On the **Appian Way (Via Appia Antica),** you can walk over what was the first and most important Roman consular road — called the **Regina Viarum (Queen of Roads).** Started in 312 B.C., the road was a main link to Capua but eventually was extended all the way to Brindisi. It was on this road that St. Peter, in flight from Rome, had his vision of Jesus (a church stands where Peter asked, *"Domine quo vadis?"* or "Lord, where are you going?") and turned back toward his martyrdom. The street was paved with large, flat basalt stones and lined with villas, tombs, and monuments, of which some ruins remain. One of the most important is the **Tomba di Cecilia Metella,** a first-century-B.C. mausoleum of a patrician gentlewoman (☎ 06-780-2465). It's open Monday through Saturday from 9 a.m. to 6 p.m. (until 3 p.m. in winter) and Sunday from 9 a.m. to 1 p.m. Admission is 2€ ($1.80). Grab a map from the main tourist office and rent a bike! To get there by public transportation, take metro line A to Colli Albani (on Sunday to Arco di Travertino) and then bus 660 to Via Appia Antica.

And on Your Left, the Colosseum: Seeing Rome by Guided Tour

The French writer Stendhal once wrote, "As soon as you enter Rome, get in a carriage and ask to be brought to the Coliseum or to St. Peter's. If you try to get there on foot, you will never arrive: Too many marvelous things will stop you along the way."

Taking a bus tour of this complicated city when you first arrive is an excellent idea. Doing so helps you get the general feeling of the place and gives you an idea of what you'd really like to see more in depth. After you decide what you want to see in more detail, you can take a walking tour of the area or areas that interest you most and do the rest by yourself.

Many organized tours in Rome cater to most every interest. Many are organized by cultural associations, and you can find them listed in various magazines like *Roma c'e* (which comes out on Thursdays at all newsstands, with a section in English at the end), *Metropolitan,* and *Wanted in Rome* (also available at most newsstands).

Bus tours

The city bus company **ATAC** gives the best bus tours of Rome. The 110 bus leaves from Piazza dei Cinquecento in front of Stazione Termini daily at 10:30 a.m. and 2:00, 3:00, 5:00, and 6:00 p.m. for a 2½-hour tour costing 7.80€ ($7) per person; the buses are new and very modern and the tour guides are professionals. The price includes an illustrated guidebook describing the more than 80 sites included in the tour. To reserve, call ☎ **06-4695-2252** or 06-4695-2256 daily 9 a.m. to 7 p.m. You can buy tickets at the ATAC bus information booth on platform C in front of Stazione Termini.

Stop 'n Go/C.S.R. (Via Ezio 12; ☎ **06-321-7054;** E-mail: csr@gisec.it) organizes a self-tailored bus tour with nine departures daily, from 9:30 a.m. to 4:30 p.m. in winter and 9:30 a.m. to 5:30 p.m. in summer. At 12€ ($10.80) per person, the tour starts in Piazza dei Cinquecento (in front of Stazione Termini) at the corner of Via Massimo d'Azeglio and makes 14 stops; you can get on or off at your leisure. (You can buy the ticket directly on the bus.) A two-day ticket is 16€ ($14.50) and a three-day ticket 22€ ($20), giving you more time to see things than a one-day ticket. The company also organizes an afternoon tour of the Castelli Romani (hill towns around Rome), which leaves at 2:30 p.m., and a morning tour of Tivoli and Hadrian's Villa, which leaves at 9:30 a.m. (see Chapter 13).

Another bus-tour possibility is **American Express** (Piazza di Spagna 38; ☎ 06-67-641; Metro: Line A to Spagna), which organizes tours of Rome and the Vatican as well as excursions to nearby sites like Tivoli (see Chapter 13). Tours start at 28€ ($25) per person and leave daily at 9:30 a.m. and 2:30 p.m. American Express also offers day tours to farther-afield destinations like Florence and Pompeii. The American Express office is open Monday through Friday from 9:00 a.m. to 5:30 p.m. and Saturday from 9:00 a.m. to 12:30 p.m.

If you're interested in Pompeii, a good choice is the day tour organized by **Enjoy Rome** (see "Walking tours," later in this chapter) with a departure at 8:30 a.m. in an air-conditioned minivan fitting eight passengers. The driver speaks English, and you're given material and maps to prepare you for your visit — all for 32€ ($29).

Walking tours

Enjoy Rome (Via Varese 39, three blocks north off the side of Stazione Termini; ☎ 06-445-1834; Internet: www.enjoyrome.com; Metro: Termini) offers a variety of three-hour walking tours, including a night tour that takes you through the *centro* and its sights, and a tour of Trastevere and the Jewish Ghetto. All tours cost 16€ ($14.50) adults and 13€ ($11.70) for those under 26, including the cost of the tour and admission to sights. The office is open Monday through Friday from 8:30 a.m. to 2:00 p.m. and 3:30 to 6:30 p.m. and Saturday from 8:30 a.m. to 2:00 p.m. Enjoy Rome also organizes a bike tour, with English-speaking guides.

For **Scala Reale** (Via Varese 52; ☎ 888-467-1986 or 06-4470-0898; Metro: Termini), American architect Tom Rankin organizes small-group walking tours with an architectural twist for 32€ ($29). He takes visitors through ancient and baroque Rome and discusses the city's most important buildings. Discounts are available for groups of four, and children under 12 are free. The tour includes a visit to neighborhood trattoria.

Boat tours

For a completely different point of view of Rome, take a tour on the **motorboat** *Tiber.* It leaves Tuesday through Sunday at 10:30 a.m. and 12:45 p.m. from Ponte Umberto I (Bus: 70, 81, or minibus 116), the bridge at the end of Via Zanardelli, off the north tip of Piazza Navona. The tour lasts 1½ hours and costs 11€ ($10). You can buy tickets directly on the boat. The boat takes you downriver on the Tiber through the heart of Rome, offering a beautiful view of Castel Sant'Angelo with San Pietro in the distance, Trastevere, and the Isola Tiberina.

Air tours

For 49€ ($44) per person for 20 minutes, **Umbria Fly** (☎ **06-8864-1441**) offers airborne tours of Rome for a minimum of two passengers. It's an unforgettable experience, giving you a panoramic view of Rome from the air; the only drawback is that the tour leaves from the Aeroporto dell'Urbe, on Via Salaria 825, just north of Rome (40 minutes or more from the center of the city by taxi or if you have a car).

Shopping

In terms of crafts, Rome isn't as rich as it was in ages past. Alas, very few workshops still practice traditional arts. On the other hand, Rome is a large city and the capital of the country, so you can find basically everything — including specialties here from places that you may not have time to visit.

Shopping hours are generally 9:00 or 9:30 a.m. (later for boutiques) to about 1:00 or 1:30 p.m., and then from 3:30 or 4:00 to 7:30 p.m. Many shops close Monday mornings, and most are closed all day Sunday. In the *centro,* however, many shops now stay open at lunchtime and on Sunday.

The best shopping areas

The best shopping area is the *centro,* the streets of medieval and Renaissance Rome between Piazza del Popolo and Piazza Venezia. Now with restricted car circulation, **Via del Corso** (also known as just the Corso) is the area's heart, lined with shops selling everything from clothing to shoes to CDs. On the east side of Piazza di Spagna lie the most elegant streets — like **Via Frattina** and **Via dei Condotti** — with designer boutiques and all the big names of Italian fashion (Bulgari, Ferragamo, Valentino, Armani, and so on). You also find interesting small shops, including stylish Italian housewares and antiques. On the west side of the Corso are intricate medieval streets hiding a variety of elegant and original boutiques and some of the oldest establishments in Rome. Here you can find even more variety of goods, from old prints to exclusive fashions, from books to antique furniture.

Another good shopping area is **Via Cola di Rienzo** and **Via Ottaviano** on the San Pietro side of the Tevere. It doesn't boast the luxury shops of Via dei Condotti, but you can find the big names of Italian fashion. This area is also excellent for shoes, with many shops of every level of price and style, and for a variety of other items.

Via Nazionale off Piazza della Repubblica near Stazione Termini and running almost to Piazza Venezia is another major shopping street. Less elegant than the others for general fashion and frequented more by Italians than tourists, it has developed a specialty in leather goods. This may be the best place to find that jacket you want.

What to look for and where to find it

If you're in the hunt for a particular item, here are the places to go to find that special something.

Antiques

If antiques interest you, the *centro* is the place to go. **Via dei Coronari** literally offers one shop after another on both sides of the street. Likewise, you can find some more refined dealers on **Via Giulia, Via del Babuino,** and **Via Margutta** nearby. For more casual shopping, try **Via del Pellegrino.**

Artworks

Artists have been coming to Rome to paint and draw for centuries, and you've no doubt seen many views of the city's ancient and baroque monuments. For prints, two well-known shops are **Nardecchia** (Piazza Navona 25; ☎ **06-686-9318**; Bus: 70, 81 or minibus 116) and **Alinari** (Via Alibert 16/a; ☎ **06-679-2923**; Metro: Line A to Spagna). **Antiquarius** (Corso Rinascimento 63; ☎ **06-688-02941**; Bus: 70, 81, or minibus 116) is a nice shop across from the Palazzo Madama. At these shops, you find higher-quality — and somewhat more reliable — articles than at the nearby **antiquarian book and print market** on Piazza Fontanella Borghese (Bus: 81 or minibus 117 or 119 to the Corso at Via Tomacelli). The market, however, is a great place to browse if you know your prints, and it offers good deals on dated art books as well as Roman prints.

Books and magazines

If you forgot to bring a book to read and don't understand Italian, go to the **English Bookshop** (Via di Ripetta 248; ☎ **06-320-3301**; Bus: minibus 117 or 119 to Piazza del Popolo). This store stocks books in English on a wide range of subjects. **Remainders** (Piazza San Silvestro 27–28; ☎ **06-679-2824**; Bus: 85 or 850 to Piazza San Silvestro) also offers a large selection of books in English at discount prices. The **Libreria Babele** (Via dei Banchi Vecchi 116; ☎ 06-687-6628; Bus: 62, 64, or minibus 116 to Via dei Banchi) is Rome's most central gay/lesbian bookstore. In addition, many of the larger newsstands in the *centro* have English-language newspapers and magazines as well as bestsellers in fiction and perhaps some classics.

Clothing

For clothing, the best strategy is to shop in the *centro* or in the area of **Via Ottaviano** and **Via Cola di Rienzo** (Vatican/San Pietro). Prices are quite competitive, and there's a good variety. For women's fashion, the hot area is around **Piazza di Spagna** (logically — this area includes the highest concentration of tourists). You can find **Fendi** (Via Borgognona 39; ☎ 06-679-4824), **Valentino** (Via dei Condotti 13; ☎ 06-67-391), **Gucci** (Via Condotti 8; ☎ 06-678-9340), **Armani Boutique** (Via dei Condotti 77; ☎ 06-6991460), and **Emporio Armani** (Via del Babuino 140; ☎ 06-3600-2197) nearby. For men's clothes, the specialists are **Battistoni** (Via dei Condotti 57 and 61/a; ☎ 06-678-6241) and **Testa** (Via Borgognona 13, ☎ 06-679-6174; Via Frattina 104, ☎ 06-679-0660). You can find all the shops that we mention in this paragraph a short walk away from the Spanish Steps (Metro: Line A to Spagna). An elegant men's store, **Davide Cenci** (Via Campo Marzio 1–7; ☎ 06-699-0681; Bus: minibus 116 to Pantheon) is popular with locals.

Although Florence is more the place for **leather clothes,** you can find some nice stores in Rome, especially on **Via Nazionale.** In Rome, though you can certainly find excellent leather gloves, the best shops are around **Piazza di Spagna.**

Eyewear

In Rome, you can hardly turn around without knocking over a display of eyewear, but one of the best places to buy eyewear is **Ottica Alessandro Spiezia** (Via del Babuino 199; ☎ **06-361-0593;** Bus: minibus 117 or 119 to Piazza del Popolo), right off Piazza del Popolo. The shop is small but the quality very high and includes Spieza's own designs. Likewise, an entire store is devoted to **Swatch watches** (Via Belsiana 64; ☎ **06-6992-0173;** Metro: Line A to Spagna) in the central shopping district. Here you may find styles that you can't find in the United States (so did Bill and Chelsea Clinton, who stopped in recently to pick up some new eyewear).

Leather accessories

For leather accessories, the two best areas are **Via dei Condotti** in the *centro* and **Via Cola di Rienzo** in the Vatican area. For leather bags and wallets (if money isn't an issue), go either to **Bottega Veneta** (Piazza San Lorenzo in Lucina 9; ☎ **06-6821-0024;** Bus: 81 or minibus 116 to Piazza San Lorenzo), famous for its beautiful woven designs, or to **Prada** (Via dei Condotti 15; ☎ **06-679-4876;** Metro: Line A to Spagna), both off the Corso.

Local crafts

If you insist on finding some typical craft, go to the medieval area of Rome around **Piazza Navona.** There you can find *vimini* (basketry) on **Via dei Sediari,** ironwork on **Via degli Orsini,** and reproductions of Roman and Pompeian mosaics in the **Opificio Romano** (Via dei Gigli d'Oro 9–10; ☎ **06-6880-2762;** Bus: 70, 81 or minibus 116 to Via Zanardelli). Another excellent neighborhood is **Trastevere.** Try the **Bottega Artigiana Ceramica Sarti** (Via Santa Dorotea 21; ☎ **06-588-2079;** Bus: 23 to Piazza Trilussa on the Lungotevere; Tram: 8 to Piazza G. Belli on Viale Trastevere), a long-established ceramic workshop, or the **Officina della Carta** (Via Santa Dorotea 26b; ☎ **06-589-5557**) for paper and leather handicrafts.

Religious apparel

One typical product that you find in Rome and nowhere else in such a large variety is religious apparel. Of course, the interest for the public at large is a little limited. However, if you're looking for religious objects, Rome is the place. Stroll around the neighborhood of **Piazza della Minerva** and **Corso Rinascimento** to find a variety of curious artifacts.

Shoes

For shoes, the two best areas are **Via dei Condotti** in the *centro* and **Via Cola di Rienzo** in the Vatican area. Among the top names are **Dominici** (Via del Corso 14; ☎ **06-361-0591**), **Ferragamo** (Via dei Condotti 73–74; ☎ **06-679-1565**), and **Ferragamo Uomo** (Via dei Condotti 75; ☎ **06-678-1130**). However, if you really want to make your friends green with envy, have a pair of shoes custom-made by **Listo** (Via della Croce 76; ☎ **06-678-4567**). These shops are all a short walk from the Spanish Steps (Metro: Line A to Spagna).

Stationery and pens

For refined stationery and paper, go to **Pineider,** founded in 1774 (Via Fontanella Borghese 22, ☎ **06-687-8369,** Bus: 81 or minibus 117 or 119 to the Corso at Via Tomacelli;Via dei Due Macelli 68, ☎ **06-679-5884,** Bus: minibus 116, 117, or 119 to Via Due Macelli). Another great place is the **Fabriano boutique** (Via del Babuino 173; ☎ **06-361-7844;** Bus: minibus117 to Via del Babuino), for quality paper from the Cartiere Fabriano (in existence as such since 1872, but with a tradition that goes back to the 13th century).

Italians are also crazy for accessories like fountain pens. At **Campo Marzio Penne** (Via Campo Marzio 41; ☎ **06-6880-7877;** Bus: 81 or minibus 116 to Piazza San Lorenzo in Lucina on the Corso), you can find every kind of writing implement, from steel nibs to antique fountain pens — the shop even does repairs.

Wine

Rome has many a fine *enoteca* (wine shop). If you want to buy wine to take home, go to the granddaddy of Roman wine stores, **Trimani** (Via Goito 20; ☎ **06-446-9661;** Bus: 60 or 62), a family business since 1821 with literally thousands of bottles in the old residential neighborhood behind the Terme di Diocleziano. Rome's most special source of intoxicants is **Ai Monasteri** (Corso Rinascimento 72; ☎ **06-6880-2783;** Bus: 70, 81, or minibus 116), off the east side of Piazza Navona. Here you can find the liqueurs, elixirs, and other alcoholic concoctions that monks in Italy have traditionally made since the early Middle Ages.

Nightlife

Romans love to stroll about their beloved city by night on what they call a *passeggiata.* All the major monuments are illuminated, and the ancient Roman ruins join the Renaissance and baroque buildings to create a fairy-tale tableau. Don't miss a tour of the Roman piazze by night. Sample Rome's wonderful ice cream (gelato — see the sidebar in Chapter 11) or sit on the outdoor terrace of a famous cafe and watch the people parade as you sip an espresso or a glass of Chianti.

The performing arts

From June through September, Roman nights come alive with **Roman Summer (the Estate Romana),** a series of musical, theatrical, and other cultural events. You can find details on the Web at www.comune.roma.it or www.romapreview.com; or call ☎ **06-6880-9505** Monday through Saturday from 10 a.m. to 5 p.m. Events include important concerts with appearances by the **Accademia Nazionale di Santa Cecilia** at the Villa Giulia (☎ **06-322-6571**) and the **summer edition of the opera** at the monumental Olympic Stadium (Stadio Olimpico), across the Tevere from Piazza Mazzini.

Among the most picturesque initiatives is the opening of some of the major ancient Roman sights by night for special guided visits (call the Villa Cecilia to make a reservation) or performances. During the summer of 2000, the **Colosseum** opened its doors to the public again after 15 centuries with a performance of Sophocles's *Oedipus.* If you're lucky, the program may include a performance in the dramatic setting of the **Baths of Caracalla (Terme di Caracalla).** You can also check out a summer season of theater in the **Teatro Romano** at Ostia Antica (see Chapter 13).

One of Italy's premier musical associations is the **Accademia Nazionale di Santa Cecilia** (Via della Conciliazione 4, just off San Pietro; ☎ **800-085-085** or 06-6880-1044; Internet: www.santacecilia.it; Bus: 23, 62, or 64). Its season runs from October through May, with symphonic concerts Saturdays through Tuesdays and soloist and ensemble chamber music on Fridays. In the summer, the association holds **outdoor concerts at the Villa Giulia** (☎ **06-322-6571**). The organization **Amici della Musica Sacra** (☎ **06-6880-5816**) sponsors free choral and other religious music concerts by mostly foreign traveling groups in the theatrical setting of Sant'Ignazio church, between the Corso and the Pantheon (Bus: 62, 85, 850, or minibus 117 or 119 to the Corso at Via Caravita or minibus 116).

Rome is famous for theater. Of course, if you don't understand Italian you won't get much out of it — but if you do, you'll be delighted by the number of performances, from classical to contemporary. Opera, how-ever, is an exception, because you may already know the story and the same operas are performed everywhere. At the newly restored **Teatro dell'Opera** (Piazza Beniamino Gigli 1, just off Via Nazionale; ☎ **06-481-601**; Internet: www.themix.it; Metro: Line A to Repubblica; Bus 60, 64, 70, or minibus 116 to Via A. Depretis), opera performances run from January to June, with a special July/August season that changes venues every year. (There's a rumor they may even start putting on *Aïda* at the Baths of Caracalla again.) The **Rome Opera Ballet** performs classical and modern ballet at this venue as well. Likewise, the **Teatro Olimpico** (Piazza Gentile da Fabriano; ☎ **06-323-4890**; Tram: 225 from Piazzale Flaminio) hosts musical performances of all kinds, and it's also the venue of the **Filarmonica di Roma**.

Cafes

Rome boasts many famous old cafes that have never lost their glamour. Very pleasant, if a little expensive, the **Antico Caffè della Pace** (Via della Pace 3–7; ☎ **06-686-1216**; Bus: minibus 116 to Piazza Navona) is one of the most popular cafes in the city. Another is the beautifully furnished **Caffè Greco** (Via Condotti 84; ☎ **06-679-1700**; Metro: Line A to Spagna); among its customers were famous writers like Stendhal, Goethe, and Keats. The **Caffè Sant'Eustachio** (Piazza Sant'Eustachio 82; ☎ **06-686-1309**; Bus: minibus 116) is a traditional Italian bar that has been serving Rome's best espresso since 1938, made with water carried into the city on an ancient aqueduct.

Also famous is the **Caffè Rosati** (Piazza del Popolo 4–5; ☎ **06-322-5859**; Bus: minibus 117 or 119), which retains its 1920s Art Nouveau decor. **Tre Scalini** (Piazza Navona 30; ☎ **06-687-9148**; Bus: 70 or 81 to Corso Rinascimento, minibus 116) is a perfect spot for a drink or an ice cream (they're famous for *tartufo* — ice cream coated with bittersweet chocolate, cherries, and whipped cream). Less famous but trendy and enjoyable is the **Bar del Fico** (Vicolo del Fico; ☎ **06-686-5205**; Bus: minibus 116 to Piazza Navona).

Jazz and other live music

Romans love jazz, and Rome offers many jazz clubs and other venues where you can hear live jazz. The most famous are the **Alexanderplatz** (Via Ostia 9, just off the Musei Vaticani; ☎ **06-3974-2171**; Metro: Line A to Ottaviano/San Pietro; Bus: 23 to Via Leone IV), where reservations are recommended and the cover is $6.20€ ($5.60), and **Big Mama** (Vicolo S. Francesco a Ripa 18 in Trastevere; ☎ **06-581-2551**; Tram: 8), with a 5.20€ ($4.70) cover. If you prefer understated modernist surroundings for cocktails and jazz, head to trendy **Chiavari** (Via dei Chiavari 4–5, near Campo de' Fiori; ☎ **06-683-2378**; Bus: 62, 64, 70, or 81 to Corso Vittorio Emanuele at Largo dei Chiavari).

The **Aldebaran** (Via Galvani 54 in Testaccio; ☎ **06-574-6013**; Bus: 23; Tram: 3 to Via Marmorata) is a quieter lounge with music and an ample choice of drinks; there's no cover. The **Caffè Latino** (Via Monte Testaccio 96; ☎ **06-5728-8556**; Bus: 23; Tram: 3 to Via Marmorata, and then walk down Via Galbani — it's best to take a taxi) is a trendy spot for a mix of live music, including funk and acid jazz. The 7.80€ to 10.30€ ($7.00 to $9.30) cover includes one drink.

Bars and pubs

On Campo de' Fiori you can find a full range of alcohol-oriented nightspots. The exceedingly popular but old-fashioned wine bar called **Vineria** at building no. 15 (no phone) still holds its own amid the nightly crowds swarming this trendy piazza. There's a crowded **Taverna del Campo** snack stop with *crostini, panini,* and beer next door at no. 16 (☎ **06-687-4402**), and a few more doors down you can groove to the live DJ-spun music (and air-conditioning) of the American-style bar the **Drunken Ship** at nos. 20–21 (☎ **06-6830-0535**). To get to these hot spots, take bus 62 or 64 to Corso Vittorio Emanuele at Largo San Pantaleo or minibus 116 to Campo de' Fiori.

For something calmer, you can try the bar at **Gusto** (see Chapter 11), which has an intimate romantic atmosphere. Or stop at the **wine bar attached to Trimani** (see the "What to Look for and Where to Find It" section in this chapter), the famous wine seller.

The Italian craze for Irish pubs hit Rome very hard. These are among the nicest ones: **Mad Jack** (Via Arenula 20, off Largo Argentina; ☎ **06-6880-8223**; Tram: 8) is the place for Guinness and a choice of light food. It also features live music on Wednesday and Thursday. The **Abbey Theatre Irish Pub** (Via del Governo Vecchio 51–53, near Piazza Navona; ☎ **06-686-1341**; Bus: 62 or 64 to Corso Vittorio Emanuele II) is in the oldest part of town and features an authentic decor and souvenirs from the famous theater. The **Albert** (Via del Traforo 132, off Via del Tritone, before the tunnel; ☎ **06-481-8795**; Bus: 62 or minibus 116, 117, or 119 to Largo del Tritone) provides a real English atmosphere and beer, with everything from the furnishings to the drinks imported from England.

Dance clubs

The **Alpheus** (Via del Commercio 36 near Via Ostiense; ☎ **06-574-7826**; Bus: 23; best to take a cab) is a very popular spot, with several rooms offering different music — from Latin to rock — for dancing and bars for sitting. The cover is 7.80€ ($7) on Friday and Saturday. The **Fonclea** (Via Crescenzio 82/a behind Castel Sant'Angelo; ☎ **06-689-6302**; Bus: 23 to Via Crescenzio) offers live music every evening, including jazz, soul, funk, and rock; the cover on Saturday is 5.20€ ($4.70). The trendy **Goa** (Via Libetta 13, off Via Ostiense near the Basilica di San Paolo; ☎ **06-574-8277**; Bus: 23; best to take a cab) is a dance club mixing ethnic elements and multimedia. The cover charge is 7.80€ to 15.60€ ($7 to $14).

Rome's attempt at a major Manhattan– or London-style disco is **Alien** (Via Velletri 13–19; ☎ 06-841-2212; Bus: 490 to Piazza Fiume). Alien features a funky sci-fi decor with underground, garage, and house music pumping and mainly 20-somethings dancing. The cover charge is 18€ ($16.30). More glitzy is the perennially packed **Gilda** (Via Mario de Fiori 97; ☎ 06-679-7396; Metro: Line A to Spagna), a disco with a pizzeria/restaurant where the beautiful — and older — people congregate. The cover charge is 21€ ($19).

Gay and lesbian bars

The hottest gay club in Rome is **Alibi** (Via di Monte Testaccio 40–44; ☎ 06-574-3448; Bus: 23 or tram 3 to Via Marmorata, and then walk down Via Galbani — taking a cab is best), with a rotating schedule of DJs and a great summer roof garden. The cover is 5.20€ to 10.30€ ($4.70 to $9.30). The **Hangar** (Via in Selci 69; ☎ 06-488-1397; Metro: Cavour) is Rome's oldest gay club, frequented by the under-30 crowd and American visitors; admission is free. At the gay disco **Angelo Azzurro** (Via Cardinale Merry del Val 13 in Trastevere; ☎ 06-580-0472; Tram: 8 to Viale Trastevere at Piazza Mastai), guys of all ages groove to the mix of dance, house, and pop. Admission is free, and Friday night is ladies only.

Lesbians get a few women-only nights at some clubs across town: **New Joli Coeur** (Via Sirte 5; ☎ 06-8621-5827; Bus: 38, 80, or 88 to Piazza Sant'Emerenziana) on Saturdays, and **L'Angelo della Notte** (Via dei Sabelli 10; no phone; Tram: 3) on Fridays with live music.

Fast Facts: Rome

American Express

The office is at Piazza di Spagna 38 (☎ 06-676-41; Metro: Line A to Spagna), open Monday through Friday 9:00 a.m. to 5:30 p.m. and Saturday 9:00 a.m. to 12:30 p.m.

ATMs

They're available everywhere in the center and near hotels. Most banks are linked to the Cirrus network, so if you need the Plus network, look for a BNL (Banca Nazionale del Lavoro) ATM.

Country Code and City Code

The country code for Italy is **39**. The city code for Rome is **06**; use this code when calling from anywhere outside or inside Italy and always include the 0.

Currency Exchange

A very good exchange bureau is located at the airport and another is inside Stazione Termini (the main train station). Otherwise, you can find change offices scattered all around town and concentrated in the *centro*.

Also, you can find automatic exchange machines that operate 24 hours a day outside many banks and at the airport.

Disabled

There is an information line for disabled persons: Rome for Everyone, at ☎ 06-2326-7695.

Doctors and Dentists

Contact your embassy or consulate to get a list of English-speaking doctors or dentists.

Embassies and Consulates

Rome is the capital of Italy and therefore the seat of all the embassies and consulates. United States: Via Vittorio Veneto 119a (☎ 06-46-741; Metro: Line A to Barberini; Bus: minibus 116); Canada: Via Zara 30 (☎ 06-445-981; Bus: 60 or 62 to Via Nomentana); United Kingdom: Via XX Settembre 80a (☎ 06-482-5441 or 06-4220-0001; Bus: 60, 62, or 490 to Porta Pia); Ireland: Piazza Campitelli 3 (☎ 06-697-9121; Bus: 81 to Via del Teatro di Marcello); Australia: Via Alessandria 215 (☎ 06-852-721; Tram: 19 or 3 to Viale Regina Margherita); New Zealand: Via Zara 28 (☎ 06-440-2928; Bus: 60 or 62 to Via Nomentana).

Emergencies

Ambulance, ☎ **118**; Police, ☎ **113**; Carabinieri (other police force), ☎ **112**; Fire, ☎ **115**; Polizia Stradale (Road Police), ☎ **06-67-691**; First Aid ☎ **06-5820-1030** or 06-482-6741.

Hospital

All large hospitals in Rome have a 24-hour *Pronto Soccorso* (first-aid) service. Two examples are the Santo Spirito on Lungotevere in Sassia 1 (☎ 06-68-351; for first aid, ☎ 06-65-0901; Bus: 23, 62, or 64) and the Fatebenefratelli on the Isola Tiberina (☎ 06-68-371; for first aid, ☎ 06-683-7299; Bus: 23; Tram: 8), both in the *centro*.

Information

The main office of the Azienda di Promozione Turistica di Roma (Agency for the Promotion of Tourism) is on Via Parigi 5 (☎ 06-4889-9255 or ☎ 06-4889-9253; Internet: www.informa roma.it), just a couple of blocks from Stazione Termini, off Piazza della Repubblica. It's open Monday through Saturday from 9 a.m. to 7 p.m. There are two tourist information desks at main points of arrival, namely Fiumicino Airport (☎ 06-6595-6074) and at the front of track 4 inside Stazione Termini (☎ 06-4890-6300), open daily from 8 a.m. to 9 p.m., and others are scattered around the city near major attractions (see Chapter 11). The tourist information hotline is ☎ 06-3600-4399.

Internet Access

The ever-expanding Easy Everything has a big Internet access point at Piazza Barberini 2/16; it's open 24 hours a day 7 days a week, and with 350 computers, it is by far the most convenient Internet source in the city (and usually the cheapest — their prices start at .50€/45¢ and rise with demand). Thenetgate has several locations around Rome and more are on the way (Piazza Firenze 25, ☎ 06-689-3445, Bus: 81 or minibus 117 or 119 to Via Tomacelli; Via in Arcione 103, ☎ 06-6992-2320, Bus: 62 or minibus 116 or 119 to Via del Tritone). You can get an updated listing of locations at www.thenetgate.it. Near Termini, behind the Terme di Diocleziano, is Freedom Traveller (Via Gaeta 25; ☎ 06-4782-3862; Internet: www.freedom-traveller.it; Metro: Line B to Castro Pretorio).

Mail

Rome has many post offices. The central post office is in Piazza San Silvestro 19 (off Via del Tritone and the Corso; Bus: 62, 81, 85, 850, or minibus 116, 117, or 119), open Monday through Friday from 9 a.m. to 6 p.m. and Saturday from 9 a.m. to 2 p.m. Another possibility is the Vatican Post Office in Piazza San Pietro (Metro: Ottaviano; Bus: 23, 62, or 64).

Maps

You can find free maps at the Azienda di Promozione Turistica di Roma (see the Information listing). If you want something more detailed, you can buy maps at newsstands and kiosks around Rome. One of the best maps is *Tutto Città,* which costs about 6.20€ ($5.60).

Newspapers and Magazines

All the newspaper kiosks in the center offer the *International Herald Tribune,* European issues of *Time, The Economist* (usually), and the *Financial Times.* Another good place for English-language periodicals is the kiosk on Via Veneto across from the U.S. Embassy (Via Veneto 119a; Metro: Line A to Barberini; Bus: minibus 116).

Pharmacies

Pharmacies are open Monday through Friday from 8:30 a.m to 7:30 p.m. They operate in rotation on evenings and Saturdays and Sundays, so that there is an open pharmacy in each neighborhood. To find out which is open, call ☎ 06-228-941. Or you can go to one of the all-night pharmacies, such as the one near Termini at Piazza della Repubblica (☎ 06-488-0410) or in Prati at Via Cola di Rienzo 213 (☎ 06-324-4476), or Piazza Barberini 49 (☎ 06-487-1195).

Police

Call ☎ 113.

Restrooms

Some public toilets are scattered around town, but not many. You can find one outside the Colosseum across the road toward Via Labicana, and a convenient one is halfway up the steps from Piazza del Popolo to the Pincio, on the left side. Facing San Pietro, you can find toilets under the colonnade on the right. Your best bet may be to go to a nice-looking cafe (though you have to buy something, like a cup of coffee).

Safety

Rome is a very safe city except for pickpockets. Pickpockets concentrate in tourist areas, on public transportation, and around crowded open-air markets like the Porta Portese. One area that gets somewhat seedy at night is behind the main rail station Termini.

Smoking

Smoking is allowed in cafes and restaurants and is very common. Unfortunately for non-smokers, finding a restaurant with a no-smoking area is virtually impossible, although some are beginning to appear.

Taxes

Rome doesn't have a local tax. Other taxes are always included in the prices quoted. You can get a refund of the 19% IVA (value-added tax) for purchases costing more than 155€ ($140). See Chapter 4.

Taxis

If you need a taxi, call ☎ 06-88-177, 06-66-45, 06-49-94, 06-55-51, or 06-65-45.

Transit/Tourist Assistance

The tourist information hotline at ☎ 06-3600-4399 will provide you with information in four languages including English from 9 a.m. to 7 p.m.

Weather Updates

For forecasts, your best bet is to look at the news on TV (there's no phone number to get weather forecasts). On the Web, check out meteo.tiscalinet.it.

Web Sites

The city's own Web site, www.comune.roma.it, is mostly in Italian, with only some parts in English. However, it maintains an English site, www.romaturismo.com, as well as www.romapreview.com. Written delightfully in "English as a second language," www.informaroma.it directs you to everything you may need to feel at home in Rome. Time Out's site (www.timeout.co.uk) lists the latest in everything from sightseeing to nighclubbing in the Eternal City. Two other sites worth checking out are www.romace.it and www.ciaoRome.com.

At www.tourome.com/tourrome.htm you can find day tours of Rome's sights and attractions, led by local tour leaders who pick you up and drop you off at your hotel. The Vatican features a multilingual site at www.vatican.va — the official site of the Holy See — while at www.christusrex.org you can find tourist information as well as a tour of the Vatican Museums. A private site where you can see a reconstruction of ancient Rome is www.ancientsites.com/users/COCCIEIUSCAESAR. Other good sites are www.virtualrome.com and www.romaonline.it.

Chapter 13

Side Trips from Rome

*L*azio, the region surrounding Rome, is rich in beautiful and interesting sites that you can easily reach from the capital. If you have the leisure, you can stay a couple extra days in Rome and branch out from there for some enjoyable day-trips.

Tivoli and Its Trio of Villas

Try not to miss the splendor of **Tivoli,** northeast of Rome. Like Rome, it's situated on a hill — actually on the pre-Apennines — and is the seat of three famous villas, one ancient Roman, one baroque, and one romantic. Here you can see Rome's architectural history as it played out over almost 2,000 years.

The ancient Tibur (Tivoli) of the Romans was the destination of choice for the wealthy and famous. Many constables and even emperors had their villas here to escape the stress of daily life in ancient Rome — not such a joke if you remember that at the height of the Empire, Rome the city counted 2 million inhabitants. The tradition of fleeing the confines of the city for Tivoli continued during the Renaissance, and even nowadays Tivoli remains a favorite retreat for Romans in search of a cool breeze, good food, and beautiful vistas.

Getting there

A short drive from the capital — only 31km (20 miles) northeast — Tivoli lies on Via Tiburtina, one of the consular roads, running northeast of Rome and just southeast of the Via Nomentana. Given the traffic and

Italian driving habits, though, you'd be better off going by public transportation. Tivoli is like a suburb of Rome, and many people commute to and from the city daily, so traffic at peak hours can be horrible.

The best idea is taking **Metro Line B** to the last stop, Rebibbia (a 15-minute trip), and then switching to a **COTRAL bus** for Tivoli (☎ **0774-720-096** in Tivoli) at the terminal outside the Metro station (a 30-minute trip). Buses depart about every 20 minutes, and tickets cost $5.20€ ($4.70). **Beware:** Buses are less frequent on Saturdays and quite infrequent on Sundays. If you want to use the bus on a Sunday, check the schedule in advance to ensure that you'll have a bus at a convenient time for your way out.

Alternatively, you could take the **train.** One train departs from Rome's Stazione Termini for Tivoli about every hour on the hour. The ticket costs about 2€ ($1.80) for the half-hour trip. Note, however, that the Tivoli train station is a little outside the town center and a bit of a walk. Of course, you can always take a taxi at the train station.

Taking a tour and getting information

If you sign up with a tour, you can avoid the hassle of driving and the trouble of dealing with transportation in a foreign language. A reliable agency that organizes excursions to Tivoli is **American Express** (Piazza di Spagna 38; ☎ **06-67-641**). Another is **Stop'n Go/C.S.R.** (Via Ezio 12; ☎ **06-321-7054**; E-mail: csr@gisec.it), which offers half-day tours (morning only). Both charge about 10.40€ ($9.40) for the tour.

The **tourist office in Tivoli** is in the central square of Largo Garibaldi (☎ **0774-334-522**); summer hours are Monday through Saturday 9 a.m. to 6 p.m. and Sunday 9 a.m. to 2 p.m. (in winter it closes an hour earlier).

Seeing the sights

The two main villas are within walking distance of the center of town and from each other. The Villa Adriana is about 5km (3½ miles) from the center of Tivoli and can be reached by the local **C.A.T. city bus no. 4** (☎ **0774-334-229**) from Largo Garibaldi, a few minutes' ride costing .77€ (69¢). A slightly more expensive option is taking a taxi from the main square in town or having one called for you by the restaurant where you had lunch; the five-minute trip will cost about 2.60€ ($2.35).

The visit to the three villas shouldn't make you forget to have a look at the town of Tivoli itself. The highlights are the second-century-B.C. **Tempio della Sibilla,** on the Roman Acropolis (on the other side of the Aniene River); the 12th-century churches of **San Silvestro** (southwest of the Villa d'Este) and **Santa Maria Maggiore;** and the 1461 **Rocca Pia,** Pope Pius II's castle, which was turned into a prison after 1870.

Rome and Environs

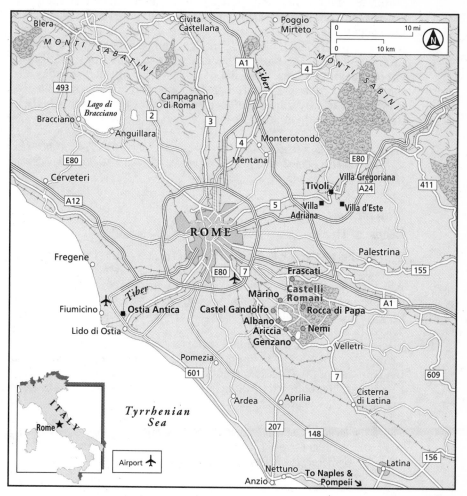

Villa Adriana

5km (3½ miles) from the center of Tivoli

Hadrian, one of Rome's "good" emperors, had this villa built between A.D 118 and 138 as his holiday home. He spent the last three years of his life here. The villa, placed on the site of a Roman villa from Republican times, is magnificent, though it has lost its marbles, so to speak — many of its sculptures are now conserved in Roman museums. Much of the marble once covering the structures has gone, because the estate was used as a "quarry" during the Renaissance, as were many other Roman buildings, like the Colosseum. Here, Hadrian wanted to be surrounded by the architectural marvels he'd seen during his trips across the

Empire: On the 300 acres of this self-contained world for his vast royal entourage, he constructed replicas of famous buildings of antiquity, such as the **Canopus** (the Egyptian round canal ringed with statues) and the **Lyceum** (the school of Aristotle), as well as temples and theaters, monumental thermal baths, fountains and gardens, and a library. Although most of the monuments are today in ruins, the effect is still impressive. For a glimpse of what the villa looked like in its heyday, see the reconstruction at the entrance. Like any ruin in Italy, the villa gets very hot at midday during summer, so the best time to visit is early in the morning or late in the afternoon.

Via di Villa Adriana, 5km (3½ miles) from the center of Tivoli. ☎ 0774-530-203. Bus: 4 to Villa Adriana. Admission: 5.16€ ($4.70) adults; children free. Open: Daily 9 a.m. to 1½ hours before sunset.

Villa d'Este
Center of Tivoli

Built in 1550 by Cardinal Ippolito d'Este of Ferrara — the son of notorious Lucrezia Borgia and Alfonso I d'Este — this villa is relatively banal. The real attractions are the magnificent gardens surrounding it, where architect Pirro Ligorio, using an underground spring and the natural slope of the land, designed a masterpiece of linked fountains and hidden rivulets. The work is really magnificent and isn't diminished by the other masterpieces in the garden: the **Fountain of the Organ (Fontana dell'Organo)** by Claude Veanard, the **Ovato Fountain (Fontana del'Ovato)** by Ligorio, and the **Fountain of the Big Glass (Fontana del Bicchierone)** by Bernini. The gardens are incredibly refreshing in summer and a perfect spot to be at midday on your visit to Tivoli.

Piazza Trento, in the center of Tivoli. ☎ 0774-312-070. Bus: COTRAL bus from Rome has a stop in Largo Garibaldi, just east of Piazza Trento. Admission: 5.16€ ($4.70) adults; children free. Open: Daily 9 a.m. to 1½ hours before sunset.

Villa Gregoriana
Center of Tivoli

The latest of the three famous villas of Tivoli, the Villa Gregoriana was built in the 19th century and isn't a villa at all. In reality, it's a beautiful garden built to enhance the natural beauty of the gorges of the Aniene — the river that meets the Tiber in Rome. Pope Gregory XVI had a path carved all the way down to the bottom of the ravine to allow him to admire the 300-foot waterfall, grottoes, and ponds. The deep slopes are covered with vegetation and mighty trees, making it a magical spot, especially in summer.

Via di Villa Adriana, in the center of Tivoli. ☎ 0774-530-203. Bus: 4. Admission: 4.13€ ($3.70) adults; children free. Open: Daily 9 a.m. to 1½ hours before sunset.

Where to dine

Tivoli has a number of trattorie and restaurants that are Sunday favorites for Romans on outings. The food is typically Roman, with such specialties as cannelloni, *saltimbocca, abbacchio,* and *trippa alla Romana* (see Chapter 11 for descriptions).

Albergo Ristorante Adriano

$$$$ Villa Adriana   ROMAN

Countryside elegance describes this tree-surrounded villa offering a variety of Roman specialties. Everything is homemade, from the delicious pastas to the desserts. And if you decide to stay overnight, you can rent one of the few guest rooms at 105€ ($95) per double.

Via di Villa Adriana 194, near the ticket booth to Villa Adriana. ☎ *0774-535-028. Reservation not necessary. Bus: 4 to Villa Adriana. Secondi: 8€–16.50€ ($7–$15). Prix-fixe menu: 39€ ($35). AE, DC, MC, V. Open: Lunch daily; dinner Mon–Sat.*

Le Cinque Statue

$$$ Villa Gregoriana   ROMAN

Decorated with marble statues — the five statues in the restaurant's name — this reliable family-run restaurant offers a number of typical Roman dishes you can enjoy with a choice of local wines, mostly from the nearby Castelli (see "The Castelli Romani and Their Wines," in this chapter).

Via Quintilio Varo 8, just off the entrance to the Villa Gregoriana. ☎ *0774-335-366. Reservations recommended on weekends. Bus: Near the last stop of the COTRAL bus from Rome. Secondi: 6.50€ ($12). AE, DC, MC, V. Open: Lunch and dinner Sat–Thurs; closed the second two weeks in Aug.*

The Castelli Romani and Their Wines

The **Castelli Romani,** the hill towns surrounding Rome to the southeast, are a favorite destination for locals (including the pope) looking for a place to cool off and relax in the summer. These towns are famous for their history and the production of excellent wine and foodstuffs. Each town is dominated by its own castle — the smallest called a *rocca* — and is surrounded by fertile countryside, the produce of which is masterly prepared and served in the many trattorie.

The Castelli towns are Albano, Ariccia, Castel Gandolfo, Frascati, Genzano, Marino, Nemi, and Rocca di Papa. Frascati may be the most familiar, for the white wine produced there.

Getting there

The best way to visit the Castelli is by **car.** Driving allows you to visit more than one of these attractive small towns. If you decide to rent a car, take the Tuscolana out of Rome and follow it to Frascati, then continue with the local road — almost a loop — to Marino on one side and Rocca di Papa on the other. It'll take you through all the other Castelli. You can also reach Marino from the Appia Nuova, taking a 4½-mile detour to the north. From the Appia, you can take another side road for Castel Gandolfo. The Appia then continues to Albano, Ariccia, and Genzano.

If you don't care for driving, a good alternative is taking an **organized tour** (see "Taking a tour and getting information" later in this chapter). Another possibility is using one of the several public transportation options. The public company **COTRAL** (☎ **800-431-784** for schedules) offers buses for each of the Castelli every 20 minutes or so. They leave from the Subaugusta and Anagnina (the last two) stops on metro Line A. There's also some service among the Castelli; Albano is the hub for this service, and you can catch COTRAL buses from Albano to Nemi, Ariccia, and Genzano. Of course, the length of the trip will vary depending on your destination, but all of them are under an hour. The price of the ride ranges from 3.10€ to 5.16€ ($2.80 to $4.70).

Some of the Castelli are also connected by **train.** A train leaves from Rome's Stazione Termini and heads to Albano, also stopping at Marino and Castel Gandolfo, and there's a separate train to Frascati. The ride will be about half an hour and cost 2.07€ ($1.90).

Taking a tour and getting information

Stop 'n Go/C.S.R. (Via Ezio 12; ☎ **06-321-7054**; E-mail: csr@gisec.it) organizes a tour of the Castelli Romani leaving at 2:30 p.m. from Rome's Piazza dei Cinquecento (at the corner of Via Massimo d'Azeglio) for 11€ ($10). The bus will bring you back to its point of departure in Rome by around 6:30 p.m.

The **central tourist office** for the Castelli Romani is in Albano (Viale Risorgimento 1; ☎ **06-932-4081**; Fax: 06-932-0040). Another large office is in Frascati (Piazza Marconi 1; ☎ **06-942-0331**). Both are open Monday through Friday 8 a.m. to 2 p.m. and 3:30 to 6:30 p.m. and Saturday 8 a.m. to 2 p.m.

Seeing the sights

The Castelli towns and the surrounding countryside are all attractive. Each of the towns could justify at least a day-long stay. We indicate in the following sections the highlights of each town. Don't forget that each one offers food specialties well worth sampling during your visit.

Albano

Though it's the most built-up of the Castelli, Albano still maintains its unique charm. It's the center of the area producing the table wine Colli Albani, a pleasant white you often find in trattorie around Rome. Albano was the site of an ancient Roman town; later, Emperor Septimius Severus housed Roman legions here; and still later, Renaissance Italians built villas here. Albano, because of its beautiful views, was a regular stop of tourists on the Grand Tour (though the 1829 earthquake and the 1867 cholera epidemic put a damper on tourism).

Ariccia

On Ariccia's main square is the 17th-century **Palazzo Chigi,** a villa still belonging to the Chigi family and surrounded by a splendid garden. Across from the *palazzo* is the **church of the Assunta,** designed by Bernini. Unfortunately, quite ugly modern buildings have been built around the historic center. The main reason to come here are the *fraschette* (small taverns), often with outdoor dining areas, where you can sample local wine and the town's specialty: *porchetta. Porchetta* is something not to be missed — it's a whole (deboned) pig carefully roasted with herbs, then sliced and served with peasant bread. A *porchetta* sandwich is one of the best "fast foods" you'll ever have.

Castel Gandolfo

On the slopes of the beautiful Lago Albano, Castel Gandolfo has a great beach — you can even swim — and a very pleasant promenade along the lake. It's the summer residence of the pope, whose 17th-century villa, surrounded by an enormous garden, was built atop the villa of the Roman emperor Domitian. Obviously, you can't visit the papal villa, but you can enjoy the rest of the town — including Bernini's **San Tommaso di Villanova church** and his **fountain** on the main square, Piazza della Libertà.

Frascati

Frascati is probably the best known town of the Castelli because of the wine of the same name, produced in the surrounding countryside. Romans come here to visit the various *cantine* (cellars), where you can sample the wine and eat simple fare — a sandwich made with local bread and salami or *porchetta* and *pecorino* (sheep's-milk cheese). The town is dominated by the imposing 16th-century **Villa Aldobrandini,** atop a steep slope above the main square. You can visit its gardens daily from 9 a.m. to 1 p.m. by getting a free ticket from the **tourist office** on Piazza Marconi 1 (see "Taking a tour and getting information" earlier in this chapter).

Genzano

Picturesquely situated above the Lago di Nemi, which is actually the crater of an extinct volcano, Genzano is a charming small town surrounded by beautiful countryside. Among the highlights are the 17th-century **Palazzo Sforza-Cesarini** and the nearby **cathedral.** Genzano's main event is the *Infiorata* (literally "flowering") — where one Sunday in spring the main street is covered with a carpet of flowers. The wine is good here, and you'll find a few nice trattorie.

Marino

The closest of the Castelli to Rome (only 15 miles), Marino is a pleasant small town — though the surroundings are modern and bland. The town is most famous for its wine, particularly enjoyable when it's fresh. On the occasion of the **harvest celebration** in October, the main fountains in town pour wine instead of water, to the great delight of all. The rest of the time, you can sample it in the various *osterie* and *cantine* in town — just look for the sign "VINO"!

Nemi

Nemi is a jewel of a small town. It has its own lake, the **Lago di Nemi,** on the slopes of which are cultivated some of the best strawberries of the world and certainly the best in Italy. Nemi also specializes in the production of salami, sausages, *pancetta* (Italian bacon), and other mouth-watering items. Alas, you can't bring meat products back into the States, but that's just one more reason to sample them here. They keep quite well, and you can include them in a future picnic on your trip.

Rocca di Papa

The town of Rocca di Papa, named after its castle, dominates the Lago di Albano and enjoys breathtaking views of the surrounding hills. It's worth climbing the hill above the town to see the great view; it's now a park, and all that's left here is the ruin of an old *albergo* (hotel) where people once came to eat and enjoy the pure air. The town below is quite picturesque. The **Chiesa dell'Assunta** is a baroque church that was reconstructed after an 1806 earthquake.

Where to dine

The Castelli contains a procession of small and big trattorie and *ristoranti*. They're all quite reliable, but keep in mind the rule of "trust the locals" (if it's dinnertime and nobody is eating in a place, there must be a reason). We give you some safe bets below, but just follow your nose to find many other great places on your own.

The food in the Castelli is typically Roman, including fresh pasta and grilled meats. People come to sample the variety of local salami and cheeses, usually served as antipasto. *Porchetta* is a specialty of Ariccia (see the previous section) but is prepared to some extent everywhere in the Castelli. The wine of the Castelli is probably the best in Lazio; particularly famous are the white Frascati and the Marino (white and red, respectively).

Antico Ristorante Paganelli

$$$$ Castel Gandolfo   ROMAN/SEAFOOD

The Roman menu here includes a variety of traditional specialties as well as more-common Italian dishes. The prix-fixe menus change in price according to what's included. As is usually the case in Italy, fish is the most expensive.

Via Gramsci 4. ☎ *06-936-0004. Reservations recommended on weekends. Secondi: 10€–21€ ($9–$19). AE, DC, MC, V. Open: Lunch and dinner Wed–Mon.*

Cacciani

$$$ Frascati   ROMAN

The renowned Cacciani is family-run and serves some of the best food and wine in the area — and that's high praise. The restaurant is modern inside and has a terrace from which you can enjoy the beautiful view over the hills. The typical Roman specialties are wonderfully prepared; go for the homemade pasta and the other pasta specialties. The meat dishes, such as the *abbacchio alla cacciatora* (lamb cooked with white wine and rosemary), are also excellent.

Via Armando Diaz 13. ☎ *06-942-0378. Reservations required on weekends. Secondi: 11€–17€ ($10–$15.30). AE, DC, MC, V Open: Lunch and dinner Tues–Sun; closed ten days in Jan and ten days in Aug.*

Cantina Comandini

$ Frascati   WINE TAVERN

Not a restaurant but a "cellar," this family-run business is the outlet of one of Frascati's vineyards. Here you'll be able to sample the famous Frascati wine and accompany it with a sandwich or a choice of local cold cuts and cheese. You can also buy wine to bring away, but you'll probably want to drink it before you go home.

Via E. Filiberto 1. ☎ *06-942-0915. Reservations recommended. Secondi: 2.60€–7€ ($2.30–$6.30). MC, V. Open: Dinner Mon–Sat.*

Ostia Antica: Rome's Ancient Seaport

Southwest of Rome, toward the sea, is **Ostia Antica,** the commercial harbor of ancient Rome. Its ruins are particularly attractive early in the morning or at sunset, when many Romans like to come for an evening *passeggiata* (stroll). It's popular also on weekends for picnics, but most popular are the shows — music and theater — held in the Roman theater, the **Teatro Romano,** in July.

The ancient city of Ostia served as a shipyard, a gathering place for the fleet, and a distribution center for ancient Rome. Founded in the fourth century B.C. as a military colony for the defense of the river Tevere, Ostia flourished for about eight centuries before being progressively abandoned as a result of the silting up of the river and the spread of malaria in the region (no longer a concern, thankfully).

Getting there

Ostia Antica is about 28km (16 miles) from Rome. It's linked by **train** from Stazione Ostiense (take Metro Line B to the Piramide stop and follow the signs for Ostia), with trains departing every half-hour and costing about 1€ (90¢) for the 25-minute trip. You can easily reach the site on foot from the train station, which is across the street.

You can also get to Ostia by **car** on Via Ostiense or Via del Mare (they run parallel to each other). You can take Via Ostiense from Piramide and Via del Mare from Eur. Note, however, that this is also the route to the beaches, so if you set off on a beautiful weekend, you may find yourself in heavy traffic heading out of Rome.

Keep in mind that the ruins are incredibly hot in summer. They're spread across a flat plain, and shade is hard to come by. If you don't like heat, come early, end your visit just before lunch, and head elsewhere to eat.

Seeing the sights

Ostia Antica includes a small village, quite cute but really small, and the major site of the archaeological area, which is what people come here to visit. Note that there is nowhere to eat inside or by the archaeological area. Bring a picnic lunch or plan to eat elsewhere. You'll find a couple of small restaurants and a bar in the village of Ostia Antica.

To take a guided tour of the sights, check out **Stop 'n Go/C.S.R.** (Via Ezio 12; ☎ **06-321-7054;** E-mail: csr@gisec.it). It organizes morning and afternoon tours of Ostia Antica for 11€ ($10).

Area Archeologica di Ostia Antica
Ostia Antica

The archaeological site covers the impressive excavations of the ancient town of Ostia. The main streets of the town have been unearthed, as well as some of the principal monuments. After entering the site, on the right you'll find **Via delle Corporazioni,** leading to the **Roman Theater (Teatro Romano).** Noting the mosaics indicating the nature of each of the businesses once housed along this street is interesting. The theater is still in use today for performances of works by modern and ancient authors during July as part of the **Estate Romana** (you can find details on the Web at www.comune.roma.it or by calling ☎ **06-6880-9505** Monday through Saturday 10 a.m. to 5 p.m.).

Returning to the main street and continuing ahead, you'll find on your left the **Forum** and behind it the **Terme (thermal baths).** There are two temples on the left, and the **Capitolinum** on the right. The site also includes many interesting houses and buildings. The tourist office in Rome has a relatively good map of the park. Remember to bring a picnic; you'll enjoy dining under a tree among the ruins. Allow a minimum of three hours for the visit, more if you visit the museum. The **Museum** — conserving all the material found during the excavations of the site — just opened its doors after a restoration that lasted several years. The entrance to the museum is within the excavations and admission is included; it observes the same hours as the site as a whole.

Via Ostiense ☎ *06-5635-8099. Admission: 5.16€ ($4.70). Open: Summer Tues–Sun 9:00 a.m.–6:30 p.m.; winter Tues–Sun 9 a.m.–5 p.m.*

Part IV
Florence and the Best of Tuscany and Umbria

The 5th Wave   By Rich Tennant

I know _how_ to ask for directions to a McDonalds in Italian, I'm just afraid to.

In this part . . .

*T*uscany is the most visited region in Italy, and for a great
reason: The concentration of attractions here—sights,
scenery, food, and wine—is beyond imagination. Practically
every hill town offers something interesting to visit. (This is
true of all of Italy, but Tuscany boasts so many more hills!)
Tuscany has a proud tradition and a unique character and
flavor, including the regional delicacies that each part of
Italy seems to offer. Umbria is a less-toured region, but it's
also famous for its cuisine and the art of its towns. Perugia,
a city on a hill (of course) with a rich artistic patrimony, is
Umbria's capital.

In the following chapters, we give you the top of the top,
the not-to-be-missed things to see and do in these regions.
Chapter 14 is dedicated to the beautiful city of Florence.
Chapter 15 covers the northern Tuscan towns of Lucca and
Pisa and detours to the Italian Riviera for a glimpse of the
Cinque Terre (five fishing villages). In Chapter 16 we take
you to southern Tuscany and explore the Chianti region
and the towns of Siena and San Gimignano. Chapter 17
covers the highlights of Umbria, including the cities of
Assisi, Perugia, and Spoleto.

Chapter 14

Florence

● ●

In This Chapter

▶ Finding your way to and around Florence

▶ Discovering the best neighborhoods, hotels, and restaurants

▶ Exploring the magnificent sights of Florence

▶ Sampling the best of Italian food

▶ Getting the scoop on the best shopping areas and nightlife attractions

● ●

*A*long with Venice and Rome, Florence (Firenze) is the top destination for Americans in Italy. So why does everyone go to Florence? Well, Venice seems a bit surreal, a beautiful but almost dead city slowly sinking into the muddy lagoon it was build upon. Rome is a crazy mix of ancient and modern, with free-wheeling Vespas careering down ancient alleyways. Florence, on the other hand, maintains its compact medieval scale and Renaissance core, and at the same time feels like a real place. But that's only part of it. Florence holds one of the world's most incredible repositories of art and architecture, home to such treasures as the Botticellis and Leonardos in the Uffizi Gallery (Galleria degli Uffizi), Michelangelo's *David* in the Accademia Gallery (Galleria dell'Accademia), Brunelleschi's dome crowning the Duomo (Santa Maria del Fiore), Giotto's Campanile, Ghiberti's "Gates of Paradise" on the Baptistry (Battistero di San Giovanni), the Ponte Vecchio.

Florence thrived from its ninth-century-B.C. beginnings, but in medieval times — when it grew to be a great banking center, dominating the European credit market — the city truly reached its apogee. Florence's riches enabled the flourishing of the arts: Dante was born here in 1265, and so was the painter Cimabue (Giotto's teacher). The Renaissance blossomed in the 1300s, despite a flood, the Black Plague, and political upheaval. The 15th century brought the rule of Lorenzo the Magnificent, head of the powerful Medici clan, and then a brief restoration of the Republic. In this, Florence's greatest period, the artists Leonardo, Michelangelo, and Raphael were producing amazing works. In 1537, the Medici family returned to power in the person of Cosimo I.

Florence has remained a center of intellectual life into the modern period; in fact, it was the capital of Italy from 1865 to 1870. By that time, it had become one of the paramount stops on the Grand Tour, and its past had been transformed into its most important asset. Tourism has exploded in recent years — this relatively small town is crammed with 6 million visitors annually. But not to worry: In the following sections, we tell you how to maneuver the city with ease and confidence.

Getting There

Located in the region of Tuscany, Florence is easy to reach by air, train, or car.

By air

There are no direct flights from the United States to Florence. If you're leaving from the States, you have to fly first to Rome or Milan — the only two international airports in Italy — and then get a connecting flight. The situation is different if you're flying from one of the European Union countries: There are direct flights between a number of European cities and Florence.

Florence is served by two airports — in addition to its own airport, the **Aeroporto Amerigo Vespucci,** the city is accessible from Pisa's nearby **Aeroporto Galileo Galilei** (for Pisa information, see Chapter 15). Both airports are easy to get around, though the Florence airport is smaller.

Arriving at Aeroporto Amerigo Vespucci/Peretola

The **Aeroporto Amerigo Vespucci (☎ 055-373-498;** Internet: www.safnet.it), is generally called the **Aeroporto di Peretola,** which is the name of the small town where it's located (like the Leonardo da Vinci/Fiumicino confusion for Rome's airport). The airport is only 4km (2½ miles) outside of Florence.

The easiest way to get from the airport to your hotel is by taking a taxi, which will take about 10 to 15 minutes and cost about 20€ ($18). You can also get into Florence by regular city bus 62, which takes about half an hour and arrives at the central train station, Santa Maria Novella, for .77€ (69¢).

The **SITA bus (☎ 055-214-721)** airport shuttle is slightly more expensive at 4€ ($3.60) but is also faster (10 to 15 minutes) because it's nonstop; about one bus leaves per hour, arriving at the Florence's SITA bus terminal, just behind the rail station of Santa Maria Novella.

Landing at Aeroporto Galileo Galilei

Pisa's well-organized **Aeroporto Galileo Galilei (☎ 050-500-707)** is just outside the city and 80km (50 miles) from Florence. From the airport, you can take a special shuttle train to Florence's Santa Maria Novella rail station, costing about 4.13€ ($3.70) and taking about an hour. Leaving Florence, you can even check your bags for your flight at the **rail station of Santa Maria Novella** (look for the sign "Air Terminal"; ☎ 055-216-073) to avoid lugging them to the airport yourself. There is a train every hour between 6 a.m. and 10 p.m.

By train

This is by far the best way to get to Florence from other destinations in Italy — there are fast connections from all major Italian cities, such as Rome, Milan, and Venice. One train about every hour arrives from both Rome and Venice. The trip takes about two hours from Rome and three from Venice, depending on the kind of train (intercity or the faster Eurostar). You'll arrive at Florence's **Stazione Santa Maria Novella,** often abbreviated **SMN Firenze** (☎ 055-288-765), from which you can get to almost anywhere in the city via a cab, via a bus, or on foot. Some trains stop at other stations on Florence's outskirts, but don't get off there.

At Santa Maria Novella, you can leave luggage at the office at the head of Track 16. The station's tourist office (see "Street smarts: Where to get information after you arrive" in this chapter) mainly arranges hotel rooms but also gives out some information, such as the free city map; this is where you can pick up your reserved tickets for the Uffizi or the Accademia (see the tip under "Exploring Florence").

By car

Florence is at the intersection of several major highways, so getting there from the north, south, east, and west is easy. After you're inside the city, however, your car will become a big pain in the neck. The city center is closed to autos except those of the residents; and the historic center — the part you're interested in — is closed to all vehicles except city buses. If you already have a hotel reservation, you're allowed to drive in to your hotel and unload, but then you have to find a place to stow your car, and city parking lots are expensive (your hotel may have one; check when you book). Rates near the center are about 1€ to 3€ (.90¢ to $2.70) per hour. You may get a daily rate, but you're still renting a space for a vehicle you can't use.

For these reasons, if you're doing a driving tour of smaller towns in Tuscany, scheduling it before or after your stay in Florence makes sense. That way, you can either dump off the car at the agency when you arrive, or you can pick it up at one of the locations on the outskirts of town when you're ready to leave. You'll spare yourself plenty of headaches this way.

Orienting Yourself in Florence

Unlike Rome and Venice, Florence has a relatively simple layout, bisected by the river Arno. The city has much expanded in recent times, but the new areas have little of historic interest. Like other Italian cities, Florence developed beyond its medieval perimeter only toward the end of the 19th century. The historic center is quite small and easy to get around.

Florence by neighborhood

Here we give you the layout of the historic districts of Florence, the part that interests you as a tourist. Most of the historic part lies on the north side of the Arno. This area is packed with monuments and museums. We don't want you to neglect the other bank of the river, however, so we describe the major attractions in that neighborhood as well.

The historic district (centro storico)

Florence began here in a square area defined by the Stazione Santa Maria Novella, Piazza SS. Annunziata, and the Arno. Most of the tourist draws are in this neighborhood, as well as the major shopping areas.

From SMN to the river is the elegant commercial district along Via dei Tornabuoni and eastward on Piazza della Repubblica and Via Roma. From Piazza SS. Annunziata — where you'll find the **Accademia Gallery (Galleria dell'Accademia)** with Michelangelo's *David* — to the Arno is the "monumental" district. Within the monumental district, Via dei Calzaiuoli leads from the **Duomo (Santa Maria del Fiore),** whose striped marblework and red-tiled dome symbolize Florence, to Piazza della Signoria, right in front of the **Palazzo Vecchio** and **Loggia dell'Orcagna** (the massive structure and soaring tower that have dominated political life since the 13th century). Next to the Duomo and also banded in pink, white, and green marble are the octagonal **Baptistry (Battistero di San Giovanni),** with its famous bronze doors and 13th-century mosaics, and **Giotto's bell tower (Campanile di Giotto),** a masterpiece from late in the painter's life.

Just behind the Palazzo Vecchio and overlooking the river is the **Uffizi Gallery (Galleria degli Uffizi)**, containing one of the most important painting collections in the world and showcasing the great Florentine painters of the Renaissance. If you turned right and walked along the riverbank, you'd come to the **Ponte Vecchio,** one of several bridges crossing the Arno and one of the symbols of the city, dating from 1345.

Oltrarno (Across the Arno)

Included within the walls of Florence only in 1173, the south side of the Arno is a quieter and more elegant residential area. The number of attractions there is limited, yet the magic of the medieval city is still

Florence Orientation

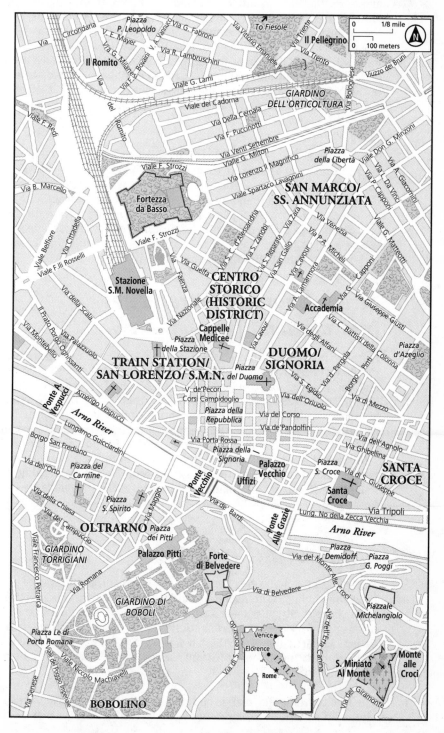

present (and with reduced crowds). Crossing the Ponte Vecchio, you arrive on Via Guicciardini, which leads to the **Palazzo Pitti,** the largest Florentine palace, built by banker Luca Pitti in the 15th century and then transformed into the grand Medici residence. It now houses seven museums, including a *pinacoteca* (picture gallery) with works by Raphael, Andrea del Sarto, and others. Behind the *palazzo* is a beautiful garden, the **Boboli Gardens (Giardino di Boboli)**. Also on this side of the Arno is the **Chiesa di Santa Maria del Carmine,** a 13th-century church famous for frescoes by Masaccio and Masolino da Panicale.

Fiesole

The one other "neighborhood" you may want to visit outside the center is actually a separate town 4.5km (3 miles) away — **Fiesole** (see "Exploring Florence") — from which you can get marvelous views of Florence and the surrounding hills. It's particularly pleasant in the summer, when it offers cooler air and a welcome break from the stuffy city. Fiesole is a preferred outing for Florentines on summer nights and is an excellent place to stay if you want to be away from the crowds (see the hotel and restaurant listings later in this chapter).

Street smarts: Where to get information after you arrive

Florence has several tourist offices. One is inside the **SMN train station** (☎ 055-212-245), open Monday through Saturday 8:30 a.m. to 7:00 p.m. and Sunday 8:30 a.m. to 1:30 p.m. Another is at **Via Cavour 1R** (☎ 055-290-832 or 055-290-833; Fax: 055-276-0383; Bus: 14, 23, or 71 to Duomo), about three blocks north of the Duomo; it's open Monday through Saturday 8:15 a.m. to 7:15 p.m. in summer (to 2:00 p.m. in winter) and Sunday 8:30 a.m. to 1:30 p.m. Yet another is at **Borgo Santa Croce 29R** (☎ 055-234-0444 or 055-224-4524; Bus: A or 14 to Piazza Santa Croce), just behind Piazza Santa Croce; it's open Monday through Friday 9 a.m. to 2 p.m. You can get information on the Web at www.firenze.turismo.toscana.it.

Getting Around Firenze

Florence's city center has long been closed to automobiles except those belonging to the residents, and the historic center is free from all traffic except city buses — no cars, no taxis, and no mopeds (the ubiquitous and very noisy *motorinis*). Although some still protest — taxi drivers in particular — we think it was a great decision, because it made the city much more pleasant for visitors (for everybody, in fact) and easier to visit.

The free tourist office map is completely adequate for most visitors. If you're an ambitious explorer and don't feel satisfied with that map, you can pick up the yellow **Studio FMB Bologna map** of the city at a news-stand for about 4.13€ ($3.70).

Florence has its own peculiar way of marking street addresses: Restaurants, agencies, and shops have numbers of their own, separate from the residential and hotel building numbers, even if the shop, restaurant, or agency is located within that building. Business numbers have the letter *R* appended to the number (for *rosso* or "red") and are painted in red, while residential numbers are painted in black or blue. For example, the address of one branch of the tourist office, Via Cavour 1R, refers to shop no. 1 on Via Cavour, whereas the address Via Cavour 1 is the private building with the entrance no. 1. Such seemingly similar addresses can be many doors away from one another.

On foot

Really, the best way to get around Florence is on foot. The full walk from the Duomo at one end of the major historic district to the Palazzo Pitti at the other takes only about 30 minutes at a leisurely pace; you'd also pass most of the major sights in town. As compact as any medieval city, Florence has a dense concentration of attractions, so you can basically walk from one sight to another.

By bus

The only sight that's far away from the center and absolutely requires a bus ride is the town of Fiesole. However, buses come as a welcome rest to the tired visitor — especially after a long day at the Uffizi — and the view on the way up to Fiesole is exquisite. Also, we found the bus particularly useful to move back and forth between the Palazzo Pitti/Giardino di Boboli and the center of town on the other side of the river Arno.

Florence's bus system is well organized and easy to use. You can get a bus map at the main ticket booth outside the SMN train station — in fact, that's the only place where you can get one. Each bus stop has a name that's neatly written on the post at the stop and is reported on the map and also has a number when there's more than one stop by the same name (for example, on the same street). This helps you figure out where you are and check your progress on the map as you ride.

A regular *biglietto* **(ticket)** is valid for an hour and costs .77€ (69¢). As elsewhere in Italy, you need to buy tickets before boarding the bus; you can buy them at most bars, tobacconist shops (signed *tabacchi* or by a white *T* on a black background), and newsstands. Tickets are also sold at the bus information booth outside the Santa Maria Novella rail station. Within the hour of validity, you can take as many buses as you want. Remember that you need to stamp the ticket at your first ride using the machine inside the bus; without the stamp, the ticket isn't valid. After hours (9 p.m. to 6 a.m.), you can buy a ticket on the bus, but the charge is double. Also available is the *multiplo* **ticket,** which is good for four one-hour rides and costs 3.90€ ($3.50), a slight savings; it can be used by up to four people. The **3-hour pass** costs 1.80€ ($1.62); the **24-hour pass** is 4€ ($3.60); the **2-day pass** is 5.70€ ($5.13); and the **3-day pass** is 7.20€ ($6.48).

Always have a ticket when boarding the bus and be sure to properly stamp it; some people may tell you that no one ever checks, but they're wrong. Within five minutes of boarding our first bus, someone was nabbed by the ticket inspector, a scene we saw repeated several times. And, come on, why try to wriggle out of a bargain 70¢ ride?

Where to Stay in Florence

Florence boasts hundreds of hotels, but because it's a medieval city filled with old buildings, lodgings can be rather cramped and their amenities limited. Another thing to consider is that Florence is dominated by tourism and, therefore, is relatively expensive. Hotels also often have complicated rate structures for high season, low season, and middle season (note that all of August is often considered low season, because it's so hot and Italians are on vacation). In the following sections, we offer a rundown of the best places to stay, followed by some acceptable alternatives if you have trouble booking a room. Unless otherwise specified, all rooms in the hotels listed come with private bathrooms.

If you arrive without a room reservation (something we advise against), remember that the **tourist office in Stazione Santa Maria Novella** offers a room-finding service. If you arrive by car, stop at the office in the **Area di Servizio AGIP Peretola** (rest area) on Highway A11 (☎ 055-421-1800) or in the office at the **Area di Servizio Chianti Est** on Highway A1 (☎ 055-621-349). Both maintain hotel databases and can tell you if rooms are available in town and can even make reservations if you like.

The top hotels

Hotel Alessandra
$$ Centro storico

Steps from the Ponte Vecchio and the Uffizi, this *pensione* offers simple guest rooms — many quite large — at moderate prices. The private bathrooms have been recently renovated; the shared ones are oldish though large and spotless. This all adds up to a very good value. Only a few rooms are air-conditioned, so reserve in advance if you must have it (and if it's August, you must).

Borgo SS. Apostoli 17. ☎ ***055-283-438.*** *Fax: 055-210-619. Internet:* www.hotel alessandra.com. *Bus: B to SS. Apostoli or 6, 11, 36, or 37 to Tornabuoni; walk right on Borgo SS. Apostoli. Parking: 16€–18€ ($14.40–$16). Rack rates: 108€–145€ ($97.20–$116) double, including breakfast. AE, MC, V.*

Hotel Bellettini
$$ Centro storico

Just west of the Duomo, this 14th-century *palazzo* has been a guesthouse for the past 300 years. The old-fashioned Bellettini offers simple, clean guest rooms — some with fantastic views — and one of the best breakfasts in town, with a buffet that includes ham and fresh fruit. The owners, two sisters, are very friendly and helpful — many of their guests keep coming back, so you'll have to reserve in advance. Some of the rooms share a bath, so be sure to ask when you reserve.

Via de' Conti 7. ☎ ***055-213-561.*** *Fax: 055-283-551. Internet:* www.firenze.net/ hotelbellettini. *Bus: 1, 6, 11, or 17 to Martelli; walk south to the Baptistry, turn right on Via de' Cerretani, and right again on Via de' Conti. Parking: 16€ ($14.40). Rack rates: 97€@124€ ($87–$112) double, including breakfast. AE, DC, MC, V.*

Hotel Boboli
$$ Oltrarno

Just south of the Palazzo Pitti and a short walk from the Ponte Vecchio, this simple, modern hotel is a nice value in a residential part of town that's full of much pricier choices. The Boboli is a good choice if you want to be in a quiet area yet near the major sights; it's convenient for families as well, because it has some triple rooms and a couple of quads. The bathrooms are really tiny but still very clean and sufficient for most people.

Via Romana 63. ☎ ***055-229-8645*** *or 055-233-6518. Fax: 055-233-7169. Bus: 11, 36, or 37 to Serragli 05; walk south on Via dei Serragli, turn left on Via Serumido, and left again on Via Romana. Parking: 7.75€–11€ ($7@$9.90). Rack rates: 108.45€–130.15€ ($98–$117) double, including breakfast. AE, DC, MC, V.*

Hotel Chiari-Bigallo
$$$ Centro storico

Just by the Duomo, this hotel has a great central location for comparatively moderate prices, but because of that location it'll be a little noisy at night, especially in summer. The view from the windows, though, will more than compensate. The recently renovated guest rooms have parquet floors and new bathrooms (some with Jacuzzis). The hotel has the same owners as the Hotel de' Lanzi. The hotel sometimes runs specials so be sure to ask.

The big splurge

In this chapter, we supply entries for several deluxe ($$$$$) hotels, among them the Helvetia and Bristol, the Hotel Monna Lisa, and the Plaza Lucchesi. If you're looking for the plushest of the plush, here are a few more suggestions:

✔ **Grand Hotel** (Piazza Ognissanti 1; ☎ **800-625-5144** in the U.S. and Canada, or 055-288781; Fax: 055-217400; Bus: 6 or 17)

✔ **Grand Hotel Villa Medici** (Via il Prato 42; ☎ **055-238-1331**; Fax: 055-238-1336; Bus: 9, 13, 16, 17, or 26)

✔ **Hotel Excelsior** (Piazza Ognissanti 3; ☎ **800-625-5144** in the U.S. and Canada, or 055-264201; Fax: 055-210278; Internet: www.starwood.com; Bus: 6 or 17)

✔ **Savoy Hotel** (Piazza della Repubblica 7; ☎ **055-27-351**; Fax: 055-273-588; Internet: www.rfhotels.com; Bus: A)

Vicolo degli Adimari 2. ☎ *055-216-086. Fax: 055-216-086. Bus: 1, 6, 11, or 17 to Martelli; walk south between the Baptistry and the Duomo at the corner with Via Calzaiuoli to Vicolo degli Adimari. Parking: 14€ ($12.60). Rack rates: 186€ ($168) double, including breakfast. DC, MC, V.*

Hotel de' Lanzi

$$$ Centro storico

This hotel a block from the Duomo has been renovated recently and offers carpeted guest rooms and new bathrooms. Owned by the same people as the Chiari Bigallo, it has the advantage of being less noisy, but fewer of the rooms have the breathtaking vista over the Duomo. The breakfast is nice too, including ham and fruit.

Via delle Oche 11. ☎ *055-288-043. Fax: 055-288-043. Bus: 1, 6, 11, or 17 to Martelli; walk south between the Baptistry and the Duomo to Via Calzaiuoli and turn left onto Via delle Oche. Parking: 14€ ($12.60). Rack rates: 186€ ($168) double, including breakfast. AE, MC, V.*

Hotel Helvetia & Bristol

$$$$$ Centro storico

A block east of Via dei Tornabuoni, this upscale 19th-century hotel is within walking distance of Via dei Calzaiuoli and the major sights. It was the elegant choice of Belle Epoque Florence, visited by Eleonora Duse, Enrico Fermi, Luigi Pirandello, and Giorgio De Chirico. After a long restoration, the Helvetia & Bristol reopened in 1989, with modernized marble baths and antique furnishings. Much original art is on the walls, even in the guest rooms. The beautiful **Winter Garden (Giardino d'Inverno),** a renowned meeting place in the 1920s, serves as the breakfast room and later as a cocktail bar (the buffet breakfast is 18.60€/$16.75). Despite the high rack rate, the hotel does run specials.

Via dei Pescioni 2. ☎ *055-287-814. Fax: 055-288-353. Internet:* www.charming hotels.it. *Bus: 6, 11, 36, or 37 to Antinori; walk east on Via del Campidoglio and turn left on Via dei Pescioni. Parking: 21€ ($18). Rack rates: 542€ ($488) double. AE, DC, MC, V.*

Hotel Loggiato dei Serviti
$$$ Centro storico

This hotel occupies a landmark 16th-century building designed by Antonio da Sangallo il Vecchio (the Elder) to match the twin buildings of the Hospital of the Innocents (Ospedale degli Innocenti) across the square — by the way, the square is the beautiful one just by the Accademia Gallery. Recently renovated and restored to its simple Renaissance beauty (it was built as a monastery and transformed into a hotel only early in the 20th century), the Loggiato dei Serviti is a hotel of character, with pleasant guest rooms and furnishings.

Piazza SS. Annunziata 3. ☎ *055-289-592. Fax: 055-289-595. Internet:* www.loggiato deiservitihotel.it. *Bus: 6, 31, or 32 to SS. Annunziata. Parking: 18€–23€ ($16–$21). Rack rates: 201.41€ ($181.27) double, including breakfast. AE, DC, MC, V.*

Hotel Monna Lisa
$$$$$ Centro storico

The Monna Lisa (no, that's not a misspelling) yearns to be a private collector's home. The guest rooms of this beautiful 14th-century *palazzo*, once home to the Neri family, vary in style and size. The antique furnishings, original coffered ceilings, inner garden and patio, modern bathrooms (some with Jacuzzis), and important artworks make this hotel very desirable. Alas, the prices are a little steep in most seasons.

Borgo Pinti 27. ☎ *055-247-9751. Fax: 055-247-9755. Internet:* www.monnalisa.it. *Bus: A, 14, or 23 to Salvemini. Parking: 11€ ($9.90). Rack rates: 325.37€ ($293) double, including breakfast. AE, DC, MC, V.*

Hotel Palazzo Benci
$$$ Centro storico

Recently opened west of the Duomo, this hotel occupies a lovingly restored 16th-century *palazzo,* the residence of the Renaissance Benc family. The guest rooms are simple but tasteful, and comfort in summer is ensured by air-conditioning; other amenities include safes and minibars. Many rooms open onto the delightful inner garden courtyard. The common spaces are absolutely gorgeous, with richly stuccoed walls, and the breakfast room boasts coffered wooden ceilings.

Florence Accommodations and Dining

ACCOMMODATIONS ■
Albergo Santa Croce **42**
Grand Hotel **11**
Grand Hotel Villa Medici **3**
Hotel Alessandra **15**
Hotel Bellettini **6**
Hotel Boboli **20**
Hotel Casci **28**
Hotel Chiari-Bigallo **31**
Hotel de' Lanzi **32**
Hotel Excelsior **12**
Hotel Helvetia & Bristol **8**
Hotel Hermitage **38**
Hotel Loggiato dei Serviti **26**
Hotel Monna Lisa **41**
Hotel Palazzo Benci **5**
Hotel Pensione Pendini **7**
Hotel Torre Guelfa **14**
Hotel Vasari **1**
Hotel Villa Aurora **24**
Hotel Villa Azalee **2**
Hotel Villa Carlotta **22**
Il Guelfo Bianco **27**
Plaza Hotel Lucchesi **44**
Savoy Hotel **30**

DINING ◆
Cammillo dal 1945 **18**
Cantinetta Antinori **9**
Coronas Café **34**
Da Ganino **36**
Don Chisciotte **23**
Enoteca Ristorante Mario **25**
Il Caffè **19**
Il Cantastorie **37**
Il Cantinone **16**
Il Cibreo **43**
Gelateria Carabè **29**
Gelateria Vivoli **40**
La Carabaccia **10**
Le Mossacce **33**
Mamma Gina **17**
Osteria del Caffè Italiano **39**
Perchè No **35**
Sabatini **4**
Trattoria Boboli **21**
Trattoria Garga **13**

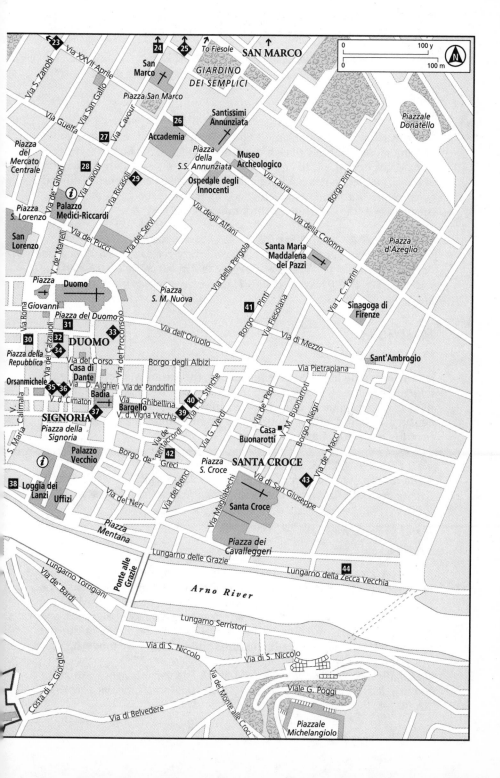

Piazza Madonna degli Aldobrandini 3. ☎ *055-213-848. Fax: 055-288-308. Bus: 1, 6, 11, or 17 to Martelli; walk west on Via dei Gori, then across Piazza San Lorenzo and around the church on Corso Tonelli into Piazza Madonna degli Aldobrandini. Rack rates: 192€ ($173) double, including breakfast. AE, DC, V.*

Hotel Pensione Pendini

$$$ Centro storico

Minutes from Via dei Calzaiuoli and the top sights, the old-fashioned Pendini is just off busy Piazza della Repubblica. This family-style *pensione* dates from the 19th century, when Florence was briefly the capital of Italy. It underwent renovations during the 1990s and offers insulated guest rooms with double-paned windows (so you won't be bothered by the nearby traffic) and new bathrooms.

Via Strozzi 2. ☎ *055-211-170. Fax: 055-281-807. Internet:* www.tiac.net/users/pendini. *E-mail:* pendini@da.it. *Bus: A to Strozzi stop or 6, 11, 36, or 37 to Antinori; walk south on Via dei Tornabuoni and turn left on Via Strozzi. Parking: 18€–21€ ($16–$18). Rack rates: 150€ ($135) double, including breakfast. AE, DC, MC, V.*

Hotel Vasari

$$ Centro storico

On the east side of the SMN train station, the Vasari is a good value for a location within walking distance of the main sights and the historic district. Once home to French poet Alphonse de Lamartine, this 19th-century building offers simple but comfortable guest rooms with recently renovated bathrooms.

Via B. Cennini 9–11. ☎ *055-212-753. Fax: 055-294-246. Bus: 7, 14, 23, 36, or 37 to FS S. Maria Novella; walk left across Piazza Adua and turn right onto Via B. Cennini. Parking: 8€ ($7.20). Rack rates: 149.77€ ($135) double, including breakfast. AE, DC, V.*

Hotel Villa Aurora

$$$ Fiesole

In Fiesole's central square, just by the terminus of the city bus from Florence, this hotel is elegant and comfortable, if a bit pretentious. The guest rooms in back enjoy the gorgeous view over Florence, while the ones on the side overlook the garden. Some rooms have balconies, and there are Jacuzzis in some bathrooms. The old-world feeling doesn't extend to the rooms, where the fixtures and furniture are modern.

Piazza Mino 39. ☎ *055-59100. Fax: 055-59587. Internet:* www.logicad.net/aurora. *Bus: 7 to last stop. Rack rates: 183.34€ ($165) double, including breakfast. AE, DC, MC, V.*

Hotel Villa Azalee
$$$ Centro storico

Just beyond the historic district to the west, the Azalee is minutes from the SMN train station, though a bit removed from the top sights. This villa offers a welcome break from the crowds and is surrounded by a flower garden; the soundproofed guest rooms are furnished in a cozy English style, with flowery fabrics and wooden floors. The stables have been converted into rooms and are among the best in the hotel. Bikes are rented at a very low 2.58€ ($2.32) per day.

Viale Fratelli Rosselli 44. ☎ *055-214-242 or 055-284-331. Fax: 055-268-264. Bus: 9, 13, 16, or 17 to Porta Prato. Parking: 18€ ($16). Rack rates: 153.90€ ($138.51) double, including breakfast. AE, DC, MC, V.*

Hotel Villa Carlotta
$$$$$ Oltrarno

This beautiful early-1900s villa, surrounded by an attractive garden, is in a residential area a short walk from the Ponte Vecchio. The guest rooms are very nicely decorated, and the hotel maintains the air of a private home. The Carlotta is an excellent choice if you arrived by car — it offers the rare luxury of free parking. Staying here is a very enjoyable way to escape the crowds in the center and yet still be close by.

Via Michele di Lando 3. ☎ *055-233-6134. Fax: 055-233-6147. Bus: 38 to Bobolino. Parking free. Rack rates: 270€ ($243) double, including breakfast. AE, DC, MC, V.*

Il Guelfo Bianco
$$$ Centro storico

North of the Duomo and a few steps from the Accademia Gallery, this recently renovated hotel occupies a 15th-century *palazzo* and a neighboring 17th-century *palazzo*. The guest rooms in the former are pleasantly furnished and come with beautiful bathrooms; many overlook the inner garden and courtyard. Don't worry about noise, though, even in rooms overlooking the street — the new windows are triple-paned! The rooms in the neighboring building boast ceiling frescoes, and some have painted wood and antique furniture.

Via Cavour 57r. ☎ *055-288-330. Fax: 055-295-203. Internet:* www.ilguelfo bianco.it. *Bus: 1, 6, or 17 to Cavour 02 or 1, 6, 7, 10, 11, 17, 25, 31, or 32 to San Marco 01; walk south on Via Cavour, the hotel is near the corner with Via Guelfa. Parking: 12.91€–21€ ($12–$19). Rack rates: 208€ ($187.20) double, including breakfast. AE, MC, V.*

Plaza Hotel Lucchesi
$$$$$ Centro storico

Near Santa Croce, the Plaza Hotel Lucchesi opened in 1860 at the eastern edge of the historic district. It's tastefully decorated and modernized, and you'll be pampered by the spacious guest rooms, modern baths, and comfortable furniture; 20 rooms have balconies. In addition to the normal amenities for a hotel of this caliber, it offers Internet access for guests.

Lungarno della Zecca Vecchia 38. ☎ *055-26-236. Fax: 055-248-0921. Internet:* www.plazalucchesi.it. *Bus: B or 13 Zecca Vecchia. Parking free. Rack rates: 387€ ($348.30) double, including breakfast. AE, DC, MC, V.*

Runner-up accommodations

Albergo Santa Croce
$$ Centro storico

This is a simple family-run hotel charging modest prices in an expensive town; just renovated, it's behind Piazza della Signoria and the Uffizi.

Via de' Bentaccordi 3. ☎ *055-217-000. Fax: 055-217-000. Internet:* www.hotelsantacroce.it. *Bus: 23.*

Hotel Casci
$$ Centro storico

Occupying a 15th-century *palazzo,* the Hotel Casci offers comfortable guest rooms and an excellent location just north of the Duomo. The breakfast room is decorated with original frescoes.

Via Cavour 13. ☎ *055-211-686. Fax: 055-239-6461. Internet:* www.hotelcasci.com. *E-mail:* info@hotelcasci.com. *Bus: 14 or 23.*

Hotel Hermitage
$$$$ Centro storico

This hotel is right off the Ponte Vecchio toward the Uffizi and has been recently renovated; many of the guest rooms have beautiful views over the river and all have antique furniture and premium bathrooms.

Vicolo Marzio 1. ☎ *055-287-216. Fax: 055-212-208. Internet:* www.hermitagehotel.com. *Bus: 23.*

Hotel Torre Guelfa
$$$ Centro storico

Near the Ponte Vecchio and the Uffizi, the Torre Guelfa offers pleasant guest rooms (many air-conditioned), good service, and a breathtaking view from the 13th-century tower. The owners of this landmark also own the Villa Rosa in Panzano, in the heart of the Chianti region (see Chapter 16).

Borgo SS. Apostoli 8. ☎ *055-239-6338. Fax: 055-239-8577. Bus: 23.*

Where to Dine in Florence

Tuscan cuisine is considered by many to be the best in Italy. It's flavorful yet light — Tuscany is poised between the north, where the food is heavier and uses butter and animal fats, and the south, where the flavors (dominated by tomato sauces) tend to be sharper. Many of the traditional dishes are farmland recipes based around plenty of fresh vegetables and game, though others were refined for the Florentine sovereigns and are fit for more modest modern stomachs.

The steak that ate Florence

The thing to order if you love meat is *bistecca alla fiorentina* (and if you like meat only once in a while, make this one of those whiles). This specialty is a 2-plus-pound steak for two — you can have it all by yourself if you feel up to it. The real *fiorentina* comes from the Chianina cow, a breed raised only in the Tuscan countryside and blessed with especially delectable meat. Most restaurants in Tuscany will have the *fiorentina* on their menus, but watch out for imitations. The real *fiorentina* used to be served on the bone, but for the moment (and until further notice) it is served boneless to safeguard against mad cow disease (steak purists have protested that the Chianina cows are local, have never mixed with imported animals, and are traditionally farmed — in other words, without suspect commercial feeds; they hope to have the ban lifted soon).

Primi, secondi, contorni, and dolce

Other Tuscan specialties are *crostini* (toasted bread with savory toppings), *affettati* (traditional cold cuts), *ribollita* (cabbage, bread, and vegetables in a thick soup), and *pappardelle al sugo di lepre* (large fettuccine with hare sauce). All of these are ***primi,*** or first courses. *Coniglio* (rabbit), *cinghiale* (wild boar), and a variety of meats grilled or fried are common for ***secondi,*** or main courses, and *fagioli all'uccelletto* (white Tuscan beans in a light tomato sauce) are a traditional ***contorno,*** or side dish. For ***dolce*** (dessert), the typical thing to have is *cantucci col vin santo* (hazelnut biscotti with a strong sweet wine) or *zuccotto* (a dome-shaped sponge cake filled with chocolate mousse, cream, dried fruits, and nuts).

And then there's the wine

To go with all of this, there's Tuscan wine. Chianti, perhaps the best-known Tuscan red, is often served as table wine *(vino della casa)* — even on tap, from huge casks — in restaurants. If you want to splurge, Vino Nobile di Montepulciano or — even better — Brunello di Montalcino are among Italy's greatest wines. For a white wine, try Vernaccia di San Gimignano, and for a dessert wine, the famous *vin santo. Buono appetito!*

Fixings for a garden picnic

For a cheap but delicious meal that'll give your wallet a rest and let you do as the locals do, drop by an *alimentari* (grocery shop) for the fixings for a picnic. You can buy some delicious Tuscan bread, country ham and cheese, fruit, mineral water, or wine. Stop by **Consorzio Agrario Pane and Co.,** Piazza S. Firenze 5R, at the corner of Via Condotta (☎ **055-213-063;** Bus: A to Condotta), where you'll find excellent *cinghiale* salami and a choice of local cheeses and cured pork delicacies, plus water, wine, and all the rest. The best place to have a picnic is in Fiesole or in the Boboli Gardens (see "The top sights" in this chapter).

The top restaurants

Cammillo dal 1945
$$$ Oltrarno   TUSCAN

This popular restaurant is housed in a *palazzo* that once belonged to the Medici family. The food is more upscale than that of the nearby Mamma Gina (listed in this section) and offers hearty and traditional dishes like fried boneless pigeon with artichokes, chicken with truffles and Parmesan cheese, and a choice of homemade fresh pastas with simple yet refined sauces.

Borgo San Jacopo 57R. ☎ 055-212-427. Reservations required. Bus: D to San Jacopo. Secondi: 13€–20€ ($12–$18). AE, DC, V. Open: Lunch and dinner Thurs–Tues; closed most of Aug and last two weeks in Dec.

Cantinetta Antinori
$$$$ Centro storico   TUSCAN

Antinori is the family name of the oldest and one of the largest producers of wine in Italy. The *cantinetta* (small wine cellar) occupies the 15th-century *palazzo* of this noble family and serves as their winery in town. Typical Tuscan dishes and many specialties from the Antinori farms are served in the restaurant to accompany the wine. Wine tasting, though, remains the top activity here, and you can stay at the counter and sample the various vintages.

They stole it from us

Italians love to remind people that French cuisine is derivative, largely descended from Tuscan specialties imported to France by the gourmet queen Caterina de' Medici in the 16th century. Not trusting Northern barbarians to cook food to her liking, she brought her cooks with her when she married Henri II of France. For example, French crêpes are derived from Florentine *crespelle,* a delightful preparation of layered dough and ham, cheese and tomato sauce, and often spinach as well.

Piazza Antinori 3R. ☎ *055-292-234. Reservations recommended. Bus: 6, 11, 36, or 37 to Antinori; Piazza Antinori is at the north end of Via de' Tornabuoni. Secondi: 13€–18€ ($12–$16). MC, V. Open: Lunch and dinner Mon–Fri.*

Il Cibreo

$$ (tavern), $$$$ (restaurant)   Centro storico   TUSCAN

This is a renowned chef's restaurant, where the dishes depend on the daily market finds and the kitchen's imagination. The backbone of the menu is historical Tuscan, with some recipes that go back to the Renaissance, but the interpretation is more modern. You won't find pasta or grilled meat, but there are soufflés, roasted and stuffed birds, and other oven-cooked specialties. On one side of the kitchen is a formal dining room and on the other a small tavern serving a smaller selection of dishes at lower prices.

Via de'Macci 118R. ☎ *055-234-1100. Reservations recommended. Bus: A to Borgo la Croce or Agnolo 04 stop; walk south on Via de' Macci from Piazza S. Ambrogio (outdoor vegetable market). Secondi: 11€ ($10) at trattoria and 23€ ($21) at restaurant. AE, DC, MC, V. Open: Lunch and dinner Tues–Sat; closed mid-July through early Sept.*

Da Ganino

$$$ Centro storico   TUSCAN

At this cozy, centrally located restaurant, you'll find ubiquitous Florentine specialties like *bistecca alla fiorentina* and *tagliatelle con tartufi* (homemade pasta with truffle sauce). In addition to the traditional menu, it offers a wide selection of daily specials. The food is deliciously prepared and served by an attentive staff.

Piazza dei Cimatori 4R. ☎ *055-214-125. Reservations recommended. Bus: A to Condotta or Cimatori; Via dei Cimatori is two short blocks north of Piazza della Signoria. Secondi: 8.26€–16€ ($7.43–$14.40). AE, DC, MC, V. Open: Lunch and dinner Mon–Sat.*

Don Chisciotte

$$$ Centro storico   TUSCAN/SEAFOOD

This restaurant is especially known for its fish dishes, like risotto with broccoli and baby squid and black squid-ink ravioli stuffed with shrimp and crayfish. The dining room is on the second floor of a typical *palazzo* and gets quite busy, especially on weekends. The food here is more creative and experimental than in other Florentine restaurants.

Via Ridolfi 4R. ☎ 055-475-430. Reservations recommended. Bus: 10, 14, or 23 to Strozzi 01 stop; northeast of the train station, walk on Via Filippo Strozzi and turn right on Via Ridolfi. Secondi: 14.46€–18€ ($13–$16). AE, DC, MC, V. Open: Lunch Tues–Sat; dinner Mon–Sat.

Enoteca Ristorante Mario

$$$$ Fiesole   TUSCAN

On Fiesole's main square, this restaurant offers a choice of excellent wines to accompany the nicely prepared Tuscan specialties. You'll find dishes that are typical of various parts of Tuscany, and the service is very good. You can start with *crostini* or *affettati misti* and follow with *pappardelle al sugo di lepre* and a wild boar stew or some delicious grilled vegetables. The restaurant occupies two floors, and the decor is stylish tavern style, with wooden ceiling beams and a small art gallery on the walls.

Piazza Mino 9R. ☎ 055-59-143. Reservations recommended on Sat. Bus: 7 to last stop in Fiesole; walk up toward the northwest side of the square, the restaurant is on the left. Secondi: 11€–16.50€ ($10–$14.40). AE, MC, V. Open: Lunch and dinner Tues–Sun.

Il Caffè

$$ Oltrarno   TUSCAN

Across from the Palazzo Pitti, this is a good spot for a quick bite during your sightseeing marathon. It's a snack bar that offers a basic choice of dishes all day long, with two prix-fixe menus at lunch and dinner. It's frequented by young crowds — especially at night, because it stays open until 2 a.m.

Piazza Pitti 9R. ☎ 055-239-6241. Reservations recommended on Sat. Bus: D to Pitti or 11, 36, or 37 to Serragli 03 or San Felice. Secondi: 6.71€–8.78€ ($6–$8). Prix-fixe menus: Lunch 6.20€ ($5.70) with appetizer and primo or 9.30€ ($8.37) with secondo as well; dinner 16€ ($14.40) or 21€ ($18.90), respectively. AE, MC, V. Open: Lunch and dinner daily.

Il Cantastorie

$$$ Centro storico   TUSCAN

Near the top sights, this pleasant country-style *ristorante* boasts wooden tables, high ceilings, and ironwork chandeliers and serves excellent wine and hearty food. It defines itself as a bit of Tuscan countryside in the heart of Florence, and you'll find all the typical specialties and some of the best Chianti you've ever had. *Ribollita, salsiccia e bietola* (sausages and green chard), *crostoni* (larger version of *crostini*), *filetto di maiale al finocchio* (pork filet in fennel sauce), Tuscan cold cuts and *sottoli* (vegetables preserved in herbs and olive oil), and homemade desserts are some of the choices you may find on a menu that changes daily. The same management runs Il Cantinone (also listed in this section).

Via della Condotta 7–9R. ☎ *055-239-6804. Reservations recommended on Sat. Bus: 14 or A to Ghibellina 01; walk west toward the Palazzo Vecchio to Via della Condotta. Secondi: 7.23€–11.36€ ($6.50–$10.22). MC, V. Open: Lunch and dinner Wed–Mon.*

Il Cantinone
$$$ Oltrarno   TUSCAN

Twin restaurant to Il Cantastorie, this has an even more convivial atmosphere, with low arched ceilings and long wooden tables. The food choice is similar, with all the best of traditional cuisine: soups, pasta, *cinghiale, coniglio, crostoni,* and delicious *affettati* and cheese, all accompanied by excellent wine. A particularly interesting offering is the prix-fixe menu *degustazione,* a meal for two including a different wine with each serving.

Looking for a gelato break?

Ice cream is certainly one of the best treats in Italy, and Florence is famous for its gelato. Of a different school from the Venetian, the Roman, or the Sicilian gelati, Florentine ice cream was invented — as were many other Tuscan gastronomic specialties — to gratify the palates of the Medicis. Alas — for our taste — the Medici family had a very big sweet tooth, judging from the result: Florentine ice cream is extremely sweet. The flavors are basically the same that you'll find all over Italy, with all kind of nuts — such as *pistacchio* (pistachio) and *nocciola* (filbert), fruits such as *limone* (lemon) and *pera* (pear), and creams such as chocolate and vanilla based. If you try it all over the country, you can practice being Italian by developing a strong opinion and defending it vociferously (we feel the best gelato is in Venice or Rome).

Try the celebrated **Gelateria Vivoli** (Via Isola delle Stinche 7R, between the Bargello and Santa Croce; ☎ 055-292-334; Bus: A or 14 to Piazza Santa Croce), which is truly a marvel for its zillions of flavors. There are many other *gelaterie* in town, such as **Coronas Café** (Via Calzaiuoli 72R; ☎ 055-239-6139; Bus: A to Orsanmichele) for good *produzione propria* (homemade) ice cream, and **Perchè No** (Via dei Tavolini 19R, just off Via Calzaiuoli; ☎ 055-239-8969; Bus: A to Orsanmichele), one of the oldest Florentine *gelaterie.* And if you can't go to Sicily on this trip, try the **Gelateria Carabè** (Via Ricasoli 60R, near the Accademia; ☎ 055-289-476; Bus: 6, 31, or 32 to S.S. Annunziata) for a typical Sicilian gelato or granita; the owner has the ingredients — lemons, almonds, pistachios — shipped from Sicily, and his ice cream has been rated among the best in Italy.

Via Santo Spirito 6R. ☎ *055-218-898. Reservations recommended on Sat. Bus: 11, 36, or 37 to Sauro or Frescobaldi; walk south to Via Santo Spirito, a block south of the river, off Ponte Santa Trinita and Ponte alla Carraia. Secondi: 7.23€–11.36€ ($6.50–$10.22). Menu degustazione: 21€ ($18.90) per person. MC, V. Open: Lunch and dinner Tues–Sun.*

La Carabaccia
$$$ Centro storico   TUSCAN

The name of this restaurant refers both to a traditional working boat that once plied the Arno and to *zuppa carabaccia,* a hearty onion soup favored by the Medicis during the Renaissance. The menu features daily choices of pasta, fresh vegetables, and fish according to what caught the chef's eye in the market, plus a variety of delicious homemade breads.

Via Palazzuolo 190R. ☎ *055-214-782. Reservations recommended on Sat. Bus: A to Moro; turn left from Via del Moro into Via Palazzuolo, west of Via de' Tornabuoni. Secondi: 7.75€–16€ ($7–$14.40). AE, MC, V. Open: Lunch Tues–Sat; dinner daily; closed two weeks in Aug.*

Le Mossacce
$$ Centro storico   TUSCAN

Between the Duomo and the Museo Nazionale del Bargello, this small *osteria* offers a choice of Tuscan specialties like *crespelle* and *ribollita* as well as *spaghetti alle vongole* (spaghetti with clams) and lasagne. Opened for a hundred years, it serves food that's excellent and moderately priced.

Via del Proconsolo 55R. ☎ *055-294-361. Reservations recommended. Bus: 14 or 23 to Proconsolo. Secondi: 6.20€–12.91€ ($5.60–$11.62). AE, MC, V. Open: Lunch and dinner Mon–Fri.*

Osteria del Caffè Italiano
$$ (tavern), $$$ (restaurant)   Centro storico   TUSCAN

With a restaurant in one room and a tavern in the other, this place allows you to choose between a complete meal or light fare. It serves the usual specialties with a fantastic choice of some of the best Tuscan wines. No wonder — thanks to the imaginative owners, this *osteria* is the urban antenna of Tuscany's ten best vineyards, which send a choice of their finest products here regularly. *Ribollita, farinata al cavolo nero* (thick black cabbage soup), *bollito misto* (mixed boiled meats), *cinghiale in salmì* (wild boar stew), *bistecca alla fiorentina,* and a great choice of *affettati misti* (Tuscan cold cuts) will more than satisfy you. The **Caffè Italiano** (Via Condotta 56R, near Via Calzaiuoli; ☎ 055-291-082) and **Alle Murate** (Via Ghibellina 52R; ☎ 055-240-618) are two other restaurants by the same owners, offering the same quality food but at higher prices.

Via Isola delle Stinche 11–13R. ☎ **055-289-080** *or 055-289-020. Reservations recommended on Sat. Bus: A or 14 to Piazza Santa Croce. Secondi: 6.20€–12.91€ ($5.60–$11.62). MC, V. Open: Lunch and dinner daily.*

Sabatini

$$$$ **Centro storico** **TUSCAN**

One of Florence's most famous restaurants and almost an institution, Sabatini is located practically in front of the rail station. The food is strictly Tuscan, and you'll be able to sample a *fiorentina* as well as a large choice of typical meat and pasta dishes, such as *bollito in salsa verde* (boiled meat with an herb sauce) and *scaloppine ai carciofi* (sautéed veal with artichokes). Typical desserts are served as well.

Via dei Panzani 9/Ar. ☎ **055-282-802.** *Reservations recommended. Bus: A, 6, 11, 36, or 37 to FS Santa Maria Novella 01; walk toward the church and turn right on Via dei Panzani on the east side of the church. Secondi: 18€–24€ ($16.30–$21). AE, DC, MC, V. Open: Lunch and dinner Tues–Sun.*

Runner-up restaurants

Mamma Gina

$$$ **Centro storico**

Just across the Ponte Vecchio, Mamma Gina is part of a chain of restaurants in Tuscany but none the worse for it.

Borgo San Jacopo 37R. ☎ **055-239-6009.**

Trattoria Boboli

$$ **Centro storico**

Near the Palazzo Pitti, this is a real mom-and-pop operation (it keeps weird hours because the chef also teaches school a few days a week in the winter) where you'll find all the specialties of Tuscan cuisine and a lot of warmth.

Via Romana 45R. ☎ **055-233-6401.**

Trattoria Garga

$$$$$ **Centro storico**

An elegant restaurant on the western edge of the *centro*, it offers contemporary interpretations of Tuscan fundamentals; the imaginative chef has become famous for his *taglierini alla Magnifico* (fresh angel-hair pasta with a mint-cream sauce flavored with lemon and orange rind and

Parmesan cheese). The secondi include game and seafood prepared with a variety of herb sauces and vegetables.

Via del Moro 48R. ☎ *055-239-8898.*

Exploring Florence

Florence is known as the birthplace of the Renaissance, as well as its heart. This city is the hometown of many of the greatest artists who ever lived. At every turn, you'll see beautiful paintings, legendary statues, and magnificent buildings. Take a look at the top sights we recommend and be sure to give yourself enough time to admire the ones that interest you the most.

Remember that to visit Florence, particularly in the high season, you will have to contend with millions of fellow visitors. The line for the Uffizi can easily be over three hours, and the one for the Accademia can be just as long. Reserving your tickets in advance is an excellent idea. If you really care about seeing the top museums and saving yourself hours of waiting in line, make reservations by calling ☎ **055-294-883** (Monday through Friday 8:30 a.m. to 6:30 p.m., Saturday 8:30 a.m. to 12:30 p.m.) or going online at www.firenzemusei.it before leaving home. You can reserve for each of the Florentine State museums — **Galleria degli Uffizi, Galleria dell'Accademia, Palazzo Pitti, Cappelle Medicee, Museo San Marco, Museo Nazionale del Bargello, Museo Archeologico,** and **Museo delle Pietre Dure.** But you probably need to reserve tickets only for the Uffizi and Accademia. How does it work? You make an appointment for a certain day and time, pay by credit card (or international bank draft if you don't have a credit card), and pick up your tickets at the Florence train station tourist office or at the Uffizi sales booth. Schedule your visit at the Uffizi first and you can pick up all your tickets there. There is a reservation fee of 1.55€ ($1.40).

Another good idea is to pick up at an information booth the photocopied sheet giving the most recent opening and closing times of museums and monuments. Florence has the most mind-boggling system of opening hours, with certain sites open on certain Saturdays, Sundays, and Mondays but not on others.

The top sights

Basilica di San Lorenzo and the Medici Chapels (Cappelle Medicee)
Centro storico

San Lorenzo, founded in the fourth century, was the parish church of the powerful Medici family, some of whom are buried in the **Medici Chapels**

(Cappelle Medicee). The church in its present form was designed by Brunelleschi (the inside of the facade was done by Michelangelo). The **Old Sacristy (Sagrestia Vecchia)** is a masterpiece of Renaissance architecture, designed by Brunelleschi and then decorated by Donatello, who executed the cherubs all around the cupola; also note the bronze pulpits from 1460 and his terra-cotta bust of St. Lawrence.

Leaving the church, you enter the Medici Chapels from Piazza Madonna. The octagonal **Chapel of the Princes (Cappella dei Principi)** is a gaudy baroque affair, decorated with marble and semiprecious stones and containing monumental tombs of Medici grand dukes. By contrast, the **New Sacristy (Sagrestia Nuova),** begun by Michelangelo and finished by the artist/author Vasari, is somber and impressive. The design reflects some of the elements of the Old Sacristy, but with bold innovations (it became one of the founding works of the Mannerist style). Michelangelo's funerary sculptures are brilliant. The **Monumento a Lorenzo Duca d'Urbino** represents the seated duke flanked by *Aurora* (Dawn) and *Crepuscolo* (Dusk). The **Monumento a Giuliano Duca di Nemours** (the son of Lorenzo the Magnificent) is shown rising, with the figures of *Giorno* (Day) and *Notte* (Night) at his sides. In front of the sacristy's altar is Michelangelo's *Madonna and Child.* Lorenzo the Magnificent is buried under this sculpture; because Michelangelo didn't live to complete his plan (he died in 1564), Lorenzo got a far less magnificent tomb than some of the lesser Medicis.

To the left of the altar is a small subterranean chamber containing some drawings attributed to Michelangelo, and you can see them by making an appointment when you enter. The place is more a tribute to Michelangelo than to the people who bankrolled the Renaissance. He also designed the 1524 **Laurentian Library (Biblioteca Laurenziana)**, where a few of the Medicis' fabulous manuscripts are displayed and which you can reach via an elaborate stone staircase from the cloister on the left of the basilica facade.

Cappelle Medicee: Piazza Madonna; and Basilica: Piazza San Lorenzo (just off from the Baptistry). Basilica ☎ 055-216-634; Cappelle Medicee ☎ 055-238-8602. Bus: 1, 6, or 17 to Martelli 02 or 36 or 37 to Olio. Open: Basilica Mon–Sat 10 a.m.–5 p.m.; Cappelle Medicee Tues–Sat 8:15 a.m.–5:00 p.m., Sun and holidays 8:15 a.m.–1:50 p.m., closed second and fourth Sun of each month and open second and fourth Mon of each month 8:15 a.m.–1:50 p.m.; Biblioteca Laurenziana Mon–Sat 9 a.m.–1 p.m. Admission: Basilica and Biblioteca Laurenziana 2.50€ ($2.25); Cappelle Medicee 6€ ($5.40).

Basilica di Santa Croce and Cappella Pazzi
Centro storico

Santa Croce, the world's largest Franciscan church, is significant both for its architecture and for what (and whom) it contains. The basilica was begun in 1294 by Arnolfo di Cambio, the first architect of the Duomo, and boasts some Giotto frescoes (not the most well preserved of his works); its

15th-century **Cappella Pazzi,** a wonderful example of early Renaissance architecture by Brunelleschi, is a museum containing Cimabue's famous *Crucifixion* among other works. You'll also find the final resting places of many notable Renaissance figures — over 270 tombstones pave the floor, and monumental tombs house luminaries like Michelangelo, Galileo, Rossini, and Machiavelli. Note that Dante's tomb is really just a *cenotaph* (an empty tomb): He died in exile in Ravenna and was buried there.

Piazza Santa Croce, just off Via de' Benci. ☎ *055-244-619. Bus: 23 or 71 to Santa Croce. Open: Summer Mon–Sat 9:30 a.m.–5:30 p.m., Sun 3:00–5:30 p.m.; winter Mon–Sat 9:30 a.m.–12:30 p.m. and 3:00–5:30 p.m., Sun 3:00–5:30 p.m. Admission: Free.*

Basilica di Santa Maria Novella and Museo di Santa Maria Novella
Centro storico

This Dominican church, built in the Gothic style from 1246 to 1360, is decorated with frescoes by Domenico Ghirlandaio, Filippino Lippi, and others. Adjoining the church is the entry to the museum, which occupies what was originally the cloisters annexed to the church. From here, you can access the **Green Cloister (Chiostro Verde),** named for the beautiful coloration of its frescoes (some by Paolo Uccello), and the **Cappellone degli Spagnoli,** named for Cosimo de' Medici's wife, Eleonora of Toledo (who permitted her fellow Spaniards to be buried here), and frescoed by Andrea di Buonaito between 1367 and 1369. The frescoes depict scenes from the lives of Christ and St. Peter, but the *Trionfo di San Tommaso* and the *Trionfo dei Domenicani* (the triumphs of St. Thomas and the Dominicans, respectively) are especially beautiful.

Piazza Santa Maria Novella. ☎ *055-215-918. Bus: 6, 11, 36, 37, or A to S.M. Novella 01 or 1, 17, and 23 to S.M. Novella 02. Open: Basilica Mon–Thurs and Sat, 9:30 a.m.–5:00 p.m., Fri, Sun, and holidays, 1–5 p.m.; Museum Mon–Thurs and Sat 9 a.m.–5 p.m., Sun 9 a.m.–2 p.m. Admission: Basilica 2.58€ ($2.32); Museum 2.60€ ($2.35).*

Baptistry (Battistero di San Giovanni)
Centro storico

Part of the tricolored marble trio on Piazza del Duomo (see also the Duomo and the Campanile di Giotto, in this section), the octagonal Baptistry is a beautiful example of the Florentine Romanesque style from the 11th and 12th centuries. It was likely built on the site of a Roman palace. The Baptistry's marvels are the exterior doors: The beautiful bronze reliefs adorning the north and east doors were the life's work of Lorenzo Ghiberti. He began the north doors in 1401 when he was 20 and finished them more than two decades later — one of the most important pieces of Renaissance sculpture, they depict Issac's sacrifice with marvelous detail. However, the east doors, completed shortly before the artist's death, are the real stars, known as the **Gates of Paradise** (when he saw them, Michelangelo supposedly said, "These doors are fit to stand at the gates of Paradise"); the ten panels show stunning scenes from the Old Testament. Alas, the panels presently in place are copies, because the originals have been moved to the **Museo dell'Opera del Duomo** (covered later in this section). The south doors were created by Andrea Pisano in the mid-14th century and show a more static Gothic style than Ghiberti's revolutionary work.

Piazza del Duomo. ☎ *055-230-2885. Bus: 14, 23, or 71 to Duomo or 36 or 37 to Olio. Open: Mon–Sat noon to 7 p.m., Sun 8:30 a.m.–2:00 p.m. Admission: 3€ ($2.70).*

Giotto's Bell Tower (Campanile di Giotto)
Centro storico

You may ask, "Wasn't Giotto a painter and not an architect?" Yes, but shortly before the end of his life he designed this beautiful, soaring bell tower banded with pink, green, and white marble, from which you have excellent views of the city and especially of the Duomo next door. Giotto had completed only the first two levels by his death in 1337, and the replacement architect had to correct the mistakes he'd made — like not making the walls thick enough to support the structure. Some of the artworks that originally graced the tower — by Donatello, Francesco Talenti, Luca della Robbia, and Andrea Pisano — are now housed in the **Museo dell'Opera del Duomo,** and copies take their place.

Note that there are 414 steps up to the top of this 84-meter tower, and the last entrance is 20 minutes before closing.

Piazza del Duomo. ☎ *055-230-2885. Bus: 14, 23, or 71 to Duomo. Open: Daily 8:30 a.m.–7:30 p.m. Admission: 6€ ($5.40).*

Chiesa di Orsanmichele
Centro storico

In the 14th century, the Orsanmichele was but a warehouse when it was the site of a miracle — an image of the Madonna supposedly appeared there. Soon afterward it was turned into a church. The original statues for the external niches were commissioned by city guilds and executed by Donatello, Ghiberti, Verrocchio, and others; most of these are displayed inside, protected from further weather damage, with copies taking their places outside. You'll find vaulted Gothic arches, 500-year-old frescoes, and an encrusted 14th-century tabernacle by Andrea Orcagna protecting a 1348 *Madonna and Child* by Bernardo Daddi. The church is connected by a second-floor walkway to the *palazzo* of the powerful wool merchants guild, built in 1308.

Via Arte della Lana, between the Duomo and Piazza della Signoria. ☎ *055-284-944. Bus: A to Orsanmichele. Open: Mon–Fri 9 a.m. to noon and 4–6 p.m., Sat, Sun, and holidays 9 a.m.–1 p.m. and 4–6 p.m.; closed the first and last Mon of each month. Admission: Free.*

Florence Attractions

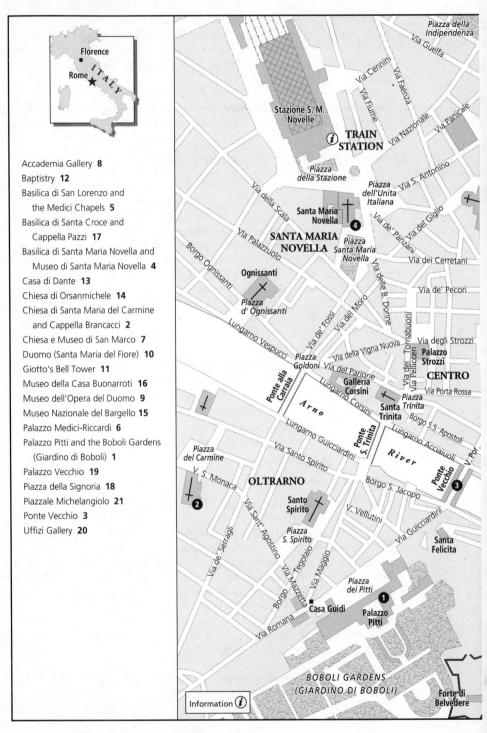

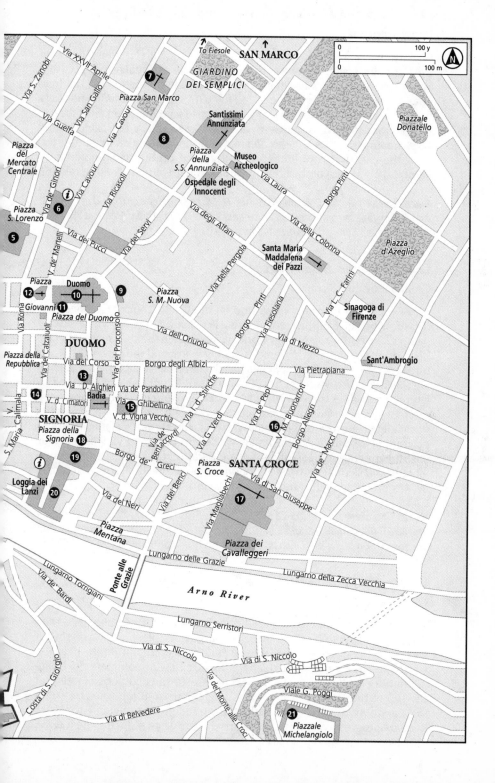

To Fiesole
SAN MARCO

GIARDINO
DEI SEMPLICI

7

Piazza San Marco

Santissimi
Annunziata

8

Piazza
della
S.S. Annunziata

Museo
Archeologico

Piazzale
Donatello

Piazza
del
Mercato
Centrale

Ospedale degli
Innocenti

Via Laura

6

Via degli Alfani

Santa Maria
Maddalena
dei Pazzi

Piazza
d'Azeglio

Piazza
S. Lorenzo

5

Via della Colonna

Piazza
Duomo

12   10   9

Giovanni   11

Piazza del Duomo

DUOMO

Piazza
S. M. Nuova

Sinagoga di
Firenze

Via dell'Oriuolo

Via di Mezzo

Piazza della
Repubblica

Via del Corso

Borgo degli Albizi

Via Pietrapiana

Sant'Ambrogio

13

Via D. Alighieri

Via de' Pandolfini

14

V. d. Cimatori

Badia

Via Ghibellina

15

V. d. Vigna Vecchia

SIGNORIA

Piazza della
Signoria   18

16

Borgo de' Greci

Piazza
S. Croce

SANTA CROCE

Loggia dei
Lanzi   20

Via del Neri

17

Via di San Giuseppe

Piazza
Mentana

Piazza dei
Cavalleggeri

Lungarno delle Grazie

Lungarno Torrigiani

Via de' Bardi

Ponte alle
Grazie

Arno River

Lungarno della Zecca Vecchia

Lungarno Serristori

Via di S. Niccolo

Via di S. Niccolo

Costa di S. Giorgio

Via di Belvedere

Viale G. Poggi

21

Piazzale
Michelangiolo

Chiesa di Santa Maria del Carmine and Cappella Brancacci

Centro storico

Luckily, the 1771 fire that devastated Santa Maria del Carmine didn't ruin the Cappella Brancacci, one of the masterpieces of Renaissance art. Here you'll find Masaccio's greatest works: Although he died at 27, the frescoes he executed here between 1424 and 1428 are remarkable not only for their perspective but also for their intense emotion, seen most clearly in the Expulsion from the Garden. Other frescoes by Masaccio are *St. Peter Healing the Sick with his Shadow* and the *Baptism of the Neophytes.* Near the end of the 15th century, the fresco cycle was completed by Filippino Lippi, son of the libertine monk and great painter Filippo Lippi.

Piazza del Carmine. ☎ *055-238-2195. Bus: 11, 36, or 37 to Serragli 01 or D to Carmine. Admission: Chiesa free; Cappella Brancacci 3.10€ ($2.79). Open: Mon and Wed–Sat 10 a.m.–5 p.m., Sun and holidays 1–5 p.m.*

Chiesa e Museo di San Marco

Centro storico

This Dominican monastery is a stop on the Grand Tour of Florence's art treasures because of the incomparable Fra Beato Angelico, whose vividly painted, exceptionally human works are early Renaissance masterpieces. The dormitory contains his famous *Annunciation,* and the part of the structure that's now a museum contains panel paintings and altar pieces, including the *Crucifixion.* Another notable work is Ghirlandaio's *Last Supper.* The church itself is decorated with works by Fra Bartolomeo and other artists. Another former resident — actually the prior — of the monastery was the passionate reformer Girolamo Savonarola. His sermons against worldly corruption brought him into conflict with Pope Alexander VI (who had four illegitimate children, including Cesare and Lucrezia Borgia). Excommunicated and betrayed by the Florentines who at one time supported him, he was executed on Piazza della Signoria in 1498.

Piazza San Marco 1. ☎ *055-238-8608. Bus: 1, 6, 7, 10, 11, 17, 20, 25, or 33 to San Marco 01. Open: Tues–Fri 8:15 a.m.–1:50 p.m., Sat 8:15 a.m.–6:50 p.m.; open second and fourth Sun 8:15 a.m.–7:00 p.m. and first, third, and fifth Mon 8:15 a.m.–1:50 p.m.*

Duomo (Santa Maria del Fiore)

Centro storico

The Duomo, surmounted by Filippo Brunelleschi's famous red-tiled dome, is the symbol of Florence. The largest in the world at the time it was built, the dome is 150 feet wide and 300 feet high from the drum — where previous builders had left off, unsure how to complete the building until Brunelleschi showed them how — to the distinctive lantern at the top of the cupola. Brunelleschi's ingenious solution was constructing the dome of two layers with a space inside and having each layer become progressively thinner toward the top, thus reducing the weight.

You can climb 463 spiraling steps to the top inside the space between the layers (the last ascent is 40 minutes before closing). The dome was finished in 1436, but other architects fiddled with it through the ages, and the facade was redone in neo-Gothic style hundreds of years later. As a whole, the Duomo is more impressive on the outside than on the inside, its alternating bands of white, green, and pink marble echoing the patterns on the Baptistry and Campanile. Inside are Paolo Uccello frescoes from the 1430s and 1440s, including his memorial to Sir John Hawkwood, an English mercenary hired by the Florentines (they promised him a statue but gave him a fresco of a statue instead). Restored in 1996, the frescoes inside the dome were begun by Giorgio Vasari and finished by Frederico Zuccari in 1579. The **New Sacristy** is where Lorenzo de' Medici hid out after he and his brother (who was murdered) were ambushed during Mass by some of their rivals in one of Florence's endless power struggles; its bronze doors are the work of Luca della Robbia.

Under the Duomo are the remains of **Santa Reparata,** the former Duomo, torn down in 1375 to build the new cathedral. Excavations, begun in 1966, uncovered a rich trove of material dating back over centuries, including walls of Roman houses and Roman ceramic, glass, and metalwork, as well as paleo-Christian and medieval objects (Brunelleschi's tombstone was also discovered here).

Piazza del Duomo. ☎ *055-230-2885. Bus: 14, 23, or 71 to Duomo. Open: Mon–Wed and Fri 10 a.m.–5 p.m., Thurs and first Sat of each month 10:00 a.m.–3:30 p.m.; other Saturdays 10:00 a.m.–4:45 p.m., Sun and holidays 1:30–4:45 p.m. Cupola: Mon–Fri 8:30 a.m.–7:00 p.m., Sat 8:30 a.m.–5:40 p.m., except first Saturday of month, 8:30 a.m.–4:00 p.m. Admission: Cathedral free; cupola 6€ ($5.40).*

Uffizi Gallery (Galleria degli Uffizi)
Centro storico

The Uffizi is mind-blowing, occupying a Renaissance *palazzo* built by Vasari to house the administrative offices (*uffizi* means "offices") of the Tuscan Duchy (Granducato di Toscana). Here you pictorially experience the birth of the Renaissance, seeing how the changing ideas about the nature of humanity (the new humanism) were translated into visual form. (The medieval artists weren't bad painters — their work reflected a holistically Christian viewpoint, with no concept of "nature" as something separate from the divine.) Start with Cimabue's great *Crucifixion,* still inspired by the flat forms and ritualized expressions of Byzantine art. With the work of his student Giotto, the human figure began to take on greater and greater realism.

The rooms devoted to Sandro Botticelli — with his *Birth of Venus* (the goddess emerging from the waves on a shell) and *Primavera* (an ambiguous allegory of spring) — show how the revival of classical (pagan) myth opened a new range of expression and subject. Don't miss, across from Botticelli's Venus, the spectacular **triptych** of Hugo van der Goes, whose

The Uffizi Gallery

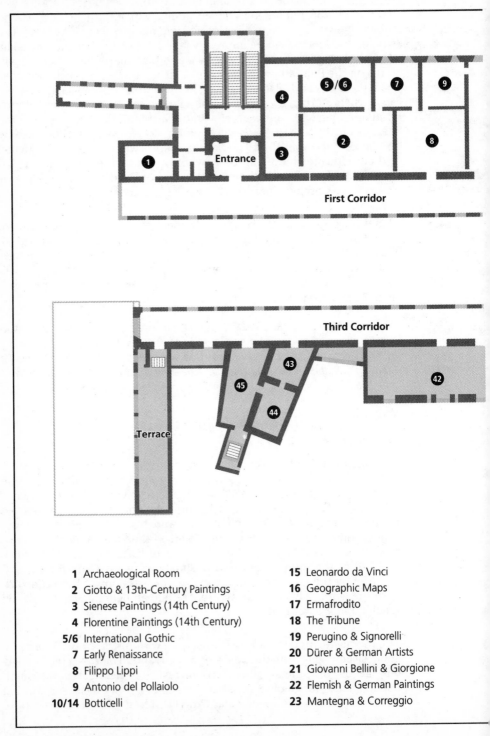

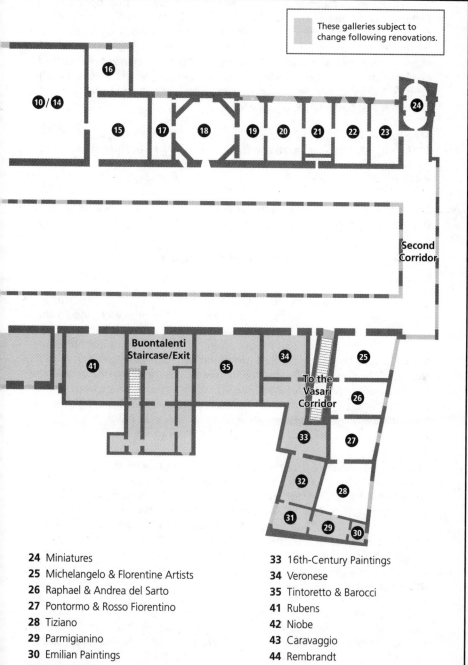

These galleries subject to change following renovations.

24 Miniatures
25 Michelangelo & Florentine Artists
26 Raphael & Andrea del Sarto
27 Pontormo & Rosso Fiorentino
28 Tiziano
29 Parmigianino
30 Emilian Paintings
31 Dosso Dossi
32 Sebastiano del Piombo & Lorenzo Lotto

33 16th-Century Paintings
34 Veronese
35 Tintoretto & Barocci
41 Rubens
42 Niobe
43 Caravaggio
44 Rembrandt
45 18th-Century Paintings

humanism emerges in the intensity of expression and powerful realism of his poor peasants (also look for the fanciful monster lurking in the right panel). Piero della Francesca's **diptych** with full-profile portraits of Federico da Montefeltro and his wife is a justly famous work painted in the third quarter of the 15th century. Francesca's luminosity is matched by the incredible detail — he brings his subjects to life, warts and all. Masaccio's **Madonna and Child with St. Anne,** Leonardo's **Adoration of the Magi** and **Annunciation,** several Raphaels, Michelangelo's **Holy Family,** Caravaggio's **Bacchus** . . . there's so much at the Uffizi that you should really come twice if you can.

Piazza degli Uffizi 6, just off Piazza della Signoria (Palazzo Vecchio). ☎ *055-38-8651 or 055-294-883 for reservations. Bus: 23 or 71 to Galleria Uffizi. Open: Tues–Sun 8:15 a.m.–6:50 p.m.; Sat June 15–Sept 15 8:15 a.m.–10:00 p.m. Admission: 6.50€ ($5.85).*

Remember to reserve your tickets for the Uffizi and the Accademia (for details, see the beginning of this section).

Accademia Gallery (Galleria dell'Accademia)

Centro storico

The Accademia's undisputed star is Michelangelo's **David** (there's often a line to go in to see him, so make a reservation or try getting to the museum just as it opens or an hour or two before closing). Michelangelo was just 29 when he took a 17-foot column of white Carrara marble abandoned by another sculptor and produced the masculine perfection of *Il Gigante (The Giant),* as *David* is nicknamed. The statue stands beneath a rotunda built expressly for it in 1873, when it was moved here from Piazza della Signoria (a copy stands in its place on the square). In 1991, *David* was attacked by a lunatic with a hammer, so you have to view him through a reinforced-glass shield (like the *Pietà* in Rome).

Many people don't realize that the gallery offers many other remarkable Florentine works as well. Among the paintings are Perugino's **Assumption** and **Descent from the Cross** (the latter done in collaboration with Filippino Lippi); **The Virgin of the Sea,** thought to have been painted by Botticelli; and Pontormo's **Venus and Cupid.** *David* isn't the only Michelangelo sculpture here — his **St. Matthew** and his interesting series of **Slaves** (which are either unfinished or were poetically left partly escaped from the original hunks of stone) also illustrate the master's remarkable skills.

Via Ricasoli 60 between the Duomo and Piazza San Marco. ☎ *055-238-8609 or 055-294-883 for reservations. Bus: 6, 31, or 32 to S.S. Annunziata. Open: Tues–Sun 8:15 a.m.–6:50 p.m.; Sat June 15–Sept 15 8:15 a.m.–10:00 p.m. Admission: 6.50€ ($5.85).*

Museo Nazionale del Bargello
Centro storico

The Bargello, built in 1255, shows what a medieval/early-Renaissance government office building looked like. The word *bargello* means "cop," and it was used to refer to the chief of police, a post created in 1574; this was his headquarters; it also housed an armory. Now the Bargello is a treasury of Renaissance sculpture, including two Donatello **Davids** (one in marble, the other in bronze) and several works by Michelangelo, including another **David** (it may also be Apollo), a **bust of Brutus,** and a **Bacchus** he executed when he was only 22. You'll also find works by Benvenuto Cellini, whose **Autobiography** offers a fascinating look at Florence during the Renaissance and is well worth reading. You can also compare two bronze panels of the **Sacrifice of Isaac,** one by Brunelleschi and one by Ghiberti, which were submitted in the famous contest to see who'd get to do the Baptistry doors (see "Baptistry" in this section). The Bargello also has impressive collections of Islamic art, majolica, and terra-cotta works by the della Robbia family.

Via del Proconsolo 4. ☎ *055-238-8606 or 055-294-883 for reservations. Bus: 23 to Galleria Uffizi or B to Loggia del Grano. Open: Tues–Sat 8:15 a.m.–1:50 p.m.; Sun and holidays 8:15 am–5:00 p.m. Open first, third, and fifth Mon each month. Admission: 4€ ($3.60).*

Museo dell'Opera del Duomo
Centro storico

This museum is where you'll need to go to see the original Renaissance works, such as Ghiberti's breathtaking bronze **Gates of Paradise panels** for the Baptistry, that were removed from their settings to avoid damage from pollution or maniacs with hammers. The museum also contains works that once graced Giotto's Campanile, like Donatello's highly realistic **sculpture of Habbakuk;** his **Maddalena (Mary Magdalen),** in polychromed wood, is perhaps equally striking for its tortured expression. Michelangelo is represented with a **Pietà;** Luca della Robbia's **cantoria** (choir loft) faces a similar work by Donatello, offering an example of the diversity of Renaissance styles. At press time, the museum was temporarily closed; ask at the tourist office if it is open when you arrive.

Piazza Duomo 9, behind the Duomo. ☎ *055-230-2885. Bus: 14, 23, or 71 to Duomo. Open: Mon–Sat 9:00 a.m.–7:30 p.m., Sun and holidays 9:00 a.m.–1:40 p.m. Admission: 6€ ($5.40).*

Palazzo Pitti and the Boboli Gardens (Giardino di Boboli)
Oltrarno

Begun in 1458 by the textile merchant/banker Luca Pitti, this golden *palazzo* was finished by the Medicis in 1549 (they tripled its size and added the Boboli Gardens). It houses an important painting collection in the **Palatine Gallery (Galleria Palatina).** Some of the greatest works are a collection of Raphaels, including his *Madonna of the Chair* and *La Fornarina* (modeled on the features of his Roman mistress); perhaps the largest single collection of works by moody psychological painter Andrea del Sarto (see Robert Browning's poem on him); and several Titians.

The *palazzo* also houses seven other museums. On the mezzanine from the left of the courtyard, the **Silver Museum (Museo degli Argenti)** houses collections of objects in precious metals, ivory, and crystal. Notable are the semiprecious stone vases of Lorenzo de' Medici and the cameos and carved precious stones of the Medici collection. The **Porcelain Museum (Museo delle Porcellane)** recently reopened, and contains a collection of precious porcelain by great European makers, including Sèvres, Chantilly, and Meissen. On the third floor is the **Modern Art Gallery (Galleria d'Arte Moderna),** with a collection of Italian paintings from the 1800s and early 1900s, including some famous paintings of the movement of the Macchiaioli (the Italian counterpart to the French Impressionists; notably the paintings of Giovanni Fattori and Telemaco Signorini). By appointment you can visit the second-floor **Royal Apartments (Appartamenti Reali),** with furnishings from various Medici villas; and the **Contini-Bonacossi Collection,** temporarily housed in the **Palazzina della Meridiana,** an 18th-century neoclassical pavilion, and including paintings by important artists like Cimabue, Veronese, and Bellini and sculpture like the famous *Martirio di San Lorenzo* (Martyrdom of St. Lawrence) by Bernini. You can make the appointment for your visit to the museum that interests you (or for all of them) at the information booth inside the Uffizi, where you can also buy your ticket (access will depend on availability of personnel, but the admission should be included in your ticket to the Uffizi).

Behind the palace is one of the most grandiose examples of an Italian garden, the **Boboli Gardens.** This expanse of 45,000 square meters (11.1 acres) of gardens was designed in the 16th century and added to in the 18th and 19th centuries. Among the highlights are several fountains and sculptures, such as the 17th-century **Artichoke Fountain (Fontana del Carciofo)** and the **Piazzale dell'Isolotto** off the Viottolone (large lane) lined with laurels, cypresses, and pines and punctuated by statues. On the *piazzale* (a small piazza) is the beautiful **Ocean Fountain (Fontana dell'Oceano).**

Piazza de' Pitti, just on the other side of the Ponte Vecchio. ☎ *055-238-8614 or 055-294-883 for reservations. Bus: D to Pitti. Open: Galleria Palatina Tues–Sun 8:15 a.m.–6:50 p.m., Saturdays June 15–Sept 15 open until 10 p.m. Giardino di Boboli daily 8:15 a.m. to one hour before sunset. Museo degli Argenti Tues–Sat 8.15 a.m.–1:50 p.m., open second and fourth Mon and first, third, and fifth Sun of each month; Museo delle Porcellane Tues–Sat 9:00 a.m.–1:30 p.m., open second and fourth Mon and first, third, and fifth Sun of each month; Galleria d'Arte Moderna and Galleria delle Costume, Tues–Sat 8:15 a.m.–1:50 p.m; open second and fourth Mon and first, third, and fifth Sun of each month. Admission: Galleria Palatina 8.50€*

($7.65); Giardino di Boboli 3€ ($2.70), including Museo delle Porcellane 2.50€ ($2.15); Museo degli Argenti 2€ ($1.80); Galleria d'Arte Moderna and Galleria delle Costume, cumulative ticket 5€ ($4.50); Royal Apartments, 10.33€ ($9.30).

Palazzo Vecchio
Centro storico

The Palazzo Vecchio (Old Palace) looks either like a fortress disguised as a palace or a palace trying to be a fort. It's actually a little bit of both, built as the town hall from 1299 to 1302. Cosimo de' Medici (that's Giambologna's equestrian statue of him in the middle of the piazza; see "Piazza della Signoria" in this section) and his family made changes to the *palazzo* in the mid-16th century. The highlight of the interior is the **Hall of the 500 (Sala dei Cinquecento),** where the 500-man council met when Florence was still a republic and before the Medicis' despotic rule. The frescoes by Vasari and others are nothing to write home about, yet those planned by Michelangelo but never painted would've been; note Michelangelo's **Genius of Victory** statue. Bronzino's **paintings in the private chapel of Eleanora di Toledo** (wife of Cosimo), Donatello's **Judith and Holofernes,** and Ghirlandaio's fresco of **St. Zenobius Enthroned** are other notable works. Some of the collections are open only at certain times (mainly in summer), such as the collection of musical instruments. In summer, you can view the city from the balustrade and hope for a breath of wind.

Piazza della Signoria. ☎ 055-276-8465. Bus: 23 or 71 to Galleria Uffizi or B to Loggia del Grano. Open: Winter, Fri–Wed 9 a.m.–7 p.m., Thurs 9 a.m.–2 p.m.; June 15–Sept 15, Tues, Wed, and Sat 9 a.m.–7 p.m.; Mon and Fri 9 a.m.–11 p.m.; Thurs and Sun 9 a.m.–2 p.m. Admission: 5.70€ ($5.13).

Piazza della Signoria
Centro storico

Florence's most famous square was built in the 13th and 14th centuries. Signoria is the name of the political system that governed the city at the time — the Medicis were the *signori* (lords) — and this was the political heart of Florence. A beautiful example of medieval architecture, the L-shaped square is flanked by the **Palazzo Vecchio** (see listing in this section) on the east side and the famous **Loggia della Signoria** on the south. The loggia is also called the Loggia dei Lanzi (after the *Lanzichenecchi*, soldiers who camped there in the 16th century) or the Loggia dell'Orcagna (after a belief it was built by Andrea di Cione, who was known as Orcagna). In fact, this Gothic structure was built from 1376 to 1382 by Benci Cione and Simone Talenti for political ceremonies. Later it was used as a sculpture workshop and is still used as a showplace for statues. The most famous piece here is Giambologna's **Ratto delle Sabine (Rape of the Sabines),** an essay in three-dimensional Mannerism; also by Giambologna are the **bronze of Duke Cosimo de' Medici on horseback** and *Hercules with Nessus the Centaur.* Also here is Benvenuto Cellini's famous **Perseus** holding up the severed head of

Medusa (the original was moved to the Uffizi in 1996 and replaced with a copy, but the original was replaced here in late 2000).

The **Fountain of Neptune (Fontana del Nettuno)**, at the corner of the Palazzo Vecchio, was built by the architect Ammannati in 1575 and criticized by many, including Michelangelo; Florentines used to mock it as Il Biancone ("big whitey"). The small disk in the ground near the fountain marks the spot where the famous Dominican monk Savonarola was executed. His efforts to purify the Florentines and rid the church of corruption (he directed the burning of jewels, books, riches, and art pieces judged too "pagan" on pyres erected in Piazza della Signoria) gave him increased political power but also led to his excommunication from the church. He was condemned as a heretic and burned on the square in 1498.

The ***David*** that you can see in the square is a copy of the original statue by Michelangelo, which was moved to the Accademia in the 19th century. The statue flanking it is ***Ercole* (Heracles)** by Baccio Bandinelli.

Off Via dei Calzaiuoli. Bus: 23 or 71 to Galleria Uffizi or B to Loggia del Grano.

Ponte Vecchio
Centro storico

The Ponte Vecchio (Old Bridge) is the only remaining original of Florence's many lovely medieval bridges spanning the Arno — the Germans blew the rest of them up during their retreat from Italy near the end of the World War II (they've since been rebuilt). This symbol of the city of Florence offers beautiful views and thrives with shops selling leather goods, jewelry, and other commodities. If you look up, you'll see the famous **Vasari Corridor (Corridoio Vasariano).** The bridge was built in 1345, but after the completion of the Palazzo Pitti in the 16th century, Cosimo de' Medici commissioned Vasari to build an aboveground "tunnel" running along the Ponte Vecchio rooftops linking the Uffizi with the Pitti. The corridor was richly decorated with art, and you can visit it from the Uffizi at certain times.

At the end of Via Por Santa Maria. Bus: B to Ponte Vecchio.

More cool things to see and do

Florence's major sites are so extensive they could easily soak up all your time, so you probably won't get to the minor ones. On the other hand, you could get sick of being inside, and museum fatigue is always a risk (especially for kids). Here are some further ways to see Florence:

- ✔ The **Casa di Dante** (Via Dante Alighieri; ☎ 055-219-516; Bus: A to Condotta) may be called Dante's House, but it isn't really. It's in the neighborhood where he lived but is actually a 1910 reconstruction and contains a museum of Dante's life and work. If you're especially interested in the man many consider the greatest European poet of any age, it contains memorabilia and objects you may find curious. The house is open Wednesday through Monday 10 a.m. to 4 p.m. (Sunday to 2 p.m.), and admission is 2.58€ ($2.33).

✔ Fiesole makes a wonderful day-trip, 8km (5 miles) north of Florence. Probably one of the nicest bus rides you'll ever take is the one through the green fields and past the villas lining the route to this hill town (take the no. 7 from SMN train station or Piazza San Marco and get off at the last stop). Fiesole existed before Florence — it started as an Etruscan settlement in the sixth century B.C. and retains the character of a small town and its independence as a municipality. In the summer, the town hosts music, theater, and other cultural events, making it a great place to escape the heat and congestion below. Be sure to visit the 1028 **Duomo (Cattedrale di San Romolo)** on the main square, Piazza Mino da Fiesole. Also definitely worth a visit is the archaeological area, which includes the **Roman Theater and Civic Museum (Teatro Romano e Museo Civico,** Via Partigiani 1; ☎ **055-59-477**). The theater, built in the first century B.C., is where outdoor concerts are held in the summer. Surrounding this picturesque ruin are the remains of baths and even some Etruscan walls from the fourth century B.C., as well as a Roman temple. They're open in the winter Wednesday through Monday 9:30 a.m. to 5:00 p.m., and in the summer daily from 9:30 a.m. to 7:00 p.m. The 6.20€ ($5.58) admission includes entrance to the **Museo Bandini** near the Duomo with its 13th– to 15th-century Tuscan art. A special ticket, the *Biglietto Fiesole Musei,* includes the roundtrip bus from Firenze, the archaeological museum, the Museo Bandini and other sites for 7.20€ ($6.48). It is sold at the train station and in bars and newsstands displaying a sticker.

✔ The **Museo della Casa Buonarroti** (Via Ghibellina 70; ☎ **055-241-752;** Bus: 14 or A to Ghibellina 01) may never have had Michelangelo as a tenant, but he and his heirs did own it. His grand-nephew got the homage going early by turning the house into a museum. Some of the holdings are very interesting; they include some of the master's earliest works, such as the *Madonna of the Steps,* which he did when only in his mid-teens. The museum is open Wednesdays through Mondays 9.30 a.m. to 2:00 p.m., and admission is 6.20€ ($5.58).

✔ The **Palazzo Medici-Riccardi** (Via Cavour 1; ☎ **055-276-0340;** Bus: 14, 23, or 71 to Duomo) is where Cosimo de' Medici and his family lived before they took over the Palazzo Vecchio. It was built by Michelozzo in 1444 and has a less-heavy feeling than later *palazzi,* such as the Pitti. Benozzo Gozzoli, a student of Fra Angelico's, decorated the chapel with marvelous frescoes. The *palazzo* gives a good idea of what upper-class Florentine life was like during the Renaissance. It's open Thursday through Tuesday 9 a.m. to 7 p.m., and admission is 4€ ($3.60).

And on your left, the Uffizi: Seeing Florence by guided tour

To get the ins and outs of Florence's sights, a guided tour may be just the ticket. We've listed a few that we feel will give you a comprehensive, enjoyable tour. Be sure to ask about the length of tours, lunch breaks, and the maximum number of participants allowed per tour.

If you want to participate in a bus tour, call **American Express** (☎ 055-50-981) or **SitaSightseeing** (☎ 055-214-721), both offering the same kinds of tours of Florence and of the major attractions in Tuscany. We feel, though, that Florence is best seen on foot because the historic center is closed to traffic. If you contact the **Ufficio Guide Turistiche** (Viale Gramsci 9a; ☎ 055-247-8188), you'll be able to organize a guided tour more tailored to your needs or even a private tour.

Shopping

Florence offers some very nice specialty products, many available at the outdoor markets, where you can make some great buys if you keep in mind a few simple shopping rules:

- ✔ **Don't expect things to be cheap.** A good leather jacket will cost a few hundred dollars, but you should be able to get a level of quality that would be difficult to find back home, especially at that price.

- ✔ **Remember that light bargaining is allowed in outdoor markets.**

- ✔ **Try to have a fair idea in your mind of what things are worth as well as what you can afford.** If you aren't an expert on the items you want to buy, shop around and find out as much as you can before making your decision.

The bottom line? Buy an item if you really like it for what sounds to you a fair price, without worrying too much about getting the best bargain in the world — being happy with what you bought matters more than saving $20.

Shops are generally open daily from 10:00 a.m. to 1:30 p.m. and 4 to 8 p.m. and closed on Monday mornings, whereas open-air markets are usually open during lunchtime but close earlier in the evening.

Remember that all crowded areas are the preferred hunting ground for pickpockets and purse-snatchers. Don't display your money too liberally and keep an eye on your pockets and purse — otherwise your shopping spree will be very short indeed.

The best shopping areas

For elegant shopping, the place to go is the area of town along **Via de' Tornabuoni** and left on **Via della Vigna Nuova;** you'll find all the big names of Italian fashion and a choice of reliable but expensive boutiques. Less luxurious is the parallel area of **Via Roma, Piazza della Repubblica,** and **Via Calimala** toward the Ponte Vecchio.

What to look for and where to find it

Florence is famous for its leather and woven straw, embroidered linen and lace, paper goods, and gold jewelry. It's also a great place to buy Italian fashions and designs, in both garments and housewares.

For browsing and also for some great gift ideas, try **Viceversa** (Via Ricasoli 53R; ☎ **055-239-8281;** Bus: 6, 31, or 32 to S.S. Annunziata) for housewares, and **Emporium** (Via Guicciardini 122R; ☎ **055-212-646;** Bus: D to Pitti) for a variety of stylish accessories. **Controluce** (Via della Vigna Nuova 89R; ☎ **055-239-8871;** Bus: 6, 11, 36, or 37 to Tornabuoni) has a beautiful assortment of designer lamps and accessories.

For special items, we cover the places to hit in the following sections.

Embroidery

Florentine embroideries are renowned around the world, but they don't come cheap. Try **Cirri** (Via Por Santa Maria; ☎ **055-239-6593;** Bus: B to Ponte Vecchio).

Gold

The **Ponte Vecchio** is the place to go for the gold: It's one shop after another, all with pretty much the same merchandise. The prices are far from as good as tradition holds — maybe after 500 years and a trillion tourists, the street has gotten a tad stale — and it's difficult to find something original. One of the best jewelry stores in town is **C.O.I.** (Via Por Santa Maria 8R, second floor; ☎ **055-283-970;** Bus: B to Ponte Vecchio), with a very large selection organized by type — bunches of bracelets, drawers of earrings, and so on. Go with a precise idea in mind; it isn't the place for browsing, the staff is overworked, and the shop is always crowded.

Leather products

Starting by the church of San Lorenzo, just northwest of the Duomo, the **Mercato San Lorenzo** (Bus: 1, 6, or 17 to Martelli 02 or 36 or 37 to Olio) is a famous open-air leather market, but the average quality of its goods has much declined over the years. Finding a really wonderful item is difficult and requires a lot of looking. On the other hand, the market is an attraction in itself, and many consider a visit to Florence incomplete without it.

If you prefer the reliability and service of a boutique, head for Via de' Tornabuoni and the side street Via del Parione. Among the dependable leather shops here are the famous **Beltrami** (Via de' Tornabuoni 48R; ☎ 055-287-779; Bus 6, 11, 36, or 37 to Tornabuoni/Via de' Panzani 1, near the church of Santa Maria Novella; ☎ 055-212-661; Bus: 6, 11, 36, 37, or A to S.M. Novella 01 or 1, 17, or 23 to S.M. Novella 02) — the first address is the main shop and the second is where to go for last season's discounted items. For gloves, cross the Ponte Vecchio and go to **Madova Gloves** (Via Guicciardini 1R; ☎ 055-239-6526; Internet: www.madova.com; Bus: D to Pitti). If you want to learn about the ancient art of leather embossing, head for **Santa Croce's leather school** (Piazza Santa Croce, enter from the church's right transept; ☎ 055-244-533; Bus: A or 14 to Piazza Santa Croce).

Stationery and paper goods

Exquisite papers, especially the marbleized kind, are another Florentine specialty. The most famous paper shop is **Pineider** (Piazza della Signoria 13R; ☎ 055-284-655; Bus: 23 or 71 to Galleria degli Uffizi or B to Loggia del Grano/Via Tornabuoni 76; ☎ 055-211-605; Bus: 6, 11, 36, or 37 to Tornabuoni). Opened in 1774, it has been a purveyor of paper to many crowned heads. Another top store, this one dating back to the 19th century, is **Giulio Giannini & Figlio** (Piazza Pitti 37R; ☎ 055-212-621; Bus: D to Pitti), where you'll find an excellent choice of stationery and marbleized paper.

Straw products

Stretching from Piazza della Repubblica to the Ponte Vecchio is the Mercato Nuovo (or della Paglia, "of straw"), where all kinds of straw products are sold (Bus: B to Ponte Vecchio). The items range from hats to bags to baskets to things you didn't know could be made out of straw.

Nightlife

As is true in the rest of Italy, the most common version of nightlife in Florence is hanging out in a pub with a group of friends, going for a drink in a trendy bar, or taking a stroll and enjoying some gelato in the historic center. The other preferred activity is listening to some music in a club or (mainly for the young) dancing in one of the popular discos out of town.

The performing arts

During the month of May, Florence blossoms with music. It's the month of the **Maggio Musicale Fiorentino,** which is Italy's oldest music festival. (For reservations, call toll-free in Italy ☎ 800-112-211, or 055-213-535; Fax: 055-277-9410; reservations accepted starting in September). Tickets are sold online, too (www.maggiofiorentino.com), and cost 20€ to

155€ ($18 to $140). Continuing until the end of June, this concert and dance series includes famous performers and world premiers. It's mainly held in the **Teatro Comunale** (Corso Italia 16; ☎ 055-211-158), which also has a regular program of ballet and opera at other times of the year.

Many churches present **evening concerts.** The easiest way to find out about these performances is to check the posters on the walls for announcements and pick up a free copy of the listing of events at the Via Cavour tourist office (see "Street smarts: Where to get information after you arrive" in this chapter). The most sought-after are the concerts of the **Florentine Chamber Orchestra** in the Chiesa di Orsanmichele during fall; tickets are available at the city's box office in Via Faenza 139R (☎ 055-210-084; Bus: A to Orsanmichele).

The **Teatro Verdi** (Via Ghibellina 99; ☎ 055-212-320) is a smaller theater that offers mainly dance and classical music performances.

Bars and pubs

The oldest *caffè* in town is **Gilli** (Piazza della Repubblica 39R/Via Roma 1R; ☎ 055-213-896; Bus: A to Orsanmichele), which dates back to the 18th century. Not only is it in a great location, but it has an elegant decor. **Giacosa** (Via de' Tornabuoni 83R; ☎ 055-239-6226; Bus: 6, 11, 36, or 37 to Tornabuoni) is known for its drinks, particularly the Negroni (the ancestor of Italian *aperitivo,* the bittersweet pre-lunch or pre-dinner drink), which apparently was invented here. Giacosa is closed on Sundays.

The upscale **Caffè degli Artisti/Art Bar** (Via del Moro 4R; ☎ 055-28-76-61; Bus: 6, 11, 36, or 37 to Antinori) is a longtime expatriate favorite. An interesting crowd comes to mingle and talk (though the music can get loud) and sample the long list of cocktails and mixed drinks that are uncommon in this wine-imbibing society. Also, there is often live music. It is closed Sundays, however.

Florence has been swept up in the Italian passion for Irish pubs. The beer is original but the atmosphere a little less so. Try the **Fiddler's Elbow** (Piazza Santa Maria Novella 7R; ☎ 055-215-056; Bus: 6, 11, 36, 37, or A to S.M. Novella 01 or 1, 17, or 23 to S.M. Novella 02), a very successful branch of the Italian chain, or the **Dublin Pub** (Via Faenza 27R; ☎ 055-293-049; Bus: A to Orsanmichele).

Gay and lesbian bars

Tabasco (Piazza Santa Cecilia 3R; ☎ 055-213-000; Bus: 23 or 71 to Galleria degli Uffizi or B to Loggia del Grano) is Florence's (and Italy's) oldest gay dance club, near Piazza della Signoria. The crowd is mostly men in their 20s and 30s. The dance floor is downstairs, while a small video room and piano bar are up top. There are occasional cabaret shows and karaoke. The club is open Thursday through Tuesday 10 p.m. to 3 a.m., with a 7.75€ to 15.50€ ($7 to $14) cover.

In summer at **Discoteca Flamingo** (Via del Pandolfini 26R; ☎ **055-243-356;** Bus: A or 14 to Piazza Santa Croce), near Piazza Santa Croce, the crowd is international. Thursday through Saturday its a mixed gay/lesbian party; the rest of the week, it's men only. It's open Sunday through Thursday 10 p.m. to 4 a.m. and Friday and Saturday 10 p.m. to 6 a.m. The bar is open year-round; the disco open only September through June. Cover, including the first drink, is 6.20€ ($5.60) Sunday through Thursday and 7.75€ to 10.33€ ($7 to $9.30) Friday and Saturday.

Fast Facts: Florence

American Express

The main office is at Via Dante Alighieri 22R (☎ 055-50-981; Bus: A to Condotta), open Monday through Friday 9:00 a.m. to 5:30 p.m. and Saturday 9:00 a.m. to 12:30 p.m.

Country Code and City Code

The country code for Italy is **39.** The city code for Florence is **055;** use this code when calling from anywhere outside or inside Italy, even within Florence itself (include the 0 every time, even when calling from abroad).

Currency Exchange

Numerous banks and exchange offices are located along Via dei Calzaiuoli, between the Duomo and the Palazzo Vecchio.

Doctors and Dentists

Call your consulate or the American Express office for a list of English-speaking doctors and dentists.

Embassies and Consulates

United States: Lungarno Amerigo Vespucci, 38 (☎ 055-239-8279 or 055-7283-780; Bus: 12 to Palestro), near the intersection with Via Palestro. United Kingdom: Lungarno Corsini, 2 (☎ 055-284-123 or 055-289-556; Bus: 11, 36, or 37 to Lungarno Corsini). For citizens of Canada, Ireland, Australia, and New Zealand, see Chapter 12 for the addresses of embassies and consulates in the capital.

Emergencies

Ambulance, ☎ **118** or 055-212-222; Polizia ☎ **113;** Carabinieri ☎ **112;** Fire, ☎ **115;** Pronto Soccorso (first aid) Careggi, Viale Morgagni 85, ☎ **055-427-7247.**

Hospitals

The Tourist Medical Service (Via Lorenzo il Magnifico 59; ☎ 055-475-411) is open 24 hours and can be reached by buses 8 and 80 (stop Lavagnini) or bus 12 (stop Poliziano). The Ospedale di Santa Maria Nuova (Piazza Santa Maria Nuova; ☎ 055-27-581; Bus: 14 or 23 to Piazza Santa Maria Nuova) is just a block northeast from the Duomo.

Information

For tourist information and assistance, call ☎ 055-276-0382 or 055-290-832. The best of the tourist offices is at Via Cavour 1R (☎ 055-290-832 or 055-290-833; Fax: 055-276-0383; Bus: 14, 23, or 71 to Duomo), about three blocks north of the Duomo; it's open Monday through Saturday 8 a.m. to 7 p.m. in summer (to 2 p.m. in winter). See "Street smarts: Where to get information after you arrive," earlier in this chapter, for the other addresses of Florence's tourist offices.

Internet Access

The Internet Train chain has five locations, the most convenient being Via Guelfa 24a (☎ 055-214-794; Bus: 7, 14, 23, 36, or 37 to FS

Santa Maria Novella) near the train station; Via dell'Oriuolo 40R (☎ 055-263-8968; Bus: 14, 23, or 71 to Duomo) near the Duomo; and Borgo S. Jacopo 30R (☎ 055-265-7935; Bus: B to Ponte Vecchio) near the Ponte Vecchio.

Mail

The main post office is the Ufficio Postale (Via Pellicceria 3, just off Piazza della Repubblica; Bus: A to Orsan-michele), open Monday through Friday 9 a.m. to 6 p.m. and Saturday 9 a.m. to 2 p.m.

Maps

The city bus and street maps available at the tourist office are adequate.

Pharmacies

There are many pharmacies in Florence, but the Farmacia Molteni (Via Calzaiuoli 7R; ☎ 055-215-472; Bus: A to Orsanmichele) is open 24 hours, as is the Farmacia Communale, inside the Santa Maria Novella train station (☎ 055-216-761).

Police

Call ☎ 113; for the Carabinieri (other police force), call ☎ 112.

Restrooms

As elsewhere in Italy, public restrooms aren't plentiful and are often closed. Your best bet is to go to a cafe; better yet, because Florence is full of museums, use one while you're inside.

Safety

Florence is quite safe; your only major worries are pickpockets and purse snatchers because of the huge concentration of tourists. Avoid deserted areas after dark (such as behind the train station and Casine Park) and exercise normal urban caution.

Smoking

Smoking is allowed in *caffès* and restaurants and is very common. Unfortunately for nonsmokers, it's virtually impossible to find a restaurant with a separate no-smoking area.

Taxes

There's no local tax in Florence. Other taxes are always included in the prices quoted. You can get a refund of the 19% IVA (value-added tax) for purchases above $160 — see Chapter 4 for detailed information.

Taxi

If you need a taxi, call ☎ 055-4390, 055-4798, or 055-4242, or 055-4499.

Transit/Tourist Assistance

The airports are Aeroporto Amerigo Vespucci (☎ 055-373-498), known as Peretola, and the Pisa airport, Aeroporto Galileo Galilei (☎ 050-500-707). For buses, call SITA (☎ 055-214-721); for trains, Stazione Santa Maria Novella, sometimes abbreviated SMN Firenze (☎ 055-288-765). The tourist office is ☎ 055-212-245.

Weather Updates

For forecasts, the best bet is to look at the news on TV (there's no phone number to get weather forecasts). On the Web, you can check http://meteo.tiscali.it.

Web Sites

The city maintains a useful site at www.comune.firenze.it. Much of it, however, is in Italian. At www.florence.ala.it, most of the places listed are ranked — hotels by luxury, restaurants by price, and museums by importance. If you're going to Florence to see its magnificent works of art, first take a peek at www.arca.net/florence.htm for a combined tour-guide and Florence art-history lesson that includes a glossary of art terms.

Chapter 15

Northern Tuscany and the Cinque Terre

. . . .

In This Chapter

▶ Exploring city ramparts

▶ Checking out leaning towers

▶ Discovering fishing villages

. . . .

*N*orthern Tuscany is an area rich in history and natural beauty. Of its many fascinating destinations, we chose to cover the two very best: **Pisa** and **Lucca.** We also cover the nearby **Cinque Terre,** a group of five picturesque villages along the coast. For each of these destinations, Pisa makes an excellent base; it's not only central but also a pleasant city to visit, with a choice of moderately priced hotels. Alternatively, you can easily visit each of the destinations in this area as a day-trip from Florence.

What's Where: Northern Tuscany and Its Major Attractions

If you travel west from Florence along the Arno River on its route toward the sea, you pass through **Lucca,** an unspoiled medieval walled town, often bypassed by tourists — to their great loss and your advantage! Lucca's architecture speaks of its past glory, and its **ancient ramparts, Duomo** (cathedral), and local **olive oil** will impress you.

Continuing on your route and shortly before you run out of land, you arrive at beautiful **Pisa.** Famous for its Leaning Tower, Pisa was one of the powerful Italian Maritime Republics from the 11th through the 13th centuries. These rival ports developed far-flung mercantile empires (see Chapter 1 for a brief history of Italy). Centuries later, the city lost its water access (the river silted up) and its power (it was defeated by Genoa's navy). You can still see evidence of Pisa's glory days, however, and the medieval buildings overlooking the curving Arno offer some of

Tuscany and Umbria

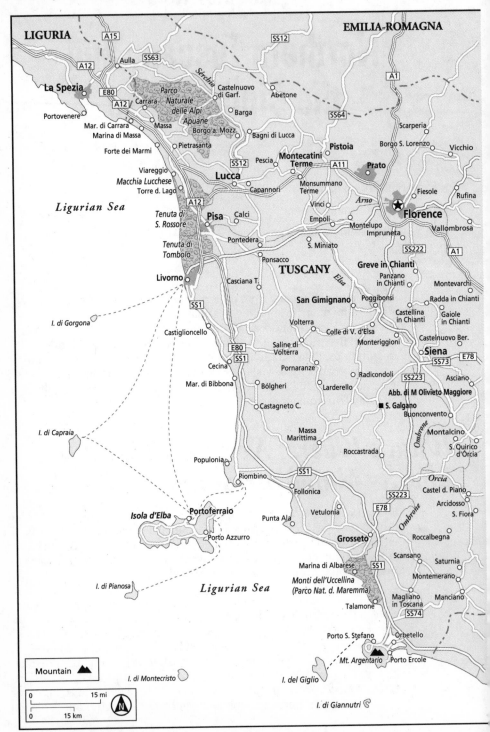

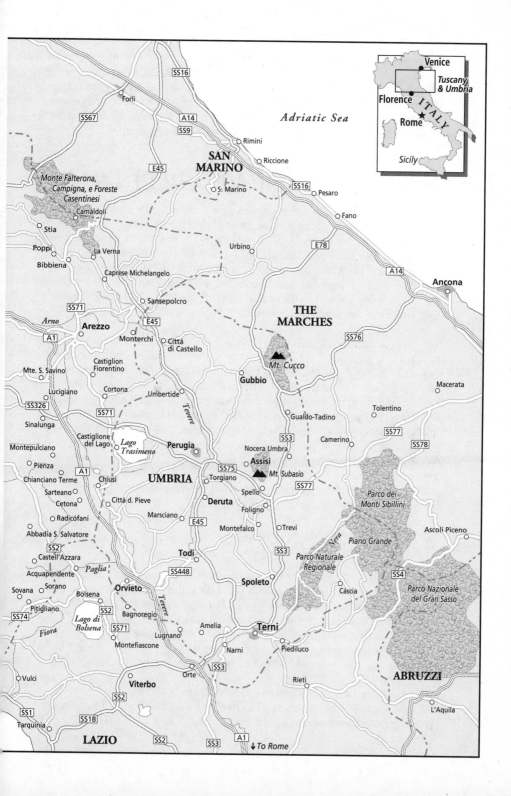

Italy's nicest riverside views. The city's highlights are the **Leaning Tower**, the **Duomo**, the **Baptistry**, and the **Camposanto cemetery.**

If you push on a bit farther along the coast, into neighboring Liguria and the Riviera di Levante (part of the Italian Riviera), you discover the **Cinque Terre (Five Lands),** a fishing and agricultural area of great natural beauty. Five small towns are perched here at the water's edge and are insulated from the inland by towering promontories: **Monterosso al Mare, Vernazza, Corniglia, Manarola,** and **Riomaggiore.**

Uncovering the Walled City of Lucca

Located west of Florence, Lucca was an important city under the Romans and later became a republic, fighting for its independence against Pisa. It was — and still is — famous for the works produced in its music school, founded in A.D. 787. A famous student of the school was Giacomo Puccini, who gave the world some of its greatest operas, such as *Madame Butterfly* and *Tosca*. The great English poet Percy Bysshe Shelley passed by here and wrote "The Baths of Lucca" about this small medieval town surrounded by powerful red ramparts.

You can easily reach Lucca from Florence and Pisa and can see everything in one day. But if you have time, it's a wonderful place to spend a couple of days leisurely strolling the walls, which are of monumental scale (cars once used the tops of the walls as roads), with projecting defense works at various points. Lucca is a city of music, and you may enjoy catching an opera at the historic **Teatro del Giglio** (☎ **0583-46531,** or 0583-467-521 for tickets; Internet: www.teatrodelgiglio.it). If you're interested in the opera, a great time to visit Lucca is during the **Settembre Lucchese,** the September music festival celebrating the memory of Puccini. The theater also has a dance season as well. At any time, Lucca is an intriguing small city that has maintained the integrity of its walls as well as its unique character.

Getting to Lucca

You can catch **trains** every hour and sometimes even more frequently between Florence and Lucca. The trip takes about 1¼ hours and costs about 4.45€ ($4). Trains from Pisa to Lucca travel as frequently, but the trip is only 20 to 30 minutes. **Lucca's rail station** (☎ **0583-467-013)** is just outside the walls, south of St. Peter's Gate (Porta San Pietro). You can walk — if you don't have luggage or if you left it at the train station — or take a taxi or bus to the center of town.

The company **Lazzi** runs **buses** to Lucca from both Pisa and Florence (☎ **050-46-288** in Pisa, 055-215-155 in Florence, 0583-584-896 in Lucca). The trip lasts about an hour and costs about 5.16€ ($4.64) from

Lucca

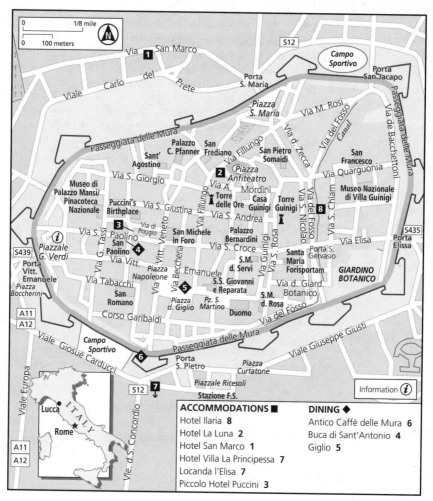

0   1/8 mile
0   100 meters

ACCOMMODATIONS ■

Hotel Ilaria **8**
Hotel La Luna **2**
Hotel San Marco **1**
Hotel Villa La Principessa **7**
Locanda l'Elisa **7**
Piccolo Hotel Puccini **3**

DINING ◆

Antico Caffè delle Mura **6**
Buca di Sant'Antonio **4**
Giglio **5**

Florence. Pisa is only about 30 minutes away (about 2.58€/$2.32).
Buses arrive in Piazzale Verdi, within Lucca's walls, on the west side.

Lucca is about 64km (40 miles) west of Florence (22km/14 miles from
Pisa) and is easy to reach by *autostrada.* If you have a **car,** from Florence
take A11 toward Prato, Pistoia, and Lucca. From Pisa, you can take A12
north toward Viareggio and turn off toward Florence on A11; Lucca is
the first exit after the junction with A11. You can also take the local road
SS12 from Pisa to Lucca — it's narrower (two lanes) but shorter. You'll
have to park your car outside the walls because only the locals are
allowed to drive inside. If you enter town at the Porta Vittorio
Emmanuele, you will see an information office in the imposing white
building to the left standing all by itself.

Getting around Lucca

Although residents' cars are allowed within the city walls, Luccans seem to prefer biking. You see a lot of them — especially the older ones — pedaling around the city and atop the walls. You can rent a bike at the **city stand** (☎ **0583-515-064** or 0583-419-689), near the walls by the tourist office in Piazzale Verdi (see "Fast Facts: Lucca"). Otherwise, the best way to visit the city is on foot. If you get tired, though, you can catch a bus; the public transport system is well organized, with small buses regularly running on schedule.

Where to stay in Lucca

If you're looking for elegance and luxury at a price, you can choose from two places that are across from each other 3km (2 miles) south of the city: the **Hotel Villa La Principessa** (☎ **0583-370-037**; Fax: 0583-379-136) and the **Locanda l'Elisa** (☎ **0583-379-737**; Fax: 0583-379-019).

Hotel Ilaria
$$$ **Via Santa Croce**

This new hotel in the historical center lies in a quiet location near the canal that crosses the city toward the east. Being new, the rooms are modern and equipped with satellite TV and all the modern comforts. Some rooms are disabled accessible. The hotel also has a parking lot and an enclosed garage.

Via del Fosso 26, off Via Santa Croce. ☎ *0583-469-200. Fax: 0583-991-961. E-mail:* info@hotelilaria.com. *Parking: Free. Rack rates: 180.75€ ($163) double. AE, DC, MC, V.*

Hotel La Luna
$$ **Anfiteatro**

This hotel offers a great value. Located in the historic center, it's divided between two buildings; some of the ceilings in the older building have 17th-century frescoes. All the guest rooms are spacious and nicely furnished, and some of the suites are quite grand, with large beds and high ceilings. The hotel is very well kept.

Corte Compagnoni 12, off Via Fillungo. ☎ *0583-493-634. Fax: 0583-490-021. E-mail:* la luna@onenet.it. *Parking: Free. Rack rates: 92.96€ ($83.70) double. AE, DC, MC, V.*

Hotel San Marco
$$ **Residential Lucca**

A relatively new hotel just outside the city walls, the San Marco is beautifully furnished with modern Italian furniture. Because it's so new, the guest rooms offer good-sized modern baths. The hotel has large common areas, including a pleasant garden, and is completely air-conditioned. If you don't mind being outside the romantic medieval town, but within walking distance, this hotel is a very good value.

Via San Marco 368. ☎ *0583-495-010. Fax: 0583-490-513. Internet:* www.hotelsan marcolucca.com. *E-mail:* hotelsanmarcolu@onenet.it. *Parking: Free. Rack rates: 95.54€ ($86) double. AE, DC, MC, V.*

Piccolo Hotel Puccini
$ Piazza San Michele

In the heart of the historic center, this hotel is housed in a small 15th-century *palazzo;* it's just across from the house where Puccini was born, hence its name. The guest rooms are small and so are the new bathrooms, but they're nicely furnished and very romantic. This popular hotel is always full, so book well in advance.

Via di Poggio 9. ☎ *0583-55-421. Fax: 0583-53-487. Internet:* www.hotelpuccini. com. *E-mail:* info@hotelpuccini.com. *Parking: Free parking available near the hotel in a garage. Rack rates: 74.88€ ($68) double. AE, DC, MC, V.*

Where to dine in Lucca

Lucca's specialty is its *olio di oliva delle Colline Lucchesi* (extra-virgin olive oil), one of the best olive oils in the world. The already good Tuscan dishes become absolutely delectable when prepared with it. You can taste the difference when you eat in Lucca's restaurants.

Antico Caffè delle Mura
$$$ City Ramparts   LUCCAN

With its fantastic location atop the city walls, this elegant restaurant is a good competitor for the Buca di Sant'Antonio (see the following listing), although its food doesn't quite reach the same heights. The food is fine, however. Try the homemade fresh pasta and some of the delectable *secondi* (main courses), including such specialties as rabbit, duck, and lamb.

Piazza Vittorio Emanuele 2. ☎ *0583-47-962. Reservations necessary. Secondi: 11€–18€ ($10–$16). AE, DC, MC, V. Open: Lunch and dinner Wed–Mon; closed three weeks in Jan.*

Buca di Sant'Antonio
$$$$ Piazza San Michele   LUCCAN

Lucca's best restaurant, the Buca di Sant'Antonio boasts excellent food (try the *capretto allo spiedo,* spit-roasted baby goat) and an interesting history (the restaurant has existed since the 18th century). The remarkable atmosphere is characterized by a labyrinthine succession of small rooms decorated with musical instruments and copper pots.

Via della Cervia 3. ☎ *0583-55-881. Reservations necessary. Secondi: 11€–19€ ($10–$17). AE, DC, MC, V. Open: Lunch Tues–Sun; dinner Tues–Sat; closed three weeks in July.*

Giglio

$$ Piazza del Giglio   LUCCAN

Less elegant and refined than the other restaurants in this section, Giglio offers excellent traditional Luccan specialties and a friendly atmosphere. Try the famed *zuppa di farro* (thick spelt soup) or the homemade tortellini. The secondi are also very tasty, and you can never go wrong with the *coniglio alla cacciatora* (rabbit) or the roasted lamb.

Piazza Puccini 2. ☎ *0583-494-058. Reservations recommended. Secondi: 9€–13€ ($8–$12). AE, DC, MC, V. Open: Lunch and dinner Thurs–Mon; closed two weeks in Feb.*

Exploring Lucca

Take advantage of the city tourist office's **Cityphone Guided Tour.** For 7.75€ ($7) — 5.16€ ($4.64) for the second person — you can rent a recorded guided tour in your own language that offers explanations and historic facts on all of Lucca's sights. Together with the free city map, it's all you need to explore the city in as much depth as you like. See "Fast Facts: Lucca," later in this chapter, for the location of the tourist office. If you prefer exploring the city without the aid of a recorded tour, we provide the highlights in the following section.

You can buy a **cumulative ticket** that includes the **Duomo and Sacristy,** the **museum of the Cathedral,** and the **church and baptistry of SS. San Giovanni e Reparata.** It costs 5.50€ ($4.95). Yet another cumulative ticket includes the **Museo Nazionale Palazzo Mansi** and the **Villa Guinigi** for 6.60€ ($5.94).

The top sights in Lucca

Chiesa e Battistero SS. Giovanni e Reparata

The 12th-century church of SS. Giovanni e Reparata was partly rebuilt in the 17th century, and it and its adjacent baptistry (with a Gothic dome) are handsome. However, the real attraction here are the excavations under the church that take you back in time through layers of history. Beneath the later constructions, you see the remains of a previous basilica, a paleo-Christian church, a Roman temple, and a more ancient Roman house. (Excavations are accessible to the public.)

Piazza San Giovanni. ☎ *0583-490-530. Admission: 2.50€ ($2.25). Open: Winter Sat–Sun 10 a.m.–5 p.m (call for reservation); summer daily 10 a.m.–6 p.m.*

Duomo (Cattedrale di San Martino)

Sitting on a medieval square, this cathedral is a perfect example of Luccan-Pisan Romanesque architecture. Made of striped green and white marble, the facade is decorated with three tiers of polychromed small columns. Take some time to walk behind the church and admire the imposing apse, surrounded by a small park. The interior is Gothic, divided into three naves, and contains several fine pieces, the most important in the **Sacristy:** Ghirlandaio's **Madonna with Saints** and **Ilaria del Carretto Guinigi's funeral monument,** a Jacopo della Quercia masterpiece that's one of the finest examples of 15th-century Italian sculpture. Ilaria was the first wife of Paolo Guinigi, ruler of Lucca, and he had the monument built to commemorate her death (she died at 26 after only 2 years of marriage) and beauty. Other interesting works are the **Last Supper** *(Tintoretto Ultima Cena),* on the third altar of the right nave, and several sculptures by 15th-century Luccan artist Matteo Civitali (among which are the two angels in the Chapel of the Sacrament [Cappella del Sacramento] and the altar dedicated to San Regolo in the adjacent chapel). Also by Matteo Civitali is the marble housing for the Duomo's relic: the **Volto Santo,** a wooden crucifix showing the real face of Christ, said to have been miraculously carved. Adjacent to the cathedral is a museum containing artworks once housed in the cathedral.

Piazza San Martino. ☎ *0583-494-726. Admission: Duomo free; Sacristy 2€ ($1.80); Museum 3.50€ ($3.15). Open: Duomo, daily 7:00 a.m.–5:30 p.m.; museum, winter Mon–Fri 10 a.m.–2 p.m., Sat and Sun 10 a.m.–5 p.m; summer daily 10 a.m.–6 p.m.*

Museo Nazionale Palazzo Mansi and Pinacoteca Nazionale

This lavish 17th-century palace is still decorated with part of the original furnishings and frescoes. Of special note are the **Music Room (Salone della Musica)** and **Nuptial Room (Camera degli Sposi).** The collection of paintings in the *pinacoteca* (picture gallery) includes Italian and foreign artists from the Renaissance to the 18th century; highlights are a portrait by Pontormo of a youth and works by a few big names, such as Andrea del Sarto, Veronese, and Domenichino.

Via Galli Tassi 43. ☎ *0583-55-570. Admission: 4€ ($3.60). Open: Tues–Sat 9 a.m.– 7 p.m. and Sun 9 a.m.–2 p.m.*

Museo Nazionale Villa Guinigi

Formerly the residence of the Guinigi family, this villa contains an interesting collection of Lucchese artworks. The Guinigi ruled Lucca during the Renaissance, and some of the furnishings dating from that period also remain.

Via del Quarquonia. ☎ *0583-496-003. Admission: 4€ ($3.60). Open: Tues–Sat 9 a.m.–7 p.m. and Sun 9 a.m.–2 p.m.*

Passeggiata delle Mura

Erected between the 16th and 17th centuries, this is the third and last set of city walls built by the independent Republic of Lucca. In fact, they're Europe's only practically undamaged set of defense ramparts from the Renaissance, measuring 115 feet thick at the base and soaring 40 feet high. The tops of the walls were transformed into a tree-lined 4.2km-long (2½-mile-long) public promenade in the early 19th century, and today the wall is a wonderful attraction overlooking the whole city, one that visitors and Luccans alike enjoy. Do as the Luccans do and rent a bike in **Piazzale Verdi** (see "Getting Around Lucca"), entering the promenade at the nearby entrance.

Surrounds the historic center, with 11 bastions and several points of access. Admission: Free. Open: 24 hours.

San Frediano

Built in the early 12th century, this church has a simple facade decorated with a beautiful Byzantine-style mosaic depicting the ascension of Christ, as well as a soaring bell tower. Among the works inside the church are noteworthy Jacopo della Quercia **carvings** in the left nave's last chapel, the 12th– and 13th-century **mosaic floor** around the main altar, and the beautifully carved **Romanesque font** at the right nave's entrance.

Piazza San Frediano. ☎ *0583-493-627. Admission: Free. Open: Mon–Sat 9 a.m. to noon and 3–6 p.m., Sun 9 a.m.–1 p.m. and 3–5 p.m.*

San Michele in Foro

Probably one of the greatest examples of Luccan-Pisan Romanesque architecture, the church of San Michele was built between the 12th and 14th centuries. The church derives its name from the fact that it was built over the ancient Roman city's **Forum (Foro).** The facade is graced by four tiers of small columns and is luxuriously decorated with different colors of marble, while the apse powerfully illustrates the Pisan influence. Inside is a beautiful **Filippino Lippi painting** on wood representing four saints — Sebastian, Jerome, Helen, and Roch. Piazza San Michele, which surrounds this wonderful church, is itself lovely.

Piazza San Michele. ☎ *0583-48-459. Admission: Free. Open: Daily 7:30 a.m.– 12:30 p.m. and 3–6 p.m.*

More cool things to see and do in Lucca

Here are some more sights to check out in and around Lucca:

Other Northern Tuscan favorites

If you have extra time and are looking for a few more interesting places to visit in the area, try the following:

- ✔ **Prato:** Among the draws of this city 17km (10 miles) northwest of Florence is a green-and-white gothic-Romanesque cathedral known for its Filippo Lippi frescoes, as well as the beautifully carved pulpit by Donatello and Michelozzo, which extends from the right side of the main entrance. The cherub bas-reliefs are copies of the originals, which are conserved in the attached Museo dell'Opera del Duomo. Prato's art treasures also include Filippo Lippi's painting *Death of St. Jerome (Morte di San Gerolamo)*, Caravaggio's *Crowning with Thorns (Incoronazione di Spine)*, and works by Paolo Uccello and Giovanni Bellini.

- ✔ **Pistoia:** This town, 35km (21 miles) northwest of Florence, lies halfway between Pisa and Florence and has kept much of its 14th-century walls. The 12th-century Duomo (cathedral), a beautiful example of the Pisan style, contains the famous Dossale di San Jacopo, a richly decorated covering for the front of the altar. The octagonal Baptistry was designed by Andrea Pisano, and, like the Duomo, is in white and green marble.

- ✔ **Montecatini Terme:** This is one of Italy's most fashionable spas, 31km (19 miles) north of Florence, drawing visitors who want to test its fine mineral water and try out its thermal centers and perhaps take a mud bath.

- ✔ **Via Guinigi** and **Via Fillungo** are the two most typical streets in town. Via Fillungo is the main street of the historic center, where shops now housed in the buildings don't dilute the strong medieval character. Via Fillungo connects to the famous **Piazza Anfiteatro** (where the Market is held in the morning): a ring of medieval houses built atop a Roman theater, the remains of which you can see in the lobbies of the buildings. Via Guinigi is smaller and is one of Lucca's most evocative streets, flanked by the houses of the Guinigi, Lucca's ruling family. The houses are a compact block of 14th-century towers and brick palaces, perfect examples of monumental Luccan Romanesque-Gothic style. Note the large palace at the corner of Via Sant'Andrea, the **Casa Guinigi.**

- ✔ Lucca is dominated by two medieval towers, **Torre Guinigi** (Via Sant' Andrea, off Via Guinigi; ☎ **0583-48-524**) and **Torre delle Ore** (Via Fillungo between Vicolo San Carlo and Via Sant' Andrea; ☎ **0583-48-524**). Torre Guinigi is topped by a garden with trees (entrance on Via Sant'Andrea), whereas the Torre delle Ore has marked the passing of time since the 14th century (the clocks have been replaced over the centuries and the current one dates from 1754). Recently restored, the towers are open Tuesday through Saturday from 9 a.m. to 7 p.m. and Sunday from 9 a.m. to 2 p.m.; admission is 3.10€ ($2.80) for one tower and 4.65€ ($4.20) for both.

✔ You can still visit the house where the famous musician Giacomo Puccini was born, today transformed into a museum: the **Casa Natale di Giacomo Puccini** (Corte San Lorenzo 9; ☎**0583-584-028**). The museum is open in the winter Tuesday through Sunday from 10 a.m. to 1 p.m. and 3 to 6 p.m., and in the summer daily from 10 a.m. to 6 p.m. It's closed January and February.

Fast Facts: Lucca

Country Code and City Code

The country code for Italy is **39**. The city code for Lucca is **0538**; use this code when calling from anywhere outside or inside Italy and even within Lucca (including the 0, even when calling from abroad).

Currency Exchange

There's a *cambio* (exchange office) in the rail station and one near the tourist office on Piazzale Verdi, as well as others around town. You can also find a number of ATMs throughout the city.

Embassies and Consulates

The nearest location is Florence for the United States and the United Kingdom (see "Fast Facts" in Chapter 14) and Rome for Canada, Ireland, Australia, and New Zealand (see Chapter 12).

Emergencies

Ambulance, ☎ **118**; fire, ☎ **115**; road assistance ☎ **116**.

Hospital

The Ospedale Campo di Marte is on Via dell'Ospedale (☎ 0583-9701 or toll-free 800-869-143).

Information

The tourist office is on Piazzale Verdi at the west side of the city walls (☎ 0583-442-944; Fax: 0583-442-505). Here you can pick up the Cityphone guide and a free map that's useful. The office is open daily from 9:30 a.m. to 6:30 p.m. (to 3:30 p.m. in winter).

Mail

One post office (ufficio postale) is at Via Vallisneri 2 (☎ 0583-43-352).

Police

Call ☎ **113**; for the Carabinieri (other police force) call ☎ **112**.

Taxi

Call ☎ 0583-492-691 (in Piazza Napoleone) or 0583-494-989 (at the train station) or 0583-581-305 (in Piazza Verdi).

Web Sites

The official Web site of the city is www. commune.lucca.it; the official site of the tourist office is www.lucca.turismo. toscana.it.

Pisa: Home of the Leaning Tower

The origins of Pisa stretch back to Roman times, when the Italic settlement that had existed since 1000 B.C. was transformed into a commercial harbor (in the second century B.C.). The city's maritime power was realized in the 11th century, when Pisa was one of the four powerful

Italian Maritime Republics, along with Venice, Amalfi, and Genoa. Pisa controlled Corsica, Sardinia, and the Balearic Islands, competing with Genoa for commerce with the Arabs. In 1284, Genoa finally won its struggle against Pisa, whose fleet was destroyed. Genoa became the dominant power in the Tyrrhenian (the sea to the west of the Italian peninsula), while Pisa shrank to a possession of Florence. During the three centuries of its splendor, however, the wealth coming from far-flung commerce funded the construction of the monumental town that you can still admire today.

You can see most of Pisa's attractions on a day-trip from Florence. However, Pisa makes a perfect base for exploring most other destinations in northern Tuscany and, like Lucca, has a good selection of moderately priced hotels and restaurants.

Getting to Pisa

Only 3km (2 miles) south of town, Pisa's **Aeroporto Galileo Galilei** (☎ **050-500-707**) is Tuscany's main airport, with daily flights from other major towns in Italy and Europe. You can take a 1€ (90¢) **train** to Pisa Centrale (Pisa's rail station), departing about every hour, or take a .77€ (69¢) ride on **city bus** no. 3, departing every 20 minutes. Bus tickets can be purchased at the information desk or from a machine outside. The trip takes about five minutes by train and a little longer by bus. You can also take a taxi for about 4€ to 8€ ($3.60 to $7.20) if you're dying to see the tower right away and want to get to the center of town as soon as possible.

The train is also an excellent way to get into Pisa, especially if you're coming from the south. It allows you to avoid the traffic along the coast road (SS1), which is terrible in summer. The junction of the two major rail lines from Rome and Florence to Genoa is at Pisa. So you can catch a train about every hour from Rome and one every half-hour from Florence. (The trip is about 3½ hours from Rome and a little over an hour from Florence.) Likewise, the trip costs about 4.70€ ($4.25) from Florence and 23.03€ ($20.70) from Rome. The rail station is Pisa Centrale (☎ **050-41-385**), toward the south end of the historic center and on the opposite side from the Duomo and its tower. Bus no. 1 brings you across town to the Duomo.

Pisa is about 96km (60 miles) west of Florence; if you have a car, count on making the drive in about an hour or less. You can easily get to Pisa by the *autostrada* (turnpike). From Florence, take A11 to Lucca and follow the signs for A12 toward Livorno; watch for the exit for Pisa shortly after the junction with A12 South. From Florence, you can also follow the directions for Empoli-Livorno to reach Pisa by the more direct but slower *superstrada* (super-road); the turnoff for Pisa is after the exit for Pontedera. From Rome and Venice, take the autostrada to Florence and then follow the directions that we provide earlier in this paragraph.

Pisa

ACCOMMODATIONS ■
Grand Hotel Duomo 9
Hotel d'Azeglio 13
Royal Victoria 14
Villa Kinzika 6

DINING ◆
Al Ristoro dei Vecchi Macelli 15
Da Bruno 8
La Grotta 11
Trattoria San Omobono 10

ATTRACTIONS ●
Baptistry 2
Campanile or Torre di Pisa
(Leaning Tower of Pisa) 5
Camposanto 3
Duomo 4
Museo delle Sinopie 1
Museo dell'Opera del Duomo 7
Museo Nazionale di San Matteo 12

Getting around Pisa

Pisa is a relatively small town, and you can easily visit everything on foot, which allows you to discover the little streets and beautiful views over the Arno River and its bridges. The town does have a system of city buses, however, and you can get tickets and a map at the train station. Chances are, though, that the only bus you may need is the no. 1 that runs between Pisa Centrale (the train station) and the Duomo for .77€ (69¢).

Where to stay in Pisa

Pisa offers a nice variety of hotels, from the deluxe to the simple but comfortable. The following are some of our favorites.

Grand Hotel Duomo
$$$ Duomo

Right off Piazza del Duomo, this hotel offers comfortable guest rooms with high ceilings and parquet floors; front rooms offer views of the piazza. A 1997 renovation gave all the rooms new baths, air-conditioning, and safes. The hotel has a covered roof garden with great views of the city and serves a buffet breakfast that includes ham and cheese.

Via Santa Maria 94. ☎ *050-561-894. Fax: 050-560-418. Bus: 1 to Duomo. Parking: 16€ ($14.40). Rack rates: 155€ ($140) double, including breakfast. AE, DC, MC, V.*

Hotel d'Azeglio
$$ Stazione

Near the train station and in the middle of the commercial area of town, this hotel offers comfortable modern guest rooms for a moderate price, air-conditioning and minibars included. The hotel has a rooftop garden with a nice view over the town.

Piazza Vittorio Emanuele II 18B. ☎ *050-500-310. Fax: 050-28-017. Bus: 1 to Piazza Vittorio Emanuele. Parking: 8€ ($7). Rack rates: 120€ ($108) double. AE, DC, MC, V.*

Royal Victoria
$ Ponte di Mezzo

Opened in 1839 as Pisa's first hotel and still run by the same family, the Royal Victoria occupies several medieval buildings, including the remains of a tenth-century tower. The guest rooms differ greatly — some have frescoes and others are rather plain — but all are kept clean and comfortable. The location on the Arno, within walking distance from all the major attractions, and moderate prices make it a great value.

Lungarno Pacinotti 12. ☎ *050-940-111. Fax: 050-940-180. E-mail:* mail@royal victoria.it. *Bus: 1, 2, 3, 4, 5, 7, or 13 to Ponte di Mezzo. Parking: 16€ ($14.40). Rack rates: 68€–102€ ($61–$92) double, including breakfast. AE, DC, MC, V.*

Villa Kinzika

$ Duomo

Named for a Pisan heroine who saved the city from the Saracens, this hotel is just across from the famous tower. There is a fine view of Pisa's main attraction from many of its air-conditioned guest rooms (some are rather small). Otherwise, the place is quite simple, with an average level of comfort but nothing exceptional.

Piazza Arcivescovado 2. ☎ *050-560-419. Fax: 050-551-204. Bus: 1 to Duomo. Parking: Free. Rack rates: 78€ ($70) double, including breakfast. AE, DC, MC, V.*

Where to dine in Pisa

Food in Pisa includes typical Tuscan fare, such as *ribollita* (here called *zuppa pisana,* or Pisan soup — old rivalries die hard), *fiorentina* steak, and excellent *coniglio* (rabbit), plus a variety of local specialties. Because the sea is nearby, you can also find lots of seafood: Typical is the *baccala* (codfish), prepared in various ways but often with chickpeas, and many other fish *secondi* (main courses). For antipasto, you can choose between the inland specialties (typical cheeses and cold cuts) and a variety of fish and seafood. The following restaurants are among the city's best.

Al Ristoro dei Vecchi Macelli

$$$$ Piazza Solferino   PISAN/SEAFOOD

A little outside the historic district, this is Pisa's best restaurant, frequented by locals. Traditional Pisan and Tuscan recipes are reinterpreted with genius and elegance. The homemade ravioli are stuffed with fish and served with shrimp sauce or stuffed with pork and served with broccoli

---

Fixings for a Pisa picnic

An excellent place to eat around town is the **food market** on **Piazza delle Vettovaglie,** just north of Piazza Garibaldi and the Ponte di Mezzo, and off Via D. Cavalca on the west side of the market. Every day from 7:00 a.m. to 1:30 p.m., food producers from the countryside offer their specialties for sale, and you may want to save a few bucks and have a great picnic — perhaps along the riverbanks — with fresh produce and Tuscan specialties. You can buy bread, salami, fruit, and everything else you'll need for a picnic.

sauce. Other inventions are gnocchi with pesto and shrimp, stuffed rabbit with truffle sauce, sea bass with onion sauce, and oysters au gratin. If you're looking for a formal dining experience and not just something to eat, this is the place to go.

Via Volturno 49. ☎ 050-20-424. Reservations necessary. Bus: 1 to Via Nicola Pisano; then turn right on Via Volturno, southwest of the Duomo. Secondi: 10.33€–18.59€ ($9.30–$16.73). AE, DC. Open: Lunch and dinner Mon–Tues and Thurs–Sat; closed two weeks in Aug.

Da Bruno

$$$ Duomo PISAN

Just outside the city walls northeast of the Duomo, this trattoria offers real homemade food in a warm atmosphere. The dishes are chosen from the traditional local cuisine and include homemade fresh pasta like the *pappardelle al sugo di lepre* (with hare sauce), *baccala coi porri* (codfish with fresh tomatoes and leeks), *coniglio* (rabbit), and lamb.

Via Luigi Bianchi 12. ☎ 050-560-818. Reservations recommended. Bus: 2, 3, or 4 to Porta Lucca. Secondi: 10.33€–15.49€ ($9.30–$13.94). AE, DC, MC, V. Open: Lunch daily; dinner Wed–Sun.

La Grotta

$$$ Ponte di Mezzo TUSCAN

A favorite among locals and visitors alike, this friendly trattoria has an interesting decor — a papier-mâché grotto — and a lively atmosphere. The traditional food is nicely prepared and includes such specialties as *tortelli* (a special kind of stuffed pasta), *pappardelle alla lepre* (in hare sauce), *gnocchi di ricotta e spinaci* (gnocchi with ricotta cheese and spinach), and a variety of *secondi* like stuffed rabbit and roasted meats.

Via Luigi Bianchi 12. ☎ 050-560-818. Reservations recommended. Bus: 2, 3, or 4 to Porta Lucca. Secondi: 8€–12.91€ ($7.20nd$11.62). AE, DC, MC, V. Open: Lunch Mon–Sun; dinner Wed–Sun.

Trattoria San Omobono

$$ Ponte di Mezzo PISAN

Near the food market, this trattoria offers traditional Pisan fare at very moderate prices. Try the homemade pasta specialties or one of the tasty *secondi,* which include *baccala alla livornese* (codfish with onion and fresh tomatoes) and pork roast.

Piazza San Omobono 6. ☎ 050-540-847. Reservations recommended. Bus: 1, 2, 3, 4, 5, 7, or 13 to Ponte di Mezzo Secondi: 7.75€ ($6.98). No credit cards accepted. Open: Lunch and dinner Mon–Sat; closed two weeks in Aug.

Exploring Pisa

The monumental **Piazza del Duomo,** also known as the **Field of Miracles (Campo dei Miracoli),** is where Pisa's top attractions are concentrated. The square was built in medieval times abutting the city walls — a quite unusual location for the city's cathedral, as far as cities in Italy go. Another unusual feature is that the piazza is covered with shining green grass — a perfect background for the carved marble masterpieces in the monumental compound.

If you want to visit several or all of the sights of Pisa, you may want to buy one of the **cumulative tickets** that are available, and which are sold at all the participating monuments — except the Leaning Tower, which has a separate admission. Note that the tickets are only available March 1 through October 31, and are valid for eight days. The most comprehensive, the *biglietto unico,* includes all the major sites we discuss and more. It's available for 12.91€ ($11.62).

Here are the other multi-site ticket options: To visit all the five top sights (minus the tower) listed here, you pay 10€ ($9); for four sights, it's 8.50€ ($7.65); and for two, 6€ ($5.40). Single-sight admissions are 5€ ($4.50).

The top sights in Pisa

Baptistry

In front of the Duomo (see "Duomo," later in this section) on Campo dei Miracoli stands the Baptistry. It was built between the 12th and 14th centuries, and its architecture reflects the passage from the Romanesque to the Gothic style during those years. This Baptistry is the largest in Italy and is actually taller — counting the statue on top — than the famous Leaning Tower. The exterior was once richly decorated with Giovanni Pisano statues, but many have been removed to the Museo dell'Opera del Duomo (see the listing, later in this chapter) and only a few were replaced with plaster casts. Inside is a **hexagonal pulpit** carved by Nicola Pisano (father of Giovanni) between 1255 and 1260 and a **baptismal font** carved and inlaid by Guido Bigarelli da Como.

Piazza del Duomo. ☎ *050-560-547. Internet:* www.duomo.pisa.it. *Admission: 5€ ($4.50). Bus: 1 to Piazza del Duomo. Open: Summer daily 8:00 a.m.–7:40 p.m.; winter daily 9:00 a.m.–4:40 p.m.*

Leaning Tower of Pisa (Campanile or Torre di Pisa)

Behind the Duomo is the famous Leaning Tower, the Duomo's Campanile (bell tower). Started in 1173 by the architect Bonnano, this beautiful eight-story carved masterpiece, with open-air arches matching those on the Duomo, was finally finished in 1360. It took so long to build because it started leaning almost from the beginning, so the Pisans stopped construction in 1185. In 1275, they started again and built up to the belfry, cleverly curving the structure as they went to compensate for the lean. The construction stopped until 1360, when the belfry was added. Later architects and engineers studied the problem — the shifting alluvial subsoil, saturated with water — but couldn't devise a solution (one attempt to fix it made it lean more). In 1990, the lean became so bad — 15 feet out of plumb — that the tower was closed to the public. Two years later, a belt of steel cables was placed around the base, and in 1993, it was decided to stop ringing the bells to prevent vibrations from shaking the tower, and visits to the tower had to be stopped. But after a $24-million restoration, engineers succeeded in reducing the tower's lean by 15 inches. It reopened in December 2001.

Note that your ticket to visit the tower has a precise time on it. (At press time, there were plans to make it possible to reserve tickets through the Web site; check online.) Also note that the stairs are very steep and narrow and the climb is physically taxing. There is a guided tour every 40 minutes.

Piazza del Duomo. ☎ *050-560-547. Bus:1 to Piazza del Duomo. Internet:* www.duomo.pisa.it. *Admission: 15€ ($13.50). Open: Daily 8 a.m.–8 p.m.*

Cemetery (Camposanto)

On the edge of the piazza stands the beautiful wall of the Cemetery (Camposanto). Designed by Giovanni di Simone and built in 1278, this monumental cemetery has been the burial ground for Pisa's constables, and you can find sarcophagi, statues, and marble bas-reliefs here. The dirt used in the cemetery isn't common dirt but holy dirt from Golgotha in Palestine — where Christ was crucified — brought back by ship after a Crusade. During the 1944 U.S. bombing of Pisa to dislodge the Nazis, the cemetery's loggia roof caught fire, and most of the magnificent frescoes were destroyed. Parts of the frescoes that were salvaged — particularly interesting are the *Triumph of Death* and the *Last Judgment* — are exhibited inside, along with photographs showing the Camposanto before the destruction.

Piazza del Duomo. ☎ *050-560-547. Bus: 1 to Piazza del Duomo. Admission: 5€ ($4.50). Open: Summer daily 8:00 a.m.–7:40 p.m.; winter daily 9:00 a.m.–4:40 p.m.*

Duomo (Cattedrale di Santa Maria Assunto)

The center of Campo dei Miracoli is occupied by the magnificent Duomo, built by Buschetto in the 11th century. However, its current facade, with four layers of open-air arches diminishing in size as they ascend, is from the 13th century. In 1595, the cathedral was heavily damaged by a fire that destroyed the three bronze exterior doors and much of the art inside. It was restored during the 16th century, integrating some baroque elements. Still original is the **monumental bronze door** at the south entrance (the Porta San Ranieri) cast by Bonanno Pisano in 1180, the Andrea del Sarto painting of *Sant'Agnese* at the choir entrance, the 13th-century mosaic of *Christ Pantocrator,* and the Cimabue *San Giovanni*

Evangelista in the apse. The **polygonal pulpit** carved by Giovanni Pisano was restored in 1926 when the original pieces were found — they had been put in storage after the fire in the 16th century.

Piazza del Duomo. ☎ 050-560-547. Bus: 1 to Piazza del Duomo. Admission: Duomo 2€ ($1.80). Open: Summer daily 10:00 a.m.–7:40 p.m.; winter Mon–Sat 10:00 a.m.– 12:45 p.m. and 3:00–4:45 p.m., Sun and holidays 3:00–4:45 p.m. only.

Museo dell'Opera del Duomo

On the south side of the Leaning Tower is the Museo dell'Opera del Duomo, which houses plans for the Duomo, ancient artifacts found on the site at the time the Duomo was constructed, illuminated books and religious paraphernalia, and original artworks that were removed from the Duomo and the other monuments for preservation. Particularly notable are the **griffin** that decorated the Duomo's cupola before being replaced by a copy (an 11th-century Islamic bronze, booty from a Crusade) and Giovanni Pisano's *Madonna col Bambino,* carved from an ivory tusk in 1299. Also interesting are the Carlo Lasinio **etchings,** which were prepared for the 19th-century restoration of the Camposanto's frescoes. Colored by Lasinio's son, they're the best record of the frescoes that were made before their destruction in World War II.

Piazza del Duomo. ☎ 050-560-547. Bus: 1 to Piazza del Duomo. Admission: 5€ ($4.50). Open: Summer daily 8:00 a.m.–7:20 p.m.; winter daily 9:00 a.m.–4:20 p.m.

Museo delle Sinopie

On the other side of the piazza, across from the Camposanto, this museum houses the *sinopie* — the preparatory sketches for frescoes — found under the charred remains of the frescoes in the Camposanto. Each *sinopia* faces an engraving that shows what the Camposanto frescoes looked like before their destruction.

Piazza del Duomo. ☎ 050-560-547. Bus: 1 to Piazza del Duomo. Admission: 5€ ($4.50). Open: Summer daily 8:00 a.m.–7:40 p.m.; winter daily 9:00 a.m.–4:40 p.m.

More cool things to see and do in Pisa

If you have more time to spend in Pisa, check out these sights:

✔ The **Museo Nazionale di San Matteo** (Piazzetta San Matteo 1, near Piazza Mazzini; ☎ 050-541-865) has a collection of paintings and sculptures from the 12th to the 15th centuries. Some of the works come from nearby churches, particularly from Santa Maria della Spina. Important masterpieces include the 1426 painting *San Paolo* by Masaccio, the two paintings of the *Madonna con i Santi* by Ghirlandaio, and the sculpture of the *Madonna del Latte* by Nino Pisano. The admission is 4€ ($3.60), and the museum is open Tuesday through Saturday from 9 a.m. to 7 p.m. and Sunday from 9 a.m. to 2 p.m.

✔ A traditional fun event is the **Gioco del Ponte,** held on the last Sunday in June, when teams from the north and south sides of the Arno fight each other. Wearing Renaissance costumes, the teams use a decorated 7-ton cart to push each other off the Ponte di Mezzo, the Roman bridge at the center of town. Contact the tourist office for more information (see "Fast Facts: Pisa").

✔ Another town celebration is the **Festa di San Ranieri,** on June 16 and 17, for Pisa's patron saint. The Arno is lit with torches all along its length, which makes quite a beautiful sight. Contact the tourist office for more information (see "Fast Facts: Pisa").

If you prefer to see Pisa via guided tour, you can contact **American Express** (☎ **055-50-981**) or **SitaSightseeing** (☎ **055-214-721**) in Florence. Both offer a tour of Pisa from Florence for about 26€ ($23.40).

Fast Facts: Pisa

Country Code and City Code

The country code for Italy is **39.** The city code for Pisa is **050;** use this code when calling from anywhere outside or inside Italy, even within Pisa (include the 0 every time, even when calling from abroad).

Currency Exchange

There's a *cambio* (exchange office) at the airport and several in town, including one on Piazza del Duomo.

Embassies and Consulates

The nearest location is Florence for the United States and the United Kingdom (see "Fast Facts" in Chapter 14) and Rome for Canada, Ireland, Australia, and New Zealand (see Chapter 12).

Emergencies

Ambulance ☎ **118;** fire ☎ **115;** road assistance ☎ **116.**

Hospital

The Ospedale Santa Chiara is at Via Roma 67 (☎ 050-992-111 or 050-923-111).

Information

The tourist office (☎ 050-929-777; Fax: 050-929-764) maintains three information booths, one outside Pisa Centrale, just to the left when you exit (☎ 050-42-291; open from 9 a.m. to 7 p.m. Monday through Saturday and Sunday from 9:30 a.m. to 3:30 p.m.); one near the Duomo at Via Cammeo 2 (☎ 050-560-464; open Monday through Saturday from 9 a.m. to 6 p.m. and Sunday from 10:30 a.m. to 4:30 p.m.); and at the airport (☎ 050-503-700; open daily from 10:30 a.m. to 4:30 p.m. and 6 p.m. to 10 p.m.).

Mail

The Central Post Office (Poste Centrali) is at Piazza Vittorio Emanuele 9 (☎ 050-519-411).

Police

Call ☎ **113;** for the Carabinieri (other police force), call ☎ **112.**

Radio Taxi

Call ☎ 050-54-1600.

Website

The city's official Web site is at www.commune.pisa.it.

Farther Afield: The Cinque Terre

Although not in Tuscany but in the neighboring region of Liguria, the five villages on this portion of rocky coast are just beyond the regional border with Tuscany and easy to reach from either Pisa or Lucca. Because of its unique character, merging land and sea in a most spectacular way, the **Cinque Terre (Five Lands)** enjoy a protected status as a national park.

A day-trip is certainly enough time to take in the sights of the Cinque Terre, unless you have time to spare and want to take a break from the noise and fast pace of modern life. The area's main attractions are beaches and scenery, not art or architecture.

Getting to the Cinque Terre

From Florence, Lucca, or Pisa, take a **train** to La Spezia, where you change to the local train line running between La Spezia and Monterosso al Mare, making stops at each of the other four villages of the Cinque Terre in between. The trains run frequently and the entire ride costs only about 2.60€ ($2.34).

Because they form a national park, you can't access the Cinque Terre by **car,** but you can get as far as Monterosso, where you can change to another type of transportation. From Pisa, take A12 toward Genova and exit at Monterosso al Mare. From Lucca, take A11 toward Genova–La Spezia and follow as it merges with A12; take the exit for Monterosso al Mare. In Monterosso, you can stow your car in the **large parking lot** (☎ **0187-802-050**) provided for visitors (about 8.25€/$7.43 per day). From there you can get a taxi to town for about 6.20€ ($5.58).

Getting around the Cinque Terre

In this magnificent but fragile land sloping steeply to the sea, there are two ways to get around: by rail (see "Getting to the Cinque Terre") or on foot. There's also a limited **boat service:** From Monterosso, you can take boats to Riomaggiore, Vernazza, and Manarola. The boats to Vernazza are run by the **Motobarca Vernazza** (look for the boat on the dock) every hour, with the last run a little before sunset. The other two are run by the **Navigazione Golfo del Porto** (☎ **01871-967-676**) about five times a day.

If you intend to travel from one village to another by train, be aware that most of the run is through tunnels — the line was excavated along the cliff. Don't expect scenic views — you'll see mostly solid rock!

The Cinque Terre

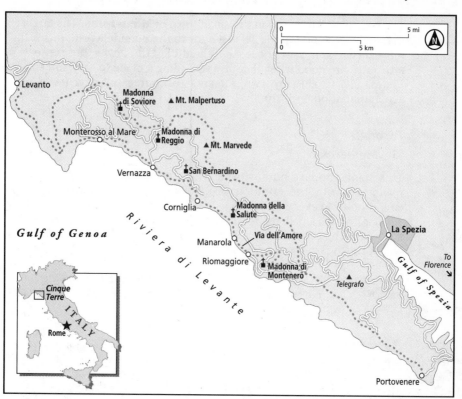

The best way to visit the Cinque Terre is on foot, which is the only way to fully enjoy the beauty of the villages and the surrounding cliffs, because some of the "roads" are actually paths over many stone steps cut into the earth. Two **trails** marked with red-and-white blazes link the five villages: The more difficult one is a mountain trail from Levanto to Portofino (difficulty level: medium), requiring a 12-hour hike; the easier one is the coastal route from Monterosso to Riomaggiore (difficulty level: easy), which requires five hours. You can also walk only one section of a trail and travel the rest of the way by train or boat. To hike from Riomaggiore to Manarola, for example, it takes only 30 minutes; this fairly flat stretch is known as the *Via del'amore* (the Path of Love). The section from Vernazza to Monterosso, however, takes about 1½ hours and is quite different, with windy ups and downs, and a precipitous descent into Monterosso.

Although the easy trail requires you to be only moderately fit, you should go with at least one companion, bring at least a quart of water per person (especially in summer, when it gets very hot), and wear sturdy walking shoes. The trail is along a cliff, and landslides are not uncommon.

Where to stay in the Cinque Terre

The best place to stay is in the small town of **Monterosso.** The largest of the villages and Cinque Terre's door to the outside world, this is the busiest (and some say the least authentic) of the towns, but those attributes are good when it comes to finding a place to stay and eat. The smaller villages are more romantic, of course, but have fewer accommodation opportunities.

Pasquale
$$ Monterosso

This small, modern hotel sits right next to the beach. It was recently revamped with the addition of satellite TVs, hair dryers, and air-conditioning in every guest room (the decor remains old-fashioned, however). Although small, the rooms offer beautiful views over the ocean and coastline. The common areas include a real bar (with a seating area, not one of those skimpy affairs) that doubles as a restaurant.

Via Fegina 4. ☎ *0187-817-477 or 817-550. Fax: 0187-817-056. Internet:* www. pasini.com. *E-mail:* pasquale@pasini.com. *Rack rates: 87.80€–129€ ($79–$116) double, including breakfast. MC, V.*

Porto Roca
$$$ Monterosso

The Porto Roca offers everything you'd find in a luxury hotel in a larger town, plus spectacular views from its high cliff location. The air-conditioned guest rooms are very spacious, bright, and comfortable, and most have large balconies. The hotel's amenities include a bar, a restaurant with an extensive cellar of Italian wines, and a private beach. The hotel accepts pets for a charge and provides a free car service to the train station.

Via Corone 1. ☎ *0187-817-502. Fax: 0187-817-692. Internet:* www.portoroca.it. *E-mail:* portoroca@cinqueterre.it. *Parking: Free. Rack rates: 161€–225€ ($144.90–$202.50) double, including buffet breakfast and beach umbrella and chairs for the day. AE, DC, MC, V.*

Villa Adriana
$$ Monterosso

This hotel is a real bargain for the area. Although it doesn't include some modern amenities (no air-conditioning), it compensates with a private beach, a garden, a good restaurant, and moderate prices. The guest rooms are modest in size though not cramped, and pets are welcome.

Via IV Novembre 23. ☎ *0187-818-109. Fax: 0187-818-128. Rack rates: 74.89€–82.63€ ($67.40–$74.37) double, including breakfast. AE, MC, V.*

Villa Steno
$$ Monterosso

This is the hotel we prefer most in the Cinque Terre. Unpretentious, it offers comfortably appointed guest rooms with a minimalist look and bright white walls. In addition, each room has a private terrace or small garden, and the view is great. However, it doesn't have air-conditioning or a restaurant. Note that the breakfast is buffet style.

Via Roma 109. ☎ ***0187-817-028*** *or 818-336. Fax: 0187-817-354. Internet:* www.pasini.com. *E-mail:* steno@pasini.com. *Parking: Free. Rack rates: 87.80€–129.11€ ($79.02–$116.20).*

Where to dine in the Cinque Terre

The cuisine of the Cinque Terre is typical Ligurian, with a lot of fish and simple produce from the surrounding almost vertical fields, sloping steeply toward the sea. Pesto sauce, now famous around the world, originated in the Cinque Terre and tastes best with linguine pasta. Another Ligurian specialty is *zuppa di pesce,* a savory, brothy fish stew. You can complete your meal with your choice of local grilled fish. For tasty treats while visiting Cinque Terre, try the following restaurants.

Al Carugio
$$ Monterosso LIGURIAN

The restaurant of this small *pensione* serves excellent food at moderate prices. You can find all the typical dishes of Ligurian cuisine proudly prepared and served in a friendly atmosphere. Go for the classic *linguine al pesto* and the *zuppa di pesce,* both delicious.

Via Roma 100. ☎ ***0187-817-453.*** *Reservations recommended. Secondi: 8.50€–13€ ($7.65–$11.70). AE, MC, V. Open: Lunch and dinner Wed–Mon.*

Marina Piccola
$$$ Riomaggiore LIGURIAN

An unpretentious restaurant, Marina Piccola is the trattoria of a nearby hotel. Liked by locals, it's known for its grilled fish — try the *spigola alla griglia* or the San Pietro.

Via Discovolo 192. ☎ ***0187-920-103.*** *Reservations recommended. Secondi: 9.30€–18.08€ ($8.37–$16.27). AE, DC, MC, V. Open: Lunch and dinner Wed–Mon.*

Ristorante l'Alta Marea
$$$ Monterosso LIGURIAN

In the center of town, this lively restaurant offers a casual atmosphere that appeals to younger crowds. Although trendy, the food is as good as in more old-fashioned, traditional restaurants. The delicious *linguine al pesto* is tangy and fresh.

Via Roma 54. ☎ *0187-817-170. Reservations recommended. Secondi: 9.50€–18.08€ ($8.55–16.27). AE, MC, V. Open: Summer lunch and dinner daily; winter lunch and dinner Thurs–Tues.*

Trattoria Gianni Franzi
$$ Vernazza   LIGURIAN

Tradition is the key word at Gianni's, where the recipes of Ligurian cuisine are prepared with care and attention to detail and include local fish, herbs, and vegetables. You can find all the classics — including *zuppa di pesce* and delicious octopus — all served in a pleasant setting.

Piazza Marconi 5. ☎ *0187-821-003. Reservations recommended. Secondi: 8.25€–14.50€ ($7.45–$13.05). MC, V. Open: Lunch and dinner Thurs–Tues.*

Exploring the Cinque Terre

The Cinque Terre region is a great place to spend some time with your kids. The breathtaking views, the sea, the swimming, and the hiking provide a great respite from all the usual cultural attractions.

If you intend to walk, take an early train from Monterosso to the last of the villages, Riomaggiore. From there you can easily walk the first three sections of the easy trail (30 minutes for the first stretch and 45 each for the two others) to have a taste of it; and then catch the boat in Vernazza back to Monterosso. If you don't want to walk, you can take a mix of boat and train, but make sure that you check the train schedule so you make it back to Monterosso (or La Spezia if you're there only for the day) at a decent hour.

If you're traveling in the hot season and you don't start your trip by 9 a.m. at the latest, you may have to walk in broiling-hot air. We don't recommend it.

The real attraction of the Cinque Terre are the splendid views over the sea and the tiny villages poking out among the rocky cliffs of the coast. It's amazing to see that the cliffs are cultivated — using terraces — and planted with luscious fruit and olive groves and grapevines. If you're lucky, during your walk you may see a local farmer standing where you'd think only goats can stand, lovingly tending to one of his plants. During the harvest, farmers secure themselves with ropes to prevent themselves from falling. Progress has come to the area, however, so here and there you may notice small lifts that look almost like monorails.

The five villages are all unique and offer a gorgeous sight from a distance, either by sea or by land. The entry to the area, **Monterosso al Mare,** is the largest of the Cinque Terre and the only town where cars are allowed. It maintains the feeling of an unspoiled seaside resort, however. It's also the only one of the villages to have a nice sandy beach (wonderful for swimming, even though most of it is divided into private swaths for the hotels lining the beachfront). Art isn't a big draw here, but in the **Church of the Capuchins (Chiesa dei Cappuccini),** in Luccan-Pisan green-and-white-striped marble, you can find a fine crucifixion attributed to Van Dyck.

Vernazza, on the other hand, is a very tiny fishing village with a strong medieval flavor. Overlooking the village is the Gothic church of **Santa Margherita di Antiochia.** The fishing harbor offers a fine view over the rest of the bay.

The only inland village of the Cinque Terre — though you can reach the sea by way of an old flight of steps — **Corniglia** is the most agricultural of the last three villages. The cobblestone streets of Corniglia wind from door to door and to its church, **San Pietro;** the whole town is like a step back in time. Its agricultural tradition goes back millennia: It was already exporting wine to Pompeii during the Roman period.

In contrast, **Manarola,** a lovely sight from a distance with its gaily colored houses, and **Riomaggiore,** the last of the Cinque Terre, are real fisherman's villages, still dependent on and closely related to the sea. In addition to its colorful houses, Manarola contains the 14th-century **church of San Lorenzo,** highlighted by a splendid rose window. In Riomaggiore you can find the **church of San Giovanni Battista,** also from the 14th century.

The most famous section of the coastal path is the **Via dell'Amore,** the romantic path between Manarola and Riomaggiore, which was excavated in the cliff and offers fabulous views. It was closed for more than five years after a landslide and has only recently reopened.

Fast Facts: The Cinque Terre

Country Code and City Code

The country code for Italy is **39.** The city code for the Cinque Terre is **0187;** use this code when calling from anywhere outside or inside Italy, even within the Cinque Terre (include the 0 every time, even when calling from abroad).

Embassies and Consulates

The nearest location is Florence for the United States and the United Kingdom (see "Fast Facts" in Chapter 14) and Rome for Canada, Ireland, Australia, and New Zealand (see Chapter 12).

Currency Exchange

You can exchange money at the Pro loco office (tourist information) in Monterosso (see "Information" in this listing) and in banks in both Monterosso and Vernazza.

Emergencies

Ambulance ☎ **118,** or in Riomaggiore, ☎ **0187-920-777,** in Manarola ☎ **0187-920-766,** in Monterosso ☎ **0187-817-475,** and in Vernazza ☎ **0187-821-078.** Fire ☎ **115;** road assistance ☎ **116.**

Hospital

The nearest hospital is San Nicolo Levanto, in the town of Levanto, just west of Monterosso al Mare (☎ 0187-800-409).

Information

In Monterosso al Mare, the Pro loco office (tourist office) is at Via Figena 38 (☎ 0187-817-506; Fax: 0187-817-825), open Monday through Saturday from 10 a.m. to noon and 5:00 to 7:30 p.m. and Sunday 10 a.m. to noon.

From June through September, there's an additional office on Via del Molo (☎ 0187-817-204), which is open the same hours. There is also a tourist office inside the train stations of the following towns: Monterosso (☎ 0187-817-059), Corniglia (☎ 0187-812-523), Vernazza (☎ 0187-812-533), and Riomaggiore (☎ 0187-760-091).

Mail

The main post office for the area is in Monterosso al Mare, on Piazza Garibaldi, in the center of town.

Police

Call ☎ **113;** for the Carabinieri (other police force), call ☎ **112.**

Taxi

In Monterosso, call ☎ 335-616-5842 or ☎ 335-616-5845.

Web Sites

Go to www.cinqueterreonline.com.

Chapter 16

Southern Tuscany

• •

In This Chapter

▶ Discovering the glorious Tuscan landscape

▶ Exploring medieval towers and walled cities

• •

*Y*ou could spend many weeks exploring the rich trove of cities and hills surrounding Florence. This region's incomparable beauty — a cultivated beauty, with terraced rows of vineyards, shimmering olive groves, and stately cypress trees — matches the richness of its artistic heritage. A castle or walled city seems to surmount each hill.

We recommend that you spend a few rewarding days exploring southern Tuscany. If, however, your time is limited, you can visit each destination in this chapter as a day-trip from Florence.

What's Where: Southern Tuscany and Its Major Attractions

Lying between Florence and Siena is the **Chianti region,** famous for its flavorful ruby-red wine. This region is an agricultural area of uncommon beauty, the soft slopes of its hills blooming with magnificent colors in every season, and the tallest hills topped by medieval walled towns and *pieve* (fortified churches). The deceptively simple cuisine of the Chianti, like its wine, is much celebrated.

South of the Chianti is **San Gimignano,** famous for its medieval towers. During the 13th century, the city experienced an economic boom, and the city's rich merchants marked their increasing wealth and pride by building palaces, each with its own tower. This started a competition, and the towers became so high that the city's government had to intervene and dictate that no tower could be higher than the tower of the municipal palace. Of the original 72 or so towers, only 15 remain, but the view is still quite impressive. Continuing southeast, you arrive at **Siena,** Italy's most beautiful medieval town, in our opinion. Famous for the Palio delle Contrade (a furiously contested horse race that has been held in the city's main square, the Piazza del Campo, since medieval times), which occurs in July and August, Siena is a jewel of a town, giving unending pleasure to those who stroll its streets and visit its monuments.

To see the scope of the entire Tuscan landscape, see the "Tuscany and Umbria" map in Chapter 15.

The Chianti: Land of Food and Wine

Break our rule about driving in Italy and put the pedal to the metal in the Chianti region (or at least take a bus tour). This gorgeous region between Florence and Siena has it all: velvety hills, tiny medieval walled towns, and acres of vineyards and olive groves. You can visit the area as a day-trip from Florence, but the area has so many breathtaking sights that you're likely to long for more travel time. The region's tourist office is in **Greve in Chianti** (see "Fast Facts: The Chianti").

Getting to the Chianti

The *strada statale* (state road) SS222 — called the **Chiantigiana** — crosses the Chianti region, linking Siena to Florence. Although it's only 66km (41.3 miles), this winding road (winding because it was established as the route to collect wine from each vineyard in the region and bring it to Florence) is the best way to explore the Chianti. It passes through each of the major points of interest in the area.

The bus company **SITA** (☎ **055-294-955**; Internet: www.sita-on-line.it) runs lines that connect Florence with most small towns in the Chianti. A good destination is Greve, the main town in Chianti, at the center of the region; the trip takes about an hour and 15 minutes and costs about 3€ ($2.70). There are also a number of buses departing from Siena with the bus company **TRA-IN** (☎ **0577-204-221** or 0577-204-245) for many of the small towns in the Chianti.

Getting around the Chianti

Driving is the best way to discover most of the Chianti's beauties; get a good map of the region from the tourist office in Florence or from newspaper stands, souvenir shops, and bookstores in Florence or Siena.

You can also move around by bus. You still get a good view of the countryside, and you can stop for some excellent meals. If you decide to explore the Chianti by bus, the best way is to go to Greve (see the previous section for information on bus companies serving the Chianti).

Alternatively, you can take a **guided bus tour** from Florence, a solution that requires less organization on your part and may allow you to see

The Chianti Region

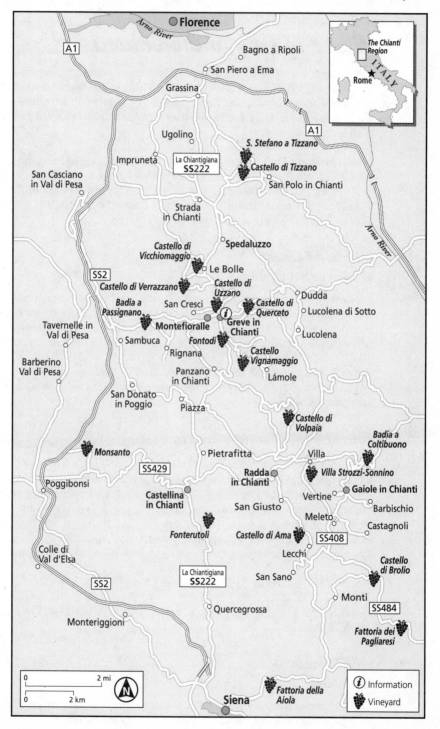

Florence

Arno River

A1

Bagno a Ripoli

San Piero a Ema

Grassina

Ugolino

Imprunetà

La Chiantigiana
SS222

S. Stefano a Tizzano

A1

Castello di Tizzano

San Polo in Chianti

San Casciano
in Val di Pesa

Strada
in Chianti

Arno River

*Castello di
Vicchiomaggio*

Spedaluzzo

Le Bolle

SS2

Castello di Verrazzano

*Castello di
Uzzano*

Dudda

San Cresci

*Castello di
Querceto*

Lucolena di Sotto

*Badia a
Passignano*

Montefioralle

**Greve in
Chianti**

Lucolena

Tavernelle in
Val di Pesa

Sambuca

Fontodi

Barberino
Val di Pesa

Rignana

*Castello
Vignamaggio*

Panzano
in Chianti

Lámole

San Donato
in Poggio

Piazza

*Castello di
Volpaia*

Monsanto

Pietrafitta

Villa

*Badia a
Coltibuono*

SS429

Poggibonsi

Radda
in Chianti

Villa Strozzi-Sonnino

Vertine

Gaiole in Chianti

**Castellina
in Chianti**

San Giusto

Meleto

Barbischio

Castagnoli

Fonterutoli

Castello di Ama

SS408

Colle di
Val d'Elsa

Lecchi

*Castello
di Brolio*

SS2

La Chiantigiana
SS222

San Sano

Monti

SS484

Quercegrossa

Monteriggioni

*Fattoria dei
Pagliaresi*

0   2 mi

0   2 km

N

Siena

*Fattoria della
Aiola*

(i) Information

Vineyard

The Chianti
Region

ITALY

Rome

more in less time (see the section on bus tours later in this chapter). It is a particularly good solution if you're pressed for time.

Where to stay in the Chianti

In this section, we give you a small selection of proven places to stay. The Chianti is rich in not only hotels and inns in the main towns but also rural accommodations (*agriturismo,* as Italians call it), some of which are luxurious agricultural villas more similar to elegant castles than farms.

Just over 5km (3 miles) from Greve is the little village of Panzano. If you want to spend the night there, contact the owners of the Torre Guelfa in Florence (☎ **055-239-6338;** Fax: 055-239-8577) and ask about the **Villa Rosa di Boscorotondo,** their newly opened hotel with 11 individually decorated double rooms with private baths.

Albergo del Chianti

$$ Greve in Chianti

On Greve's main square, this hotel offers a great value. The guest rooms are comfortable, very clean, and moderately priced. The service is excellent, and you can enjoy the hotel's garden and pool. The restaurant serves all the specialties of the region and a superb *fiorentina* steak.

Piazza A. Matteotti 86. ☎ *055-853-763. Fax: 055-853-764. Internet:* www.albergo delchianti.it. *Parking: Free. Rack rates: 92.96€ ($83.66) double, including breakfast. AE, DC, MC, V.*

Hotel Tenuta di Ricavo

$$$$ Ricavo

If you have a car and want to splurge, you can stay on this beautiful estate with all its comforts and an excellent restaurant, **La Pecora Nera** (see the restaurant listings for Chianti, later in this chapter). This 15th-century villa built out of medieval houses boasts two tennis courts, a golf course, an 8km (5-mile) horse-riding path, bike paths, a pool, a terrace, and a garden. The guest rooms are elegant and comfortable, with country-style antiques.

Ricavo (3.2km/2 miles north of Castellina in Chianti). ☎ *0577-740-221. Fax: 0577-741-014. E-mail:* ricavo@ricavo.com *or* ricavo3iantinet.it. *Internet:* www.ricavo.com. *Parking: Free. Rack rates: 170€–256€ ($153–$230.40) double. AE, DC, MC, V.*

Villa Miranda

$$ Radda

The old inn — housing an excellent restaurant — is the center of a large complex that includes two pools and open, grassy spaces. You can stay in a room in the old inn, but they're, well, *old.* The new units are beautiful, with large rooms and antique furnishings. The baths are a little small but have modern fixtures and bright decoration.

Neighborhood of Villa (1.1km/0.7 miles east of Radda in Chianti) ☎ 0577-738-021. Fax: 0577-738-668. Parking: Free. Rack rates: 61.97€–144.61€ ($55.77–$130.14) double. MC, V.

Where to dine in the Chianti

The fruits (and foodstuffs) of this magnificently fertile land include not only milk and honey but some of the most famous wines in the world — the famous **Chianti Classico.** You can stop to sample wines in the region's many wineries, accompanied by tasty local specialties.

The milk of this region comes from a special variety of cow, the Chianina. Cheese-makers turn the milk into delicious **caciotta cheese,** while the cow itself, poor beast, is made into some of the best steak you'll ever eat, the *bistecca alla fiorentina.* A bona-fide *fiorentina* is a minimum of 1-inch thick (that's more than 2 pounds of meat) — a problem if you're alone, but perfect if you're a couple famished after a day of sightseeing and walking.

The Chianti also offers all the specialties of typical Tuscan cuisine, with an emphasis on fresh vegetables and game, here executed as beautifully as in any restaurant in Florence — and closer to the source to boot. (See Chapter 14 for a detailed description of Tuscany's cuisine.)

Bottega del Moro
$$$ Greve   TUSCAN

In Greve's center, this restaurant is a perfect place for a not-too-heavy lunch. The cooks prepare Tuscan specialties with an eye to tradition but also to modern health standards (less fat). This restaurant is a favorite with locals, who come for the grilled or stewed meats and fresh pastas — including scrumptious ravioli.

Piazza Trieste 14R ☎ 055-853-753. Reservations necessary. Secondi: 10€–15.50€ ($9–$14). AE, MC, V. Open: Lunch and dinner Thurs–Tues; closed Nov and one week in June.

La Cantinetta
$$ Spedaluzzo   TUSCAN

In this two-centuries-old farmhouse surrounded by a garden, you can taste real Tuscan countryside food. Savor the regional specialties, including some that are more difficult to find, such as *involtini* (veal rolls) and stuffed pigeon. The Tuscan equivalent of prime rib, known as *tagliata,* is excellent.

Via Mugnano 93, in Spedaluzzo (2.25km/1.4 miles north of Greve). ☎ **055-857-2000.** *Reservations necessary. Secondi: 6.30€–13€ ($5.85–$12.60). AE, DC, MC, V. Open: Lunch and dinner Tues–Sun.*

La Pecora Nera

$$$$ Ricavo TUSCAN

The dining room of this luxurious farm-villa measures up to what you'd expect of a fine country inn in this region. It has a fireplace, white walls and red bricks, arched passageways, and wooden beams. The excellent food includes traditional Tuscan dishes prepared in the classic manner.

At the Hotel Tenuta di Ricavo, in Ricavo (3.2km/2 miles north of Castellina in Chianti). ☎ **0577-740-221.** *Reservations recommended on weekends. Secondi: 10.50€–21€ ($9.45–$18.90). AE, DC. Open: Lunch and dinner Mon–Tues and Thurs–Sat; closed two weeks in August.*

Villa Miranda

$$$ Radda TUSCAN

Inside an old roadside inn (see "Where to stay in the Chianti"), this restaurant is intensely atmospheric and decorated with country-style furniture. The food is well-prepared traditional Florentine. You can't go wrong with the grilled meat (like the *fiorentina*) or the homemade pastas. If you're in the mood for typical vegetable soup, the *ribollita* is wonderful.

Villa (1.12km/0.7 miles east of Radda in Chianti). ☎ **0577-738-021.** *Reservations recommended. Secondi: 7.75€–19€ ($7–$17.10). MC, V. Open: Lunch and dinner Tues–Sun.*

Exploring the Chianti

A rural agricultural area dotted with small towns, the Chianti is a perfect place to do some leisurely exploring. It'll give you a different feeling for Italy than you'd ever get in the cities, as well as show you more of the country's natural assets.

The top sights in the Chianti

Aside from its sheer physical beauty, the Chianti's major attractions are food and wine. The Tuscan cuisine combines fresh, high-quality ingredients with centuries-old country recipes. Hundreds of Italians and foreigners come each year to comb the area's dusty roads in search of the ultimate trattoria. They come to buy some of the best olive oils and herbed vinegars in the world. And they visit the local vineyards whose signs — DEGUSTAZIONE or VENDITA DIRETTA — beckon the public to taste their wines.

The Chianti is also a region to visit for art. You can find small treasures in the abbeys and *pieve* (fortified churches surrounded by farms) that were the fabric of society during the Middle Ages. Many *pieve* hide interesting works of art.

The three main towns in Chianti — Greve, Radda, and Castellina — are all worth a visit. On the river Greve, **Greve in Chianti** (on SS222, 30km/19 miles from Florence, about halfway to Siena) is a medieval town that began developing during the 13th and 14th centuries and today is the capital of the Chianti. Thanks to its central location, it hosts the annual **Rassegna del Chianti** (☎ 055-854-243), a market fair of producers and sellers of Chianti Classico — the highest in the hierarchy of Chianti wines — during the second week of September. The picturesque center of town has a unique triangular main square, **Piazza Matteotti,** surrounded by arcades full of shops, restaurants, and hotels. The church of **Santa Croce,** in a small square farther west, is another focus of activity.

Just 1.28km (0.8 mile) east of Greve is a detour well worth making: **Montefioralle,** a tiny hamlet that's one of the few remaining perfectly preserved medieval fortified villages. Built on a steep hill and surrounded by walls, Montefioralle's houses and diminutive cobblestone squares are decorated with bright red geraniums; walking around the circular main road during the good weather months is a real delight. Just northeast of Greve (on a side road from the SS222; about 5km/ 3 miles or an hour on foot) is the **Castello di Uzzano** (☎ 055-854-032; Fax: 055-854-375), an 11th-century castle that in the 16th century was transformed into an imposing villa. The surrounding estate produces both wine and olive oil. In addition to visiting the cellars (4.13€/$3.71), you can tour the famous Italianate Renaissance gardens (5.16€/$4.64). From Easter through October, the gardens are open daily from 8:30 a.m. to 6:00 p.m. (by reservation only in winter).

Built on a steep hill about 20km (12.5 miles) from Greve, **Radda in Chianti** is much smaller than Greve, with parts of its defense walls still standing. The town conserves a more definite medieval character. The **city hall (Palazzo Comunale)** boasts an interesting 15th-century fresco under its portico.

But it's in **Castellina in Chianti,** 10km (6.25 miles) from Radda, that the medieval flavor is the most strong. Still surrounded by most of its walls and dominated by a fortress with crenellated walls known as the *Rocca*), Castellina has a typical vaulted street — **Via delle Volte** — once used by the soldiers for defense purposes during the wars between Florence and Siena.

No visit to the Chianti is complete without a stop at the **Castello di Brolio** (☎ 0577-7301 or 0577-749-066), about 11.2km (7 miles) southeast of Radda. Owned by the Baron Ricasoli, this is one of the region's oldest wine-producing estates (the vineyards trace back to at least the 11th century) and the inventor of the Chianti Classico as it's known today, a masterly mix of grapes finalized in the mid-19th century. You can visit part of the spectacular grounds and gardens (2.58€/$2.32) Monday through Saturday from 9 a.m. to noon and 2:30 to 5:30 p.m. or take a wine-tasting tour of the cellars on Mondays at 3 p.m. (March through September only). The on-site store (open year-round) sells the estate's award-winning wines.

Seeing the Chianti by guided tour

If you don't have a car, you can take a guided tour of the Chianti organized by **SITA bus lines** (☎ 055-214-721; Internet: www.sita-on-line.it) or **American Express** (☎ 055-50-981). Tours leave from Florence for about 31€ ($27.90). These trips allow you to get a good taste of the region without having to drive the snaking back roads.

Fast Facts: The Chianti

Country Code and City Code

The country code for Italy is **39**. The city code for towns within the province of Florence is **055**, and the city code for towns within the province of Siena is **0577**; use these codes when calling from anywhere outside or inside Italy, even within the same town (include the 0, even when you call from abroad).

Embassies and Consulates

See "Fast Facts: Florence," in Chapter 14.

Currency Exchange

Although we recommend that you get your cash before coming to the Chianti (it's a farming area with few services), you can exchange currency at banks in the major urban centers. Note, however, that you'll probably receive a better rate using ATMs — try the towns of Greve, Castellina, and Radda.

Emergencies

Ambulance ☎ **118**; fire ☎ **115**; road assistance, ACI ☎ **116**.

Hospital

The Ospedale Castellina is on Via Ferruccio (☎ 0577-740-897) in Castellina in Chianti.

Information

The tourist office for the region is in Greve in Chianti (Via Luca Cino 1; ☎ 055-854-5243; open daily from 8 a.m. to 1 p.m. and 3 to 6 p.m. in summer and 8 a.m. to 2 p.m. in winter) and Radda in Chianti (Piazza Ferrucci 1; 0577-738-494, open daily from 9 a.m. to 1 p.m. and 3 to 5 p.m.).

Mail

A post office (ufficio postale) is at Via Chiantigiana (☎ 0577-741-000) in Castellina in Chianti.

Police

Call ☎ **113**; for the Carabinieri (other police force), call ☎ **112**.

Web Sites

Good sites that have an English version are www.chianti.it and www.greve-in-chianti.com.

Siena: Stunning City of the Palio delle Contrade

Siena is a magnificent medieval city surrounded by sun-drenched countryside. What makes the city so unique is that it's extremely well preserved — almost museum-like — and yet still alive as a town. The traditional Palio horse race (see "More cool things to see and do in Siena") is far from just a tourist attraction; it's a deeply felt and hotly contested competition among the city's 17 districts *(contrade)* — trust us, the Super Bowl doesn't incite as much passion as this race.

The same kind of passion pervades Sienese life, and you should set aside a couple of days to steep yourself in the local flavors. Siena developed a unique artistic style during the Renaissance — as in all things, in opposition to its archrival, Florence. Some consider its Duomo the most beautiful in Italy. For information on Siena's tourist office, see "Fast Facts: Siena," later in this chapter.

Getting to Siena

Siena is 62km (37 miles) south of Florence, so you can easily reach it via **car** on the Florence/Siena highway or on one of the older and more scenic roads. From Rome, take the A1 (the coast road) north toward Florence and exit at Val di Chiana for SS326, or alternatively take the Via Cassia from Rome (one of Italy's old consular roads). When you arrive in Siena, park for the duration of your stay — traffic in the historic district is heavily restricted (it's also a shame to drive around a medieval town when you can see so much more on foot). You can find pay parking lots at the various gates of town, particularly around the north entrance. You can park for free outside the town walls, but you shouldn't leave cars alone for too long in Italy — they tend to get broken into or disappear.

Siena is on a secondary rail line, so if you take the **train,** you have to change in Empoli (from Florence and Venice) or Chiusi (from Rome). The trip from Rome takes about 3 hours and costs 17€ ($15), the trip from Florence takes about 1¾ hours and costs about 15€ ($13.50), and the trip from Venice takes about 5 hours and costs 28.50€ ($25.60). Siena's rail station (☎ 0577-280-115) is on Piazza Fratelli Rosselli, about 2.5km (1½ miles) from the town center. Minibus C takes you from the train station to Piazza Gramsci, the northern tip of the historic district, a pedestrian-only area.

The **TRA-IN company** (Piazza San Domenico 1, northwest of the historic district; ☎ 0577-204-221 or 0577-204-245) offers **bus runs** to many other Tuscan cities and, in particular, to Florence about every

Siena

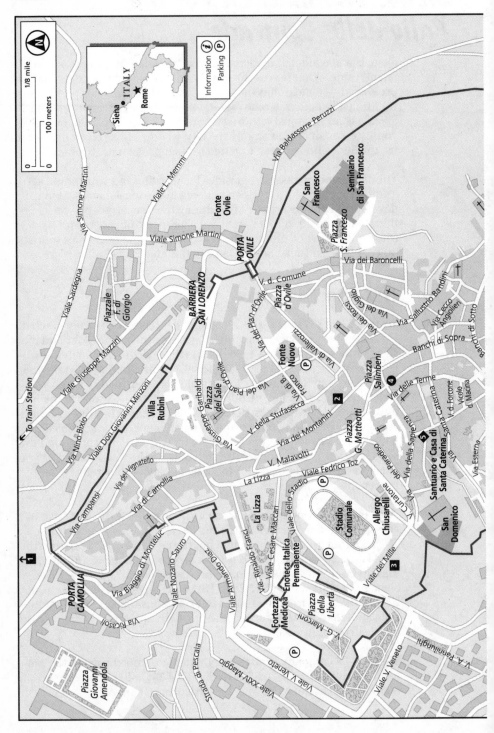

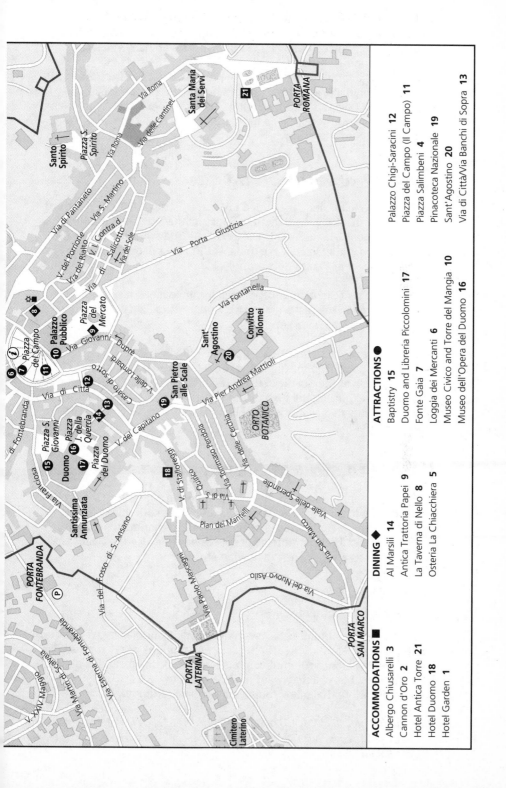

ACCOMMODATIONS ■

Albergo Chiusarelli **3**
Cannon d'Oro **2**
Hotel Antica Torre **21**
Hotel Duomo **18**
Hotel Garden **1**

DINING ◆

Al Marsili **14**
Antica Trattoria Papei **9**
La Taverna di Nello **8**
Osteria La Chiacchiera **5**

ATTRACTIONS ●

Baptistry **15**
Duomo and Libreria Piccolomini **17**
Fonte Gaia **7**
Loggia dei Mercanti **6**
Museo Civico and Torre del Mangia **10**
Museo dell'Opera del Duomo **16**

Palazzo Chigi-Saracini **12**
Piazza del Campo (Il Campo) **11**
Piazza Salimbeni **4**
Pinacoteca Nazionale **19**
Sant'Agostino **20**
Via di Città/Via Banchi di Sopra **13**

hour. The ride lasts about 1¼ hours (less than the train) and costs 4.13€ ($3.72). The **SENA company** (Via Montanini 92, ticket booth at Piazza San Domenico; ☎ **0577-247-934**) runs seven daily rides to Rome's Stazione Tiburtina (five on Sunday) for 12.91€ ($11.62). Reservations are obligatory from Rome to Siena, but not from Siena to Rome. You can make a reservation and buy a ticket by phone at **Eurolines** (☎ **06-4425-2461**), which will deliver your ticket by messenger service to your hotel. (In Siena, the SENA company provides the same delivery service.)

Getting around Siena

Built on three hills, Siena is divided in *terza* (districts that cover a third of town). North, along Via Banchi di Sopra, is the **Terza di Camollia;** southwest, along Via di Città, is the **Terza di Città** (with the Duomo); and southeast, along Via del Porrione, is the **Terza di San Martino.** The three *terza* meet at Piazza del Campo.

You can best visit Siena **on foot,** especially since motorized traffic has been restricted in the historic district. And most of Siena's attractions are very close to one another.

Siena runs a system of **minibuses** (☎ **0577-204-246**; Fare: 0.77€/69¢) daily from 6 a.m. to 9 p.m., including the C from the train station to Piazza Gramsci at the northern tip of the historic district, a good starting point for exploring the town. Note that the buses are color-coded; hence the funny names in the hotel listings that we give you later in this chapter.

Where to stay in Siena

Siena has a number of hotels in town, but we can guarantee they'll all be full during the Palio delle Contrade (see "More cool things to see and do in Siena," later in this chapter). If you're planning to visit during the Palio, remember that hotels accept reservations for the Palio period as far as a year in advance. Plan ahead!

Albergo Chiusarelli
$$ Piazza San Domenico

This 19th-century building, a five-minute walk from Piazza del Campo, has been renovated and features plain but modern guest rooms. The facade displays Ionic columns and a second-floor loggia and is shaded by palm trees, but you may want to get a room toward the back to avoid street noise. Note that a few rooms may remain unrenovated.

Viale Curtatone 9. ☎ *0577-280-562. Fax: 0577-271-177. Internet:* www. chiusarelli.com. *Bus: C to Piazza San Domenico. Parking: Free. Rack rates: 108.46€ ($97.61) double. AE, MC, V.*

Cannon d'Oro

$ Piazza Salimbeni

This 15th-century *palazzo* is on a commercial street. It's a nice mix of the once grand and the now economical. Its guest rooms are simple but large, furnished with old pieces that make you feel as if you've stepped back in time. The bathrooms are small but have modern fixtures.

Via Montanini 28. ☎ **0577-44-321.** *Fax: 0577-280-868. Bus: C to Piazza Salimbeni. Rack rates: 85.50€ ($76.95) double. AE, MC, V.*

Hotel Antica Torre

$$ Porta Romana

You can't find a much more romantic room than in this hotel's 16th-century tower (*torre* — hence the name). This family-run hotel is elegant, from the marble staircase and floors to the attractive old furniture. A few of the guest rooms offer views of Siena and the countryside. Because it's a tower, however, don't expect huge rooms.

Via di Fieravacchia 7. ☎ **0577-222-255.** *Fax: 0577-222-255. Bus: A, B, or N to the Porta Romana. Rack rates: 118.79€ ($106.10) double. AE, MC, V.*

Hotel Duomo

$$ Duomo

You can't beat this hotel's location halfway between Piazza del Campo and the Duomo. As in many other hotels occupying ancient *palazzi* — this one from the 12th century — you get charm outside but sparse amenities inside. In the basement is an atmospheric breakfast room. The redone guest rooms are fairly good sized, but the baths are very small. Ask for a room with a Duomo view.

Via Stalloreggi 38. ☎ **0577-289-088.** *Fax: 0577-43-043. Internet:* www.hotel duomo.it. *Bus: A to Duomo. Parking: 8.26€ ($7.43). Rack rates: 130€ ($117) double. AE, DC, MC, V.*

Hotel Garden

$$$ North of Siena

Just north of the city, this elegant 1700 villa is 1.5km (1 mile) up a hill among vineyards, olive groves, and a park full of oaks. (The walk is very pleasant if you feel up to it, but take a taxi if you arrive with your luggage.) Some of the guest rooms are in the villa but most are in the modern annex; there are even some four-star rooms with additional amenities. Guests have access to a tennis court and an outdoor pool (nice on really hot days). The terrace affords panoramic views over Siena and the countryside.

Via Custoza 2. ☎ *0577-47-056. Fax: 0577-46-050. E-mail:* garden@venere.it. *Parking: Free. Rack rates: 185.92€ ($167.33) double, including breakfast. AE, MC, V.*

Where to dine in Siena

Sienese cuisine shares many of the specialties of Florentine cooking (see Chapter 14), with few fish dishes but plenty of game and prepared meats. Among the *primi* (first course) are *pici* (hand-rolled spaghetti), usually prepared with bread crumbs and tomato sauce, and *pappa col pomodoro* (a soup of tomatoes and bread). Among the cold cuts are *finocchiona,* a fennel-flavored salami famous all over Italy.

Al Marsili
$$$ Duomo   SIENESE

If you've come to Siena for a getaway with your significant other or you just feel like splurging on a great dinner, Al Marsili is a superb romantic choice. The service is formal, the atmosphere is elegant, and the food lives up to its reputation. Here you can find staples of Sienese cuisine, such as the ubiquitous *pici,* but also specialties like *faraona alla Medici* (guinea hen with pine nuts, almonds, and prunes), and an excellent selection of wines.

Via del Castoro 3. ☎ *0577-47-154. Reservations recommended. Bus: A to Duomo; then walk past the Museo dell'Opera Metropolitana toward Via di Città. Secondi: 9.30€–15.50€ ($8.37–$13.94). AE, DC, MC, V. Open: Lunch and dinner Tues–Sun.*

Antica Trattoria Papei
$ Piazza del Mercato   SIENESE

This charming trattoria, close to Piazza del Campo, is a favorite with the Sienese. The food is good and sometimes remarkable (like the *anatra alla Tolomei* — duck stewed with tomatoes). You can also try the Tuscan favorite *al sugo di cinghiale* (pasta with wild boar sauce).

Piazza del Mercato 6. ☎ *0577-280-894. Reservations suggested. Bus: A to Piazza del Campo; then walk behind the Palazzo Pubblico. Secondi: 4.13€–7.75€ ($3.72–$6.98). DC, MC, V. Open: Lunch and dinner Tues–Sun.*

La Taverna di Nello
$$ Duomo   SIENESE

In this rustic tavern off Piazza del Campo, you find a real country atmosphere and excellently prepared food using fresh local vegetables and homemade pasta. Try the green lasagna (the pasta is made with spinach) with the very nice local wine.

Via del Porrione 28–30. ☎ *0577-289-043. Reservations necessary. Bus: A, B, and N to Via del Porrione. Secondi: 8.26€–14.46€ ($7.43–$13). AE, DC, MC, V. Open: Summer, lunch and dinner daily; closed Sun–Mon in Dec and Feb; closed in Jan.*

Osteria La Chiacchiera

$ San Domenico   SIENESE

This *osteria* is cheap, with a minimum of decor and really good peasant food, dishes like *pici* and *salsicce e fagioli* (sausages cooked with beans). Anything on the daily menu is good and recommended.

Costa di Sant'Antonio 4. ☎ *0577-280-631. Reservations recommended. Bus: A to San Domenico; then walk up Via di Sapienza and turn right. Secondi: 4.65€–6.20€ ($4.19–$5.58). No credit cards accepted. Open: Lunch and dinner daily.*

Exploring Siena

Siena's main sight isn't a site but an event. The famous **Palio delle Contrade** (see "More cool things to see and do in Siena") is a medieval-style derby in which riders representing the city's neighborhoods compete on horseback for top honors. Siena is a small town, but during the Palio it's literally crammed with excited and noisy crowds.

With its rich orange tones and myriads of tiled roofs baking in the strong sun, Siena is a sculpture in its own right. Although strolling the narrow medieval streets is one of Siena's great pleasures, there's plenty to see indoors, from the Duomo to the collections of Siena's unique Renaissance school of art.

Buy the **cumulative ticket** for the Museo dell'Opera del Duomo, Libreria Piccolomini, and Battistero for 7.75€ ($6.98) to save some money on the price of admission for these sights.

The top sights in Siena

The heart of Siena is the shell-shaped **Piazza del Campo (Il Campo)**, described by Montaigne as "the finest of any city in the world." This is where the famous Palio is held. Pause to enjoy the **Fonte Gaia,** which was inaugurated to great jubilation throughout the city, with embellishments by Jacopo della Quercia. (The present sculptured works are reproductions. You can find the badly beaten originals in the Museo Civico, which we describe later in this chapter.)

Baptistry of St. John (Battistero di San Giovanni)

Built in the 14th century, the Baptistry's unfinished Gothic facade is by Domenico di Agostino. But you won't care about the facade when you're inside admiring the lavish frescoes, most of which depict the lives of

Christ and St. Anthony. In addition, the Baptistry boasts a splendid masterpiece: a baptismal font made of several panels, each cast by one of the best artists of the time.

Piazza San Giovanni, behind the Duomo. ☎ *0577-283-048. Bus: A red or A green to Piazza del Duomo. Admission: 2.07€ ($1.86). Open: Summer daily 9:00 a.m.–7:30 p.m.; winter daily 10 a.m.–1 p.m. and 2:30–5:00 p.m.*

Duomo and Piccolomini Library (Libreria Piccolomini)

Decorated with contrasting colored marble both inside and out, Siena's cathedral was built during the first half of the 13th century in Romanesque and Gothic styles. It contains many artworks, including a superb **13th-century pulpit** carved by Nicola Pisano — the artist who crafted the magnificent pulpit in Pisa's Baptistry and father of Giovanni Pisano (who carved the pulpit in Pisa's Duomo). Another masterpiece inside the Duomo is the **Piccolomini Library (Libreria Piccolomini),** founded by Cardinal Francesco Piccolomini (later Pius III) to honor his uncle, Pope Pius II. Inside the library is the *Three Graces,* an exquisite Roman sculpture designed after a Greek model of the third century B.C.

Piazza del Duomo. ☎ *0577-283-048. Bus: A red or A green to Piazza del Duomo. Admission: Duomo free; Library 1.55€ ($1.40). Open: Duomo summer Mon–Sat 7:30 a.m.–7:30 p.m., Sun 7:30 a.m.–2:30 p.m.; winter Mon–Sat 7:30 a.m.–1:00 p.m. and 2:30–5:00 p.m., Sun 7:30 a.m.–2:30 p.m.; Library summer Mon–Sat 9:00 a.m.–7:30 p.m. and Sun 9:00 a.m.–2:30 p.m.; winter Mon–Sat 10 a.m.–1 p.m. and and Sun 9:00 a.m.–2:30 p.m.*

Museo Civico and Torre del Mangia

The Museo Civico is housed in the beautiful 13th-century Palazzo Pubblico, the seat of the government in Siena's republican period. Its richly frescoed rooms host some of Siena's important artworks. On the second floor, the loggia is the showcase for the eroded panels from the masterpiece fountain that decorated Piazza del Campo — the 14th-century **Gaia Fountain (Fonte Gaia)** was carved by Jacopo della Quercia and replaced by a replica in the 19th century. In the **Globe Room (Sala del Mappamondo),** just off the chapel, are two important pieces by 14th-century Sienese painter Simone Martini: the *Maestà* and the magnificent fresco of *Guidoriccio da Fogliano,* captain of the Sienese army (though there's been debate about the attribution of the latter work to Martini). In the **Peace Room (Sala della Pace),** the meeting room of the Council of Nine (Siena's government), is a famous series of frescoes by another 14th-century Sienese painter, Ambrogio Lorenzetti: the secular medieval *Allegory of the Good and Bad Government and Its Effects on the City and the Countryside.* From the *palazzo*'s 14th-century **Torre del Mangia** — accessible from the courtyard — is a breathtaking view of the town and the surrounding hills (if you're up to climbing the 503 steps). At 335 feet, the Torre del Mangia is the second-tallest medieval tower in Italy (the tower in Cremona is taller).

Piazza del Campo. ☎ *0577-292-226. Bus: A pink, B, or N to Piazza del Campo. Admission: Museo 6.20€ ($5.58); Tower 5.16€ ($4.64). Open: Summer daily 10 a.m.– 7 p.m.; winter daily 10:00 a.m.–6:30 p.m. (tower open in winter 10 a.m.–4 p.m. only).*

Museo dell'Opera del Duomo

This museum occupies a part of the originally projected Duomo, which was never built; the current Duomo would have been just the transept (this ambitious plan was reworked because of engineering problems and the plague of 1348). The gallery contains artworks that were removed from the Duomo for safekeeping and to prevent further decay. The main works are the statues that Giovanni Pisano carved for the facade; Duccio di Buoninsegna's painting of the Virgin, the *Maestà* (Duccio was a forerunner of Martini); and sculpture by Jacopo della Quercia.

Piazza Jacopo della Quercia, adjacent to Duomo. ☎ *0577-283-048. Internet:* www.operaduomo.it. *Bus: A red or A green to Piazza del Duomo. Admission: 5.15€ ($4.64). Open: Summer daily 9:00 a.m.–7:30 p.m.; winter daily 9:00 a.m.–1:30 p.m.*

Pinacoteca Nazionale

This picture gallery is housed in the 15th-century Palazzo Buonsignori and contains an expansive collection of art showing the unique Sienese style, which retained Greek and Byzantine influences long after realism came into play elsewhere (notably Florence), and emphasized rich coloration. Guido da Siena, an early developer of the Sienese school, is well represented, along with the more famous Duccio, the real founder of the style; his painting of the Virgin is a marvel of delicacy and pathos. Also represented is Giovanni di Paolo — don't miss his beautiful little painting of the Virgin.

Via San Pietro 29. ☎ *0577-286-143. Bus: A red or A green to Piazza del Duomo. Admission: 4.13€ ($3.72). Open: Tues–Sat 8:15 a.m.–7:15 p.m., Mon 8:30 a.m.– 1:30 p.m., and Sun 8:15 a.m.–1:15 p.m.*

More cool things to see and do in Siena

Here are some more things to experience in Siena:

✔ The best thing to do in Siena, besides visiting its monuments, is watching the **Palio delle Contrade** (June 29 through July 3 and August 13 to August 17). This frantic horse race has been going on since the Middle Ages and is still a Sienese passion. The town's 17 *contrade* (neighborhoods) fight dearly to win the race around Piazza del Campo, which is temporarily filled with dirt for the event. Perhaps not surprisingly, this is the world's most difficult horse race, and to some the most brutal — injuries aren't uncommon. A number of colorful parades in medieval costumes — each *contrada* has its own colors — accompany the race; particularly famous is the flag juggling.

If you want to attend the Palio, don't bother buying expensive tickets for the day of the race unless you really want to see the horse racing (as opposed to the pageantry) up close. Standing in the middle of the piazza is free — and a lot more fun. Get to Piazza del Campo very early and bring lots of refreshments (and a hat if it's sunny and hot). The square quickly fills to capacity. Note that if you do seat yourself in the middle, you won't be able to get out until the race is over.

If standing in the middle of the Campo doesn't appeal to you, you can try to buy a ticket for a seat in the grandstands or at a window of one of the buildings surrounding the piazza. These are controlled by the building owners and the shops in front of which the stands are set up and cost anywhere from 77€ to 155€ ($75 to $150). **Palio Viaggi,** Piazza Gransci 7 (☎ **0577-280-828**) can help you score a seat, and the tourist office has all the contacts for the individual shops if you want to negotiate directly for a seat. Call early; they often sell out months in advance.

✔ Not far from the Pinacoteca Nazionale (see "The top sights in Siena"), the **church of Sant'Agostino** (Via Mattioli 6) was built in the 13th century and renovated in the 17th, and it features a baroque interior. It houses several art treasures, such as Perugino's *Adorazione di Cristo in Croce* (Adoration of the Crucifix), as well as works by Lorenzetti, Sodoma, and other Sienese masters. The church is open only in summer, daily 10:30 a.m. to 1:30 p.m and 3:00 to 5:30 p.m., and admission is 1.55€ ($1.40).

✔ Running like a main artery through the heart of Siena, **Via di Città,** and its continuation, **Via Banchi di Sopra,** are lined with medieval and Renaissance palaces. To truly experience Siena, stroll along these streets, which still have their original flagstone pavement. The buildings along these streets continue to serve important functions, like the beautiful Gothic Palazzo **Chigi-Saracini,** today the academy of music, and the **Loggia dei Mercanti,** now a court building.

And on your left, the Campo: Seeing Siena by guided tour

If you want to participate in a bus tour, call **American Express** (☎ **055-50-981**) or **SITA bus lines** (☎ **055-214-721**; Internet: www.sita-on-line.it) in Florence. Both offer similar tours of the major attractions in Tuscany, visiting the most important places and monuments, and give a tour of Siena for about 47€ ($42.30).

Shopping in Siena

Siena offers a variety of elegant and interesting shops. Besides the usual Italian shops, where you find clothing, shoes, leather goods, and

personal and home accessories, Siena has a few shops that sell specialized Sienese crafts. Included among the city's specialties is the wine of
the surrounding hills, which you can find at *enoteche* (wine stores).
Note that like all spirits, *grappa* (clear Italian brandy) travels better
than wine, which "bruises" and has to be left to sit for months after
being carried on a plane. Try the **Enoteca San Domenico** (Via del
Paradiso 56; ☎ **0577-271-181**), which offers a good selection of local
wines as well as an assortment of the region's food specialties.

Local products include embroidery, and you can find a variety of hand-
embroidered goods at **Siena Ricama** (Via di Città 61; ☎ **0577-288-339**),
where you can also place an order for custom-made items fashioned
after Renaissance patterns. Another interesting shop is **Ceramiche
Santa Caterina** (Via di Città 51; ☎ **0577-280-098**), the showcase of an
important producer of Sienese ceramics.

Fast Facts: Siena

Country Code and City Code

The country code for Italy is **39**. The city
code for Siena is **0577**; use this code when
calling from anywhere outside or inside
Italy, as well as within Siena. Include the 0
every time, even when calling from abroad.

Embassies and Consulates

See "Fast Facts: Florence" in Chapter 14.

Currency Exchange

There are many exchange offices in town,
near major attractions. You can also change
money at banks or get cash from ATMs.

Emergencies

Ambulance ☎ **118**; fire ☎ **115**; road assistance ACI ☎ **116**.

Hospital

The Policlinico Le Scotte is at Viale Bracci
16 (☎ 0577-585-111).

Information

Before your trip, write to Siena's main tourist
office at Via di Città 43, 53100 Siena (☎ 0577-
42-209; Fax: 0577-281-041). Pick up

brochures at the tourist booth at Piazza del
Campo 56 (☎ 0577-280-551). Summer hours
are Monday through Saturday from 8:30 a.m.
to 7:30 p.m. Winter hours are Monday
through Friday from 8:30 a.m. to 1:00 p.m. and
3:30 to 6:30 p.m. and Saturday from 8:30 a.m.
to 1:00 p.m.

Internet Access

The Internet Train chain of shops has a
branch at Via Pantaneto 54, near the Campo
(☎ 0577-247-460).

Mail

The main post office is at Piazza Matteotti 37
(☎ 0577-42-178).

Police

Call ☎ **113**; for the Carabinieri (other police
force), call ☎ **112**.

Taxi

Call ☎0577-49-222 (radio taxi) or ☎ 0577-
289-350 (in Piazza Matteotti).

Web Site

Visit www.siena.turismo.toscana.it.

San Gimignano: The Manhattan of Tuscany

A perfectly preserved medieval town, San Gimignano is one of southern Tuscany's most famous destinations and is known for its lofty medieval towers. The city actually began as a small Etruscan village in the third century B.C., but it was only centuries later that it became an important town. The medieval "Francigena," the main route from Italy to France, went right through San Gimignano and accounted for much of its wealth.

San Gimignano has been called "The Manhattan of Tuscany" because of its soaring towers, but the comparison is really not apt, because San Gimignano is a city of the past. Unlike Florence or even Siena, San Gimignano is too small to have survived as a thriving center into the modern period. So although it is very dependent on tourism (in the winter, many restaurants and hotels close for lack of business), the atmosphere is still magical.

Try to visit San Gimignano in the off-season so you won't be overwhelmed by tourists from all over the world. (Note, however, that in the low season of January and February, there may be only one hotel open in town; four of the hotels take turns staying open so there is always a place to stay.) San Gimignano is an easy day-trip from Siena or even Florence, but it can be a romantic place to spend the night, with its view of the twinkling lights of other Tuscan hill towns.

Getting to San Gimignano

With a **car,** you can reach San Gimignano (which is on a secondary route southwest of Florence and northwest of Siena) using the *autostrada* Florence-Pisa. There are two ways to proceed: San Gimignano is signed from the Colle di Val d'Elsa exit, which takes you along picturesque small roads through the countryside. It's also the slow way. Alternatively, you can exit at Poggibonsi, a busy industrial town. The sign on the highway doesn't say San Gimignano, but after you exit, the way to San Gimignano is well-marked; follow the directions for San Gimignano on S324. The trip takes about 1½ hours from Florence and slightly less time from Siena.

The companies **TRA-IN** (☎ 0577-204-111 or 0577-204-245) in Siena and **SITA** (☎ 055-294-955; Internet: www.sita-on-line.it) in Florence offer regular **bus service** to San Gimignano, with a transfer at Poggibonsi. The bus ride from Siena takes about 50 minutes and costs 3.62€ ($3.26); the trip from Florence takes half an hour longer and costs approximately 4.13€ ($3.72).

San Gimignano

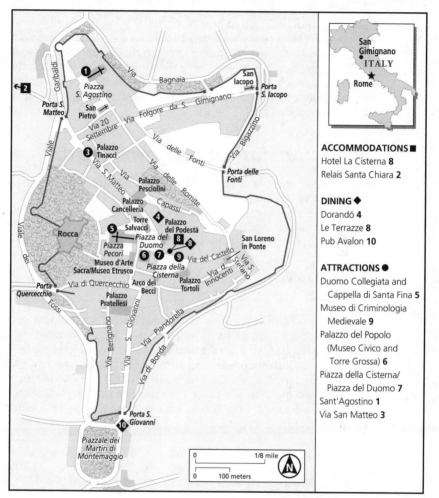

San Gimignano
ITALY
Rome

ACCOMMODATIONS ■
Hotel La Cisterna **8**
Relais Santa Chiara **2**

DINING ◆
Dorandó **4**
Le Terrazze **8**
Pub Avalon **10**

ATTRACTIONS ●
Duomo Collegiata and
  Cappella di Santa Fina **5**
Museo di Criminologia
  Medievale **9**
Palazzo del Popolo
  (Museo Civico and
  Torre Grossa) **6**
Piazza della Cisterna/
  Piazza del Duomo **7**
Sant'Agostino **1**
Via San Matteo **3**

You can also utilize the regular **train service** from Siena to Poggibonsi. The ride takes only about 30 minutes and costs 4.13€ ($3.72). From Florence to Poggibonsi, the trip is a little longer because you must change trains in Empoli (the whole trip takes about an hour and a half and costs 4.65€/$4.19). If you're traveling from Venice or Rome, you must go to Florence first. From Poggibonsi, a regular bus service starts from outside the train station and arrives in the center of San Gimignano in about 20 minutes, but be aware that there's little service on Sundays (only two runs — one in the early morning and one around noon).

Getting around San Gimignano

San Gimignano is closed to private traffic. Only public buses and taxis are allowed in the center of town. The only exception is for tourists, who are allowed to use their cars to reach their hotels and deposit their luggage, but you need to have the authorization arranged by the hotel (ask when you make your reservation, and allow enough time for the paperwork to go through). The town is quite small, and you can explore it easily on foot.

Where to stay in San Gimignano

Stop by the **Protur Siena Hotels Promotion booth** on Piazza San Domenico (☎ **0577-288-084**; Fax: 0577-280-290; E-mail: shpnet@nova media.it) for help in finding a room (they'll reserve it for a 1.55€/$1.40 fee). The booth is open Monday through Saturday from 9 a.m. to 7 p.m. (until 8 p.m. in summer). They also change money.

Hotel La Cisterna
$$ Duomo

Opening onto San Gimignano's most picturesque square, this old hotel offers large rooms and baths as well as a sweeping panoramic view from some of the rooms (and from the breakfast room at the top of the building). The rooms are furnished with a mixture of reproduction antique furniture and more modern furnishings. The balconies are large enough for a table and chair and make a nice place to relax. The hotel's restaurant is the renowned **Le Terrazze** (see "Where to dine in San Gimignano," later in this chapter).

Piazza della Cisterna 23. ☎ *0577-940-328. Fax: 0577-942-080. Internet:* www.san gimignano.com/lacisterna. *E-mail:* lacisterna@iol.it. *Parking: 12.91€ ($11.61) outside the walls of town. Rack rates: 88€–112€ ($80–$103) double, including breakfast. AE, DC, MC, V.*

Relais Santa Chiara
$$$ Duomo

This beautiful hotel/resort is a ten-minute walk outside the town walls. Overlooking the luscious countryside and surrounded by private gardens, it's the grand way to see San Gimignano, and yet it isn't really that expensive. The guest rooms and public areas are beautifully decorated, and some rooms have private terraces. There's also a pool and Jacuzzi. The broad range of rates reflects different levels of rooms classed from "small" to "superior."

Via Matteotti 15. ☎ *0577-940-701. Fax: 0577-942-096. Internet:* www.rsc.it. *E-mail:* rsc@rsc.it. *Parking: Free. Rack rates: 87€–215€ ($79.20–$193.50) double, including buffet breakfast. AE, DC, MC, V.*

Where to dine in San Gimignano

You can dine very well indeed in San Gimignano. The cuisine is classic Tuscan and always with a heavy accent on game. For example, you can find roasted wild boar and hare, both of which are also used to season the *pappardelle* (homemade ribbon-like flat pasta). The famous local wine is the white Vernaccia di San Gimignano.

Dorandó
$$$ Duomo SIENESE

On a tiny street near the Duomo, this excellent restaurant is a popular destination for locals and Italian tourists alike. The food is classic Tuscan, with all the local specialites, including an excellent Vernaccia wine.

Vicolo dell'Oro 2; off Piazza del Duomo, turn right at the beginning of Via San Matteo. ☎ *0577-941-862. Reservations recommended. Secondi: 9.30€–16.53€ ($8.37–$14.87). MC, V. Open: Lunch and dinner Tues–Sun; closed two weeks in Jan.*

Le Terrazze
$$$ Duomo TUSCAN

Located in **Hotel La Cisterna** (see "Where to stay in Siena," earlier in this chapter), this restaurant is one of the classiest places to dine in San Gimignano. It features two dining rooms, one of which is original from the 13th century and has a classic Tuscan countryside feeling, with medieval beamed ceilings and wooden furniture. Both rooms have large windows that provide a breathtaking view of the surrounding valley. Try the *crostini,* grilled meat, or game *ragù.*

Piazza della Cisterna 24. ☎ *0577-940-328. Reservations recommended. Secondi: 10.33€–13.94€ ($9.29–$12.54). AE, DC, MC, V. Lunch and dinner daily.*

Pub Avalon
$$ San Giovanni TUSCAN

Located just outside the main entrance to town, the cavernous Pub Avalon offers a little of everything. The first thing you'll see is the outdoor beer garden, a popular hangout in summer. Inside, live music often starts around 10 p.m. The food runs the gamut from the Tuscan equivalent of "pub grub" (*crostini, bruschetta,* and other finger food) to substantial entrees like grilled chicken, risotto, and steak with porcini mushrooms.

Viale Roma at Porta S. Giovanni. ☎ *0577-940-023. Internet:* www.avalon-pub.com. *Reservations recommended in summer. Secondi: 7.25€–13.43€ ($6.52–$12). AE, DC, MC, V. Lunch and dinner daily.*

Exploring San Gimignano

A **cumulative ticket** includes the Palazzo del Popolo/Pinacoteca, the Torre Grossa, and the archaeological museum and other minor attractions. It costs 7.50€ ($6.75).

The top sights in San Gimignano

The **medieval towers** attached to the local *palazzi* have become the symbol of the town and the source of its nickname, San Gimignano delle Belle Torri (San Gimignano of the Beautiful Towers). Once the symbol of the palace owners' wealth, the towers flourished in San Gimignano during the city's period of great economic success in the 13th century. So much competition existed in tower-building — always taller and taller — that the government made a law forbidding any tower taller than the tower on the Palazzo del Popolo — the seat of the government.

The town's economic boom was suddenly wiped out by the plague (which hit San Gimignano several times between the 14th and the 17th centuries), a disaster that ultimately preserved the town, allowing it to remain basically intact as a typical walled medieval town, with no modern additions. Obviously, time has taken its toll, and some of the buildings have collapsed. Of the original 72 or so towers, only 15 remain today, including the tower on the Palazzo del Popolo (177 feet, 3 inches).

The triangular **Piazza della Cisterna,** together with the attached **Piazza del Duomo,** constitutes the heart of the town. **Piazza della Cisterna,** an elegant example of medieval architecture, is one of the most attractive sights in San Gimignano. At the center of the square (beautifully paved with bricks) is the well that gives access to the underlying cistern. Surrounding the square are some of the town's important palaces, such as the Palazzo Tortoli-Treccani at no. 22, with its elegant double row of *bifora* ("bifold," divided by a stone arch) windows.

Duomo Collegiata (Basilica di S. Maria Assunta) and Cappella di Santa Fina

Still called the Duomo by locals — long ago, the town lost its bishop and the cathedral was downgraded to a Collegiata — the basilica opens onto a beautiful square connected to Piazza della Cisterna. Built in the 12th century, the Collegiata has a very plain unfinished facade but a gorgeously decorated Romanesque interior with tiger-striped arches and a galaxy of gold stars. Among the treasures inside are the wooden statues of *Gabriele* and *Annunziata* by Jacopo della Quercia and the 14th-century frescoes decorating the naves. The right nave's last chapel is the **Chapel of St. Fina (Cappella di Santa Fina),** one of the most beautiful from the Tuscan Renaissance. Designed by Giuliano and Benedetto da Maiano — Benedetto also carved the panel of the altar — its glorious cycle of frescoes by Domenico Ghirlandaio describes the life of a local girl named Fina, who became the town's patron saint.

Piazza del Duomo. ☎ *0577-940-316. Admission: 3.50€ ($3.15). Open: Summer Mon–Fri 9:30 a.m.–7:30 p.m., Sat 9:30 a.m.–5:00 p.m., and Sun 1–5 p.m.; winter Mon–Sat 9:30 a.m.–5:00 p.m., Sun 1–5 p.m. Closed Jan 21–Feb 28.*

Palazzo del Popolo (Museo Civico and Torre Grossa)

The Palazzo del Popolo (the government's palace) was built between 1288 and 1323 — the crenels were added in the 19th century. Its tower, the **Torre Grossa (Big Tower)** — the tallest in town — was added in 1311. Visiting the Torre Grossa awards you with a superb view over the town. The interior of the palace is decorated with great frescoes and furnishings from the 14th and 15th centuries. Particularly worth visiting in the **Museo Civico** inside the palace is the *Sala di Dante (Dante's Room),* which you reach via an external staircase from the courtyard. (This external staircase is decorated with splendid frescoes by Lippo Memmi — his *Maestà* is considered a masterpiece.)

Piazza del Duomo 1. ☎ *0577-990-312. Admission: 3.62€ ($3.26); Torre Grossa 4.13€ ($3.72). Open: Summer daily 9:30 a.m.–7:30 p.m.; Winter daily 10:00 a.m.–5:30 p.m.*

More cool things to see and do in San Gimignano

San Gimignano is a small town but rich in sights. If you have more time, you may want to explore more of the medieval delights of this once very important artistic and commercial center. Here are a few more choices:

- ✔ **Sant'Agostino** (Piazza Sant'Agostino; ☎ 0577-940-383) is a beautiful 13th-century Romanesque-Gothic church. Its plain facade hides a superb cycle of frescoes by Benozzo Gozzoli on the life of St. Augustine; also interesting is his fresco of St. Sebastian on the third altar to the left. The church is open daily from 7 a.m. to noon and 3 to 6 p.m. (until 7 p.m. in summer), and admission is free.

- ✔ **Via San Matteo** is a section of the Via Francigena, the medieval highway to France. Besides its historic interest — it was the most important communication path between northern and southern Europe — it's a beautiful section of medieval San Gimignano, lined with palaces and towers.

- ✔ The **Museo di Criminologia Medievale (Medieval Criminology Museum)** is housed in the Torre del Diavolo (Devil's Tower) and contains an ample choice of torture instruments as well as a collection of drawings and etchings concerning their use, complete with descriptions in English. These displays are horrifying but soberingly relevant, especially considering that modern versions of these instruments are still used today. *Note:* We designate this museum with the Kid Friendly icon because teenagers may be interested in these ghoulish instruments; this museum is definitely not appropriate for young children. To visit the museum, go to Via del Castello 1, off Piazza della Cisterna. Call ☎ 0577-942-243 for more information.

And on your left, another tower: Seeing San Gimignano by guided tour

If you want to participate in a bus tour, call **American Express** (☎ 055-50-981) or **SITA** (☎ 055-214-721; Internet: www.sita-on-line.it) in Florence. Both companies offer tours of the major attractions in Tuscany, including San Gimignano, for about 47€ ($42.30).

Fast Facts: San Gimignano

Country Code and City Code

The country code for Italy is **39**. The city code for San Gimignano is **0577**; use this city code when calling from anywhere outside or inside Italy, even within San Gimignano, and always include the 0 whether you are calling from Italy or from abroad.

Embassies and Consulates

The nearest are in Florence; See "Fast Facts: Florence" in Chapter 14.

Currency Exchange

You can exchange money at the tourist office (see the tourist office information, later in this section) and in banks or the Protur office (see "Where to stay in San Gimignano" in this chapter).

Emergencies

Ambulance and Pronto Soccorso (first aid) ☎ **118**; fire ☎ **115**; road assistance, ACI ☎ **116**.

Hospital

The nearest hospital is the Ospedale Poggibonsi (Via Pisana 2; ☎ 0577-915-555).

Information

The Pro Loco office (tourist office) is at Piazza Duomo 1 (☎ 0577-940-008; Fax: 0577-940-903). Summer hours are daily 9 a.m. to 1 p.m. and 3 to 7 p.m. Winter hours are 9 a.m. to 1 p.m. and 2 to 6 p.m. daily.

Mail

The post office (ufficio postale) is at Piazza delle Erbe 8 (☎ 0577-941-983).

Police

Call ☎ **113**; for the Carabinieri (other police force), call ☎ **112**.

Web Site

Visit www.sangimignano.com.

Chapter 17

Umbria

● ●

● ●

***U**mbria* is a small region tucked away between Lazio (the region in which Rome is located); Tuscany (Toscana), where Florence is located; and the Marches, with no access to the sea. Famous for its deep green hills and natural beauty, it's also the land of San Francesco (St. Francis) and Santa Chiara (St. Clare), as well as of painter Pietro Vannucci, who brought fame to himself and his town under the name "Il Perugino." Like other parts of Italy, Umbria has its own food specialties, including *tartufi* (truffles) and porcini mushrooms.

Perugia and Spoleto make excellent starting points from which to visit the rest of this region. Keep in mind, though, that you can reach all destinations in Umbria as day-trips from Florence or Rome.

What's Where: Umbria and Its Major Attractions

Umbria is traversed north-to-south by the river **Tiber (Tevere),** the river of Rome that ends at the sea near Ostia Antica (see Chapter 13). In its early segment, the river goes through ravines and steep valleys, which explains why **Perugia,** the region's capital, wasn't built along the river. At the heart of Umbria, this delightful city is rich in art and historic sights and is a lively university town. The city's highlights are the **Palazzo dei Priori** and its magnificent art and the famous **Fontana Maggiore** — and nowhere else will you find a Perugina chocolate as big as your rental car!

Not far away to the east is **Assisi,** hometown of San Francesco, Italy's patron saint. The 1997 earthquakes and aftershocks luckily didn't destroy the town's monuments entirely and spared most of the masterpieces by the major artists of the Renaissance. The highpoints of Assisi are the **Basilica di San Francesco** and its frescoes, the **Basilica di Santa Chiara,** and the **Eremo delle Carceri**.

Spoleto is famous for its music and art festivals — the **Festival di Spoleto** and the **Stagione Lirica** — but it's also a delightful small medieval town offering beautiful vistas, a majestic **Duomo,** and the **Ponte delle Torri.**

To see the scope of the entire Umbrian landscape, see the "Tuscany and Umbria" map in Chapter 15.

Enticing Perugia: Home of Perugina

Etruscan in origin, Perugia developed as an important urban center during the Middle Ages and the Renaissance. It was infamous during the Renaissance for its fierce battles and was finally subjugated by the popes, who imposed a few hundred years of steady rule. Today the city is renowned for its universities and art — and for its chocolate. It's the home of the famous chocolate house of Perugina.

Getting to Perugia

Because Perugia lies on a secondary line, only a few **direct trains** connect it to Florence or Rome. From Rome, the ride takes about 2¾ hours and costs around 13€ ($11.70); from Florence, it's 2½ hours and 12€ ($10.80), and you have to change trains in Terontola. From Venice, you have to go to Florence first; the whole trip takes around six hours and costs 36€ ($32.40). Trains arrive at the **Stazione FS Perugia (☎ 075-500-6865)** on Piazza Vittorio Veneto. From there you can catch one of many buses to Piazza Italia in the town center (a trip of about 15 minutes). Perugia is also on a privately run line connecting Sansepolcro to Terni with a frequent schedule. These trains arrive and depart from the **Stazione Sant'Anna (☎ 075-572-9121)** in the center of town.

The company **SULGA (☎ 075-500-9641)** has three daily **bus runs** from Rome and one from Florence; the trip from Rome takes 2½ hours and costs about 14€ ($12.60); the trip from Florence is 1¾ hours and costs about 13€ ($11.70). The company **SITA (☎ 055-214-721;** Internet: www. sita-on-line.it) also makes one daily run to and from Florence for about the same price. The company **ASP (☎ 075-573-1707)** connects Perugia with Assisi on a daily basis for 2.58€ ($2.32) and with other cities in Umbria. Buses arrive in Perugia in Piazza Partigiani, an escalator ride from Piazza Italia at the center of town.

Perugia is 180km (115 miles) from Rome and 150km (94 miles) from Florence. If you're **driving** from Florence, take A1 to the Val di Chiana Bettolle-Sinalunga exit and switch to SS75bis to Perugia. From Rome,

Perugia

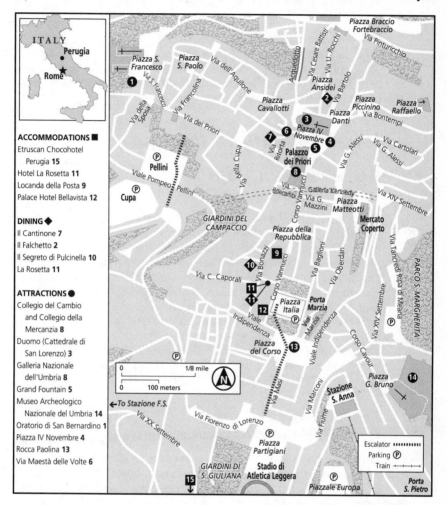

ITALY
Perugia •
Rome ★

ACCOMMODATIONS ■
Etruscan Chocohotel
   Perugia **15**
Hotel La Rosetta **11**
Locanda della Posta **9**
Palace Hotel Bellavista **12**

DINING ◆
Il Cantinone **7**
Il Falchetto **2**
Il Segreto di Pulcinella **10**
La Rosetta **11**

ATTRACTIONS ●
Collegio del Cambio
   and Collegio della
   Mercanzia **8**
Duomo (Cattedrale di
   San Lorenzo) **3**
Galleria Nazionale
   dell'Umbria **8**
Grand Fountain **5**
Museo Archeologico
   Nazionale del Umbria **14**
Oratorio di San Bernardino **1**
Piazza IV Novembre **4**
Rocca Paolina **13**
Via Maestà delle Volte **6**

take A1 to Orte and then SS204 to SS36 to Perugia. The center of the
historic town is at the top of a steep hill; because the center has
restricted traffic, you have to leave your car in one of the numerous
parking lots — a convenient one is Piazza Partigiani's underground
parking lot, just south of the historic center, but they're all linked to
the center by elevators or escalators.

You're allowed to drive up into town to bring your luggage to your
hotel before parking — but keep an eye on it (someone broke the
window of our rental car in the few minutes we left it unattended).
Maybe because of its bloody past, Perugia has a reputation for having a
slightly violent edge (though, as elsewhere in Italy, physical violence
isn't as much a concern as theft).

Getting around Perugia

The historic center has a relatively simple layout along **Corso Vannucci,** with the bus and train arrivals at one end (at the bottom of a public escalator) in **Piazza Italia** and the major sites on **Piazza IV Novembre** at the other end. As often in small medieval Italian towns, Perugia is easily visited on foot; however, the city maintains a system of buses with the central hub in Piazza Italia. If you want a **taxi,** call ☎ **075-500-4888.**

Where to stay in Perugia

Etruscan Chocohotel Perugia
$$ Piazza dei Partigiani

This almost glitzy (for Italy) hotel offers style at a moderate price. All the air-conditioned guest rooms have modern Italian-style furniture and large baths. The real draw, though, is staying in a "chocohotel": Each floor is dedicated to a type of chocolate (milk, dark, gianduia) and each room has a "chocodesk" . . . we'll leave you to discover that surprise. The restaurant features a cocoa-based menu, and in the chocostore you can sample many concoctions. Non-chocolate amenities include a large roof deck with a panoramic view and a good-sized swimming pool.

Via Campo di Marte 134. ☎ *075-583-7314. Fax: 075-583-7314. Internet:* www.choco hotel.it. *E-mail:* etruscan3ocohotel.it. *Parking: Free. Rack rates: 84€–116€ ($75.60–$104.40). AE, DC, MC, V.*

Hotel La Rosetta
$$ Piazza Italia

Considered one of the best hotels in town, La Rosetta is very convenient and boasts a national historic landmark in one of its guest rooms (Suite 55, which is richly decorated with frescoes). The rooms vary widely in furnishings but are uniformly comfortable, airy, and well kept.

Piazza Italia 19. ☎ *075-572-0841. Fax: 075-572-0841. Parking: 15.50€ ($14). Rack rates: 115€ ($103.50) double, including buffet breakfast. AE, DC.*

Locanda della Posta
$$$ Corso Vannucci

The first hotel to open in Perugia — it counts Goethe among its past guests — the Locanda is an old-fashioned place. Although the atmosphere is very classic, the hotel was revamped with modern amenities, and the commodious guest rooms have up-to-date baths and air-conditioning. The management is friendly and available.

Corso Vannucci 97. ☎ **075-572-8925.** *Fax: 075-572-2413. E-mail:* locanda@assind. perugia.it. *Bus: 1 to Piazza Vittorio Emanuele. Parking: 10.33€ ($9.30) Rack rates: 123.95€–75.60€ ($111.60–$158) double, including buffet breakfast. AE, DC, MC, V.*

Palace Hotel Bellavista
$$ Piazza Italia

Once part of Perugia's most expensive hotel — which still exists next door — the Bellavista has a curious but charming layout. The public areas are grand and bestow a feeling of timeless elegance, but the rest of the hotel is modern. The spacious guest rooms have contemporary furnishings and functional baths, and the service is excellent.

Piazza Italia 12. ☎ **075-572-0741.** *Fax: 075-572-9092. Parking: 13€ ($11.70). Rack rates: 113.62€–134.28€ ($102.26–$120.85) double, including breakfast. AE, DC, MC, V.*

Where to dine in Perugia

Landlocked Umbria developed a cuisine that relies heavily on regional produce. Particularly famous for its truffles, both black and white, it uses them lavishly in its cuisine, usually under the label *alla Norcina* (in the manner of Norcia). Another specialty of Umbria — and Norcia — is wild boar (the famous *cinghiale*), so *alla Norcina* may also refer to a sauce prepared with the wild boar sausages that make Norcia famous (if you're lucky, you may even get both).

A university town, Perugia has a lot of *pizzerie* and cheap trattorie where you can have a bite in a lively, casual atmosphere; you'll often see crowds of young people waiting to get into these places.

Il Cantinone
$$$ Piazza Italia   UMBRIAN

Just off Piazza IV Novembre, in the medieval district, this restaurant has vaulted ceilings and a·simple decor. The food is traditional and excellent; try the grilled meats or the *torello alla Perugina* (veal with chicken livers), one of Perugia's specialties.

Via Ritorta 6. ☎ **075-573-4130.** *Reservations recommended. Secondi: 7.23€–15.49€ ($6.51–$14). AE, DC, MC, V. Open: Lunch and dinner Wed–Mon.*

Il Falchetto
$$$$$ Duomo   UMBRIAN

With a real medieval atmosphere (one dining room is from the 14th century) and a traditional menu, Falchetto is an excellent place for discovering Umbrian cuisine — especially if you're in the mood for a splurge.

Try the *lepre alle olive* (hare with olives). The terrace is particularly in demand during the summer Umbria Jazz concerts (see "More cool things to see and do in Perugia," later in this chapter).

Via Bartolo 20. ☎ 075-573-1775. Reservations recommended. Secondi: 15.49€– 30.99€ ($13.94–$27.89). AE, DC, MC, V. Open: Lunch and dinner Tues–Sun.

Il Segreto di Pulcinella
$$ Piazza Italia   PIZZA

To give your wallet a breather, sample the tasty pizza prepared in this popular hangout. It's located just a couple of blocks off the most crowded street of the historic center.

Via Larga 8. ☎ 075-573-6284. Reservations recommended on weekends. Pizza: 5.15–8.26€ ($4.64–$7.43). No credit cards accepted. Open: Lunch and dinner Wed–Mon.

La Rosetta
$$$ Piazza Italia   UMBRIAN

In the hotel of the same name, La Rosetta is a famous restaurant in Perugia, offering a large choice of dishes prepared according to the best Umbrian tradition. Try the *spaghetti alla Norcina* (spaghetti with truffles) or the *scaloppine alla Perugina* (veal sautéed with wine and chicken livers).

Piazza Italia 19. ☎ 075-572-0841. Reservations recommended. Secondi: 8.26€– 20.66€ ($7.43–$18.59). AE, DC, MC, V. Open: Lunch and dinner daily.

Exploring Perugia

Although having a couple of days to really savor the treasures of the capital of Umbria — both the visual and the edible arts — would be best, Perugia is a small town you can easily visit as a day-trip from Rome or Florence. For the location of the tourist office, see "Fast Facts: Perugia."

The top sights in Perugia

Once a Roman reservoir, **Piazza IV Novembre** is the heart of Perugia. On one side is the 15th-century facade of the **Duomo (Cattedrale di San Lorenzo)** — a beautiful face on an otherwise dull baroque church. On the other side is the magnificent 13th-century **Palazzo dei Priori,** created as the seat of the government and one of the finest examples of Gothic architecture in Italy. Built between 1298 and 1353, the *palazzo* is a striking travertine building with white and red marble inlays. The main portal — accessible by a wide semicircular staircase — is off-center in the facade; it leads to the spacious **Hall of the Notables (Sala dei Notari).** There are two bronzes over the door, of the griffin and the lion, symbols of the city. You can visit the *palazzo*'s many frescoed rooms (☎ 075-577-2339; open summer daily from 9 a.m. to 1 p.m. and 3 to

7 p.m.; winter Tuesday through Sunday from 9 a.m. to 1 p.m. and 3 to 7 p.m.); admission is free. It also houses the Collegio del Cambio and the Galleria Nazionale dell'Umbria (see descriptions in the following paragraphs). In front of the palace, the **Grand Fountain (Fontana Maggiore),** a Gothic masterpiece carved by the famous Pisan sculptors Nicola and Giovanni Pisano, was under restoration for many years and is now visible once again. It has been called the most beautiful fountain in the world. Carved from white and pink marble, it has an allegorical panel representing each of the months of the year. Departing from the piazza is **Via Maestà delle Volte,** a typical medieval street with covered passages.

Collegio del Cambio and Collegio della Mercanzia

On the Palazzo dei Priori's ground floor, the Collegio del Cambio was the city's goods exchange in Renaissance times. This section of the palace is very interesting for its architecture and also for its magnificent frescoed ceilings, in particular those of the **Hall of the Audience (Sala dell'Udienza)** by Perugino and his assistants, one of whom was a young Raphael. These frescoes illustrate the life of Christ; there's also a **self-portrait of Perugino** himself. Also of interest is the **Chapel of Saint John the Baptist (Cappella di San Giovanni Battista),** with frescoes by Giannicola di Paolo. If you enter at Corso Vannucci 15, you'll find the **Merchant's Guild (Collegio della Mercanzia),** decorated with intricately carved wood paneling and beautiful vaulted ceilings.

Collegio del Cambio, Corso Vannucci 25. ☎ 075-572-8599. Collegio della Mercanzia, Corso Vannucci 15. ☎ 075-573-0366. Admission: Cambio 2.60€ ($2.34); Mercanzia 1.03€ (93¢); combined ticket to both 3.10€ ($2.79). Open: Cambio, Mon–Sat 9:00 a.m.–12:30 p.m. and 2:30–5:30 p.m., Sun 9:00 a.m.–12:30 p.m.; Mercanzia, Tues–Sat 9 a.m.–1 p.m. and 2:30–5:30 p.m., Sun 9 a.m.–1 p.m.

Galleria Nazionale dell'Umbria

On the Palazzo dei Priori's third floor, this gallery is remarkably well organized, with explanatory material for each work. The collection of Umbrian art from the 13th to the 19th centuries is indeed rich, including a number of marvelous Peruginos, a Gentile da Fabriano *Madonna and Child,* and a famous (and stunning) Piero della Francesco polyptych. This museum is strong in the late-medieval/early-Renaissance period, documenting the important phase during which Giotto and Cimabue revolutionized painting techniques. It's probably the most enjoyable Italian museum after the more famous ones in the larger cities.

Palazzo dei Priori, Corso Vannucci 19. ☎ 075-574-1257. Admission: 6.50€ ($5.85). Open: Daily 8:30 a.m.–7:30 p.m.; closed the first Mon of every month.

Museo Archeologico Nazionale del Umbria

Founded at the end of the 18th century, this museum occupies a former convent and is divided into a prehistoric section and an Etruscan-Roman section. The latter includes jewelry, funerary urns, statues, and other objects. Of particular interest are the sets of objects that, according to Etruscan custom, were entombed with the dead; these come from the necropoli of Frontone and Monte Luce. You can also see the **Cippo Perugino,** the stone that marked the boundary of Perugia in Etruscan times — it's important for its long inscription in Etruscan (a language still not fully deciphered).

Piazza G. Bruno 10. ☎ *075-572-7141. Admission: 2.07€ ($1.86). Open: Mon 2:30–7:30 p.m. and Tues–Sun 8:30 a.m.–7:30 p.m.*

Oratorio di San Bernardino

Built in 1461 and designed by Agostino di Duccio, this oratory is a particularly attractive example of northern Italian Renaissance architecture. Constructed of multicolored marble, the church has a facade decorated with intricate reliefs illustrating the life of the saint. A paleo-Christian sarcophagus (fourth century) is now the main altar.

Piazza San Francesco al Prato, at the end of Via dei Priori. Admission: Free. Open: Daily 9:00 a.m.–12:30 p.m. and 3–6 p.m.

More cool things to see and do in Perugia

If you have some extra time to spend in Perugia, check out some of these other sights:

✔ The **Rocca Paolina,** built in 1540 by Pope Paul III (hence the name) and designed by the famous architect Antonio da Sangallo the Younger, is a fortress that was constructed on top of medieval buildings and even earlier structures (you can still see an arch from the original Etruscan city walls). The upper part of the Rocca was demolished in 1860, but the lower sections were preserved, and the archaeological site has now been excavated. By a series of escalators, you can see the inside, viewing the fortification's huge walls, parts of dwellings and ancient streets, and even fragments of the ancient stadium where a forerunner of soccer was played. The Rocca is open daily from 6:15 a.m. to 1:45 a.m. (the information office is open from 9 a.m. to 1 p.m. and 4 to 7 p.m.; ☎ **075-506-781**), and admission is free.

✔ Perugia owes its fame to the world-famous chocolate manufacturer **Perugina,** and Perugina's claim to fame is its brilliant creation of Baci ("kisses"). You may have seen these bonbons — wrapped in silver paper speckled with purple-blue stars — in your country. They're delicious balls of soft chocolate mixed with finely chopped hazelnuts, each topped by a whole toasted hazelnut and dipped in dark chocolate. Call ☎ **075-52-761** in advance to schedule a free tour of the **Perugina chocolate factory,** in the neighborhood of San Sisto, 6km (3 miles) west of the city center (take a cab). A delicious experience! Inside the factory is a **Museo Storico,** the historic

museum of the Perugina factory (☎ **075-527-6796**); it's open
Monday through Friday from 9 a.m. to 1 p.m. and 2:30 to 5:00 p.m.
(Saturday and Sunday by appointment only), and admission is free.

✔ Because of its role in the chocolate world, Perugia is the seat of
many an event involving the dark delicacy. The most important is
the international **Eurochocolate** (☎ **075-572-3327**; Internet: www.
chocolate.perugia.it), showcasing the latest developments in
the centuries-old art of making chocolate (held in October). You can
buy chocolate by weight in huge pieces in Perugia — and at Easter
they make a giant Bacio weighing hundreds of kilos and let children
and chocolate-mad adults hack away at it!

✔ The **Umbria Jazz Festival,** one of Europe's major jazz festivals,
attracts big names from all over the world. It takes place in the
second half of July and has a mini winter version over the New
Year's holiday. Contact the Associazione Umbria Jazz (Piazza
Danti 28, Casella Postale 228; ☎ **075-573-2432;** Fax: 075-572-2656;
Internet: www.umbriajazz.com).

Fast Facts: Perugia

Country Code and City Code

The country code for Italy is **39.** The city
code for Perugia is **075;** use this code when
calling from anywhere outside or inside Italy,
even within Perugia itself (include the 0
every time, even when calling from abroad).

Embassies and Consulates

See "Fast Facts: Florence" in Chapter 14 and
"Fast Facts: Rome" in Chapter 12.

Currency Exchange

You can change money at the F.S. Piazza
Vittorio Veneto rail station and Genefin at
Via Pinturicchio 14–16 and also at the
numerous banks that have ATMs.

Emergencies

Ambulance and first aid (Pronto Soccorso),
☎ **118;** fire, ☎ **115;** road assistance, ☎ **116.**

Hospital

The Ospedale Monteluce is on Piazza
Monteluce (☎ 075-57-81).

Information

You can write for information to Perugia's
main tourist office: APT (Via Mazzini 21;
☎ 075-572-3327; Fax: 075-573-6828). Once in
town, visit its tourist booth just off the stairs
of the Palazzo dei Priori at Piazza IV
November 3 (☎ 075-573-6458), open daily
from 9 a.m. to 1 p.m. and 4 to 6 p.m. The
tourist info line is ☎ 199-101-330.

Mail

The post office (ufficio postale) is on Piazza
Matteotti.

Police

Call ☎ **113;** for the Carabinieri (other police
force), call ☎ **112.**

Web Sites

Visit www.perugiaonline.com.

Visiting Assisi: An Artistic and Religious Pilgrimage

The hometown of Italy's patron saint, St. Francis (San Francesco), Assisi is famous around the world for its art and religious monuments. Many of its visitors are actually pilgrims who come to honor the humble man who was said to speak to animals and who created the Franciscan order. San Francesco was born in 1182 to a wealthy merchant family and died in 1226 in a simple hut. How he traversed the social scale and caused a revolution in Christianity is a remarkable story.

In 1209, after a reckless youth and even imprisonment, Francis experienced visions that led him to sell his father's cloth and give away the proceeds. He tried to follow the Bible literally and live the life of Christ, publicly renouncing his inheritance and rejecting wealth absolutely (this didn't endear him to the rich medieval church hierarchy). Two years before his death, he received the stigmata on a mountaintop — this and other scenes from his life were popular subjects for painters of the late medieval period and the Renaissance.

Assisi is only a small town of about 3,000 souls, though millions flock to it every year. You can easily visit it on a day-trip from Florence or Rome, but you can also stay overnight. For the location of the tourist office, see "Fast Facts: Assisi," later in this chapter.

Getting to Assisi

Assisi lies on a spur track of the main **train line** so you'll have to switch trains to get here. If you're coming from Perugia or Rome, you'll have to change at Foligno; from Florence, you'll have to change in Terontola. Trains for Assisi are frequent from each of these stations. A ticket from Rome and Florence costs about 12.91€ ($11.62) and from Perugia (a half-hour away) about 1.55€ ($1.40). Figure on 3½ hours from Rome and 3 hours from Florence, depending on connections. Trains arrive at the rail station of Santa Maria degli Angeli, a small town 6km (3¾ miles) from Assisi. The station is well connected to the historic center of Assisi by a shuttle bus departing every half-hour and stopping in Piazza Matteotti, within Assisi's walls; the price is 1.29€ ($1.16). Taxis are also available at the station, but they cost much more.

The **bus company ASP** (☎ 075-573-1707) connects Perugia with Assisi on a frequent schedule — about every half-hour. Buses leave Perugia from Piazza Partigiani and arrive at Piazza Matteotti behind the Duomo for 2.60€ ($2.34). There are also daily runs from Florence and Rome — one a day from Rome (a 3-hour trip costing 15.49€/$13.94) and two from Florence (a 2½-hour trip costing 12.91€/$11.62).

Assisi

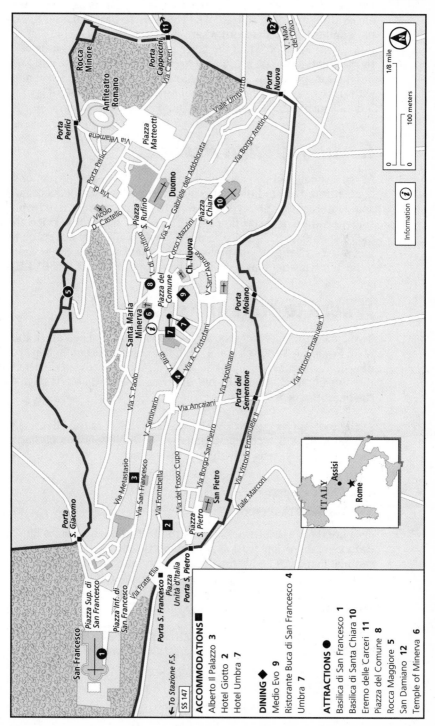

Information

ACCOMMODATIONS ■
Alberto Il Palazzo **3**
Hotel Giotto **2**
Hotel Umbra **7**

DINING ◆
Medio Evo **9**
Ristorante Buca di San Francesco **4**
Umbra **7**

ATTRACTIONS ●
Basilica di San Francesco **1**
Basilica di Santa Chiara **10**
Eremo delle Carceri **11**
Piazza del Comune **8**
Rocca Maggiore **5**
San Damiano **12**
Temple of Minerva **6**

Assisi is 27km (16.9 miles) from Perugia. If you're **driving,** take SS3 in the direction of Foligno, then look for the exit for Assisi. The town is almost totally closed to traffic, so you have to park outside. You can park under Piazza Matteotti where there's a large lot — but "large" doesn't mean much when the place is packed with thousands of tourists and pilgrims. If you're going in summer, get there early or use public transportation. All parking lots outside the walls are connected with the town center by public minibuses costing .62€ (56¢); you can buy tickets at bars, tobacconists, and newsstands.

Getting around Assisi

Assisi is small and you can see it on foot — the town's attractions are concentrated around the main square. However, outside Assisi are some interesting sights you can walk to — but getting there by public transportation or taxi is far easier. The public **minibus service** links all major sites (see "Getting to Assisi"). You can also buy tickets on the bus at a surcharge. If you prefer to take a **taxi,** look for the several stations in town where taxis wait for their fares or call ☎ **075-813-193.**

Where to stay in Assisi

If you want to come to Assisi for religious holidays like Easter, the Feast of St. Francis (October 3 and 4), and the Calendimaggio in May, you'll have to reserve as much as half a year or more in advance. Otherwise, the only choices left may be big, ugly hotels in Santa Maria degli Angeli, the nearby little town.

At the tourist office (see "Fast Facts: Assisi" later in the chapter) you can get help with accommodations — but don't count on finding a room in the high season without a reservation.

Albergo Il Palazzo
$$ Via San Francesco

This hotel occupies the left wing of the 16th-century Palazzo Bindangoli-Bartocci (the other wing is still inhabited by the descendants of the original family). The beamed ceilings, antique furnishings, and original paintings that decorate the halls give the *albergo* a uniquely authentic feeling. The rooms have wrought-iron four-poster beds and bright white walls; some afford a view over the surrounding valley.

Via San Francesco 8. ☎ *075-816-841. Fax: 075-812-370. Rack rates: 90€–110€ ($81–$99) double including buffet breakfast. Closed Nov–Feb. AE, DC, MC, V.*

Hotel Giotto

$$ Porta San Francesco

This big hotel caters to groups but is still a good choice, and you may have a chance of finding a room here if you didn't plan ahead. The guest rooms are modern, even though the building isn't (a work of the centuries). Built on the side of a hill, it offers sweeping vistas, terraces, and a garden.

Via Fontebella 41. ☎ *075-812-209. Fax: 075-816-479. Parking: Free. Rack rates: 118.79€ ($106.91) double, including breakfast. AE, DC, MC, V.*

Hotel Umbra

$$ Piazza del Comune

Like many other hotels in Umbria and Tuscany, this one is housed in an old *palazzo,* but the Umbra has more of the nice touches people look for — old or even antique furniture, views of the surrounding hills and valleys, renovated bathrooms, and balconies. The Umbra's **restaurant** (see "Where to dine in Assisi") is particularly good and is popular with locals as well as guests. The walled garden is an especially nice place to take a meal if you're in town in summer.

Via degli Archi 6, just off Piazza del Comune (west side). ☎ *075-812-240. Fax: 075-813-653. E-mail:* humbra@mail.caribusiness.it. *Parking: 7.75€ ($6.98). Rack rates: 103.29€–129.11€ ($92.96–116.20) double. Closed mid-Jan to mid-Mar. AE, DC, MC, V.*

Where to dine in Assisi

Assisi's food is basically the same as that of Perugia. There are lots of restaurants in town — some very touristy, others more authentic. Prices in general are above average.

Medio Evo

$$$ Piazza del Comune   UMBRIAN/ITALIAN

A little south of Piazza del Comune, this family-run restaurant may be the town's most interesting place to eat. It combines traditional Umbrian cuisine with accents from other cultures. The building rests on 1,000-year-old foundations (note the name, which means "Middle Ages") and has vaulted medieval ceilings. For a *primo,* try the *tortelloni* (large ravioli) or pasta with truffles; for a *secondo,* try one of the variety of grilled and roasted meats.

Via dell' Arco dei Priori 4/b. ☎ *075-813-068. Reservations recommended. Secondi: 9.30€–14.46€ ($8.37–$13.01). AE, DC, MC, V. Open: Lunch and dinner Thurs–Tues; closed a month in Jan/Feb and three weeks in July.*

Ristorante Buca di San Francesco

$$$$ Piazza del Comune   UMBRIAN

In the center of town, this restaurant is housed in a medieval building and serves traditional, if pricey, food. The menu is excellent and changes with the seasons and what's available at the market. One dish we particularly like is the *cannelloni* (homemade pasta tubes filled with cheese or meat and served with tomato sauce). The garden provides a view of Assisi's historic center.

Via Brizzi 1. ☎ 075-812-204. Reservations recommended. Secondi: 12.91€–20.66€ ($11.62–$18.59). AE, DC, MC, V. Open: Lunch and dinner Tues–Sun; closed two weeks in July.

Umbra

$$$ Piazza del Comune   UMBRIAN

In the hotel of the same name, this popular restaurant opened nearly 80 years ago and is an institution. Don't miss the garden if the weather is fine. Umbra serves traditional dishes from the countryside, including *primi* with truffles (like the coveted white ones, when in season) and well-prepared *secondi*.

Via degli Archi 6. ☎ 075-812-240. Reservations recommended. Secondi: 8.78€– 15.49€ ($7.90–$13.94). AE, DC, MC, V. Open: Lunch and dinner Mon–Sun; closed mid-Jan to mid-Mar.

Exploring Assisi

The 1997 earthquakes and multiple aftershocks that rocked Umbria had tragic consequences for Assisi. Two Franciscan friars and two surveyors examining the damage right after the first quake were killed when pieces of the ceiling fell on them. The main quake did severe damage to the Basilica di San Francesco, and the beautifully decorated church and the monastery were greatly endangered. Further tremors did more damage.

Restoration was immediately started with an ambitious (breakneck) schedule of repairs and was completed by the Papal Jubilee in 2000 (pretty amazing, given that one fresco was in 50,000 pieces and had to be put back together). Through the generosity of donors all over the world, Assisi was rebuilt — the total cost of repairing the destruction in the region was estimated at more than $1 billion. The upper basilica had severe structural damage; in addition to the loss of the art inside, it was in danger of collapse, imperiling the lower basilica. Frescoes that fell from a great height were completely pulverized and beyond repair; all that was left were small chips of colored dust. Other frescoes crumbled into pieces the size of a dime, which had to be painstakingly catalogued and reassembled over full-size copies of the frescoes or scanned and input into a computer and then positioned. The basilica's ceiling and walls have been reinforced and its columns braced with steel.

The top sights in Assisi

Piazza del Comune is in the heart of Assisi, at the end of Via San Francesco, and at the junction with Corso Mazzini. With so much religious art to see in Assisi, many people forget it was actually a Roman town. Graced with Renaissance fountains, this medieval piazza was built over the Roman Forum and the **Temple of Minerva** from the first century B.C., the latter still standing with its portico of six Corinthian columns. Later, Christians converted the temple into a church (and later gave it a baroque overhaul), which saved it from the destruction of time and accounts for why it's one of the best-preserved Roman temples in Italy. Adjoining the temple is the 13th-century **Torre (Tower),** built by the Ghibellines. The site is open daily from 7 a.m. to noon and 2:30 p.m. to dusk.

Basilica di San Francesco

Begun in 1228 to house the bones of St. Francis, the basilica is not one church but two churches — an upper basilica and a lower basilica. The scaffolding that covered the church has been removed, and although the quake destroyed some frescoes beyond repair, some have been reassembled — from immense puzzles of thousands of pieces. The **Upper Basilica** contains Cimabue's *Crucifixion* and Giotto's celebrated cycle of frescoes on the life of the saint, including *St. Francis Preaching to the Birds.* The **Lower Basilica** is a somber Gothic monument to Francis's life, from which stairs descend to the crypt where his coffin was hidden (rediscovered in the 19th century). The **Magdalen Chapel (Cappella della Maddalena)** was frescoed by Giotto and his followers. Pietro Lorenzetti's beautiful *Deposition* is in the left transept; on the right is Cimabue's *Madonna Enthroned with Four Angels and St. Francis.* Friars assist visitors and even give church tours, some of them in English (though the tour is free, making a donation is customary because the order exists only on alms).

Piazza Superiorie di San Francesco/Piazza Inferiore di San Francesco. ☎ *075-819-001. Admission: Basilica free; Treasury and Perkins Collection 2.07€ ($1.86). Open: Basilica summer daily 8:30 a.m.–7:00 p.m. (winter to 6 p.m.; no visiting Sundays and holidays during morning mass); Treasury and Perkins Collecton summer Mon–Sat 9:30 a.m. to noon and 2–6 p.m.*

Basilica di Santa Chiara

Pilgrims come to this cavernous 1260 church to see the **tomb of Santa Chiara (St. Clare).** Canonized in 1255, she was the founder of the order of the Poor Clares. Chiara left her family to follow St. Francis, abandoning wealth and worldly pretensions as he did and cutting off her hair to symbolize her renunciation of the world. A number of miracles are attributed to her, one of which, a vision, led to her being proclaimed the patron saint of TV (saints don't get asked whether they want these honors). The other object attracting pilgrims is in the **Oratorio** — the crucifix that miraculously spoke to St. Francis and led him to start on his difficult path in the face of family, church, and society. Only some of the church's original frescoes remain. Note that Santa Chiara was closed at press time but should be open by the time you arrive.

Piazza di Santa Chiara. ☎ *075-812-282. Admission: Free. Open: Summer daily 6:30 a.m. to noon and 2–7 p.m.; winter daily 6:30 a.m. to noon and 2–6 p.m.*

Eremo delle Carceri

Eremo means "hermitage," and this is the site where St. Francis retired to meditate and pray, on the peaceful slopes of Mount Subasio. The name of the site comes from the fact that Francis and his followers withdrew here as though to a prison *(carcere)*. Several of his miracles occurred here, and you can still see the sites — such as the ancient tree believed to be the one where he preached his sermon to the birds (see Giotto's fresco of this scene in the Basilica di San Francesco). Also here are the unforgiving stone bed where he slept and the dried-out stream he quieted because its noise was interrupting his prayers. If you want to partake of the silence of Mount Subasio yourself, stroll the marked trails in the park.

4km (2½ miles) east of Assisi, out the Porta Cappuccini. ☎ *075-812-301. Bus: A minibus links the major sights (see "Getting around Assisi"). Admission: Voluntary by donation. Open: Summer daily 6:30 a.m.–7:30 p.m., winter only until 5 p.m.*

More cool things to see and do in Assisi

If you still haven't gotten your fill of the sights of Assisi, here are some more you can visit:

✔ At the end of Via della Rocca is the **Rocca Maggiore** (☎ 075-815-292), a monument to a spirit opposite that of St. Francis's. With foundations going back to ancient times, this 14th-century fort was built by the papacy when it subdued Assisi and brought the area under Roman rule. It's somber and dark inside, but from the top you have a fabulous view of the walls and the town. In the spring of 2000, a bolt of lightning struck the Rocca and a tower partially collapsed, so the site is closed until further notice.

✔ The **convent of San Damiano** (☎ 075-812-273), 2.5km (1.6 miles) from Assisi out the Porta Nuova, was built around the place of worship where St. Francis, praying before a wooden crucifix (today in the Basilica di Santa Chiara), had his first vision. This simple convent and its oratory, refectory, and cloister are beautifully decorated with frescoes from the 14th to the 16th centuries. You can also visit the dormitory where St. Clare died. It's open daily from 10:00 a.m. to 12:30 p.m. and 2 to 6 p.m., and admission is free.

And on your left, the Basilica di San Francesco: Seeing Assisi by guided tour

Free tours of Assisi are given by the Franciscan order in town, starting from the office just outside the entrance to the lower basilica on the left in Piazza Inferiore di San Francesco (☎ **075-819-0084**; Fax: 075-819-0035; E-mail: chiu@krenet.it). Tours last about an hour and take place Monday through Saturday from 9 a.m. to noon and Monday through Sunday from 2:00 to 5:30 p.m. (winter to 4:30 p.m.).

Fast Facts: Assisi

Country Code and City Code
The country code for Italy is **39**. The city code for Assisi is **075**; use this code when calling from anywhere outside or inside Italy, even within Assisi itself (include the 0 every time, even when calling from abroad).

Embassies and Consulates
See "Fast Facts: Florence" in Chapter 14 and "Fast Facts: Rome" in Chapter 12.

Currency Exchange
You can change money in the ticket office at the rail station in Santa Maria degli Angeli.

Emergencies
Ambulance and Pronto Soccorso, ☎ **118**; fire, ☎ **115**; road assistance ACI, ☎ **116**.

Hospital
The Ospedale di Assisi is just outside town in the direction of San Damiano (☎ 075-81-391).

Information
The main tourist office is APT at Piazza del Comune 27 (☎ 075-812-450; Fax: 075-813-727). It's open Monday through Friday 8 a.m. to 2 p.m. and 3:30 to 6:30 p.m., Saturday 9 a.m. to 1 p.m. and 3:30 to 6:30 p.m., and Sunday 9 a.m. to 1 p.m. It also maintains a seasonal tourist booth outdoors at Largo Properzio, just off Piazza del Comune (☎ 075-812-534), where you can get brochures and maps; April through October, it's open daily 9 a.m. to 6 p.m.

Mail
The Ufficio Postale is at Largo Properzio 4 (☎ 075-812-355).

Police
Call ☎ **113**; for the Carabinieri (other police force), call ☎ **112**.

Enjoying Spoleto and the Spoleto Festival

A small medieval city in the shadow of an imposing fortress, Spoleto is one of the most picturesque towns in Umbria as well as one of the most famous. The city's development began in pre-Roman times, with the Umbri people who founded it. During the Roman period, Spoleto valiantly resisted the advances of Hannibal; under the emperors it was the resort of wealthy Romans. In the Middle Ages, Spoleto was devastated by the black plague and an earthquake; still, this jewel set among the Umbrian hills was a coveted prize fought over by Perugia and the Papacy. Today it is known the world over as a city of music and culture.

Spoleto is surrounded by the countryside that has made Umbria famous: olive groves, green hills, and beautiful mountains. Small enough to be visited as a day-trip from Rome or Florence, it's also a wonderful place to spend some days of leisure, especially during one of its art and music festivals. For the location of the tourist office, see "Fast Facts: Spoleto."

Getting to Spoleto

Spoleto is well connected by **rail** to all major destinations. There's direct service from Rome (the trip takes 1½ hours and costs about 14€/$12.60); you need to change in Foligno if you're traveling to and from Perugia (a trip of less than an hour, costing about 8€/$7.20). Trains arrive at Spoleto's **Stazione FS** on Piazza Polvani (☎ **0743-48-516**), across the river Tessino to the north of the city's center. The station is well connected with the town by bus (circolare A, B, C, or D).

The **bus company SSIT** (☎ **0743-212-211**) has two daily runs to Perugia (a 90-minute trip for about 7€/$6.30) and many daily runs to Terni, where you can switch to one of the two daily trips to Rome (the whole thing takes about 2½ hours).

Spoleto lies about 130km (80 miles) from Rome on the Flaminia (SS3), the scenic but narrow consular road heading north from Rome. If you're **driving,** a faster possibility is A1; you exit at Orte and take the *superstrada* for Terni (follow the directions for Terni). The *superstrada* merges back into SS3 right after Terni; then just follow the directions for Spoleto.

Getting around Spoleto

Spoleto is a small town on the slope of a mountain. Although the city developed on two levels (a lower one around the river Tessino and an upper one toward the fortress), the historic center *(centro storico),* with most of Spoleto's attractions, is on the upper level, and you can easily visit it on foot — easily, that is, if you are in relatively good shape, for some of the streets are quite steep. However, you can also make use of the well-organized **bus service;** tickets cost .62€ (55¢) and are sold at the usual places (tobacconists and bars). As in other medieval towns, some of the narrower or stepped streets are closed to traffic.

Where to stay in Spoleto

Because of its festivals, Spoleto offers a large range of accommodations; if you're in need of a room, the local tourist office can arrange one for you. Consider, though, that reservations for the Spoleto Festival are made as much as a year in advance, and if you just breeze into town without a reservation at that time you probably won't find accommodations.

Spoleto

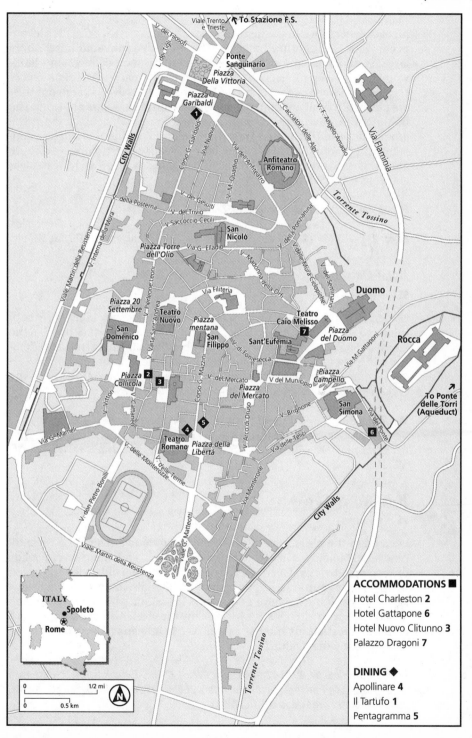

ACCOMMODATIONS ■
Hotel Charleston **2**
Hotel Gattapone **6**
Hotel Nuovo Clitunno **3**
Palazzo Dragoni **7**

DINING ◆
Apollinare **4**
Il Tartufo **1**
Pentagramma **5**

Hotel Charleston
$$ Centro

An excellent choice in the historic center *(centro storico),* the Charleston occupies a 17th-century building. The recently renovated hotel offers large, comfortable guest rooms with wood-beamed ceilings and hardwood floors. Each room is decorated differently, many with bright colors recalling the Renaissance. The bathrooms are not always large but they are nicely tiled and appointed; some have bathtubs, others showers. The public areas have terra-cotta floors, and an open fireplace is on the ground floor in the lounge area. The family that runs this hotel is constantly upgrading it; most rooms now have air-conditioning, and there are designated no-smoking rooms. The breakfast is buffet style, with meat and eggs if you want them.

*Piazza Collicola 10. ☎ **0743-220-052.** Fax: 0743-221-244. Internet: www.hotel charleston.it. E-mail: info@hotelcharleston.it. Parking: Free. Rack rates: 74€–108.46€ ($66.60–$97.61) double, including breakfast. AE, DC, MC, V.*

Hotel Gattapone
$$$ Rocca

Named after the architect who built the Rocca Albornoz (see "More cool things to see and do in Spoleto," later in this section), this hotel is the nicest in Spoleto. The two 17th-century buildings forming the hotel dominate the town from a splendid location on the side of the Rocca. The guest rooms — furnished with antiques — are spacious and offer all the comforts, including good beds and modern baths.

*Via del Ponte 6. ☎ **0743-223-447.** Fax: 0743-223-448. Internet: www.caribusiness. it/gattapone. E-mail: gattapone@mail.caribusiness.it. Parking: Free. Rack rates: 139.44€–201.42€ ($125.50–$181.28) double, including breakfast. AE, DC, MC, V.*

Hotel Nuovo Clitunno
$$ Centro

Located in the older part of town, the Clitunno is housed in a recently renovated building, has a large number of rooms, and offers several kinds of accommodations. The rooms are divided between old style (decorated with antique reproduction furnishings in Renaissance style) and new style (modern but tasteful and comfortable). In addition, some small apartments with kitchens are rentable by the week, which may appeal to families. A restaurant and bar as well as a handicapped-accessible room have recently been added.

*Piazza Sordini 6. ☎ **0743-223-340.** Fax: 0743-222-663. E-mail: hotelclitunno @oletol.com. Parking: Free. Rack rates: 51.65€–92.96€ ($46.49–$83.66) double, including buffet breakfast. AE, DC, MC, V.*

Palazzo Dragoni
$$$ Centro

This hotel is housed in a 15th-century *palazzo* built over older structures (in the basement you can see the remains of tenth-century houses and a medieval street). From its magnificent lobby and common areas you ascend to rooms (no two alike) elegantly decorated with antiques. Some have balconies overlooking the Duomo and a panoramic view as far as Assisi. Book early — the hotel only has 15 rooms.

Via del Duomo 13. ☎ *0743-222-220. Fax: 0743-225-225. Parking: Free permit parking in nearby piazza. Rack rates: 119€–145€ ($107–$131) double, including buffet breakfast. AE, DC, MC, V.*

Where to dine in Spoleto

More famous for its art than for its food, Spoleto nonetheless offers a number of good places to sample Umbrian cuisine, including the famous *tartufo* (truffle) — which you should try. Truffles exist in white and black varieties; the former, which has a milder flavor, is the most coveted.

Apollinare
$$$ Teatro Romano   NOUVELLE UMBRIAN

One of the best restaurants in town, the Apollinare is situated underneath the hotel Aurora, across the square from the Sant'Agata monastery. The food is excellent and includes traditional Umbrian dishes as well as imaginative — and delicious — interpretations of the classics. Be prepared for the crowds, especially if you're coming on a weekend.

Via S. Agata 14. ☎ *0743-223-256. Reservations necessary. Secondi: 9.30€–14€ ($8.37–$12.60). AE, DC, MC, V. Open: Lunch and dinner Wed–Mon; closed two weeks in Jan or Feb and in Aug.*

Il Tartufo
$$$ Piazza Garibaldi   UMBRIAN

Il Tartufo — as its name suggests — specializes in dishes based on truffles. Its other specialties are mushrooms — especially porcini, a specialty of the region. You can taste them in various preparations, including as a sauce for fresh pasta or grilled meat. This is traditional Umbrian cuisine at its best.

Piazza Garibaldi 24. ☎ *0743-40-236. Reservations necessary. Secondi: 9.30€–13.43€ ($8.37–$12.09). AE, DC, MC, V. Open: Lunch and dinner Tues–Sun; closed two weeks in July and Aug.*

Pentagramma

$$ Teatro Romano UMBRIAN

The area of expertise of this restaurant is pasta, homemade or not. You have a choice of sauces and — of course — truffles and porcini mushrooms when in season. In addition, it serves a variety of soups, like the *zuppa di farro* (spelt soup), and a delicious risotto with radicchio.

Via Martani 4. ☎ 0743-223-141. Reservations recommended. Secondi: 7.23€–12.91€ ($6.50–$11.61). DC, MC, V. Open: Lunch and dinner Thurs–Tues; closed two weeks in Jan or Feb and in Aug.

Exploring Spoleto

Created by Gian Carlo Menotti, the **Festival di Spoleto** (also known as the Festival dei Due Mondi/Festival of Two Worlds) opened in 1958 as a way to bring together the best of "two worlds," Europe and America. Definitely a resounding success, the festival today, held two weeks from the end of June to the beginning of July, attracts major performing-arts figures from around the world and is famous for its great performances. This international event includes theater, dance, music, and even cinema (Spoletocinema); art exhibits are put on for the occasion as well. Performances are held all over town, including in the **Teatro Romano** (Piazza della Libertà; ☎ 0743-223-419), the Rocca, and the scenic Piazza del Duomo, but mainly in the **Teatro Nuovo** (Via Filetteria 1; ☎ 0743-223-419) and the **Teatro Caio Melisso** (Piazza del Duomo; ☎ 0743-222-209). Tickets run 5€ to 40€ ($4.50–$36), depending on the event, and the **ticket office** is at Piazza del Duomo 8 (☎ 0743-220-320; Fax: 0743-220-321; E-mail: info@oletofestival.it or tickets@oletofestival.it; Internet: www.spoletofestival.net or www.spoletofestival.it). Once in Spoleto, you can get tickets at the Teatro Nuovo.

The top sights

Duomo (Santa Maria Assunta)

This 12th-century Romanesque cathedral has a majestic facade, graced by rose windows and a beautiful 1207 mosaic by Solsterno depicting Christ in typical Byzantine style, flanked by saints against a magnificently gilded background. Because of the position of the church in a declivity on the slope of the hill, you can get a spectacular view looking down on the Duomo and its piazza. The Duomo's **campanile (bell tower)** was pieced together using stone looted from Roman temples. The church's interior, refurbished in the 17th century, still has the original mosaic floor in the central nave. In a niche at the entrance is the bronze bust of Urban VIII by Gian Lorenzo Bernini. Among all the treasures inside, the most important are in the **apse,** which was decorated in the 15th century with great Filippo Lippi frescoes, including the brooding and powerful *Morte della Vergine (Death of the Virgin Mary)*. The fresco cycle was restored in 1990, bringing Lippi's gorgeous palette to life again. The painter died in Spoleto in 1469 and was buried in the Duomo under a stone monument in the right nave — though his bones were stolen from the tomb a few centuries later. The final concert of the Spoleto Festival is held every year in the piazza in front of the Duomo.

Piazza del Duomo. Admission: Free. Open: Summer daily 8 a.m.–1 p.m. and 3:00–6:30 p.m.; winter daily 8 a.m.–1 p.m. and 3:00–5:30 p.m.

Teatro Romano

This theater dates back to the first years of the Roman Empire and is one of numerous vestiges of ancient Spoleto that are still visible. It was uncovered by a local archaeologist under Piazza della Libertà at the end of the 19th century and excavated in the 1950s, revealing some well-preserved structures. A little farther east is the first-century **Arco di Druso (Via Arco di Druso)**, once the monumental arched entry to the Forum (now Piazza del Mercato). The impressive **baroque fountain** in the piazza was built on the site of the facade of a Romanesque church, of which a few pieces survive. Nearby are the remains of a temple with six marble columns. Up a narrow lane is the **church of Sant'Ansano,** which was built on the site of a Roman temple (first century A.D.) and contains the crypt of Sant'Isacco, which has some interesting early frescoes.

Piazza della Libertà. ☎ 0743-223-277. Admission: 2.07€ ($1.86). Open: Daily 9:00 a.m.–1:30 p.m., Mon–Sat 2:30 p.m. to sunset.

More cool things to see and do in Spoleto

Haven't gotten enough of Spoleto? Check out these other sights:

✔ Overlooking the city to the east, the **Rocca Albornoz** was built in the 14th century by master architect Gattapone to establish the power of the popes over the city. The Rocca has six square towers, the tallest being the Torre Maestra. Among the castle's governors was Lucrezia Borgia, who was appointed by pope Alexander VI (another Borgia) in 1499. The Rocca has retained its usefulness through the centuries: It was used as a prison up until 1982, and it currently houses the European school of book and manuscript restoration, as well as an open-air theater. The Rocca can only be visited by guided tour (4.65€/$4.19) and is open Monday through Friday from 10 a.m. to 8 p.m. and Saturday and Sunday from 10 a.m. to 9 p.m. in summer; in winter it closes earlier, at 5 p.m., and is also closed between noon and 3 p.m.

✔ From Piazza Campello at the east end of town, you can take Via del Ponte, which goes around the southern side of the fortress and brings you to the famous **Ponte delle Torri,** a bridge/aqueduct over the river Tessino. The ten arches of this gigantic bridge — 264 feet tall and 760 feet long, built in the 12th century to bring water to the Rocca — offer a majestic view. The bridge was refurbished by Gattapone during the construction of the Rocca. On the other side of the bridge is a beautiful woods (considered sacred in Etruscan and Roman times — an inscription from the third century B.C. has been found outlawing the cutting of its trees).

✔ The 12th-century **church of Sant'Eufemia** (Via Saffi, between Piazza del Duomo and Piazza del Mercanto; ☎ 0743-23101) is a small gem. Note the gallery above the nave, where women were required to sit, a holdover from the Eastern Church; it's one of the few such galleries in Italy. In the courtyard, double stairs lead to the **Diocese Museum (Museo Diocesano),** noted for its paintings of the Madonna, one from 1315. One room contains Filippino Lippi's 1485 *Madonna and Child with Sts. Montano and Bartolomeo.* Admission is 2.60€ ($1.86) and by reservation only, daily 10:00 a.m. to 12:30 p.m. and 3:30 to 7:00 p.m. (to 6:00 p.m. November through February).

Fast Facts: Spoleto

Country Code and City Code

The country code for Italy is **39**. The city code for Spoleto is **0743**; use this code when calling from anywhere outside or inside Italy — you must add the codes even within Spoleto itself (and you must include the 0 every time, even when calling from abroad).

Embassies and Consulates

See "Fast Facts: Florence" in Chapter 14 and "Fast Facts: Rome" in Chapter 12.

Currency Exchange

You can exchange money at banks and ATMs in town.

Emergencies

Ambulance and Pronto Soccorso (first aid), ☎ **118**; fire, ☎ **115**; road assistance ACI, ☎ **116**.

Hospital

There's an Ospedale on Via San Matteo (☎ 0743-21-01).

Information

The tourist office is on Piazza della Libertà (☎ 0743-220-311). Summer hours are Monday through Friday 9 a.m. to 1 p.m. and 4 to 7 p.m. and Saturday and Sunday 10 a.m. to 1 p.m. and 4 to 7 p.m.; winter hours are Monday through Saturday 9 a.m. to 1 p.m. and 3:30 to 6:30 p.m. and Sunday 10 a.m. to 1 p.m.

Mail

The Posta Centrale is on Piazza della Libertà (☎ 0743-40-231).

Police

Call ☎ **113**; for the Carabinieri (other police force), call ☎ **112**.

Part V
Venice and the Best of the Pianura Padana

The 5th Wave   By Rich Tennant

PROGRAM
THE THREE
TENORS

"Funny—I just assumed it would be Carreras too."

In this part . . .

American poet Mark Rudman once wrote, "Venice is anti-simile; it isn't like any other place." It may be one of the few cities where you'll never hear an automobile (though the growling diesel motors of boats are never very far away). Venice, arguably the world's most romantic city, has grown up over thousands of years on marshy ground where people once hid in the reeds from barbarian hordes. From those humble beginnings, Venice became one of the greatest maritime empires history has ever seen and gave birth to great art, great institutions, and a unique architecture. And still, when you think of Venice, you first think of water—beguiling, mesmerizing, relaxing. The artistic and cultural influence of Venice spread to the surrounding region of the Pianura Padana, whose towns offer many splendid sights.

In Chapter 18, we take you through the watery roads and alleys of Venice and the most interesting of the nearby lagoon islands. In Chapter 19, we introduce you to the Pianura Padana's other three important cities: Padua and Verona, with their own beauties and treasures, and Milan, the business and industrial capital of Italy.

Chapter 18

Venice

● ●

In This Chapter

▶ Getting around without getting your feet wet

▶ Finding the best in Venice lodging and food

▶ Experiencing the sights, smells, and tastes of Venice

● ●

*V*enice (Venezia) feels important — its massive public structures
and elegant private *palazzi* lining the canals show a city of
tremendous wealth, power, and culture. It's truly a magnificent human
achievement. And yet people have been calling Venice a dead city for a
century and a half. Henry James wrote, "She exists only as a battered
peep-show and bazaar." Just 70,000 people actually live in Venice, but if
you're ever alone anywhere for more than five minutes, consider yourself lucky. The crowds are unbelievable: Everywhere you go, someone
is already there.

And yet . . . the Grand Canal at sunset, St. Mark's Square, the Academy
Gallery, the lagoon, the Lido, the Canaletto skies, and the stillness
beneath the hubbub are sights you just have to experience. And Venice's
famous serenity (the republic was called *La Serenissima,* the "serene
one") is as seductive as ever. Cranky Henry James and many other
famous travelers have succumbed to Venice before you. James conceded
that "the only way to care for Venice as she deserves it is to give her a
chance to touch you often — to linger and remain and return."

Venice became independent from Bisance (Constantinople, the capital
of the Eastern Roman Empire) in the eighth century A.D. with its first
doge (the head of the government). The word *doge* is the Venetian
mutation of the Latin word *dux* ("leader"). Venice became a harbor of
international importance in the tenth century, when the Republic
started regulating commerce between Europe and the Orient. The city
we know today started developing around St. Mark's Basilica (Basilica
di San Marco), constructed to house the relics of the saint. The group
of islands in the lagoon was built up, the canals drained, and their
edges reinforced. The city had begun its metamorphosis.

The Venetian Republic was a great experiment in government. Over the
centuries, a complicated network of institutions and checks and balances was built to limit the power of the *doge* and all the other political

institutions that governed the city-state. At the heart was the *Maggior Consiglio* (Great Council) who elected the *doge*. Originally elective, membership to the Maggior Consiglio became hereditary in 1297. The smaller Council of Ten was established in 1310 to judge conspirators in a failed plot, but it became permanent (the *doge* and his counselors were also members). It became so powerful that the Maggior Consiglio passed legislation to limit its powers in 1582, 1628, and 1762. Most powerful of all, perhaps, was the Grand Chancellor, who, as the head of the secret police, knew all the dark secrets of the nobility, so other institutions were established to limit his power. The experiment was successful: Venice remained a republic until May 12, 1797, when Napoleon invaded northern Italy and established a new European order.

Venice has weathered wars, dictators, and conspiracies and enjoyed more than a thousand years of democracy. But its most treacherous foe may be the very ground beneath it. The increase in the sea levels registered all over the planet in recent years has had especially dramatic consequences for Venice, and the city is literally sinking into the muddy lagoon on which it was built. In spite of advice from experts all over the world, cement injections, and the ongoing work of restoration and solidification of the canals, the city continues to sink. The search for ways to save one of the most beautiful and extraordinary cities ever built continues.

Getting There

Regardless of Venice's unique location, it is easily accessible by plane, train, ship, or car.

By air

Small but not too small, Venice's **Aeroporto Marco Polo** (☎ 041-260-9260) is situated in a mainland locality called Tessera, about 10km (6¼ miles) from the city. **Alitalia** (☎ 041-258-1333) has several flights a day to Venice from other Italian cities. The hour-long flight from Rome is about 140€ ($126) round-trip.

Note that you can't fly directly to Venice from outside Italy — first you must go through Rome or Milan.

From the airport, you can reach the city by bus or water. The *moto-scafo* **(shuttle boat)** to Piazza San Marco run by **Cooperativa San Marco** (☎ 041-522-2303) takes about 50 minutes and costs 8.78€ ($7.20) per person. Though romantic, a **water taxi** (☎ 041-541-5084) costs a whopping 67.14€ ($60.43); perhaps this is for honeymooners only. A less expensive option is to take the **shuttle bus** to Piazzale Roma (Venice's car terminal on the mainland) operated by **ATVO** (☎ 041-520-5530). It runs every hour and costs 2.60€ ($2.34) per person. The trip takes about a half-hour. You can also take the regular city bus no. 5; it runs every half-hour and brings you to Piazzale Roma for .77€ (69¢). When you arrive at Piazzale Roma, you have to switch to another form of transportation.

By train

Venice's rail station is the **Stazione Ferroviaria Santa Lucia.** Many trains head directly to **Santa Lucia,** but sometimes you have to change in **Mestre,** Venice's inland rail hub. The trip from Mestre to Santa Lucia takes about ten minutes, with connections every few minutes. The fastest train to Venice is the **Eurostar,** getting you to Venice in about 5 πhours from Rome and 3½ from Milan; the **Intercity** takes just a little longer (both will take you directly to Santa Lucia). Try to avoid the slower regular train that makes many stops. A one-way ticket from Rome costs about 34€ ($33.57), depending on the category of train you choose. In Santa Lucia, you can find a branch of the tourist office, the hotel association (in case you don't have a reservation), and, just in front of the exit, the ticket booth for the *vaporetto* (see "By vaporetto" later in this chapter), as well as water taxis.

By ship

Traditionally, Venice was accessible only by water — the bridge to the mainland was built only in 1846. You can still get to Venice by ship, but pleasant as it is, it's also rare. Several international cruising companies offer cruises to Venice; your travel agent can help you sort through the options. Remember that it's a long way to Venice from most international ports of call, usually a minimum of a month (most travelers don't have that kind of time). Your ship arrives at the **Marine Terminal (Stazione Marittima)** in Santa Croce, in the heart of Venice. From there, the regular city transportation is at your disposal.

By car

If you drive to Venice from Rome, take A1 to Bologna, then A13 to Padua and A4 to Venice. The distance is 530km (327 miles). The A1 passes through Florence, so you also follow these directions if you're starting from there (though Florence is 287km/179 miles closer to Venice than Rome).

No cars are allowed to enter Venice. The closest you can get is the car terminal in Piazzale Roma, where you have to say goodbye to your mechanical pet. Expect to pay 33€ ($25) or more per day for a garage, depending on the size of your car. (Don't even think about leaving your car on the street for a day or two.) The **Garage Comunale** (Piazzale Roma 496; ☎ **041-522-2308** or 041-523-7763) and the **Garage San Marco** (Piazzale Roma 467/f; ☎ **041-523-5101** or 041-523-2213; Fax:

041-528-9969) are convenient to boat stops. A cheaper alternative is on the island of Tronchetto, where the **Parcheggio del Tronchetto** (☎ 041-520-7555) costs about 11€ ($9.90).

But all these parking places are hard to get to in summer and on weekends because of humongous traffic jams. Leaving your car on the mainland, in Mestre, where there are parking lots at the train station or on Via Stazione, is a better (and cheaper) idea. There are two garages in the city of Mestre: **Garage Serenissima** (☎ 041-938-021) and **Crivellari** (☎ 041-929-225). You can also find parking in Merghera. From Mestre or Marghera you have to take a train (see "By train" earlier in this chapter) or a bus. For the bus, you have to buy a ticket in advance at a tobacconist or a bar; ask the parking officer for directions. Note, however, that the bus can get stuck in the same traffic jams we mentioned earlier.

Orienting Yourself in Venice

Venice grew haphazardly over a period of centuries, one of the reasons why it's a wonderful maze of canals and tiny streets, with small squares scattered all around. Larger groupings did form, however, and these determine the main neighborhoods. Each has a character of its own, which we describe in this section.

Venice by neighborhood

Venice is composed of three major areas: the *centro storico* (historic district), the **mainland development on the coast** (where a large part of the city's population actually lives), and **the islands of the *laguna* (lagoon).** The parts you may be most interested in are the historic district and the lagoon.

The centro storico (historic center)

The group of islands forming the heart of Venice is divided into *sestieri* (meaning a sixth of the city, these are, in effect, boroughs or districts; the singular form is *sestiere*), three on each side of the **Grand Canal (Canal Grande).** The Grand Canal is the central canal, S-shaped (but reversed) and crossed by only three bridges: the Accademia, the famous Rialto, and the Ponte degli Scalzi at the rail station. The canal divides the historic district in two — *de citra* ("this side" of the canal) and *de ultra* (across the Grand Canal), as the locals say.

St. Mark's (San Marco) is the central tourist destination, with **St. Mark's Basilica (Basilica di San Marco), Ducal Palace** and the **Bridge of Sighs (Palazzo Ducale and Ponte dei Sospiri), Correr Museum (Museo Correr), Teatro La Fenice** (the opera house not yet rebuilt after a 1996 fire), and **Palazzo Gritti.** San Marco is a neighborhood with lots of hotels — including some of the most expensive in the city — and a number of city offices. The many restaurants tend to be "touristy" and

Venice Orientation

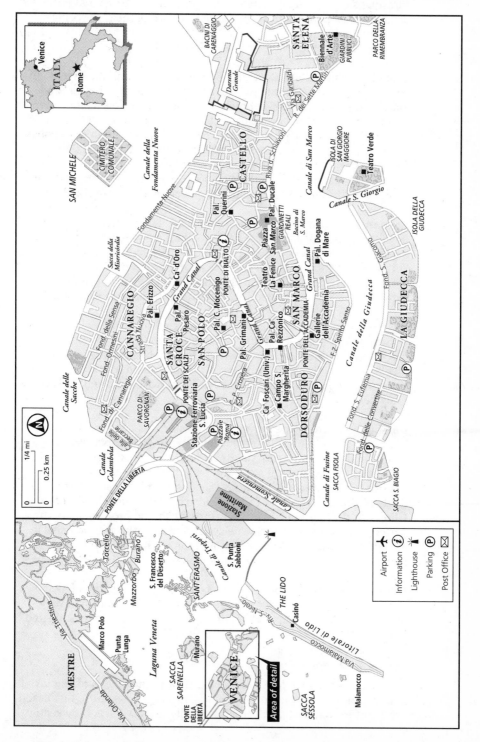

the *calli* (streets; singular is *calle*) overcrowded. To appreciate its picturesque side, explore the area at night, when the crowds have receded. San Marco is connected to other *sestieri* by two of the three bridges crossing the Grand Canal: the **Rialto,** connecting San Marco to San Polo, and the **Accademia,** connecting San Marco to Dorsoduro.

Castello begins behind **St. Mark's Basilica.** Inland from the **Riva degli Schiavoni** — the grandiose promenade overlooking the bay of San Marco with some expensive hotels and restaurants — is a much more popular district, in the original sense. "Real" Venetians still live and work here, particularly between the **Arsenale** and the **Public Gardens (Giardini Pubblici).** Running through the heart of **Castello is Via Garibaldi,** with its many shops, outdoor market, and *osteria* offering Venetian fare. More toward the center of the quarter is the grand Gothic **Basilica of Sts. John and Paul (Basilica dei Santi Giovanni e Paolo).**

Cannaregio is also a popular neighborhood. The painter Tintoretto was born here, near the Madonna dell'Orto church, not far from the Ghetto. On the Grand Canal end are the **Ca' d'Oro,** and, farther up, the **Stazione Ferroviaria Santa Lucia.** It's from this borough, on the lagoon side, that you find the **Fondamenta Nuove station,** from which you can take the *vaporetto* (ferry) to the islands of **Murano, Burano,** and **Torcello.**

San Polo, just across from the rail station and over the Rialto Bridge from San Marco, is a less touristy neighborhood. San Polo was the main market in Venice at the time when Rialto was the marine terminal of the medieval city; it is still a commercial neighborhood with many shops. You can also find the **Scuola Grande di San Rocco** and the **Basilica dei Frari** here.

Dorsoduro is where the university is located. It's a more artsy and trendy neighborhood, where you can find the **Academy Gallery (Gallerie dell'Accademia), Ca' Rezzonico,** and the **Peggy Guggenheim Collection;** you can stroll along the beautiful promenade of the **Zattere** — famous for its outdoor cafes — to the majestic church of **Santa Maria della Salute.** This area also includes the **Island of the Giudecca (Isola della Giudecca),** across from the promenade of the Zattere, separated by the Canale della Giudecca, the second canal in importance after the Grand Canal, and the main water route to the maritime terminal.

Santa Croce is the borough in which you arrive when you come by car. It has the marine and automobile terminal but also some very interesting churches and a beautiful promenade. It's the least visited part of Venice.

The laguna (lagoon)

The lagoon stretches from the Adriatic Sea to the mainland, enclosing Venice proper and many other islands. Among those not to be missed are **Murano, Burano,** and **Torcello.** Smaller than Venice, they keep exactly the same spirit but in a quieter way. Murano is the island of the glassmakers, famous for centuries. It has the **Glass Museum (Museo Vetrario di Murano)**, and you can find a few glassworks that still produce artistic glass. Burano is the island of fishermen and is still a major producer of lace and embroidered linen. Torcello was actually the urban center of the lagoon before Venice, but the population decamped to the present site of Venice after Torcello started to get too swampy. But Torcello's past glory remains in the magnificent cathedral, **Santa Maria Assunta.**

The **Lido** is the long barrier island that protects the lagoon from the open sea. Inhabited since ancient times, it bloomed at the end of the 19th century with the development of an elegant Art Nouveau resort that includes the **Excelsior Palace,** the **Hotel des Bains,** and the **casino.** It's here that Venetians come to swim and tan on the long beaches. Many tourists choose to stay here because it's only a short *vaporetto* ride from San Marco and you get much better hotels for your money.

Venice by address

You'll find that the names of things are different in Venice — different even from other parts of Italy. That's because Venice developed its own unique dialect and words to deal with its very unique geography. A *calle* (pronounced with a hard l) is a narrow street; a paved road is a *salizzada* or a *calle larg;* a *rio terà* is a canal that was filled in to make a street; a *fondamenta* is a long street running alongside a canal; and a *sottoportico* is a passage under a building. Note that there's only one piazza in Venice and that's **St. Mark's Square (Piazza San Marco)** — all the others are either a *campo* (square) or a *campiello* (a smaller square).

As if that weren't enough, buildings are numbered differently from the way you're probably used to seeing them: You may need to find addresses like "2534 San Marco" and "2536 San Marco," and they may be on two different streets — oops, *calli!* So, if you're looking for a particular street number, don't expect sequential numbers. Just use the building numbers as Boy Scout marks on a forest path and always ask directions according to street names and recognizable sites. That's why all hotels and restaurants have small maps printed on the back of their business cards and why even Venetians call for directions before going to an address they haven't been to before.

This rule applies to postal addresses. However, because Venetians understand the difficulty, when asked, they will give you the name of the street or square, as you're used to (no number, though). So, for example, the address "Hotel Bernardi-Semenzato, Calle dell'Oca, 4366 Cannaregio" means the hotel is in building no. 4366 on Calle dell'Oca in the borough of Cannaregio. Always make sure you have the name of the *sestiere* (borough): Venice has many streets of the same name!

As you wander, look for those ubiquitous signs with arrows (some-times a little old, but still readable) that, just like trailblazers, direct you toward major landmarks: **Ferrovia (the train station), Piazzale Roma,** the **vaporetto,** the **Rialto Bridge, Piazza San Marco,** and the **Accademia Bridge,** and so on. If you decide to ask someone for direc-tions, be aware that people are more likely to know the name of the actual place you're looking for than the name of a small street, often unmarked.

Street smarts: Where to get information after you arrive

The tourist board operates several offices around town and is planning to open a few small booths at the main tourist spots. But the best place to get your information is at the arrival points: the **Stazione Ferroviaria Santa Lucia** (☎ and Fax **041-719-078**), open in summer daily from 8 a.m. to 8 p.m. and in winter Monday through Saturday from 8 a.m. to 7 p.m.; and the **Aeroporto Marco Polo** (☎ **041-541-5887**), open daily from 8 a.m. to 7 p.m. If you arrive by car, you can find an information point in Marghera at the *nuova rotatoria autostradale* (new highway traffic circle), where the highway ends.

The tourist offices are worth a visit if only to get the latest opening hours of churches and museums — they change all the time, as in the rest of Italy. If you need wheelchair access, special maps are available. The office at the **train station** (☎ and Fax **041-719-078**) is the most logical place to get this material.

Getting Around Venice

Made up of over 100 islands linked by 354 bridges over 177 canals, Venice can be quite confusing to the visitor. These waterways have always been the main means of access to houses, which is why the facades of buildings are on the canals. Crossing these canals are small bridges with steps up and down — a major difficulty for anything on wheels. You can just imagine how difficult loading and unloading for shops and catering places must be.

On foot

Walking is the best way to visit Venice, and you'll be doing a lot of it. The only things you need are a good map (try the smartly folded Falk map, available at many bookstores and newsstands), comfortable shoes, and perhaps good foot balm (an end-of-the-day treat for your faithful "wheels"). We've seen many a tourist, unprepared for the rigors of walk-ing Venice, slumped in dismay in front of the steps of yet another bridge.

The famous *acqua alta* (high water) shouldn't be a concern. From November through March, in periods of high tides, many streets of the historic district are inundated with water. To facilitate walking, wooden platforms are placed around, so you don't have to pack your waders, unless you want to wander in the smallest or out-of-the-way streets. Many hotels ($$$ and above) actually provide plastic boots in an ample choice of sizes for you to borrow (ask when you reserve if you're planning your visit for the *acqua alta* season).

When you're walking around Venice, remember two things:

✔ **Venice isn't dangerous.** No matter how narrow a *calle* may be or how poor a place may look, there's no "bad neighborhood" in the historic district, even at night. That shouldn't induce you, though, to do foolish things such as display large quantities of money or leave your expensive camera unattended. Plenty of pickpockets are still around, and some bag snatchers, too.

✔ **Don't let people scare you with "It's impossible not to get lost there" or "Venice is like a maze, and you'll never find your way."** The city is, indeed, like a maze, but you really can't get lost — at worst, you may arrive at a canal and have to backtrack and then try the next turn. Big deal — you'll have discovered yet another fantastic view of the city you came to visit.

By vaporetto

The bus system of the historic district is the *vaporetto* (water bus). Riding these strange motorboats — something between a small barge

How to get around if you're wheelchair-bound

Although the city has made big efforts, Venice still isn't easy for wheelchair-bound visitors. The only real problem, but a major one, are the bridges over the canals, all with steps up and down. Any longish route passes over a canal, hence the steps; otherwise, you're condemned to go around in circles on the same tiny island. Still, the main attractions are all accessible by water (boats are boarded by gangways, which have no steps), you can take strolls without crossing a bridge, and a few bridges have been equipped with motorized lifts (alas, we saw a number that were inoperable).

Fortunately, the tourist board has prepared a **city map with yellow-highlighted wheelchair-accessible itineraries.** The lifts on the few bridges equipped with them require a key to work, and the key is available free at the tourist office (see "Street smarts: Where to get information after you arrive"). Keep in mind that the lifts are sometimes out of order, so ask the tourist office for the latest details.

The big splurge

Venice is the lap of luxury, with palatial hotels at every turn. In this chapter, we supply entries for the deluxe hotels **Londra Palace** and **Hotel des Bains**. If you're looking for the plushest of the plush, here are a few more suggestions, many of which, like the famous Gritti, have been swallowed up by the Starwood resorts chain:

- ✔ **Danieli Royal Excelsior** (Riva degli Schiavoni, Castello 4196; ☎ **800-325-3535** in the U.S. and Canada, or 041-522-6480; Fax: 041-520-0208; Internet: www. ittsheraton.com; Vaporetto: San Zaccaria)

- ✔ **Excelsior Palace** (Lungomare Marconi 41; ☎ **800-325-3535** in the U.S. and Canada, or 041-526-0201; Fax: 041-526-7276; Internet: www.ittsheraton.com; Vaporetto: Lido, then bus A, B, or C)

- ✔ **Gritti Palace** (Campo Santa Maria del Giglio, San Marco 2467; ☎ **800-325-3535** in the U.S. and Canada, or 041-794-611; Fax: 041-520-0942; Internet: www.starwood.com/redir/luxurycollection/grittipalace; Vaporetto: Santa Maria del Giglio)

- ✔ **Hotel Bauer/Bauer Palace** (Campo San Moisè, San Marco 1459; ☎ **041-520-7022**; Fax: 041-520-7557; Internet: www.bauervenezia.it; E-mail: bauer@bauervenezia.it; Vaporetto: San Marco)

- ✔ **Hotel Cipriani** (Isola della Giudecca 10; ☎ **800-223-6800** in the U.S., or 041-520-7744; Fax: 041-520-7745; Internet: www.orient-expresshotels.com; E-mail: cipriani@gipnet.it; Vaporetto: Zitelle)

and a ferry — is great fun: *Vaporetti* are relatively slow, but what a view you get! One must-do experience is the ride down the Grand Canal, both by day and by night (see "Exploring Venice").

See the Cheat Sheet at the front of this guide for a map of Venice's *vaporetto* lines.

The cost is quite high for a *vaporetto* — 3.10€ ($2.79) for the minimal ride, more for special rides to the far islands — so if you plan to stay more than a day, go for one of the long-term tickets: a *giornaliero* (daily pass) at 9.33€ ($8.40), a *biglietto tre giorni* (three-day pass) at 18.08€ ($16.27), and a *settimanale* (weekly pass) at 30.99€ ($27.89). The pass gives you access to the whole public transportation system, including the beautiful islands of Torcello, Murano, and Burano (see "More cool things to see and do") as well as the Lido.

A cost-effective way to tote the family around town is by purchasing a family pass. The daily pass for a family of three is 23.24€ ($20.91), for a family of four 30.99€ ($27.89), and for a family of five 38.73€ ($34.85). The **Rolling Venice three-day pass** for people under 30 is 12.91€ ($11.62).

By gondola

Yes, we know, gondolas are for, ahem, *tourists* . . . but really, don't they look fun? And what can be more romantic than being rowed in a gondola along the Grand Canal? Alas, a gondola ride is also very expensive: The official rates are 61.97€ ($55.77) for 50 minutes for a maximum of six people during the day and 77.47€ ($69.72) during the night. This isn't likely to be the price you'll pay, however: Many *gondolieri* (the guys who row) contend that they'd be underpaid if they respected those rates. That said, rates have rarely gone up in the past few years — as a result, they try to charge whatever the market will bear. So be sure to establish the price in advance before you get in the boat! Your chances of getting a good deal at any of the many gondola stations along the Grand Canal are about equal. What really makes the difference is how busy the *gondolieri* are.

Many people don't know that a traditional type of boat is still used as public transport: the *traghetto,* very similar to the gondola, only it's moved by two rowers instead of one and is much less fancy in decoration. Because only three bridges span the Grand Canal, *traghetti* take you across at various points for a mere .41€ (37¢) per person. You just walk down to the small wooden dock, indicated by a sign saying "TRAGHETTO" (often the street leading to the dock is called Calle del Traghetto), and wait for the boat to come. Note that Venetians ride *traghetti* standing, proudly displaying their sea legs. The only drawbacks are that the *traghetti* operate for limited hours (most only mornings, a few also in the afternoon) and that the ride won't last more than five minutes.

By water taxi

Though a little expensive, *taxi acquei* (water taxis) are a great way to get to and from your hotel with your luggage or to have a taste of luxury. They cost 13.94€ ($12.55) for the first seven minutes and then .26€ (23¢) for each additional 15 seconds; a ride from Piazzale Roma to Piazza San Marco is about 42€ ($37.80) for up to four passengers. Remember that certain locations — and hotels — even water taxis can't reach, in which cases you have to walk the rest of the way. Among the several companies in town are the **Cooperativa San Marco** (☎ 041-522-2303), **Cooperativa Veneziana** (☎ 041-766-124), and **Cooperativa Serenissima** (☎ 041-522-1265).

Where to Stay in Venice

Because Venice is such a major tourist attraction, it has a wide variety of hotels to choose from. The ones we've chosen to list offer nice amenities in a good location and will serve you well as a home base.

Most of our choices are accessible by water or by a short walk without crossing bridges.

Remember that luggage is your enemy in Venice. Pack as light as you can. No vehicles are allowed in the city, so whatever you bring with you you'll have to carry. Beware also that the bridges over the canals have steps — not many of them, but enough to transform that luggage with wheels into an unbearable load.

If you want to see Venice during Carnevale (Carnival, better known in the U.S. as Mardi Gras), reserve your hotel room way in advance.

If you don't have a reservation when you get to Venice, stop at one of the three locations of the **Hotel Association of Venice, AVA** (Associazione Veneziana Albergatori), at the Aeroporto Marco Polo (☎ **041-541-5133**), the Stazione Ferrovia Santa Lucia (☎ **041-715-016** or 041-715-288), or the Garage San Marco on Piazzale Roma (☎ **041-520-6335**).

A helpful small publication to pick up in all major hotels is *Un Ospite a Venezia,* a guide on everything useful, from public transportation to the program of special events and to addresses of all kinds.

You can get special discounts for youths (under 30) if you have the **Rolling Venice card** (see "Exploring Venice," in this chapter).

The top hotels

Albergo La Meridiana
$$$ Lido di Venezia

Here's a way to factor out many of Venice's special difficulties. Staying on the Lido in the hot weather gets you near the beach and away from the smelly canals. There's a ferry to the Lido from Tronchetto (where the parking lots are) every hour, and you can bring your car. La Meridiana is a member of the Logis hotel association, a guarantee of quality and excellent service. All the guest rooms have air-conditioning, minibars, and safes; they're generally spacious, and most are decorated with simple but comfortable furniture. The nicest are those that have rows of casement windows and look out over the garden. The hotel also has a private beach and offers such perks as free bicycles and free entrance to the casino.

Via Lepanto 45, Lido di Venezia. ☎ *041-526-0343. Fax: 041-526-9240. Internet: www.lameridiana.com. E-mail: info@lameridiana.com. Parking: Free. Vaporetto: 62 to Casino; walk left on Via Dardanelli, turn left on Via Lorenzo Marcello, and right on Via Lepanto. Rack rates: 98€–165€ ($88.20–$148.50) double, including breakfast. AE, DC, MC, V. Closed Nov 15–Jan 31.*

Al Sole Palace
$$$ Santa Croce

Away from the tourist crowds near the university and Ca' Foscari (see "More cool things to see and do"), this hotel occupies a delightful 15th-century *palazzo* that was originally the home of the prominent Marcello family. The rooms have old Venetian furniture and beamed ceilings, but there are modern comforts as well, such as hair dryers, satellite TV, and (most important) air-conditioning. Ask for one of the rooms with a view over the canal. A restaurant is on the premises. Note that the hotel sometimes runs specials and affordable package deals including sightseeing tours.

Fondamenta Minotta, 136 Santa Croce. ☎ *041-710-844. Fax: 041-714-398. Internet:* www.alsolepalace.com. *E-mail:* info@alsolepalace.com. *Vaporetto: 1, 82, 41, 42, 51, or 52 to Piazzale Roma; follow the Fondamenta Croce to your left, turn right on Fondamenta dei Tolentin along the Canali, and continue to Fondamenta Minotta on your left. Rack rates: 176€–233€ ($158.40–$209.70) double, including buffet breakfast. AE, DC, MC, V.*

Hotel Bernardi-Semenzato
$ Cannaregio

Renovated in 1995, this hotel a few minutes from the Ponte di Rialto combines an antique look with modern amenities and includes an annex three blocks away. The air-conditioned guest rooms are good sized and the baths mostly new; but you can get a really cheap room if you're willing to do without a private bath. Nearby Strada Nuova is a busy shopping street where Venetians actually outnumber tourists and linger for a chat, a coffee, or an ice cream. The hotel has a 40%-off deal with a parking lot in Tronchetto.

Calle dell'Oca, 4366 Cannaregio. ☎ *041-522-7257. Fax: 041-522-2424. Vaporetto: 1 to Ca' d'Oro; walk up to Strada Nuova, turn right, then turn left on Calle del Duca and right on Calle dell'Oca. Rack rates: 61.97€–103.29€ ($55.77–$92.96) double. MC, V.*

Hotel Campiello
$$$ Castello

This pink 15th-century building is easy to find — just off posh Riva degli Schiavoni — and is a bargain for the area. It's somewhat quieter than the nearby Riva, and the location is just about perfect. The recently renovated guest rooms are decorated either in Venetian Liberty (Art Nouveau) style or in a mod Italian look. The expert staff of this family-run hotel is friendly. The buffet breakfast is more substantial than many and is served in a rather glitzy hall. The hotel also has suites and quads.

Campiello del Vin, 4647 Castello, ☎ *041-520-5764. Fax: 041-520-5798. Internet:* www.hotelcampiello.it. *E-mail:* campiello@hcampiello.it. *Vaporetto:*

Venice Accommodations and Dining

ACCOMMODATIONS ■

Albergo La Meridiana **38**
Al Sole Palace **3**
Boston Hotel **28**
Danieli Royal Excelsior **25**
Excelsior Palace **38**
Gritti Palace **36**
Hotel Bauer/
  Bauer Palace **32**
Hotel Bernardi-
  Semenzato **16**
Hotel Campiello **39**
Hotel Casanova **29**
Hotel Cipriani **37**
Hotel des Bains **38**
Hotel Do Pozzi **34**
Hotel Flora **33**
Hotel Geremia **8**
Hotel Locanda
  Remedio **23**
Hotel Marconi **21**
Hotel Metropole **41**
Hotel Pantalon **5**
Hotel San Cassiano
  Ca' Favretto **17**
Hotel Tivoli **6**
Londra Palace **40**
Pensione Accademia
  Villa Maravegie **9**
Pensione La Calcina **10**
Pensione Seguso **10**

DINING ◆

Algiubagiò **11**
A La Vecia Cavana **13**
Al Pantalon **4**
Antica Besseta **1**
Antico Gatoleto **14**
Antica Ostaria Ruga
  Rialto **19**
Antico Martini **30**
Bar Pizzeria di Paolo
  Melinato **42**
Da Raffaele **35**
Do Forni **24**
Fiaschetteria
  Toscana **15**
Locanda Cipriani **12**
Ostaria ai Vetrai **12**
Ostaria a la
  Campana **26**
Ostaria à la
  Valigia **27**
Osteria da Fiore **2**
Ostaria da Franz **22**
Ostaria Enoteca
  Vivaldi **18**
Pasticceria Tonolo **7**
Trattoria alla
  Madonna **20**
Trattoria Busa alla
  Torre **12**
Trattoria da
  Romano **12**
Vino Vino **31**

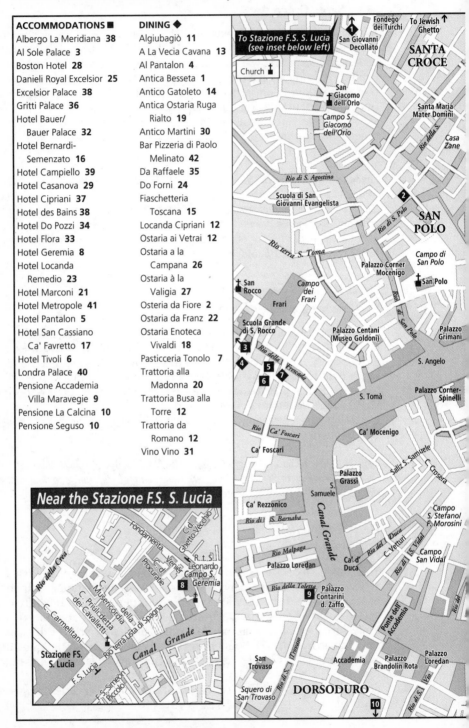

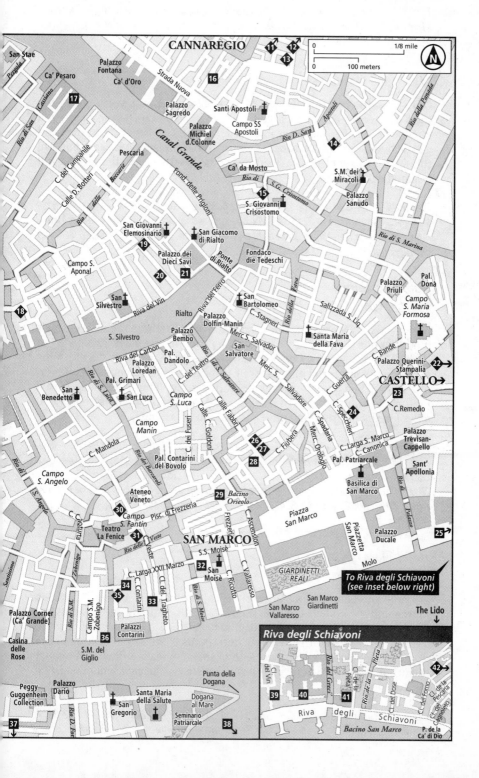

CANNAREGIO

San Stae

Palazzo
Fontana

Ca' Pesaro

Ca' d'Oro

Strada Nuova

16

11 **12**

13

0   1/8 mile

0   100 meters

N

17

Palazzo
Sagredo

Santi Apostoli

Campo SS
Apostoli

Rio D. Savi

14

Palazzo
Michiel
d.Colonne

Canal Grande

Pescaria

Ca' da Mosto

S.M. dei
Miracoli

Fond. delle Prigioni

Rio di

S.G. Crisostomo

15

S. Giovanni
Crisostomo

Palazzo
Sanudo

C. del Campanile

Calle D. Botteri

San Giovanni
Elemosinario

19

San Giacomo
di Rialto

Fondaco
die Tedeschi

Rio di S. Marina

Palazzo
Priuli

Pal.
Donà

Campo S.
Aponal

Palazzo dei
Dieci Savi

20 **21**

Ponte
di Rialto

Campo
S. Maria
Formosa

18

San
Silvestro

Riva del Vin

San
Bartolomeo

Salizzada S. Lio

Rialto

Palazzo
Dolfin-Manin

C. Stagneri

Santa Maria
della Fava

C. Bande

Palazzo Querini-
Stampalia **22**

S. Silvestro

Palazzo
Bembo

Merc. S. Salvador

San
Salvatore

CASTELLO

23

Riva del Carbon

Pal.
Dandolo

Merc. S.

C. Guerra

C.Remedio

Palazzo
Loredan

C. del Teatro

C. Spadaria

Palazzo
Trevisan-
Cappello

Pal. Grimari

San
Benedetto

San Luca

Campo
S. Luca

C. del Fuseri

Calle C. Goldoni

Calle Fabbri

24

C. Larga S. Marco

Pal. Patriarcale

C. Canonica

Sant'
Apollonia

Campo
Manin

26 **27**

28

Basilica di
San Marco

C. Mandola

Pal. Contarini
del Bovolo

Merc. Orologio

Campo
S. Angelo

Ateneo
Veneto

29 Bacino
Orseolo

Piazza
San Marco

Piazzetta
San Marco

Palazzo
Ducale

25

30

Campo
S. Fantin

Pisc. di Frezzeria

Teatro
La Fenice

31

Rio delle Veste

SAN MARCO

S.S. Moisè

Molo

To Riva degli Schiavoni
(see inset below right)

The Lido

C. Larga XXII Marzo

32 San
Moisè

C. Ricotto

GIARDINETTI
REALI

San Marco
Giardinetti

34

35

C. Contarini

33

San Marco
Vallaresso

Palazzo Corner
(Ca' Grande)

Campo S.M.
Zobenigo

Palazzi
Contarini

Casina
delle
Rose

36

S.M. del
Giglio

Riva degli Schiavoni

Punta della
Dogana

42

Peggy
Guggenheim
Collection

Palazzo
Dario

Santa Maria
della Salute

Dogana
al Mare

39 **40** **41**

37

San
Gregorio

Seminario
Patriarcale

38

Riva   degli   Schiavoni

Bacino San Marco

P. de la
Ca' di Dio

1, 14, 41, 42, 51, 52, 71, 72, or 82 to San Zaccaria; walk up Calle del Vin. Rack rates: 115€–170€ ($103.50–$153) double. AE, MC, V.

Hotel Casanova

$$$$ San Marco

Only 20 yards from Piazza San Marco, this hotel puts you right in the touristic heart of the city. If you reserve in advance and are lucky, you may be able to get the *mansarda* (attic room) with a private terrace and a view over Venice's rooftops. The furnishings are adequate and modern, though the guest rooms vary in size; some have exposed brick walls and beamed ceilings.

Frezzeria, 1284 San Marco. ☎ **041-520-6855.** *E-mail:* hotel.casanova.ve@ iol.it. *Vaporetto: 1 or 82 to San Marco–Vallaresso; walk up Calle Vallaresso, turn left on Salizzada San Moisè, then right on the Frezzeria. Rack rates: 185.92€ ($167.32) double, including breakfast. MC, V.*

Hotel des Bains

$$$$$ Lido

Now owned by Starwood, this grand Art Nouveau hotel is one of Venice's most famous. Everybody who was anybody in the early 1900s stayed here (Thomas Mann's *Death in Venice* was set here). The guest rooms boast handsome furnishings as well as modern conveniences too numerous to list. The amenities include baby-sitting, laundry service, and a motorboat shuttle between the Lido and Venice, plus tennis courts and a pool in the surrounding park and horseback riding.

Lungomare Marconi 17, Lido di Venezia. ☎ **800-325-3535** *in the U.S. or 041-526-5921. Fax: 041-526-0113. Internet:* www.starwood.com/redir/sheraton/des bains. *Vaporetto: 1, 6, 14, 51, 52, 61, 62, or 82 to the Lido; walk up Gran Viale Santa Maria Elizabetta and turn right (the hotel is in the park) or take bus A, B, or C. Rack rates: 296€–380€ ($266.40–$342) including buffet breakfast. AE, DC, MC, V. Closed Nov–Mar.*

Hotel Flora

$$$ San Marco

Friendly and handicapped accessible, this hotel lies between Piazza San Marco and the still-unrepaired Teatro La Fenice. All the guest rooms are furnished Venetian style; many have views of the beautiful private garden (a rare treasure in Venice) and rooms 3 and 47 have views of the dome of La Salute — try to get one of these, because they're the most beautiful. Another amenity for hotel guests is a private launch service to Murano.

Calle dei Bergamaschi, 2283/A San Marco. ☎ **041-520-5844.** *Fax: 041-522-8217. Vaporetto: 1 to Giglio; walk up Calle Gritti, turn right on Calle delle Ostriche, cross* the bridge and continue onto Calle Larga XXII Marzo, then turn right on Calle dei Bergamaschi. Rack rates: 160€–220€ ($144–1198) double, including breakfast. MC, V.

Hotel Locanda Remedio
$$$ Castello

In the calm residential borough of Castello, this quiet hotel is actually just behind St. Mark's Basilica. The building dates from the early 16th century, and the atmosphere is Old World; you can even see some remnants of ceiling frescoes. The air-conditioned guest rooms have been upgraded with modern amenities and new baths.

Calle de Remedio, 4412 Castello. ☎ **041-520-6232**. Fax: 041-521-0485. Vaporetto: 1, 14, 41, 42, 51, 52, 71, 72, or 82 to San Zaccaria; walk up Calle del Vin, continue toward the left along the canal on Fondamenta del Vin and then turn left, crossing the bridge onto Salizzada San Provolo, and turn right on Calle della Chiesa, go left around the side of the church, bear right along the canal, and turn left on Calle de Remedio. Rack rates: 118.79€–144.61€ ($106.91–$130.15) double, including breakfast. MC, V.

Hotel Marconi
$$ San Polo

At the foot of the Ponte di Rialto and overlooking the Grand Canal, the Marconi has an understated elegance. Refurbished in 1999, the building dates from the 1500s and is in a beautiful — particularly at night — part of Venice that has many cafes and restaurants. All the guest rooms have air-conditioning, safes, and Venetian-style furniture; only four open onto the canal, so reserve early. Whichever room you get, you can eat breakfast in fair weather at the tables outside by the canal.

Riva del Vin, 729 San Polo.☎ **041-522-2068**. Fax: 041-522-9700. Internet: www.hotel marconi.it. E-mail: info@hotelmarconi.it. Vaporetto: 1 and 82 to Rialto; walk to the Rialto Bridge and cross over and turn left along the canal on Riva del Vin. Rack rates: 68€–310€ ($61.20–$279) double, including breakfast. AE, MC, V.

Hotel Pantalon
$$ Dorsoduro

In the nice neighborhood between San Polo, the Accademia, and Santa Maria de' Frari, this hotel has been renovated with care and is a good alternative to the more pricey ones around San Marco. All the moderate-sized guest rooms have air-conditioning, minibars, and safes; one has a handicapped-accessible bathroom, and a few have terraces. They're decorated with tasteful reproductions. The decor in the common areas has a French feel (the place is popular with French tourists).

Crosera San Pantalon, 3941 Dorsoduro. ☎ **041-710-896**. Fax: 041-718-683. Internet: www.venere.com. Vaporetto: 1 or 82 to San Tomà; walk up to Campo San Tomà, *turn left on Calle Campanièl, cross a bridge onto Calle Balbi, turn right on Fondamenta del Fornèr, then left onto the bridge and Calle Larga Foscari and right on Crosera. Rack rates: 134.28€–201.42€ ($120.85–$181.28) double, including breakfast. MC, V.*

Hotel San Cassiano Ca' Favretto
$$$$ Santa Croce

This moderately priced (comparatively) hotel occupies a 14th-century *palazzo* on the Grand Canal — what more can you ask for? It's just across from the Ca' d'Oro and left of the Ca' Corner della Regina. The building has been completely renovated (which explains why the prices shot up), and all the guest rooms have massive, dark wood furniture, relieved by the light-colored paper on the walls and large windows. Many have views of the Ca' d'Oro or the smaller canal on the side.

Calle della Rosa, 2232 Santa Croce. ☎ 041-524-1768. Fax: 041-721-033. Internet: www.venere.com. Vaporetto: 1 to San Stae; walk to the left of Campo San Stae, cross the canal and turn right on Fondamenta Rimpetto Mocenigo, then left on Calle del Forner, cross the bridge, continue on Calle del Ravano, cross the bridge, and turn left on Calle della Rosa. Rack rates: 134€–284€ ($120.60–$255.60) double, including breakfast. AE, V.

Hotel Tivoli
$$ Dorsoduro

This simple family-run hotel is between the Frari and the Scuola Grande di San Rocco and the Accademia. Some of the guest rooms overlook the sunny garden courtyard where breakfast is served in warm weather. The two ground-floor rooms are more accessible. The continental breakfast is a bit more substantial than many — fruit, yogurt, and cheese are available. Though the Mediterranean-style furnishings may seem a bit dated, at this price and in this location the Tivoli is a good deal.

Calle Larga Foscari, 3838 Dorsoduro. ☎ 041-524-2460. Fax: 041-522-2656. Vaporetto: 1 or 82 to San Tomà stop; walk up to Campo San Tomà, turn left on Calle Campanièl, cross a bridge onto Calle Balbi, turn right on Fondamenta del Fornèr, then left onto the bridge and Calle Larga Foscari at the intersection with Crosera. Rack rates: 77.41€–160.10€ ($69.67–$144.09) double, including breakfast. No credit cards.

Londra Palace
$$$$$ Castello

You can't miss the Londra Palace — it has a hundred windows facing the lagoon and is only steps from St. Mark's Square. Tchaikovsky stayed here several times and wrote some of his works here during his stays. All the guest rooms are gorgeously furnished, and two attic rooms boast beamed ceilings and Regency furniture. The bar is almost like an English pub, and there's a comfortable reading room. The ground-floor restaurant is the famous **Do Leoni;** like the hotel, it's pricey. The hotel is wheelchair-accessible.

Riva degli Schiavoni, 4171 Castello. ☎ *041-520-0533. Fax: 041-522-5032. Internet:* www.hotelondra.it. *E-mail:* info@hotelondra.it. *Vaporetto: 1, 14, 41, 42, 51, 52, 71, 72, or 82 to San Zaccaria; walk right on Riva degli Schiavoni. Rack rates: 270€–370€ ($243–$333) double, including buffet breakfast. AE, DC, MC, V.*

Pensione Accademia Villa Maravegie

$$$ Dorsoduro

This whole place has a wonderfully old-fashioned feeling. In a beautiful location two steps from the Accademia, the hotel occupies a 17th-century villa with a garden. The guest rooms contain 19th-century furnishings, and all have private bathrooms. It's very popular, so you have to reserve well in advance to secure a room with a view over the garden.

Fondamenta Bollani, 1058 Dorsoduro. ☎ *041-521-0188. Fax: 041-523-9152. E-mail:* pensione.accademia@flashnet.it. *Vaporetto: 1 or 82 to Accademia; turn right on Calle Corfù, left on Fondamenta Priuli, right on the first bridge, and then again right on Fondamenta Bollani. Rack rates: 113.62€–206.58€ ($102.26–$185.92) double, including breakfast. AE, DC, MC, V.*

Pensione La Calcina

$$$ Dorsoduro

This is where Victorian writer John Ruskin stayed in 1876. The location overlooking the Canale della Giudecca is both beautiful and less hectic than the area around San Marco. Nicely restored, it's an excellent value. All the guest rooms have parquet floors and air-conditioning, and some furnishings are original. In warm weather, the buffet breakfast is served on the large terrace by the water. The hotel also has a *solarium* (roof terrace). Note that you can't have an extra bed placed in a double and you need to reserve six months in advance for summer. La Calcina now also rents small apartments.

Zattere ai Gesuati, 780 Dorsoduro. ☎ *041-520-6466. Fax: 041-522-7045. Vaporetto: 51, 52, 61, 62, or 82 to Zattere; turn right along the Canale della Giudecca to the Rio di SanVio. Internet:* www.venere.com; www.warmhospitality.com *for apartments. Rack rates: 119€–147€ ($108–$162) double, including breakfast. AE, DC, MC, V.*

Pensione Seguso

$$ Dorsoduro

If you want to stay where Victorian writer John Ruskin stayed, stay at La Calcina; if you want to *feel* like Ruskin, stay here. From the bull's-eye glass-front windows to the antique furnishings, glass chandeliers, and marble floors, this old-fashioned *pensione* transports you back in time. (On the other hand, it may feel a little long in the tooth for some people.)

The corner guest rooms are very large and have balconies, but their bathroom is across the corridor and in some cases is shared by two rooms. Note that in low season you have to take — or at least pay for — half-board: breakfast and your choice of dinner or lunch.

Zattere ai Gesuati, 779 Dorsoduro. ☎ *041-528-6858. Fax: 041-522-2340. Vaporetto: 51, 52, 61, 62 or 82 to Zattere; turn right along the Canale della Giudecca to the little campiello at Rio di San Vio. Rack rates: 82.63€–154.94€ ($78.30–$139.44) double, including breakfast. AE, MC, V.*

Runner-up accommodations

Boston Hotel
$$$ San Marco

The Boston Hotel isn't too expensive (for its area) and is a good alternative just off St. Mark's Square. Some of the guest rooms have views of the canal from their balconies (you have to stand, however; they're very small) and about half have air-conditioning.

Ponte dei Dai, 848 San Marco. ☎ *041-528-7665. Fax: 041-522-6628. Vaporetto: 1 or 82 to San Marco–Vallaresso.*

Hotel Do Pozzi
$$$ San Marco

The Hotel Do Pozzi has a quiet yet central position between St. Mark's Square and the Teatro La Fenice. The guest rooms have been renovated but are still furnished in antique style; guests get a 10% discount at the **Ristorante Da Raffaele** (see "Where to Dine in Venice").

Corte dei Do Pozzi, 2373 San Marco. ☎ *041-520-7855. Fax: 041-522-9413. Vaporetto: 1 to Giglio.*

Hotel Geremia
$$ Cannaregio

The Hotel Geremia is within walking distance of the rail station — a nice hotel in an area where many are not. A lot of care has been put into the renovation, especially the baths, and the service is good.

Campo San Geremia, 290/A Cannaregio. ☎ *041-716-245. Fax: 041-524-2342. Vaporetto: 1, 82, 71, 72, 51, 52, 41 or 42 to Ferrovia.*

Hotel Metropole
$$$$ Castello

The Metropole is a romantic hotel with an entrance on a canal and baroque furnishings.

Riva degli Schiavoni, 4149 Castello. ☎ *041-520-5044. Fax: 041-522-3679. Internet: www.hotelmetropole.com. E-mail: Venice@hotelmetropole.com. Vaporetto: 1, 82, 41, 42, 51, or 52 to San Zaccaria.*

Where to Dine in Venice

Fish and shellfish from the lagoon and the Adriatic served on rice, pasta, or *polenta* (corn meal) are the staples of Venetian cuisine. Typical dishes are *risi e bisi* (rice and peas), *risotto* (creamy rice cooked with fish or vegetables), *bigoli in salsa* (whole-wheat spaghetti with anchovy-and-onion sauce), *sarde in saor* (sardines in a sauce of vinegar, onions, and pine nuts), *baccalà mantegato* (creamed cod fish served cold), and the famous *fegato alla veneziana* (liver sautéed with onions and wine). For dessert, visit one of the many pastry shops for one of the local cakes or the famous *Bussolai* and *S e' Buranei* — O- and S-shaped cookies, respectively, originally from the small island of Burano (see "More cool things to see and do"). Or go for a delicious gelato, the best in Italy after Rome (see the sidebar "Taking a sweet break").

The best local wines are Amarone and Valpolicella (red) or, if you prefer it white and fizzy, try Cartizze or Prosecco. The wine is as important as — more important than, some locals would say — the food in Venice.

Although Venice has the reputation of having an inordinate number of bad and expensive restaurants, you can eat really well here. (It's our personal theory that the more a restaurant advertises, the worse the place is likely to be.) The most traditional places to dine are small *osterie* and *bacari,* which look on the inside as if you've just stepped into somebody's house. In general, these simple places, often with wooden tables and paper atop the tablecloths (or directly on the tables), are the best bet. At the other end of the spectrum, Venice has a number of well-established restaurants that serve excellent fare, but at much higher prices. Both of these kinds of restaurants have steady customers.

If you want to seek out your own finds, the best places to hunt are along **Via Garibaldi** in Castello, **Strada Nuova** in Cannaregio, and **Rialto** in San Polo.

The top restaurants

A La Vecia Cavana
$$$$ Cannaregio VENETIAN

This renowned restaurant is housed in a 17th-century building where *gondole* (more than one gondola) were once repaired and stationed. The cuisine is typically Venetian; among the dishes is *granchio al forno* (oven-roasted crab), an excellent antipasto. The prices are high but well worth it, given the quality of the food.

Rio Terrà dei Franceschi, 4624 Cannaregio. ☎ *041-528-7106. Reservations recommended. Vaporetto: 1 to Ca' d'Oro; walk straight ahead to Strada Nuova and turn right, bear left around Campo dei Apóstoli and the church, take Rio Terrà SS Apóstoli, and turn left at Rio Terrà dei Franceschi. Secondi: 20.66€–30.99€ ($18.59–$27.89). AE, DC, MC, V. Open: Lunch and dinner Fri–Wed.*

Al Pantalon

$$ Dorsoduro   VENETIAN

This is a great place for lunch in the busy area near the university, and lots of Venetians know it — go early if you want to avoid the line. The food is traditional, extremely fresh, and served by a friendly young staff. Try the *antipasto di pesce* (mixed seafood appetizer) or the *baccalà mantegato* as a starter and continue with one of the many *secondi* (main courses). You can have a pasta dish, like excellent *spaghetti alle vongole* (spaghetti with clams), for less than 9€ ($8).

Campo San Fantin, 3958 Dorsoduro. ☎ *041-710-849. Reservations not accepted. Vaporetto: 1 or 82 to San Tomà; follow the red signs to the Scuola di San Rocco but just before the Scuola turn left on Sottoportego San Rocco and cross the bridge. Secondi: 10.33€–20.66€ ($9.30–$18.59). No credit cards. Open: Lunch and dinner daily.*

Antica Besseta

$$$$ Santa Croce   VENETIAN

This small trattoria from 1700 is very popular with locals, so making a reservation is a good idea. Try one of the many excellent *risotti*. With the fish *secondi,* you have an opportunity to try delicious versions of the main dishes of Venetian cuisine.

Salizzada de Ca' Zusto, 1395 Santa Croce, ☎ *041-721-687. Reservation recommended. Vaporetto: 1 to Riva de Biasio; walk up Calle Zen, turn left, and make an immediate right on Salizzada de Ca' Zusto. Secondi: 15.49€–18.08€ ($13.94–$16.27). AE, MC, V. Open: Lunch Thurs–Mon; dinner Wed–Mon.*

Antica Ostaria Ruga Rialto

$$ San Polo   VENETIAN

Italians who don't have a lot of money still manage to eat well at places like this, where the decor is minimal, the tablecloth is likely to be a piece of paper, and all the food is local and fresh. Popular with students, this *ostaria* serves an excellent antipasto, specialties like *baccalà mantegato,* and abundant and tasty pastas. There's lots of space, lots of people, and (sometimes) lots of noise, but you never have a bad meal.

Taking a sweet break

Venetians definitely have a sweet tooth! They not only make scrumptious pastries but, together with Rome, Florence, and Sicily, are contenders for the best *gelato* (ice cream) in Italy and maybe in the world. One of the best places for gelato is **Algiubagiò** (☎ 041-523-6084; Internet: www.algiubagio.com), on Fondamenta Nuove right in front of the *vaporetto* stop of that name. It also has a coffee shop and restaurant. (Twenty yards down the *fondamenta*, it has a little storefront selling just ice cream.) You should definitely sample the delicious flavors — try the fantastic *crema Veneziana,* a cream-flavored ice cream with chunks of chocolate (the recipe is a secret). For typical and delicious pastries, a good address is **Pasticceria Tonolo** (San Pantalon, 3764 Dorsoduro; Vaporetto: San Tomà). Of course, Venice has many, many other ice cream and pastry shops. Don't be afraid to stop and sample; you'll rarely find a bad one.

Ruga Vecchia San Giovanni, 692 San Polo. ☎ *041-521-1243. Reservations recommended for large parties. Vaporetto: 1 or 82 to Rialto; walk to the Rialto Bridge and cross over, continue straight through the arcades and make your first left on Ruga Vecchia San Giovanni. Secondi: 7.23€–10.33€ ($6.51–$9.30). No credit cards. Open: Lunch and dinner Tues–Sun.*

Antico Gatoleto

$$ Castello   VENETIAN

Although this restaurant is in Castello, it's in the northwest corner and so isn't far from the Ponte di Rialto. It's on a quiet little square and has some tables outside. In addition to Venetian specialties and seafood, you can get inexpensive pasta dishes and even pizza.

Campo Santa Maria Nova, 6055 Castello. ☎ *041-522-1883. Reservations recommended on Sat. Vaporetto: 1 or 82 to Rialto; turn left and pass the bridge, make a right when you can't go any farther, take your first left on Salizzata San Giovanni Crisóstomo, follow it, and immediately after the second bridge take a right on Salizzata San Canciano; when you reach Campo San Canciano, take the dogleg to the right that leads to Campo Santa Maria Nova. Secondi: 6.21€–12.91€ ($5.58–$11.62). DC, MC, V. Open: Lunch and dinner daily.*

Antico Martini

$$$$$ San Marco   VENETIAN

This elegant restaurant on the site of an 18th-century cafe is one of the city's best, and as such comes with a high price. You can sample Venetian specialties as well as other innovative dishes. This gourmet spot is famous for its *involtini di salmone al caviale* (salmon rolled up and stuffed with caviar).

Campo San Fantin, 1983 San Marco. ☎ *041-522-4121. Reservations recommended. Vaporetto: 1 to Giglio; walk up Calle Gritti, turn right on Calle delle Ostreghe, continue into Calle Larga XXII Marzo, turn left on Calle delle Veste and follow it to Campo San Fantin. Secondi: 18.08€–25.82€ ($16.27–$23.24). AE, DC, MC, V. Open: Lunch Thurs–Mon; dinner Wed–Mon.*

Bar Pizzeria di Paolo Melinato
$$ Castello   PIZZA

Pizza? In Venice? After two or three days of nonstop meat and shellfish consumption, your body may be asking for a break. This pizzeria, in front of the Arsenale, is simple to find and has really good pizza, especially for the north of Italy. You can get all the classics — *margherita, capricciosa,* and so on. The small campo with the Arsenale and its canal in the background are especially quiet and picturesque at night.

Campo Arsenale, 2389 Castello. ☎ *041-521-0660. Reservations not necessary. Vaporetto: 1, 41, or 42 to Arsenale; follow Calle dei Forni to its end, turn left on Calle di Pegola, and turn right into Campo Arsenale. Secondi: 6.21€–10.33€ ($5.58–$9.30). No credit cards. Open: Lunch Tues–Sat; dinner Mon–Sat.*

Da Raffaele
$$$ San Marco   VENETIAN

Go to this canal-side restaurant for excellent fresh fish and other specialties. If you're tired of seafood, try the very tasty pastas and grilled meats. Everything on the menu is reliable — which is why this place has been a major tourist magnet for years (make a reservation). A nice plus is the terrace, so you can dine outdoors in the summer.

Ponte delle Ostreghe, 2347 San Marco. ☎ *041-523-2317. Reservations recommended on weekends. Vaporetto: 1 or 82 to San Marco–Vallaresso; walk up Calle Vallaresso, turn left on Salizzada San Moisè, and continue into Calle Larga XXII Marzo and Calle delle Ostreghe. Secondi: 12.91€–19.63€ ($11.62–$17.67). AE, DC, MC, V. Open: Lunch and dinner Wed–Mon.*

Do Forni
$$$$ San Marco   VENETIAN

A very popular restaurant especially with younger people, Do Forni is constantly busy. It has made it into many guidebooks, so don't expect to be alone among the locals. The food, however, justifies the wait. The room in back has a casual coziness. The specialties of the house are *risi e bisi* and *bigoli in salsa.*

Calle degli Specchieri, 457–468 San Marco. ☎ *041-523-0663. Reservations recommended. Vaporetto: 1 or 82 to San Marco–Vallaresso; cross Piazza San Marco, turn* right in Piazzetta dei Leoni on the left side of the Basilica di San Marco, and turn left on Calle degli Specchieri. Secondi: 15.49€–25.82€ ($13.94–$23.24). AE, DC, MC, V. Open: Lunch and dinner daily.

Fiaschetteria Toscana
$$ Cannaregio   TUSCAN/ITALIAN

The Venetian-Tuscan merging has given birth here to a refined cuisine, making this one of Venice's best restaurants. You can get steaks in true Tuscan style, as well as seafood in various faultless preparations, all served amid an elegant decor.

Salizzada San Giovanni Crisostomo, 2347 Cannaregio. ☎ *041-528-5281. Reservations required. Vaporetto: 1 or 82 to Rialto; walk past the Rialto Bridge along the Canal Grande, then turn right and left onto Salizzada San Giovanni Crisostomo. Secondi: 9.30€–19.63€ ($8.37–$17.67). AE, DC, MC, V. Open: Lunch and dinner Wed–Mon.*

Locanda Cipriani
$$$$ Torcello   VENETIAN

If you have to eat in one of the Cipriani restaurants — there's the Ristorante Cipriani in the luxurious hotel of the same name on the Isola della Giudecca, and Harry's Bar on Calle Vallaresso just off Piazza San Marco — do it here. From its Venetian base, this family has gained world renown, but it's in this traditional venue that you find the best food. The menu is simple yet refined; the only drawback is the high-season crowds. (You can stay overnight in one of the several guest rooms, newly renovated and reopened in 2001.)

Piazza Santa Fosca 29, Torcello. ☎ *041-730-150. Reservations recommended. Vaporetto: 12 from Fondamenta Nuove to Torcello; walk right and up the Fondamenta dei Borgognoni along the canal and turn left. Secondi: 15.49€–20.66€ ($13.946–$18.59). AE, DC, MC, V. Open: Lunch Wed–Mon; dinner Fri–Sat; closed winter.*

Ostaria ai Vetrai
$$ Murano   VENETIAN

If you're on Murano and looking for lunch, this *ostaria* serves excellent seafood at a more affordable price than many comparable restaurants in Venice. It prepares every type of local fish and also serves pastas with seafood. The huge antipasto for two at 12.91€ ($11.62) contains all the Venetian seafood specialties — it's virtually a meal in itself — and you can eat it at a canalside table.

Fondamenta Manin 29, Murano. ☎ *041-739-293. Reservations not necessary. Vaporetto: 41, 42, 71, or 72 to Colonna; walk along the canal to the right until you* *come to the first bridge, then cross over to Fondamenta Manin and turn left. Secondi: 8.78€–18.08€ ($7.90–$16.27). DC, MC, V. Open: Lunch Wed–Sun.*

Ostaria a la Campana
$ San Marco   VENETIAN

It's hard to find a place that's dirt cheap without the dirt. This *ostaria* is really small but neat and simple, and you can get a plate of steaming pasta with a delicious sauce for the equivalent of about $5. A half-liter of wine runs another $1.75. This is good hearty food with a complete absence of tourist ambience. The place is convenient because it's on Calle dei Fabbri, the main drag (very straight, for Venice) between Piazza San Marco and the Ponte di Rialto.

Calle dei Fabbri, 4720 San Marco. ☎ *041-528-5170. Reservations not accepted. Vaporetto: 1 or 82 to Rialto; turn right and walk along the canal, then turn left on Calle Bembo, which turns into Calle dei Fabbri. Secondi: 4.13€–7.75€ ($3.72–$6.98). No credit cards. Open: Lunch and dinner Mon–Sat.*

Ostaria Enoteca Vivaldi
$$ San Polo   VENETIAN

This charming *ostaria/enoteca,* with its wood interior and bar, low ceilings, and rustic feeling, is a cozy place for dinner. It offers typical Venetian cuisine and, as the name suggests, excellent wine. It has a faithful following and may be hard to get into because it's not that large; calling ahead is a good idea.

Calle Madonnetta, 1457 San Polo. ☎ *041-523-8185. Reservations necessary. Vaporetto: 1 to San Silvestro; follow the narrow street behind the Palazzo Barzizza to Campo Aponàl, turn left toward Campo San Polo, and cross the bridge onto Calle Madonnetta. Secondi: 7.23€–12.91€ ($6.51–$11.62). No credit cards. Open: Lunch and dinner Mon–Sat.*

Osteria da Fiore
$$$$ San Polo   SEAFOOD/VENETIAN

One of the city's most popular restaurants, this *osteria* offers excellent traditional cuisine but at high prices. Among the specialties are risotto with scampi and fried calamari. Though it's a bit difficult to find and also crowded, this is one of the best places to sample Venetian cuisine.

Calle del Scaleter, 2202/A San Polo. ☎ *041-721-308. Reservations required. Vaporetto: 1 or 82 to San Tomà; walk straight ahead to Campo San Tomà, continue straight on Calle larga Prima toward Santa Maria dei Frari and the Scuola di San*

Rocco and a block before the Scuola and behind the Frari, turn right on Calle del Scalater. Secondi: 23.24€–28.41€ ($20.92–$25.57). AE, DC, MC, V. Open: Lunch and dinner Tues–Sat.

Trattoria alla Madonna
$$ San Polo   VENETIAN

Seafood and more seafood! In this local trattoria, celebrated by both locals and tourists, you find all the bounty the Adriatic has to offer, some existing only in the Venetian lagoon, prepared in various traditional ways — grilled, roasted, fried, or served with pasta, risotto, or polenta. The moderate prices attract crowds, so be prepared for a long wait.

Calle della Madonna, 594 San Polo. ☎ 041-522-3824. Reservations accepted only for large parties. Vaporetto: 1 or 82 to Rialto; cross the Rialto Bridge, turn left on Riva del Vin along the Canal Grande, and turn right onto Calle della Madonna. Secondi: 9.30€–11.56€ ($8.37–$10.22). AE, MC, V. Open: Lunch and dinner Thurs–Tues.

Trattoria da Romano
$$ Burano   VENETIAN

A very busy address in Burano, this restaurant is renowned for its *risotti*. You may choose among squid risotto, mixed seafood risotto, and other delicious combinations. If you're still hungry after one of these dishes, try the excellent fish *secondi*.

Via Baldassarre Galuppi 221, Burano. ☎ 041-730-030. Reservations recommended. Vaporetto: 12 from Fondamenta Nuove to Burano; walk up and then left onto Via Baldassarre Galuppi. Secondi: 9.30€–12.91€ ($8.37–$11.62). AE, MC, V. Open: Lunch and dinner Wed–Mon.

Runner-up restaurants

Ostaria à la Valigia
$$ San Marco   VENETIAN

The Ostaria à la Valigia caters to tourists, but the food is good, from the pasta with seafood to the more expensive Venetian *secondi*. The restaurant has lots of room, making it a good fallback, and there's seating outside on the quieter side street.

Calle dei Fabbri, 4696 San Marco. ☎ 041-521-2526. Vaporetto: 1 or 82 to San Marco Vallaresso.

Trattoria Busa alla Torre

$$$ Murano VENETIAN

On a broad piazza, the Trattoria Busa alla Torre is open every day for lunch only. You can find the typical range of pastas and Venetian specialties, well prepared and relatively cheap.

Campo San Stefano 3, Murano. ☎ *041-739-662. Vaporetto 41, 42, 71, 72, 12, or 13.*

Vino Vino

$ San Marco VENETIAN

Vino Vino is a Venetian *bacaro* (wine bar) just behind the remains of the Teatro La Fenice; the service is simple but the food is very good. You can find traditional Venetian fare and a large choice of wines.

Calle del Cafetier, 2007/A San Marco. ☎ *041-523-7027. Vaporetto: 1 or 82 to San Marco–Vallaresso.*

Exploring Venice

In Venice, every side street leads to another wonderful view of the city. But the main sights — such as St. Mark's Square — are truly remarkable, and you'll be glad you took the time to visit this one-of-a-kind city.

If you're under 30, buy a **Rolling Venice card** to get substantial discounts — from 10 to 40% — on hotels, restaurants, museums, public transportation, and shops. Working on the premise that young people are put off by schlepping around the famous sights at the end of a long line of tourists (very uncool), Rolling Venice provides alternative itineraries, places to meet and be seen, and a more lively approach to the "dead" city. To have access to the discounts you need only register and pay 2.60€ ($2.34) at one of the Rolling Venice information points, the easiest being the **Stazione Ferroviaria Santa Lucia booth** (☎ 041-524-2852; July through October, open daily 8 a.m. to 8 p.m.) and the **Transalpino booth,** also in the station (☎ 041-524-1334; Fax: 041-716-600; open Monday through Friday 8:30 a.m. to 12:30 p.m. and 3 to 7 p.m. and Saturday 8:30 a.m. to 12:30 p.m.).

Besides the card (it helps if you bring an ID photo for the card or you may have to show another picture ID with the card when you present it), you get a map of Venice charting the location of all the participating hotels, restaurants, clubs, and shops, as well as a small guidebook including facts about Venetian history and culture and smart itineraries. You can also get the **ACTV Rolling Venice Rover ticket,** a three-day pass for all public boats and buses for 12.91€ ($11.62). A booklet — the *agenda* — gives a load of useful information, from cultural listings to locations of supermarkets and emergency numbers (2.60€/$2.34). You can even get a T-shirt (5.16€/$4.64) with the Rolling Venice logo and a canvas bag (6.21€/$5.58).

Older travelers can buy a 7.75€ ($6.98) **three-day pass** to 14 churches in Venice at any of the participating churches. It allows you to visit 6 churches of your choice out of the 14, saving time at the ticket booth (but not necessarily money — it depends on where you go). The sights included are the Treasury of the Basilica di San Marco, the Basilica dei Frari, the Chiesa della Madonna dell'Orto, the Chiesa di San Sebastiano, San Polo, San Stae, San Giacomo dall'Orio, Santa Maria del Giglio, San Stefano, Santa Maria Formosa, San Pietro di Castello, Sant'Alvise, Santa Maria dei Miracoli, and the Chiesa del Redentore. All are rich in paintings and works by famous artists of the 15th and 16th centuries.

There is a bewildering variety of other combo tickets: one for the Ca' d'Oro and the Museo d'Arte Orientale Ca' Pesaro for 4.13€ ($3.72) and one for the Ca' d'Oro, Museo d'Arte Orientale Ca' Pesaro, and Gallerie dell'Accademia for 9.30€ ($8.37), as well as a MuseumCard that admits you to the museums on the Piazza San Marco (9.50€/$8.55), including the Palazzo Ducale and the Correr Museum.

The Museum Pass includes the Piazza San Marco museums, several of the most famous 16th-century *palazzi* on the Grand Canal (including the Ca' Rezonico and the Casa di Goldoni), and the lace museum and the glass museum on the islands of Burano and Murano, all for 15.50€ ($13.95). Or you can buy a combo ticket for the 16th-century *palazzi* (8€/$7.20) or just for the Burano and Murano museums (6€/$5.40).

The period before Lent — celebrated as Mardi Gras in New Orleans — is celebrated as **Carnevale** all over Italy, but Venice's celebrations are spectacular, beginning the week before Ash Wednesday (usually in February) and culminating on the last day, *martedi grasso* (Fat Tuesday). In 1797, Napoleon suppressed Carnevale, which had grown into a months-long bacchanal. But this festive holiday was revived in 1980 and has become a big deal in Venice, famous for the elaborateness of its costumes and masks, which are historic and elegant rather than Halloween-ish (no Darth Vader or Mutant Ninja Turtles). Music events take place at all times, and crowds — big crowds — surge all over. Some of the events are reserved only for those who are disguised, such as the Gran Ballo in Piazza San Marco, with prizes given for the best costume. Other events include a Children's Carnevale daily on Piazza San Polo, a cortege of decorated boats on the Grand Canal, and a market of Venetian costumes at Santo Stefano (see "Shopping" for other sources of masks and authentic Venetian getups). You can also rent a costume at **Tragicomica di Gualtiero dell'Osto** (Campiello dei Meloni, 2800 San Polo; ☎ 041-721-101; Vaporetto: 1 to San Staè).

Venice Attractions

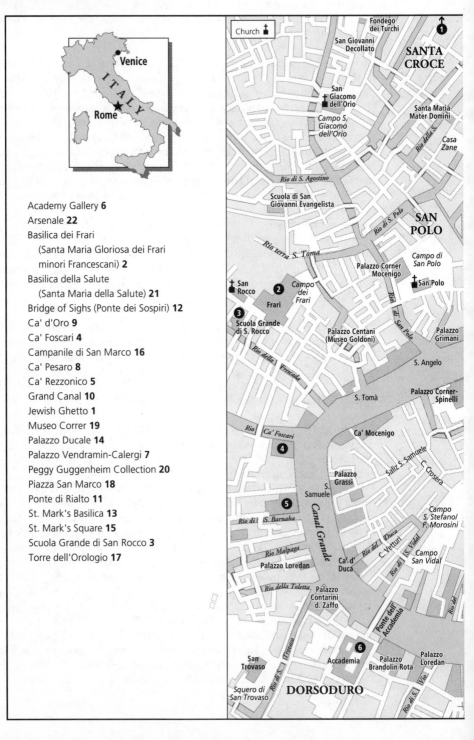

Academy Gallery **6**

Arsenale **22**

Basilica dei Frari
(Santa Maria Gloriosa dei Frari
minori Francescani) **2**

Basilica della Salute
(Santa Maria della Salute) **21**

Bridge of Sighs (Ponte dei Sospiri) **12**

Ca' d'Oro **9**

Ca' Foscari **4**

Campanile di San Marco **16**

Ca' Pesaro **8**

Ca' Rezzonico **5**

Grand Canal **10**

Jewish Ghetto **1**

Museo Correr **19**

Palazzo Ducale **14**

Palazzo Vendramin-Calergi **7**

Peggy Guggenheim Collection **20**

Piazza San Marco **18**

Ponte di Rialto **11**

St. Mark's Basilica **13**

St. Mark's Square **15**

Scuola Grande di San Rocco **3**

Torre dell'Orologio **17**

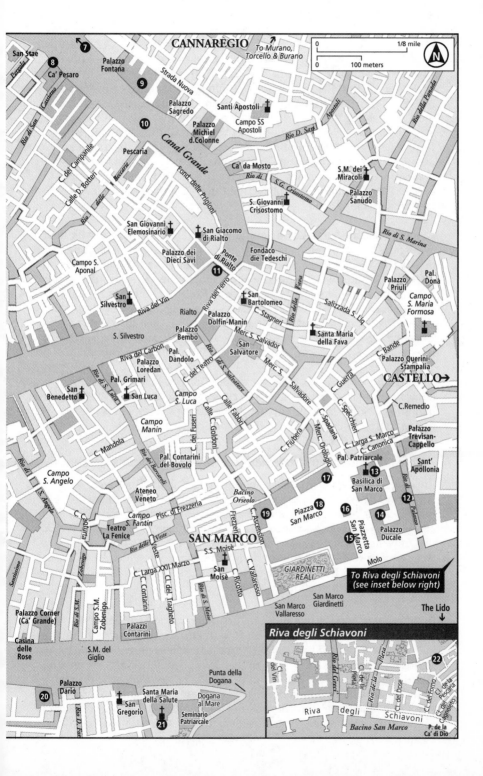

CANNAREGIO
To Murano,
Torcello & Burano

San Stae
Ca' Pesaro
Palazzo Fontana
Strada Nuova
Palazzo Sagredo
Santi Apostoli
Campo SS Apostoli
Palazzo Michiel d.Colonne
Pescaria
Canal Grande
Fond. delle Prigioni
Ca' da Mosto
Rio di
S.G. Crisostomo
S.M. dei Miracoli
Palazzo Sanudo
S. Giovanni Crisostomo
C. del Campanile
Calle D. Botteri
Beccarie
Rio di San Cassiano
Pescaria
San Giovanni Elemosinario
San Giacomo di Rialto
Rio di S. Marina
Campo S. Aponal
Palazzo dei Dieci Savi
Fondaco die Tedeschi
Ponte di Rialto
Palazzo Priuli
Pal. Dona
Campo S. Maria Formosa
San Silvestro
Riva del Vin
Rialto
Riva del Ferro
San Bartolomeo
Salizzada S. Liq
S. Silvestro
Palazzo Dolfin-Manin
C. Stagneri
Rio della Fava
Merc S. Salvador
Santa Maria della Fava
C. Bande
Palazzo Querini-Stampalia
Riva del Carbon
Palazzo Bembo
San Salvatore
Merc. S. Salvador
C. Guerra
Palazzo Loredan
Pal. Dandolo
C. del Teatro
Merc. S.
CASTELLO→
San Benedetto
Pal. Grimari
San Luca
Campo S. Luca
Calle Fabbri
Merc. Orologio
C. Specchieri
C.Remedio
C. Mandola
C. dei Fuseri
Calle C. Goldoni
C. Filbera
C. Spadaria
C. Larga S. Marco
Palazzo Trevisan-Cappello
Campo Manin
Pal. Contarini del-Bovolo
C. Canonica
Sant' Apollonia
Campo S. Angelo
Rio di S. Luca
Rio dei Barcaroli
Pal. Patriarcale
Basilica di San Marco
Ateneo Veneto
Bacino Orseolo
Piazza San Marco
C. Coltrera
C. dei Frezzeria
Piazzetta San Marco
Palazzo Ducale
Teatro La Fenice
Campo S. Fantin
Pisc. di Frezzeria
Frezzeria
C. Ascension
Rio di Palazzo
Rio delle Veste
Veste
SAN MARCO
S.S. Moisè
Molo
Rio dei S.M.
Campo S.M. Zobenigo
C. Larga XXII Marzo
San Moisè
C. Vallaresso
To Riva degli Schiavoni
(see inset below right)
Palazzo Corner (Ca' Grande)
Cl. del Traghetto
C. Contarini
C. Ricotto
GIARDINETTI REALI
The Lido
Casina delle Rose
S.M. del Giglio
Palazzi Contarini
San Marco Vallaresso
San Marco Giardinetti
Palazzo Dario
Santa Maria della Salute
Punta della Dogana
Rio di S. Moise
San Gregorio
Dogana al Mare
Seminario Patriarcale
Rio D. Toia

Riva degli Schiavoni
Cl. del Vin
Rio del Greci
Cl. de la Pietà
Rio de la Pietà
Cl. del Dose
Cl. del Forno
Cl. de la Pescaria
Riva degli Schiavoni
Bacino San Marco
P. de la Ca' di Dio

0 — 1/8 mile
0 — 100 meters
N

7 8 9 10 11 12 13 14 15 16 17 18 19 20 21 22

The top sights

The **Grand Canal (Canal Grande)** was and still is the heart of Venice. Whether you're riding in a *vaporetto* packed as tight as a can of tuna or whispering along in a gondola with just your significant other by your side, you will find the procession of buildings stunning — nowhere else is the feeling of the past so bittersweet and mesmerizing. One of the most interesting things to do is catch a ride on a *vaporetto*. It's the best way to admire the city's showcase of Venetian Gothic architecture — the delicate marble decorations of the *palazzi* opening onto the canal are best seen from the water. These were once the residences of Venice's wealthiest families. Many have been transformed into museums or hotels, others are still lived in (lucky tenants!), and a few seem forlorn and abandoned.

Leaving Stazione Santa Lucia behind you, be on the lookout for (in this order) the **Palazzo Vendramin-Calergi** (hosting the casino in winter) on the left; the **Ca' Pesaro** on the right; the famous and delightful **Ca' d'Oro** (a Gothic jewel built at the beginning of the 15th century) on the left; the beautiful red-and-white **Ponte di Rialto** as you pass beneath it; the **Ca' Foscari** (one of the best examples of Venetian Gothic, today the seat of the university) farther down on the right; then the **Ponte Accademia.** You know you're coming out to the lagoon when you see the imposing white dome of the **Basilica della Salute** to your right.

The best *vaporetto* is no.1: Slower than others (making every stop), it allows a more leisurely perusal and runs at night under the letter N (for *notturno*). For the busy or impatient, the express *vaporetto* is no. 82 (same route, fewer stops).

Academy Gallery (Gallerie dell'Accademia)

Rivaling Florence's Uffizi Gallery and Rome's Galleria Borghese, Venice's Academy Gallery contains great paintings from the 13th through the 18th centuries. Its 24 rooms are housed in a former church (deconsecrated in 1807), its monastery, and its **Scuola Grande di Santa Maria della Carità,** one of Venice's religious associations. The complex also houses Venice's **Academy of Fine Arts.** You can follow the development of art from the medieval period to the Renaissance through the galleries, while also walking through the history of Venetian art.

In room 1 you find the luminous, influential works of Veneziano, still very medieval in feeling. Then you pass into the totally different world of the 15th century, marked by greater naturalism, fuller figures, and the introduction of perspective. For example, Jacopo Bellini's **Madonna and Child** shows the figures in three-quarter view rather than head-on, giving an intimate feeling. In succeeding rooms are Mantegna's **St. George,** works by Mantegna's brother-in-law Giovanni Bellini, and examples of Tintoretto's revolutionary work (radical postures, greater looseness, and theatricality, as well as an instantly recognizable palette).

There's too much in the Accademia to even give an adequate summary, but don't miss Lorenzo Lotto's striking **portrait of a young man** watched by a small lizard on a table; Giorgione's haunting **portrait of an old woman;** and the Tiepolo **ceiling paintings** rescued from a now destroyed building. One of the most famous works is Veronese's incredible, enormous *Last Supper.* Its frenzied energy and party atmosphere (with wine flowing and dwarf figures in the foreground) brought a charge of heresy (and a hasty change of title to *The Banquet in the House of Levi*). At the end of room 15 is Palladio's gravity-defying **staircase.** Room 20 contains a fascinating series of paintings by Carpaccio, Bellini, and others, all commissioned to illustrate miracles of the True Cross, a fragment of which was brought to Venice in 1369, but also illustrating Venice as it once was.

Campo della Carità, Dorsoduro, at the foot of the Accademia Bridge. ☎ *041-522-2247. Vaporetto: 1 or 82 to Accademia. Admission: 6.21€ ($5.58). Open: Tues–Sat 9 a.m.–9 p.m. (Sun–Mon to 2 p.m.).*

Basilica dei Frari (Santa Maria Gloriosa dei Frari minori Francescani)

This church is a magnificent example of the Venetian Gothic, built in the first half of the 14th century and enlarged in the 15th. Beside it is the 14th-century **campanile (bell tower).** The Frari contains many significant artworks, none more so than Titian's *Pala Pesaro (Pesaro altarpiece)* and *L'Assunta (Assumption)* over the main altar, a glorious composition that combines billowing forms with exquisite colors and a feeling of serenity. Also important are Giovanni Bellini's triptych *Vergine con il Bambino e Quattro Santi (Virgin and Child with Four Saints)* and Donatello's *San Giovanni Battista (St. John the Baptist),* a rare sculpture in wood. Be sure to visit the original wooden choir, where monks participated in Mass — this is the only extant choir of its kind in Venice. The triangular marble monument dedicated to sculptor Antonio Canova was actually designed by Canova to be a monument to Titian (Canova's followers appropriated the design for their master after he died in 1822). A bit of trivia: If you look carefully at the walls near the monument, you see an **Austrian bomb** that was dropped on the church during World War I but miraculously failed to explode.

Campo dei Frari, San Polo. ☎ *041-522-2637. Vaporetto: 1 or 82 to San Tomà; walk up to Calle Campaniel, turn right, turn left on Campo San Tomà, continue onto Calle larga Prima, and turn right. Admission: 1.55€ ($1.40). Open: Mon–Sat 9 a.m.–6 p.m., Sun 1–6 p.m.*

Basilica della Salute (Santa Maria della Salute)

Built after the 1630 black plague epidemic as an *ex-voto* (thanks offering to God), the octagonal St. Mary of Good Health is an enduring baroque landmark at the end of Dorsoduro, almost across from Piazza San Marco. On the main altar is a 13th-century **Byzantine icon** and Titian's *Discesa dello Spirito Santo (Descent of the Holy Spirit);* in the Sacristy are three Titian **ceiling paintings** as well as Tintoretto's wonderful *Le Nozze di Cana (Wedding at Cana).* If you happen to be in town on November 21, you can see the feast of the Madonna della Salute, a centuries-old commemorative pageant in which a pontoon bridge is constructed across the Canal Grande, linking La Salute with the San Marco side.

Campo della Salute, Dorsoduro. ☎ *041-523-7951. Vaporetto: 1 to Salute. Admission: Church voluntary offering; Sacristy 1.03€ (93¢). Open: Summer daily 9 a.m. to noon and 3–6 p.m. (winter to 5:30 p.m.).*

Ca' d'Oro

The Ca' d'Oro (Gold House), as its name suggests, was once richly decorated with gold, now worn away to reveal the pink and white marble beneath. Begun in 1422, it's one of the most beautiful of the *palazzi* fronting the Grand Canal. Its elegant tracery of carvings, even without the gold, are evocative of the Venetian spirit — ornate without being gaudy, Gothic but without the broodingly morbid feel of north European Gothic. The building was bought in 1895 by musician/art collector Giorgio Franchetti, who donated the Ca' d'Oro and his collections to the public in 1916. The collection's primary works are Mantegna's *San Sebastian,* Titian's *Venus at the Mirror,* works by Carpaccio and Tintoretto, and **Venetian ceramics** from as far back as the 12th century.

Calle Ca' d'Oro, Cannaregio. ☎ *041-523-8790. Vaporetto: 1 to Ca' d'Oro. Admission: 3.10€ ($2.79); children 16 and under free. Open: Daily 9:00 a.m.–1:30 p.m.*

Ca' Rezzonico

Despite its name, the Ca' Rezzonico was begun in 1649 for the Bon, an important Venetian family. The Rezzonico acquired it a hundred years later and completed the structure — now one of the most magnificent *palazzi* on the Grand Canal. The most famous resident, however, was the English poet Robert Browning, who died here in 1889. The Ca' Rezzonico contains the **Museum of the 1700s in Venice (Museo del Settecento Veneziano),** and among its elegant rooms is the Throne Room, whose ceilings were painted by Giovanni Battista Tiepolo. You can step out onto the balcony and gaze down at the Grand Canal like a tortured lover or brooding poet and get a feel for the life of a Venetian aristocrat.

Fondamenta Rezzonico, Dorsoduro. ☎ *041-241-0100. Vaporetto: 1 to Ca' Rezzonico. Admission: 6.50€ ($5.85). Open: Summer Wed–Mon 10 a.m.–6 p.m.; winter Wed–Mon 10 a.m.–5 p.m.*

Correr Museum

The Correr, which gets less press than the more famous Venetian museums, offers an interesting and eclectic collection, including not only art but also items that make up a history of daily Venetian life, like games, cards, coins, and weapons. Among the clothing are robes worn by the *doges.* The artwork highlights are Canova **bas-reliefs;** a Cosmé Tura *Pietà* from 1460, a fanciful and in some ways surreal painting with a red Golgotha in the background; the famous Carpaccio *Two Venetian Ladies* (familiarly called *The Courtesans* but now known to be a pair of respectable Venetian ladies, a fragment from a larger painting); and a strange Lucas Cranach, with Christ rising from the tomb and two bearded soldiers looking trollish. Hugo van der Goes's emotional small *Crucifixion* is striking.

Procuratie Nuove in Piazza San Marco, San Marco. ☎ *041-522-5625. Vaporetto: 1 or 82 to San Marco–Vallaresso. Admission: See the Palazzo Ducale entry. Open: Summer daily 9 a.m.–7 p.m. (winter until 5 p.m.).*

Palazzo Ducal and the Bridge of Sighs (Ponte dei Sospiri)

Once the private home of the *doges* (elected for life), the seat of the govern-ment, and a court of law, the pink-and-white marble Palazzo Ducale was the Republic's heart. The present Gothic-Renaissance building was begun in 1173 and integrated walls and towers of an A.D. 810 castle. The *palazzo* was enlarged in 1340 with the addition of the new wing housing the **Great Council Room (Sala del Maggior Consiglio),** a marvel of architecture for the size of the unsupported ceilings. On the left side of the courtyard is the **Scala dei Giganti,** guarded by two giant stone figures. After you reach the top of these steps, you enter the loggia, from which departs the famous **Golden Staircase (Scala d'Oro);** it leads to the doges' apartments and government chambers, where are conserved beautiful paintings by the major artists of the 16th century (all the work by 15th-century artists decorating the older wing was destroyed by fires at the end of the 16th century), such as Titian, Tintoretto, Veronese, and Tiepolo. Tintoretto's *Paradiso,* in the Great Council Room, is said to be the largest oil painting in the world (not Tintoretto's best, however). A little-known part of the palace's collection is a group of paintings bequeathed by a bishop, including interesting works by Hieronymous Bosch.

From the palace you continue your visit on the famous **Bridge of Sighs (Ponte dei Sospiri),** which didn't get its name from the lovers who met under it. The bridge connects the palace to the 16th-century **New Prisons (Prigioni Nuove),** and those condemned to death had to pass over this bridge (supposedly sighing heavily) both on their way into the prison and eventually on their way out to be executed in Piazzetta San Marco. The two red columns in the facade of the Ducal Palace mark the place where the death sentences were read out.

If you're interested in the dark history of these ages, you'll love the special guided tour, the **Secret Itineraries (Itinerari Segreti)** offered: It takes you into the doges' hidden apartments and the **Palace of Justice (Palazzo di Giustizia),** where the most important decisions were made. You also visit the famous **Piombi** ("leads"), the prisons under the lead roof of the palace; horribly hot in summer and cold in winter — this is where Casanova was held and from where he made his illustrious escape.

You then visit the **Prigioni Nuove,** built when the palace's limited facilities became insufficient. The guided tour is available in English, and you need to book in advance by calling the number at the end of this listing; the admission includes the guided visit and the regular ticket.

Don't be misled by the exterior; the Palazzo Ducale is huge, especially when you count the labyrinthine prison next door, through which you can wander (and shudder at the medieval conditions — the place was used into the 1920s). You can easily spend four hours inside, especially if you take one of the special tours.

When you pay admission to the Palazzo Ducale, you get a **package ticket** including same-day admission to the *palazzo* as well as the Biblioteca Marciana and Museo Archeologico (Piazzetta San Marco), Correr Museum, Museo Vetrario di Murano, Scuola di Merletti di Burano (on Burano), and Palazzo Mocenigo (on Salizzada di San Stae in San Polo, housing a museum of fabric and costumes).

Piazza San Marco; the entrance to the palace is from the Porta del Frumento on the water side. ☎ 041-522-4951. Fax: 041-528-5028. Advance reservations recommended (with your reservation you go directly to the booth and buy your ticket without standing in line). Vaporetto: 1, 14, 41, 42, 51, 52, 71, 72, or 82 to San Zaccaria. Admission: 9.30€ ($8.37). "Secret Itineraries" tour Thurs–Tues 10:30 a.m. in English (in Italian at 10 a.m. and noon) 12.39€ ($11.15). Open: Daily summer 9 a.m.–7 p.m. (winter until 5 p.m.); ticket booth closes 1½ hours before the palace.

Peggy Guggenheim Collection

In the Palazzo Venier dei Leoni on the Grand Canal, this museum holds one of Italy's most important collections of avant-garde art. The reason the building looks so short is that it's the ground floor of a 1749 *palazzo* that was never completed. American expatriate collector Peggy Guggenheim lived here for 30 years; after her death in 1979, the building and collection became the property of New York's Guggenheim Foundation. Peggy G.'s protégés included Jackson Pollock, represented by ten paintings, and Max Ernst, whom she married. From dada and surrealism to expressionism and abstract expressionism, the collection is rich and diverse, with works by Klee, Magritte, Mondrian, De Chirico, Dalí, Kandinsky, Picasso, and others. The sculpture garden includes works by Giacometti. Temporary exhibits are also mounted.

Calle San Cristoforo, 701 Dorsoduro. ☎ 041-540-6288 or 041-520-6288. Vaporetto: 1 or 82 to Accademia; walk left past the Accademia, turn right on Rio Terrà A. Foscarini, turn left on Calle Nuova Sant'Agnese, continue on Piscina Former, cross the bridge, continue on Calle della Chiesa and then Fondamenta Venier along the small canal, and turn left on Calle San. Cristoforo. Admission: 6.21€ ($5.58). Open: Wed–Mon 10 a.m.–6 p.m. (Sat until 10 p.m.).

Ponte di Rialto

The original wooden bridge here started rotting away, and the citizens of Venice couldn't decide what to do. Finally, in 1588, they decided to replace it with the current stone marvel. The bridge opens onto the Rialto district in San Polo, the merchant area of the past. Ships arrived here after stopping at the *Dogana* **(Customs house)** at the tip of Dorsoduro and discharged their merchandise in the large warehouses. Goods were then sold at the market surrounding the warehouses. The fish and vegetable market had survived until 1998, when it was moved to the current merchant and maritime area of Venice, near the Stazione Ferroviaria Santa Lucia.

Across the Canal Grande, between Riva del Vin and Riva del Carbon. Vaporetto: 1 or 82 to Rialto.

St. Mark's Basilica (Basilica di San Marco)

Dedicated to St. Mark, the city's patron saint, the basilica dominates St. Mark's Square (see listing in this section). It was built in A.D. 829 to house the remains of St. Mark (martyred by the Turks in Alexandria, Egypt), burned down in 932, was rebuilt, and was rebuilt again in 1063, taking its present shape.

The five portals of the basilica are topped by domes that were originally gilded; above the portals is the loggia from which the *doges* (the elected heads of the Venetian Republic) presided over the public functions held in the square, under the shade of the famous gilded bronze horses brought from Constantinople in 1204 after the Fourth Crusade. (If you ascend to the loggia, you find multilingual audio boxes giving a brief description of the sites around the piazza.) The horses (the *Triumphal Quadriga*) outside are copies, but you can admire the originals in the museum within the basilica (see the Marciano Museum, later in this listing); it's estimated they date from the fourth century B.C. Also from the Fourth Crusade are the bronze doors of the main portal and of the **Zen Chapel (Cappella Zen),** named for a family, not the religion. Only one of the mosaics above the doorways is original — the one in the first doorway to the left. The others are 17th- and 18th-century reproductions.

You can take advantage of a free English-language tour of the basilica on Wednesdays, Thursdays, and Fridays at 11 a.m.

Entering the portal, you may be overwhelmed by the luxury of the decorations: gold mosaics and colored inlaid marble. The lower part of the basilica is decorated in Byzantine and Venetian style and the second story in Flamboyant Gothic. The atrium's ceiling mosaics date from 1225 to 1275 and depict Old Testament scenes. The floors are in geometric marble mosaics of typical Byzantine style from the 11th and 12th centuries. The inner basilica mosaics, depicting scenes from the New Testament, were begun in the 12th century and finished in the 13th.

St. Mark's Basilica

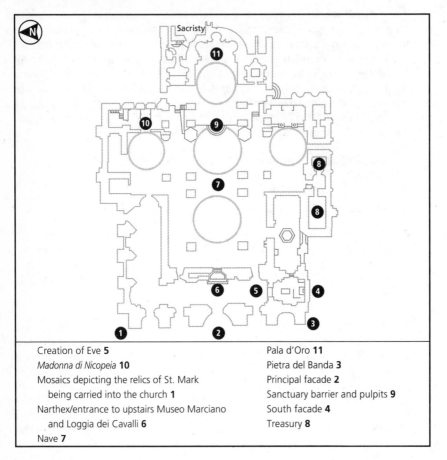

Sacristy

Creation of Eve **5**
Madonna di Nicopeia **10**
Mosaics depicting the relics of St. Mark
being carried into the church **1**
Narthex/entrance to upstairs Museo Marciano
and Loggia dei Cavalli **6**
Nave **7**

Pala d'Oro **11**
Pietra del Banda **3**
Principal facade **2**
Sanctuary barrier and pulpits **9**
South facade **4**
Treasury **8**

The **Treasury (Tesoro)** holds the basilica's riches, and its masterpiece is the famous **Pala d'Oro**, a magnificent altarpiece in gold, finely chiseled in Byzantine-Venetian style. You have to pay 1.55€ ($1.40) in order to see it up close. Inside the basilica is also the small **Marciano Museum** (on the right after you enter, up a long and steep flight of stone steps); the main attraction is the original *Quadriga,* but there are also mosaics, altarpieces, and other works. The **Presbytery** features some beautiful mosaics depicting scenes from the life of Jesus, including the Resurrection.

As in Rome's Basilica di San Pietro, bare shoulders, halter tops, tank tops, shorts, and skirts above the knee all lead to your being turned away from the Basilica di San Marco — no kidding.

Piazza San Marco, San Marco. ☎ *041-522-5205. Vaporetto: 1 or 82 to San Marco–Vallaresso. Admission: Basilica free; Treasury 2.40€ (2.15); Museo Marciano 1.55€ ($1.40); Presbytery 1.55€ ($1.40). Open: Basilica summer Mon–Sat 9:30 a.m.–5:30 p.m., Sun 2:00–5:30 p.m.; winter Mon–Sat 9:30 a.m.–5:00 p.m., Sun 2:00–4:30 p.m. Treasury*

St. Mark's Square (Piazza San Marco)

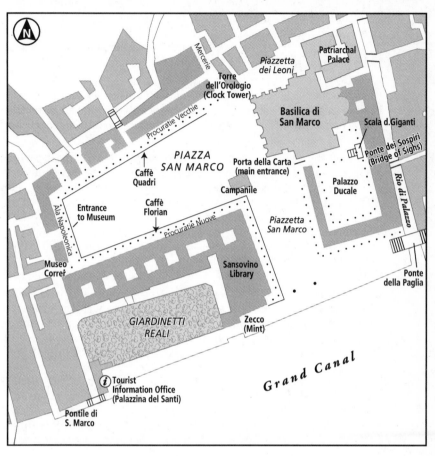

Mon–Sat 9:45 a.m.–4:30 p.m., Sun 2:00–4:30 p.m. Museo Marciano summer Mon–Sat 10:00 a.m.–5:30 p.m., Sun 2:00–4:30 p.m.; winter Mon–Sat 10:00 a.m.–4:45 p.m.

St. Mark's Square (Piazza San Marco)

The symbol of Venice, its center past and present, this piazza is the site richest in monuments in the whole city. The square itself is majestic. Obviously, **St. Mark's Basilica (Basilica di San Marco)** represents its main attraction (see earlier listing), but there's much more to see. Outside the basilica is the **Torre dell'Orologio,** a clock tower built in 1496. This is a Venetian masterpiece: The clock indicates the phases of the moon and signs of the zodiac, while above it a complicated mechanism propels statues of the Magi (the three kings bringing offerings to Jesus) guided by an angel to come out at the striking of the hour and pass in front of the Virgin and Child. Above this, yet another mechanism propels two bronze Moors to strike a bell on the hour. A gruesome legend has it that when the clock was completed, it was such a wonder that the workman who designed and built it was blinded so he could never duplicate it anywhere else. The whole tower was completely restored for the new millennium, and the delicate mechanisms have been undergoing restoration by the renowned watchmaker Piaget (the clock tower is scheduled to reopen for visitors in 2004). An exhibit in the tower explains how this magnificent timepiece works.

Next to the basilica is the **Ducal Palace (Palazzo Ducale)** (see listing earlier in this section). Its exterior, though beautifully carved in marble, gives little hint of the vast spaces and many treasures inside (and a few horrors).

Also on the square is the **Campanile di San Marco (bell tower)** from which you can admire a 360-degree panorama of the city — and you can do so without climbing hundreds of steps because there's an elevator. The campanile is only about a century old — the original fell down in 1902 and had to be rebuilt. On the other end of the square is the Correr Museum (see listing earlier in this section). As you approach the museum, on your left you see the famous **Caffè Florian** and on the right the **Caffè Quadri** (see "Nightlife").

The smaller square between St. Mark's and the water is known as the **Piazzetta San Marco,** once a little harbor that was later filled in. The piazzetta has been modified in various ways since the ninth century, and one of its public functions was executions, carried out between the two granite columns topped by Venetian-Byzantine capitals.

Piazza San Marco. ☎ *041-522-4951 (Torre dell'Orologio).* ☎ *041-522-4064 (Campanile). Vaporetto: 1 or 82 to San Marco–Vallaresso. Admission: Torre dell'Orologio free; Campanile 4.13€ ($3.72). Open: Campanile summer daily 9 a.m.– 8 p.m.; winter Tues–Sun 9:45 a.m.–4:00 p.m. Torre dell'Orologio daily 9:45 a.m.–5:30 p.m.*

Scuola Grande di San Rocco

San Rocco is Jacopo Tintoretto's Sistine Chapel. From 1564 to 1587, Tintoretto, a brother of the school, decorated the **Sala dell'Albergo**, the *sala inferiore* **(lower hall)**, and the *sala superiore* **(upper hall)** with an incredible series of paintings on biblical and Christian subjects. There are 21 paintings on the upper hall ceiling alone (mirrors are available so you don't have to strain your neck). The most impressive is his *Crucifixion,* a painting of almost overpowering emotion and incredible detail (the tools used to make the cross are strewn in the foreground); the painter shows the moment when one of the two thieves' crosses is raised. The upper hall is also decorated with a fascinating collection of Francesco Pianta **wood sculptures** from the 17th century; some depict artisans and the tools of their trade with an amazing realism. Works by Bellini, Titian, and Tiepolo are also on display.

Campo San Rocco, 3058 San Polo. ☎ *041-523-4864. Vaporetto: 1 or 82 to San Tomà; walk up to Calle Campaniel, turn right, turn left on Campo San Tomà, continue onto*

Calle Larga Prima and Salizzada San Rocco, and turn left. Admission: 4.65€ ($4.19). Open: Summer daily 9:00 a.m.–5:30 p.m.; winter daily 10 a.m.–4 p.m.

More cool things to see and do

No matter how long you decide to stay in Venice, you'll discover that the length of your visit is always too short. There are so many interesting things to see and do that time is never enough. Here are some more sights you can check out in and around Venice, many of these geared toward children, who can stand only so many hours in a museum:

✔ Built in the 13th century, the **Arsenale** (Vaporetto: 1, 41, or 42 to Arsenale; follow Calle dei Forni to its end, turn left on Calle di Pegola, and turn right into Campo Arsenale) was the Venetian Republic's shipyard, the largest in the Mediterranean. At its heyday, crews could assemble a vessel from prefab timbers in a single day! Although you can't visit the Arsenale — it's still a restricted military area — the portal is beautiful and so is the view of the canal flowing into the Arsenale's large pond. The lions decorating the entrance were brought back to Venice as spoils of war; the standing lion was taken in the Crusades and once overlooked the harbor of Piraeus in Greece.

✔ The word *ghetto* has been used to name the neighborhood once set apart for Jews in European cities, but the **Venetian Ghetto (Ghetto Novo)** was Europe's first. It was established in 1516 on a small island accessible by only one bridge that was closed at night (you can still see the grooves in the marble *sottoportico* (portico interior) where the iron bars fitted). In 1541, when groups of Jews from Germany, Poland, Spain, and Portugal fled to Venice, the government allowed the community to expand into the **Old Ghetto (Ghetto Vecchio),** the area between the Ghetto Novo and the Rio di Cannaregio, which has the two largest places of worship — the Levantine and Spanish synagogues **(Scola Levantina** and **Scola Spagnola).** To accommodate the growing population, buildings were made taller and taller, so that this area has some of the tallest buildings in Venice. Every hour daily beginning at 10:30 a.m., guided tours of the Ghetto (6.20€/$5.58) start at the **Museo Ebraico** (Campo del Ghetto Novo; ☎ 041-715-359; Vaporetto: 1 or 82 to San Marcuola); the museum is open daily from 10 a.m. to 7 p.m. in summer and Sunday through Friday from 10:00 a.m. to 4:30 p.m. in winter; admission is 2.60€ ($2.34).

✔ A visit to Venice isn't complete without a trip to the lagoon. Of the three famous islands near Venice, **Murano** is the closest and largest (connected via a *navetta* direct from the rail station and vaporetti nos. 41, 42, 71, 72, 12, and 13). This community of more than 6,000 contains about 70 glass factories, some of which allow you to sit and watch glass being blown. You'll find many shops selling glass of all kinds and several good seafood restaurants (see "Where to Dine in Venice"). Glassmaking was moved from Venice to Murano by a 1291 decree because of the danger of fire. One indicator of just how important Murano's wealth has been over the centuries is that aristocrats could marry the daughters of the island's glass masters without compromising their noble titles. Some people think Murano is industrial and not exactly "picturesque"; we like Murano because it has real people doing real things (and eating real good food). At the **Museo Vetrario di Murano** (Fondamenta Giustinian; ☎ 041-739-586), you can see a wonderful selection of glass. Summer hours are Thursday through Tuesday from 10 a.m. to 5 p.m. (winter until 4 p.m.), and admission is 4.13€ ($3.72). The Venetian-Byzantine **Chiesa di Santa Maria e Donato** is really one of the wonders of the whole Venetian region. Founded in the 7th century, it was rebuilt in the 12th. The floor is decorated with a mosaic of birds and animals dating from 1140. In the apse is a dramatic and simple mosaic of the Virgin Mary, from the first half of the 13th century; she wears a deep blue gown and is pictured against a shimmering gold background. The church also has a Paolo Veneziano *Madonna and Child with Saints.*

✔ The second island of the trio (vaporetto no. 12 from Fondamenta Nove), **Torcello** is where the civilization of the lagoon began. In 639, the diocese of Altino was moved here because of the barbarian invasions. It grew into a town of 20,000 inhabitants and was the focus of the lagoon — until this area became more and more marshy and the population center shifted to Venice. Torcello today is abandoned, and because Venice used it as a quarry, few buildings are left. The **Cattedrale di Santa Maria Assunta,** however, is magnificent, founded in 639 and added to over the centuries (in 824 and in 1004). The **campanile** is one of the lagoon's highest, but the real attractions are the 13th-century **Byzantine mosaics** inside — a striking *Madonna and Child* and an almost Boschian *Last Judgment* full of demons and beasts. Open daily from 10:00 a.m. to 12.30 p.m. and 2:00 to 6:30 p.m., the church sits in the middle of a grassy plain reached by a canal from the dock; you can do the walk in 15 minutes or so, but there may be gondoliers hanging around to convince you to make the trip by boat.

✔ The farthest island from Venice — about half an hour by vaporetto no. 12 from Fondamenta Nove — **Burano** is a fishing village renowned for its lacemaking. The typical craft is still alive, and a few fishermen are left, too, but a lot of boats seem to be lying unused in people's backyards. The houses on Burano are famous for their bright colors, ranging from purple to mustard to bright yellow. The town itself is almost wholly given up to lace shops, and the **Scuola di Merletti di Burano** (San Martino Destra 183; ☎ 041-730-034) is right in the middle of town on Piazza Baldassare Galuppi. It has a lace museum where you can study some of the amazing creations of this world-renowned center at leisure (without people pressing you to buy). Summer hours are Wednesday through Monday from 10 a.m. to 5 p.m. (winter until 4 p.m.), and admission is 4.13€ ($3.72). The **Duomo** is just across the street and features a Tiepolo *Crucifixion;* it's open daily from 9:00 a.m. to 12:30 p.m. and 3 to 6 p.m. You can observe the radical tilt of the campanile from almost anywhere on the island — it's truly frightening from some angles!

✔ The island of **Lido** (take vaporetto no. 1, 6, 14, 41, 42, 61, 62, or 82 to Lido) is the stretch of sand protecting the lagoon from the open sea. It's called *Lido* (beach) because it's here that Venetians come to enjoy the beaches on the open-water side. On the lagoon side, you have a fantastic view of Venice. The Lido is also the seat of some of the most elegant hotels from the early 1900s, such as the Art Nouveau **Hotel des Bains** (see "Where to Stay in Venice"). The two best things to do here are spend a decadent evening at the elegant casino (in summer) after dinner in a fancy restaurant (see "Where to Dine in Venice") and bike around this barrier island, which extends for 11km (6.9 miles). If you choose the second option, you can rent a bike at the shop on Piazzale Santa Maria Elisabetta where the ferry arrives or in the three shops on Gran Viale leading away from the vaporetto station (**Gardin Anna Vallè,** Piazzale Santa Maria Elisabetta 2/a, ☎ **041-276-0005; Lazzari Bruno,** Gran Viale Santa Maria Elisabetta 21/b, ☎ **041-526-8019;** or **Barbieri Giorgio,** Via Zara 5, ☎ **041-526-1490**). You can take either of the two parallel roads, the one running on the lagoon side or the one running on the sea side. If you go left from the *vaporetto* station, you soon arrive at the end of the island and can take a ride along the narrow sandbar leading to the lighthouse. It overlooks one of the three entry channels to the lagoon. If you prefer a more urban landscape, go toward the right and the sea; you come to the casino and the Art Nouveau buildings. If you're in good shape, you can reach **Malamocco** (one of the lagoon's oldest settlements) and, even farther, **Alberoni** (a fishing village protected by dikes).

And on your left, San Marco: Seeing Venice by guided tour

Many travel agencies organize tours of Venice, but the best are offered by **American Express** (Salizzada San Moisè, 1471 San Marco; ☎ **041-520-0844;** Vaporetto: 1 or 82 to San Marco–Vallaresso). At about 20€ ($18) for a half day and 31€ ($27.90) for a full day, a guide walks you around the sights and keeps you from getting lost. American Express also has the best prices — half that of other guide services.

Shopping in Venice

Venice's most renowned wares reflect the city's aura of delicate, shimmering beauty. Where else would you find exquisite goblets tinged with gold and lace as fine as snowflakes? Where else would fine paper be fashioned from molds from the 18th century? The good stuff is definitely here, but so is the not so good, so be careful to buy only from reputable merchants; see our recommendations in this section.

Remember that shopping hours generally are daily from 9 a.m. to 1 p.m. and 3.30 to 7.30 p.m. (only local neighborhood shops close on Sunday).

The best shopping areas

For glass, the best shops are in **Murano** and around **St. Mark's Square,** and for lace you need to go to **Burano** or to the area between St. Mark's Square and the Ponte di Rialto. For these two specialized items and paper, see the reliable shops we list.

For browsing, the best streets are the **Mercerie** (the zigzag route from the Piazza San Marco clock tower to the Ponte di Rialto) and the path leading from Piazza San Marco to Campo Santo Stefano and includes **Calle Larga XXII Marzo.** Here you can find big-name Italian stores specializing in everything from shoes to housewares to clothing. Of course, you'll also find these kinds of shops in Florence or Rome.

The **Ponte di Rialto** is famous for its shops, which spill over into the surrounding neighborhood, particularly on the Dorsoduro side. Many of these merchants, however, aren't selling Murano chandeliers and Burano tablecloths, but T-shirts with pictures of Piazza San Marco and plastic Campaniles. Don't count on finding much more here than a few souvenirs and trinkets for the folks back home.

What to look for and where to find it

Venice is known for its exquisite blown glass, lace, fabric, antiques, and fine paper. Here are the best places to find them.

Getting the goods in Venice

Don't part with your money too quickly. In a place with as many tourists as this, a ten-minute walk away from St. Mark's Square can yield a significant price reduction. Be sure to examine whatever you buy with care — there are many cheapo versions of the genuine article that aren't worth a thing. Our philosophy is, "If I like it, and I have X euro to spend on it, then I won't be disappointed." Some people, on the other hand, want not only something they like but something they can feel is valuable to others and would've cost more back home. If you're hoping to find a bargain — like what the Dutch paid for Manhattan — consider that the Venetians have been merchants for more than a thousand years and there's not much they don't know about bargaining. 'Nuff said?

Glass

In Venice, you feel like a bull in a china shop — there's glass here, there, and everywhere. Some of it is low quality, however, and some isn't even from Venice! If you already know a lot about glass, you're okay. If not, be very careful.

Here are a couple of recommended, reputable glass shops. **Venini** (Piazzetta dei Leoncini, 314 San Marco; ☎ **041-522-4045;** Vaporetto: 1 or 82 to San Marco–Vallaresso) is just to the left of the basilica and near the clock tower. This emporium is world-renowned and has its own furnace, so it's not just a store. Prices are what you'd expect for works of art; one drinking glass could cost up to $1,000. **Marco Polo** (Frezzeria, west of Piazza San Marco, 1644 San Marco; ☎ **041-522-9295;** Vaporetto: 1 or 82 to San Marco–Vallaresso), has some small and, therefore, more affordable items. Its selection of Murano glass is exceptional. Another option, of course, is to go to Murano itself and shop around; a huge array of glass shops and showrooms lines both sides of the **Rio dei Vetrai,** which means "the small canal of the glassmakers" (see "More cool things to see and do"). Prices will be the same as in town, but the selection will be much larger.

Lace

The deal with lace is the same as with glass: You may find something handmade in Venice, not handmade in Venice, or not handmade and actually produced thousands of miles away. You can go to **Burano** — go there anyway just for the experience (see "More cool things to see and do") — but some of the shops there feel very fake and others subject you to heavy sales pressure, and we hear rumors about lace coming from other parts of Italy or even the Far East. Again, if you know your linens and laces, you can tell what you're buying. If not, going to a reputable shop in Venice may be better. For example, **Jesurum** (Mercerie del Capitello, 4857 San Marco; ☎ **041-520-6177;** Vaporetto: 1 or 82 to San Marco–Vallaresso) is a reliable lace shop that's been in business since the 1870s. High quality is expensive, but the range of items, from cocktail napkins to bed linens, means that you stand a good chance of finding something within your budget.

Masks and costumes

If you're in town to enjoy Carnevale and didn't pack your 18th-century finery, you're going to need a mask at the very least. The **Laboratorio Artigianale Maschere,** just a short way from SS. Giovanni e Paolo (Barbaria delle Tole, 6657 Castello; ☎ **041-522-310;** Vaporetto: 41, 42, 51, or 52 to Ospedale) has some of the most beautiful costumes. Another good shop is the more affordable **Mondonovo** (Rio Terra Canal, 3063 Dorsoduro; ☎ **041-528-7344;** Vaporetto: 1 or 82 to Accademia). Still, expect to pay 16€ ($14.40) for a basic mask; for the beautiful and artful masks, prices run much higher.

Paper

Handmade marbleized paper is a specialty of Venice. **Piazzesi** (Campiello della Feltrina, just off Santa Maria del Giglio, 2511 San Marco; ☎ 041-522-1202; Vaporetto: 1 to Giglio) is said to be one of the oldest in the business — founded in 1900. The marbleizing is produced by blowing the ink onto the paper by hand (or rather by mouth). Some of the molds used here are from the 1700s. Note that Piazzesi's paper is for sale all over Italy.

Nightlife

As often in Italy, nightlife for the locals means visiting pubs, sitting at outdoor terraces in well-placed cafes, going to concerts, and dancing at discos — usually for the youngest. Night ends early in Venice, finding places that stay open much past midnight is rare. For the big discos you have to go to the mainland.

The performing arts

Venice is famous for music; it seems there are always a dozen performances and concerts going on, whether in the major theaters or in a former church. The **Orchestra di Venezia,** which performs in period costumes, is one of the most entertaining ensembles. Performances are held in the **Scuola Grande di San Giovanni Evangelista** (Campo San Giovanni Evangelista, 2454 San Polo; vaporetto: 1 or 82 to San Tomà), near the Frari church. Prices range from 20.66€ to 30.99€ ($18.59 to $27.89). For information, call ☎ 041-522-8125, fax 041-523-5807, or check the Web site at www.orchestra.venezia.it.

The **Teatro Goldoni** (Calle Goldoni, 4650/B San Marco; ☎ 041-520-7583; Vaporetto: 1 or 82 to Rialto) is one of Venice's premier theaters, especially with the sad demise of the La Fenice. Indeed, Venice's largest opera theater, the **Teatro La Fenice** (Campo San Fantin, 1965 San Marco) is still being reconstructed after the fire that gutted it in 1996. The theater has a temporary site at the **Palafenice** (☎ 041-786-501; Fax: 041-786-580; Internet: www.palafenice.it; E-mail: fenice@inter business.it; Vaporetto: 72 or 82 to Tronchetto), an outdoor tent on the Tronchetto island. Tickets are 15.49€ to 41.30€ ($13.94 to $37.20). You can also book online at www.tin.it/fenice.

The best way to find music is to keep your eyes peeled for poster ads, which are plastered everywhere there's a free wall.

Bars and pubs

Since Hemingway's days in Venice, one of the classic things for visitors to do is head to **Harry's Bar** (Calle Vallaresso, 1323 San Marco;

☎ 041-528-5777; Vaporetto: 1 to San Marco–Vallaresso) for a martini or a Bellini (made with Prosecco, a champagne-like white wine, and the juice of white peaches). Harry's also has great food, but the prices are as huge as the reputation — figure on about 45€ ($40.50) as the base price for a main dish. Even the simplest cocktail costs around $10.

If you're looking for relaxed nightlife, Dorsoduro is the place to go. Among the many pubs, we like **Senso Unico** (Calle della Chiesa, just off Campo S. Vio, 684 Dorsoduro; ☎ 041-241-0770; Vaporetto: 1 or 82 to Accademia), where you can have a drink in a cheerful ambience and listen to music; the beer isn't bad either. Senso Unico stays open until 1 a.m., too. Another place where you can hear music and have a drink is **Caffè Blue** (San Pantalon, 3778 Dorsoduro; ☎ 041-523-7227; Vaporetto: 1 or 82 to San Tomá), which stays open until 2 a.m.

In Castello, the American Bar **Lanterna Blu** (Campo San Lorenzo, 5063 Castello; ☎ 041-523-5571; Vaporetto: 1, 14, 41, 42, 51, 52, 71, 72, or 82 to San Zaccaria) offers live music and cabaret. Closer to the heart of things is the **Devil's Forest Pub** (Calle Stagneri, 5185 San Marco; ☎ 041-520-0623; Vaporetto: 1 or 82 to Rialto), which is very popular and often crowded.

You won't find any gay or lesbian bars in Venice, but you can find some in nearby Padua, a lovely old city about 35 minutes from Venice by train (see Chapter 19).

Cafes

Right on St. Mark's Square are two cafes that square off (sorry!) against each other with classical music groups. They've been there for centuries: **Caffè Florian** (☎ 041-528-5338) since 1720 and **Caffè Quadri** (☎ 041-522-2105) since 1638. You won't find a more central place in Venice (Byron, Wagner, and other famous people used to hang out here), and these cafes are always packed with visitors admiring the basilica, watching the clouds of pigeons take off and land, and sipping expensive drinks.

If you want something a little more authentic, **Le Cafe** (Campo San Stefano, 2797 San Marco; ☎ 041-523-7201; Vaporetto: 1 or 82 to Accademia, then cross the bridge) serves at its outdoor tables a large assortment of drinks, good coffee, and salads (the last, at 11.88€/ $10.69, are a bit expensive but cheap compared with anything you can get on Piazza San Marco). More than just a poor man's St. Mark's experience (here you can enjoy a martini for about 5.50€/$4.95), the campo is a place where you see many Italians stopping on their way to the train station after work. Le Cafe is easy to find because the statue in the campo looks straight at it.

If you happen to be out at Murano, a nice place to have a beer, a coffee, or a light snack is **Ai Pianta Leoni** (Riva Longa 25; ☎ **041-736-794;** Internet: www.datanduo.it; Vaporetto: 41, 42, 71, or 72 to Museo), a bright, modern bar and snack restaurant where you can rest and relax out of the heat.

Fast Facts: Venice

Country Code and City Code

The country code for Italy is **39.** The city code for Venice is **041;** use this code when calling from anywhere outside or inside Italy and even within Venice itself (including the 0, even when calling from abroad).

American Express

The office is at Salizzada San Moisè, 1471 San Marco (☎ 041-520-0844; Vaporetto: 1 or 82 to San Marco–Vallaresso). Summer hours are Monday through Saturday 8 a.m. to 8 p.m. (currency exchange) and 8:00 a.m. to 5:30 p.m. (everything else); winter hours are Monday through Friday 9:00 a.m. to 5.30 p.m. and Saturday 9:00 a.m. to 12.30 p.m.

ATMs

You can find banks with ATMs all around town, especially in the commercial areas of Mercerie, Campo Santo Stefano, Calle Larga XXII Marzo, and Strada Nuova.

Currency Exchange

You can change currency at banks or specialized exchange offices, such as the many on the north side of Piazza San Marco. Remember you can get cash from ATMs that have Cirrus or Plus signs.

Doctors and Dentists

See the "Hospital" entry or call the U.K. consulate or the American Express office for a list of English-speaking doctors and dentists.

Embassies and Consulates

The U.K. Consulate is at Campo della Carità, 1051 Dorsoduro (☎ 041-522-7207). All other consulates are in Milan, three hours away by train.

Emergencies

Ambulance, ☎ **118;** fire, ☎ **115;** First Aid (Pronto Soccorso), ☎ **041-520-3222.**

Gondola Stands (Gondole)

Molo San Marco (☎ 041-520-0685, Vaporetto: 1 or 82 to San Marco–Vallaresso); Ponte di Rialto (☎ 041-522-4904; Vaporetto: 1 or 82 to Rialto).

Hospital

The 24-hour Ospedali Civili Riuniti di Venezia (Campo SS. Giovanni e Paolo; ☎ 041-260-711; Vaporetto: 41, 42, 51, or 52 to Ospedale) has doctors who speak English.

Information

See "Street smarts: Where to get information after you arrive" in this chapter.

Internet Access

Venetian Navigator (www.venetiannavi gator.com) has three locations (Vaporetto: 1, 14, 41, 42, 52, 52, 71, 72, or 82 to San Zaccaria, for all three): Casselleria, 5300 Castello (☎ 041-277-1056); Calle delle Bande, 5269 Castello (☎ 041-522-6084); and Spadaria, 676 San Marco (☎ 041-241-1293). You can also try Omniservice (Fondamenta dei Tolentini, 220 Santa Croce; ☎ 041-710-0470; Vaporetto: 41, 42, 51, 52, 71, 72, or 82 to Piazzale Roma).

Mail

You can find many post offices around town, but the central one is the Ufficio Postale

(Fontego dei Tedeschi, 5550 San Marco; ☎ 041-271-7111; Vaporetto: 1 or 82 to Rialto).

Maps

One of the best maps is Falk, especially because of the smart way it folds, but many other maps are available at most bookstores and newsstands around town.

Newspapers and Magazines

Most newsstands in town sell English papers. One of the largest is in the Stazione Santa Lucia.

Pharmacies

A centrally located one is the International Pharmacy (Calle Larga XXII Marzo, 2067 San Marco; ☎ 041-522-2311; Vaporetto: 1 or 82 to San Marco–Vallaresso). If you need a pharmacy after hours, ask your hotel or call ☎ 192 to get a list of those open near you.

Police

Call ☎ 113; for the Carabinieri (other police force), call ☎ 112.

Restrooms

There are few public toilets in town. Clean public toilets are at the foot of the Accademia Bridge (you need change) and inside the Stazione Santa Lucia. Your best bet is to go to a nice-looking cafe (though you have to buy something, like a cup of coffee).

Safety

Venice is very safe, even in the off-the-beaten-path solitary areas. The only real danger are pickpockets, always plentiful in areas with lots of tourists: Watch your bags and cameras and don't display wads of money or jewelry.

Smoking

Smoking is allowed in cafes and restaurants and is very common. Unfortunately for non-smokers, finding a restaurant with a separate no-smoking area is virtually impossible.

Weather Updates

For forecasts, your best bet is to look at the news on TV (there's no "weather number" by telephone as there is in the States). On the Internet, you can check http://meteo.tiscalinet.it.

Web Sites

The city maintains a useful site at www.comune.venezia.it, and the official tourist board site is at www.provincia.venezia.it/aptve. At www.carnivalofvenice.com/uk, you can find out what's planned for Carnevale each year and get details on transportation and other basics. Two other good general sites are www.meetingvenice.it and www.doge.it. You can also try www.v4u.it, or www.venicebanana.com, which is a very comprehensive *Time Out*–style site (but in Italian).

Chapter 19

Padua, Verona, and Milan

In This Chapter

▶ Discovering Padua and the famous Giotto frescoes

▶ Thrilling to Verona, the setting for the legend of Romeo and Juliet

▶ Shopping 'til you drop in bustling Milan

Though Venice towers over all other cities of northern Italy for its art and unique setting, some of the smaller towns are well worth seeing. For example, many visitors stop at Padua just to see Giotto's famous chapel full of newly restored frescoes, and Verona attracts both romantics (it was the setting for Shakespeare's *Romeo and Juliet*) and architecture buffs. Milan is different: It offers some incredible art (the *Last Supper,* painted by Leonardo da Vinci, for instance), but it is more renowned as Italy's sizzling fashion center and for its incredible shopping opportunities.

What's Where: The Pianura Padana and Its Major Attractions

The economic heart of northern Italy is the **Pianura Padana (the plain of the Po),** which stretches west from Milan all the way to the Adriatic, where the river flows out into the sea south of Venice. Just inland of Venice lies **Padua (Padova),** with its wealth of churches and museums. Although it's only a medium-sized town, Padua is an important contemporary center of art and business — and yet it manages to retain a laid-back, pleasant feeling. Reopened in 2002 after a major renovation is Padua's star sight: the **Chapel of the Scrovegni (Cappella degli Scrovegni),** where you find Giotto's famous frescoes. In fact, the fame of the chapel's frescoes dwarfs the other worthy sights of the city, such as the **Duomo** and its **Baptistry,** the **Basilica di Sant'Antonio,** and the **Palazzo della Ragione.**

Farther inland, to the west, is pleasant **Verona,** an ancient city whose development dates back to the Romans, as the famous theater in the middle of town attests. Known for its Romanesque churches, beautiful squares, and attractive Renaissance architecture, Verona also draws visitors from all over the world who want to see the **House of Juliet** with its balcony, where people like to believe that the tragic Juliet once lived. Farther to the west is Italy's main industrial and manufacturing region, and at the center of it all is **Milan.** As heavy industry lost its relative importance, Milan has progressively grown as the business capital of the country, an important center for modern services and technologies as well as the headquarters of the Italian fashion industry.

Exciting Padua: Home of Giotto's Fabulous Frescoes

Padua (Padova) is a bustling modern town and the Veneto's economic heart. Padua has been around since time immemorial, however — it began as a fishing village and became a Roman *municipium* (municipality) in 45 B.C. Ever prosperous, Patavium (the ancient Roman name of Padova) was the site of great public buildings and an amphitheater, but much was destroyed by the barbarian Longobards in A.D. 602. Padua rose from the ashes in the late Middle Ages and early Renaissance, and the university was founded in 1222, making it the second university in Italy.

Padua is a nice town where everything is on a human scale, and you can enjoy its magnificent attractions in relative calm (most of the time). The presence of the university makes for an active cultural life, open to whomever wants to take advantage of it. Padua is also linked to St. Anthony, who's buried in the basilica bearing his name. For the location of the tourist office, see "Fast Facts: Padua" later in this chapter.

Getting there

On the main line from Rome to the northeast, Padua enjoys excellent **rail connections.** The city is only 30 minutes from Venice, with trains running as frequently as every few minutes at rush hours for about 3€ ($2.70). The train trip from Rome lasts about five hours and costs about 30€ ($27). The **Stazione F.S.** is on Piazza Stazione (☎ 049-875-1800), only minutes north of the historic center. If you don't feel like walking, use the excellent bus service for .77€ (69¢).

If you're **driving,** Padua lies at the convergence of the *autostrada* **A4** (east-west) and **A13** (north-south), so you can easily reach it via car from any direction.

Buses leave for Padua about every half-hour from Venice. The ride lasts less than an hour and costs 3€ ($2.70). Padua's **bus station** is on Via Trieste (☎ 049-820-6844), off Piazza Boschetti, not far from the train station.

The Pianura Padana and Milan

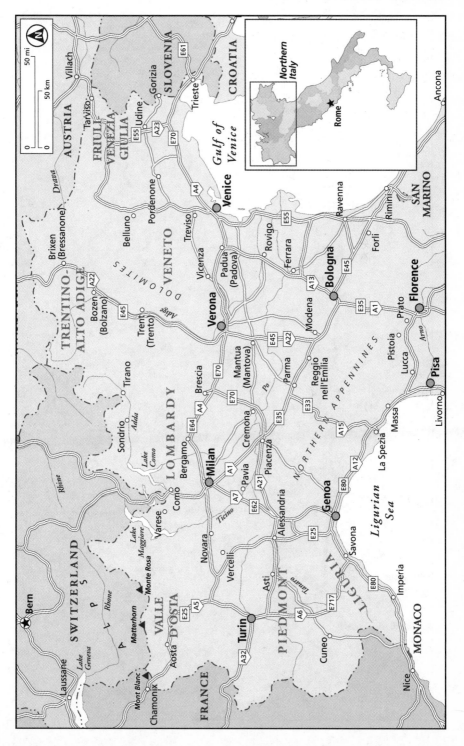

Padua

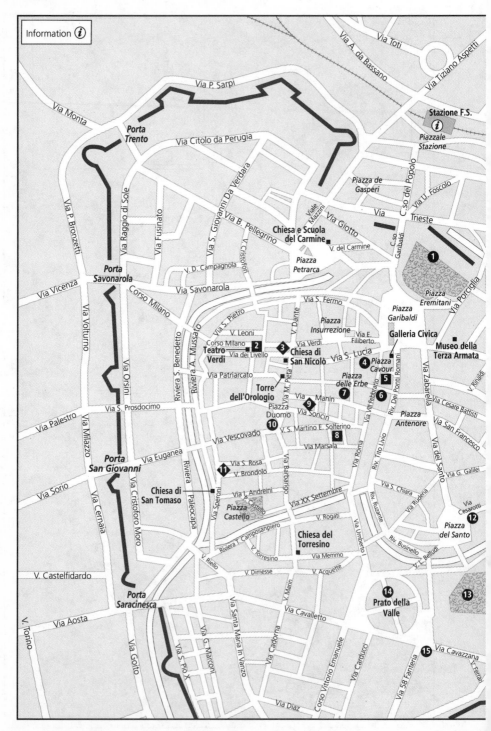

Information ⓘ

Via A. da Bassano

Via Toti

Via Tiziano Aspetti

Via P. Sarpi

Via Monta

Porta Trento

Via Citolo da Perugia

Stazione F.S. ⓘ
Piazzale Stazione

Via S. Giovanni Da Verdara

Via B. Pellegrino

Via Giotto

Piazza de Gaspéri

Via P. Bronzetti

Via Raggio di Sole

Via Fusinato

Via S. Giovanni Da Verdara

Via C. Cristofori

Via Trieste

Via U. Foscolo

C.so del Popolo

C.so Garibaldi

Porta Savonarola

Via Vicenza

Via V. D. Campagnola

Chiesa e Scuola del Carmine
V. del Carmine

Piazza Petrarca

❶

Piazza Eremitani

Via Porciglia

Via Savonarola

Corso Milano

Via S. Fermo

Piazza Garibaldi

Via Voltumo

Via Orsini

Riviera S. Benedetto

Riviera A. Mussato

Via S. Pietro

V. Leoni

Via Dante

Piazza Insurrezione

Via E. Filiberto

Galleria Civica

Museo della Terza Armata

Corso Milano

❷

❸

Chiesa di San Nicolò

Via Verdi

Via S. Lucia

Teatro Verdi

Via del Livello

Via Patriarcato

Via M. Pietà

❹ Piazza Cavour

❺

Piazza delle Erbe

Via VIII Febbraio

Riv. Dei Ponti Romani

Via Zabarella

Via Cesare Battisti

Via Rinaldi

Via S. Prosdocimo

Torre dell'Orologio

Via Manin

Piazza Duomo

❼

❾ Via Soncin

❻

Piazza Antenore

Via San Francesco

Via Palestro

Via Milazzo

❿

Via Vescovado

V.S. Martino E. Solferino

❽

Via Roma

Riv. Tito Livio

Via del Santo

Via G. Galilei

Porta San Giovanni

Via Euganea

Riviera Paleocapa

Via Marsala

Via Barbarigo

Riv. S. Chiara

Via S. Rosa

⓫

V. Brondolo

Via Sorio

Chiesa di San Tomaso

Via I. Andreini

Via XX Settembre

Riv. Ruzante

Via Rudena

Via Cesarotti

⓬

Via Cernaia

Via Cristoforo Moro

Riviera T. Camposanpiero

Piazza Castello

V. Castello

V. Sberoni

V. Rogati

Piazza del Santo

⓭

V. Castelfidardo

Chiesa del Torresino

Via Umberto I

Riv. Businello

V. Torino

Porta Saracinesca

Via Aosta

V. Riello

V. Torresino

V. Dimesse

Via Memmo

V. Acquette

⓮
Prato della Valle

V. L. Belludi

⓯

Via Cavazzana

V. Ferari

Via Santa Maria In Vanzo

V. Mainı

Via Cavalletto

V. Cadorna

Corso Vittorio Emanuele

Via Carducci

Via 58 Fanteria

Via S. Pio X

Via G. Marconi

Via Diaz

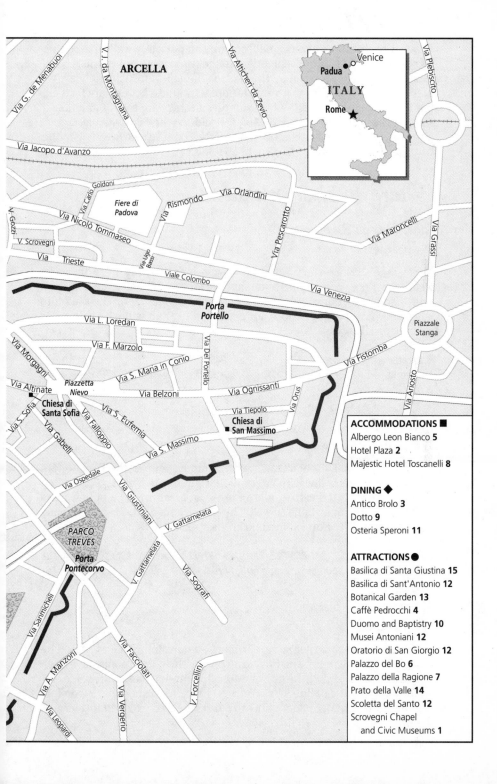

ARCELLA

Via G. de Menabuoi
V.J. da Montagnana
Via Altichieri da Zevio
Via Plebiscito

Venice
Padua
ITALY
Rome ★

Via Jacopo d'Avanzo

Goldoni
Via Catto
Fiere di Padova
Via Rismondo
Via Orlandini
Via Pescarotto
Via Maroncelli
Via Grassi

V. Gozzi
Via Nicolò Tommaseo
V. Scrovegni
Via Trieste
Via Ugo Bassi
Viale Colombo
Via Venezia
Piazzale Stanga

Porta Portello

Via L. Loredan
Via F. Marzolo
Via S. Maria in Conio
Via Del Portello
Via Fistomba
Via Ariosto

Via Morgagni
Piazzetta Nievo
Via Belzoni
Via Ognissanti
Via Orus
Via Altinate
Chiesa di Santa Sofia
Via S. Eufemia
Via Tiepolo
Chiesa di San Massimo

Via S. Sofia
Via Fallopio
Via Gabelli
Via S. Massimo

Via Ospedale
Via Giustiniani
V. Gattamelata

PARCO TREVES
Porta Pontecorvo
V. Gattamelata
Via Sograti

Via Sanmicheli
Via A. Manzoni
Via Facciolati
V. Forcellini
Via Vergerio
Via Leopardi

ACCOMMODATIONS ■
Albergo Leon Bianco **5**
Hotel Plaza **2**
Majestic Hotel Toscanelli **8**

DINING ◆
Antico Brolo **3**
Dotto **9**
Osteria Speroni **11**

ATTRACTIONS ●
Basilica di Santa Giustina **15**
Basilica di Sant'Antonio **12**
Botanical Garden **13**
Caffè Pedrocchi **4**
Duomo and Baptistry **10**
Musei Antoniani **12**
Oratorio di San Giorgio **12**
Palazzo del Bo **6**
Palazzo della Ragione **7**
Prato della Valle **14**
Scoletta del Santo **12**
Scrovegni Chapel
   and Civic Museums **1**

Getting around

Padua's center is relatively small, so you can certainly walk among the sights. The train station is slightly outside the center, but nothing is terribly remote. For example, the Giotto chapel is approximately a 10– or 15-minute walk from the train station. (Other attractions are farther, but in the same direction — for example, it'll take another 20-minute walk to reach the Prato della Valle.) If you don't feel like walking, the city has a good bus system. Get a bus map from the tourist office in the train station. For a **taxi**, call ☎ **049-651-333**.

Where to stay in Padua

Albergo Leon Bianco
$$ Center

This small 19th-century hotel is very romantic. Stay here in warm weather for the rooftop garden or anytime for its convenient central location. The guest rooms are all modernized and renovated: They're quite large and have parquet floors, air-conditioning, and white or pale color washes on the walls.

*Piazzetta Pedrocchi 12. ☎ and Fax **049-657-225**. E-mail:* leonbianco@ toscanelli.it. *Parking: 12.91€ ($11.62). Rack rates: 103€ ($92.70) double. AE, MC, V.*

Hotel Plaza
$$$ Center

The most popular hotel in town with businesspeople, the Plaza offers accommodations in line with international standards. The large, carpeted rooms are decorated with modern European furniture. The public areas are stylish and comfortable as well. The amenities include air-conditioning and minibars. The hotel sometimes runs specials.

*Corso Milano 40. ☎ **049-656-822**. Fax: 049-661-117. Parking: 13€ ($11.70). Rack rates: 170€ ($153) double, including buffet breakfast. AE, DC, MC, V.*

Majestic Hotel Toscanelli
$$$ Center

Just off of an old market square, this is a charming place to stay. The lobby has marble floors and fine furnishings. The guest rooms have been renovated with stylish furniture and offer modern amenities like air-conditioning and satellite TVs. You won't lack for atmosphere, comfort (the beds are large), or something to eat (there's an excellent pizzeria in the hotel).

Via dell'Arco 2. ☎ *049-663-244. Fax: 049-876-0025. E-mail:* `majestic@ toscanelli.it`. *Parking: 12.91€ ($11.62). Rack rates: 145€–161€ ($130.50– $144.90) double, including buffet breakfast. AE, DC, MC, V.*

Where to dine in Padua

Padua's cuisine is typical Italian, with a Venetian influence. As a university town, it offers a variety of cheap lunch spots (particularly on Piazza Cavour and Via Matteotti) where you can enjoy anything from pasta and pizza to sandwiches.

Antico Brolo

$$$$ Teatro Verdi   ITALIAN

This beautiful restaurant — with a 16th-century dining room and a terrace garden — is Padua's best. The menu includes an excellent choice of Italian recipes as well as specialties of the Veneto, such as grilled fish. In the stone-walled basement is a *taverna* (tavern) serving a much simpler but still delicious menu (like pastas and pizzas). Try the local wine.

Corso Milano 22. ☎ *049-664-455. Reservations recommended. Secondi: 12.91€–20.66€ ($11.62–$18.59). AE, DC, MC, V. Open: Lunch and dinner Tues–Sun.*

Dotto

$$ Center   ITALIAN

If you don't want to spend as much as you would at Antico Brolo (see preceding listing) but you still want more than a pizza, Dotto is an excellent choice. The menu includes a great selection of pasta dishes, wines of the Veneto, and good *secondi* (all homemade).

Via del Soncin 8. ☎ *049-875-1490. Reservations recommended. Secondi: 7.23€–12.91€ ($6.51–$11.62). MC, V. Open: Lunch Tues–Sun; dinner Tues–Sat.*

Osteria Speroni

$$ Center   SEAFOOD

Just down the street from the Basilica di Sant'Antonio, this restaurant offers an excellent antipasto buffet with a variety of fish and vegetable preparations. The regular menu includes regional dishes from coastal Veneto, with an accent on fish. Try the *capitone* (a special kind of eel) when it's in season.

Via Speroni 32–36. ☎ *049-875-3370. Reservations recommended. Secondi: 7.75€–12.91€ ($6.98–$11.62). AE, MC, V. Open: Lunch and dinner Mon–Sat.*

Exploring Padua

Padua is a wonderful place to walk. Many of the buildings have *portici* (porticoes, meaning that they overhang the street and are supported by columns), and the sidewalk runs along beneath them. This provides for picturesque views, as well as ample space for pedestrians, who have room to stroll without worrying about being mowed down by motor scooters. The town also has a few canals and bridges, giving it a Venetian feel.

If you have time for an extensive visit, buy the **biglietto unico Padova Arte (cumulative ticket)** available at the tourist booths and all participating sights. It costs 13€ ($11.70) and includes admission to the Musei Civici Eremitani, Cappella degli Scrovegni, Baptistry, Scoletta del Santo, Orto Botanico, Musei Antoniani, and the Palazzo della Ragione.

The top sights

Basilica di Sant'Antonio

Built in the 13th century, this basilica houses the remains of St. Anthony of Padua (including his tongue, still amazingly undecayed). Its distinctive Romanesque-Gothic style reveals Eastern influences, most visible in the eight round domes and the several *campanili* (bell towers) vaguely reminiscent of minarets. Several prominent Renaissance artists worked on the interior: The basilica's treasures include Donatello's **bronze crucifix, reliefs,** and **statues** on the high altar (1444–1448), as well as **frescoes** by 14th-century artists Altichiero and Giusto de' Menabuoi. In the square in front of the church is Donatello's **equestrian statue of Gattamelata** (considered one of his masterpieces). Attached to the basilica is the **Oratory of St. George (Oratorio di San Giorgio),** which opened for the Jubilee after a period of restoration; here you find a fine cycle of frescoes by Altichiero.

Piazza del Santo 11. Basilica ☎ 049-878-9722; others 049-875-5235. Admission: Basilica free; Oratorio di San Giorgio 1.55€ ($1.39); Scoletta 1.55€ ($1.39); Musei Antoniani 2.60€ ($2.34). Open: Basilica summer daily 7:00 a.m.–7:45 p.m., winter daily 6:30 a.m.–7:00 p.m.; Oratorio and Scoletta summer daily 9:00 a.m.–12:30 p.m. and 2:30–7:00 p.m., winter daily 9:00 a.m.–12:30 p.m. and 2:30–5:00 p.m.; Musei Antoniani summer Tues–Sun 9 a.m.–1 p.m. and 2:30–6:30 p.m., winter Tues–Sun 10 a.m.–1 p.m. and 2–5 p.m.

Scrovegni Chapel (Cappella degli Scrovegni) and Civic Museums (Musei Civici Eremitani)

The **Scrovegni Chapel (Cappella degli Scrovegni)** is surrounded by the archaeological remains of the **Roman Arena** — hence its other name, the **Arena Chapel (Cappella dell'Arena).** You can enter the chapel from the courtyard of the **Civic Museums (Musei Civici Eremitani),** which are well worth a visit as well. These museums house a large collection of paintings, as well as artifacts documenting the history of Padua. Artists showcased here include Giorgione, Titian, Veronese, and other Venetian masters.

But it is the Scrovegni Chapel that makes Padua an artistic pilgrimage site. In 1267, Giotto di Bondone was born in a village not far from Florence and went on to become an apprentice of the great painter Cimabue. The frescoes Giotto executed in the chapel are masterpieces. Construction of the chapel itself began in 1303 by banker Enrico Scrovegni, partly as an act of contrition because of his family's ill-gotten (in Christian terms) wealth. (In his *Inferno,* Dante put Enrico's father, Reginaldo, in the circle of hell reserved for usurers, because usury was considered sinful.) Ironically, the jewel that the chapel became under Giotto's hands led local monks to complain about the excessive luxury of the Scrovegni family. Sometimes you just can't win.

The Scrovegni Chapel reopened in March 2002 after a major renovation. You now need to make a reservation in advance (at the number that we give you at the end of this listing) because of the crowds. You'll be charged a fee of 1€ (90¢) for the reservation in addition to the ticket price.

The chapel is an early example of a complex project that reflects the vision of a single artist. The unusual design — windows on one side but not the other, no internal architectural decorations — made it a perfect canvas for Giotto's work. The stories that he depicts move from left to right. The top row or band contains scenes from the life of Joachim and Anna, parents of the Virgin Mary. The middle and lower levels of the chapel contain scenes from the life of Jesus. Giotto also painted allegorical figures representing six virtues and six vices.

Giotto's frescoes broke with tradition in a number of ways, making them striking and important in art history. His composition is dramatic rather than static, as in Byzantine art; he chose scenes that weren't usually depicted; and, above all, he represented human beings with much greater psychological realism, which a glance at these beautiful faces shows. Note that a sign outside says that visits to the chapel are limited to 20 minutes; if the crowds aren't large, however, this rule isn't strictly enforced.

Piazza Eremitani 8, off Corso Garibaldi. ☎ *049-820-4550. Admission: 11€ ($9.90), including both the chapel (by reservation only) and museums. Open: Summer daily 9 a.m.–7 p.m., winter daily 9 a.m.–6 p.m.*

Duomo

Built between the 16th and 18th centuries, the Duomo was partly designed by Michelangelo. Behind the unfinished facade, the two points of interest are the paintings in the **Sacristy (Sagrestia dei Canonici)** and the statues by Florentine artist Giuliano Vangi in the new **Presbetery.** Attached to the Duomo, the beautiful Romanesque **Baptistry** from 1075 is especially remarkable. The interior is decorated with Giusto de' Menabuoi frescoes; among the masterpieces of the 14th century; they have been recently restored and illustrate scenes from the lives of John the Baptist and Christ. A vision of paradise is gloriously depicted on the domed ceiling.

Piazza del Duomo. ☎ 049-662-814. Admission: Duomo free; Battistero 1.55€ ($1.39). Open: Duomo Mon–Sat 7:30 a.m. to noon and 3:45–7:30 p.m., Sun 7:45 a.m.–1:00 p.m. and 3:45–8:30 p.m.; Battistero summer daily 9:30 a.m.–1:30 p.m. and 3–7 p.m., winter daily 9:30 a.m.–1:00 p.m. and 3–6 p.m.

Palazzo della Ragione

Known as **Il Salone (the Great Hall),** this elegantly colonnaded structure was built in 1218 and an upper level was added in 1306. It served as the seat of the city's courts of law. On the ground floor, it divides the **Piazza delle Erbe (green market)** from the **Piazza della Frutta (fruit market).** (These markets still occupy the squares today and are lively affairs.) The top floor is the *salone,* one huge open hall. The rich wall frescoes, illustrating religious and astrological themes, date from the 13th century. The *palazzo*'s largest conversation piece is a giant 15th-century wooden horse for jousting events. *Note:* The *palazzo* reopened in June 2002 after a restoration.

Via VIII Febbraio, between Piazza delle Erbe and Piazza della Frutta. ☎ 049-820-5006. Admission: 6€ ($5.40) adults. Open: Summer Tues–Sun 9 a.m.–7 p.m., closes an hour earlier in winter.

More cool things to see and do

If you're able to spend more time in Padua, check out these other sights:

- ✔ **Caffè Pedrocchi** (Piazza Pedrocchi, just off Piazza Cavour; ☎ 049-820-5007) has been the main intellectual gathering place of the city's intelligentsia. The cafe opened in 1831, when Padua was under Austrian rule, and it still had political importance as late as 1948, when it was the scene of a student uprising. There are two porches (one outside and one inside), a bar of travertine marble and elegant 19th-century furniture, and a pub. The cafe has recently undergone a renovation, and an admission fee of 3€ ($2.70) is now charged. Open Tues—Sun 9:30 a.m.–12:30 p.m. and 3:30–6:00p.m.

- ✔ The seat of the University of Padua, the **Palazzo del Bo** (Via VIII Febbraio, just off Piazza delle Erbe; ☎ 049-820-9773) was built in the 16th century and later enlarged. Founded in 1222, the University of Padua is Italy's second oldest and counted among its scholars

Galileo Galilei. It was the first university in the world to have an **Anatomy Theater (Teatro Anatomico),** an architectural master-piece by G. Fabrici d'Acquapendente, built in 1594. Here medical students observed dissections of cadavers (sometimes in secret, for it was long forbidden by the church) in order to learn about the human body. You can visit only by free guided tour (Tuesday, Thursday, and Saturday at 9, 10, and 11 a.m.; Monday, Wednesday, and Friday at 3, 4, and 5 p.m.). Call for reservations or show up at one of the listed times.

✔ Padua boasts the world's first **Botanical Garden (Orto Botanico;** off Via San Michele, behind the Basilica di Sant'Antonio; ☎ **049-656-614**). It was founded in 1545 as the garden for the university's faculty of medicine, where medicinal plants and herbs were grown. Today it houses a very important collection of rare plants. You can also visit the old library and the university's collection of botanical specimens. There's nothing dusty and academic about this garden, however; it's organized as a Renaissance garden and is very pleas-urable to stroll through. Summer hours are daily 9 a.m. to 1 p.m. and 3 to 6 p.m., and winter hours are Monday through Saturday 9 a.m. to 1 p.m. Admission is 2.60€ ($2.34).

✔ The **Prato della Valle** (between Via Umberto I and Via Belludi) is a traditional recreational area for Paduans. This monumental park was built in 1775, reclaiming an ancient Roman theater that had degenerated into a swampy pond. Majestic statues line both sides of a large canal that runs around a grassy island. Opening on the Prato is the **Basilica di Santa Giustina** (☎ **049-875-1628**), a 16th-century church built over ancient temples. Inside, over the main altar, is Veronese's painting *Martyrdom of St. Justine.* The basilica is open daily from 8.30 a.m. to noon and 3 to 6 p.m.

Fast Facts: Padua

Country Code and City Code

The country code for Italy is **39**. The city code for Padua is **049;** use this code when calling from anywhere outside or inside Italy, even within Padua, and include the 0 every time.

Embassies and Consulates

See "Fast Facts: Venice" in Chapter 18.

Currency Exchange

You can change money at the train station as well as in the exchange office at Via Belludi 15 (☎ 049-660-504).

Emergencies

Ambulance, ☎ **118**; fire, ☎ **115**; road assis-tance ☎ **116**; First Aid (Pronto Soccorso), ☎ **049-821-2856** or 049-821-2857.

Hospital

The Ospedale Civile is at Via Giustiniani 1 (☎ 049-821-1111).

Information

You can write to the main tourist office before your trip: APT (Riviera dei Mugnai 8; ☎ 049-875-0655 or 876-2911; Fax: 049-650-794). After you arrive, visit the tourist booth inside the train station (☎ 049-875-2077).

Summer hours are Monday through Saturday 9 a.m. to 7 p.m. and Sunday 8:30 a.m. to 12:30 p.m. Winter hours are Monday through Saturday 9:20 a.m. to 5:45 p.m. and Sunday 9 a.m. to noon.

Mail

The post office (ufficio postale) is at Corso Garibaldi 33 (☎ 049-820-8511).

Police

Call ☎ **113**; for the Carabinieri (other police force), call ☎ **112.**

Taxi

Call ☎ 049-651-333.

Romancing Verona: City of Juliet and Her Romeo

Like Padua, **Verona** was a Roman city whose historic center is now surrounded by a bustling modern urban area (Verona, too, is a major economic hub). After its glory during the reign of Augustus, Verona suffered under barbarian invasions and went into decline. The Scaliger family ruled it in the 13th and 14th centuries much as the Medici family ruled Florence. Venice absorbed Verona in 1405, and Venetian rule lasted until Napoleon made everybody equal (sort of). Austrian domination followed, which continued until 1866 and the unification of Italy.

Today Verona is a popular destination — even though Romeo and Juliet may never have existed, there's plenty to see here — but because of its contemporary vitality, it's not as overwhelmed with tourists as Venice. For the location of the tourist office, see "Fast Facts: Verona."

Getting there

The **train** to Verona takes two hours from Venice and six from Rome. The fare is approximately 6€ ($5.40) from Venice and 22€ ($20) from Rome. Trains arrive at the **Stazione Porta Nuova** on Piazza XXV Aprile (☎ **045-590-688**).

Verona's **Aeroporto Valerio Catullo,** in Villa Franca, is 16km (10 miles) from the center. **Meridiana** offers hour-long flights daily from Rome (☎ **06-4780-4222** or 02-864-771) for about 135€ ($122) round-trip. You can take a taxi from the airport (about 15 minutes), or you can take a regular city bus running from the airport to the town center (.77€/69¢) in about 20 minutes.

If you're **driving** from Rome, take **A1** to Campogalliano and then **Autostrada del Brennero (A22)** to the Verona Sud exit (about six hours). The trip is a total distance of 505km (315 miles). From Venice,

Verona

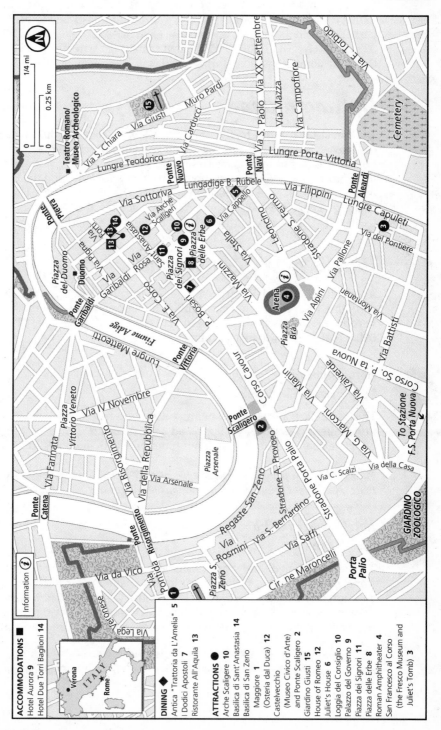

N

1/4 mi
0   0.25 km

Teatro Romano/
Museo Archeologico

ACCOMMODATIONS ■
Hotel Aurora **9**
Hotel Due Torri Baglioni **14**

Information ⓘ

DINING ◆
Antica "Trattoria da L'Amelia" **5**
I Dodici Apostoli **7**
Ristorante All'Aquila **13**

ATTRACTIONS ●
Arche Scaligere **10**
Basilica di Sant'Anastasia **14**
Basilica di San Zeno
Maggiore **1**
Castelvecchio
(Museo Civico d'Arte)
and Ponte Scaligero **2**
Giardino Giusti **15**
House of Romeo **12**
Juliet's House **6**
Loggia del Consiglio **10**
Palazzo del Governo **9**
Piazza dei Signori **11**
Piazza delle Erbe **8**
Roman Amphitheater **4**
San Francesco al Corso
(the Fresco Museum and
Juliet's Tomb) **3**

(Osteria dal Duca) **12**

take **A4** heading west; the drive requires approximately two hours (it's about 110km/68 miles). When you get to Verona, however, you'll have to leave your car in a parking garage — the center is closed to private cars. The main parking lot is **Arsenale** (Piazza Arsenale 8, ☎ **045-830-3281**), which costs 1.30€ ($1.15) for overnight (11 p.m. to 7 a.m.) but the same amount *per hour* during the day.

Getting around

You can easily reach Verona's main attractions on foot, or you can use **city buses.** Tickets cost .77€ (70¢), and you must purchase them before boarding, either from *tabacchi* (tobacconists) or inside the station. The main bus hubs are the train station (Stazione Ferroviaria) and the Roman Arena (Piazza Brà, see "Exploring Verona" later in this chapter). The winding river Adige flows through Verona much like the Tiber does in Rome. Most of the city's attractions lie in the river's southern bend.

Where to stay in Verona

As a lively commercial center, Verona has many hotels. If you arrive without a reservation, you can contact the **Cooperativa Albergatori Veronese** (Via Patuzzi 5, parallel to Via Leoncino off the Arena; ☎ **045-800-9844**), which will help you find a room.

Hotel Aurora

$$ Piazza delle Erbe

This good basic hotel, a 15th-century structure resting on older foundations, offers views over a piazza and a great location for exploring the city. The guest rooms are small but functional with modern furnishings.

Piazzetta XIV Novembre 2, off Piazza delle Erbe. ☎ *045-594-717. Fax: 045-801-0860. Rack rates: 75€–110€ ($68–$99) double, including breakfast. AE, MC, V.*

Hotel Colomba d'Oro

$$$ Arena

This is a good medium-range choice. A couple of steps from the Roman Arena (see "Exploring Verona" later in this chapter), this hotel occupies an impressive old building, with 15th-century frescoes decorating the hall. It's been an inn since the 19th century, and in a previous incarnation was a monastery. The guest rooms are comfortable and tasteful.

Via C. Cattaneo 10. ☎ *045-595-300. Fax: 045-594-974. E-mail:* info@colomba hotel.com. *Parking: 14€ ($13). Rack rates: 90€–160€ ($81–$144) double. AE, MC, V.*

Hotel Due Torri Baglioni
$$$$$ Center

This is the elegant place to stay in Verona. Situated in the town center, the hotel was once the home of the powerful Scaligeri family. In 1990, a major chain took it over and totally restored it. The beautiful antique furniture remains, and the public areas are decorated in grand hotel style. We recommend the hotel's **Ristorante All'Aquila** (see the listing later in this chapter).

Piazza Sant'Anastasia 4. ☎ ***045-595-044.*** *Fax: 045-800-4130. E-mail:* duetorri. verona@baglionihotels.com. *Parking: 24€ ($22). Rack rates: 175€–440€ ($158–$396) double, including buffet breakfast. AE, DC, MC, V.*

Where to dine in Verona

Verona offers plenty of cheap places to eat, as well as elegant restaurants that cater to business travelers and well-heeled visitors. You'll find good food as well as good wine: The important wine-growing region of the Veneto supplies Verona with an interesting assortment of fine wines.

Antica "Trattoria da L'Amelia"
$$ Center   ITALIAN

This old trattoria by the river has been open since 1876. It serves typical food of the Veneto, and in particular has a great selection of desserts. The trattoria's interior is a cozy and warm refuge. Choose something to accompany your meal from the excellent, large wine list.

Lungadige B. Rubele 32, near the Anfiteatro. ☎ ***045-800-5526.*** *Internet:* www. trattoriaamelia.com. *Reservations recommended. Secondi: 10€–18€ ($9–$16). Open: Lunch Tues–Sat, dinner Mon–Sat.*

I Dodici Apostoli
$$$ Center   ITALIAN

This restaurant has existed for more than two centuries, and its interior is decorated with frescoes. I Dodici Apostoli specializes in regional cuisine, but the chef has added many innovative twists to traditional recipes (marinated salmon stuffed with scallops, for example).

Vicolo Corticella San Marco 3. ☎ ***045-596-999.*** *Reservations recommended. Secondi: 14€–18€ ($13–$16). AE, DC, MC, V. Open: Lunch Tues–Sun; dinner Tues–Sat; closed two weeks in June.*

Ristorante All'Aquila
$$$ Center   ITALIAN

This is a place to go for a real dinner, not just something to sate your appetite. Inside the town's most elegant hotel (see the listing for Hotel Due Torri Baglioni), the restaurant offers a Liberty-style decor and a menu that includes regional and seasonal specialties. The pastas are prepared with a variety of creamy sauces, and you can order such unusual items as smoked horsemeat.

Piazza Sant'Anastasia 4 in the Hotel Due Torri Baglioni. ☎ *045-595-044. Reservations recommended. Secondi: 16€–20€ ($14.50–$18). Open: Lunch and dinner daily.*

Exploring Verona

A harmonious mix of Roman, medieval, and Renaissance architecture, Verona is one of the preferred destinations of international tourism in northern Italy. Here we detail its most famous and worthwhile attractions.

The top sights

Basilica di San Zeno Maggiore

A wonderful example of the Romanesque style and the most beautiful in northern Italy, this church and campanile were built between the 9th and 12th centuries above the tomb of Verona's patron saint (the original church dates from the 4th and 5th centuries). Some of its most fascinating artworks are the 11th- and 12th-century **bronze door panels** illustrating San Zeno's miracles. Like other works in this part of Italy (notably Venice), they reflect a mix of Byzantine, Gothic, and Turkish influences. The interior has a 14th-century **timbered roof,** and over the entrance is the famous **Wheel of Fortune (Ruota della Fortuna) rose window** from the early 12th century. Note particularly the Romanesque capitals on the columns and the frescoes (dating from the 12th to 14th centuries). Also don't miss the Romanesque **cloister** at the north end of the church.

Piazza San Zeno, just west of the Arena. ☎ *045-800-4325. Admission: 1.55€ ($1.40). Open: Summer Mon–Sat 9 a.m.–6 p.m. and Sun. 1–6 p.m.; winter Mon–Sat 10 a.m.–4 p.m. and Sun 1–4 p.m.*

Castelvecchio (Museo Civico d'Arte) and Ponte Scaligero

The 14th-century **Castelvecchio,** perched on the Adige River, was the fortress of the Scaligeri family but now houses an art museum containing paintings by artists of the school of the great Renaissance painter Paolo Veronese. Veronese is represented, as well as Venetian artists like Tiepolo and Tintoretto. The castle is worth a visit, with its labyrinthine passageways and the tower from which you can see sweeping vistas of the city and its environs. The bridge linking the castle with the other side of the river is the famous **Ponte Scaligero** (built between 1355 and 1375), which was destroyed by the Nazis during their retreat at the end of World War II and rebuilt using the pieces that remained in the river.

Corso Castelvecchio 2, at the western end of Corso Cavour. ☎ *045-594-734. Admission: 3.10€ ($2.80). Free the first Sun of each month. Open: Tues–Sun 8:30 a.m.–7:30 p.m. and Mon 1:30 p.m.–7:30 p.m. Ticket booth closes at 6:45 p.m.*

Piazza dei Signori and Arche Scaligere

One of northern Italy's most beautiful piazze, surrounded by beautiful palaces, this square was the center of Verona's government during its heyday. The **Palazzo del Governo** is where Cangrande della Scala (one of the first Scaligeri) extended the shelter of his hearth and home to the fleeing Florentine poet Dante Alighieri. A marble statue of Dante stands in the center of the square. The **Palazzo della Ragione,** on the south side of the piazza, was built in 1123 but underwent changes many times in later centuries, including receiving a Renaissance facade in 1524. From its courtyard rises a tower, the majestic **Torre dei Lamberti** (84m/277 feet), also called the Torre del Comune. An elevator takes you to the top, and the views are magnificent. On the north side of the piazza is the 15th-century **Loggia del Consiglio,** which was the town council's meeting place; it's surmounted by five statues of famous Veronese citizens. Five arches lead into Piazza dei Signori.

Just off Piazza dei Signori are the **Arche Scaligere,** the outdoor tombs of the Scaligeri princes, enclosed behind wrought-iron gates bearing the representation of ladders, the family's heraldic symbol. The grandest of the monuments is that of Cangrande I (he was certainly top dog — his name means "Big Dog"), which stands apart from the other tombs. Some of the other Scaligeri were Cansignorio (more or less "Sir Dog") and Mastino ("Mastiff"). Adjoining is the 12th-century **Santa Maria Antica,** through which you can access the Arche. The mausoleum contains many Romanesque features and is crowned by a copy of an **equestrian statue** of Cangrande (the original is at the Castelvecchio). Tickets for both the Arche and the Torre are sold at the booth by the Torre's entrance. Note that you can't visit the Arche during the winter.

Arche Scaligere: Via Arche Scaligere, off Via Sant'Anastasia and Via P. Bosari; Torre dei Lamberti: Cortile Mercato Vecchio. ☎ *045-803 2726. Admission: Winter, Torre 1.50€ ($1.40) on foot and 2.10€ ($1.90) by elevator; summer, Torre and Arche 2.10€ ($1.90) by foot, 2.60€ ($2.34) by elevator. Open: Tues–Sun 9:30 a.m.–7:30 p.m., Monday 1:30–7:30 p.m. (ticket booth open to 5:30 p.m.).*

Piazza delle Erbe

The piazza (its name means Square of the Herbs) was built where the Forum stood in Roman times. Today, it's the fruit-and-vegetable market where Veronese shoppers and vendors mill about, surrounded by

Renaissance palaces. In the center is the **Berlina,** a canopy supported by four columns where the election of the town's *signore* (elected prince) and the *podestà* (the governor) took place. On the north side is a 14th-century **fountain** and the *Madonna Verona,* which is actually a restored Roman statue. Important buildings on the piazza include the early-14th-century **House of the Merchants (Casa dei Mercanti),** restructured in 1870 to restore its original 1301 form; the baroque **Palazzo Maffei;** the adjacent **Torre del Gardello,** a tower built in 1370; and the **Casa Mazzanti,** another Scaligeri palace, decorated with frescoes.

Intersection of Via Mazzini and Via Cappello.

Roman Amphitheater (Arena di Verona)

This famous elliptical Roman arena dates from the reign of Diocletian (it was built around A.D. 290) and remains in surprisingly good condition. The inner ring is basically intact, though a 12th-century earthquake destroyed most of the outer ring (only four of the arches remain). This was Italy's third-largest Roman amphitheater and the second most important to have survived after Rome's Colosseum.

The arena's overall length was 152m (470 feet) and its height 32m (97½ feet). Its 44 rows of seats could originally hold as many as 20,000 spectators, who watched gladiators and animals sparring. These days, however, the arena hosts more civilized entertainments: One of the greatest experiences in Verona is attending an opera or a ballet here during July or August. The setting speaks for itself. Tickets cost from about 20€ to 160€ ($18 to $144); for schedule and ticket information, call ☎ 045-800-5151. To make a reservation in the United States, call the **Global Tickets agency** (☎ 800-223-6108 or 914-328-2150; Fax: 914-328-2752), and the company will mail or fax a voucher to you. You can also make reservations and buy tickets online at www.arena.it.

Piazza Brà. ☎ 045-800-3204. Admission: 3.10€ ($2.80) adults. Open: Tues–Sun 8:30 a.m.–7:30 p.m., Monday 1:30–7:30 p.m., free first Sun of every month. On performance days, arena closes at 1:30 p.m.

More cool things to see and do

Verona is a small city, but it offers a number of interesting sights. You can **rent a bicycle** in Piazza Bra' (☎ 0338-955-0056 or 045-582-389) near the arena and take yourself for an exhilarating tour of the city. If you still have time after visiting the city's main attractions, try some of these other points of interest:

✔ The small **Juliet's House (Casa di Giulietta),** at Via Cappello 23 (☎ 045-803-4303), is a 12th-century house that the city bought in 1905 and turned into a tourist site (the famous balcony was added in 1935). Shakespeare's Capulets and Montagues (from his famous play *Romeo and Juliet*) were indeed versions of two historic

Veronese families, the Cappuletti (or Cappello) and the Montecchi. No proof exists that a family of Capulets ever lived in this house, but that doesn't stop people from flocking here to see the balcony where Juliet would've stood, if she'd been here at all. Tradition calls for you to rub the right breast of the bronze statue of Juliet for good luck. The house is open Tuesday through Sunday from 8:30 a.m. to 7:30 p.m., and Monday from 1:30 to 7:30 p.m.; admission is 3.10€ ($2.80). Of course, you can't have a Juliet without a Romeo, and there's a so-called **House of Romeo (Casa di Romeo)**, at Via Arche Scaligeri 2 (east of Piazza dei Signori), which is said to have been the home of the Montecchi family and now houses a small, cute restaurant called the **Osteria dal Duca** (☎ **045-594-474;** closed on Sunday; reservations recommended; prix-fixe menu 13€/$11.70).

✔ The **Fresco Museum (Museo degli Affreschi G. B. Cavalcaselle)** and **Juliet's Tomb (Tomba di Giulietta)** are housed in the 12th-century complex of **San Francesco al Corso** (Via Shakespeare; ☎ **045-800-0361**). It was inaugurated in 1935 with the display of a sarcophagus that, according to legend, holds the bodies of Romeo and Juliet. The museum also displays an interesting collection of frescoes from a number of buildings in Verona, as well as 19th-century sculptures. The church of San Francesco houses several paintings from the 15th, 16th, and 17th centuries and a large collection of Roman amphoras in the vaults. The complex is open Tuesday through Sunday from 8:30 a.m. to 7:30 p.m., Monday from 1:30 to 7:30 p.m.; admission is 2.60€ ($2.40).

✔ The **Basilica di Sant'Anastasia** (Piazza Sant'Anastasia; ☎ **045-800-4325**) is Verona's largest church. Built between 1290 and 1481, it is graced by an unfinished Gothic facade adorned by a beautiful arched portal and an ornate campanile. Although the architecture (rather than the contents of the church) is its noblest feature, it does contain a Pisanello fresco of San Giorgio pictured with a princess in the Giusti Chapel (Cappella Giusti) and terra cotta works by Michele da Firenze in the Pellegrini Chapel (Cappella Pellegrini). Admission to the church is free, and it's open Monday through Saturday from 10 a.m. to 1 p.m. and 1:30 to 4:00 p.m. (to 5 p.m. on Sunday).

✔ The **Giardino Giusti** (Via Giardino Giusti 2; ☎ **045-803-4029**) is a perfect example of an Italian garden. It has survived for many centuries (it was built in the 14th century and given its current layout in the 16th) more or less intact. Crossed by a main alley lined with secular cypress trees, the garden is embellished with grottoes, statues, and fountains. From a balcony at one end of the garden, known as the "monster balcony," you can enjoy a panoramic view of the city. The garden is open daily from 9 a.m. to 8 p.m. in summer (to sunset in winter), and admission is 4.50€ ($4.00).

Fast Facts: Verona

Country Code and City Code

The country code for Italy is **39**. The city code for Verona is **045**; use this city code when calling from anywhere outside or inside Italy, even within Verona and always include the 0.

Embassies and Consulates

See "Fast Facts: Venice" in Chapter 18.

Currency Exchange

You can change currency inside the rail station or at numerous banks around town (for example, on Corso Cavour, where you can also find ATMs).

Doctor

At night and during weekends and holidays, you can reach a doctor by calling ☎ 045-807-5627.

Emergencies

Ambulance, ☎ **118**; fire, ☎ **115**; road assistance, ☎ **116**; first aid (Pronto Soccorso, ☎ 045-807-2120.

Hospital

The Ospedale Civile Maggiore Borgo Trento is at Piazzale Stefani 1 (☎ 045-807-1111).

Information

The tourist office is at Via degli Alpini 9 (☎ 045-806-8680); open 9 a.m.–3 p.m. There are also tourist booths in the train station (☎ 045-800-0861) and the airport (☎ 045-861-9163).

Mail

The post office (ufficio postale) is at Piazza Viviani 7 (☎ 045-805-1111).

Police

Call ☎ **113**; for the Carabinieri (other police force), call ☎ **112**.

Milan: Italy's Business and Fashion Center

Milan (Milano) is a large industrial city that has deep roots in Italy's history. It is the capital of Lombardy, a region of rich agricultural plains that have often been fought over in the past (the area was long occupied by Austria). Although it has much to offer from both historic and artistic points of view, the life of this busy city is defined by commerce, the newest technologies, and international influences. As a tourist destination, it isn't up there with Rome, Venice, and Florence, but it does have several gems that you should make a detour to see.

For the location of the tourist office, see "Fast Facts: Milan."

Getting there

The main international airport of Milan is **Malpensa** (☎ **02-7485-2200**), located 50km (31 miles) to the north of the city. There is a **shuttle train,** the Malpensa Express, to the rail station **Cadorna Ferrovie Nord,** which runs every 20 minutes, and a **shuttle bus** (the Airpullman) to the railway station FS Milano Centrale every 30 minutes.

The **Linate Airport** (☎ **02-7485-2200**) is 10km (6.2 miles) to the east of town. There is a **city bus** (bus 73) every ten minutes, which connects to the subway (M1). There is also a **shuttle** (☎ **02-669-0351**).

Milan is an important transportation hub in Italy, second only to Rome. The train trip from Rome lasts about five hours and costs about 40€ ($36). The **Stazione Centrale,** Piazza Duca d'Aosta (☎ **1478-88-088** toll-free in Italy), is the city's main rail station for arrivals.

If you're **driving,** Milan is at the intersection of the following high-ways: **A1** (Milano-Napoli); **A4** (Torino-Trieste); **A7** (Milano-Genova); **A8** (Milano-Varese); and **A9** (Lainate-Chiasso). Take the exit "Milano centro" for the center of the city. Avoid driving into Milan, however — it has a lot of traffic, and parking is expensive. If you choose to do so anyway, use the public parking marked by blue lines on the ground: You have to buy a card from a news kiosk or a tobacconist (or from an attendant when available) and display it inside your car.

Getting around

Although walking is always the best way to see a town, you may want to use public transportation to get yourself to more distant corners of Milan. The city is well served by a system of three **subway lines** and several **buses and tramways.** The **Metro (subway)** is the fastest and simplest means to get around, but you'll see more from buses and tramways. Be sure to pick up a public transportation map from the information booth in the Duomo subway station (open Monday through Saturday from 7:45 a.m. to 8:15 p.m.) if you intend to use the buses and tramways.

Buses, tramways, and subways use the same tickets, which are sold at newsstands, tobacconists, and bars. A **75-minute ticket** costs 1€ (90¢), but you can also buy a **carnet of ten tickets** for 9.20€ ($8.28), a **one-day travel card** for 4€ ($3.60), or a **two-day travel card** for 5.50€ ($4.95).

Where to stay in Milan

As Italy's business center, Milan has many hotels. Consider, however, that big business often means big prices, and hotel rates may be keyed to the business traveler on an expense account. Also keep in mind that business travelers tend to go home on weekends, so weekend rates

Milan

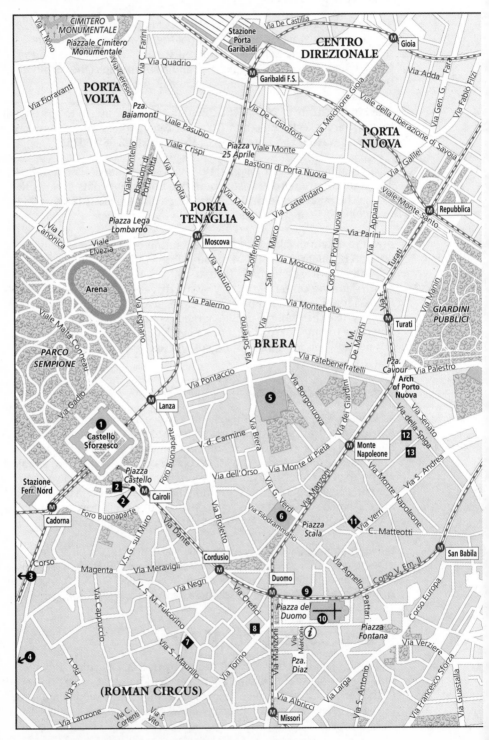

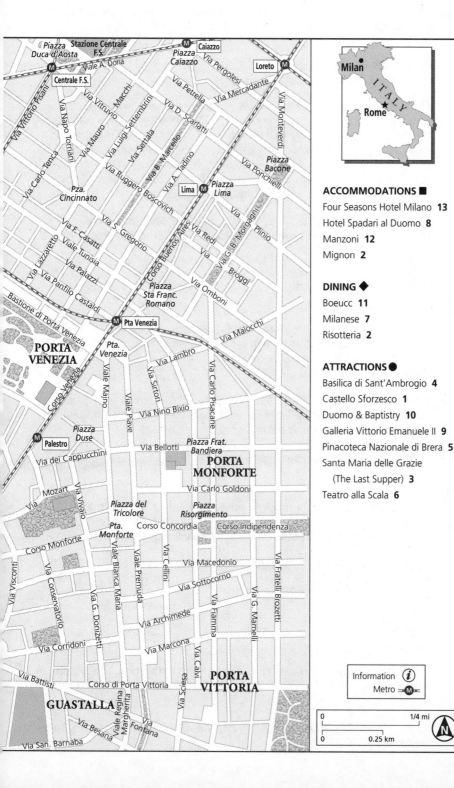

ACCOMMODATIONS ■
Four Seasons Hotel Milano **13**
Hotel Spadari al Duomo **8**
Manzoni **12**
Mignon **2**

DINING ◆
Boeucc **11**
Milanese **7**
Risotteria **2**

ATTRACTIONS ●
Basilica di Sant'Ambrogio **4**
Castello Sforzesco **1**
Duomo & Baptistry **10**
Galleria Vittorio Emanuele II **9**
Pinacoteca Nazionale di Brera **5**
Santa Maria delle Grazie
   (The Last Supper) **3**
Teatro alla Scala **6**

Information ⓘ
Metro Ⓜ

0   1/4 mi
0   0.25 km

may be much more economical than weekday for the leisure traveler. The following options run the gamut from luxury to economy.

Four Seasons
$$$$$ **Center**

This luxury hotel is housed in a 15th-century convent, whose columned cloister now forms an inner courtyard. The rooms are large and tastefully decorated, and you get the kind of amenities you'd expect in a major-city hotel frequented by business travelers: air-conditioning, refrigerator, safe, multi-line phone, in-room Internet access — the works. And you're right in the center of everything. It comes at a price, of course, but the hotel does run weekend and other specials.

Via Gesù 8. ☎ *02-77088 or 02-791-490. Fax: 02-77088-5004. Internet:* www.four seasons.com. *Parking: Valet parking. Rack rates: 470€ ($423) double. AE, DC, MC, V.*

Hotel Spadari al Duomo
$$$$ **Duomo**

Not far from La Scala, this modern hotel is decorated in the chic and contemporary styles Milan is known for. The rooms are spacious and have large beds, modern baths, and sofas and desks. A few rooms have balconies.

Via Spadari 11. ☎ *02-7200-2371. Fax: 02-861-184. Internet:* www.spadari hotel.com. *Parking: 20.66€ ($18.59). Rack rates: 208€ ($187.20) double. AE, DC, MC, V. Specials on weekends and in August.*

Manzoni
$$ **Center**

The Manzoni occupies a modern postwar building and is an affordable choice in an expensive city. With large beds and tasteful modern or reproduction furniture, the rooms are comfortable and attractive.

Via Santo Spirito 20. ☎ *02-7600-5700. Fax: 02-784-212. Internet:* http://hotel manzoni.com. *E-mail:* info@hotelmanzoni.com. *Rack rates: 134.28€– 144.61€ ($114–$120.85) double. AE, DC, MC, V.*

Mignon
$ **Center**

Located just outside the center and near the train station, the Mignon is an inexpensive option — but it also offers clean, nicely decorated simple rooms.

Corso 0. ☎ *and Fax: 02-331-1407. Rack rates: 75€ ($67.50) double, including buffet breakfast. AE, DC, MC, V.*

Where to dine in Milan

The most typical dish of Milanese cuisine is *risotto,* Italian rice seasoned and slowly cooked and served with grated *Parmigiano Reggiano* (Parmesan cheese). The classic risotto is *allo zafferano,* with saffron and bone marrow. Other dishes include *cotoletta alla Milanese* (breaded and deep-fried tender meat) and a variety of stews that stay true to the peasant traditions of the surrounding region. The weather in Milan is bad (for Italy), meaning often foggy and cold. The traffic, noise, and pollution are what you find in any metropolitan region the world over. If you find yourself doubting that you're still in Italy, just duck into one of these restaurants for a reminder that you're in the right place!

Boeucc
$$$$ **Center** **MILANESE**

This renowned restaurant serves typical Milanese cuisine in high style. The restaurant is elegant, the service is perfect, and the food is extremely well prepared. Of course, expect to pay for all this perfection.

Piazza Belgioioso 2. ☎ 02-7602-2880 or 02-7602-0224. Reservations recommended. Secondi: 13.43€–20.66€ ($12.09–$18.59). AE, DC, MC, V. Open: Lunch and dinner Mon–Sat.

Milanese
$$$ **Duomo** **MILANESE**

This traditional trattoria offers a choice of typical Milanese dishes in a pleasantly old-fashioned ambience. Their risotto is excellent, but you can also enjoy some of the very good meats for a *secondo,* and the vegetable dishes are also recommended.

Via Santa Marta 11. ☎ 02-8645-1991. Metro: M1 to Cordusio. Reservations recommended. Secondi: 7.75€–15.49€ ($6.98–$13.94). AE, DC, MC, V. Open: Lunch and dinner Wed–Mon.

Risotteria
$$ **Center** **MILANESE**

This is a simple restaurant specializing in — you guessed it — Milan's traditional staple dish. Risotto is prepared here in many varieties, prices are moderate, and the service is professional.

Via Dandolo 2. ☎ 02-5518-1694. Secondi: 6.20€–12.91€ ($5.58–$11.62). MC, V. Open: Lunch and dinner Mon–Sat.

Exploring Milan

Rome may be hectic, but Milan is at another level (think New York City). A thriving economy and international business reputation (the Italian stock exchange is here) comes at a price. The traffic is bad, and so is the air quality, and you're fighting for space with hordes of business travelers as well as tourists. That said, the city offers much to the resourceful and the persistent. Public transportation is an excellent way to get around this huge city, and you'll find many areas that are pleasant and somewhat removed from the bustle of modern life.

The top sights

Duomo

This grandiose cathedral (often compared to a sand castle), covers about 108,000 square feet, is 356 feet high, and is decorated with about 3,400 statues; its 15,000 square feet of windows feature about 3,600 different characters! It was founded in 1386, and the construction lasted for centuries: The facade was completed at the beginning of the 19th century, and the last bronze portal was posed in 1965. Some of the best artists of all periods have participated in the project, a history illustrated by the very interesting collection in the **Museo del Duomo.** The museum is on the first floor of the **Royal Palace,** by the cathedral, and houses a huge collection of artwork assembled over the centuries of construction and ongoing restoration. An important sculpture collection is organized chronologically and offers a unique panorama of Italian sculpture from the late 14th to the 19th centuries. There is also a fascinating array of stained-glass windows.

Cathedral Piazza Duomo; Museum Piazza Duomo 14 (inside Palazzo Reale). ☎ *02-860-358. Metro: M1 and M3 to Duomo. Tram: 2, 3, 4, 12, 14, 15, 23, 24, 27. Bus: 60, 65. Open: Cathedral daily 7:15 a.m.–6:45 p.m.; crypt daily 9 a.m.–12 p.m. and 2:30–6:00 p.m.; Baptistry Tues–Sun 10 a.m.–12 p.m. and 3–5 p.m.; roof daily 9:00 a.m.–4:30 p.m.; Museum daily 9:30 a.m.–12:30 p.m. and 3–6 p.m. Admission: Cathedral free; crypt 1.03€ (93¢); Baptistry 1.55€ ($1.40); roof 4.13€ ($3.72); museum 5.16€ ($4.64).*

Castello Sforzesco

The castle embraces centuries of the history of Milan, from its construction as a small defensive *rocca* by the Visconti family in the 14th century to its enlargement as a palace by the Sforza family, who dominated Milan during the Renaissance, and finally to its military development under the Austrian domination. Badly damaged during the Italian wars for independence in the 19th century, the castle seemed doomed, but the powers that be finally decided to restore it to its original Renaissance design. Kids will love the storybook crenellated walls, the underground passages, and the towers. The former ducal public apartments now house the **Museo d'Arte Antica,** whereas the private apartments house the **Pinacoteca** (with its collection of Italian art from the 13th to the 18th centuries, including the *Madonna in Gloria con Santi* by Andrea Mantegna and the *San Benedetto* by Antonello da Messina). Underground is the **archaeological collection.** Inside the inner castle, around which later circles of defenses were added, is the beautiful **Argo,** with frescoes probably by Bramante. Note that the Museum was still closed at press time for restoration, but it is scheduled to reopen in August 2002.

Porta Umberto. ☎ *02-8846-3700 or 02-8846-3703. Internet:* www.creval.it/ sforzesco. *Metro: M1 Cairoli or M2 Lanza/Cadorna. Tram: 1, 4, 12, 14, 20, 27. Bus: 43, 57, 61, 70, 94. Open: Castle Tue–Sun summer 7 a.m.–7 p.m., winter 7 a.m.–6 p.m.; museums daily 9:00 a.m.–5:30 p.m.; Civica Biblioteca d'Arte Mon–Fri 9:15 a.m.– 12:15 p.m. and 2:00–4:30 p.m. Admission: Free.*

Santa Maria delle Grazie and Leonardo's Last Supper

Built in the 15th century, this church was supposed to be the burial place of Ludovico il Moro and his descendants; the beautiful sculpted cover for the tomb is still here. But it's not tombs that draw tourists from all over the world.

In the refectory of the church is the famous Leonardo da Vinci painting the *Ultima Cena,* or *Last Supper.* Painted by the master with an experimental technique (tempera over a plaster preparation) over four years of work. The fresco was already looking quite bad by the end of the 16th century, so it required continuous repainting and restoration during the following centuries. The most recent restoration lasted 20 years and was completed in 1999; it removed the many previous restorations, revealing Leonardo's original work. Unfortunately, there are many gaps, but what remains is still a wonderful example of Leonardo's artistic achievement. Audioguides are available. *Note:* Reservations are mandatory.

Piazza S. Maria delle Grazie 2, off Corso Magenta. ☎ *02-8942-1146. Metro: M1 Conciliazione. Tram: 20, 24, 29, 30. Open: Tues–Sun 8:15 a.m.–6:45 p.m. Admission: 6.20€ ($5.58) plus 1.03€ (93¢) for mandatory reservation.*

Pinacoteca Nazionale di Brera

Open since 1809 and housed in a beautiful 18th-century palace, this art museum was started by the Austrian Hapsburgs in the late 18th century as a small collection for the use of the students at the attached Art Academy. During the Napoleonic period, though, it was vastly enlarged with artworks confiscated by the French from museums as well as from the churches and monasteries that were shut down all over northern Italy. This already rich art collection was further enlarged with two private collections of modern art. It includes paintings by famous masters from the 14th to the 18th centuries, as well as important 19th- and 20-century paintings by artists such as Carrà and Morandi.

Via Brera 28 (at the Accademia di Brera). ☎ *02-894-2146. Metro: M2 to Lanza. Open: Tues–Sun 8:30 a.m.–7:00 p.m. Admission: 6.20€ ($5.58).*

More cool things to see and do

If you're able to spend more time in Milan, here are a few other interesting sights:

- Originally built in 386 by the Roman Magistrate Ambrogio on the burial site of two martyrs, Gervaso and Protaso, the **Basilica di Sant'Ambrogio** is an interesting example of a Romanesque church (Piazza S. Ambrogio 15; ☎ **02-8645-0895;** Metro: MM2 S. Ambrogio; Bus: 50, 58, or 94; Open: Church daily 9:00 a.m.–12:30 p.m. and 3:30–5:00 p.m.; museum Wed–Sun 10 a.m.–12 p.m. and 3–5 p.m.; closed August; Admission: church free, museum 2.07€/$1.86). Under the main altar is a ninth-century masterpiece housing the church's relics and decorated with scenes from the life of Jesus in gold, toward the front, and the life of St.Ambrose in silver, toward the back. You can still view the remains of the two martyrs, together with those of Ambrogio. The **chapel of San Vittore in Ciel d'Oro (St.Victor in the Golden Sky)**, in the apse area, is the only visible part of the church that dates from the fifth century. The **Museum of the Basilica** was recently reopened after a complete overhaul and is also worth a visit. Of particular interest is the **Urna degli Innocenti,** a jewelery masterpiece from the 15th century and a **stucco portrait of Saint Ambrose** from the 11th century.

- The famous **Teatro della Scala** (see "Nightlife") is a landmark in the history of Milan and Italian opera; if you love theater and opera you shouldn't miss the interesting **Museo Teatrale della Scala** (☎ 02-805-3418; Palazzo Busca, Collegio San Carlo, Corso Magenta 71; Metro: M1 Conciliazione or M2 Cadorna; Open: Tues–Sun 9 a.m.–6 p.m.). *Note:* La Scala will be closing for renovations in the near future and will not reopen until 2004.

- Take a stroll under the **Galleria Vittorio Emanuele II** (off Piazza Duomo), a beautiful construction of wrought iron and glass covering four streets, built in the 1870s. Under the elegant canopy you'll find a number of shops, cafes, and small boutiques.

Shopping

The heart of Italy's fashion industry, Milan is prêt-à-porter galore. Do not leave without doing at least a bit of window shopping.

The most famous shopping street for clothes and accessories is the world-renowned **Via Montenapoleone;** also worthy is the nearby **Via della Spiga.** You'll find all kinds of shops and boutiques along with some of the top names of Italian fashion (Valentino and Versace are in Via Montenapoleone, Dolce & Gabbana is in nearby Corso Venezia, and Armani is in Via Manzoni).

If you aren't interested in haute couture or you already bought your Armani suit in a discount outlet back home, another excellent shopping

area for Italian goods is the **Brera district.** Here you'll find elegant boutiques and open-air market stalls.

Nightlife

If you have the time, viewing an opera performance at the grand **Teatro
della Scala** (Piazza della Scala; ☎ 02-7200-3744; Internet: www.la
scala.milan.it) is an unforgettable experience. You need to reserve
well in advance, though. Tickets cost from about 6€ to 90€ ($5.40 to
$81). At press time, La Scala was still open, but a planned renovation
will keep its doors shut until 2004.

For a simpler evening out, you may want to head for one of the two
major nightlife destinations in Milan, the more elegant Brera district
(Metro M2 to Lanza or M3 to Montenapoleone) or the more casual
Navigli district. Both offer a large choice of restaurants, bars, and clubs.

Brera is a trendy district of Old Milan, with narrow streets and alleys (the
name Brera comes from ancient German, meaning "meadows"). It used to
be the artsy neighborhood of Milan, but of late it has become much more
classy and established. Having undergone a transformation similar to
New York's SoHo, it's still where you'll find some of the major art galleries
of the city, but it is also home to some top fashion boutiques.

The **Navigli** is a charming neighborhood of canals and narrow streets to
the southwest of the city center. Places are open late here and attract a
more mixed crowd, with lots of hangouts for young people, trendy bars,
small restaurants, and clubs with live music.

If dance clubs are your thing, here are two of the hottest addresses in
town: **Magazzini Generali** (Via Pietrasanta 14; ☎ 02-5512-1313; closed
Monday and Tuesday); and **Propaganda** (via Castelbarco 11; ☎ 02-
5831-0682; closed Wednesday and Thursday).

For live jazz try **La Salumeria della Musica** (Via Pasinetti 2, off Via
Pipamonti; ☎ 02-5680-7350; Internet: www.lasalumeriadella
musica.com; closed Sunday and Monday); for jazz, blues, or rock, as
well as a good restaurant, head to **Le Scimmie** (Via Ascanio Sforza 49,
☎ 02-840-2200; Internet: www.scimmie.it).

Milan is also the center of the gay scene in Italy, and it has plenty of specialized venues for both gays and lesbians. A popular disco is **Plastic**
(Viale Umbria 120; ☎ 02-733-996; closed Monday), but you'll have to
wait till 2 a.m. for things to liven up, and gay night is Thursday. A lesbian
stop is **Sottomarino Giallo** (Via Donatella 2; ☎ 02-2940-1047), which is
also open to gays Wednesday through Friday. Otherwise, check with the
association ArciGay (Via Torricelli 19; ☎ 02-5810-0399 or 02-8940-1749)
for information on the latest goings-on.

Fast Facts: Milan

Country Code and City Code

The country code for Italy is **39**. The city code for Milan is **02**; use this code when calling from anywhere outside or inside Italy, even within Milan, and always include the 0.

Embassies and Consulates

Australia: Via Borgogna 2 (M1 to San Babila), ☎ 02-777-041; Canada: Via V. Pisani 19 (M2 and 3 to Centrale), ☎ 02-67581 or for emergency ☎ 02-6758-3994; United Kingdom: Via San Paolo 7 (M1 and 3 to Duomo) ☎ 02-723-001, or for emergency ☎ 02-862-490; Ireland: P.Zza S. Pietro In Gessate 2 (Bus 60), ☎ 02-5518-7569; U.S.A.: Via Principe Amedeo 2/10 (M3 to Turati) ☎ 02-290-351 or 02-2900-1841; New Zealand: Via Guido D'Arezzo 6 (M1 to Pagano) ☎ 02-4801-2544.

Currency Exchange

An exchange bureau is located at the airport and another is inside Stazione Centrale (the main train station). Otherwise, you can find change offices scattered all around town and concentrated in the *centro.*

Also, outside many banks and at the airport are automatic exchange machines that operate 24 hours a day.

Doctors and Dentists

Call ☎ 34567 for a doctor at night or during the weekend. For a dentist call ☎ 282-9808 from 9 a.m. to 12 a.m. (Piazzale Loreto 11).

Emergencies

Ambulance, ☎ **118**; fire, ☎ **115**; road assistance, ☎ **116**; Carabinieri (other police), ☎ **112**; Polizia, ☎ **113**; Croce Rossa (Red Cross), ☎ **3883**; Polizia Municipale, ☎ **77271**; First Aid (Pronto Soccorso), ☎ **02-5503-3209**.

Hospital

Ospedale Policlinico (☎ 02-5503-3209) is in Via Francesco Sforza 35.

Information

The APT (Azienda di Promozione Turistica) is in via Marconi 1, off Piazza Duomo, ☎ 02-809-662, 02-809-663, or 02-7252-4300; Monday through Friday 8:45 a.m.–1:00 p.m. and 2:00–5:45 p.m., Sat and Sun 9 a.m.–1 p.m. and 2:00–4:45p.m. An information booth is inside the Stazione Centrale (central Railway Station), near the "Gran Bar" (☎ 02-7252-4360; open Monday through Saturday 8 a.m.–7 p.m., Sun 9:00 a.m.–12:30 p.m. and 1:30–6:00 p.m.).

Police

Call ☎ **113**; for the Carabinieri (other police force), call ☎ **112**.

Pharmacies

Carlo Erba (Piazza Duomo 21) is open all night.

Taxi

Radio Taxi ☎ 02-8585, 02-4040, 02-5353, 02-8383, or 02-6767.

Part VI
Naples, Pompeii, and the Amalfi Coast

The 5th Wave   By Rich Tennant

©RICHTENNANT

"He had it made after our trip to Italy. I give you Fontana di Clifford."

In this part . . .

*N*aples is the capital of Campania, a beautiful region south of Rome. Campania is in many ways the heart of Italy—warm, welcoming, and mysterious. Naples borrows some of its character from Mount Vesuvius, the unpredictable volcano in whose shadow the city lies.

Chapter 20 covers the best of Naples, a city rich in art (often overlooked by visitors) that has undergone a marked resurgence after years of having a bad reputation. Chapter 21 guides you to nearby excursions, including the Roman ruins of Herculaneum and Pompeii, which are really more than just ruins. In fact, their violent instant destruction by Vesuvius's eruption gives them a poignancy that peaceful ruins, eroded over centuries, don't have. Another day-trip is to the beautiful isle of Capri, which has entranced the artistic and well-to-do since the Roman Emperor Tiberius rioted here with his playthings. And Chapter 22 leads you along the most celebrated stretch of Italian coast, the justly renowned Amalfi Coast.

Chapter 20

Naples

● ●

In This Chapter

▶ Finding your way to and around the city

▶ Choosing where to stay and where to eat

▶ Soaking up the Neapolitan atmosphere and activities

● ●

*U*rban **Naples (Napoli),** former capital of the Kingdom of the Two Sicilies, is rich in art, churches, and historic sights and may be daunting or seductive, depending on who you are. Naples is one of the most vital cities anywhere, legendary for its craziness, terrible drivers, thieves, and dirt (a cholera outbreak occurred in the 1970s). The city gets a bad rap from the rest of Italy because of its poverty and grunginess, but major improvements have been made in recent years. Naples definitely has marvelous things to see and do, but above all, it's the city's character that is incredibly vivid — it has its own dialect that's indecipherable to outsiders, and the place is bursting with life. In a sense, if you haven't seen Naples, you haven't seen Italy. And the city underwent a real renaissance during the 1990s, with monuments refurbished and the main squares cleaned up and reclaimed for pedestrians.

Naples is an excellent starting point for exploring sites nearby (see Chapters 21 and 22) and is the jumping-off point for Sicily if you go by boat (see Chapter 23). But don't make the mistake of using the city as merely a departure point for sights south: Take the time to explore this vivid, intense destination.

Getting There

Although Naples may feel like a world apart from Rome or Florence, it is quite convenient to reach in a variety of ways: by rail, air, sea, or road.

By train

One or more trains per hour leave Rome for Naples; the trip takes about 2½ hours and costs about 15€ ($13.50). The trip from Florence is about 4½ hours and costs about 35€ ($31.50), and the trip from Venice

7½ hours and 50€ ($45). Naples's **Stazione Centrale** (☎ 081-554-3188) is on Piazza Garibaldi, in the city center. (Naples's other train station, **Stazione Mergellina,** on Piazza Piedigrotta, is convenient to the western part of town.) Piazza Garibaldi is a major hub for city buses and the subway line and also has a taxi station. The city center lies only a few blocks west, but the area around the station is grungy, so you may want to catch some form of public transportation to get to the city center; walking through the station area could spoil your first impression of this otherwise beautiful town.

By plane

About 7km (4 miles) from the city center, the small **Aeroporto Capodichino** (☎ 081-789-6111) receives daily flights from other cities in Italy. The easiest way to get into town is by taking a taxi directly to your hotel. However, expect to pay up to 30€ ($27) for the 15-minute trip. Much cheaper is taking the regular ATAN city bus no. 14. The trip to the **Stazione Centrale** in Piazza Garibaldi, at the center of town, takes only 15 minutes and costs 1.81€ ($1.63).

By ferry

Naples's harbor is the major port of central Italy, with ferries and cruise ships pulling in and out from various destinations. Coming into the **Stazione Marittima** (seaport, just off Via Cristoforo Colombo) is the best way to arrive in Naples, not only because of the legendary beauty of the bay but also because you arrive in the heart of town, where most of the historic attractions lie. One of the most interesting possibilities is taking a ferry to or from Sicily, saving many hours of driving. The company **Tirrenia** (☎ 081-761-3688) leaves from the Stazione Marittima for the overnight trip to Palermo. A faster ferry, the **SNAV** (☎ 081-761-2348), takes about half the time; see Chapter 23 for complete details on rates and schedules.

By car

Driving in Naples is challenging, even for Italians. The best thing to do is put your car in a garage when you get there and continue by foot and bus. (By the way, when we say a garage, we mean it; Naples is infamous for prevalent car theft.) All roads lead to Rome, and your road to Naples from the north passes by Rome. From Rome, take or continue on *autostrada* **A1,** which ends in Naples. You can find parking lots just off the highway at the exit Corso Malta (behind the Stazione Centrale), on Piazza Garibaldi (in front of the Stazione Centrale), and at the Stazione Marittima by the harbor.

The Gulf of Naples and Salerno

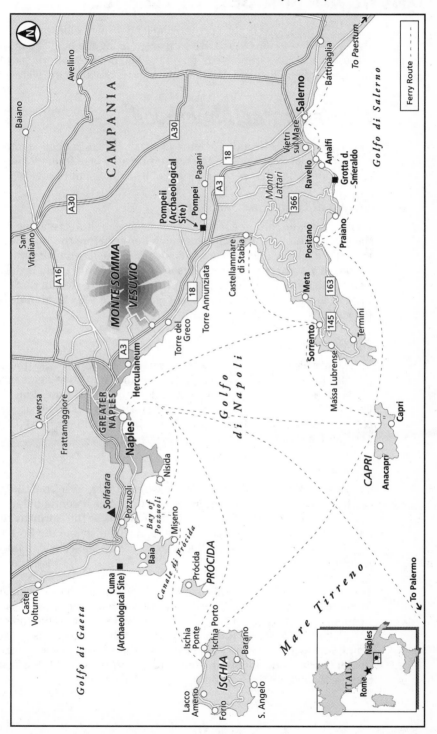

Orienting Yourself in Naples

Forced by the shape of the surrounding land — high cliffs overlooking the sea — Naples developed like a crescent along the bay. The more fashionable neighborhoods are up on the hill, but the historic part of town, where you'll spend most of your time, is down by the water.

Naples by neighborhood

Developed along a beautiful stretch of coast, Naples is divided into four major parts, of which one — the *centro storico* — is of foremost interest to the tourist because of the richness of its artistic endowment.

Riviera di Chiaia and Santa Lucia

Along the water, this area is famous for its elegant hotels and view over the bay — which, by the way, was much better before the 19th century, when they filled the waterfront and advanced the *lungomare* (promenade) of **Via Partenope** to its present position. **Santa Lucia** is the area right behind the **Castle of the Egg (Castel dell'Ovo);** west of that is the **Riviera di Chiaia,** along the pleasant green of the **Villa Comunale** and the gardens of the **Villa Pignatelli.**

The Vomero

The higher part of town, the **Vomero,** is where the *Napoli bene* (the city's middle and upper classes) live. There are some interesting sights up on the Vomero for everybody, however, such as the **Castel Sant'Elmo,** the **Certosa di San Martino,** and the villa **La Floridiana.** Also a hill above the city but distinct from the Vomero is **Capodimonte,** with its royal palace, park, and museum.

The centro storico

The **centro storico** is the city's heart, where it was born from the two original Greek colonies of Partenope and Neapolis. It continued to grow under successive dominations, from the Romans to the Normans to the Angevins (house of Anjou) and finally to the Spanish and the Borbone (the Bourbons). Each group left its mark, making Naples one of the richest art cities in Italy.

The city's central part was historically turned toward the sea. Inland from the **seaport (Stazione Marittima)** are the major monuments of the Neapolitan political establishment: the **Palazzo San Giacomo,** today the city hall; the **New Castle (Castel Nuovo),** built by the Angevins as the center for their two-century-long kingdom; the **Royal Palace (Palazzo Reale)** on Piazza del Plebiscito, built under the Spanish; and the **Teatro San Carlo,** built by the Borbone.

Naples

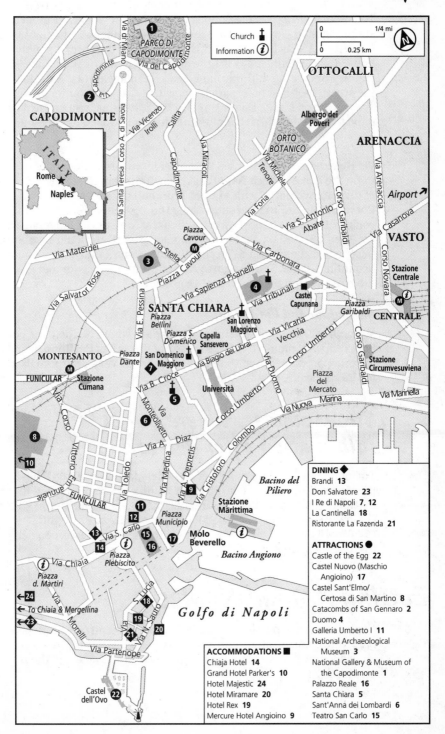

Church ✝
Information ⓘ

0   1/4 mi
0   0.25 km

PARCO DI
CAPODIMONTE

OTTOCALLI

CAPODIMONTE

Albergo dei
Poveri

ORTO
BOTANICO

ARENACCIA

Airport ↗

ITALY

Rome ★
Naples ●

VASTO

Via Materdei

Piazza
Cavour

Via Carbonara

Via S. Antonio
Abate

Stazione
Centrale

SANTA CHIARA

Piazza Cavour

Via Sapienza Pisanelli

Castel
Capuana

Piazza
Garibaldi

CENTRALE

Piazza
Bellini

Via Tribunali

San Lorenzo
Maggiore

Via Vicaria
Vecchia

MONTESANTO

Piazza S.
Domenico

Capella
Sansevero

Piazza
Dante

San Domenico
Maggiore

Via Biagio dei Librai

Stazione
Circumvesuviana

FUNICULAR   Stazione
Cumana

Via B. Croce

Università

Piazza
del
Mercato

Via Marinella

Via Nuova Marina

Via A. Diaz

Via Toledo

FUNICULAR

Bacino del
Piliero

DINING ◆
Brandi **13**
Don Salvatore **23**
I Re di Napoli **7, 12**
La Cantinella **18**
Ristorante La Fazenda **21**

Stazione
Màrittima

Piazza
Municipio

Molo
Beverello

Bacino Angiono

ATTRACTIONS ●
Castle of the Egg **22**
Castel Nuovo (Maschio
  Angioino) **17**
Castel Sant'Elmo/
  Certosa di San Martino **8**
Catacombs of San Gennaro **2**
Duomo **4**
Galleria Umberto I **11**
National Archaeological
  Museum **3**
National Gallery & Museum of
  the Capodimonte **1**
Palazzo Reale **16**
Santa Chiara **5**
Sant'Anna dei Lombardi **6**
Teatro San Carlo **15**

Via S. Carlo

Piazza
Plebiscito

Piazza
d. Martiri

To Chiaia & Mergellina

Golfo di Napoli

Via Partenope

ACCOMMODATIONS ■
Chiaja Hotel **14**
Grand Hotel Parker's **10**
Hotel Majestic **24**
Hotel Miramare **20**
Hotel Rex **19**
Mercure Hotel Angioino **9**

Castel
dell'Ovo

Beginning in Piazza del Plebiscito, **Via Toledo** is Naples's main street, lined with elegant palaces and fashionable shops. Opening from Via Toledo on the right is the famous glass-and-iron **Galleria Umberto I shopping mall.** On the left are the **Quartieri Spagnoli,** the tight grid of narrow streets built by the Spanish in the 16th century, mainly to house their troops; today it's the embodiment of "Neapolitanness" — laundry drying at windows, mammas screaming at their kids down in the street, motor scooters rushing past, and so on. Continuing on Via Toledo across Piazza Dante and into Via E. Pessina, you arrive at the important **National Archaeological Museum (Museo Archeologico Nazionale).**

Via Benedetto Croce and Via Biagio dei Librai are colloquially referred to by the name **Spacca Napoli** because they seem to divide the center of town in two parts, with **Via dei Tribunali** parallel to the north and **Corso Umberto I** to the south. Along those streets are concentrated some of the most important attractions, as well as the university. There are churches and palaces galore, including **Sant'Anna dei Lombardi** (also called the **Chiesa di Monteoliveto**), **Santa Chiara** with its unique beautiful cloister, **San Gregorio Armeno** with its cloister and view of the bay, the **Duomo,** and **Castel Capuano.**

Mergellina and Via Posillipo

Mergellina is the pleasure harbor of Naples, where Neapolitans come for a romantic dinner by the sea. West of this is **Via Posillipo,** along the towering promontory, at the tip of which is the very pretty small square of **Marechiaro.**

Street smarts: Where to get information after you arrive

The main tourist office is **APT** (Piazza dei Martiri 58; ☎ 081-405-311; Bus: R3 to Riviera di Chiaia). **Tourist booths** can also be found in the Stazione Centrale on Piazza Garibaldi (☎ 081-268-799; Metro: Piazza Garibaldi) and in the Stazione Mergellina on Piazza Piedigrotta (☎ 081-761-2102; Metro: Mergellina). These booths are open daily from 8:30 a.m. to 8:30 p.m.

Getting Around Naples

Naples is a large, bustling city. But the parts that attract tourists are relatively concentrated, and you can cover a lot of this ground on foot. You will, however, welcome public transportation now and then.

On foot

Naples offers beautiful walks, particularly near the major sights. All the areas we describe in the preceding sections are safe to walk on foot.

Outside the central district are scattered pockets of poverty, and you may want to avoid walking in these neighborhoods (the only one close to the area of tourist interest, though, is in the vicinity of the Stazione Centrale). Although sociologically interesting, they're potentially dangerous for visitors (don't flash expensive cameras and jewelry), but if you dress unobtrusively and look like a local, nobody should bother you. These neighborhoods may also be unpleasant for lone young women, who'll get whistled at and approached. Brushing off these attentions isn't too difficult, but sometimes it can be a bit much. If you're a woman alone, stick to the sightseeing areas; if you want to explore farther, join forces with another visitor.

By subway

The **Metropolitana (subway)** line makes a few widely spaced stops but is quite useful for avoiding the city traffic. Surprisingly, little of it is actually underground; it's an urban railroad more than a subway and is, in fact, linked to the rail system. It runs daily from 5:00 a.m. to 11:30 p.m., and you can use the same tickets as on the bus (see the next section).

By bus or tramway

ANM is the city bus system (☎ **081-7000-1000**), which is quite complete and includes a few lines of tramway and the funicular described in the next section. You can get an excellent map at the information booth at Stazione Centrale on Piazza Garibaldi. Tickets cost .77€ (69¢) and are valid for 90 minutes. You can buy them at bars, tobacconists, and newsstands around town. You can also buy a one-day ticket offering unlimited travel for 2.32€ ($2.08) — if you plan to do Naples and see a number of sites, you'll probably break even on this ticket before lunch. Both tickets are labeled **GiraNapoli.**

Because of traffic, regular buses are slow and crowded, but most tourist destinations are served by special fast lines *(linee rosse,* red lines, marked by a letter *R)* running much more frequently. Each bus and tram line has its own schedule — this is Italy after all! The *linee rosse* run daily from roughly 5:30 a.m. to midnight; other buses stop earlier, some as early as 8:30 p.m. A number of *linee notturne* (night lines) usually start around midnight and run with an hourly frequency.

By Funivia

Given the city's development over the cliffs surrounding the bay, Naples enjoys a special kind of transportation: the funicular (railway pulled up and over hills by cables) — here called the *Funivia*. Three funiculars connect the lower town to the higher one: **Montesanto** (at the metro station Montesanto, running daily from 7 a.m. to 10 p.m.), **Chiaia** (from Piazza Amedeo, running Monday through Thursday from 7 a.m. to 9 p.m., Friday through Sunday from 7 a.m. to 1 a.m.), and **Centrale** (from Via Toledo, off Piazza Trieste e Trento, running daily from 6 a.m. to 1 a.m.). Mergellina also has a funicular, from Via Mergellina by the harbor (running daily from 7 a.m. to 10 p.m.). The Funivia accepts regular bus tickets (see the preceding section).

By taxi

Naples has a number of taxi stations, where taxis wait in line for customers, near major hubs and attractions. You can also call a **radio taxi** at ☎ **081-556-4444.** Beware, though, that the driving in Naples is reckless — even if you're in a taxi — and Neapolitans are known for rounding up their fares to make a little extra money (it's a bad town in which to go around looking gullible). Although things have changed a lot, a few taxi drivers still pretend their meter is broken in order to charge you a little more. If so, take another cab.

A number of destinations have fixed fares, and *not* using the meter is therefore legal. For example, if you're traveling from the airport to your hotel, or to the Museo Capodimonte, you're charged a set fare. Ask the price before boarding.

Beware of illegal taxis, from which most of the bad reputation of Naples's cabs stems. Always take a taxi from an official taxi stand or make sure you only get in marked vehicles, painted white (or yellow for the older models) and sometimes with a *Comune di Napoli* (Naples municipality) mark.

Where to Stay in Naples

Like other large Italian cities, Naples offers a big selection of hotels — the city is a thriving commercial center, so you can find glitzy tourist hotels as well as places for the traveling salesperson. The only thing we don't recommend are really cheap places — frankly, it's not worth staying in a marginal area just to save a little, and you can economize in other ways if you want to balance things out.

Chiaja Hotel
$$ Piazza Plebiscito

This new hotel is housed in the restored residence of the Marquis Lecaldano Sasso La Terza, steps from all the majors attractions in Naples. The decor manages to be both elegant (in an ornate Neapolitan style) and cozy; service is excellent. Rooms have all the modern comforts including satellite TV, air-conditioning, Jacuzzi bath, and soundproofed windows. You can even get someone to sing a real Neapolitan serenade to your loved one!

Via Chiaja 216 (second floor). ☎ *081-415-555. Fax: 081-422-344. E-mail:* info@ hotelchiaia.it. *Internet:* www.hotelchiaia.it. *Bus: R2 to Piazza Municipio. Parking: 15.49€ ($13.49). Rack rates: 124€ ($111.60) double, including buffet breakfast. AE, DC, MC, V.*

Grand Hotel Parker's
$$$$ Vomero

Dating from 1870, this historic residence is the top hotel in Naples. It sits on the hill above the harbor and offers grand views of the city and the sea; its neoclassical interior and ornate Liberty (Italian Art Nouveau) plasterwork have been completely preserved. The large, elegant guest rooms are decorated in period furniture. The roof garden houses a restaurant, where you can enjoy regional specialties and a magnificent view. Parker's also features some less common (for Naples) amenities, such as a business center.

Corso Vittorio Emanuele 135. ☎ *081-761-2474. Fax: 081-663-527. E-mail:* info@ grandhotelparkers.it. *Internet:* www.grandhotelparkers.com. *Metro: Piazza Amedeo. Parking: 11€ ($10.90). Rack rates: 223€–976€ ($200–$878.85) double, including buffet breakfast. AE, DC, MC, V.*

Hotel Majestic
$$$ Riviera di Chiaia

A modern hotel favored by locals, the Majestic is located in a pleasant area of town. The guest rooms are of a fairly good size and look like tasteful modern apartments, with hardwood floors, dark wood furniture, and walls painted in earth tones. They have all the comforts, including air-conditioning. We highly recommend **La Giara,** the hotel's restaurant.

Largo Vasto a Chiaia 68. ☎ *081-416-500. Fax: 081-410-145. E-mail:* info@ majestic.it. *Internet:* www.majestic.it. *Metro: Piazza Amedeo. Parking: 15.49€ ($13.49). Rack rates: 202€ ($181.80) double, including buffet breakfast. AE, DC, MC, V.*

Hotel Miramare
$$$ Santa Lucia

Built in 1914, this charming hotel right on the water was once a villa and then became the American consulate before being converted into a hotel. The public areas are still decorated in Liberty style; the renovated guest rooms have beautiful baths, air-conditioning, and minibars. Guests at the hotel get a 10% discount at the restaurant **La Cantinella** (see the description of this restaurant later in this chapter).

Via Nazario Saura 24. ☎ 081-764-7589. Fax: 081-764-8775. E-mail: info@hotel miramare.com. *Internet:* www.hotelmiramare.com. *Bus/Tram: Bus R3 or tram 4 to Via Acton. Parking: 20.66€ ($18.60). Rack rates: 147€–190€ ($132.30–$171) double, including buffet breakfast. AE, DC, MC, V.*

Hotel Rex
$$ Santa Lucia

The Rex is well known as a moderately priced hotel in the waterside neighborhood of Santa Lucia near the Castle of the Egg. Not all the guest rooms are big, but each has all the necessary comforts — and some have a view over the harbor or the Vesuvio and balconies. Baths are good-sized, and the room furniture is simple (many rooms are decorated in a 1960s style) but in good repair. The location and the price of the hotel (and its lavish exterior, not matched by the rooms) make it much in demand.

Via Palepoli 12. ☎ 081-764-9389. Fax: 081-764-9227. Bus/Tram: Bus R3 or tram 4 to Via Acton. Parking: 20.66€ ($18.60). Rack rates: 110€ ($99) double, including breakfast. AE, DC, MC, V.

Mercure Hotel Angioino
$$ Piazza Municipio

This hotel is within sight of the Angioino castle and is both modern and convenient. Housed in a beautiful renovated 19th-century building, the Mercure has a large number of rooms, and one whole floor is nonsmoking. Rooms are simple, with large beds, satellite television, and air-conditioning. You can also plug in your computer in your room.

Via Depretis 123. ☎ 081-552-9500. Fax: 081-552-9509. E-mail: commerciale. mercurenapoliangioino@accor-hotels.it. *Bus: R2 to Piazza Municipio. Parking: 15€ ($13.50). Rack rates: 135€ ($121.50) double, including buffet breakfast. AE, DC, MC, V.*

Where to Dine in Naples

Neapolitan food has been made famous by **pizza** — the Neapolitans invented it, and everyone agrees theirs is the best (thicker and with better mozzarella than anywhere else). But this city has more to offer than just pizza; you'll want to try the many seafood dishes, including one of our favorites, *pasta alle cozze* (pasta with mussels), and grilled seafood.

If you have a sweet tooth, try Naples's specialty: the *sfogliatella,* a fragrant, crisp, crusty triangular pocket filled with sweet ricotta. We've never had them anywhere else as good as here, and they're the perfect counterpart to a Neapolitan coffee — justly famous as the best in Italy (we know some Romans who drive to Naples for coffee). Another specialty is the *babá,* a soft brioche soaked in rum and sugar syrup and often filled with cream — it's addictive, and it's not the alcohol. You can sample these treats at the **Pasticceria Scaturchio** (Piazza San Dominico Maggiore 19–24; ☎ **081-551-6944;** Bus: R2), one of the oldest pastry shops in town, established in 1903. Besides wonderful pastries, you may also want to sample the *Ministeriale,* a medallion of dark chocolate with a liqueur cream filling.

Brandi
$$ Centro storico   PIZZA

Literally fit for a queen, this pizzeria opened in the 19th century and is the place where *pizza margherita* was invented. It takes its name from Margherita di Savoia, first queen of Italy, who graciously accepted having a pizza named after her (how many sovereigns can say that?). The pizza comes with tomato, basil, and mozzarella — red, green, and white, not coincidentally the colors of the united Italy. Brandi's menu includes many dishes other than pizza, all well prepared.

Salita Sant'Anna di Palazzo. ☎ *081-416-928. Reservations required. Bus: R2 or R3 to Piazza Trieste e Trento. Secondi: 6.21€–15.49€ ($5.58–$13.94). No credit cards accepted. Open: Lunch and dinner Tues–Sun.*

Don Salvatore
$$$ Mergellina   NEAPOLITAN/SEAFOOD

On the Mergellina waterfront, near the dock where the ferries leave for Capri, Don Salvatore is an excellent example of a Neapolitan seaside trattoria. The grilled fish is fresh, accompanied by local vegetables, and served on pasta or rice. The restaurant also features an excellent choice of wine.

Strada Mergellina 4/a. ☎ *081-681-817. Reservations recommended. Metro: Mergellina. Secondi: 7.75€–18.08€ ($6.98–$16.27). AE, DC, MC, V. Open: Lunch and dinner Thurs–Tues; daily in summer.*

1 Re di Napoli
$$$ Piazza Plebescito   NEAPOLITAN/PIZZA

With a view of the open space and grand buildings of the Piazza Plebescito, and with outdoor dining in good weather, this is a nice place to sample Naples's greatest contribution to cuisine. In addition to pizza, it has a full range of *antipasti* and vegetable dishes. Another good thing about I Re di Napoli is that it's open continuously from lunchtime until 1 a.m. A second location is near the archaeological museum (Piazza Dante 16, off via Toledo), which is open all day long till 1 a.m.

Piazza Trieste e Trento 7. ☎ *081-423-013. Internet:* www.netlab.it/redi napoli. *Reservations recommended. Bus/Tram: Bus R3 or R2 to Piazza Trieste e Trento. Pizza: 2.58€–5.16€ ($2.32–$4.64). AE, DC, MC, V. Open: Lunch and dinner daily.*

La Cantinella
$$$ Santa Lucia   ITALIAN/NEAPOLITAN/SEAFOOD

One of the best restaurants in Naples, this waterfront spot has plenty of style. It feels like a 1930s nightclub or something out of a movie, but the food is pure Neapolitan, with excellent *antipasto* and grilled seafood.

Via Cuma 42. ☎ *081-764-8684. Reservations required. Bus/Tram: Bus R3 or tram 4 to Via Acton. Secondi: 12.91€–24.79€ ($11.62–$22.30). AE, DC, MC, V. Open: Lunch and dinner Mon–Sat, daily in summer; closed two weeks in Aug.*

Ristorante La Fazenda
$$$$ Santa Lucia   NEAPOLITAN/SEAFOOD

With a beautiful view over the bay and an informal atmosphere, La Fazenda pleases both locals and visitors. The terrace is popular in summer (don't go then without a reservation). The place is famous for its fish specialties, including *pasta alle vongole* (pasta with clams) and fresh grilled seafood.

Via Mare Chiaro 58/a. ☎ *081-575-7420. Reservations required. Bus/Tram: Bus R3 or tram 4 to Via Acton. Secondi: 11.36€–20.66€ ($10.22–$18.59). AE, MC, V. Open: Lunch Tues–Sun, dinner Mon–Sat; closed one week in Aug.*

Exploring Naples

Visiting Naples's major attractions is one of the best ways to understand the city's spirit. Entering the museums, palaces, and churches will put you in tune with the city's history, which is very much imprinted in the soul of its inhabitants. Here is a list of the best that Naples offers.

The top sights

Castle of the Egg (Castel dell'Ovo)

The Castle of the Egg sits on a promontory projecting into the harbor. The first Greek colonists landed here in the ninth century B.C. In Roman times, it's believed that Lucullus (the celebrated gourmet) had his villa here. A symbol of the city and an important landmark, the current fortress was built by Frederick II and enlarged by the Angevins. The name originated in the Middle Ages: One explanation has it that Virgil (author of the *Aeneid* and reputed magician) placed a sacred egg under the castle's foundations to protect it; this ploy apparently wasn't too successful, because the castle collapsed and the present one was built over the site. You have a beautiful view of the castle from **Via Partenope,** the promenade overlooking the sea, which merges into the **Riviera di Chiaia** farther west. The castle houses the **Ethno-Prehistoric Museum (Museo Etno-Preistorico),** with a collection of artifacts and objects dating back 700,000 years (call for reservations; see the next paragraph). The castle itself is very interesting — see the **Hall of the Columns (Sala delle Colonne),** for example — and from it you can enjoy a superb view over the city.

Porto Santo Lucia, off Via Partenope. ☎ *081-246-4334 for castle or 081-764-5343 for museum reservations. Bus/Tram: Bus R3 or tram 4 to Via Acton, Porto Santa Lucia. Admission: Free. Open: Mon–Sat 9 a.m.–3 p.m.*

Castel Nuovo (Maschio Angioino)

Built in the 12th century by Carlo d'Angió (Angevin dynasty) as the new royal residence — the Castel dell'Ovo and Castel Capuano didn't fit the needs of the new kingdom — this castle was renovated in the 15th century. The inland facade is graced by the **Triumphal Arch of Alfonso (Arco di Trionfo di Alfonso),** a splendid example of early Renaissance architecture, the work of Francesco Laurana to commemorate the 1442 expulsion of the Angevins by the forces of Alphonso I. Inside, note the **Hall of the Barons (Sala dei Baroni),** a monumental room with a star-shaped vaulted ceiling (today the seat of the Municipal Council), and the **Civic Museum (Museo Civico),** with a nice collection of sculpture and other art.

Piazza del Municipio. ☎ *081-795-2003. Bus: R1 or R4 to Piazza del Municipio. Admission: 5.16€ ($4.64). Open: Mon–Sat 9 a.m.–7 p.m.*

Duomo

The 14th-century Duomo may not be the most interesting church in town, but it houses the **Chapel of St. Gennaro (Cappella di San Gennaro),** named after the patron saint of Naples. The chapel is richly decorated with goldwork, including a gold bust of the saint that contains his relics. Also here is the famous relic of San Gennaro containing vials of his blood — the blood is said to become liquid each May and September, and it's a sign of great misfortune for the whole town if the miracle doesn't take place. In the left nave is the original paleo-Christian basilica of **Santa Restituta;** it and its adjoining baptistry are decorated with beautiful mosaics and were absorbed into the Duomo and refurbished in the 17th century.

Via del Duomo 147. ☎ *081-449-097. Metro: Piazza Cavour. Admission: 2.60€ ($2.34). Open: Mon–Sat 9 a.m.–12 p.m. and 4:30–7:00 p.m; Sun and holidays 9 a.m.–12 p.m.*

The National Archaeological Museum (Museo Archeologico Nazionale)

The National Archaeological Museum contains one of the greatest collections of treasures from antiquity in Europe and probably the world. If you want to visit just one archaeological museum in Italy, make it this one. Among the holdings is a superb collection of **Roman sculptures** copied from Greek originals of the fourth and fifth centuries B.C. and reflecting the Roman incorporation of Hellenism into its art. The most stunning is the massive *Toro Romano,* which depicts several warriors trying to harness the surging figure of a bull — a dramatic scene come to life in marble. In addition, the museum is the repository for objects from archaeological excavations in southern Italy, particularly Pompeii and Herculaneum. The vast collection of mosaics and frescoes on display include a huge mosaic of the victory of Alexander the Great over the Persians. Other mosaics naturalistically depict fish, animals, birds, and themes from mythology. The diversity of other objects in the museum is amazing; whether it's a **gladiator's helmet, exquisite cameo vases,** or the tiny **head of a centurion carved in bone** with great psychological realism, you will marvel at the artistic heights Rome achieved. The **Gabinetto segreto (secret room)** is a historic collection of Roman erotica (famous already in Goethe's day). It is now housed in a special room and documents the ancient attitude toward sexuality (guilt-free and frank, to say the least).

Piazza Museo Nazionale 18–19. ☎ 081-440-166. Metro: Piazza Cavour. Admission: 6.50€ ($5.85). Open: Wed–Mon 9:00 a.m.–7:30 p.m.

National Museum & Gallery of the Capodimonte (Museo e Gallerie Nazionali di Capodimonte)

Recently restored and reorganized, this museum holds a first-class painting collection that contains several masterpieces On the second floor, the Farnese collection includes Masaccio's *Crucifixion,* Perugino's *Madonna and Child,* Bruegel's *Misanthrope,* and Filippino Lippi's *Annunciation and Saints,* plus works by Mantegna, Raphael, Titian, and Botticelli; on the third floor the *pinacoteca* **Borbonica D'Avolos** (a 16th-century family) includes the famous 16th-century **tapestry series** of the Battle of Pavia as well as important paintings such as Simone Martini's *San Ludovico di Tolosa,* Tiziano's *Annonciation,* and Caravaggio's *Flagellation.* The building is itself a masterpiece: The **Palazzo Capodimonte** and the surrounding park were built in the 18th century as a royal hunting residence and museum, situated to afford beautiful views over the city and bay. You can also see what the palace was like originally in the **royal apartments** on the second floor, full of priceless objects, tapestries, and statuary.

Palazzo Capodimonte, Via Miano 2 and Via Capodimonte. ☎ 081-749-9111. Bus: 24 to Parco Capodimonte. Admission: 7.50€ ($6.75); 6.50€ ($5.85) from 2 to 5 p.m. Open: Tues–Sun 8:30 a.m.–7:30 p.m.

Palazzo Reale

The imposing neoclassical Royal Palace was designed by Domenico Fontana and built by the Bourbons in the 17th century; the eight statues on the facade are of Neapolitan kings. Inside you can visit the **royal apartments,** richly appointed with marble floors, tapestries, frescoes, and baroque furniture. The **library,** established by Charles de Bourbon, is one of the greatest in the south, with more than 1,250,000 volumes. The *palazzo* retains its glamour to this day and was used as the venue for a G7 summit meeting in 1994.

Piazza del Plebiscito 1. ☎ 081-794-4021. Bus: R2 or R3 to Piazza Trieste e Trento. Admission: 4.13€ ($3.72), courtyard and gardens free. Open: Thurs–Tues 9 a.m.– 8 p.m.

Sant'Anna dei Lombardi

Built in the 15th century and renovated in the 17th, Sant'Anna dei Lombardi (also called the Chiesa di Monteoliveto) is famous for its rich collection of Renaissance sculpture. Noteworthy are the **Piccolomini Chapel (Cappella Piccolomini),** with the tomb of Maria d'Aragona by Antonio Rossellino and Benedetto da Maiano; the **Terranova Chapel (Cappella Terranova);** the **Cappella Mastro Giudice,** with the *Annunciazione* by Benedetto da Maiano; and the Tuscan-influenced **Tolosa Chapel (Cappella Tolosa),** decorated in the styles of Brunelleschi and della Robbia. In the **sacristy** are frescoes by Giorgio Vasari and helpers, as well as the spectacular wood inlay work by Giovanni da Verona (1506–1510). These incredibly intricate works depict classical panoramas, musical instruments, and other scenes with thousands of tiny slivers of wood of various kinds and colors.

Note that the main nave is under reconstruction but will be reopened by the end of 2003. In the meantime, you can still visit the right-hand nave and the sacristy. There are plans (not executed at press time) to create a passageway to the left-hand nave to give access to the Cappella Piccolomini, Cappella Terranova, and the Cappella Tolosa.

Via Monteoliveto. ☎ 081-551-3333. Metro: Montesanto. Admission: Free. Open: Mon–Sat 9:30 a.m. to noon.

Santa Chiara

Built in the 14th century as the burial church for the d'Angió dynasty, Santa Chiara was once the center of a large monastic complex for the order of the Clarisse. The church was severely damaged by World War II bombing and an ensuing fire, but it has been restored somewhat to its original look. Although damaged, the monumental **tomb of Roberto d'Angió** at the end of the nave is still a magnificent example of Tuscan-style Renaissance sculpture. Also interesting is the **Choir of the Clarisses (Coro delle Clarisse),** where the nuns can sit protected from the public during mass. The key attraction is the **Chiostro delle Clarisse,** the uniquely beautiful cloister behind the church (turn around the church to the left). On the piazza outside the church is one of Naples's several baroque spires, the **Guglia dell'Immacolata,** a tall pile of statues and reliefs from 1750.

Via Santa Chiara. ☎ *081-552-6209. Metro: Montesanto. Admission: Church free, cloister 4€ ($3.60). Open: Church Mon–Sat 8:30 a.m.–12:30 p.m. and 4:30–7:00 p.m., Sun 8:30 a.m.–12:30 p.m.; cloister Mon–Sat 9:30 a.m.–1:00 p.m. and 2:30–5:30 p.m., Sun 9:30 a.m.–1:00 p.m.*

More cool things to see and do

Here are some more sights to explore:

- ✔ Built at the end of the 19th century (20 years after its larger Milanese counterpart), the **Galleria Umberto I** (Bus: R2 or R3 to Piazza Trieste e Trento) is a splendid example of the Liberty style (Italian Art Nouveau). Opening to the right of Via Toledo as you come from Piazza del Plebiscito, the glass-and-iron galleria is an enormous airy space with a soaring glass ceiling, and is lined with graciously decorated buildings and elegant shops. Come to marvel at the architecture and even to shop (see "Shopping" later in this chapter).

- ✔ Built by the Borbone at the beginning of the 18th century, the **Teatro San Carlo** (Via San Carlo 98/f; ☎ **081-797-23311** or 081-797-2412; Bus: R2 or R3 to Via San Carlo) is among Europe's most beautiful opera houses, a neoclassical jewel with an ornate gilded interior. It's said to have even better acoustics than Milan's famous La Scala. You can come during the day to appreciate its architecture and decoration, but of course you can also come for a performance (see "Nightlife") and hear the building in its full glory.

- ✔ If you want an excuse to visit the Vomero and take the funicular (take the *Funivia* Centrale from Piazza Trento e Trieste to the last stop), head to the **St. Elmo Castle (Castel Sant'Elmo)** and **Carthusian Monastery of St. Martin (Certosa di San Martino),** which lie in a beautiful park that has great views over the city from terraced gardens. The monastery was built in the 14th century but rebuilt in the 17th; the church is considered the most important baroque church in the city. The monastery houses the **National Museum of St. Martin (Museo Nazionale di San Martino;** ☎ **081-578-1769),** displaying maps, *presepi* (crèches), and a collection of images. The monastery, museum, church, cloister, and gardens are open Tuesday through Saturday from 8:30 a.m. to 7:30 p.m. and Sunday from 9:00 a.m. to 7:30 p.m. Admission is 5.68€ ($5.11). Near the Certosa is the St. Elmo Castle, a 14th-century castle restored in the 16th century and now used for special exhibits (Largo San Martino; ☎ **081-578-4030;** open Tuesday through Sunday from 9 a.m. to 7 p.m.; admission 1.29€/$1.16).

✔ In use between the second and ninth centuries, the **Catacombs of St. Gennaro (Catacombe di San Gennaro,** entrance Via di Capodimonte 13, down a small alley running alongside the church Madre del Buon Consiglio; ☎ **081-741-1071;** Bus: 24 to Via Capodimonte) are particularly famous for the well-maintained frescoes covering the whole period of the use of the catacombs. Also buried in these catacombs is San Gennaro, the patron saint of Naples — hence the name — whose remains were moved here in the fifth century. At press time, the catacombs were closed for restoration; call the tourist office for information.

Seeing Naples by guided tour

The agency **Every Tours** (Piazza del Municipio 5; ☎ **081-551-8564;** Metro: Garibaldi) is the American Express antenna in Naples and organizes tours of the city as well as day excursions to Vesuvio and other sights. It's open Monday through Friday from 9:00 a.m. to 1:30 p.m. and 3:30 to 7:00 p.m., and Saturday from 9 a.m. to 1 p.m.

Shopping

Although not a shopping mecca, Naples does offer some serious possibilities. In the elegant area behind the **Riviera di Chiaia** are all the big names of Italian fashion, such as Valentino, Versace, Ferragamo, and Prada. The best places for this kind of shopping are **Via dei Mille, Piazza dei Martiri,** and **Via Calabritto.**

Another good area for shopping is **Via Roma,** the animated street leading into Via Toledo. From Via Roma you can catch the funicular to the **Vomero,** where you can find many pedestrian streets and plenty of moderately priced shops, away from the most touristed areas downtown. If you're looking for specialty items, check out the following.

Antiques

Naples is an excellent place to buy antiques, with a major antiques fair and many major stores. But beware that some Neapolitans are reputed to be experts in the tricky art of *antiquing* — making something new look antique. If you know a lot about antiques, try the important antiques market, the **Fiera Antiquaria** in the Villa Comunale di Napoli on Viale Dohrn, held every third Saturday and Sunday of each month 8 a.m. to 2 p.m. (except in August). Nearby is **Via Domenico Morelli,** home of the city's most established antiques dealers, specializing in 18th-century furniture and paintings. Two fine choices are **Regency House** (Via D. Morelli 36; ☎ **081-764-3640**) and **Navarra** (Piazza dei Martiri; ☎ **081-764-3595**). For these shops, take bus R3 to Riviera di Chiaia.

Chocolate

The **Gay-Odin Fabbrica di Cioccolato** has two locations, at Via Toledo 214 and up the street at no. 427–428. They make delicious, 100% pure chocolate, and even experiment with such daring concoctions as chocolate *con peperoncino* (with hot pepper).

Crafts

Naples used to be famous for its crafts, and you can still find some specialized crafts typical of the region. Among them, the most dear to Neapolitans probably is the carving of figurines for the *presepio* (crèche). **Via San Gregorio Armeno** is lined with historic workshops that still produce the vividly painted figurines — or perhaps figurines is the wrong word, because some are life-sized. A small figurine is a beautiful souvenir of Naples and Italy, but these carvings don't come cheap.

Porcelain

Also typical of Naples is porcelain — from the tradition of the royal plant of Capodimonte — and hand-painted majolica. You can find some shops in the **Galleria Umberto I,** off Via Toledo (see "More cool things to see and do" earlier in this chapter).

Nightlife

Seeing an opera at the **Teatro San Carlo** (Via San Carlo 98/f; ☎ **081-797-2412** or 081-797-2331; Fax: 081-400-902; Internet: www.teatrosan carlo.it; E-mail: biglietteria@teatrosancarlo.it; Bus: R2 or R3 to Via San Carlo) is an unforgettable experience. This is a world-class venue; for example, the 2001–2002 season included performances conducted by the well-known stars James Levine and Riccardo Muti. The acoustics are excellent, and the program always includes some grandiose production. The season opens in December and closes in June, with shows Tuesday through Sunday and tickets at 45€ to 90€ ($40.50 to $81). Call the number given for reservations or contact the tourist office (see the "Fast Facts" section at the end of this chapter).

As a real harbor town, Naples offers a lively nighttime scene with discos and clubs. One of the most popular is **Chez Moi** (Via del Parco Margherita 13; ☎ **081-407-526**), a small, chic hangout in the Riviera di Chiaia. Nearby is **La Mela** (Via dei Mille; ☎ **081-401-0270**), where the best night is Thursday. For both of these clubs, take bus R3 or tram 2 or 4 to Riviera di Chiaia or the Metro to Amadeo.

The best local jazz is often heard at **Riot** (Via San Biagio 38; ☎ **081-552-32-31;** Bus: E1 to Via Duomo), which attracts students from the nearby university.

For a gay atmosphere, go to **Tongue** (Via Manzoni 202; ☎ **081-769-0888;** Metro: Mergellina, then take a cab), where you'll find a mixed crowd but with a large proportion of gays and lesbians.

If you feel like relaxing over a nice glass of wine, **Berevino** (Via Sebastiano 62; ☎ **081-290-313**) is an *enoteca* with lots of room and wines to sample. With its beamed ceiling and warm interior, it will make you feel as if you've stepped into the countryside. Berevino also serves food and has a full bar. Best of all, maybe, is that it has a no-smoking room — not an easy thing to find in Italy.

Like other Italians, Neapolitans like to stroll in the evening, maybe having an ice cream or sitting on the terrace of a popular cafe, such as the oldest cafe in Naples, the **Gran Caffè Gambrinus** (Via Chiaia 1; ☎ **081-417-582;** Bus: R2 or R3 to Piazza Trieste e Trento). The cafe has been beautifully restored to its full glory; the ornate gilded interior dates from the 1860s. If Gambrinus is too full, the nearby **Caffè del Professore** (Piazza Trieste e Trento 46; ☎ **081-403-041**) serves an excellent coffee, and you'll rub shoulders with locals taking an espresso break.

Fast Facts: Napoli

American Express

American Express business is handled by Every Tours (Piazza del Municipio 5; ☎ 081-551-8564; Bus: R2 or R3 to Piazza del Municipio). It's open Monday through Friday 9:00 a.m. to 1:30 p.m. and 3:30 to 7:00 p.m., and Saturday 9 a.m. to 1 p.m.

ATMs

ATMs are available everywhere in the city center and near hotels. Most banks are linked to the Cirrus network; if you have access only to the Plus system with your card, look for a BNL (Banca Nazionale del Lavoro), with several locations in Naples.

Country Code and City Code

The country code for Italy is **39**. The city code for Naples is **081**; use this code when calling from anywhere outside or inside Italy, even within Naples itself (include the 0 every time, even when calling from abroad).

Currency Exchange

There are three exchange offices on Piazza Garibaldi (Metro: Piazza Garibaldi) and four on Corso Umberto at nos. 44, 92, 212, and 292 (Bus: R2 to Corso Umberto); Thomas Cook is on Piazza del Municipio (Bus: R2 or R3 to Piazza del Municipio).

Doctors

Call the 24-hour Guardia Medica Specialistica at ☎ 081-43-1111, or contact any consulate to get a list of English-speaking doctors.

Embassies and Consulates

The U.S. Consulate is at Piazza della Repubblica (☎ 081-583-8111); the U.K. Consulate is at Via Francesco Crispi 122 (☎ 081-663-511). For other embassies and consulates, See "Fast Facts: Rome" in Chapter 12.

Emergencies

Ambulance, ☎ **118**, 081-780-4296, or 081-584-1481; fire, ☎ **115**; first aid (pronto soccorso), ☎ **081-752-0696.**

Hospital

The Ospedale Fatebenefratelli is at Via Manzoni 220 (☎ 081-769-7220).

Information

The tourist office is in Via San Carlo 9 (☎ 081-402-394). Open Monday through Saturday 9 a.m. to 8 p.m., and Sunday 9 a.m. to 3 p.m. There is another office in Piazza del Gesu (☎ 081-552-3328) operating the same hours. There is also the provincial office (APT), which maintains the tourist booths in the Stazione Centrale at Piazza Garibaldi (☎ 081-268-799; Metro: Piazza Garibaldi) and the Stazione Mergellina (☎ 081-761-2102; Metro: Mergellina). The station booths are open daily 8:30 a.m. to 8:30 p.m.

Internet Access

Try the ClickNet Internet Café (Via Toledo 393; ☎ 081-552-9370; E-mail: clicnet@mbx.clicnet.it; Bus: R1 or R4 to Via Toledo) on one of the main streets in the city center.

Mail

The post office (Ufficio Postale) is at Piazza Matteotti (☎ 081-551-1456; Bus: R3 to Piazza Matteotti).

Pharmacies

A good one is the large one near the Stazione Centrale, Farmacia Helvethiam (Piazza Garibaldi 11; ☎ 081-554-8894; Metro: Piazza Garibaldi).

Police

Call ☎ **113**; for the Carabinieri (other police), call ☎ **112.**

Restrooms

There are very few public toilets in town, so your best bet is to go to a nice-looking cafe (though you'll have to buy something, like a cup of coffee).

Safety

Naples is considered less safe than other cities in Italy, although notable efforts have been made in recent years, with tremendous improvement. Still, pickpocketing and car theft are popular. In dark alleys off the beaten track, getting mugged is also possible, but that's quite rare in the city center or in the areas we describe in this book. Definitely seedy at night is the area around the train station.

Smoking

Smoking is allowed in cafes and restaurants and very common. Unfortunately for non-smokers, finding a restaurant with a separate no-smoking area is virtually impossible.

Taxes

Naples has no local tax. Other taxes are always included in the prices quoted.

Taxi

There are five radio taxi companies: ☎ 081-570-7070, 081-551-5151, 081-556-4444, 081-556-0202, or 081-552-5252.

Transit/Tourist Assistance

Call ☎ 147-888-088 daily 7 a.m. to 9 p.m. for the FS, the state railroad.

Weather Updates

For forecasts, the best bet is to watch the news on TV (there's no "weather number" by telephone as there is in the U.S.). On the Internet, you can check http://meteo.tiscalinet.it.

Web Sites

For a virtual-reality tour of Naples, try ww2.webcomp.com/virtuale/us/napoli/movie.htm. Other useful sites are www.thecity.it/napoli and www.ept.napoli.it (the site of the regional tourist office).

Chapter 21

Side Trips from Naples

Campania lies just south of Lazio, the region where Rome is. Naples is the capital of Campania, which has mountainous inland areas as well as a beautiful coastline. Its beauty and its nearness to Rome made Campania a favorite resort of the ancient Romans (even though Mount Vesuvius ultimately destroyed Herculaneum and Pompeii). Ancient historians reported that Caligula had a bridge of ships built the entire 4 or so miles across the nearby Bay of Pozzuoli — maybe there's always been something a little nutty about this place! Tiberius retreated to the nearby island of Capri to concentrate on his decadent pleasures. Today, Campania is a wonderful place to visit that offers very different destinations, some easily reached as day-trips from Naples.

Mount Vesuvius: The Sleeping Monster

From Naples, you can visit **Mount Vesuvius (Vesuvio),** the volcano that swallowed Herculaneum and Pompeii in its A.D. 79 eruption. Neapolitans live below a sleeping monster: Of the two major kinds of volcanoes — some slowly ooze magma, like the ones on Hawaii; others build and build and build the pressure inside and then blow their tops — Vesuvius is a top-blower. Although Vesuvius has belched only a few puffs of smoke since the last real eruption in 1944, no one really knows whether the volcano is losing its punch or just biding its time — although it did send out a puff of smoke in 1999, in case anyone thought it was sleeping. Luckily, one of the best (and the first) observatories for the study of vulcanology is right there on the mountain, taking its pulse daily.

Getting there

You can reach Vesuvius from Naples via the **Circumvesuviana Railway,** which leaves from the Stazione Circumvesuviana on Corso Garibaldi, off to the right from Piazza Garibaldi (Metro: Garibaldi). After about 15 minutes, the train stops at Herculaneum, where you can catch a bus for the crater. The trip costs about 1.50€ ($1.35).

By car, you can take the *autostrada* **Naples-Salerno (Napoli Salerno)** and exit at Herculaneum, where the windy road going up to the crater begins. The road is 13km (8 miles) long and reaches a height of 1,017m (3,106 feet).

Seeing the volcano

Mount Vesuvius is the only continental volcano still active in Europe, and is now a national park. Rising 1,281m (3,944 feet), the slopes of Vesuvius are green with vineyards — the Tears of Christ (Lacrima Christi) wine made here is very famous — and they become more rugged only as you approach the top. Before the top, at 608m (1,994 feet), you can make a short detour to visit the **Vesuvian Observatory,** which has observed the volcano's activity day by day since around 1850. Closer to the top, the path becomes lava, the typical black-and-purple rough pieces of stone. From the top on a good day, you can enjoy a fantastic view over the Bay of Naples. *Note:* An alert issued in June 2002 warned about a possible upcoming explosion of Vesuvius. Check with the park to find out if the monitors of the volcano are issuing a warning. For more information, call the **national park office** at ☎ **081-771-7549.** Admission is 2.07€ ($1.86); a guided tour costs 3€ ($2.70). It's open daily from 9 a.m. until one hour before sunset.

Pompeii and Herculaneum: Buried Alive

Few archaeological sites are as moving as the towns that shared a similar catastrophic destiny. Each is still unique: **Pompeii (Pompei)** was buried beneath volcanic ash and pumice stone, transforming Pompeiians taking flight into human statues that remain to this day. **Herculaneum (Ercolano)** was buried beneath volcanic mud that preserved its houses to a remarkable extent. In the 1990s, a boat was found near the water at Herculaneum, still filled with the corpses of victims caught in frantic postures. These are unforgettable sights, and the towns have yielded great numbers of artifacts and sculptures as well. You can see many of the finds on display in Naples's National Archaeological Museum.

Touring the crater, up close and personal

You can take a tour of the crater — indeed, you can closely approach the crater only with a guide — for 3€ ($2.70); sign up at the site's entrance. You can also join a tour group organized from Naples — for example, by the agency that handles American Express business, **Every Tours** (Piazza del Municipio 5; ☎ 081-551-8564).

You can visit either — or both — of these towns as a day-trip from Naples. Consider spending several hours at each.

Getting there

The **Circumvesuviana** (☎ **081-772-2444**) leaves from Naples's Stazione Circumvesuviana on Corso Garibaldi (between Piazza Nolana and Piazza G. Pepe), off to the right of Piazza Garibaldi. For Herculaneum, get off at the Ercolano stop, where you can catch a shuttle bus for the site. For Pompeii, take the **Sorrento train** (not the train going to modern Pompeii, on the Poggiomarino line) and get off at the Pompei Scavi stop, from which you can walk to the site. The one-way fare is about 1.50€ ($1.35), and trains leave every half-hour. The ride to Herculaneum takes 20 minutes and to Pompeii 45 minutes.

If you have a car, take the *autostrada* toward Salerno (which becomes A3); Ercolano (Herculaneum) and Pompei Scavi (Pompeii) each have an exit. It's about 8km (4½ miles) to Herculaneum and 24km (14½ miles) to Pompeii.

Taking a tour

At each sight, when you get your ticket at the ticket office, you can ask for an official guide. Doing so is a good idea, because the guide can show you those houses that are protected by gates. If you're on your own, you can't enter these locked structures and you'll have to squint between the iron frames.

Seeing the sights

Unless you're visiting in the dead of winter, remember to bring a hat, plenty of sunscreen, and water. There are no trees among the ruins, and it can get really hot. Remember to wear comfortable shoes as well, especially if you're visiting larger Pompeii.

If you have time to visit both Herculaneum and Pompeii, you can get a special ticket, the *biglietto scavi,* for 13.50€ ($12.50).

Herculaneum

Herculaneum is the smaller of the two ancient towns; much of it still lies under the present-day town and has never been excavated (digging into the solidified volcanic mud is quite a chore). Many of Herculaneum's buildings were more elaborate than Pompeii's — this was, after all, a seaside resort for rich Romans. Although all the streets and buildings of Herculaneum hold interest, some ruins merit more attention than others. Among the most interesting are the two sets of *terme* **(thermal baths)** — particularly the smaller but more elegantly decorated **Suburban Baths (Terme Suburbane).** The **Palestra** was a kind of sports arena, where games were staged to satisfy the spectacle-hungry denizens.

The average townhouse was built around an uncovered atrium. Herculaneum also had the forerunner to the modern apartment house. Important private homes to seek out are the **House of the Bicentenary (Casa del Bicentenario),** the **House of the Latticework (Casa a Graticcio),** the **House of the Wooden Partition (Casa del Tramezzo di Legno),** and the **House of Neptune (Casa di Nettune),** which contains the most striking mosaic found in the ruins. The finest example of how the aristocracy lived is the **House of the Stags (Casa dei Cervi),** named because of the sculpture found inside. Note that several houses are locked and opened only with permission. For this reason, taking a guided tour is a good idea. Herculaneum is easier to see because it's smaller, but it's less impressive than Pompeii — though the sites share the feeling of having been abandoned not very long ago.

Ufficio Scavi di Ercolano, Corso Resina, Ercolano. ☎ *081-857-5347. Admission: 8.50€ ($7.65). Open: Daily 8:30 a.m.–7:30 p.m.; in winter, closes at 5:00 p.m.*

Pompeii

Pompeii was a commercial town as well as a residential resort, and its urban fabric was a mix of elegant villas, shops, and more modest housing. The town was buried under volcanic ash and pumice stone that then solidified, which allowed the residents who had escaped to come back and salvage some of their treasures. Of course, this same situation also made it easier for the treasure hunters of later centuries to loot the place. Yet even though the site was picked over by scavengers, the city was very well preserved, and the archaeological excavations have uncovered much about the life of the times.

The most elegant of the patrician villas is the **House of the Vettii (Casa dei Vettii),** boasting a courtyard, statuary, paintings, and a black-and-red Pompeiian dining room known for its frescoes. The house was occupied by two brothers named Vettii, both of whom were wealthy merchants. Another treasure is the **House of the Mysteries (Casa dei Misteri),** near the Porto Ercolano outside the walls, decorated with frescoes of mythological scenes related to the cult of Dionysus (Bacchus), one of the cults that flourished in Roman times. The most famous and the largest of the

Herculaneum

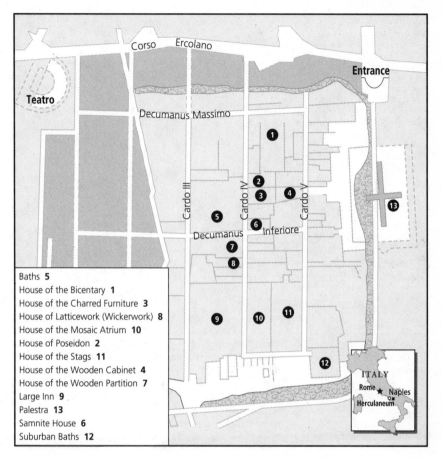

Corso Ercolano

Entrance

Teatro

Decumanus Massimo

Cardo III

Cardo IV

Cardo V

Decumanus Inferiore

Baths **5**
House of the Bicentary **1**
House of the Charred Furniture **3**
House of Latticework (Wickerwork) **8**
House of the Mosaic Atrium **10**
House of Poseidon **2**
House of the Stags **11**
House of the Wooden Cabinet **4**
House of the Wooden Partition **7**
Large Inn **9**
Palestra **13**
Samnite House **6**
Suburban Baths **12**

ITALY
Rome ★ ■ Naples
Herculaneum ○■

houses is the **House of the Faun (Casa del Fauno),** so called because of
the bronze statue of a dancing faun that was found there; the house takes
up a city block and has four dining rooms and two spacious gardens.

Also interesting are the public areas of the ancient city. In the center of
town is the **Forum** — parts were severely damaged in an earthquake 16
years before the eruption of Vesuvius and had not been repaired when
the final destruction came. Three buildings surrounding the Forum are
the **basilica** (the city's largest single structure) and the **Temple of Apollo
(Tempio di Apollo)** and **Temple of Jupiter (Tempio di Giove).** The
Terme Stabiane (baths) are in good condition, among the finest baths to
survive from antiquity. Other buildings of interest are the **Teatro Grande,**
built in the fifth century B.C.; the **House of the Gilded Cupids (Casa degle
Amorini Dorati),** a flamboyant private home; and the **House of the
Tragic Poet (Casa del Poeta Tragico),** which gets its name from a mosaic
discovered here (later sent to Naples). It depicts a chained watchdog on
the doorstep with this warning — CAVE CANEM ("Beware of the dog").

Pompeii

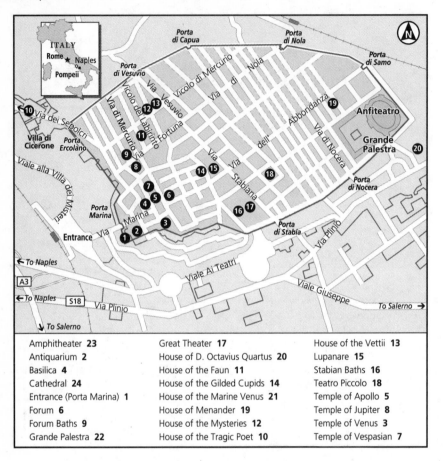

Amphitheater **23**	Great Theater **17**	House of the Vettii **13**
Antiquarium **2**	House of D. Octavius Quartus **20**	Lupanare **15**
Basilica **4**	House of the Faun **11**	Stabian Baths **16**
Cathedral **24**	House of the Gilded Cupids **14**	Teatro Piccolo **18**
Entrance (Porta Marina) **1**	House of the Marine Venus **21**	Temple of Apollo **5**
Forum **6**	House of Menander **19**	Temple of Jupiter **8**
Forum Baths **9**	House of the Mysteries **12**	Temple of Venus **3**
Grande Palestra **22**	House of the Tragic Poet **10**	Temple of Vespasian **7**

Particularly evocative — and disturbing — are the "statues" of the victims: The ash hardened on the dead bodies and became a shell that preserved all the details, including agonizing facial expressions. The archaeologists were then able to make casts of these bodies by pouring plaster into the cavities.

Pompeii is some four times larger than Herculaneum, and visiting the whole thing is somewhat laborious. Count on a minimum of four hours just to get a general idea of the place and have a quick look at most of the attractions. You can now get a guided tour of the **suburban thermal baths (Terme Suburbane).** Make a reservation at the ticket booth of Porta Marina between 10:00 a.m. and 1:30 p.m. On Saturdays and Sundays, the tour also includes a visit to two Roman houses, the Casa di Polibio and Casa Menandro.

Ufficio Scavi di Pompei, Piazza Esedra. ☎ *081-857-5347. Admission: 8.50€ ($7.65). Open: Daily 8:30 a.m.–7:30 p.m.; in winter, closes at 5:00 p.m.*

Where to dine

There's little to eat at the excavations, so packing a picnic lunch to bring with you is a good idea (don't forget plenty of water during the summer). If you want to eat in a restaurant, you have to head for the modern town. Herculaneum is relatively poor, but it has a few snack bars near the center; Pompeii offers better options.

Il Principe

$$$ Pompeii   NEAPOLITAN

This is one of the best restaurants in the whole region, serving the height of Neapolitan cuisine, such as grilled fish and pasta with seafood. The decor is quite funny, giving a local interpretation of ancient Pompeian life (including mosaics and frescoes).

Piazza Bartolo Longo, near the basilica in the center of town. ☎ *081-850-5566. Reservations necessary. Bus: From the excavations to the rail station of the town of Pompeii. Secondi: 12.91€–20.66€ ($11.62–$18.59). AE, DC, MC, V. Open: Lunch and dinner Tues–Sun; daily in summer.*

Capri and the Blue Grotto: Sunny Island Getaway

Idyllic — now only in the off-season — **Capri** (pronounce it *Cap*-ree), with its famous Blue Grotto and emerald water, makes a perfect getaway from busy Naples. It's just a ferry ride south of the city off the peninsula of Sorrento, and you can visit it in a day-trip, thus avoiding high hotel charges.

Should you want to take a romantic break by the sea, however, Capri is well worth a longer stay. Ever since Emperor Tiberius sought amusement at Villa Jovis here, the island has been a haunt for eccentric characters (such as movie stars hiding out, artists in exile, and the like). Norman Douglas's *South Wind* is a very funny novel about various strange people living on Capri who engage in long philosophical debates and repartee. Douglas also wrote *Siren Land,* about Sorrento and Capri, where he lived for many years.

Whether you stay for a day or a year, remember to bring very little luggage: The island is quite steep and you may have to walk up many steps. At the more exclusive hotels, you can find staff to carry your stuff, but otherwise plan on having to lug your suitcases yourself.

Getting there

Ferries leave Naples frequently for Capri. There are several competing companies, and schedules change all the time. Contact **ALILAURO** (☎ **081-761-1004;** Internet: www.alilauro.it), **Tirrenia** (☎ **081-761-3688;** Internet: www.tirrenia.it), **Carremar** (☎ **081-551-3882**), SNAV (☎ **081-761-2348**), and **NLG** (☎ **081-552-7209**) for schedules. The trip with the *aliscafo* (hydrofoil) takes 45 minutes and costs about 23€ ($20.70) round-trip. The conventional ferry, for example, with Carremar, costs half as much and takes twice as long. They all leave from Molo Beverello at Naples's Stazione Marittima several times a day.

From the ferry terminal you can also catch a **funicular** (in summer) or a **bus** (in winter) that brings you up the steep coast to the town of Capri. From there, you can reach Anacapri — the second town on the island, higher up on the promontory — by **taxi,** by **bus,** or **on foot.** A bus also links Capri to Marina Piccola, a village by the sea (see "Seeing the sights," later in this chapter).

While you're in Capri, you can get information from the **tourist office** at Piazza Umberto I 19 (☎ **081-370-686**). Summer hours are Monday through Saturday 8:30 a.m. to 8:30 p.m. and Sunday 8:30 a.m. to 2:30 p.m.; winter hours are Monday through Saturday 9:00 a.m. to 1:00 p.m. and 3:30 to 6:30 p.m.

Taking a tour

Boat tours of the island leave from **Marina Grande** (where the ferry and hydrofoil from Naples arrive). The cost is about 20€ ($18) per person for the whole tour.

Seeing the sights

This legendary island has been the chief destination for the rich and famous since antiquity. It has two main urban centers: the town of **Capri** (where you can find the most glamorous hotels, cafes, and shops) and the smaller town of **Anacapri** (up a steep climb from Capri through the old **Scala Fenicia** staircases — read on for details — or via a hair-raising bus ride). From Anacapri you can take the chairlift up to **Monte Solaro,** the highest point on the island. On the south shore is the **Marina Piccola,** a tiny harbor with a beach offering views over the famous **Faraglioni,** the tall rocks off the island's southeastern tip. The windy roads climbing up the promontory are picturesque, though less entertaining when clogged with tourists. Capri boasts beautiful cliffs and views of the sea and out over the Bay of Naples and Vesuvius.

If you're moderately fit, you may enjoy exploring the island on foot. Most of the footpaths offer fantastic views. One of the musts is climbing the **Scala Fenicia,** the steep path linking Anacapri to Capri that was begun by Greek colonists thousands of years ago. It's so steep that it is actually a staircase (*scala* means "stairs") with over 500 steps.

If your real reason for coming to Capri is to swim, you won't be disappointed: The water is beautiful and marvelously refreshing under the hot sun. Because Capri is very rocky, though, the **beaches** are small. The easy-to-reach beaches are often crowded, but you can walk to several others that have fewer crowds. The best idea, however, is to avail yourself of one of the small boats that take you to a difficult-to-reach beach for about 8€ ($7.20).

The **Bagni di Tiberio** is a nice sandy beach on the north side of the island, near the ruins of an ancient villa. You can take a boat there from Marina Grande or walk (it takes about half an hour). The beach is freely accessible.

The Blue Grotto (Grotta Azzurra)

Kids will love visiting the **Blue Grotto (Grotto Azzurra)** — an underwater cave that can be reached only by small boats. This natural wonder conjures up visions of pirates and buried treasure.

The Blue Grotto is also Capri's top attraction, and as such it has been overexploited by entrepreneurs. When you board that big boat going there, don't think that's how you'll see the grotto. You have to get off onto a rowboat that takes you into the grotto, which is reached by a narrow passage — so narrow and low that if you're not limber or have claustrophia you won't like it. The slow sinking of the grotto over time has reduced the opening to slightly more than 3 feet above sea level. Another way to see the grotto is the old-fashioned way: Swim to it. However, we strongly advise against this option during peak season because of the incessant boat traffic. If you insist upon swimming, doing it toward evening is best.

When you get inside, you'll understand the reason for all the commotion and even forget about the outrageous money you've paid to see it. The grotto was known to the ancients but was later lost to the world until an artist stumbled upon it in 1826. Inside the cavern, light refraction (the sun's rays entering from an opening under the water) creates incredible colors and a magical atmosphere — stunning, indeed. Alas, chances are you won't be able to stay as long as you'd like, because at the height of tourist season no lingering is allowed. For all these reasons, we think that the grotto, like Capri in general, should be seen in the off-season if possible. Then you at least get a feeling for what it was like in the old days.

Near the northwestern tip of the island. Admission: Boat tour 14€ ($12.60) plus 10€ ($9) "tip" to be rowed inside the grotto. Open: Daily 9 a.m. to one hour before sunset.

Capri

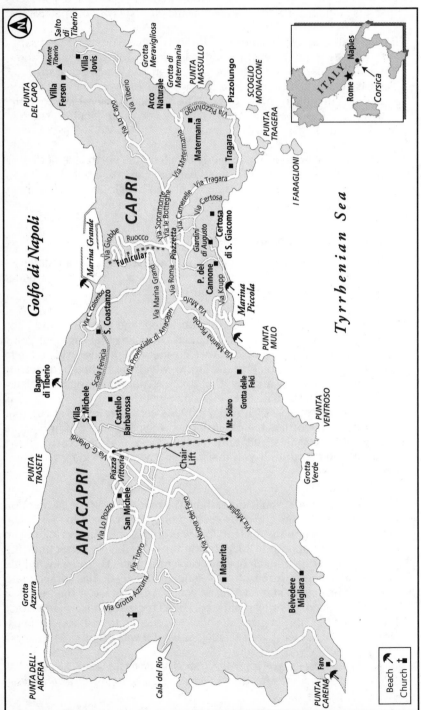

Villa Jovis
Capri

Capri has long been a haunt of eccentrics and sometimes degenerates: Emperor Tiberius built several villas on the island during his self-imposed exile here, where he could enjoy all sorts of illicit pleasures far away from the prying eyes of the Roman Senate. The Villa Jovis, the palace where Tiberius lived, extended over several levels for an estimated 63,000 square feet (just a modest summer home) but is now only a romantic ruin from which you get beautiful views.

Via Tiberio, at the eastern tip of the island. Admission: 3€ ($2.70). Open: Daily 9 a.m. to one hour before sunset.

Where to stay

If you want to stay overnight, be forewarned that Capri town isn't cheap. Hotels in Anacapri are a little cheaper, and you may like to be away from the bustling crowds of Capri town.

Grand Hotel Quisisana Capri
$$$$$ Capri

At the top of the scale, the Grand Hotel Quisisana is the chic place to stay on Capri — Georgio Armani has been a regular for years. What was a sanatorium in the 19th century is today the most popular place in Capri. If you can't afford one of the ritzy guest rooms, lounge in the terrace of the hotel cafe, maybe sipping the blue-colored house cocktail, or take a sauna or a swim in the pool. The room furnishings are stylish, and some of the more expensive ones have fine antiques, marble columns, and extravagant baths.

Via Camerelle 2. ☎ *081-837-0788. Fax: 081-837-6080. E-mail:* info@quisi.com. *Internet:* www.quisi.com. *Rack rates: 245€–498€ ($220.50–$448.20) double, including buffet breakfast. Closed Nov–mid-March.*

Hotel Luna
$$$$ Capri

A less pricey choice than the Grand Hotel Quisisana but still upscale, Hotel Luna offers beautiful vistas over the Faraglioni and the bay from its location atop a cliff. Most guest rooms have private terraces overlooking the cliffs or gardens, and all are quite luxurious; you even get a phone in the bathroom.

Viale Matteotti 3. ☎ *081-837-0433. Fax: 081-837-7459. Internet:* www.lunahotel. com. *E-mail:* luna@capri.it. *Rack rates: 157€–335€ ($141.30–$301.50) double, including breakfast. Closed end of Oct–Easter.*

Hotel San Michele
$$ Anacapri

A beautiful pool (the largest on Capri), gardens overlooking the sea, and pleasant guest rooms make Hotel San Michele an excellent moderately priced (for Capri) choice. The atmosphere is more relaxed and the hotel much quieter than one of the more expensive ones in Capri. Every room has some kind of view, whether of the sea, the mountain, or the gardens. The furnishings are contemporary and functional.

Via G. Orlandi 1–3. ☎ *081-837-1427. Fax 081-837-1420. E-mail:* smichele@ capri.it. *Rack rates: 135€–170€ ($121.50–$153) double, including breakfast. AE, MC, V. Closed Nov–March.*

Where to dine

Restaurants on Capri can be excellent although expensive. One of the specialties is *zuppa di cozze* (mussel soup) with beans; another is the Caprese, the simple salad of fresh mozzarella, basil leaves, and tomatoes sprinkled with extra-virgin olive oil. Don't be afraid to explore — some very nice small trattorie are tucked away among the rocks of this magnificent island.

Casanova
$$$ Capri   NEAPOLITAN/CAPRESE

Quite central, this restaurant offers a good choice of seafood and pasta dishes to satisfy the hungriest customers. If you're thirsty as well, you'll be pleased that it also has an excellent wine cellar, with a good selection of local wines. The Casanova features two dining rooms: the main one with arched ceilings, trestle tables, and tiled floors, and a smaller tavern room. The antipasto buffet is excellent; for a secondo, try the *totanetti affogati* (a type of squid, "drowned" — that is, stewed — in herbs and wine).

Via le Botteghe 46, just off Piazza Umberto. ☎ *081-837-7642. Reservations necessary for dinner. Secondi: 10.33€–19.63€ ($9.30–$17.67). AE, DC, MC, V. Open: Lunch and dinner daily; closed Dec–mid-March.*

Grottino
$$$$ Capri   NEAPOLITAN

Of historic importance — the preferred spot for the celebrities of the 1950s — Grottino still deserves its popularity. You can taste some true Caprese specialties, such as *zuppa di cozze,* and the old-fashioned Neapolitan everyday delicacy (think of it as old-world junk food) *mozzarella in carrozza* (deep-fried mozzarella), here prepared in four varieties.

Via Longano 27. ☎ *081-837-0584. Reservations necessary for dinner. Secondi: 12.91€–18.08€ ($11.62–$16.27). AE, MC, V. Open: Lunch and dinner daily; closed Nov–March.*

Chapter 22

The Amalfi Coast

. . . .

In This Chapter

▶ Living the good life in Positano

▶ Sunning and swimming on the beaches of the Amalfi Coast

▶ Taking in the sights in lovely Ravello

. . . .

The **Amalfi Coast (Costiera Amalfitana)** is a stretch of shore famous for its natural beauty. Its terraced cliffs overlooking the sea are blanketed with lemon trees, olive groves, and vineyards interspersed with small villages and historic towns, among which the queen is Amalfi. It was one of the four Italian historic maritime republics, along with Siena, Genoa, and Venice.

The Amalfi Coast is only a couple of hours from Naples, so you can choose to visit this famous area as a day-trip. Given the difficult driving, however — the road is narrow and winding, sometimes without a guardrail — and the beauty of the place, you may be tempted to extend your stay and spend at least one night.

Getting There

There are several ways to get to and to see the Amalfi Coast. Some are more adventurous than others — read on for more about cliffside roads and breathtaking vistas.

By bus

The bus company **SITA** (☎ **089-871-016** or 089-871-009 in Amalfi) makes daily runs from Sorrento to Positano and Amalfi. The fare is 1.14€ ($1.03) to Positano and 2.07€ ($1.86) to Amalfi. The ride can be hair-raising at times, but it's certainly panoramic. From Naples, get the 2.07€ ($1.86) express train to Sorrento on the **Circumvesuviana** (☎ **081-772-2444**), then switch to the bus. Trains leave Naples from the Stazione Circumvesuviana, on Corso Garibaldi (between Piazza Nolana and Piazza G. Pepe) off to the right of Piazza Garibaldi. The train ride takes about an hour; the bus a little more, depending on the traffic. SITA also has frequent runs between Amalfi and Ravello.

The Amalfi Coast

By ferry

The company **Alicost** (☎ **089-871-483** or 089-873-301 in Amalfi and ☎ **089-875-032** or 089-811-164 in Positano) has daily runs to Capri from Positano and from Amalfi, by ferry and hydrofoil. A one-way ticket from Amalfi is 10.50€ ($9.45) for the regular ferry and 13.50€ ($12.15) for the hydrofoil, and the trip lasts 80 minutes; from Positano the one-way ticket is 10€ ($9) for the regular ferry and 13€ ($11.70) for the hydrofoil, and the trip lasts 50 minutes. In order to take the ride, you need to make a reservation at least 24 hours in advance. Using this ferry, you could take ferries from Naples to Capri and then from Capri to Positano, thus avoiding all driving.

By car

If you have a car, take the *autostrada* Napoli-Salerno and exit either at Vietri — the southern limit of the Costiera Amalfitana — and follow the windy *strada statale* SS163 back toward Sorrento, or do it the other way around, taking the exit for Sorrento and then following the signs for Positano and Amalfi east on SS163, which actually starts before Sorrento at the village of Meta. The road cuts from Meta across the peninsula, avoiding Sorrento, but if you continue on toward Sorrento, you can take an extra piece of windy road around the promontory (SS145), which then merges back with SS163. Farther along, note that Ravello is inland off SS163, posted from Amalfi.

Road maps are flat, of course, and show little topography. On the Amalfi Coast, something that's slightly inland is more up than it is in. And it may be *way* up the cliffs. This lack of correspondence between maps and reality is why you sometimes think you're lost but really you aren't. The other thing to remember is that when driving west to east, you're in the outside lane and, thus, close to the plunging cliff edge; if the prospect makes you nervous, you can drive the Amalfi Coast east to west, so you're on the inside lane.

Getting Around

Each of the towns along the Amalfi Coast is small and easily visited on foot. Especially in Positano, though, you may prefer to wear comfortable shoes without heels, to climb the steep alleys and many ramps of steps. To move among the attractions, you can use a **SITA bus** (☎ **089-871-016** or 089-871-009 in Amalfi), connecting Positano to Amalfi and Amalfi to Ravello.

Where to Stay on the Amalfi Coast

If you're looking for another splurge choice, try the famous **Hotel Le Sirenuse** (Via Cristoforo Colombo 30; ☎ **089-875-066;** Fax: 089-811-798; E-mail: sirenuse@macronet.it; Internet: www.sirenuse.it), in a villa a few minutes' walk up from the bay. It's owned by the Marchesi Sersale family and was their residence until 1951. You may have seen the hotel featured in the film *Only You* with Marisa Tomei and Robert Downey, Jr.

Albergo L'Ancora
$$$ Positano

Not one of the most elegant choices in Positano, this moderately priced hotel still offers good value. Most guest rooms have air-conditioning, and each boasts comfortable beds, some antiques, and a private terrace. Open only to guests, the hotel's restaurant serves meals on the terrace.

Via Colombo 36. ☎ *089-875-318. Fax: 089-811-784. Parking: Free. Rack rates: 129.11€–164.94€ ($116.20–$148.45) double, including breakfast. AE, DC, MC, V. Closed Nov–Mar.*

Hotel Cappuccini Convento
$$$$ Amalfi

One of Amalfi's most beautiful hotels, this 12th-century landmark is a convent turned into a hotel, and the "cells" are now luxuriously appointed guest rooms with dark wood furniture. Accommodations are accessed by elevator and a glass-walled corridor with sweeping views. The magnificent hotel's restaurant is only rivaled by the terrace, open in the good season and renowned for its view over the cliffs.

Via Annunziatella 46. ☎ *089-871-877. Fax: 089-871-886. E-mail:* cappuccini@ amalfinet.it. *Internet:* www.hotelcappuccini.it. *Parking: 15.50€ ($13.95). Rack rates: 156€–208€ ($140.40–$187.20) double, including breakfast. Additional charges are 15.50€ ($13.95) per day for air-conditioning and 3€ ($2.70) for frigobar. AE, DC, MC, V.*

Hotel Lidomare
$$ Amalfi

This moderately priced hotel near the beach is housed in a 13th-century building. The guest rooms are brightly decorated in typical Amalfitan style (tiling, strong colors, lots of sparkling white). Most rooms have air-conditioning; the baths are small but very clean, and the staff is extremely friendly.

Largo Duchi Piccolomini 9. ☎ *089-871-332. Fax: 089-871-394. Parking: 10€ ($9). Rack rates: 70€–85€ ($63–$76.50) double, including breakfast. AE, MC, V.*

Hotel Poseidon
$$$$ Positano

A villa from the 1950s, this hotel offers luxury accommodations at moderate prices. Each guest room has a terrace and unique decor. In addition to a beautiful garden and terrace with a spectacular view, the hotel has a pool and a small spa with a sauna, a Jacuzzi, and a choice of massages. The hotel's restaurant is not only convenient but up to the standards of the area.

Via Pasitea 148. ☎ *089-811-111. Fax: 089-875-833. E-mail:* poseidon@starnet. it. *Internet:* www.hotelposeidonpositano.it. *Parking: 21€ ($18.90). Rack rates: 181€–263€ ($162.90–$236.70) double, including breakfast. AE, DC, MC, V. Closed Jan to mid-March.*

Villa Cimbrone
$$$$ Ravello

This villa, home to the Vuillemier family, who are the owners, offers hospitality to a small number of guests (20 maximum) in great luxury and privacy. Each of the rooms is unique and decorated with antiques. From Ravello, call the hotel; they'll send a porter to carry your luggage to the villa. The villa is an attraction in itself (see "The Top Sights," later in this chapter).

Via Santa Chiara 26. ☎ *089-857-459. Fax: 089-857-777. Internet:* www.villa cimbrone.it. *Rack rates: 155€–310€ ($139.50–$279) double, including breakfast. AE, DC, MC, V. Closed Dec–March.*

Where to Dine on the Amalfi Coast

On the Amalfi coast, the sea reigns: It's a paradise for seafood — grilled, fried, or prepared in the local version of *zuppa di pesce* (fish stew). Similar to the Neapolitan cuisine, Amalfitan cuisine is rich in the flavors of the local countryside — ripe tomatoes, fresh herbs, and citrus fruits. The mussel-bound coast is also known for *zuppa di cozze* (mussel soup), and mussels are used in pasta dishes as well. For cheese, the winner is the *mozzarella di bufala* (buffalo mozzarella), the delicious specialty from the nearby Salerno region.

Buca di Bacco
$$$$ Positano   AMALFITAN

At this popular restaurant right on the beach, you find local cuisine at its best, with a large array of flavorful seafood dishes. The tables are set on the large, shaded terrace with a great view over the sea. Try the *zuppa di cozze* or the grilled fish.

Via Rampa Teglia 8. ☎ *089-875-699. Reservations necessary. Secondi: 20.60€– 30.99€ ($18.59–$27.89). AE, DC, MC, V. Open: Lunch and dinner daily; closed Nov–March.*

Cumpà Cosimo
$$ Ravello   AMALFITAN

At this great family-run restaurant, you can order all the local specialties prepared home-style but at a lower price than in the more "resorty" restaurants. The pasta is very good, and so are the *secondi* (main dishes of meat or fish), among which you'll find a good *zuppa di pesce* and a fine *fritto misto*.

Via Roma 44. ☎ *089-857-156. Reservations recommended. Secondi: 9.30€–28.41€ ($8.37–$25.57). AE, DC, MC, V. Open: Lunch and dinner daily.*

Da Adolfo
$$$ Positano   AMALFITAN

If you're here in the right season, this restaurant provides you with an extra experience: Its motorboat (with a red fish on the side) waits for customers at the dock in Positano and carries them to the small resort. For the price of an excellent lunch — including fish, *zuppa di cozze* (mussel soup), and *pasta con cozze e vongole* (pasta with mussels and small clams) — you get access to the private beach and facilities (you have to pay extra, though, if you want to rent a beach umbrella and chair). In July and August, the resort is open daily from 10 a.m. to midnight (to about 7:30 p.m. in June and September); the boat leaves the Positano dock every 30 minutes.

Laurito, just off Positano. ☎ **089-875-022.** *Reservations recommended. Secondi: 7.75€–13.94€ ($6.98–$12.54). No credit cards. Open: Lunch daily, dinner Sat in July and Aug only; closed Oct–May.*

Da Gemma
$$$ Amalfi AMALFITAN

One of the best restaurants on this stretch of coast, Da Gemma serves all the typical regional dishes. The *zuppa di pesce per due* (fish stew for two) is definitely a winner; the *fritto misto* is one of the lighter fried mixed seafoods you've ever tasted, and the *polipo* (tender octopus) is great. The homemade *crostata* (a thick crust topped with jam, a typical Italian home-style dessert) also deserves a mention, prepared with local citrus fruit jam.

Via Fra Gerardo Sassi 9. ☎ **089-871-345.** *Reservations necessary. Secondi: 11.36€–28.41€ ($10.22–$25.57). AE, DC, MC, V. Open: Lunch and dinner Thurs–Tues; closed Jan.*

Ristorante Luna Convento
$$$ Amalfi AMALFITAN/ITALIAN

Across from the hotel of the same name (which was once a convent), this is a popular and fashionable rendezvous. It's housed in a 16th-century tower and includes both a restaurant and a bar. Just underneath is a pool and the beach. Besides charming surroundings, you get great food. The ample menu includes pasta and seafood but also several meat dishes. The hotel also has a dining room with a nice terrace and views over the sea.

Via Pantaleone Comite 33. ☎ **089-871-002.** *Reservations recommended. Secondi: 15.49€–18.08€ ($13.94–$16.27). AE, DC, MC, V. Open: Lunch and dinner daily.*

Exploring the Amalfi Coast

The Amalfi Coast's three most famous towns vary: Positano is mainly a resort, while Amalfi retains more art and architecture from the area's glory days (about 800 years in the past); Ravello is somewhere in between — it offers some art but is mostly a tranquil, elegant resort. Each is well worth a visit.

The top sights

The attractions of the Amalfi Coast are mainly natural; people come to drive along the spectacular cliffs, play in the sea, and eat delicious seafood. Here are our favorite things to see.

Positano

The westernmost of the three towns, **Positano** is also the most dramatic. Built in the narrow gap between two mountains, the village slopes steeply to the Tyrrhenian Sea. Just off its coast are the legendary Sirenuse Islands, Homer's siren islands in the *Odyssey,* which form the privately owned mini-archipelago of Li Galli (The Cocks). Don't expect white Caribbean beaches here: The beach is gray and rather pebbly; however, the sea is splendid.

Aside from the town, the big attraction here — as you see as soon as you step into town — is the swimsuits. Whether maillot, bikini, or thong, all have colorful and unique patterns. Because people here spend two-thirds of their time in swimsuits, this local industry has exploded. We know someone who buys her bikinis only in Positano, no matter how far she has to travel to get them! The town is an exclusive resort, and its small alleys and ramps are filled with boutiques, restaurants, and hotels.

The topography of the town, you'll soon discover, is impossibly steep. Wear comfortable walking shoes — no heels!

Amalfi

Having known its moment of glory between the 10th and the 12th centuries — it was the first of Italy's maritime republics, before Genoa and Venice — the city of **Amalfi** is rich in monuments and mementos from the past. The grandiose **Duomo,** Piazza del Duomo (☎ **089-871-059**) — named in honor of St. Andrew (Sant'Andrea) — has a black-and-white facade that was redone in the 18th century; inside is the original tenth-century cathedral integrated into the Duomo as the **Chapel of the Crucifixion (Cappella del Crocifisso).** The Duomo is open daily from 7:30 a.m. to 8:00 p.m., and admission is free. To the left of the Duomo is the **Paradise Cloister (Chiostro del Paradiso),** the 13th-century cloister that was once the cemetery for the city's religious and political elite. From it, you can gain access to the crypt containing the remains of St. Andrew. An interesting detail is that his face is missing — it was donated to St. Andrew's in Patras, Greece. Admission to the cloister is 3€ ($2.70), and it's open daily from 9 a.m. to 7 p.m. From July through September, concerts are held in the cloister on Friday nights.

The once-powerful republic was famous for its paper industry, and paper from Amalfi was shipped all around Europe. This art has been preserved in town, where one of the descendants of the ancient master papermakers is still at his work: **Antonio Cavaliere** (Via Fiume; ☎ **089-7871-954**). You can visit his workshop — complete with the traditional equipment of the trade, where he produces paper of an almost forgotten quality. The shop is open for regular business hours. Cavaliere's products are sold to the most exclusive paper shops in Italy and Europe. The water for this craft still comes from the covered river that crosses town and was the key resource in the development of the paper industry in Amalfi.

If you follow the river out of town toward the hills (start at Piazza del Duomo and head up Via Genova), you can explore the **Valle dei Mulini,** the path stretching down the narrow valley of the river, along which the old paper mills that were the town's main economic resource are still visible. You can find out more details about the industry at the **Museum of Paper (Museo della Carta)** (Via Valle dei Mulini; ☎ 089-872-615), filled with antique presses and yellowing manuscripts. It's open Tuesday, Thursday, Saturday, and Sunday from 9 a.m. to 1 p.m., and admission is 1.55€ ($1.40).

Besides paper, Amalfi is famous today for its lemons. Unique in size, sweetness, flavor, and color, the lemons of Amalfi are exported as rare gems to markets around Italy. Here you can see them turned into the famous *limoncello,* a yellow-colored sweet lemon liqueur, but also into delicious confections like candied lemons, jams, and lemon ice cream.

Limoncello has a very nice taste, but few people can drink it straight. If you buy a bottle, you will probably want to use it to flavor cakes, cookies, and other sweet preparations.

Ravello

The only one of the major towns not on the coast, **Ravello** opens into a splendid valley with intensive cultivation — vineyards and lemons and other fruit grow on its steep terraced flanks. The town has a feeling of subdued elegance, the evidence of its magnificent past. Indeed, Ravello continued, after the fall of Amalfi, to be an important center for commerce with the East during the 13th century. Celebrities and writers favor this town, and the reigning celeb of the moment is Gore Vidal, who purchased a villa as a writing retreat.

The 11th-century **Duomo,** on Piazza Vescovado, has a beautiful portal from the 12th century, a campanile from the 13th century, and interesting treasures in the crypt. The **Chapel of St. Pantaleone (Cappella di San Pantaleone),** the patron saint of Ravello, contains a relic of the saint (a cracked vessel with his blood, which miraculously fails to leak away); it's to the left of the main altar. The blood is a symbol of the saint's violent demise: He was beheaded in Nicomedia on July 27, 290. Ravello holds a festival on that day every year. The Duomo is open daily from 8 a.m. to 7 p.m., and admission is free.

Also on Piazza Vescovado is the entrance to **Villa Rufolo** (☎ 089-857-657), founded in the 11th century, though today it's a jumble of styles, from imitation Moorish to pretend Norman. But you can still see memories of its past splendor. Among its illustrious guests was Richard Wagner, who is said to have composed an act of *Parsifal* during his residence here. The big attractions are the gardens, filled with flowers in spring and offering beautiful views over Salerno Bay. In summer, the villa is open daily from 9 a.m. to 8 p.m. (winter until 6 p.m.), and admission is 3€ ($2.70).

Going farther inland, you can reach the **Villa Cimbrone** (Via Santa Chiara 26; ☎ **089-857-459**), built in the 19th century by an eccentric Englishman over a preexisting 15th-century villa. The views and the gardens are very beautiful, and spending the night there is well worth it (some of the rooms have been opened as a hotel accommodation — see "Where to Stay," earlier in this chapter). The villa is accessible only on foot after a somewhat steep walk of about ten minutes. If you ring the bell at the entrance, a member of the staff lets you in and even takes you inside the building to admire the strange architecture. The villa is open daily from 9 a.m. to 7 p.m., and admission is 4.13€ ($3.72).

More cool things to see and do

Many people drive the Amalfi Coast and stop at only one or two of the towns, usually Amalfi or Positano. But the smaller towns and destinations are worth exploring, too. Here are a few recommendations:

✔ At 5km (3.1 miles) west of Amalfi on SS163, the **Emerald Grotto (Grotta di Smeraldo)** is a good alternative to Capri's Blue Grotto. This cave is accessible only from the sea and costs 3€ ($2.70), which includes the elevator ride from the road down to sea level and the boat ride to and inside the cave. From Amalfi, you can take the SITA bus toward Sorrento (ask the driver to stop at the grotto) or take a boat from the dock in the harbor (about 8€/$7.20 round-trip). What's unique about this grotto is its ancient formation of stalactites and stalagmites, which have been partially invaded by sea water. As a result, some of the formations are submerged, creating fantastic effects of light and shade. The boat takes you inside and around this bizarre world. It's open daily from 9 a.m. to 4 p.m., weather permitting.

✔ Of course, the **Amalfi Coast** is a seaside resort and you can enjoy the beach. Amalfi has a nice sandy beach, but even better are the beaches at the small towns of Maiori and Minori, farther east. There you can sunbathe and swim in the blue **Mediterranean Sea.**

✔ At the southeastern end of the Amalfi Coast, the little town of **Vietri sul Mare** is on your way to the *autostrada* Salerno-Napoli and is worth the detour if you're a ceramics lover. Vietri is one of the famous Italian centers for artistic ceramics — with Deruta, Fienza, Sciacca, Santo Stefano, and Caltagirone — and the industry here is still very much alive. The streets are lined with ceramics of all kinds, characterized by bright colors and semi-geometric patterns. Some of the shops sell products by different artists, but others are the marketplace of individual workshops, each with its individual pattern and colors. It's a perfect place to find a small gift for someone back home. We're especially fond of D'Amore, for the quality of his ceramics and the funny little goats that are his trademark and are imitated by many — or so he says.

Fast Facts: The Amalfi Coast

Country Code and City Code

The country code for Italy is **39**. The city code for the towns along the Amalfi Coast is **089**; use this code when calling from anywhere outside or inside Italy, even within the towns themselves (include the 0 every time, even when calling from abroad).

Consulates and Embassies

See "Fast Facts: Naples" in Chapter 20.

Currency Exchange

You can change currency at banks in the three main towns, which also have ATMs.

Emergencies

Ambulance, ☎ **118**; Fire, ☎ **115**; Police, ☎ **113**; road assistance ACI, ☎ **116**.

Hospital

The Ospedale Generale is in Amalfi, 2 Localita Pogerola (☎ 089-830-065).

Information

Each of the three main towns has a tourist office. The Positano office is on Via del Saraceno 4 (☎ 089-875-067); it's open Monday through Friday 8:30 a.m. to 2:00 p.m. (in summer also Saturday 8:30 a.m. to noon). The Amalfi office is on Corso delle Repubbliche Marinare 19 (☎ 089-871-107); it's open Monday through Friday 8 a.m. to 2 p.m. and Sat. 8 a.m. to noon. The Ravello office is on Via Santa Chiara 26 (☎ 089-857-096); it's open Monday through Saturday 8 a.m. to 7 p.m. (until 8 p.m. in summer).

Mail

Ravello, Positano, and Amalfi each has an Ufficio Postale in the center of town.

Police

Call ☎ **113**; for the Carabinieri (other police), call ☎**112**.

Web Sites

There are plenty of Web sites for the Amalfi coast. Two of the good ones are www.amalfiweb.it and www.amalficoast.it.

Part VII
Sicily

The 5th Wave   By Rich Tennant

"I appreciate that our room looks out onto several baroque fountains, but I had to get up 6 times last night to go to the bathroom."

In this part . . .

"You cannot get a true idea of Italy without seeing Sicily. Sicily is where you can find the key to everything." These words, which Goethe wrote in 1787, still hold true. Sicily is a more intense version of Italy, where things from the past are preserved with a magic vitality and hit you with strength and clarity. As you'll see from reading this part of the guide, visiting Sicily is a unique experience if you abandon yourself to the task.

In Chapter 23, we tell you everything you need to know to explore Palermo, Sicily's capital and southern Italy's largest art center. In Chapter 24, we recommend two very interesting destinations that you can easily visit as day-trips from Palermo: Cefalù, a fishing port and lovely seaside resort, and Segesta, famous for its remarkable Doric temple. To round out Part VII, in Chapter 25, we guide you through the highlights of Taormina and the rest of this wonderful region, which is rich in art and attractions.

Chapter 23

Palermo

The perfect word to describe Sicily is *unique* — it has unique architecture, unique cuisine, and a unique people, distinct from the rest of the Italian nation.

Why go to Sicily, you ask? Well, if you don't, you'll be missing out on a big chunk of Italy — bigger than Tuscany, bigger than Lombardy. In fact, Sicily is the largest of the Italian regions. The island's central position in the Mediterranean — Africa is only a day's sail away — has made it a strategic base since ancient times, and its rich volcanic soil has attracted colonizers and pillagers for just as long. No wonder Rome and Carthage used the island as a battleground. Though Sicily's northeast corner is separated from the mainland only by the sliver of the Straits of Messina, at its southernmost points it stretches farther south than Tunis.

Palermo is a busy modern port and is the political center of "new" Sicily — meaning from about 1060 onward. The invasions of the Arabs and then of the Normans, who ruled from Palermo for centuries, brought about a cultural mix that's still apparent in the fabulous works of art that have been preserved and in the traditions that have been handed down. (The Sicilian Parliament meets in the building that was the Norman palace.) Palermo was severely damaged by earthquakes in the early 20th century and was bombarded in World War II, and much of it seems to have never recovered. Although most visitors to Sicily arrive here, you'll find it easier to understand and appreciate Palermo after having seen other parts of the island.

The capital of Sicily since Norman times, Palermo boasts some of the region's finest art. Its churches alone are worth the visit, and its museums, in a region where museums are rather inadequate, are very good. Under a decaying facade, treasures await you, and a people bursting with energy and kindness are ready to help you enjoy your visit. Remember, though, that *respect* is the key word here, as well as *reserve* and *composure*.

Sicily

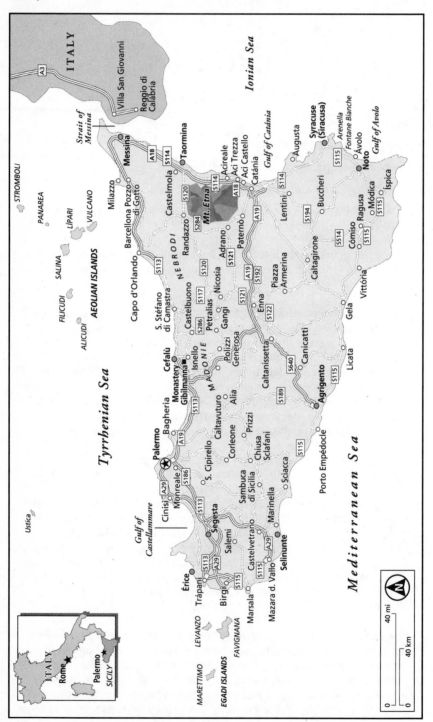

Palermo is a good starting point for exploring Sicily, especially if you're planning to take a guided tour. Indeed, tours start from here for each of the major attractions on the island. The other good starting point is Taormina (see Chapter 25).

Getting There

There are many ways to get to Sicily, but the best way, in our opinion, is to take the ferry.

By ferry

One of the newest and best ferries is the **SNAV SiciliaJet** (Via Giordano Bruno 84; ☎ **081-761-2348;** Fax: 081-761-2141; Internet: www.snavali. com), which takes only four hours between Naples and Palermo. It runs once a day, leaving from Palermo around 9:00 a.m. and from Naples around 5:30 p.m. The one-way fare is 52€ to 77.50€ ($46.80 to $69.75) for adults depending on the season; a car with two adults is 155€ to 253€ ($139.50 to $227.70) depending on the car size and the season, plus 2.17€ ($1.95) per person and 4.80€ ($4.32) per car in harbor taxes. The boat has 200 car and bus slots and takes 800 passengers. Ticketing offices are in the harbors of Naples (☎ **081-761-2348**) and Palermo (☎ **091-611-8525**).

The regular old-fashioned ferry run by **Tirrenia** (☎ **091-333-300** in Naples and 06-474-2041 in Rome; Internet: www.tirrenia.com) goes between Naples and Palermo overnight (ten hours) — a good deal because you save on a hotel for the night and don't use up daylight hours traveling. It's also cheap: A one-way adult fare is 62.49€ to 79.53€ ($56.24 to $71.57) for a double cabin (with bunk beds — very comfortable); a car costs 66.87€ to 100.96€ ($60.18 to $90.86). Note that Naples is about a two-hour train ride from Rome for about 18€ ($16.20).

By air

Flying is less romantic than taking the ferry but is still an excellent way to get to Sicily. Remember, though, that you can't fly directly in and out of Italy from Sicily — you have to fly into Rome or Milan first. **Air Sicilia** (☎ **06-6501-1046**) offers fares for about 150€ ($135) round-trip on its daily flights from Rome to Sicily. Alitalia (☎ **1478-65643** or 06-65643) has several flights a day and is slightly more expensive at about 175€ ($157.50). The flight lasts just over an hour. To find out about national departures, call ☎ **091-702-0302.**

Like Rome's Fiumicino, Palermo's airport, **Aeroporto Civile Punta Raisi** (☎ **091-591-414**), is referred to by its location and not by its actual name, the Aeroporto Falcone Borsellino. The airport is open daily from 8 a.m. to 11 p.m.

The bus company **Prestia & Comande** (☎ 091-580-457) runs the bus service between the airport and the Hotel Politeama and Stazione Centrale in Palermo. The bus runs every 30 minutes, and the fare is 4€ ($3.60). To get to the airport in a hurry if you're traveling light, you can take a helicopter from **Elitaxi** (☎ 091-227-350 or 091-227-068), leaving from Viale Regione Siciliana 544. The cost is 40€ ($36), double that if you have more than hand luggage. Regular helicopter flights are bunched in the early morning and the evening to correspond with the usual plane departures.

By train

The train (☎ 147-888-088 toll-free in Italy or 091-616-1806 or 091-616-7514) from Rome takes 11 to 13 hours and costs 40€ to 80€ ($36 to $72) per person, depending on whether it's a local or an express. A *cuccetta* (sleeping berth) runs about 20€ ($18). You don't save much, obviously, over the ferry, and the train takes longer. The train is put on a train ferry at Messina and continues on to Palermo. The train arrives at Palermo's **Stazione Centrale FS** (☎ 091-616-5914) on Piazza Giulio Cesare, very near the center of town.

By car

We don't recommend driving from Rome to Palermo, because the trip is a total of 1,050km (651 miles). In fact, we don't think you really want to go to Sicily by car at all, but if you must, take **A1** from Rome to Caserta, **A30** from Caserta to Salerno, and **A3** from Salerno to Villa San Giovanni, where you take the *traghetto* (ferry) for Messina. When in Messina, pick up **A18** to Catania and then **A19** from Catania to Palermo. The ferry from Villa San Giovanni to Messina is cheap at 12€ ($10.80) for the car, but when you add some tanks of gas at about $50 a pop and 10 or 11 hours of driving (much of the highway is narrow and constantly under construction), we don't think it makes sense.

While in Palermo, you can park in the lot on Via Spinuzza, in front of the Teatro Massimo; it costs 1.03€ (93¢) per hour from 8 a.m. to 8 p.m., then it's free overnight. You can buy the access card to the lot in most bars. **AMAT** (☎ 091-690-2690) manages this lot.

Orienting Yourself in Palermo

Palermo is a seaside city, organized around its busy port. Although the modern town sprawls between the mountains and the sea, the historic center and its sights are fairly concentrated; its neighborhoods reflect the various cultures that have dominated the city through history.

Palermo

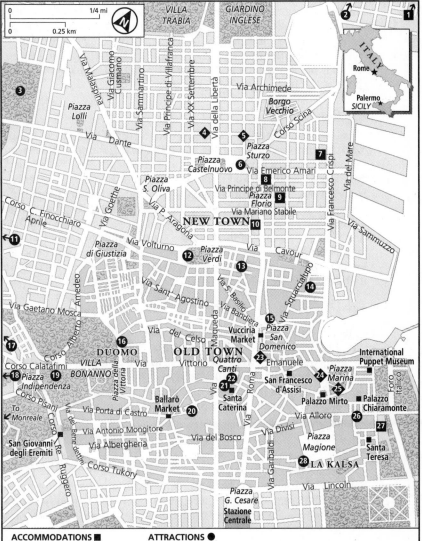

ACCOMMODATIONS ■
Cristal Palace Hotel **8**
Grand Hotel et des Palmes **10**
Grand Hotel Villa Igiea **1**
Joli Hotel **9**
Jolly Hotel **27**
President Hotel **7**

DINING ◆
Capricci di Sicilia **5**
Casa del Brodo **23**
Gourmand's **4**
I Beati Paoli **25**
La Cambusa **24**

ATTRACTIONS ●
Catacombe dei Cappuccini **17**
Casa Professa
    (Chiesa del Gesù) **20**
Chiesa di Santa Maria
    dell'Ammiraglio
    (La Martorana) **21**
Duomo **16**
Fontana Pretoria **22**
Galleria Regionale Siciliana
    (Palazzo Abatellis) **26**
La Cuba **18**
La Kalsa **28**

La Zisa **11**
Monte Pellegrino and
    Santuario di Santa Rosalia **2**
Museo Archeologico Regionale **13**
Oratorio del Santissimo Rosario
    di San Domenico **15**
Oratorio di Santa Cita **14**
Palazzo dei Normanni and
    Cappella Palatina **19**
Teatro Massimo **12**
Teatro Politeama Garibaldi **6**
Villa Malfitano **3**

Palermo by neighborhood

The historic part of Palermo is where most of the attractions are con-centrated. Although it's not that small, you can visit it on foot, pro-vided you make a logical plan — as usual, avoiding the up and down, east and west itineraries is best. The historic part can be divided into an older one (going back to the Arabian rulers) and a more recent one (built at the turn of the 20th century).

The Old Town

This is where Palermo's development started. The heart of the old city stretches from the old harbor, the **Cala,** to the **Palazzo dei Normanni,** the castle and royal residence of the various powers that reigned over Palermo (from the Arab Emirs to the current Regional Assembly of Sicily), along **Corso Vittorio Emanuele.** Cutting Corso Vittorio Emanuele at a right angle is **Via Maqueda,** the "new" avenue leading west to the modern part of the city. The crossing of these two arteries is the beau-tiful baroque square of the **Quattro Canti (four corners).** Here are such important monuments as **La Martorana,** the **Duomo,** the famous **Vucciria open-air market,** the **Regional Gallery (Galleria Regionale della Sicilia),** and the Arab neighborhood of **La Kalsa.**

The New Town

Of lesser interest, this part of town was developed in the late 19th cen-tury. Important here are the **Teatro Massimo,** the **Teatro Politeama** (its full name is the Teatro Politeama Garibaldi, but it's usually shortened), and **Via Libertà** with its Liberty (Italian Art Nouveau) palaces. This is central Palermo's most pleasant area, very popular with locals — the Politeama is the rendezvous place for people of every age — and boast-ing boutiques, restaurants, and hotels.

Monreale

A separate town yet so close it's almost a neighborhood, Monreale is to Palermo what Fiesole is to Florence, dominating the city from a beauti-ful hill. The great attraction here, sufficient alone to justify your whole trip to Sicily, is the **Duomo** with its cloister.

Street smarts: Where to get information after you arrive

The walk-in public office of the **Azienda Autonoma Provinciale per l'Incremento Turistico** is at Piazza Castelnuovo 34, across from the Teatro Politeama (☎ **091-583-847** or 091-605-8351; E-mail: aapit@ gestelnet.it; Internet: www.aapit.pa.it). It's open Monday through Friday from 8:30 a.m. to 2:00 p.m. and 2:30 to 6:00 p.m., and Saturday from 8:30 a.m. to 2:00 p.m. You can also find **tourist booths** at the airport (☎ 091-591-698) and at the train station (☎ 091-616-5914), both open daily from 9 a.m. to 6 p.m.

Getting Around Palermo

Palermo is an interesting city to discover on foot, and the only real safety problems are the purse snatchers (particularly effective and dangerous ones operate from *motorini,* or motor scooters) and pickpockets — be very careful, especially in the crowded Vucciria open-air market. Small backpacks are particularly attractive to these skilled thieves. This relative safety extends even to areas that by our standards may be a bit scary, such as the forlorn blocks with partially destroyed buildings — some by World War II bombings, others by earthquakes — that are visible in many parts of the old town.

When you're too tired to walk, you can easily take an **AMAT bus** (☎ 091-321-333), with single tickets costing .77€ (69¢) and day tickets 2.60€ ($2.34). Monreale is the one place where you really have to take a bus, unless you're traveling with a mule.

When you need to reach sights out of town, note that the *provincia* of Palermo is served by **AST** (☎ 091-688-2906).

Taxis are also a good way to get around, especially considering the traffic and the heat, which can make waiting for a bus uncomfortable. The basic charge for a taxi is 3.10€ ($2.80), and then small increments are added for every minute or kilometer. For a radio taxi, call ☎ 091-225-455, 091-512-727, or 091-682-5441.

We once got a taxi driver who awarded himself an inflation increase to 5€ ($4.50) because "rates haven't been adjusted since 1991." To avoid such problems, confirm up front where you're going and what the base price is (a long trip obviously costs more than the basic fee).

Where to Stay in Palermo

Because most of the sights are within walking distance of the center, having a central base is a good idea. In addition, because tourism isn't as highly developed here as it is in other major centers in Italy of comparable importance, hotels are much more old-fashioned than what you may be used to. Modern conveniences and private baths are definitely not the norm. On Sicily, even more than anywhere else in Italy, family-run hotels tend to feel as if you stepped into someone's home. But never fear: For better or worse, things are changing.

For the same reasons we just explained, if you're planning to pick a hotel that's not from our listing, remember that going for an el cheapo choice in Sicily doesn't pay in the long run.

The top hotels

Cristal Palace Hotel
$$ Politeama

Opened in 1990 as a member of the Hotels and Resorts Club, this central hotel occupies a converted bank building (a modern glass box but comfortable). The air-conditioned guest rooms have refrigerators/bars, hair dryers, and well-designed small baths. The furnishings are modern and streamlined (with an IKEA feel). The hotel has a restaurant, and the breakfast buffet includes ham and cheese as well as the usual pastries.

Via Roma 477/D, two blocks northeast of the Teatro Politeama. ☎ *091-611-2580. Fax: 091-611-2589. Rack rates: 118.68€ ($106.81) double, including buffet breakfast. AE, DC, MC, V.*

Grand Hotel et des Palmes
$$$ Via Roma

Once a private home, the Grand Hotel opened in 1874 and has since been the hotel to go to in central Palermo. Wagner finished writing his *Parsifal* here, and one of the guests in more recent times was Bill Clinton. The classically inspired lobby has marble floors, Greek columns, chandeliers, marble staircases, and Art Nouveau furnishings. Though the air-conditioned guest rooms can't match the level of the public spaces, they're well furnished and large. Meals are served in **La Palmetta Restaurant,** and the Hall of Mirrors (Sala degli Specchi) is used not only for receptions but also as the breakfast room — the breakfast is great, with eggs, meat, *cornetti* (Italian croissants), juices, and good coffee.

Via Roma 398, four blocks northeast of the Teatro Politeama. ☎ *091-583-933. Fax: 091-331-545. E-mail:* des-palmes@cormorano.net. *Parking: Garage $13.93€ ($12.55). Rack rates: 167.85€–191.09€ ($151.07–$171.98) double, including buffet breakfast. AE, DC, MC, V.*

Grand Hotel Villa Igiea
$$$$ North of the port area

This is one of the best hotels not only in Palermo but also on the whole island. Housed in a former private villa on the outskirts of town, the Grand Hotel Villa Igiea is a masterpiece of the Sicilian Liberty (Italian Art Nouveau) architect Ernesto Basile, who also designed the furnishings. The spacious guest rooms are as glamorous as the public areas, and the hotel is surrounded by splendid terraced gardens overlooking the bay. The two restaurants feature local and regional cuisine; in summer, meals are served on the elegant terrace overlooking Palermo. Other features include a piano bar, a seawater pool, and a meeting center for those with an entourage.

Salita Belmonte 43. ☎ ***091-543-744.*** *Fax: 091-547-654. E-mail:* villaigea-agent@cormorano.net. *Bus: 139 to Villa Igiea. Parking: Free. Rack rates: 177€–295€ ($159.30–$265.50) double, including breakfast. AE, DC, MC, V.*

Joli Hotel
$ Piazza Florio

This modest hotel, on a quiet square just north of the port, has been renovating one floor after another, and by the time you read this, the Joli should have doubled its size to 30 rooms and added a bar. All the air-conditioned guest rooms have small but functional baths and private terraces; some have views of Monte Pellegrino, the mountain overlooking Palermo. Although the hotel is small, it offers a pleasant lounge for guests.

Via Michele Amari 11, two blocks southeast of the Teatro Politeama. ☎ *and Fax:* ***091-611-1765*** *or 091-611-1766. Parking: Free. Rack rates: 72.30€ ($65.07) double. AE, DC, MC, V.*

Runner-up accommodations

Jolly Hotel
$$ Foro Italico

This pleasant modern place is surrounded by a garden with a pool. Although the guest rooms are moderate in size, some have balconies.

East of the harbor, near the train station. ☎ ***091-616-5090.*** *Fax: 091-616-1441.*

President Hotel
$$ Via Francesco Crispi

Across from the port where the ferries arrive, this hotel was renovated in 1999. All the guest rooms have air-conditioning, and rates include a buffet breakfast served in the restaurant with sunny views of the port and mountains.

Via Francesco Crispi 230, west of the harbor. ☎ ***091-580-733.*** *Fax: 091-611-1588.*

Where to Dine in Palermo

Sicily has a unique cuisine, even for Italy, which has so many regional variations. You can find dishes like Italian-looking pasta with pistachio nuts and North African spices — the Sicilians perfected multiculturalism centuries ago. And because Sicily is an island, its cuisine is full of things from the sea.

Typical Sicilian dishes are *pasta con le sarde* (pasta with shredded fresh sardines), *caponata* (cubed eggplant with other vegetables, spiced and sautéed), *tonno con aglio e menta* (fresh tuna with garlic and mint), and fish dishes with *finocchietto* (small fresh fennel, a common herb). If you want only a sandwich, go for *focacce,* the typical Palermo sandwich. Fill it with any number of things, from the excellent *caciocavallo* (typical cheese) to fried spleen. Yes, spleen, plus a little lung as well to make it better. We tried it and we have to say it was okay, especially if you're very hungry (it's definitely an acquired taste). Also excellent on the "fast food" side are *arancini* (deep-fried flavored rice balls) and *panelle* (chickpea fritters).

Sicilian desserts and pastries are famous. *Cassata* is a fabulous creation — the heart is ricotta mixed with sugar and candied fruit, which is covered with a layer of cake and then almond paste. Some say that gelato was even invented in Palermo.

The top restaurants

Casa del Brodo
$$ Vucciria SICILIAN

This trattoria, opened in 1890, claims to be the oldest in Palermo. If you choose to have the *antipasto,* you'll select from a buffet with a large variety of traditional specialties, all freshly prepared. The fresh fish dishes are great, as are the traditional *primi (pasta alla Norma, pasta con le sarde,* and so on). The old-fashioned ambience isn't a bit ruined by the air-conditioning. The restaurant is in a busy area of town and gets quite full at lunch.

Corso Vittorio Emanuele 175. ☎ 091-321-655. Reservations recommended on weekends. Bus: 104 to Quattro Canti or 105 to Corso Vittorio Emanuele, east of Via Roma. Secondi: 6.20€–10.30€ ($5.58–$9.30). MC, V. Open: Lunch and dinner Wed–Mon.

Gourmand's
$$$ Politeama SICILIAN

One of the best restaurants in Palermo, Gourmand's attracts foreigners and less adventurous customers for its tamer cuisine and reasonable prices. The *antipasti* are excellent, as is the grilled fish. In addition to typical Sicilian specialties, the menu includes a choice of dependable Italian dishes like *risotto al salmone* (risotto with salmon).

Viale della Libertà 37/A. ☎ 091-323-431. Reservations recommended on weekends. Bus: 101 and 102 to Via della Libertà. Secondi: 7.75€–15.49€ ($6.98–$13.94). AE, DC, MC, V. Open: Lunch and dinner Mon–Sat.; closed Aug.

La Cambusa
$$ **Piazza Marina** **SICILIAN**

Here you find excellent homemade-style typical fare. La Cambusa is very popular with the people of La Cala (the marina across the street) and other Palermitans, so come early — Sicilians eat at 9:00 or even 9:30 p.m. in summer — or be prepared to wait. Try the superb *pasta con le sarde* (pasta with sardines, fennel, and tomato sauce) or the *pasta alla carrettiera* (the Sicilian version of pesto sauce, with capers, almonds, and tomato).

Piazza Marina 16. ☎ *091-584-574. Reservations recommended on weekends. Bus: 105 to Piazza Marina. Secondi: 6.20€–12.91€ ($5.58–$11.62). MC, V. Open: Lunch and dinner Tues–Sun.*

Runner-up restaurants

Two excellent areas to find restaurants are the ones most popular with locals. Attracting younger crowds is the area around Piazza Marina, behind the recreational harbor of **La Cala;** the area around the **Teatro Politeama,** on Piazza Sturzo/Piazza Castelnuovo, is favored by slightly more mature customers. Two good examples follow.

Capricci di Sicilia
$$ **Piazza Sturzo**

In the more elegant part of the center, Capricci di Sicilia is an excellent restaurant offering typical recipes of the Sicilian tradition.

Via Istituto Pignatelli 6, off Piazza Sturzo to the northwest of the Teatro Politeama. ☎ *091-327-777.*

1 Beati Paoli
$$ **Piazza Marina**

Open only for dinner, this popular pizzeria has a lively young atmosphere. The menu also features a number of Sicilian specialties.

Piazza Marina 50. ☎ *091-616-6634.*

Exploring Palermo

Palermo has a depth and breadth of sights to suit every taste. Just walking around is fascinating in itself. You never know what you're going to stumble upon next as you stroll through the city, which has been the crossroads of the Mediterranean for centuries.

The top sights

Duomo (Cattedrale)

Palermo's Duomo was built in 1185 atop a mosque that was itself built atop a Byzantine church. In this mixed-up sandwich, some material was reused — in the portico is a column with an engraved inscription from the Koran (first on the left), an unusual feature for a Catholic church. In the 15th century, the south side became the main entrance, with a portico in Gothic-Catalan style. In the 18th century, the whole interior was redone in neoclassical style, and the lateral naves were added along with the dome. The apse is the original part of the church. The outside is a magnificent Romanesque in warm, pale ochres, but the inside is a shock of white and gray baroque. Look for the bas-reliefs by Vincenzo and Fazio Gagini on the altar and the *Madonna with Child* by Francesco Laurana in the seventh chapel of the left nave (Laurana's famous sculpture of Eleanora d'Aragona is in the Galleria Regionale Siciliana — see the description later in this chapter). The **imperial and royal tombs** include those of Frederick II and Roger II. The **Chapel of St. Rosalia (Cappella di Santa Rosalia)** contains the saint's remains, which are carried through the streets in a procession every July (see "More cool things to see and do" later in this chapter).

Piazza della Cattedrale, on Via Vittorio Emanuele. ☎ *091-334-376. Admission: Free. Open: Mon–Sat 7 a.m.–7 p.m., Sun and holidays 8:00 a.m.–1:30 p.m. and 4–7 p.m.*

Casa Professa (Chiesa del Gesù)

Most commonly called the Casa Professa, this is the first church in Sicily founded by the Jesuits. Its interior is rich in **stuccowork** by the Serpotta (famous 17th- and 18th-century Palermitan sculptors), and beautiful **marble inlays** in a large range of colors decorate the altar and walls. The original Renaissance church, in the form of a Latin cross (a nave and two short aisles), was designed by Giovanni Tristano in 1564. It was much changed in the following century by the Jesuit Natale Masuccio, who made it into one of the most ostentatious churches of the Sicilian baroque. A large part of the church was destroyed in 1943, but it was later restored.

Piazza Casa Professa, off Via Ponticello from Via Maqueda. ☎ *091-511-880. Admission: Free. Open: Mon–Sat 7:30–11:30 a.m. and 5:00–6:30 p.m., Sun 7:00 a.m.– 12:30 p.m.; no visits during mass.*

Chiesa di Santa Maria dell'Ammiraglio (La Martorana)

This church was built by the admiral of Ruggero II, Giorgio di Antiochia, in 1143, but it was transformed during later centuries. However, the original structure's beautiful **Byzantine mosaics** remain. The central scene depicts the heavenly hierarchy; in a bit of artistic politicking, a mosaic on the balustrade shows Roger II getting his crown directly from Christ and not from the pope. Other scenes are from the life of Mary. The name *Martorana* comes from the nearby convent, founded by the Martorana family. Tradition says that the nuns there invented the little marzipan fruits that today are a typical — and delicious — souvenir from Sicily. They still sell the original creations: sculptures of bunches of grapes made of almond paste, each grape delicately painted with sugar and the stems made of candied orange peel covered in dark chocolate — a bit expensive, yes, but a treat fit for a king.

Piazza Bellini 3, off Via Maqueda, near the Quattro Canti. ☎ *091-616-1692. Admission: 2.07€ ($1.86). Open: Mon–Sat 9:30 a.m.–1:00 p.m. and 3:30–5:30 p.m., Sun and holidays 8:30 a.m.–1:00 p.m.*

Duomo di Monreale

This 12th-century Romanesque church in Monreale is one of the most breathtaking in existence. It may not be exceptional for its Norman exterior — the Duomo in Palermo is more interesting — but the interior is extraordinary. The church is decorated with 6,000 square meters (55,000 square feet) of fabulous **Byzantine school mosaics,** whose subjects come from the Old and New Testaments, with the stories of Noah, Isaac, and Jacob most prominent. In the dome is a **Christ Pantocrator** icon (an image of Christ as the ruler of the universe, with his fingers making the Greek symbol of his divine and human nature). The apse's decorations show an Islamic influence. The floors are comprised of remarkable marble mosaics, and the bronze portals are masterpieces. Annexed to the church is the **cloister** from 1180, one of the most beautiful in Italy. It has 228 double columns, some with mosaic inlay and each with an individual pattern; the carved stone capitals are amazingly intricate renderings of scenes such as battles, the punishment of the damned, and stories of obscure meaning.

Piazza del Duomo in Monreale. ☎ *091-640-4413 or 091-640-4403 (cloister). Bus: 389 from Piazza Indipendenza, off the Palazzo dei Normanni, to Piazza del Duomo, running every 20 minutes. Admission: Duomo free, cloister 2.60€ ($2.34). Open: Duomo daily 8 a.m.–6 p.m.; cloister Mon–Sat 9 a.m.–12 p.m. and 3:30–5:30 p.m., Sun and holidays 9:00 a.m.–12:30 p.m.*

Fontana Pretoria

This magnificent 16th-century fountain was created for a Florentine villa, but when the villa's owner died, his son sold the fountain to the Palermo Senate. The nudes created a big scandal in town, and for a while it was called the "fountain of shame." The succession of concentric circular platforms are connected by stairways and balustrades. There are 4 basins on which 24 heads of monsters and animals face outward, 56 channels of water, 37 statues portraying mythological characters, and 4 large statues representing the rivers that fertilize the countryside around Palermo.

Piazza Pretoria, off the Quattro Canti, where Via Vittorio Emanuele crosses Via Maqueda.

Galleria Regionale Siciliana (Palazzo Abatellis)

In late Catalan Gothic style, the 1490 Palazzo Abbatellis houses the principal museum of Sicilian art from the 13th to the 18th centuries. The 15th-century *Triumph of Death* is a powerful and intriguing fresco that came from the hall of the 1330 Palazzo Sclafani. A skeleton on horseback fires arrows at pleasure seekers, rich prelates, and other sinners as the poor and ill look on (the two artists who did the fresco painted themselves in this group). The faces are incredible and expressive; Picasso could have done the horse's head. Antonello da Messina's *Madonna Annunziata,* looking out from under a blue mantle, displays Antonello's uncanny ability to portray more than one emotion at the same time. Francesco Laurana's **bust of Eleonora d'Aragona** is another masterpiece. These works are definitely worth the visit, even if many other pieces are of minor importance or in poor condition.

Via Alloro, near Piazza Marina. ☎ 091-623-0011. From Piazza Marina, cross the garden and take Via Quattro Aprile two blocks to Via Alloro; turn right and walk two blocks. Admission: 5.16€ ($4.64). Open: Mon–Sat 9:00 a.m.–1:30 p.m. (Tues and Thurs also 3:00–7:30 p.m.), Sun 8 a.m.–1 p.m.

La Kalsa

One of the city's oldest neighborhoods (it was built by the Arabs as the emir's citadel), La Kalsa developed around **Piazza Magione,** southeast of **Piazza Marina.** The grandiose battle scene between Garibaldi and the Bourbons in the famous Visconti movie *Il Gattopardo (The Leopard)* was filmed on Piazza Magione. Piazza Marina is one of La Kalsa's main features, with its beautiful garden enclosed by elegant Liberty-style iron railings and graced by an impressive giant ficus. **Via Alloro** was the central street of La Kalsa, as you can see from the once-elegant palaces lining the street. The nearby **Cala** is Palermo's original harbor.

Unfortunately, the rest of the neighborhood is quite grungy. Much of the Arabs' fine work was destroyed when the Spanish viceroys took over, adding their own architectural interpretations, and much of the later *palazzi* were damaged or destroyed by earthquakes and World War II, and are mostly semi-abandoned. For an idea of what they looked like in their former splendor, visit the restored 15th-century **Palazzo Abatellis,** seat of the Galleria Regionale Siciliana (see the description earlier in this chapter) and the early-20th-century **Palazzo Mirto** (Via Merlo 2; ☎ 091-616-4751); the latter is open Monday through Friday 9 a.m. to 1 p.m. and 3 to 7 p.m., and Saturday and Sunday 9:00 a.m. to 12:30 p.m., with a 3€ ($2.70) admission. Among the neighborhood's churches, visit **Santa Teresa** (Piazza Kalsa; ☎ 091-616-1658), a good example of the irrepressible Sicilian baroque, and the 13th-century **San Francesco d'Assisi** (Piazza San Francesco d'Assisi, off Via Merlo; ☎ 091-616-2819), with a superb 14th-century portal and handsome carvings inside. Both churches are closed in the early afternoon.

Unless you're a diehard urbanite, check out La Kalsa during the daytime. Its dark alleys and decaying buildings can be intimidating at night.

Defined by Via Maqueda, Corso Vittorio Emanuele, Via Lincoln, and the sea.

La Zisa

Also called Castello della Zisa, this building dates from 1165 to 1167 and is more a home than a castle. The castle is known for its elegant columns and mosaics and may have belonged to an Arab noblewoman, Azisa, or may have been built for King Guglielmo I (William) using Arab techniques and named Al-Aziz, the Magnificent. The palace was surrounded by a park with an artificial lake in which the building was reflected (a few hundred years before the Taj Mahal) and with small rivers and ponds for fish. The surrounding garden has disappeared, and the building suffered partial collapse in 1971 but was then restored. The second floor opens onto a beautiful courtyard. La Zisa also houses a collection of **Islamic art,** including the characteristic carved wooden screens known as *musciarabia.*

Piazza Guglielmo il Buono. ☎ *091-652-0269. Bus: 124 to Zisa, from Via Ruggero Settimo. Admission: 2€ ($1.80). Open: Mon–Sat 9:00 a.m.–1:30 p.m. and 3–6 p.m., Sun and holidays 9 a.m.–1 p.m.*

Monte Pellegrino and Santuario di Santa Rosalia

Rosalia is Palermo's patron saint. The young girl, niece of Guglielmo II, abandoned the riches of her royal family and took refuge in a cave on the mountain, where she prayed until her death (not unlike St. Francis, who also spurned his family's wealth in order to live a purer religious life). After her body was found, the cave became the site of a shrine/convent. An unforgettable view is offered from this 2,000-foot promontory — labeled by Goethe the most beautiful in the world — separating the bay of Palermo from the gulf of Mondello and its beaches. From its top, in good weather, you can see all the way to Etna and the Aeolian Islands. Toward the interior is a plain with beautiful villas. The flanks of Monte Pellegrino are filled with caves, some of which have Paleolithic carvings. The mountain is reached by Via Pietro Bonnano; the road to the top was finished only in the 1920s.

Monte Pellegrino, northeast of Palermo. Sanctuary: ☎ *091-540-326. Bus: 812 from Piazza Sturzo, off the Teatro Politeama.*

Museo Archeologico Regionale

This museum, built on the site of a monastery, is a good introduction to Sicily's ancient history. The best collections are on the ground floor, which has major art finds from Greek sites in southern Italy and some Roman art (as you pass through the cloister, you see a collection of Roman objects, including pieces from Pompeii). Remains from Selinunte, the site of an ancient Greek colony on Sicily's southwestern tip and today much damaged by looters, have an important place in the display. The collection was begun during the 19th century when the first *metope* (part of the frieze) from the site were found. The main salon has important finds from several of the temples, including the famous **head of Medusa.** The basement houses a reconstruction of the **clay decorations of Temple "C"** (a Greek temple built in 500 B.C. in Selinus, Italy), and in the Sala Marconi there's a partial reconstruction of the **cornice moldings** with lion heads from the Temple of Victory in Himera. There are beautiful **bronze statues** as well as a number of **Etruscan and Phoenician objects.**

Piazza P. Olivella 24, between Via Roma and Via Maqueda, near Via Cavour. ☎ *091-611-6805. Admission: 5.16€ ($4.3.64). Open: Daily 9:00 a.m.–1:15 p.m., Sun and holidays 9:00 a.m.–12:45 p.m.*

Oratorio del Santissimo Rosario di San Domenico

Sicilian sculptor Giacomo Serpotta belonged to this small chapel (oratory); though he excelled in the use of marble and polychrome, he chose stucco to lavishly decorate the oratory from 1714 to 1717, making it his masterpiece. Another member of the oratory was Pietro Novelli, who painted many of the walls and ceilings. The painting on the altar is a masterpiece by Anthony van Dyck, a *Madonna of the Rosary (Madonna del Rosario)* commissioned during his stay in Palermo in 1624 but painted four years later in Genoa.

Via dei Bambinai 2, off Via Roma, between La Cala and Via Maqueda. Admission: Free. Open: Mon–Fri 9 a.m.–1 p.m. and 2:00 p.m.–5:30 p.m., Sat 9 a.m.–1 p.m.

Palazzo dei Normanni and Cappella Palatina

The seat of the Sicilian Parliament, this *palazzo* boasts foundations going back to Punic and Roman times. In the 12th century, the Normans remodeled the palace, which had been the residence of the Arab Emir. It had four towers, of which only one remains today, the **Torre Pisana.** It was remodeled again in the 16th century to become the residence of the Spanish viceroy. The royal apartments are open to the public, but because of the parliamentary meetings, access is restricted (see details in the following paragraph). On the third floor is the **Sala di Ruggero,** originally Ruggero's bedroom, with mosaics representing hunting scenes and striking animals and plant forms. On the second floor is the famous **Palatine Chapel (Cappella Palatina),** with its impressive decorations. The chapel, started by Ruggero II in 1132, took over ten years to complete and is a harmony of masterwork from different cultures — Arab artisans made the inlaid wooden ceilings, Sicilians did the stonecutting, and the mosaics are Byzantine. The walls and dome are completely covered with rich mosaics representing scenes from the Old Testament (the nave), Christ's life (the southern transept), and scenes from the lives of Peter and Paul (the aisles). Note by the entryway the monolithic (made out of a single piece of stone) **candlestick,** intricately carved and over 13 feet tall.

Piazza Indipendenza, off Corso Calatafimi, through the Porta Nuova, on the other side of Piazza della Vittoria. ☎ 091-705-4879. Admission: Free. Open: Cappella Palatina Mon–Fri 9:00–11:45 a.m. and 3:00–4:45 p.m., Sat 9:00 a.m.–11:45 a.m., Sun 9:00–9:45 a.m. and 12:00–12:45 p.m.; royal apartments, call the Questura at ☎ 091-656-1737 to arrange a visit Mon, Fri, and Sat 9:00–11:45 a.m.

Teatro Massimo

Begun in 1875 but not completed until 1897, this building cost a fortune and was Italy's largest and most splendid theater at a time when Palermo didn't even have a good hospital. The theater is a masterpiece of Liberty style (Italian Art Nouveau) and was designed by Gian Battista and Ernesto Basile, the famous Sicilian father-and-son Art Nouveau stylists. The stage and back stage measure 1,280 square meters (12,000 square feet), the second largest in Europe after the Opéra Garnier in Paris. Its greatest marvel is a **painted ceiling** with 11 panels that open like flower petals to let heat escape from the interior during intermissions. The only change that has been made since the building's conception has been to lay a wood floor for better acoustics. The building was not only a theater but also a meeting place, and these rooms were used for important business and political meetings. The most famous is the **Sala Pompeiana,** at the level of the second loggia, where the men would meet; it's designed so that the sound of voices would keep bouncing from wall to wall and not get out of the room and disturb the performance. After 23 years of closure for restoration, the theater reopened in 1997.

Piazza Verdi, west on Via Maqueda. ☎ 091-334-246 to make an appointment for a visit to the theater or ☎ 091-605-3515 for tickets. Admission: Free.

Villa Malfitano

This great Liberty-style villa lies within one of the city's most spectacular gardens. It was built in 1886 by Joseph Whitaker, who arranged to have trees shipped here from all over the world and planted around his villa. High society in Palermo flocked here for lavish parties, and royalty from Great Britain visited. The villa today is lavishly furnished with antiques and artifacts from all over the world. The **Summer Room (Sala d'Estata)** is particularly stunning, with trompe-l'oeil frescoes covering the walls and ceiling.

Via Dante 167. ☎ 091-681-6133. Admission: 2.60€ ($2.34). Open: Mon–Fri 9:00 a.m.– 12:30 p.m.

More cool things to see and do

The major sites of Palermo are stunning, but there's still much more to see and do — as well as things to eat. Here are a few recommendations:

✔ If you happen to be in Palermo in July, the **Festa di Santa Rosalia** (July 11 through July 15) is an interesting event celebrating the anniversary of the discovery of the saint's remains many centuries after her death. Niece of Norman King Guglielmo II, Rosalia abandoned the palace for a cave on Monte Pellegrino (see the description earlier in this chapter) to live a life of prayer. During the terrible plague epidemic of 1624, her bones were found and brought down the mountain. As the procession bringing her remains traversed the city, the epidemic miraculously stopped (a good reason to keep celebrating her!). During the festival, a religious procession with a beautifully decorated, huge triumphal carriage carrying an orchestra wends through the town. There's also a spectacular candlelit procession up Monte Pellegrino to Santa Rosalia's cave. The end of the festival is marked by great fireworks.

✔ If you're into catacombs, or you're just a tad morbid, go to the **Catacombe dei Cappuccini** (Piazza Cappuccini; ☎ 091-212-117) to see 8,000 mummified bodies of aristocratic Sicilians and priests, still dressed in the costumes of their time. The catacombs were used as a burial spot, or rather a repository, for mummified remains until 1920. It's open Monday through Saturday from 9 a.m. to noon and 3:00 to 5:30 p.m., with a 1.03€ (93¢) admission charge.

✔ The city has three much-visited traditional **food markets,** where fruits, vegetables, meat, and fish provide an explosion of colors and flavors. **La Vucciria,** whose name comes from the French word *boucherie* ("meat store"), is in La Kalsa and goes along Via Argenteria to Piazza Garraffello. The **Ballarò** is our preferred market — Palermo's oldest, running from Piazza Casa Professa to Corso Tukory toward Porta Sant'Agata. It's connected to the market of Casa Professa (selling shoes and secondhand clothes); this market was called the *mercato americano* because, for a long time, secondhand clothes came to Italy from the United States in huge bundles, with everything from swimsuits to nightgowns to ski clothes and fur coats! Smaller and less lively, **Il Capo** covers Via Carini and Via Beati Paoli, crossing Via Sant'Agostino and Via Cappuccinelle. The three markets are shown in blue on the free city map you find in hotels and at the tourist office. In all the markets, beware of potential purse snatchers and pickpockets riding *motorini.*

✔ **La Cuba** (Corso Calatafimi 100, inside the Caserma Tukory; ☎ 091-590-299), a dome surrounded by gardens, is a striking example of Arab and early Norman architecture. It was built by Guglielmo II in 1180 in the Park of Genoardo; its beauty was so famous that Boccaccio used it in the Decameron. The building is only one floor, organized around a central space with a star-shaped fountain. Today only the external walls and giant arches remain. It's open Monday through Saturday from 9:00 a.m. to 1:30 p.m. and 3 to 6 p.m. and Sunday from 9 a.m. to 1 p.m., with a 2.60€ ($2.34) admission.

✔ If you fell in love with the work of Giacomo Serpotta, you should add to your schedule a visit to the **Oratorio di Santa Cita** (Via Valverde 3, off Via Squarcialupo, between Via Cavour and Via Roma, on the left of the church; ☎ 091-332-779). Famous for his stucco *putti* (cherubs), the Sicilian sculptor worked here between 1687 and 1718, creating a whole world of stucco figures and reliefs. The church is open Monday through Friday from 8 a.m. to 12 p.m. and Saturday from 9 a.m. to 1 p.m.; admission is free.

Seeing Palermo by guided tour

Palermo's city bus company, **AMAT** (Via Alfonso Borrelli 16; ☎ 091-350-415; Fax: 091-350-415; E-mail: amat.ced@ita.flashnet.it; Internet: www.amat.pa.it), offers seven sightseeing tours daily. All tours are bilingual, last three hours, cost 10.33€ ($9.29), and start at Via Mariano Stabile at the corner of Via Ruggero Settimo at 9 a.m. (a few have a second round at 3 p.m.). You can buy tickets from travel agencies and hotels, at the AMAT office, or directly on the bus. The entrance fees to attractions visited along the way aren't included. Tour 1 includes the Museo Archeologico, the Duomo, and the Cappella Palatina. Tour 6 includes La Zisa, the Catacombe dei Cappuccini, and the Duomo di Monreale. A longer itinerary of the historic center of Palermo and Monreale leaves daily at 9 a.m.

CST (Via A. Amari 124; ☎ **091-582-294**; Fax: 091-582-218; 24-hour service at 0348-343-6104) offers a one-day tour of Palermo and Monreale for 23.24€ ($20.92), leaving Saturdays at 9 a.m. It also offers a choice of day-trips from Palermo to all other major destinations in Sicily: The trip to Etna/Taormina is 61.97€ ($55.77), leaving Tuesdays at 7 a.m.; to Segesta/Erice/Trapani 46.48€ ($41.83), leaving Sundays at 8 a.m.; and to Agrigento/Piazza Armerina 46.48€ ($41.83), leaving Thursdays at 7:30 a.m.

Carriage tours of Palermo (☎ **0338-755-9021**) leave from the following locations in town: Piazza Marina, Piazza San Domenico, Piazza Massimo, Stazione Centrale SF, and Palazzo delle Aquile. The price is 30€ ($27) per hour for a maximum of four people.

The city-sponsored organization **Palermo Open Doors** (☎ 091-350-415) offers free guided tours. On every weekend for a month (usually May), students accompany visitors around Palermo as guides. A shuttle bus is available to connect the sights. Call for an appointment.

Shopping

Shopping isn't Palermo's strong suit, unless you're buying **swordfish, tuna,** or **almond paste.** The city has some of Italy's best open-air food markets (see "More cool things to see and do," earlier in this chapter), notable for the freshness and quality of their produce, and they offer some great deals. Alas, visitors can't take advantage of this fact: How are you going to explain that pound of homemade Sicilian pesto or that bunch of dried red peppers to Customs back home? Of course, you can buy things for a picnic (great for one of the out-of-town excursions or for a snack in the gardens of Piazza Marina).

Palermitans are very keen on dressing up — with a somewhat different style than you find in other Italian cities but always quite refined — and the center of town offers some nice clothes shops. For the best shopping, try the streets south of the Politeama, especially **Via Ruggero Settimo** (which becomes **Via Maqueda**) and **Via Roma** and the smaller streets in between, such as **Via Principe di Belmonte.**

Regarding other typical Sicilian goods, besides the **models of Sicilian carts** and **puppets** that you find in stands at most tourist sites, Sicily is famous for its **pottery.** In Palermo are works from the three Sicilian schools of Santo Stefano di Camastra, Caltagirone, and Sciacca. Try **Via E. Amari,** running from the Politeama to the port; it has a number of very reliable ceramic shops. **De Simone** has two shops, one at Via Gaetano Daita 13/B (☎ 091-584-876) and one at Via Principe de Scalea 698 (☎ 091-671-1005), where they also have their factory; **Verde Italiano** at Via Principe di Villafranca 42 (☎ 091-320-282) also has a shop and a factory that you can tour.

Nightlife

Nightlife in Palermo has been picking up steadily after the dark years of the 1980s, when people were almost too afraid to walk the streets. Like all Italians, Sicilians like to eat out, especially at an outdoor terrace in the good season, as evening entertainment. Sicilians, especially young ones, love to dance, and Palermo is home to dozens of discos.

The performing arts

Opera and ballet performances take place in the **Teatro Politeama Garibaldi** (Piazza Ruggero VII; ☎ 091-605-3315). Like everything else in Sicily, tickets are reasonably priced at about 20€ to 30€ ($18 to $27). The revived **Teatro Massimo** (Piazza Verdi; ☎ 091-605-3315) also hosts concert and opera performances. The season runs from October through June.

Another interesting entertainment is the traditional **Puppet Theater (Teatro dei Pupi).** The *pupi* became popular in the 18th century and, dressed in armor and bright-colored fabrics, tell tales of Orlando and the Paladins of France (who, however, think and act in a perfectly

Sicilian way). They usually stage fights against the Saracens, in which the audience participates actively. A few decades ago, Palermo boasted more than ten companies, but today the companies that are left perform only on request or on weekends in summer. The best is at the **Teatro Arte Cuticchio — Opera dei Pupi e Laboratorio** (Via Bara all'Olivella 95; ☎ 091-323-400). November through June, shows are Saturday and Sunday at 5:30 p.m. and cost 6€ ($5.40) adults and 3€ ($2.70) children; the theater also contains a museum with a collection of *pupi,* machines, and special effects you can see for 1.50€ ($1.35). In Monreale, there's the **Compagnia Munna** (Cortile Manin 15; ☎ 091-640-4542), with shows Sundays at 5 p.m. for the same price.

Discos, bars, and pubs

A popular disco is **Il Cerchio** (Viale Strasburgo 312; ☎ 091-688-5421), which is only open Fridays and Saturdays; two others are **Kandinsky** (Discesa Tonnara 4; ☎ 091-637-6511) and **Dancing Club** (Viale Piemonte 16; ☎ 091-348-917). If you want to have a drink in a piano bar, try **Escargot** (Via Generale Magliocco 15; ☎ 091-321-366).

Pubs have also swept through Palermo (like other Italian cities) and have really funny names. Try **Hot Dog** (Piazza Amendola, four blocks west of — and up from — the Teatro Politeama; ☎ 091-328-756), **Kovacs** (Via della Libertà 6; ☎ 091-611-5151), or **The Navy** (Via della Cala 46, off the marina; ☎ 091-323-032) for a good beer.

A more Italian trend is the *enoteche,* the Italian answer to an English pub. Very popular all over Italy, they are places where you can sample some nice wine and have a light snack — sometimes a real dinner. A good one of these *enoteche* is **Ai Vini d'Oro** (Piazza Nascé 11; ☎ 091-585-647).

Fast Facts: Palermo

Country Code and City Code

The country code for Italy is **39.** The city code for Palermo is **091;** use this code when calling from anywhere outside or inside Italy, even within Palermo itself (include the 0 every time, even when calling from abroad).

Currency Exchange

You can find exchange booths in the airport and scattered around town, especially in the center. You can also exchange currency at the many banks in town or use their ATMs.

Doctors

The emergency doctor for tourists (Guardia Medica Turistica) is at ☎ **091-532-798.**

Embassies and Consulates

The U.S. Consulate is at Via Vaccarini 1 (☎ 091-305-857) and the U.K. Consulate is at Via Cavour 117 (☎ 091-326-412); for other embassies and consulates, see "Fast Facts: Naples" in Chapter 20 and "Fast Facts: Rome" in Chapter 12.

Emergencies

Ambulance, ☎ **118**; Red Cross Ambulance, ☎ **091-306-644**; Fire, ☎ **115**; Road Police (Polizia Stradale), ☎ **091-656-9111**.

Hospital

The Ospedale Civico is at Via Carmelo Lazzaro (☎ 091-606-2207 or 091-606-2207).

Information

The Azienda Autonoma Provinciale per l'Incremento Turistico is at Piazza Castelnuovo 34, across from the Teatro Politeama (☎ 091-583-847 or 091-605-8351; E-mail: aapit@gestelnet.it; Internet: www.aapit.pa.it). Hours are Monday through Friday 8:30 a.m.–2:00 p.m. and 2:30 p.m.–6:00 p.m., and Saturday 8:30 a.m.–2:00 p.m. There are also information booths at the train station (☎091-616-5914; same hours) and the airport (☎091-591-698; open Monday through Friday 8 a.m. to midnight and Saturday and Sunday 8 a.m.–8 p.m.; closed holidays).

Pharmacy

Several pharmacies are open at night in Palermo. Among the most central are Farma Taxi (Via Libertà 54; ☎ 091-309-8098) and Farmacia Pensabene (Via Mariano Stabile, off Teatro Massimo; ☎ 091-334-482).

Police

Call ☎ **113**; for the Carabinieri, call ☎ **112**.

Restrooms

Museums have public toilets. The best bet for a restroom is to go to a nice-looking cafe (though you'll have to buy something, like a cup of coffee).

Safety

Palermo's historic districts are quite safe except for the pickpockets and purse snatchers on *motorini*. They concentrate in tourist areas, public transportation, and crowded open-air markets like the Vucciria.

Smoking

Smoking is allowed in cafes and restaurants and is very common. Unfortunately for non-smokers, finding a restaurant with a no-smoking area is almost impossible, though some are beginning to appear.

Taxes

Palermo has no local tax. Other taxes are always included in the prices quoted. You can get a refund of the 19% IVA (value-added tax) for purchases above 163€ ($160). See Chapter 4.

Transit/Tourist Assistance

The 24-hour tourist assistance hotline is toll-free ☎ 167-234-169. You can call ☎ 147-888-088 daily 7 a.m. to 9 p.m. for the FS, the state railroad.

Weather Updates

For forecasts, the best bet is to watch the news on TV (you can't call to get weather forecasts as you can in the U.S.). On the Web, you can check http://meteo.tiscalinet.it.

Web Sites

Try the tourist office site, www.aapit.pa.it, or the city's own Web site, www.comune.palermo.it (although much of the information is in Italian, you can find all kinds of information on the city).

Chapter 24

Side Trips from Palermo

In This Chapter

▶ Visiting Greek ruins in Segesta

▶ Basking in the Mediterranean Sea in Cefalù

You can reach many interesting places as day-trips from Palermo. In this chapter, we describe two of the closest and best: one choice for those who are insatiable explorers of antiquity and another for those who like a mix that includes more epicurean pleasures.

Segesta: Home of a Remarkable Doric Temple

Segesta contains one of the best-preserved Doric temples in existence and is set in wonderful surroundings. It was the most important town in this part of Sicily in ancient times and was long in conflict with Athens and Syracuse. Segesta was allied to Carthage but was sacked by the Siracusans and later fell into the hands of the Romans. The origin of the people who founded Segesta is a mystery, however; known as the Elyminians, they may have been related to the Trojans and came to Sicily in the 13th century B.C. Small enough to be visited in half a day, Segesta is a perfect break from Palermo and a trip farther back in time.

Getting there

One **train** per day leaves at 6:42 a.m. from Palermo and stops at Segesta Tempio; the return train comes through around 1 p.m. The trip from Palermo lasts about 45 minutes and costs about 6€ ($5.40). You then have to walk about 20 minutes uphill to get to the temples. If this sounds awfully early to get up to see ruins, consider that the temperatures in Sicily are on a level with those of North Africa. In the hot months, many people do nothing but stay inside with the shutters closed to block out the heat for most of the afternoon.

Segesta is about 75km (47 miles) from Palermo. If you're **driving,** take **A29** to Trapani/Mazara del Vallo and stay on the branch that goes to Trapani; Segesta is the first exit.

The bus company **Segesta** (☎ **091-616-7919**) has a regular service between Segesta and Palermo. During the theater season (see the listing for Teatro Greco, later in this chapter), **Noema Viaggi** (Via di Marzo 13; ☎ **091-625-4221**) runs buses to the site for 5€ ($4.50).

Taking a tour

A number of companies organize excursions to Segesta from Palermo. One, **CST** (Via A. Amari 124; ☎ **091-582-294;** Fax: 091-582-218; 24-hour service at ☎ 0348-343-6104) offers a tour of Segesta, Erice, and Trapani for 46.48€ ($41.83), leaving Palermo at 8 a.m. on Sundays.

Seeing the sights

Little remains of Segesta today, but what's left is worth seeing. On a beautiful — and unfortunately steep — hill rise the two symbols of Greek culture: a temple and a theater.

Tempio Greco

An impressive sight amid the greenery, the Doric temple is on the top of the hill, commanding a superb vista over the countryside. Built in the fifth century B.C., the temple was never quite finished, but it still stands and is exceptionally well preserved. Its 36 columns are topped by the entabulature with two fronts. All the parts are smooth, without decorations.

Teatro Greco

Near the temple, on the side of the hill, is this third-century-B.C. theater, the site of classical performances in summer. The season alternates yearly with the one in the Greek theater of Syracuse (see Chapter 25); dramas are performed in Segesta in odd-numbered years. During the season, special buses run from Palermo (see "Getting There," earlier in this chapter). Contact the **Istituto Nazionale del Dramma Antico** (Corso G. Matteotti 29, 96100 Siracusa; ☎ **0931-67-415** or 1478-82-211 toll-free in Italy) for a schedule of events, or call Palermo's tourist office (see Chapter 23).

Soaking Up Rays in Cefalù

Just a few miles from Palermo, **Cefalù** is a popular day trip. Young people from the capital like to come here for a romantic dinner by the sea or a day at the beach. The reverse is also true, and young people from Cefalù like to go for a wild night in Palermo. A small fishing village today transformed into a quiet seaside resort, Cefalù has many an attraction to offer (you may recognize it if you saw the Oscar-winning film *Cinema Paradiso*), such as its splendid location and its cathedral.

Getting there

Frequent **trains** run to Cefalù from Palermo (about once an hour); the trip lasts about an hour and costs about 4€ ($3.60).

Cefalù is 81km (51 miles) from Palermo. If you have a **car,** take **A20** toward Bagheria, Termini Imerese, and Messina and get off at the exit for Cefalù. Alternatively, take the coastal *strada statale* **SS113,** a panoramic roadway but narrow and much slower.

Seeing the sights

Dominated by the *rocca* **(clifftop fort),** Cefalù has been famous for its beauty since Greek times. Nature graced it with a nice sandy beach, scenic rocks, and a promontory, and the Normans made it over in splendid style. After Roger II survived a terrible storm at sea, he promised to build a cathedral that would be visible from the water — and he built it at Cefalù, where he landed after the storm. The best views are from the cliff. If you have some time and dare the steep ascent, the *rocca* is just above the village, surrounded by walls.

Duomo

Begun in 1131, the cathedral is a perfect fusion of Norman architecture, Arab craftsmanship and art, and Byzantine principles. After a period of abandonment, it was restored in 1240 and reconsecrated in 1267. Inside, the church is dominated by the golden mosaics, particularly the one in the apse: a beautiful example of a Byzantine **Christ Pantocrator.** Outside, the imposing facade is typically Norman and characterized by two powerful towers. Note that the dress code is strictly enforced: No bare legs above the knee or bare shoulders are allowed (they sometimes very kindly hand out shawls).

Piazza del Duomo, off Corso Ruggero. ☎ *0921-922-021. Admission: Free. Open: Daily 8:30 a.m. to noon and 3:30–6:30 p.m.*

Lavatoio Medievale

Another interesting sight is the medieval washing place, fed by a rich spring flowing from the mountains. It was an important meeting place in medieval times, but the spring has been used since time immemorial. Sailors (going back to the Phoenicians) have always stopped here to get water.

Off Via Vittorio Emanuele, indicated by a sign. Admission: Free. Open: Daily sunrise to sunset.

Museo Mandralisca

This museum is not really worth the detour, even though it has the famous **Ritratto di Ignoto,** the portrait of a man smiling an almost drunken grin, by Antonello da Messina. Yes, it's a great work of art, but it's currently displayed so inaccessibly that you may get a better view from a postcard. The rest of the collection is odd: very detailed displays of Greek ceramics, stuffed birds and mammals of the region, and many paintings in poor condition.

Via Mandralisca 13. ☎ 0921-21-547. Admission: 2.58€ ($2.32). Open: Daily 9:30 a.m.– 12:30 p.m. and 4–6 p.m.

Where to stay in Cefalù

Cefalù is a popular seaside resort, so it has many hotels. If you want to stop for a dip, the beach is beautiful and easily accessible. If you're on a driving tour of Sicily, Cefalù may be a convenient place to stop, swim, and rest. If you decide to stay over rather than continue, the Hotel Villa Belvedere is one good place to stay without paying spa prices.

Hotel Villa Belvedere
$ Cefalù

The hotel is just a walk away from the beach and from the town, it has a nice outdoor terrace, and parking is free. The guest rooms are simple and clean, with all the basics.

Via dei Mulini 13. ☎ 0921-21-593. Fax: 0921-21-845. Parking: Free. Rack rates: 51.85€–103.29€ ($46.66–$92.96) double. No credit cards accepted.

Where to dine in Cefalù

The town has many restaurants from which to choose. One of the nicest is the following.

Lo Scoglio Ubriaco
$ Cefalù SICILIAN/PIZZA

This restaurant has a great terrace overlooking the sea and the "drunken rock" after which it's named. One of the legends explaining the origin of the name is that a ship carrying wine broke apart on that rock; another says that the shape of the rock makes it seem as if it moves when you stare at it, therefore inducing the impression that you're drunk. The place serves pizza and typical Sicilian fare — and some great local wine. The rock moved, indeed.

Via Bordonaro 2. ☎ 0921-423-370. Secondi: 6.20€–12.91€ ($5.58–$11.62). Open: Lunch and dinner Tues–Sun.

Chapter 25

Taormina and the Rest of Sicily

● ●

In This Chapter

▶ Touring Taormina

▶ Viewing the past and present in Syracuse

▶ Visiting the Valley of the Temples in Agrigento

● ●

*I*nhabited since prehistoric times, Sicily has always been a coveted —
and conquested — land. The Sicani and Siculi (the people of Italic
origin who gave the name to the island) traded with the Phoenicians,
who established colonies along the coast. The Phoenicians shared the
island with the Greeks during the eighth century B.C., but the Greeks
eventually took over, and Sicily became a shining center for their art
and philosophy. The Carthaginians, Romans, and Byzantines followed,
each leaving their mark on Sicily's culture.

The Arabs landed in 827 and ruled Sicily for more than two centuries.
In 1060, they were displaced by the Normans, who established a feudal
kingdom — and reigned until they too were eclipsed, in favor of the
French dynasty of the d'Angió. After only 20 years of this government,
a revolution started in Palermo (the Vespri Siciliani of 1282) and ended
French power, opening a short period of political autonomy under the
local feudal families (particularly the Chiaramonte). Sicily was brought
under the Spanish Crown in 1415 (first Aragona, and later the
Bourbons, who ruled from 1735 until the unification of Italy in 1860).

Thus, Sicily has been shaped, culturally and physically, by each of its
rulers. The ancient ruins (Phoenician sites, Greek amphitheaters and
temples, Roman theaters and villas) mingle with stern Norman palaces
and cathedrals, softened and embellished by Byzantine and Arab art.
No complete Arab building remains — the 500 mosques that existed
under their rule were destroyed — but they left a permanent mark with
their introduction of citrus fruits, one of the symbols of Sicily.

Sicily offers some of Italy's most splendid examples of baroque architecture. After the ravages of World War II and decades of neglect, most
of these jewels are in bad need of repair. Luckily, a slow process of
recuperation has started, bringing glory back to Sicilian architecture.

What's Where: Sicily and Its Major Attractions

Sicily is roughly triangular in shape, with one corner — the city of Messina — almost touching the boot of Italy. And it feels like a mini-continent, with mountains, beautiful beaches, central agricultural plains, and the giant volcano **Etna.** In Chapter 23, we talk about the region's capital **Palermo,** on the northern shore of the island.

On the eastern shore, near Etna and south of Messina, is **Taormina,** founded by Andromachus in 358 B.C. This Greek city-state changed hands many times during the following millennium and was sacked by Arabs and Normans before sinking into obscurity for several hundred years. Fortunately, tourists like the German writer Goethe (see Chapter 27 for more on his Italian travelogues) rediscovered it in the 18th and 19th centuries.

Taormina backed the Romans in the Punic Wars, which resulted in a glorious period between the third century B.C. and the end of the Roman Empire. The **Greco-Roman Theater (Teatro Greco-Romano)** that remains is one of the great archaeological treasures of the island. Taormina makes an excellent starting point for visiting the rest of the region, so much so that many travel agencies are based in Taormina and offer guided tours to most destinations in Sicily. (See "And on your left, Etna: Seeing Taormina's environs by guided tour," for more information.)

South of Taormina and close to the island's southeast corner is **Syracuse (Siracusa),** an ancient Greek colony that once rivaled the great cities of the mother country (like Athens). The island on which Syracuse began, **Ortigia,** was the home of Calypso, who kept Odysseus captive for seven years. The Corinthians founded Syracuse in the eighth century B.C. Like the rest of Sicily, the city was swept up in the Punic Wars between Rome and Carthage, but despite the genius of Archimedes, who died in the Roman siege, it wound up on the losing side. Syracuse's **Archaeological Zone (Zona Archeologica)** contains two theaters and the quarries where stone was excavated to build the monuments in town. The city's beautiful harbor, perfectly positioned to trade with and control the eastern and western Mediterranean, has seen many tyrants (like Dionysius I) and invaders come and go. Today Syracuse is a beautiful stone city shimmering somewhat sleepily by the sea (the summer heat is unbelievable). Nearby is the unique baroque city of **Noto.**

Between Syracuse and Agrigento, along the southern shore of Sicily, is a vast and mainly agricultural area. Dominating the southern shore, **Agrigento** was another important Greek city, one of the most beautiful of the ancient world; the Greek poet Pindar admired it deeply.

Agrigento reached great heights in art and culture in the third century B.C. but saw its fortunes wax and wane with those of the Roman Empire. The **Valley of the Temples (Valle dei Templi),** where the ancient city once stood, is one of the most dramatic classical ruins anywhere in the Mediterranean. Farther up the hill from the ruins stands modern Agrigento, a small town that most visitors bypass.

Taormina: The Ideal Vista

Taking its name from Monte Taurus, the cliff dominating the sea over **Taormina,** this small town was a forgotten medieval village until the end of the 18th century, when European artists began to celebrate it as the "ideal vista." Indeed, Taormina is a unique panorama, with the sea on one side and snow-capped Etna smoking on the other.

Taormina is actually the second town built at this location. In the fifth century B.C., Dionysius I of Syracuse destroyed the first, Naxos (today the seaside resort of Giardini Naxos), which lies below, near the water. The residents prudently moved to the top of the cliffs, though that didn't save them from further invasions. Taormina flourished during the Roman period and received the coveted status of Roman colony under Augustus. After the empire ended, the city of Taormina declined and was twice laid waste by the Arabs. Roger II took over the city in 1078 for the Normans.

Today, Taormina counts about 10,000 residents and 900,000 visitors per year, which averages about 2,500 visitors per day. Consider that 80% of these visitors are non-Italians and that this figure includes only those visitors who stay overnight; many others just pass through for the day (you may find it odd that crowded Taormina was a haunt of Greta Garbo, who "wanted to be alone"). Taormina isn't a stranger to wealth and glamour, with many magnificent villas and famous visitors past and present.

Getting there

You can get to Taormina via **train,** from Palermo (with one change in Messina), as well as from Catania and Syracuse (direct, no change). The ride from Palermo is approximately 4½ hours at 12€ ($10.80), the ride from Catania is 50 minutes at 3.25€ ($2.92), and the ride from Syracuse is 2¼ hours at 7€ ($6.30).

Trains arrive at the **Stazione F.S. di Taormina** (Via Nazionale; ☎ **0942-51-026** or 0942-51-511), located a little down the hill, below Taormina's center, in Villagonia. From the station, you can catch a bus to the center of town every 15 to 45 minutes, depending on the season and hour of the day, for 1.17€ ($1.30).

Taormina

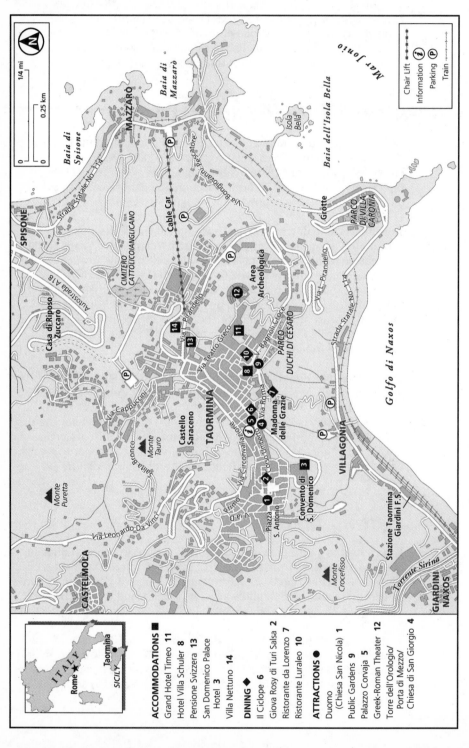

ACCOMMODATIONS ■
Grand Hotel Timeo **11**
Hotel Villa Schuler **8**
Pensione Svizzera **13**
San Domenico Palace
Hotel **3**
Villa Nettuno **14**

DINING ◆
Il Ciclope **6**
Giova Rosy di Turi Salsa **2**
Ristorante da Lorenzo **7**
Ristorante Luraleo **10**

ATTRACTIONS ●
Duomo
(Chiesa San Nicola) **1**
Public Gardens **9**
Palazzo Corvaja **5**
Greek-Roman Theater **12**
Torre dell'Orologio/
Porta di Mezzo/
Chiesa di San Giorgio **4**

Taormina is 250km (150 miles) from Palermo, 50km (30 miles) from Catania, and 41km (22 miles) from Messina. If you're **driving** from Catania or Messina, take the **A18** and exit at Taormina. From Palermo, the fastest route is **A19,** which runs briefly along the coast and then cuts cross-country to Catania, where you pick up A18. Taormina's center is pedestrian only, so you have to leave your car at the entrance of town. The best place to leave your car is just after the highway exit for Taormina, in the large city parking lot **Parcheggio Lumbi** at the base of the hill. A shuttle bus runs from the parking lot to town every few minutes. If your hotel has parking, then park your car there.

The **bus company SAIS (☎ 090-625-301**) runs a regular connection from Messina to Taormina. The trip takes 1½ hours and costs 3.50€ ($3.15).

Getting around

The center of town is pedestrian only, but because Taormina is very small, the best — and only — way to get around is on foot. Of course, if you get tired or need to go a little farther than the city center, you can call a **taxi (☎ 0942-51-150** or 0942-23-800). If you want to reach your hotel by car you can, but remember that it's very difficult (indeed impossible) to find parking around town and that driving in the very narrow and steep streets of Taormina is tricky.

From the center of town starts the *funivia* (funicular; **☎ 0942-23-906**), which connects Taormina with the beach down below. There are runs every 15 minutes all day long for 2.58€ ($2.32) round-trip or 1.55€ ($1.40) one-way. It goes until 3 a.m. in the summer.

Where to stay in Taormina

Grand Hotel Timeo
$$$$$ Centro

The first hotel opened in Taormina dates back to the 18th century. This beautiful villa sits just below the Greek theater, surrounded by its own garden. As you'd expect for this kind of money, the guest rooms are spacious and come with every amenity, including large marble baths. All have terraces or balconies. Old-fashioned elegance is updated with modern comforts, and the hotel offers a private beach as well as a sophisticated restaurant and bar.

Via del Teatro Greco 59, just off the Greek theater. ☎ 0942-23-801. Fax: 0942-24-838. Parking: Free. Rack rates: 260€–420€ ($234–$378) double, including breakfast. AE, DC, MC, V.

Hotel Villa Schuler
$$ Centro

Lovely gardens and terraces surround this moderately priced hotel, which is very close to Corso Umberto I (Taormina's main street). The good-sized guest rooms are attractively furnished, and many have balconies overlooking the sea. You can also check out the hotel's library, 24-hour bar, and laundry facilities. On top of these perks, the hotel is a member of the Catena del Sole group: After you stay in one of this group's hotels, you receive a 10% discount at the second Catena del Sole group hotel in which you stay.

Piazzetta Bastione, off Via Roma. ☎ *0942-23-481. Fax: 0942-23-522. Parking: 9€ ($8.10) in covered garage; free outside. Rack rates: 110€ ($99) double, including breakfast. AE, DC, MC, V.*

Pensione Svizzera
$ Centro

This centrally located hotel offers decent guest rooms at a moderate price. It offers a few frills, such as breakfast in the lovely garden when the weather is good. Other pluses are that it's conveniently close to the beach, and the owners speak English and are very friendly.

Via Piradello 26, just off Porta Messina. ☎ *0942-23-790. Fax: 0942-625-906. E-mail:* info@pensionesvizzera.com. *Parking: 5€ ($4.50). Rack rates: 72€–88€ ($64.80–79.20) double, including breakfast. AE, DC, MC, V. Closed in Jan.*

San Domenico Palace Hotel
$$$$$ Centro

In a converted monastery amid magnificent terraced gardens, the San Domenico was the second hotel built in Taormina and has long been a haunt of the rich and famous. The eclectically furnished guest rooms feature fine furniture from various Mediterranean lands, and the superb **Bougainvillées** restaurant serves regional specialties on the terrace with a breathtaking view. The hotel has a piano bar and a conference center housed in the church of the original convent and also boasts a heated pool with a view.

Piazza San Domenico 5, south of the Duomo. ☎ *0942-23-701. Fax: 0942-625-506. Parking: 16€ ($14.40). Rack rates: 274€–423€ ($246.60–$380.70) double, including breakfast. AE, DC, MC, V.*

Villa Nettuno
$ Centro

This small hotel is in an attractive villa that's near the center of Taormina and the *funivia* to the beach. The villa was built in 1860 and converted into a hotel in the 1950s. The furnishings are modest and modern, and some of the guest rooms feature terraces and ocean views.

Via Pirandello 23, just off Porta Messina. ☎ *0942-23-797. Fax: 0942-626-035. Parking: 5€ ($4.50). Rack rates: 61.97€ ($55.77) double, including breakfast. MC, V.*

Where to dine in Taormina

Il Ciclope
$$$ Centro   SICILIAN

This busy trattoria is popular with visitors and Italians alike, serving hearty Sicilian food at relatively inexpensive prices for Taormina. Dishes include fish soup, calamari, and grilled fish, just to name a few. The *antipasti di mare* (seafood appetizers) are very tasty as well.

Corso Umberto 203. ☎ *0942-23-263. Reservations not accepted. Secondi: 9.81€–18.08€ ($8.82–$16.27). AE, MC, V. Open: Lunch and dinner Thurs–Tues; closed one month in Jan/Feb.*

Giova Rosy di Turi Salsa
$$$ Centro   SICILIAN

On Taormina's main street, this restaurant has been around for a long time but is still dependable. Among its specialties are *spiedini* (skewers) with shrimp and lobster and *pesce spada* (swordfish). You can request a table with a view of the Greco-Roman Theater.

Corso Umberto I 38. ☎ *0942-24-411. Reservations recommended. Secondi: 9.30€–20.60€ ($8.37–$18.59). AE, DC, V. Open: Lunch and dinner daily; closed Jan and Feb.*

Ristorante da Lorenzo
$$$ Centro   SICILIAN

This excellent restaurant is a bit away from the crowds. It has a pleasant terrace, notable for the ancient tree that has given shade for some 800 years, or so they say. The food lives up to the setting and includes fresh fish, an excellent *antipasto,* and such unusual dishes as *spaghetti ai ricci di mare* (spaghetti with sea urchins), considered a real delicacy by Italians.

Via Roma, near via Michele Amari. ☎ *0942-23-480. Reservations necessary. Secondi: 8.78€–23.24€ ($7.90–$20.92). AE, DC, MC, V. Open: Lunch and dinner Thurs–Tues; closed one month in Nov/Dec.*

Ristorante Luraleo

$$$ Centro   SICILIAN

The romantic atmosphere and a terrace help ensure a pleasant experi-
ence at this restaurant, which serves a variety of Sicilian specialties.
You're always safe choosing the grilled fish if you don't want to try some-
thing more adventurous, like *risotto al salmone e pistacchi* (risotto with
salmon and pistachios).

*Via Bagnoli Croce 27. ☎ 0942-24-279. Reservations recommended. Secondi: 9.30€–
18.08€ ($8.37–$16.27). DC, MC, V. Open: Summer lunch and dinner daily; winter
lunch and dinner Thurs–Tues.*

Exploring Taormina

As reported by travelers in the 18th century, Taormina's main attrac-
tion is its location on a cliff, offering breathtaking views over the sur-
rounding sea. Centuries of history, though, have left many other
interesting sights, and we list the best.

The top sights

Taormina's central street, **Corso Umberto I** stretches between the
town's two main gates, the **Porta Catania** and the **Porta Messina.** In the
Middle Ages, the city shrank to the area between the Porta Catania and
the **Torre dell'Orologio (clock tower).** Also called the Porta di Mezzo
(Middle Gate), the Torre dell'Orologio was built during the early Middle
Ages as the gate to the medieval village. After its partial destruction,
the clock tower was rebuilt in 1679 and is attached to the **Chiesa di
San Giorgio** with its 17th-century baroque facade. During the
Renaissance, the city started expanding again, and it has reoccupied
the whole hourglass-shaped area of the Greek city only in modern
times. Along Corso Umberto are some of Taormina's most interesting
monuments, such as the **Palace of the Dukes of St. Stephen (Palazzo
dei Duchi di Santo Stefano),** the best preserved of the town's Norman
buildings, and the **Chiesa di Sant'Agostino,** the 16th-century church
opening on its nice square, **Largo IX Aprile,** above the sea. The church
is today closed to worship and used as the town library.

Duomo (Chiesa San Nicola)

Built in the 12th century in a Latin cross plan, this church was later
remodeled. The central portal dates from 1633, while the lateral portals
date from the 15th and 16th centuries, respectively. Half a dozen mono-
lithic pink marble columns — the fish-scale decoration on their capitals
recalls Sicily's maritime tradition — hold up the nave. In front of the
Duomo is the beautiful baroque **Fontana Monumentale,** built in 1635 with
two-legged female centaurs.

*Piazza del Duomo, just off Corso Umberto. Admission: Free. Open: Daily for mass,
usually early morning and early evening.*

Palazzo Corvaja

This *palazzo* consists of three structures built between the 11th and 15th centuries, around a preexisting Arab structure (probably a fortress). The center of the palace is the cubic tower built by the Arabs. During the 14th century, the crenellated structure and beautiful entrance staircase were added to the tower. And in the 15th century, the right wing was built to serve as the meeting place for the Sicilian Parliament. This *palazzo* also houses the tourist office on the ground floor.

Piazza Santa Caterina off Corso Umberto. ☎ *0942-23-243. Admission: Free. Open: Mon–Sat 8 a.m.–2 p.m. and 4–7 p.m.*

Greek-Roman Theater (Teatro Greco-Romano)

With a capacity of 5,000 people, this theater carved out of rock is second in Sicily only to Syracuse's (see later in this chapter) in size and importance. It's the best preserved of all Greek and Roman theaters in Italy. Unusual for a Greek theater, the backdrop scene was a fixed structure: It represented a two-story house, part of which is still visible. As was the case for many buildings of antiquity, part of the theater's materials were taken to build other buildings, in this case by the Arabs and Normans. During its glory days, the walls of the theater (only a portion in the back remains) were covered with marble and frescoes. Although the theater was Greek in origin, the Romans modified it for gladiator battles. For example, a tunnel connected the cellar of the Roman arena with the outside; the orchestra of the theater was enlarged and closed off by a high podium in order to protect spectators. The theater is famous for the summer performances held there (see "Nightlife").

Via del Teatro Greco. ☎ *0942-23-220. Admission: 3€ ($2.70). Open: Tues–Sun 9:00 a.m.–5:30 p.m.*

More cool things to see and do

Many visitors come to Taormina only for a day. If you have more time to spend in the city, check out these other events and sights:

✔ If you're in Taormina during summer, enjoy the **Taormina Arte,** a festival of cinema, theater, music, ballet, and video started in 1983. Included are shows at the Greek-Roman Theater (see the listing under "Exploring Taormina," earlier in this chapter). For the schedule, contact **Taormina Arte** (Via Pirandello 31, 98039 Taormina; ☎ 0942-21-142; Fax: 0942-23-348). You can also get information from the **tourist office** (Azienda Autonoma di Soggiorno e Turismo, Palazzo Corvaja, 98039 Taormina; ☎ 0942-23-243; Fax: 0942-24-941) or the **Comune di Taormina–Assessorato Turismo** (Piazza Municipio, 98039 Taormina; ☎ 0942-610-218; Fax: 0942-610-216).

✔ Just below Corso Umberto, lower on the hillside on Via Bagnoli Croce, the **Public Gardens (Giardini Pubblici)** were built by Miss Florence Trevelyan, who arrived in 1882, fell in love with the town, and bought a piece of land sloping toward the sea. She worked at transforming the land into a garden, training and employing local workers as gardeners. Taorminians were fond of her, and when she died in 1902, they threw flowers at her passage in the funeral procession. Her will forbade her heirs from building or industrially cultivating the land. Within the gardens, she designed and built the **Victorian Follies** — bizarre structures like toy houses built with red bricks and light-colored stone containing inlaid archaeological materials.

✔ By the sea below Taormina lies the town of **Mazzarò,** with its beautiful beach and restaurants specializing in fish. It's easy to reach by funicular from Taormina. In front of Mazzarò is the **Isola Bella,** with its marine grottoes.

✔ If you have the time, take a day-trip to visit the great **Etna,** which dominates the background of Taormina. Europe's biggest and most active volcano is 3,300m (10,000-plus-feet) tall and growing. Vulcanologists have charted its eruptions back to the Middle Ages and even to ancient eruptions, which were usually far more dramatic and catastrophic. Though these mega-eruptions ceased centuries ago, Etna's littlest grumbles and oozings can wipe out vast areas and human settlements. The 1669 eruption not only took out some of the not-so-close-by town of Catania (amazingly, the deposits by the side of the highway south of town look as if they were made yesterday) but also extended the coastline about a kilometer (more than half a mile) into the sea. Many of Etna's eruptions, including some of the most violent, didn't originate from the snow-capped summit but from dozens of vents and secondary craters that mark the sides of this giant. But Etna isn't all lava and debris; parts of its north slopes are covered with a soaring conifer forest that took root in the rich soil.

The easiest way to visit Etna is to take an organized tour from Taormina (see "And on your left, Etna: Seeing Taormina's environs by guided tour"). However, if you have a car, you can go by yourself. From Taormina, follow the directions for Linguaglossa and then Zafferana, where you take the small winding road to the Rifugio Sapienza. If you're starting from Catania, follow the directions to Belpasso and then Nicolosi, where you take another windy road up to the Rifugio Sapienza, from which you can take a cable car to the summit.

Climbing Etna is more regulated than it used to be after a group of tourists were killed by a sudden explosion several years ago. If you want to see the craters up close and personal, you need an authorized guide. Book one at **Guide Alpine Etna Sud (☎ 095-791-4755)**.

✔ In the mountains above Taormina are the unique **Gorges of the Alcantara River (Gole dell'Alcantara),** a series of gorges carved by one of Italy's coldest rivers. Taking an organized trip from Taormina (see "And on your left, Etna: Seeing Taormina's environs by guided tour") is the best way to see them. If you want to drive, take the Catania-Messina SS114 in the direction of Catania and get off at the Giardini exit for SS185 (right, going inland), in the direction of Francavilla. After the small town of Gaggi, the road turns left (leaving at your right the road for Graniti) and arrives at the Gole dell'Alcantara. You can park in the large parking lot by the **Bar-Restaurant Meeting** (☎ 0942-985-010). The site is open daily from 9 a.m. to 5 p.m., but access is restricted during the winter. Admission is 3€ ($2.70). The climb takes about an hour but it isn't difficult; you're liable to get wet, so wear a swimsuit or other proper clothing (you can rent a wetsuit on-site; the site also supplies rubber boots).

And on your left, Etna: Seeing Taormina's environs by guided tour

Because Taormina is so small, there are no tours of the village itself. However, excellent tours depart from the town for some of the other major attractions in Sicily.

SAT Sicilian Airbus Travel (Corso Umberto 73; ☎ 0942-24-653; Fax: 0942-21-128; Internet: www.sat-group.it) offers some good tours of Etna, including a nice bus-and-jeep sunset tour on Tuesdays and Thursdays for 55€ ($49.50). This tour leaves at 3:00 p.m. in June and July and at 2:30 p.m. in August and September. The company also offers a day-trip to Etna, leaving Mondays at 8:30 a.m. for 25€ ($22.50). It includes only the bus and the guide for the trekking, but you can arrange a tour by jeep if you want. This company also organizes tours to Agrigento and the Valley of the Temples for 38€ ($34.20), leaving at 6.30 a.m. on Tuesdays and Thursdays, as well as to Syracuse for 35€ ($31.50), including Ortigia and the Archaeological Zone, leaving at 7 a.m. on Mondays and Thursdays.

CST (Corso Umberto 99–101; ☎ 0942-626-088; Fax: 0942-23-304; 24-hour service ☎ 0348-343-6104) also offers tours of Etna, ranging from a basic one for about 25€ ($22.50) to their sunset tour for about 50€ ($45). The company also runs tours to the Gole dell'Alcantara for 20€ ($18) and to Agrigento for about 40€ ($36).

Fast Facts: Taormina

Country Code and City Code

The country code for Italy is **39**. The city code for Taormina is **0942;** use this code when calling from anywhere outside or inside Italy, including within Taormina. (Include the 0 every time, even when calling from abroad.)

Currency Exchange

There are banks with ATMs on Corso Umberto, just before the Porta Messina to the north. You can also find banks in Giardini Naxos, the town next to Taormina.

Emergencies

Ambulance, ☎ 118; Fire, ☎ 115; road assistance ☎ 116; first aid *(pronto soccorso)*, ☎ 0942-625-419.

Hospital

The Ospedale Sirina is on Piazza San Francesco di Paola (☎ 0942-53-745).

Information

The tourist office is inside the beautiful Palazzo Corvaja on Piazza Santa Caterina off Corso Umberto to the west (Azienda Autonoma di Soggiorno e Turismo, Palazzo Corvaja, 98039 Taormina; ☎ 0942-23-243;

Fax: 0942-24-941). Hours of operation are Monday through Saturday 8 a.m. to 2 p.m. and 4 to 7 p.m.

Pharmacy

Visit Dr. Verso at Piazza IX Aprile 1 (☎ 0942-625-866).

Mail

The post office (Ufficio Postale) is on Piazza Medaglie d'Oro (☎ 0942-23-010).

Police

Call ☎ 113; for the Carabinieri (other police force), call ☎ 112.

Web Sites

Some useful Web sites are www.cormorano.net/taormina and www.taormina-network.it.

Syracuse: The Archaeological Zone

The island of Ortigia sticks out into the large natural harbor of **Syracuse (Siracusa)** as if designed to be a fortress city. This geographical feature wasn't lost on the Greek colonists from Corinth who settled on Ortigia in the eighth century B.C. Although Greek colonies were never subservient to the hometowns of the settlers, Syracuse rose to become the Mediterranean's greatest power under its forceful tyrants (particularly Dionysius I). However, during the Punic Wars, Syracuse was caught between a rock and a hard place — the Romans and the Carthaginians. The Roman siege lasted two years, and in 215 B.C. they finally overwhelmed the city, despite the clever devices that Archimedes, the city's most famous son, constructed to thwart them and their siege engines.

Syracuse's glory days ended more than 1,000 years ago. Since then, it's been battered by invaders — from the Saracens to the Nazis to the Allied bombs of 1943 — but its Archaeological Zone miraculously survived. Today, Syracuse is a small, busy modern center, while the original island of Ortigia has an indescribable feeling — or maybe it's the blinding light off the water and the heat of the sun.

You can easily visit Syracuse in one day, but there's enough to do for an overnight stay, especially if you plan to visit nearby Noto.

Getting there

To get to Syracuse from Catania, you can take advantage of the frequent direct **train service** (the trip takes about 1½ hours). However, from Taormina and Palermo, you usually must transfer in Catania, and from Agrigento, you need to change in Ragusa. The ride from Taormina is two hours at about 7€ ($6.30), the ride from Palermo takes five to seven hours at 15€ ($13.50), and the ride from Agrigento is six hours at about 15€ ($13.50). Syracuse's train station **(Stazione FS)** is on the west side of town; it is approximately a 20-minute walk from there to either Ortigia or the Archaeological Zone. From the train station, city buses connect to the main sights.

Syracuse is 259km (162 miles) from Palermo, 154km (96 miles) from Messina, and 218km (136 miles) from Agrigento. If you're **driving** from Palermo, take **A19** to Catania, where this road ends. Follow the signs for Syracuse and take **SS114,** also labeled **E14** on European maps. From Agrigento, a highway is under construction but not yet completed; until it is, you'll have to take the state road **SS115,** which is picturesque but a long haul — about five hours.

If you're driving south from Catania to Syracuse, exercise caution on the stretch where it reduces to a two-lane road (about 21km/13 miles) — much too small for the amount of traffic on it. You really have to pay attention to who's passing whom in both directions. Avoid it at night if at all possible.

Getting around

The island of **Ortigia,** connected to the modern town of Syracuse by a bridge, is where the city began and is still its heart. Most of the ancient ruins on the island were displaced by or incorporated into the baroque city that developed there, particularly after the 1693 earthquake. Ortigia is a small area that you can easily tour **on foot**. Most of the tourist sights are on Ortigia, except for the Archaeological Zone (see the next paragraph).

On the edge of Syracuse's modern part is the **Archaeological Zone (Zona Archeologica).** The city **bus system** connects Ortigia to this zone. In between the zone and Ortigia lies some of modern Syracuse. Most buses stop at Piazza Archimede, the heart of Ortigia; in Largo XXV Luglio, just before the bridge to the mainland; and on Corso Umberto, which runs between the bridge to Ortigia and the train station.

Where to stay

Forte Agip Siracusa
$$$ **Archaelogical Park**

A modern hotel near the amphitheaters, the Forte Agip offers all the modern comforts, including air-conditioning (a godsend after May). The guest rooms are plain but have contemporary furnishings. The restaurant is popular with locals and serves good fish dishes.

Via Teracati 30–32. ☎ *0931-463-232. Fax: 0931-67-115. Parking: Free. Rack rates: 130.90€–179€ ($117.81–161.10) double, including buffet breakfast. AE, DC, MC, V.*

Gran Bretagna
$$ **Ortigia**

This small hotel, recently upgraded (it now has air-conditioning), has the great advantage of being on Ortigia, the main historic center of town. It's very popular with Italian and foreign tourists alike. The guest rooms are still basic, but comfortable; a few rooms still have the orginal ceiling frescoes from the 19th century.

Via Savoia 21. ☎ *0931-68-765. E-mail:* info@hotelgranbretagna.it. *Rack rates: 96€ ($86.40) double, including breakfast. AE, MC, V.*

Hotel Bella Vista
$$ **Center**

In the modern section of Syracuse, the Bella Vista is a well-kept family-run hotel. The furniture in the bright guest rooms is modern, and many rooms offer balconies with ocean views. The hotel restaurant, reserved for guests, serves tasty Sicilian fare. The Bella Vista is a member of the Catena del Sole group, which means that after you've stayed in one of the group's hotels, you receive a 10% discount for the second one in which you stay.

Via Diodoro Siculo 4. ☎ *0931-411-355. Fax: 0931-37-927. Internet:* www.sistemia.it/bellavista. *E-mail:* bellavista@sistemia.it. *Parking: Free. Rack rates: 70€–90€ ($63–$81) double, including breakfast. AE, MC, V.*

Where to dine

Gambero Rosso
$$$ **Corso Umberto   SICILIAN**

In an old tavern near the harbor, this restaurant is known for its seafood and has a terrace overlooking the port. Try the *cannelloni* (tubes of pasta filled with fish or meat, cooked in the oven with a sauce and cheese, in the manner of lasagna) or one of the fish soups.

Via Eritrea 2, on the right after the bridge leaving Ortigia. ☎ **0931-68-546.** *Reservations recommended. Secondi: 9€–18€ ($8.10–$16.20). AE, DC, MC, V. Open: Lunch and dinner Fri–Wed.*

Ristorante Jonico
$$$ Latomia dei Cappuccini   SICILIAN

On the main street running along the coast north of Ortigia, this elegant place overlooks the sea. The roof garden serves pizza, and down below is the upscale dining room. The seafood is particularly good, such as the *antipasto misto* and the *pesce spada alla pizzaiola* (swordfish in tomato-and-garlic sauce). You can also choose from a large selection of home-made pastas.

A Rutta e Ciauli, Riviera Dionisio Il Grande 194, just off Piazza dei Cappuccini. ☎ **0931-65-540.** *Reservations recommended. Secondi: 9.30€–15.49€ ($8.37–$13.94). AE, MC, V. Open: Lunch and dinner Wed–Mon.*

Ristorante Rossini
$$$ Ortigia   SICILIAN

This intimate restaurant, run by a renowned chef, offers a menu based mainly on seafood prepared in both traditional and imaginative ways. One specialty is *pesce alla stimpirata,* which creatively combines mint, garlic, and olive oil with fish. More familiar Sicilian-style preparations include roasted swordfish. The buffet *antipasto* is excellent.

Via Savoia 6. ☎ **0931-24-317.** *Reservations recommended. Secondi: 10.33€–18.08€ ($9.30–$16.27). AE, DC, MC, V. Open: Lunch and dinner Wed–Mon.*

Exploring Syracuse

You can easily visit Syracuse on foot, where there are some beautiful strolls, whether by the harbor or amid the ancient ruins. But beware of the sun in the hot months — walking around the ruins at high noon will quickly exhaust and dehydrate you. Also keep in mind that the old town of Syracuse on the island of Ortigia is made of stone, though you can find a little more shade here than in the Archaeological Zone.

The top sights

Museo Archeologico Regionale Paolo Orsi

This is the best archaeological museum in Sicily. The large, well-organized collection covers every time period, from prehistoric objects to an extensive Hellenistic collection from Syracuse's heyday. The most famous single piece is the second-century B.C. ***Venus Anadyomene*** that — though headless — powerfully evokes the birth of the goddess from the sea. The pre-Greek vases are lovely too. Other collections relate to the cities of Naxos, Lentini, Zancle, and Megara Iblea.

In the gardens of the Villa Landolina, Viale Teocrito 66, near the Zona Archeologica.
☎ *0931-464-023. Bus: 4, 5, 12, or 15 to Viale Teocrito. Admission: 5€ ($4.50). Open: Tues–Sat 9 a.m.–1 p.m., and Mon and Wed 3:30–6:30 p.m.*

Ortigia

This is the island in Syracuse's harbor that is the heart of the historic city. At the end of the 19th century, Ortigia was still all there was of Syracuse; the land side contained only the rail station and the Greek ruins. The mainland part of Syracuse has changed much since, but not Ortigia. As you cross the Ponte Nuovo, the first ruin you see is the **Temple of Apollo (Tempio di Apollo),** built in the sixth century B.C.; it is now just a few columns. If you walk up Via Savoia, you come to the **Porta Marina,** from which you can enter the old town. Farther along the stone border of the harbor is the **Aretusa Fountain (Fonte Aretusa),** where the nymph of classic mythology allegedly turned into a spring. From here, turn left and head to the center of Ortigia to see the seventh-century **Duomo,** Piazza del Duomo, built on the remains of a Greek temple to Athena (Minerva for the Romans) and including 12 of the temple's columns; it's open daily from 8 a.m. to noon and 4 to 7 p.m., with free admission. Head down toward the tip of Ortigia to the 13th-century **Palazzo Bellomo,** Via Capodieci 14, which houses the **Galleria Regionale** (☎ **0931-69-617**); its main claim to fame is Antonello da Messina's famous *Annunciation.* The museum is open Monday through Saturday from 9:00 a.m. to 1:30 p.m., and Sunday from 9:00 a.m. to 12:30 p.m., with an admission charge of 5€ ($4.50).

Off Largo XXV Luglio by the Ponte Nuovo.

The Archaeological Zone (Zona Archeologica)

The Archaeological Zone contains two theaters and the quarries from which stone was excavated to build all the monuments in town. Actually a giant sculpture because it's carved out of the rock on the hillside, the **Greek Theater (Teatro Greco),** from the fifth century B.C., is a beautiful example of an ancient theater. The tunnels you see in the stage area aren't original; they were dug later by the Romans so that they could use the theater for their blood sports. At the back of the theater are Byzantine tombs and a fountain to which water was brought by the Greeks from 40km (25 miles) away via a system of aqueducts.

In even-numbered years, the theater comes to life again when ancient dramas by Greek authors are presented as they were 2,500 years ago. Contact the **Istituto Nazionale del Dramma Antico** (Corso G. Matteotti 29, 96100 Siracusa; ☎ **0931-67-415** or 1478-82-211 toll-free in Italy;

Internet: www.indafondazione.org), which sponsors the plays. Tickets run from around 15.30€ to 31€ ($13.77 to $27.90). Call or write to the institute for information on programs and dates.

On the other side of the hill is the **Latomia del Paradiso (stone quarry).** What you see is a huge hole covering many acres, with a few pillars sticking up and giant stones scattered here and there. The central pillar held up the roof of the quarry, and the big blocks of stone were once the roof, which collapsed in the 1693 earthquake. One of the excavated caves, the **Grotto of the Ropemakers (Grotta dei Cordari),** was used in later centuries for ropemaking; it has been closed for years for safety reasons. After descending into the quarry, you can visit **Dionysius's Ear (Orecchio di Dionisio),** a deep, very tall, pitch-black cave. The story that Dionysius used the cave to eavesdrop on conversations is a myth; the painter Caravaggio was said to have given the cave its name (perhaps he made up the story, too). Nearby is another important structure, the **Roman Amphitheater (Anfiteatro Romano),** built during the reign of Augustus and partially carved from the rock. Like other Roman theaters, it was used for life-and-death battles between humans as well as animals and was sometimes flooded and filled with crocodiles and other friendly creatures for water fights.

What you see today is only the bottom story — try to imagine how it looked when the top of the theater reached the present height of the surrounding trees. Holy Roman Emperor Charles V is the bad guy of many stories about Italy, and Syracuse is no exception. He did more damage than the earthquake and is responsible for turning this theater into a quarry. During his North African campaigns, he destroyed much of the Roman ruins for material to build fortifications.

Via Augusto, near the intersection of Corso Gelone and Viale Teocrito. ☎ *0931-66-206. Bus: 4, 5, or 6 to Parco Archeologico. Admission: 3€ ($2.70). Open: Daily 9 a.m. until one hour before sunset.*

More cool things to see and do

Here are a few sights just outside Syracuse:

✔ To the north of the city, the **Forte (Fort) di Eurialo** is a masterpiece of Greek military defensive architecture, connected to walls running far up into the hills behind Syracuse and protecting the land side of the city. The fort has four powerful towers and a network of subterranean passages where cavalry could gather for an attack. You can reach it driving north on Riviera Dionisio il Grande toward Catania or take the 9, 10, or 11 bus from the modern city center. The fort is open Monday through Saturday from 9 a.m. until two hours before sunset, and Sunday from 9 a.m. to 2 p.m. Admission is 3€ ($2.70).

✔ Only 32km (20 miles) south of Syracuse is the famous town of **Noto,** a wonderful example of Sicilian baroque. It was reduced to rubble by the 1693 earthquake, which also destroyed the whole southeast of Sicily, but the town's notables decided to rebuild it 10 miles south of its original location. The reconstruction happened very rapidly — in about 45 years — and the result was a town remarkably uniform in style. Faithful to pure baroque standards, Noto was built on a regular street grid. Many important Sicilian artists contributed to the reconstruction. Carvings of grotesque animals and figures support the balconies, and the whole town is built in golden-yellow stone. Noto underwent a restoration that started in 1997. The **tourist office,** where you can also get a map of the town, is in the center at Piazza XIV Maggio (☎ **0931-573-779**); summer hours are daily from 9 a.m. to 1 p.m. and 3:30 to 6:30 p.m.; winter hours are Monday through Saturday from 8 a.m. to 2 p.m. and 3:30 to 6:30 p.m.

Fast Facts: Syracuse

Country Code and City Code

The country code for Italy is **39**. The city code for Syracuse is **0931**; use this code when calling from anywhere outside or inside Italy. Add the codes even when calling within Syracuse itself, and include the 0 every time, even when calling from abroad.

Emergencies

Ambulance, ☎ **118**; fire, ☎ **115**; road assistance ☎ **116**.

Information

The tourist office maintains two booths, one at Piazza San Sebastiano (☎ 0931-67-710) and one at the Zona Archeologica (Via Augusto); both are open Monday through Saturday 8:30 a.m. to 2:00 p.m. and 4:30 to 7:30 p.m. in summer (3:30 to 6:30 p.m. in winter).

Mail

The post office (Ufficio Postale) is on Piazza Riva della Posta 15, to the left of the main bridge in Ortigia (☎ 0931-68-973). It's open Monday through Friday 8:10 a.m. to 6:30 p.m. (Saturday to 1:00 p.m.).

Police

Call ☎ **113**; for the Carabinieri (other police force), call ☎ **112**.

Web Sites

Visit www.insiracusa.net.

Agrigento and the Valley of the Temples

Agrigento was founded in 581 B.C. on a gentle slope toward the sea shaped as a natural amphitheater and protected by two hills and two rivers. A prosperous city in antiquity, it was progressively abandoned during the decline of the Roman Empire. The Arabs and then the Normans later occupied the site, and the population moved up the hill to the current site of town. During the 13th and 14th centuries, the feudal Chiaramonte family promoted the construction of walls around the town, as well as numerous churches and monasteries.

You can easily visit Agrigento in one day as a day-trip from Palermo. However, it also makes a good base for exploring some other interesting sights, such as Syracuse and Segesta.

Getting there

Eleven **trains** a day run from Palermo to Agrigento; the trip takes 1½ hours and costs about 7€ ($6.30). The trip from Syracuse is six hours, with a change in Ragusa, costing about 16€ ($14.40). Agrigento's rail station is the **Stazione Centrale** (Piazza Guglielmo Marconi; ☎ 0922-725-669).

The company **Licata** (Via XXV Aprile 142, 92100 Agrigento; ☎ 0922-401-360) runs a **bus** from Palermo's airport to Agrigento daily at 11:30 a.m. and 8:00 p.m.; the trip takes about 2½ hours and costs around 7€ ($6.30). **Omnia** (Via Ragazzi del '99 10, 92100 Agrigento; ☎ 0922-596-490) runs four buses daily between Palermo and Agrigento, which take approximately two hours and cost about 7€ ($6.30).

Agrigento is 126km (79 miles) from Palermo by regular road or 180km (112 miles) by *autostrada,* 191km (119 miles) from Taormina, and 218km (136 miles) from Syracuse. If you're driving from Palermo, take **A19** to Caltanissetta, and then follow the directions to Agrigento and take **SS640** for the remaining 60km (37 miles). If you don't mind narrower roads, you can take **SS121/189** all the way from Palermo to Agrigento, which is shorter. To Agrigento from Syracuse, you take a scenic five-hour drive on **SS115 (E45 and E931)**; follow the directions for Noto, Ragusa, Gela, and Agrigento. From Taormina, take **A18** to Catania, then **A19** to Caltanissetta, then **SS640** to Agrigento.

Getting around

Agrigento isn't very big, so you can easily visit it **on foot.** The Valley of the Temples (see "The top sights," later in this section) is 3km (2 miles) south of the center, and city buses connect the valley with the train station in Agrigento (nos. 8 through 11). For a **taxi,** call ☎ 0922-21-899 or 0922-26-670.

The archaeological area where the temples are located is quite wide and, as is often the case, has very few trees. Remember to bring very comfortable shoes, a hat, sunscreen, and at least a quart of water per person. If you're planning to visit only as a day-trip, we recommend that you pack a picnic lunch to eat near the ruins — it's a nice spot, and you'll have more time to visit.

Where to stay

Hotel Belvedere
$ Agrigento

If you travel by public transportation or prefer to stay in town, the Belvedere is conveniently located behind Piazza Vittorio Emanuele near the station. The exterior isn't the most beautiful we've ever seen, but the hotel is well run and comfortable. It offers basic guest rooms, which aren't large but are adequate given the price.

Via San Vito 20, not far from the train station. ☎ *0922-20-051. Parking: Free. Rack rates: 62€ ($55.80) double, including breakfast. No credit cards accepted.*

Hotel Costazzurra
$$ San Leone

If you're going to stay in Agrigento, why not stay near the beach and swim in the beautiful water? Only 2.5km (1.4 miles) from the Valley of the Temples, this hotel is modern, and, although you won't get antique charm, you get air-conditioning, a restaurant, and a bar. The spacious guest rooms are furnished in modern Mediterranean style, with bright white walls and well-appointed baths. The Costazzurra is a member of the Catena del Sole group, which means that after you've stayed in one of its hotels, you receive a 10% discount at the next group hotel in which you stay.

Via delle Viole 2, off Viale dei Giardini in San Leone (off SS115 toward the sea from the Valle dei Templi). ☎ *0922-411-222. Fax: 0922-414-040. Parking: Free. Rack rates: 80€–154.94€ ($72–$139.45) double, including breakfast. AE, MC, V.*

Hotel Kaos
$$$ Caos

This hotel was originally a *casale* (farm) but was completely transformed into a major resort with all the modern conveniences (including wheelchair accessibility). The huge grounds include a courtyard, fountains, a giant swimming pool, tennis courts, gardens, and terraces with palm trees. The air-conditioned guest rooms are modern and comfortable; it also has a bar and a good restaurant. The Kaos is only minutes by car from the Valley of the Temples and from the beach.

Via Pirandello, in Caos (off SS115 to the right going to Porto Empedocle from the Valle dei Templi). ☎ *0922-598-622. Fax: 0922-598-770. Parking: Free. Rack rates: 154.94€ ($139.45) double, including breakfast. AE, DC, MC, V.*

Hotel Villa Athena
$$$ Valle dei Templi

This hotel — with all the modern comforts, including an open-air pool —
is right in the Valley of the Temples. Housed in an 18th-century villa, the
Athena is comparable to the Kaos but offers a little classier atmosphere.
The guest rooms are large and airy, with reproduction or modern furni-
ture. You can eat outdoors with a view of the Temple of Concorde (see
later in this chapter).

Via dei Templi 35 (off SS115 toward the Valle dei Templi). ☎ *0922-596-288. Fax:*
0922-402-180. Parking: Free. Rack rates: 206.58€ ($185.92) double, including break-
fast. AE, DC, MC, V.

Where to dine

Like the rest of Sicily, the cuisine of Agrigento is heavily based on
seafood. A distinction of Agrigento, however, is that it's at the center
of the almond-growing industry, so almonds are used in a variety of
preparations.

Le Caprice
$$$$ Valle dei Templi   SICILIAN

Although expensive, this is *the* restaurant in Agrigento. Locals come for
special celebrations, and visitors gather to sample the delicious seafood
specialties and to enjoy the typical Sicilian *antipasto* buffet. The *involtini*
di pesce spada (stuffed swordfish) is superb.

Strada Panoramica dei Templi 51. ☎ *0922-26-469. Reservations necessary.*
Secondi: 12.91€–19.63€ ($11.62–$17.67). AE, DC, MC, V. Open: Lunch and dinner
Sat.–Thurs.; closed two weeks in July.

Ristorante Corte degli Sfizi
$$ Agrigento   SICILIAN

In this small restaurant and pizzeria, you can get excellent pasta dishes
(including some traditional Sicilian specialties) and pizzas at very moderate prices. It's a popular place at night, particularly with the young
crowd.

Corte Contarini, Via Atenea 3, just left from the train station. ☎ *0922-595-520.*
Reservations recommended on weekends. Secondi: 5.16€–9.30€ ($4.64–$8.37). No
credit cards accepted. Open: Lunch and dinner Tues–Sun.

Ristorante Il Casello

$$$ Valle dei Templi   SICILIAN

Near the Valley of the Temples, this restaurant that doubles as a pizzeria offers well-prepared Sicilian fare, including a variety of traditional dishes like *pasta alla Norma* (with eggplant, tomato, and ricotta) and grilled fish.

Viale Emporium 1, just off SS115 in the direction of San Leone and the sea. ☎ *0922-26-208. Reservations not necessary. Secondi: 8.78€–15.49€ ($7.90–$13.94). AE, MC, V. Open: Lunch and dinner Thurs–Tues.*

Exploring Agrigento

Agrigento is most famous for its ancient Greek temples, but it has several other sights worth seeing. They cover the area's history from the decline of the ancient town to its rebirth in later centuries. There's also a house museum related to Agrigento's most famous son, playwright Luigi Pirandello.

The top sights

Chiesa di San Nicola

Built in the 12th century, this church is the first sight you encounter descending to the Valley of the Temples from Agrigento and offers a perfect view over the temples. Inside, at the center of the second chapel, is the famous third-century **Sarcofago di Fedra,** one of the most gracious examples of Greek sculpture, evoking the myth of Phaedra and Ippolyte (a sad story of unrequited love in which the rejected Phaedra is delirious while Ippolyte goes hunting; he is killed in an accident).

Contrada San Nicola, Via dei Templi, Zona Archeologica. Bus: 8, 9, 10, or 11 from Agrigento's train station. Admission: Free. Open: Daily 8 a.m.–1 p.m.

Museo Archeologico Regionale

This museum contains a large collection of Greek artifacts, many of which were found during the excavations in Agrigento. Besides the ample collection of Greek vases, an interesting piece is one of the Telamons (human figures supporting a structure) from the Tempio di Giove (see the description under the Valley of the Temples listing), which is in much better shape than the one on the ground at the temple.

Contrada San Nicola, Via dei Templi, Zona Archeologica. ☎ *0922-401-565. Bus: 8, 9, 10, or 11 from Agrigento's train station. Admission: 4.13€ ($3.72). Open: Daily 9 a.m.–1 p.m. and Tues–Sat 2 to 6 p.m.*

Agrigento and the Valley of the Temples

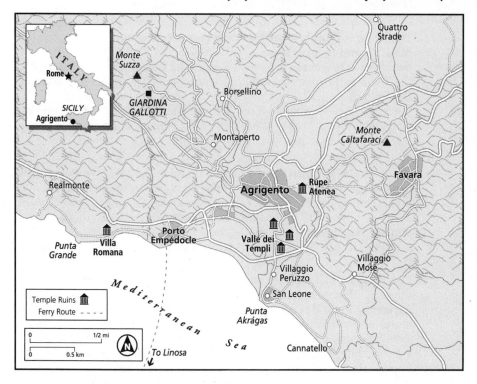

The Valley of the Temples (Valle dei Templi)

The Valley of the Temples is the reason that most people come to Agrigento, and it's the most impressive Greek ruin outside Greece. It covers a large area, so you need about three hours to see everything (excluding the museum).

You won't find shade near the largest of the temples, so you definitely need to bring a hat and sunscreen. Many books recommend that you see the valley at sunrise or sunset; this is indeed dramatic, but at sunset there isn't time to see everything before dark. However, the temperature at this time is cooler, which reduces your risk of sunburn and heatstroke in summer.

If you're coming from Agrigento, Via dei Templi brings you to **Piazzale Posto di Ristoro,** the large parking lot with several vendors and a bar (Posto di Ristoro, or rest stop) at the **Porta Aurea,** a gate in the Greek walls of ancient Agrigento. This is the center of the archaeological zone, with the three best-conserved temples on one side (Tempio di Ercole,

Tempio della Concordia, and Tempio di Giunone) and the Tempio di Giove and Tempio dei Dioscuri and the river on the other.

The massive **Temple of Jove or Zeus (Tempio di Giove)** was built to celebrate the gratitude of the people of Agrigento for their 480–479 B.C. victory over the Carthaginians at Himera. One of the largest temples of antiquity, the Tempio di Grove covered approximately 68,000 square feet and was 108 feet tall. Each of the columns rose 55.4 feet and measured 13.8 feet at the base. The Telamons — also called Atlases (human figures supporting a structure) — probably alternated with columns. Each of these giants measured 25 feet high, and one is now lying flat on the ground.

The **Temple of Castor and Pollux (Tempio di Castore e Polluce)** is believed to have been built between 480 and 460 B.C. to honor Castor and Pollux (the twin sons of Leda, queen of Sparta, and Jupiter), protectors of athletes, hospitality, and sailors in difficulty. Of the 34 columns, only 4 remain standing (at the corner of the temple), and they were restored in the 19th century. Nearby are the few remains of the **Tempio di Vulcano.**

The **Temple of Hercules (Tempio di Ercole)** is one of the most beautiful temples. Hercules was highly revered in Sicily and particularly in Agrigento; the god of strength, he was thought to free people from nightmares and unwanted erotic stimuli. The largest of the temples on this side, it occupied an area of about 22,000 square feet. Only nine columns are standing, and they were raised by the generosity of the English Captain Hardcastle in the 1920s. The columns were painted white to simulate marble, and the cornice was decorated in red, blue, and turquoise; there was also a rich decoration of sculptures.

The **Temple of Concordia (Tempio della Concordia),** built around 430 B.C., is remarkably well preserved, because in A.D. 597, it was transformed into a church. Twelve arches were opened in the walls of the temple, and the space between the columns was walled in to make it a church with three naves. These alterations were reversed in 1743 when the temple was declared a national monument and restored. It's one of the best-conserved temples of this period, together with the one of Hera in Paestum (see Chapter 22) and the Theseion in Athens.

Juno (Hera), the mother goddess, was the protectress of marriage and fertility. The 450–440 B.C. **Temple of Juno or Hera (Tempio di Giunone)** has 34 columns and a maximum height of 15.31 meters (50.2 feet). If you visit this monument, note that there's a tree just below the temple!

Piazzale dei Templi/Posto di Ristoro, at the crossroad with SS115 Siracusa–Trapani.
☎ *0922-26-191. Bus: 8, 9, 10, or 11 to the Posto di Ristoro. Admission (ticket booth is at the entrance for the Tempio di Giove) 6.20€ ($5.58), including admission to the museum. Open: Tempio di Giove archaeological area, daily 8:30 a.m.–5:00 p.m.; Tempio della Concordia archaeological area, daily 8:30 a.m.–7:00 p.m. The town of*

Agrigento makes a point to keep the area open at sunset, when the Valle dei Templi is at its best; however, as everywhere in Italy, closing times may vary, so check with the tourist office near the entrance.

More cool things to see and do

Agrigento has more to offer. Here are a couple more things you may want to check out:

✔ Held between the first and second Sunday in February, the **Festival of the Almond Flowers (Sagra del Mandorlo in Fiore)** was first held in 1938 as a celebration of spring — symbolized by the almond tree in blossom — accompanied by traditional dances and songs. Immediately successful, it was continuously improved, and today the week-long festival features folklore groups from around Sicily as well as from the rest of Italy and neighboring countries. Other events include painting shows, research meetings, cinema, and a market of almond products.

✔ The **Casa Natale di Pirandello** (Contrada Caos; ☎ **0922-511-102**) is the house where the writer Luigi Pirandello was born in 1867. The house contains the author's memorabilia, and his ashes are buried under a pine on the property. Pirandello received the Nobel Prize for Literature in 1934. In works such as *Six Characters in Search of an Author,* he explored the theme of the mask that everyone must wear to have a role in society. To visit, take the no. 11 bus. The house is open daily from 8 a.m. to 7 p.m. Admission is 2.60€ ($2.34).

And on your left, the Valle dei Templi: Seeing Agrigento by guided tour

You can take guided tours of the Valley of the Temples from both Palermo and Taormina. From Taormina, **SAT Sicilian Airbus Travel** (Corso Umberto 73; ☎ **0942-24-653;** Fax: 0942-21-128; Internet: www.tao.it/sat; E-mail: sat@tao.it) organizes tours to the Valley of the Temples for 38€ ($34.20), leaving at 6.30 a.m. on Tuesdays and Thursdays. Check out Chapter 23 for tours departing from Palermo.

The Greek temple

The Greek temple was conceived as the habitation of a god and always opened to the east because the god's statue had to look at the rising sun (symbol of the beginning of light and life) and never the sunset (symbol of the night and death). Over a high rectangular platform with steps, the classic temple has a perimeter of columns and an inside wall enclosing three rooms: the *pronaos* (entrance), the *naos* (the cell with the statue of the god), and the *opistodomos* (where the treasure, the votive gifts, and the archives of the temple were kept). In fact, temples were so sacred that citizens used to leave their valuables there, thus using them as safes.

Fast Facts: Agrigento

Country Code and City Code

The country code for Italy is **39**. The city code for Agrigento is **0922**; use this code when calling from anywhere outside or inside Italy, even within Agrigento. Make sure that you include the 0 every time, even when calling from abroad.

Currency Exchange

There's an exchange office at Piazzale Posto di Ristoro, Valle dei Templi, near the tourist booth.

Emergencies

Ambulance, ☎ **118** or 0922-401-344; fire, ☎ **115**; road assistance, ☎ **116**; first aid *(pronto soccorso)*, ☎ **0922-401-344.**

Hospital

The Ospedale San Giovanni di Dio is on Via Rupe Atenea (☎ 0922-492-111).

Information

The main tourist office is AAPIT (Viale della Vittoria 255; ☎ 0922-401-352 or 0922-20-454;

Fax 0922-35-185). There's also an AAPIT branch on Piazzale Posto di Ristoro, at the entrance to the Valle dei Templi (☎ 0922-20-391). Both are open Monday through Friday 8:30 a.m. to 1:45 p.m. and 4 to 7 p.m.

Mail

The post office (Ufficio Postale) is on Piazza Vittorio Emanuele, to the left of the Stazione Centrale (☎ 0922-26321). It's open Monday through Friday 8:10 a.m. to 7:40 p.m.

Police

Call ☎ **113**; for the Carabinieri (other police force), call ☎ **112.**

Taxi

Piazzale Aldo Moro ☎ 0922-21899; train station, ☎ 0922-2670.

Web Sites

Check out www.sicily4you.it and www.agrigentoweb.it.

Part VIII
The Part of Tens

The 5th Wave   By Rich Tennant

"So far you've called a rickshaw, a unicyclist and a Zamboni. I really wish you'd learn the Italian word for taxicab."

In this part . . .

This part is a list, a resource, and a reminder. Here you can find tips to help you make the most of your vacation. Think you can't possibly make do in Italy knowing only ten Italian words? Believe it or not, you can, and in Chapter 26 we give you the few key words that will help you converse with the natives. In Chapter 27, we give you a choice of wonderful books (besides this one) that'll get you excited about your trip before you go.

Chapter 26

Non Capisco: The Top Ten Expressions You Need to Know

● ●

In This Chapter

▶ Using salutations

▶ Asking questions

▶ Knowing lifesavers

● ●

Traveling in a country where you don't know the language can be intimidating, but trying to speak the language can be amusing, at the very least. Local people often appreciate it if you at least make the effort. And you'll find that Italian is a fun language to try to speak.

Per Favore

Meaning "please," *per favore* (*per* fa-*voe*-ray) is the most important phrase you can know. With it you can make useful phrases such as *Un caffè, per favore* ("A coffee, please") and *Il conto, per favore* ("The bill, please"). There's no need for verbs, and it's perfectly polite!

Grazie

Grazie (*gra*-tziay) means "thank you"; if you want to go all out, use *grazie mille* (*mee*-lay), meaning "a thousand thanks." Say it clearly and loudly enough to be heard. Saying *grazie* is always right and puts people in a good mood. *Grazie* has other uses as well: Italians often use it as a way to say goodbye or mark the end of an interaction. It's particularly useful when you don't want to buy something from an insistent street vendor: Say, *"Grazie,"* and walk away.

Permesso

Meaning "excuse me" (to request passage or admittance), *permesso* (per-*mess*-ow) is of fundamental importance on public transportation. When you're in a crowded bus and need to get off, say loudly and clearly, *"Permesso!"* and people will clear from your path (or feel less irritated as you squeeze your way through). The same thing applies in supermarkets, trains, museums, and so on. Of course, you may be surrounded by non-Italians and the effect may be a little lost on them.

Scusi

Scusi (*scoo*-sy) means "excuse me" (to say you're sorry after bumping into someone) and is more exactly *mi scusi,* but the shortened form is the one more people use. Again, it's a most useful word in any crowded situation. You'll note that Italians push their way through a narrow passage with a long chain of *"Scusi, permesso, mi scusi, grazie, permesso. . . ."* It's very funny to hear. *Scusi* has another important use: It's the proper beginning to attract somebody's attention before asking a question. Say *"Scusi?"* and the person will turn toward you in benevolent expectation. Then it's up to you.

Buon Giorno and Buona Sera

Buon giorno (bwon *djor*-know), meaning "good day," and its sibling *buona sera* (*bwon*-a *sey*-rah), meaning "good evening," are of the utmost importance in Italian interactions. Italians always salute one another when entering or leaving a public place. Do the same, saying it clearly when entering a store or restaurant. Occasionally, these words can also be used as forms of goodbye.

Arrivederci

Arrivederci (ah-rree-vey-*der*-tchy) is the appropriate way to say goodbye in a formal occasion — in a shop, in a bar or restaurant, or to friends. If you can say it properly, people will like it very much: Italians are aware of the difficulties of their language for foreigners.

You'll hear the word *ciao* (chow), the familiar word for goodbye, used among friends (usually of the same age). Note that using the word *ciao* with someone you don't know is considered quite impolite!

Dov'è

Meaning "where is," *dov'è* (doe-*vay*) is useful for asking for directions. Because the verb is included, you just need to add the thing you're looking for: *Dov'è il Colosseo?* ("Where is the Colosseum?") or *Dov'è la stazione?* ("Where is the train station?"). Of course you need to know the names of monuments in Italian, but don't worry! We always give you the Italian names in this book. It makes things much easier when you're there!

Quanto Costa?

Meaning "How much does it cost?", *Quanto costa?* (*quahnn*-tow *koss*-tah) is of obvious use all around Italy for buying anything from a train ticket to a trinket.

Che Cos'è?

Meaning "What is it?", *Che cos'è?* (kay *koss*-ay) will help you buy things, particularly food, and know what you're buying. But it could also be useful in museums and other circumstances. But then the real work begins — to understand the answer. If you don't understand the answer, you can get the person to repeat it by saying the next phrase on our list. . . .

Non Capisco

Non capisco (nonn kah-*peace*-koh) means "I don't understand." There's no need to explain this one: Keep repeating it and Italians will try more and more imaginative ways to explain things to you.

Chapter 27

Ten (Or so) Authors to Help You Understand More about Italy

● ●

In This Chapter

▶ Reading the classics

▶ Enjoying a romantic read

▶ Reliving Italy's past adventures

● ●

*Y*ou could read thousands of books in preparation for your trip to Italy, starting with the classics. In this chapter, we provide you with a varied selection of great books of various kinds from different periods, with a balance of heavy and light reading. Whether you want to bone up on history or read an entertaining story that will put you in the mood, this chapter has something for you.

Polybius

Polybius was a Greek hostage in Rome for 16 years in the second century B.C. During this time, he wrote his *Histories* (reprint Regnery/ Gateway 1987 as *Polybius on Roman Imperialism* or Penguin 1980 as *The Rise of the Roman Empire*) to explain "by what means and under what kind of constitution, almost the whole inhabited world was conquered and brought under the dominion of the single city of Rome, and that, too, within a period of not quite fifty-three years" (219–167 B.C.).

Robert Graves

Graves's two novels *I, Claudius* (1934) and the sequel *Claudius the God* (1934) are a highly entertaining way to find out about the glory and decadence of Imperial Rome. You can also buy or rent the 1970s BBC TV series to see for yourself just who did what to whom.

Eric Newby

Newby was a British soldier during World War II and was made a prisoner of war in Italy. He captures the spirit of the land and people in the vivid and romantic *Love and War in the Apennines* (1999), in which he recounts how he escaped and was hidden by Italians (one of whom he fell in love with and later married).

Tacitus

This classical author's *Annals* is one of our primary sources of information — and lurid stories — about the early emperors, including Augustus, Tiberius, Caligula, and Nero. It was published in the Penguin classics series as *The Annals of Imperial Rome* (1956) and has been reprinted many times since.

Giorgio Vasari

Painter, architect, and (literally) Renaissance man, Giorgio Vasari is best known for *Lives of the Most Eminent Painters and Sculptors* (1550; expanded 1568), commonly referred to as *Lives of the Painters*. Although *The Lives . . .* has been criticized for inaccuracy, it's a foundational work of art history and contains much interesting information about the great painters of the Renaissance, some of whom were the author's personal friends. The Oxford edition (1998) is one of the many abridgments in translation of this huge work.

Benvenuto Cellini

This talented Florentine sculptor/goldsmith painted himself as a larger-than-life figure in his famous *Autobiography* (1728). It doesn't matter what lies he told about himself — the book presents a vivid picture of Renaissance Italy. Among those whom it influenced was Goethe (see the listing in this chapter), who translated it into German.

Edward Gibbon

If you read 25 pages a day, it'll take you only about 4 months to get through Gibbon's *History of the Decline and Fall of the Roman Empire* (begun in 1776), one of the monuments of English prose (a less monumental Penguin abridged version [1983] is available in paperback). Gibbon described history as "little more than the crimes, follies, and misfortunes of mankind," and he gives you 13 centuries' worth, up until the collapse of the Empire and the founding of the Holy Roman Empire.

Novel works for your reading pleasure

Besides the works listed in this chapter, you may want to read one or two of the following novels (or sets of short stories) set at least partially in Italy:

- ✔ *The Agony and the Ecstasy* by Irving Stone
- ✔ *Christ Stopped at Eboli* by Carlo Levi
- ✔ *Death in Venice* by Thomas Mann
- ✔ *The Innocents Abroad* by Mark Twain
- ✔ *Roman Fever and Other Stories* by Edith Wharton
- ✔ *Roman Tales* and *The Woman of Rome* by Alberto Moravia
- ✔ *A Room with a View* and *Where Angels Fear to Tread* by E. M. Forster
- ✔ *The Talented Mr. Ripley* by Patricia Highsmith

Goethe

Johann Wolfgang von Goethe was the first great modern literary visitor to Italy. His *Italian Journey* (1816) embodies his profound love of the country and culture and recounts his varied travels from one end of the country to the other.

Henry James

Henry James lived most of his life in Europe and contributed travel pieces on art and culture to *Harper's* and other journals. Some of these essays are collected in *Italian Hours* (1907). The pieces on Venice are particularly good. You may also want to read his novella *The Aspern Papers* (1888), set in Venice.

D. H. Lawrence

Lawrence wrote several books about Italy, including *The Sea and Sardinia* (1921) and *Etruscan Places* (1927); a selected edition, *D. H. Lawrence and Italy,* has been published by Penguin (1997).

Ignazio Silone

Silone was an important socialist writer who had to go into exile during Mussolini's reign. *Bread and Wine (Pane e Vino;* 1937) is a vivid novel set during the Fascist period — a modern classic.

Giuseppe Lampedusa

Lampedusa was actually Giuseppe Tomasi, prince of Lampedusa. His novel *The Leopard* (*Il Gattopardo;* 1958) is about the effect on a noble Sicilian family of Garibaldi's invasion and the war to unify Italy as a state. It was made into a tremendous film by Luchino Visconti, starring Burt Lancaster.

Mary McCarthy

Critic/novelist Mary McCarthy, author of *The Group* (1963), also wrote entertaining nonfiction works about the places in Italy she loved: *Venice Observed* (1956) and *The Stones of Florence* (1959).

Karl Ludwig Gallwitz

Gallwitz's *Handbook of Italian Renaissance Painters* (1999) gives you an at-a-glance guide to 1,200 Italian painters; it also has some nice reproductions, brief essays on the major schools of painting, and weird charts that show who influenced whom. You may want to peruse it before you go if you're really into art — it's softcover and not very thick, so you may even want to bring it along.

Appendix

Quick Concierge

Italy Facts at Your Fingertips

Automobile Club

Contact the Automobile Club d'Italia (ACI) at
☎ 06-4477 for 24-hour information and assistance. For **road emergencies** in Italy, dial
☎ **116.**

American Express

The Rome office is at Piazza di Spagna 38
(☎ 06-676-41; Metro: Line A to Spagna); the
Florence office is at Via Dante Alighieri 22R
(☎ 055-50-981); and the Venice office is
at Salizzada San Moisè, 1471 San Marco
(☎ 041-520-0844). The Milan office is Via
Brera 3 (☎ 02-876-674); in Naples, Piazza
Municipio 5 (☎ 081-551-2007); in Palermo,
Via E. Amari 40 (☎ 091-587-144).

ATMs

ATMs are available everywhere in the centers of towns. Most banks are linked to the
Cirrus network. If you require the Plus network, your best bet is the BNL (Banca
Nazionale del Lavoro), but ask your bank for
a list of locations before leaving on your trip.

Business Hours

Normal banking hours are Monday through
Friday 8:30 a.m. to 1:00 or 1:30 p.m. and 2:00 or
2:30 p.m. to 4:00 p.m. Banks are closed
Saturday and Sunday. Merchant hours are
Monday through Saturday 8:30 or 9:00 a.m. to
1:00 or 1:30 p.m. and 4:00 or 4.30 p.m. to 7:00,
7:30, or 8:00 p.m. Food stores are usually
closed on Thursday afternoon; all other
shops close Monday morning. Some supermarkets and an increasing number of stores
in large cities don't close at lunchtime and
are also open Sundays.

Currency Exchange

You can find very good exchange bureaus
(marked *cambio/change/wechsel*) at airports
and at major train stations. Otherwise, there
are exchange offices in most towns but the
smallest, usually concentrated near major
tourist attractions. Most banks exchange
currency as well.

Customs

U.S. citizens can bring back $400 worth of
merchandise duty-free. You can mail yourself
$200 worth of merchandise per day and $100
worth of gifts to others — alcohol and
tobacco excluded. You can bring on the
plane 1 liter of alcohol and 200 cigarettes or
100 cigars. The $400 ceiling doesn't apply to
artwork or antiques (antiques must be 100
years old or more). You're charged a flat rate
of 10% duty on the next $1,000 worth of purchases. Make sure that you have your
receipts handy. Agricultural restrictions are
severely enforced: no fresh products, no
meat products, no dried flowers; other foodstuffs are allowed only if they're canned or
in air-tight sealed packages. For more information, contact the U.S. Customs Service,
1301 Constitution Ave. (P.O. Box 7407),
Washington, DC 20044 (☎ 202-927-6724) and
request the free pamphlet *Know Before You
Go,* which is also available on the Web at
www.customs.ustreas.gov/travel/
travel.htm.

Canadian citizens are allowed a $750 exemption and can bring back duty-free 200 cigarettes, 2.2 pounds of tobacco, 40 imperial ounces of liquor, and 50 cigars. In addition, you're allowed to mail gifts to Canada from abroad at the rate of Can$60 a day, provided they're unsolicited and don't contain alcohol or tobacco (write on the package "Unsolicited Gift, Under $60 Value"). Declare all valuables on the Y-38 form before your departure from Canada, including serial numbers of valuables that you already own, such as expensive foreign cameras. You can use the $500 exemption only once a year and only after an absence of seven days. For more information, write for the booklet *I Declare,* issued by Revenue Canada, 2265 St. Laurent Blvd., Ottawa K1G 4KE (☎ 613-993-0534).

There's no limit on what U.K. citizens can bring back from an EU country, as long as the items are for personal use (this includes gifts), and the necessary duty and tax has already been paid. However, Customs law sets out guidance levels. If you bring in more than these levels, you may be asked to prove that the goods are for your own use. Guidance levels on goods bought in the EU for your own use are 800 cigarettes, 200 cigars, 1kg smoking tobacco, 10 liters of spirits, 90 liters of wine (of this not more than 60 liters can be sparkling wine), and 110 liters of beer. For more information, contact HM Customs and Excise, Passenger Enquiry Point, 2nd Floor Wayfarer House, Great South West Road, Feltham, Middlesex, TW14 8NP (☎ 0181-910-3744; from outside the U.K. ☎ 44-181-910-3744), or consult their Web site at www.ukonline.gov.uk.

Australian citizens are allowed an exemption of A$400 or, for those under 18, A$200. Personal property mailed back home should be marked "Australian Goods Returned" to avoid payment of duty. On returning to Australia, you can bring in 250 cigarettes or 250 grams of loose tobacco, and 1,125ml of alcohol. If you're returning with valuable goods you already own, such as foreign-made cameras, you should file form B263.

A helpful brochure, available from Australian consulates or Customs offices, is *Know Before You Go.* For more information, contact Australian Customs Services, GPO Box 8, Sydney NSW 2001 (☎ 02-9213-2000).

New Zealand citizens have a duty-free allowance of NZ$700. If you're over 17, you can bring in 200 cigarettes, 50 cigars, or 250 grams of tobacco (or a mix of all three if their combined weight doesn't exceed 250 grams); plus 4.5 liters of wine and beer, or 1.125 liters of liquor. New Zealand currency doesn't carry import or export restrictions. Fill out a certificate of export, listing the valuables you're taking out of the country. (That way, you can bring them back without paying duty.) You can find the answers to most of your questions in a free pamphlet available at New Zealand consulates and Customs offices: *New Zealand Customs Guide for Travelers, Notice no. 4.* For more information, contact New Zealand Customs, 50 Anzac Ave., P.O. Box 29, Auckland (☎ 09-359-6655).

Doctors

Contact any of the embassies and consulates to get a list of English-speaking doctors (see later in this listing and the "Fast Facts" sections in the chapters on the larger cities). Your hotel will be able to help you find a doctor and urgent medical assistance. In an emergency, go to or call the Pronto Soccorso of the nearest hospital (see "Fast Facts" sections in the chapters on the larger cities) or call the **police emergency (☎113 and 112).**

Electricity

Electricity in Italy is 220 volts. To use your appliances, you need a transformer. Remember that plugs are different, too: The prongs are round, so you also need an adapter. You can buy an adapter kit in many electronics stores before you leave.

Embassies and Consulates

Rome is the capital of Italy and, therefore, the seat of all the embassies and consulates, which maintain a 24-hour referral service for emergencies: United States (☎ 06-46741), Canada (☎ 06-445-981), Australia (☎ 06-852-721), New Zealand (☎ 06-440-2928), United Kingdom (☎ 06-7-482-5441), Ireland (☎ 06-697-9121). For more information on embassies and consulates around Italy, see the "Fast Facts" sections in the chapters on the larger cities.

Emergencies

For an **ambulance or first aid,** call ☎ **118;** for the **police,** call ☎ **113;** for the **Carabinieri (other police force),** call ☎ **112;** for the **fire department,** call ☎ **115;** for **road emergencies,** call ☎ **116** (road emergencies and first aid of the Italian Automobile Club).

Information

See "Where to Get More Information," later in this listing.

Language

Italians speak Italian. You can survive with very little knowledge of the Italian language (see Chapter 26 and the glossary later in this Appendix), especially because Italians are very friendly and ready to help foreigners in difficulty. However, you'll greatly enhance your experience if you master more than a dozen basic expressions. A good place to start your studies is *Italian For Dummies* by Francesca Romana Onofri and Karen Antje Möller (published by Wiley)!

Liquor Laws

There are no liquor laws in Italy. However, there are laws against disturbing the *quiete pubblica* (public quiet) — getting drunk and loud in bars, streets, and so on. Italians consider public drunkenness disgraceful, and though they love wine, they very much frown upon drinking to excess. You can buy alcohol in all supermarkets and grocery stores, open usually from 9 a.m. to 1 p.m. and 4 to 7 p.m.

Mail

Each town has at least one post office, usually in the center. Mail in Italy is notoriously unreliable but getting better. In fact, many tourists in Rome prefer to use the Vatican post office while they're visiting St. Peter's (it's the same price as other Italian post offices, but faster). A letter to the U.S. with regular mail costs .67€ (60¢), to Australia and New Zealand .72€ (65¢), and to the U.K. and Ireland .62€ (56¢). For valuable packages, use a private carrier like UPS or DHL. Technically, you're supposed to mail international mail either inside the post office or in one of the blue international mail boxes, not the red ones that you see everywhere. However, if you use a red mailbox, your mail will probably still reach its destination.

Maps

You can find free good maps at information booths. If you want something more detailed, you can buy one at a newsstand or kiosk, they all carry a good selection.

Newspapers and Magazines

All the newspaper kiosks in the center of major cities carry the *International Herald Tribune,* European issues of *Time,* and usually *The Economist* and *Financial Times.* Kiosks near foreign embassies and consulates usually carry a selection of that country's newspapers and magazines.

Pharmacies

Pharmacies are open on a rotation schedule, so there's always a pharmacy *di turno* (on call) over the 24 hours. Ask your hotel to find the closest open pharmacy for you.

Prices

Italians readily accepted the euro when it was introduced in January 2002, but there has been confusion. Some prices were converted exactly, yielding numbers like 11.29€. Some merchants rounded prices up, but were accused of using the euro to raise prices. So until Italians get used to the new currency, you will find a range of prices. Also, a euro cent (the equivalent of 20 lira) is still considered a significant amount of money by Italians — true to the old saying that every penny counts — further hampering rounding.

Restrooms

You can find restrooms in public buildings like train stations and airports and at major sights. You can also use restrooms in bars and cafes, but because these are for patrons (and not a public service), buy something before you ask. A glass of bottled water *(acqua minerale)* is the cheapest item. Some cities offer public toilets, which are marked with a "WC" sign. For these, travel with a supply of 50-cent euro coins in case there's an attendant, and bring your own toilet paper in case the restroom is out.

Safety

Italy is very safe, not considering petty theft. Pickpockets abound in tourist areas, public transportation, and crowded open-air markets. Bag snatchers on motor scooters are less frequent than they used to be, and Palermo is the only city where they're still common. Keeping your bag on the wall side of a sidewalk or between you and your companion is a good rule to follow, however. There are areas of poverty where a wealthy-looking tourist with an expensive camera may be mugged after dark. (Seedy areas are often behind rail stations.)

Smoking

Smoking is allowed in cafes and restaurants and is very common. Unfortunately for non-smokers, finding a restaurant with a separate no-smoking area is not easy, but their number is growing. If dining in a no-smoking area is very important to you, call beforehand to make sure the restaurant or cafe you'll be visiting offers one.

Taxes

Italy doesn't have a local tax, and other taxes are always included in the prices quoted. You can get a refund of the 19% IVA (value-added tax) for purchases costing more than 155€ ($140). See Chapter 4 for details.

Telephone

All public pay phones in Italy take a *carta telefonica* (telephone card), which you can buy at a *tabacchi* (tobacconist, marked by a sign with a white T on a black background), bar, or newsstand. The cards are precharged with value (2.58€/$2.30, 5.16€/$4.60, or 7.75€/$7). Tear off the perforated corner, stick the card in the phone, and you're ready to go.

To call Italy from the U.S., dial the **international access code, 011;** then Italy's **country code, 39;** and then the city code for the city you're calling (06 for Rome, 055 for Florence, 041 for Venice, and so on); and then the regular phone number.

To make a call within Italy, remember to always dial city codes (including the 0) for every call, even local calls: Dial the city code of the city that you're calling and then the phone number. A local call in Italy costs .10€ (9¢). To make an international call from Italy, dial the **international access code, 00;** then the **country code** of the country that you're calling (**1 for the United States and Canada, 44 for the United Kingdom, 353 for Ireland, 61 for Australia, 64 for New Zealand);** and then the phone number. Make sure that you have a high-value *carta telefonica* before you start; your 5€ won't last long when you call San Diego at noon. Lower rates apply after 11 p.m. and before 8 a.m. and on Sundays.

The best option for calling home, though, is using your own calling card linked to your home phone. Some calling cards offer a toll-free access number in Italy, others do not and you must put in a *carta telefonica* to dial the access number (you're usually charged only for a local call). Check with your calling card provider before leaving on your trip. You can also make collect calls. For AT&T, dial ☎ 172-1011; for MCI, dial ☎ 172-1022; and for Sprint, dial ☎ 172-1877.

To make a collect call to a country other than the United States, dial ☎ 170. Directory assistance for calls within Italy is a free call: Dial ☎ 12. International directory assistance is a toll call: Dial ☎ 176.

Remember that calling from a hotel is convenient but usually very expensive.

Time Zone

In terms of standard time zones, Italy is six hours ahead of eastern standard time in the United States. Daylight saving time goes into effect in Italy each year from the end of March to the end of September.

Tipping

Tipping is customary as a token of appreciation as well as a polite gesture. A 15% service charge is usually included in your restaurant bill (check the menu when you order — it will be marked at the beginning or at the end), but it is customary to leave a few more euro if you appreciated the meal. You also must tip bellhops who carry your bags (about 1€/90¢ per bag); cab drivers get a small tip, like waiters in those restaurants where service is already included (about 5%).

Transit/Tourist Assistance

For 24-hour assistance, call the tourist hotline ☎ 167-234-169. In Rome, the tourist hotline is ☎ 06-3600-4399. For train information call ☎ 147-888-088 (toll-free in Italy) daily 7 a.m. to 9 p.m.

Weather Updates

For forecasts, your best bet is to watch the news on TV (there's no telephone weather number as there is in the U.S.). On the Internet, check `http://meteo.tiscali net.it`.

Toll-Free Numbers and Web Sites for Airlines, Car-Rental Agencies, and Hotel Chains

Airlines that fly to Italy and in Italy

Air Canada
☎ 888-247-2262
Internet: www.aircanada.ca

Air France
☎ 800-237-2747
Internet: www.airfrance.com

Air New Zealand
☎ 800-737-000
Internet: www.airnewzealand.com

Air One
☎ 06-488-800 or 478-48-880 toll-free in Italy
Internet: www.flyairone.it

Air Sicilia
☎ 06-6501-1046

Alitalia
☎ 800-223-5730 in the U.S.; ☎ 800-361-8336 in Canada; ☎ 0990-448-259 in the U.K. and 020-7602-7111 in London; ☎ 1300-653-747 or 1300-653-757 in Australia; ☎ 06-65643 in Italy or 1478-65-643 toll-free in Italy
Internet: www.alitalia.it or http://alitaliausa.com

American Airlines
☎ 800-433-7300
Internet: www.aa.com

British Airways
☎ 800-AIRWAYS (800-247-9297) in the U.S.
Internet: www.british-airways.com

Cathay Pacific
☎ 131-747 toll-free in Australia or 0508-800454 in New Zealand
Internet: www.cathaypacific.com

Continental Airlines
☎ 800-525-0280
Internet: www.continental.com

Delta Airlines
☎ 800-241-4141
Internet: www.delta.com

KLM
☎ 800-374-7747
Internet: www.klm.nl

Lufthansa
☎ 800-645-3880 in the U.S.
Internet: www.lufthansa-usa.com

Meridiana
☎ 06-874-081 or 199-111-333 in Italy
Internet: www.meridiana.it

Qantas
☎ 13-13-13
Internet: www.qantas.com

United
☎ 800-538-2929
Internet: www.ual.com

US Airways
☎ 800-428-4322
Internet: www.usairways.com

Car-rental agencies

AutoEurope
☎ 800-334-440 toll-free in Italy or 800-223-5555 in the U.S.
Internet: www.autoeurope.com

Avis
☎ 06-41-999 in Italy or 800-331-1212 in the U.S.
Internet: www.avis.com

Europe by Car
☎ 800-223-1516 in the U.S.
Internet: www.europebycar.com

Europcar
☎ 800-014-410 toll-free in Italy or 06-6501-0879
Internet: www.europcar.it

Hertz
☎ 199-112-211 in Italy or 800-654-3001 in the U.S.
Internet: www.hertz.com

Kemwel
☎ 800-678-0678 in the U.S.
Internet: www.kemwel.com

National/Maggiore
☎ 1478-67-067 toll-free in Italy or 800-227-7368 in the U.S.
Internet: www.maggiore.it

Hotel chains in Italy

Best Western
☎ 800-780-7234 in the U.S. and Canada, ☎ 0800-39-31-30 in the U.K., ☎ 131-779 in Australia, ☎ 0800-237-893 in New Zealand
Internet: www.bestwestern.com or www.bestwestern.it

Hilton Hotels
☎ 800-HILTONS
Internet: www.hilton.com

Holiday Inn
☎ 800-HOLIDAY
Internet: www.holiday-inn.com

Jolly Hotels
☎ 800-017-703 toll-free in Italy, ☎ 800-221-2626 toll-free in the U.S., ☎ 800-247-1277 toll-free in New York state, ☎ 800-237-0319 toll-free in Canada, ☎ 0800-731-0470 toll-free in the U.K.
Internet: www.jollyhotels.it.

ITT Sheraton
☎ 800-325-3535
Internet: www.sheraton.com

Sofitel
☎ 800-SOFITEL in the U.S. and Canada, ☎ 020-8 283-4570 in the U.K., ☎ 02-2951-2280 in Italy, ☎ 800-642-244 in Australia, ☎ 0800-44-44-22 in New Zealand
Internet: www.sofitel.com or www.accor-hotels.it/sofitel.htm.

(Sofitel is part of the giant Accor group, representing 3,400 hotels in several chains. You can connect to all of them through ☎ 800-221-4542 in the U.S. and Canada and ☎ 0208-283-4500 in the U.K.; Internet: www.accor.com).

Where to Get More Information

Visitor information

If you want to get some information before you leave, you can visit the central Web site of the Italian National Tourist Board (ENIT), www.enit.it, or contact one of the following offices (they're all open Monday through Friday from 9 a.m. to 5 p.m. local time):

✔ **New York** (630 Fifth Ave., Suite 1565, New York, NY 10111; ☎ 212-245-5618 or 212-245-4822; Fax: 212-586-9249; E-mail: enitny@italiantourism.com)

✔ **Chicago** (500 N. Michigan Ave., Suite 2240, Chicago, IL 60611; ☎ 312-644-0996 or 312-644-0990; Fax: 312-644-3019; E-mail: enitch@ italiantourism.com)

✔ **Los Angeles** (12400 Wilshire Blvd., Suite 550, Los Angeles, CA 90025; ☎ 310-820-9807 or 310-820-1898; Fax: 310-820-6357; E-mail: enitla@earthlink.net)

✔ **Toronto** (175 Bloor St., Suite 907, South Tower Toronto M4W3R8 Ontario; ☎ 416-925-4822; Fax: 416-925-4799; E-mail: enit.canada@on.aibn.com)

✔ **London** (1 Princes St., London, WIB 2AY; ☎ 0207-399-3562; Fax: 0207-493-6695; E-mail: italy@italiantouristboard.co.uk)

✔ **Sydney** (Level 26, 44 Market St. NSW 2000 Sydney; ☎ 02-9262-1666; Fax: 02-9262-1677; E-mail: enitour@ihug.com.au)

For more information about specific destinations, you can contact the following tourist offices in Italy:

✔ **APT Roma** (Via Parigi 5, 00100 Roma; ☎ 06-4889-9255)

✔ **APT Firenze** (Via A. Manzoni, 16, 50121, Firenze; ☎ 055-23-320; Fax: 055-234-6286)

✔ **APT Venezia** (Castello 4421, 30100 Venezia; ☎ 041-529-8711; Fax: 041-523-0399)

✔ **APT Napoli** (Piazza dei Martiri 58, 80100 Napoli; ☎ 081-405-311)

✔ **APT Palermo** (Piazza Castelnuovo 35, 90141 Palermo; ☎ 091-586-122; Fax: 091-582-788; Internet: www.aapit.pa.it; E-mail: aapit@gestelnet.it)

For 24-hour assistance call the tourist hotline at ☎ 167-234-169.

Crawling the Web

The following sites provide a variety of cultural and visitor information for your trip to Italy:

✔ **ABC's of Italy** (www.italiaabc.com). This is a good site for cultural details on the country. It's comprehensive and also offers good links and hotel listings.

✔ **Dolce Vita** (www.dolcevita.com). The site is all about style — as it pertains to fashion, cuisine, design, and travel. Dolce Vita is a good place to stay up to date on trends in modern Italian culture.

✔ **FS On-line** (`www.fs-on-line.com`). This official site of the Italian rail system gives you station descriptions, train timetables, and ticket costs for Italy. (This site can help you find practical information to help you organize your trip.)

✔ **In Italy Online** (`www.initaly.com`). This extensive site helps you find all sorts of accommodations (country villas, historic residences, convents, and farmhouses) and includes tips on shopping, dining, driving, and viewing art.

✔ **Italian Tourist Web Guide** (`www.itwg.com`). Each month, this site recommends new itineraries for art lovers, nature buffs, wine enthusiasts, and other Italiophiles. It features a searchable directory of accommodations, transportation tips, and city-specific lists of restaurants and attractions.

✔ **Italy Hotel Reservation** (`www.italyhotel.com`). With almost 10,000 listings solely for Italy, this functional site is an ideal place to research and reserve lodgings.

✔ **ItalyTour.com** (`www.italytour.com`). Check out this vast directory for coverage of the arts, culture, business, tours, entertainment, restaurants, lodging, media, shopping, sports, and major Italian cities. See photo collections and videos in the "Panorama" section.

✔ **Sharelook Italy** (`www.sharelook.it`). At this site, you find some information (historical and cultural) on most destinations in Italy, plus some tourist links (hotels and restaurants).

✔ **Welcome to Italy** (`www.wel.it`). This site is a good source for all kinds of visitor information about Italy — from cultural (monuments and history) to practical (hotels and restaurants) to curiosities.

Molto Italiano: A Basic Vocabulary

You can't become fluent in Italian in one day, but you can still know enough to get by without much trouble. In the following sections are the few essential words that will make things a lot easier for you during your vacation.

Useful words and phrases

English	Italian
Excuse me	Permesso (per-*mess*-ow)
Goodbye	Arrivederci (ah-rree-vey-*der*-tchy)
Hello (Good day)	Buon giorno (bwon *djor*-know)

continued

Useful words and phrases (continued)

English	Italian
Hello (Good evening)	Buona sera (bwon-a *sey*-rah)
Please	Per favore (per fa-*voe*-ray)
Sorry	Scusi (*scoo*-sy)
Thank you	Grazie (*gra*-tziay)
Where is . . .	Dov'è. . . (doe-*vay*)

Useful expressions

English	Italian
A coffee, please	Un caffè, per favore (oon ka-*ffay* per fa-*voe*-ray)
How much does it cost?	Quanto costa? (*quahnn*-tow *koss*-tah?)
I don't understand	Non capisco (Nonn kah-*peace*-koh)
The bill, please	Il conto, per favore (eel *kon*-tow per fa-*voe*-ray)
What is it?	Che cos'è? (kay koss-*ay*?)
Where is the Colosseum?	Dov'è il Colosseo? (doe-*vay* eel ko-low-*ssay*-o?)
Where is the train station?	Dov'è la stazione? (doe-*vay* lah stah-*tziow*-nay?)

Numbers

1	uno (*oo*-no)
2	due (*doo*-ay)
3	tre (tray)
4	quattro (*kwa*-troh)
5	cinque (*cheen*-kway)
6	sei (say)
7	sette (*set*-tay)
8	otto (*oht*-toh)
9	nove (*no*-vay)

10	dieci (dee-*ay*-chee)
11	undici (*oon*-dee-chee)
12	dodici (*doe*-dee-chee)
13	tredici (*tray*-dee-chee)
14	quattordici (kwa-*tor*-dee-chee)
15	quindici (*queen*-dee-chee)
16	sedici (*say*-dee-chee)
17	diciassette (dee-chay-*set*-tay)
18	diciotto (deech-*oht*-toh)
19	diciannove (deechay-*nno*-vay)
20	venti (*vehn*-ti)
100	cento (*chen*-toh)
1,000	mille (*meel*-leh)

Making Dollars and Sense of It

Expense	Daily cost	x	Number of days	=	Total
Airfare					
Local transportation					
Car rental					
Lodging (with tax)					
Parking					
Breakfast					
Lunch					
Dinner					
Snacks					
Entertainment					
Baby-sitting					
Attractions					
Gifts & souvenirs					
Tips					
Other					
Grand Total					

Fare Game: Choosing an Airline

When looking for the best airfare, you should cover all your bases — 1) consult a trusted travel agent; 2) contact the airline directly, via the airline's toll-free number and/or Web site; 3) check out one of the travel-planning Web sites, such as www.frommers.com.

Travel Agency_____ Phone_____
    Agent's Name_____ Quoted fare_____

Airline 1_____ Quoted fare_____
    Toll-free number/Internet_____

Airline 2_____ Quoted fare_____
    Toll-free number/Internet_____

Web site 1_____ Quoted fare_____

Web site 2_____ Quoted fare_____

Departure Schedule & Flight Information

Airline_____ Flight #_____ Confirmation #_____

Departs_____ Date_____ Time_____ a.m./p.m.

Arrives_____ Date_____ Time_____ a.m./p.m.

Connecting Flight (if any)

Amount of time between flights_____ hours/mins

Airline_____ Flight #_____ Confirmation #_____

Departs_____ Date_____ Time_____ a.m./p.m.

Arrives_____ Date_____ Time_____ a.m./p.m.

Return Trip Schedule & Flight Information

Airline_____ Flight #_____ Confirmation #_____

Departs_____ Date_____ Time_____ a.m./p.m.

Arrives_____ Date_____ Time_____ a.m./p.m.

Connecting Flight (if any)

Amount of time between flights_____ hours/mins

Airline_____ Flight #_____ Confirmation #_____

Departs_____ Date_____ Time_____ a.m./p.m.

Arrives_____ Date_____ Time_____ a.m./p.m.

Sweet Dreams: Choosing Your Hotel

Make a list of all the hotels where you'd like to stay and then check online and call the local and toll-free numbers to get the best price. You should also check with a travel agent, who may be able to get you a better rate.

Hotel & page	Location	Internet	Tel. (local)	Tel. (Toll-free)	Quoted rate

Hotel Checklist

Here's a checklist of things to inquire about when booking your room, depending on your needs and preferences.

- ❏ Smoking/smoke-free room
- ❏ Noise (if you prefer a quiet room, ask about proximity to elevator, bar/restaurant, pool, meeting facilities, renovations, and street)
- ❏ View
- ❏ Facilities for children (crib, roll-away cot, baby-sitting services)
- ❏ Facilities for travelers with disabilities
- ❏ Number and size of bed(s) (king, queen, double/full-size)
- ❏ Is breakfast included? (buffet, continental, or sit-down?)
- ❏ In-room amenities (hair dryer, iron/board, minibar, etc.)
- ❏ Other_____

Places to Go, People to See, Things to Do

Enter the attractions you would most like to see and decide how they'll fit into your schedule. Next, use the "Going 'My' Way" worksheets that follow to sketch out your itinerary.

Attraction/activity	Page	Amount of time you expect to spend there	Best day and time to go

Going "My" Way

Day 1

Hotel_____ Tel._____

Morning_____

_____

Lunch_____ Tel._____

Afternoon_____

_____

Dinner_____ Tel._____

Evening_____

_____

Day 2

Hotel_____ Tel._____

Morning_____

_____

Lunch_____ Tel._____

Afternoon_____

_____

Dinner_____ Tel._____

Evening_____

_____

Day 3

Hotel_____ Tel._____

Morning_____

_____

Lunch_____ Tel._____

Afternoon_____

_____

Dinner_____ Tel._____

Evening_____

_____

Going "My" Way

Day 4

Hotel_____ Tel._____

Morning_____

_____

Lunch_____ Tel._____

Afternoon_____

_____

Dinner_____ Tel._____

Evening_____

_____

Day 5

Hotel_____ Tel._____

Morning_____

_____

Lunch_____ Tel._____

Afternoon_____

_____

Dinner_____ Tel._____

Evening_____

_____

Day 6

Hotel_____ Tel._____

Morning_____

_____

Lunch_____ Tel._____

Afternoon_____

_____

Dinner_____ Tel._____

Evening_____

_____

Going "My" Way

Day 7

Hotel_____ Tel._____

Morning_____

_____

Lunch_____ Tel._____

Afternoon_____

_____

Dinner_____ Tel._____

Evening_____

_____

Day 8

Hotel_____ Tel._____

Morning_____

_____

Lunch_____ Tel._____

Afternoon_____

_____

Dinner_____ Tel._____

Evening_____

_____

Day 9

Hotel_____ Tel._____

Morning_____

_____

Lunch_____ Tel._____

Afternoon_____

_____

Dinner_____ Tel._____

Evening_____

_____

Notes

Notes

Notes

Index

• *E* •

• *F* •

• *G* •

• *M* •

• N •

FOR

DUMMIES®

TRAVEL

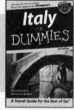

0-7645-5453-0

0-7645-5438-7

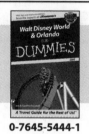

0-7645-5444-1

Also available:

America's National Parks
For Dummies
(0-7645-6204-5)

Caribbean For Dummies
(0-7645-5445-X)

Cruise Vacations For
Dummies 2003
(0-7645-5459-X)

Europe For Dummies
(0-7645-5456-5)

Ireland For Dummies
(0-7645-6199-5)

France For Dummies
(0-7645-6292-4)

Las Vegas For Dummies
(0-7645-5448-4)

London For Dummies
(0-7645-5416-6)

Mexico's Beach Resorts
For Dummies
(0-7645-6262-2)

Paris For Dummies
(0-7645-5494-8)

RV Vacations For
Dummies
(0-7645-5443-3)

EDUCATION & TEST PREPARATION

0-7645-5194-9

0-7645-5325-9

0-7645-5249-X

Also available:

The ACT For Dummies
(0-7645-5210-4)

Chemistry For Dummies
(0-7645-5430-1)

English Grammar For
Dummies
(0-7645-5322-4)

French For Dummies
(0-7645-5193-0)

GMAT For Dummies
(0-7645-5251-1)

Inglés Para Dummies
(0-7645-5427-1)

Italian For Dummies
(0-7645-5196-5)

Research Papers For
Dummies
(0-7645-5426-3)

SAT I For Dummies
(0-7645-5472-7)

U.S. History For Dummies
(0-7645-5249-X)

World History For
Dummies
(0-7645-5242-2)

HEALTH, SELF-HELP & SPIRITUALITY

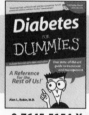

0-7645-5154-X

0-7645-5302-X

0-7645-5418-2

Also available:

The Bible For Dummies
(0-7645-5296-1)

Controlling Cholesterol
For Dummies
(0-7645-5440-9)

Dating For Dummies
(0-7645-5072-1)

Dieting For Dummies
(0-7645-5126-4)

High Blood Pressure For
Dummies
(0-7645-5424-7)

Judaism For Dummies
(0-7645-5299-6)

Menopause For Dummies
(0-7645-5458-1)

Nutrition For Dummies
(0-7645-5180-9)

Potty Training For
Dummies
(0-7645-5417-4)

Pregnancy For Dummies
(0-7645-5074-8)

Rekindling Romance For
Dummies
(0-7645-5303-8)

Religion For Dummies
(0-7645-5264-3)